The Supreme Court's Federal Tax Jurisprudence

An Analysis of Fact Finding Methods and Statutory Interpretation from the Court's Tax Opinions, 1801–Present

Second Edition

By Jasper L. Cummings, Jr.

Printed in the United States of America.

Published by the American Bar Association Section of Taxation
1050 Connecticut Avenue, NW, Suite 400, Washington, D.C. 20036; www.americanbar.org/tax.

Print 13-Digit ISBN: 978-1-63425-582-0
E-book 13-Digit ISBN: 978-1-63425-583-7

Table of Contents

Foreword

Jasper (Jack) Cummings is one of the more prolific authors today in the field of tax, writing with a point of view supported by careful research and thoughtful analysis. Whether or not one agrees with his point of view, his work is an invaluable resource. The Second Edition of *The Supreme Court's Federal Tax Jurisprudence* continues in that tradition, coming at a time when Congress is pushing the tax law into new and uncharted territory while we all hold out hope for the fundamental reform of the Internal Revenue Code that is long overdue.

Since 1803, when Chief Justice Marshall stated in *Marbury v. Madison* that "[i]t is emphatically the province and duty of the judicial department to say what the law is," the decisions of the Supreme Court have held a role second in importance only to the acts of Congress in establishing the law. The relationship between the Internal Revenue Code and its judicial constructions and interpretations is, however, a complicated one. As Jack notes, "Codes are a particular type of integrated statutes, and for that reason are seen as 'special', which is often said of the Internal Revenue Code." Yet unlike what Jack calls the "extreme purposivism" of the Uniform Commercial Code, the Internal Revenue Code has no overarching principles or stated rules of construction. For tax, this creates "a curious regime that both establishes many rigid rules to which taxpayers must conform, provides virtually no grace for slight and meaningless errors, and applies anti-taxpayer doctrines (substance over form) that stem from the rules of equity."

The Supreme Court has often been called on to step into the void created by the "curious regime," so having this book as a form of restatement of its jurisprudence is a useful resource for all. While the Court's tax cases total over nine hundred, Jack organizes them into a manageable framework. In doing so, he makes the observation—surprising perhaps to those who have focused on the Court's jurisprudence over only the last several decades—that "[t]ax cases have occupied a far larger part of the Court's output than any other single area of the law, and dominated it in some decades." Measured by volume, much of the Court's tax jurisprudence came in the years after ratification of the 16th Amendment, when the Court was called upon to explain broad concepts like the meaning of "income." From a historical perspective, that early case law remains important, and the Second Edition of Jack's book builds on the First in explaining both the Court's early case law in the field of tax and its evolution through the New Deal and beyond.

The Supreme Court's more recent decisions will be more relevant for practitioners and others in weighing and debating current unsettled tax issues. In that context, in updating the First Edition Jack does an excellent job of synthesizing recent developments in two key areas: economic substance and related "anti-abuse" rules and deference to administrative rule making. The Second Edition connects these issues to what the Supreme Court has—and perhaps more importantly has not—said on these topics over time.

On economic substance and related rules that courts apply when considering "intentional tax reduction," Jack notes that "the location of the line between permitted intentional tax reduction and the tax reduction efforts that can lead to the denial of tax benefits" is "[t]he most debated issue in federal taxation." Yet the Supreme Court has not spoken on the topic directly since 1978, an eternity when measured against intervening developments in the tax law. When the First Edition of this book was published in 2010, the ink was not yet dry on one of the more noteworthy developments in this area—codification (or at least partial codification) of the economic substance "doctrine," with "doctrine" being a description that Jack notes the Supreme Court has never embraced.

To the casual observer, codification of economic substance and a review of recent appellate court decisions applying economic substance and related rules might suggest an evolution in Supreme Court jurisprudence over time into a positive rule of law. While codification was a major development, it left many questions open and unanswered. The codified rule also leans heavily on prior case law for resolution of threshold questions like whether the "doctrine" should apply in the first place. As a result, the Supreme Court's decisions remain more relevant than ever. Building on his work in the First Edition, Jack approaches the subject with a more refined, in-depth perspective, cautioning against construing Supreme Court precedent as supporting the positive rule of law that many assume it has become. For example, he describes several of the Court's "boundary decisions" that should be viewed as limiting the scope and application of economic substance (and similar rules), rather than as supporting the expansive evolution that is conventionally assumed. Jack also helps the reader understand the scope and limits of the Supreme Court's jurisprudence in this area by analyzing cases in thirteen "factual clusters." In these "cluster areas," Jack notes that the Court's decisions should be viewed as simply an exercise in judicial fact-finding unique to the common fact patterns in these cases, rather than supportive of a broader positive rule of law.

For those arguing for or against application of economic substance and related rules, Jack's tracing of the law from *Gregory* v. *Helvering* in 1935 to codification in 2010 should be required reading, showing that even with codification (and perhaps even more so because of codification), the tax law is not a Code-based set of rules that can be navigated by turning well-defined corners. Unfortunately (or not, depending on one's perspective), the law in this area is, as Jack summarizes, now reflective of a "policy of vagueness" that provides an *in terrorem* effect against aggressive tax planning, however the Internal Revenue Service may decide to define it. Although responsibility for that policy may have shifted from the appellate courts to Congress with codification, the policy itself remains the same. Regardless, we now have a paradigm where economic substance and related rules are often the first resort, rather than the last, when the government seeks to challenge what it considers to be an unwarranted tax benefit. Jack's analysis demonstrates that this may not be the paradigm that the Supreme Court intended.

Deference to administrative rule making is a second key area of tax law that has evolved significantly since publication of the First Edition of this book in 2010. It is also an area where the role of the courts is much different than it is when they are called on to find facts or to interpret a statute in isolation. In contrast to economic substance and related rules of law, where the Supreme Court has been largely silent in recent years, its decisions in *Mayo Foundation for Medical Education & Research v. United States* and *United States v. Home Concrete & Supply, LLC*, among others, have fundamentally reshaped thinking on how the courts, practitioners and the government view administrative rulemaking in the field of tax. The Second Edition provides useful context for and explanations of these decisions.

Until recently, most practitioners and commentators thought they understood there to be a defined line between "legislative" and "interpretive" regulations arising from the landmark Supreme Court decisions in *Skidmore v. Swift & Co.* in 1944 and *Chevron U.S.A., Inc. v. Natural Resources Defense Council, Inc.* in 1984. They also thought, with some support from the Court's 1979 decision in *National Muffler Dealers Association, Inc. v. United States*, that tax regulations were treated differently from other areas of administrative law. But in just the last few years, *Mayo* and *Home Concrete* have shifted this thinking significantly, creating a more muddled framework that looks to vagaries in the statute using, as Jack notes, traditional tools of statutory construction that render ambiguous whether a statute is in fact ambiguous to begin with. Since publication of the First Edition, the Court has also marked an outer limit to administrative rulemaking, holding in *King v. Burwell* that, as Jack summarizes, the "statutory conundrum may be so great that it is above the political power of an agency to resolve." By ruling in favor of the Administration's position anyway, *King v. Burwell* highlights a practical limitation on administrative deference arguments: Defeating a rule on deference grounds may not translate into winning the case.

The Second Edition examines the scope and limits of administrative deference by reaching back to before enactment of the Administrative Procedures Act (APA) in 1946, noting that courts then did what they wanted to in construing and interpreting statutes, while mouthing some degree of deference to administrative rule making. Notwithstanding enactment of the APA and more than a half-century of case law interpreting it, that is effectively where we remain today, with some refinement of the analysis (and limit on a court's flexibility) based on the size of the hole the rule maker is trying to fill. Stating it differently, Jack explains that deference is really just a tool that courts use to protect their "turf;" when Treasury and the Internal Revenue Service attempt to perform what looks like a judicial function, the courts will rein them in. Rather than looking for bright lines between "legislative" and "interpretive" regulations, we now have a more fluid distinction that turns on how large an interpretive gap is left by the statute, the resulting need for administrative guidance, and any Congressional indication (however discerned) that guidance would be issued to fill such gaps. From a practitioner's perspective, this provides a helpful framework in an area of law that has, as Jack notes, "reached a level of abstraction that places its current resolution beyond the realm of practical applicability by the lower courts."

After deciding more than nine hundred tax cases, recent developments in the areas of economic substance and judicial deference illustrate that the Supreme Court's tax jurisprudence is more important than ever in understanding what the law is. Having moved beyond "grand issues of the tax law" like defining income or reading a "business purpose" requirement into the corporate reorganization provisions of the Code, the Court will continue to play the key role in interpreting and construing tax statutes.

Over the course of my career, I have viewed the field of tax through a number of different lenses, ranging from a Justice Department Trial Attorney riding circuit through Eastern California, to serving as the Administration's representative in Congressional tax hearings, to now handling, as a sole practitioner, matters ranging from individual income tax audits to complex circuit court appeals.

The First Edition of *The Supreme Court's Federal Tax Jurisprudence* has served as a *vade mecum* for me in the varied aspects of my practice and the Second Edition will no doubt be the same. It is a must read for anyone practicing or with an interest in the field of tax.

Michael J. Desmond
Santa Barbara, California
October 21, 2016

Preface to Second Edition

This book is for practitioners and other students of the federal tax laws. It addresses all issues arising in the application of the Internal Revenue Code that are outside of the operation of the substantive law, constitutional law,1 and tax procedure. Therefore, this book explores statutory interpretation and construction and methods of fact finding used in applying the Code to taxpayers' facts. In addition, it collects, categorizes, and explains the significant statements of the Supreme Court of the United States on these subjects.

Many of the subjects here addressed have escaped careful analysis; for them this book provides such analysis, with surprising results in many cases. For other more discussed subjects this book collects and organizes sources that can be hard to find, and states truisms established in those sources that have been overlooked. This book makes existing knowledge accessible and organizes and presents the disparate but integrated issues in a way not elsewhere available, somewhat akin to a restatement, or at least a very thorough Note by a student editorial board. Some subjects may seem obvious when presented, but are not necessarily part of many tax lawyers' tool kits simply because they have never focused on them; this book identifies such subjects and places them in familiar context. Therefore, this book has some of the characteristics of a (very long) law review article, and also aspires to be a black letter law treatise.

This book is organized with a detailed Table of Contents and is heavily footnoted so that it can serve as a resource. In the age of electronic word searches, it is easy to forget that not all useful information can be found that way.

---

[1] *See* Jasper L. Cummings, Jr., The Supreme Court, Federal Taxation, and the Constitution (ABA 2013) (addressing all Supreme Court federal tax decisions not addressed in this book because they deal primarily with constitutional issues).

This book is organized around three premises: (1) the federal tax laws are not different from the rest of the law, and do not require special legal processes, apart from standard statutory interpretation and fact finding; (2) a wealth of usually untapped guidance can be derived from the Supreme Court's extensive federal tax opinions; and (3) rather than episodically picking out phrases from Supreme Court (and other) opinions for citation, practitioners and students need a firm grasp of the progress of the Supreme Court's federal tax jurisprudence and the meaning of certain high profile decisions of the Court, including particularly those that have established base line concepts of interpretation and fact finding, such as *Eisner v. Macomber*, *Gregory v. Helvering*, *Higgins v. Smith*, *Court Holding*, *Knetsch*, and *Frank Lyon*.

The lower federal courts have developed what they consider to be special legal processes for federal tax cases (called herein "tax specific doctrines"), which with one exception are only applications of standard law methods of fact finding or legal interpretation; the one exception is the economic substance doctrine, which since the 1990's has come to be treated as a positive rule of law, seemingly enacted by the lower federal courts. The tax specific doctrines are variously described as assessing business purpose, substance over form, economic substance, step transactions, sham transactions, and related tax specific concerns. The economic substance doctrine functions like an uncodified preamble to the Code, albeit applied in episodic and unpredictable ways. Bittker & Lokken applied the term "preamble" to these doctrines generally and overstated their effect: "[T]ransactions are to be taken at face value for tax purposes only if they are imbued with a 'business purpose or reflect economic reality' ...."[2] Throughout, this book contrasts and compares what the Supreme Court actually has done versus tax specific doctrines, and otherwise comments on the doctrines' wisdom. Many of the doctrines are just names for common fact finding techniques (for example, stepping related transactions together for analysis), although the economic substance doctrine has evolved into a positive rule of law.

Moreover, a careful focus on the Supreme Court's tax opinions is justified by its huge federal tax caselaw of well over 900 opinions (not counting the constitutional decisions). That body of opinions is sufficiently large and authoritative to be the principal source of guidance on the application of the Code. Advocates can and will always find and cite the recent relevant opinions of the lower courts; this book helps them find the better Supreme Court authority that can overcome adverse lower court rulings.

This book is an objective reference book with two differences: its analyses aim to go deeper than the standard reference works by identifying the most pertinent among competing authorities and questioning spurious authorities; also, it has a stated point of view.

---

[2] Boris Bittker & Lawrence Lokken, Federal Taxation of Income, Estates and Gifts (WG&L), 4.3.1.

In going deeper, this book integrates three sources of information not directly related to tax: (1) general legal principles as applied outside the tax law, (2) legal history both generally and in the tax law, and (3) academic viewpoints on statutory interpretation. Ordinarily tax treatises do not attempt to integrate any, much less all, of these sources. They are included here because they are useful to the understanding of the current tax law, because they are often hard to find, and because the tax law has suffered from isolation and from ignoring its own history. Thus, the summaries of academic debates (for example, about *Chevron* deference and strict construction) may seem abstract, but should serve the purpose of alerting the practitioner to otherwise foreign territory and permitting an evaluation of the debates.

As a reference this book contains in-depth analyses of several subtopics related to the application of the Code, such as section 269, the *Chevron* doctrine, the economic substance doctrine in the lower courts, and the several most frequently cited Supreme Court tax opinions. In addition, the discussions of some court opinions and certain issues (like *Chevron* deference and tax equity) are quite detailed and heavily footnoted. That unusual detail is provided either to support a counterintuitive point or as evidence of one of the fundamental assumptions that underpins this book: too often the real tax law is overwhelmed by gloss and cliché, thus necessitating a careful and discerning reading of the apt authorities.

The book's point of view is one of not necessarily assuming that the current state of the law is the most advantageous, or that current understandings of the law are correct, or that (in some cases) even Supreme Court opinions are correct in all of their reasoning. This book aims for a fresh look at many accepted truths in the tax laws.

This book draws inspiration from the three volumes of *Studies in Federal Taxation* written by Randolph E. Paul between 1937 and 1940. Paul was the consummate practitioner, administrator, and scholar, who had little patience for the inscrutable. He set a matchless standard in extracting concrete meaning from tax case law, and in stating both what the law was and what it should be.

I urge you to use this book to understand the origin and place in the tax law of the tax specific doctrines, to understand the role and views of the Supreme Court in interpreting the Internal Revenue Code, and to find support for more lawyerly approaches to legal interpretation and fact finding in tax cases. That notwithstanding, in the end it may be necessary to develop systemic changes to address the more intractable difficulties of the interpretation and construction of the Code.

Finally, I thank Professor Michael Mulroney for reading the original manuscript and offering many useful suggestions, and Anne Dunn and the American Bar Association Section of Taxation for publishing and republishing this book.

Jasper L. Cummings, Jr.
Raleigh, North Carolina
June 2016

Terms and Frequently Cited Books

Chapter. References to Ch. refer to subdivisions of this book.

Cluster rules. This book shows that the tax law develops more reliably in relation to factual clusters. Ch. VI.F. discusses the principal factual clusters and the legal and fact finding rules that have coalesced around them, and to which they should be limited. In contrast, the ESD attempts to impose a universal rule on all types of factual and legal cases that arise under the tax laws.

Code. Since 1954 the Internal Revenue Code, currently title 26 of the United States Code, restated as the 1986 Code. Previously there was a Code of 1939 and biannual Revenue Laws, all of which can be referred to as the Code.

Court. When capitalized refers to the Supreme Court of the United States.

ESD. ESD, which stands for the economic substance doctrine, is a court made rule of law that Chapter V addresses extensively, but which also appears throughout the book. Ch. V.F.2. contains a partial list of cases forming the origins of the ESD as a positive rule of law. The authorities listed in the Appendix to the first edition of this book, which is omitted in this edition, are an amplification of that list.

Section. References to a "section" are to a section of the Internal Revenue Code of 1986, as amended (the "Code"), unless otherwise indicated.

Service. The Internal Revenue Service or IRS.

Tax specific doctrines. The ESD is one of a group that this book terms "tax specific doctrines:" *economic substance doctrine, step transaction doctrine, substance over form doctrine, economic substance [without doctrine], sham transaction doc-*

trine, and *business purpose doctrine.* Ch. V discusses these in detail, as well as Ch. VI.E and F. They have in common the potential to be applied to any tax issue, at the insistence of the Service. In contrast, another group of more targeted tax doctrines exists, for examples, the *open transaction doctrine* and the *relation back doctrine*, are discussed as cluster rules in Ch. VI.A.

Frequently Cited Books

The following sources are cited frequently throughout the book by use of the abreviations below:

P. S. Atiyah & Robert S. Summers, *Form and Substance in Anglo-American Law: A Comparative Study of Legal Reasoning, Legal Theory, and Legal Institutions* (Clarendon Press 1987) – "ATIYAH & SUMMERS"

Boris Bittker & Lawrence Lokken, *Federal Taxation of Income, Estates and Gifts* (WG&L) – "BITTKER & LOKKEN"

Boris Bittker & James Eustice, *Federal Income Taxation of Corporation and Shareholders* (WG&L) – "BITTKER & EUSTICE"

Jasper L. Cummings, Jr., *The Supreme Court, Federal Taxation, and the Constitution* (ABA 2013) – "CUMMINGS, CONSTITUTION"

William S. McKee, William F. Nelson & Robert L. Whitmire, *Federal Taxation of Partnerships & Partners* (WG&L) – "MCKEE, NELSON & WHITMIRE"

Randolph E. Paul, *Studies In Federal Taxation* (Callaghan 1937) – "PAUL, STUDIES I"

Randolph E. Paul, *Studies in Federal Taxation* (2d Ed. 1938) – "PAUL, STUDIES II"

Randolph E. Paul, *Studies in Federal Taxation* (3d Ed. 1940) – "PAUL, STUDIES III"

Randolph E. Paul, *Taxation for Prosperity* (Bobbs-Merrill 1947) – "PAUL, PROSPERITY"

Richard J. Pierce, Jr., *Administrative Law Treatise* (5th Ed. 2015) (Wolters Kluwer) – "PIERCE"

William D. Popkin, *Statutes In Court* (Duke 1999) – "POPKIN"

John N. Pomeroy, *A Treatise on Equity Jurisdiction as Administered in the United States* (Lawyers' Coop. 5th Ed. 1941) – "POMEROY"

Richard A. Posner, *How Judges Think* (Harvard 2008) – "Posner"

Michael I. Saltzman & Leslie Book, *IRS Practice and Procedure* (Thomson Reuters) – "Saltzman & Book"

Ch. I. Tax Principles Addressed and the Interpretive Context

I.A. Tax Application Principles Addressed

The following subchapters summarize the principles of application of the federal tax laws that later chapters will expound.

I.A.1. *Evolution of the Application of the Federal Tax Laws*

The methods of applying the United States tax laws have evolved since the early days of customs duties and stamp taxes, through the early income tax period, to today. But the stages of evolution are mostly overlooked, resulting in continuing references to outmoded authorities and incomplete understanding of others.

Most disputes about the application of the federal tax laws involve relatively straightforward uncertainties about facts and the meaning of tax statutes, which are recognized and treated as issues of fact and law. But a substantial number of tax disputes are analyzed on bases other than standard law and fact finding. These cases generally start with what can best be called a feeling on the part of the Service, then urged on a court, that the taxpayer's claimed tax benefit just cannot be allowed. That feeling, administratively well intentioned though it may be, has spawned a large body of unorganized, episodic applications of the tax laws that defies structure. Nevertheless, it encourages the view that tax is special, that the courts discern some grand truths that underlie, but are not written in, the statutes, and that there is a third legal process to be applied to tax, apart from standard fact and law finding. This book is based on the premise that tax law is not special,[3] that there are no such grand truths, nor is there a third process.

Instead, in the early days of taxation by statute in England and America there existed the common law and the effort of the judges to accommodate the new statutes to the common law. Initially in this effort the common law was exalted and statutes were strictly interpreted, except when they were intended to remedy the shortcomings of the common law (called remedial statutes); penal statutes also were strictly construed. Tax statutes were hard to pigeonhole, but because they clearly were not remedial of the common law and frequently were enforced by the criminal law, they tended to fall in the penal category and to be strictly construed against the government.

By the time of the enactment of the 1913 income tax, the tendency to view statutes generally in terms of their relation to the common law had waned and faith in the legislatures increased. The courts began to view themselves in partnership with legislators, and tried to carry out the purposes of Congress in their rulings. Thus, the paradigm of taxation shifted from being viewed as a penal law to being like a remedial law, but with a peculiar twist: the person in need of the remedy was the government. This shift appears most prominently in the opinions of the New Deal Supreme Court, with government victories peaking at least in corporate tax cases in the 1950s.[4] Particularly in the New Deal period, in tax cases the federal courts applied methods of fact finding that had developed in the courts of equity: for example a core principle of equity jurisprudence is that substance should control over form in order that right should be done. Initially the Supreme Court applied such approaches in favor of taxpayers, but the New Deal Supreme Court applied them more in favor of the government. In addition, federal courts began to construe tax statutes as they would a remedial statute like the usury statutes, to achieve the intent or purposes of Congress. For example, the Supreme Court construed several statutorily unstated requirements into the definition of a corporate reorganization, thus further limiting taxpayers' ability to literally apply the statute to obtain gain nonrecognition.

Although it was frequently stated that there should be a balanced approach to interpretation of taxing statutes, during the New Deal period the federal courts made two defining and interrelated pro-government choices in interpreting the revenue statutes: (1) they came to define income very broadly; and (2) they generally applied a rule of construction that deductions and allowances should be strictly interpreted. These two presumptions or canons do or can constitute a heavy thumb on the scales of the tax law in favor of the

---

[3] *Cf.* Livingston, *Practical Reason, Purposivism and the Interpretation of Tax Statutes*, 51 Tax L. Rev. 677, 679 (1996) (agreeing that tax is not unique in the law as to statutory interpretation, though it is on one end of a spectrum of general to specific statutes). *But see, e.g.*, Puckett, *Structural Tax Exceptionalism*, 49 Ga. L. Rev. 1067, 1120 (2014-2015).

[4] *See* Blank & Staudt, *Corporate Shams*, 87 N.Y.U. L. Rev. 1642, 1682 (2012).

government as the person needing the remedy, wholly apart from equitable fact finding in favor of the government.

However, no one seems to have observed, understood or explained these shifts in tax application toward favoring the government in the New Deal period. Grasping for an explanation of the new status quo, the lower federal courts developed tax specific explanations for their pro-government tendencies in fact finding and legal construction. They strove mightily to drain every ounce of support from a handful of Supreme Court opinions—*Gregory, Smith, Knetsch, Frank Lyon*—which frequently do not provide that support and are better explained in more traditional terms of legal construction and fact finding.

Initially the Board of Tax Appeals took a relatively literal view of the tax statutes, which academics now would call "textualist." However, over time the Board (and later the Tax Court) shifted to a "purposive" approach that both gave relatively more weight to Congress' presumed purpose, but also gave relatively less weight to the transaction's form. The likely explanation is that the Tax Court came more and more to view itself as the steward of the tax laws, and its members felt the need to protect that law. The appellate courts picked up their cues from the Tax Court (as well as from a series of well-regarded tax opinions by Second Circuit Judge Learned Hand),[5] and in concert they created several tax specific doctrines, sometimes justified with miscitations of Supreme Court decisions mostly from the 1930's and 1940's. The flowering of these doctrines in the lower courts mostly occurred after 1960 (and accelerated in the 1980's) when the courts otherwise generally were trending away from the purposive approach to statutory interpretation back toward a sort of second generation textualism.

As a result of these shifts lower federal courts commonly commence their analyses of tax disputes by stating baldly several doctrines: that in the tax law substance rather than form always determines the result (which rightly understood is no more than an assertion of common law fact finding), a bona fide business purpose is always a prerequisite for respecting a transaction for tax purposes (which is a lower court extension of the construction of a business purpose requirement into a specific statute in *Gregory v. Helvering*), and the economic substance of a transaction will always be discerned and will control the tax result despite the intervention of entities, or contracts, or other legal rights (which is either another way to assert common law fact finding, or is a positive rule of law when it appears as part of the economic substance doctrine). The availability of such doctrines obscures the fact that courts are frequently applying equitable fact finding tools and standard construction of ambiguous statutes based on the purposes of Congress. Moreover, a statistical

---

[5] *But see* Cummings, *Quote Learned but Cite Gus*, 142 TAX NOTES (TA) 993 (Mar. 3, 2014) (arguing that Hand's tax opinions are overrated).

analysis of Supreme Court opinions in corporate tax shelter cases concludes that lack of business purpose is not a major factor in the outcomes.[6]

The better way, indeed the more lawyerly way, may be to codify these doctrines in the statute or regulations, if they are to be the law.[7] But in addition we need to understand (1) the true origins and meaning of these doctrines and the more fundamental legal methods from which they derive, (2) that tax law is not special, and (3) that courts have known for centuries how to determine that an ass bearing the label "horse" is still an ass.

I.A.2. *Fact Finding, Statutory Interpretation, and the Supreme Court*

This book focuses on the two core processes of the law—statutory interpretation and construction and fact finding—as they have been applied by the Supreme Court of the United States in federal tax cases. The book employs these two categories not only as an organization tool, but also because the relatively simple step of recognizing which process is being applied can go far in clarifying what a court has done. Many denigrate the fact and law distinction, particularly in the tax area; whatever limitations it may have for purposes of appellate review, it well serves the purposes identified here.[8] A secondary focus of this book is on certain judge made doctrines, the tax specific doctrines, sometimes thought generally to govern the interpretation and application of the Code. This book will show that the tax jurisprudence of the Supreme Court does not embody the doctrines, or at least not to the extent usually thought.[9]

Although the words "interpretation" and "construction" now appear to be used interchangeably,[10] they are epistemologically different and maintaining the distinction is useful.[11] Interpretation discerns meaning from the words of the statute, possibly as influenced by a variety of extrinsic sources; construction fills a gap and sometimes reads the statute contrary to its words, and is similarly influenced. Thus, these two processes match up with two of the problem areas this book addresses: ambiguous sections of the Code and unambiguous sections that produce benefits for taxpayers that the Service finds unintended.

---

[6] *See* Blank & Staudt, *Corporate Shams*, *supra* note 4, at 1642, 1690.

[7] *See infra* Ch. V.F. (on the incomplete codification of the economic substance doctrine).

[8] *See* Pietruszkiewicz, *Economic Substance and the Standard of Review*, 60 ALA. L. REV. 339, 359 (2009).

[9] The idea for this book's focus on the Supreme Court's tax opinions took form in Cummings, *Statutory Interpretation and* Albertson's, 66 TAX NOTES (TA) 559 (Jan. 23, 1995).

[10] For three Tax Court opinions using the terms interchangeably, see Liddle v. Commissioner, 103 T.C. 285 (1994); Hesselink v. Commissioner, 97 T.C. 94 (1991); Estate of Keller v. Commissioner, 39 B.T.A. 1047 (1939).

[11] The distinction has been traced to LIEBER, LEGAL AND POLITICAL HERMENEUTICS 23 (Boston, Little Brown 1839). *See* POPKIN. *But see* Barnett, *Interpretation and Construction*, 34 HARV. J.L. & PUB. POL'Y 65 (2011) (describing a new distinction between determining meaning of text and applying text to concrete facts).

Statutory interpretation and construction may be either liberal or purposive or intentionalist, or it may be strict and literal and textualist.[12] The choice between these two poles frequently is treated as the choice answered by the tax specific doctrines, but it is not.[13] Although the doctrines may depend somewhat on purposive statutory interpretation, more generally they set up a false choice between a blinkered view of facts and an integrated view, sometimes invoking the "step transaction doctrine" or "substance over form doctrine" or "economic substance doctrine." There is no such choice: the law has always known how to find facts, despite fraud and lesser methods of obscuring facts. When law and fact finding processes are disentangled, many cases based on the doctrines can be seen as law cases or fact cases or as otherwise reflecting standard legal processes, not necessarily peculiar to the tax laws and not dependent on a judge made positive rule of law.

The judge made doctrines referred to above try to substitute for normal purposive interpretation of statutes and for doing the hard work of finding facts using common law and equity tools. This book makes, and will support, the following points.

- *Tax specific doctrines*: The lower federal courts, the Service and most taxpayer representatives have come to believe that the Service can deny a tax benefit to a taxpayer if (a) the substance of the transaction does not comport with its form, or (b) the transaction does not have economic substance, or (c) the transaction has no business purpose (generally some variation of the *economic substance doctrine*).[14]
- *Lack of balance:* These doctrines do not reflect a general application of purposive interpretation to the Code because they operate in only one direction: they deny benefits that the courts presume Congress did not intend, while not extending benefits that the Congress presumably did intend.
- *Partially debunking the doctrines:* In fact, the most authoritative sources of federal tax law, Congress, the Supreme Court,[15] and Treasury regulations, have not adopted generally applicable positive rules of Code application,

---

[12] *See* SCALIA & GARNER, READING LAW: THE INTERPRETATION OF LEGAL TEXTS (2012) (an immense volume setting forth a strict constuctionist view).

[13] *See, e.g.*, McLeod, *Collecting Taxes*, 33 VICTORIA UNIV. WELLINGTON L. REV. 371, 379 (2002) (discussing the British tax law's evolution after the Duke of Westminster case and reciting British judge's views on the twin aspects of tax law process).

[14] One summary statement of the judicial doctrines says "[T]ransactions are to be taken at face value for tax purposes only if they are imbued with a 'business purpose or reflect economic reality' . . ." BITTKER & LOKKEN, at 4.3.1. These are rules that dictate how other rules should be applied, interpreted, and construed. The Treasury has almost described them as such, stating that they "overlay the rules [referring to the Code, regulations and other administrative pronouncements]." *Treasury White Paper on Corporate Tax Shelters (Part 1 of 2)*, 1999 TAX NOTES TODAY 127-12 (July 1, 1999) (also referring to the doctrines as "standards").

[15] *See* Madison, *The Tension Between Textualism v. Substance Over Form*, 43 SANTA CLARA L. REV. 699, 749 (2003) (agreeing that the Supreme Court is likely to reject one or more of the doctrines if asked).

although the Supreme Court has adopted methods of fact finding in cluster areas; but see Ch. V.F. on codification of the economic substance doctrine.

- *Lack of synthesis of principles of application of the income tax:* The doctrines have arisen without those three sources of authority principally because of the over abundance of case law that has been poorly synthesized, and because inherent features of a progressive income tax tend to promote the development of anti-taxpayer doctrines to meet the needs of the Service, of which these are the handiest.
- *Proper synthesis:* Despite debates over textualism versus purposivism, the two courts most relevant to the application of the tax laws, the Tax Court and the Supreme Court, tend (1) to interpret the Code to carry out the purposes of Congress, (2) to do so more readily in favor of the government, and (3) to use equitable fact finding methods that have been given tax-specific names (economic substance doctrine, etc.) but have deep historic roots in common law and equity.
- *Building a synthesis out of Supreme Court tax opinions:* In lieu of doctrines, Code users can observe as more authoritative the methods used by the Supreme Court in applying the Code, on which this book focuses.
- *Cluster rules:* In place of generally applicable positive rules like the economic substance doctrine (ESD), the study of the Supreme Court's methods suggests a more modest set of truly tax specific doctrines that this book calls cluster rules; they can form a more orderly template for Code application, which will be readily accessible to users and can avoid misapplication of authorities; specifically, the ESD properly is a cluster rule that originated to assist fact finding in the area of leveraged leases, but has metastasized into a general purpose rule of positive law.
- *Agency and equity*: Principles of agency and equity (and step transaction concepts) are the fundamental tools that the law normally uses to cause substance to override form; the tax law has woefully disregarded these tools.
- *Alternatives for law reform*: Despite the vast store of Supreme Court tax guidance, the Court's waning ability to provide, or show any interest in providing, ongoing oversight in the federal tax area may lead to a need for systemic changes of which the codification of the ESD may unfortunately be an example.

The rise of the judge made doctrines roughly coincides with the rise of the tax shelters of the 1970's and later, when combined with the absence of an authorized pro-taxpayer or pro-government tilt in the interpretation of the tax laws (aside from the broad definition of income and the strict construction of deductions and allowances). Others have addressed many of these subjects, but usually with one or more of three major limitations: (1) failure to question the historical roots of various doctrines;[16] (2) more concern with relating the subject to some one rule,[17] or one case,[18] instead of the broader problem of Code application; and (3) a bias against tax avoidance.[19] Also, at least one major empirical study of the Supreme Court's tax jurisprudence exists, which provides invaluable evidence on which this book relies, but does not relate the Court's approaches to the doctrines or attempt to synthesize a method of Code application.[20]

The only tax law that is of parallel legitimacy to the Code is the tax law made by the Supreme Court. This book chooses to rely solely on the Supreme Court's tax jurisprudence for several reasons in addition to its primacy: (1) the body of its tax decisions is sufficiently large (over 900) to form a useful body of law; (2) the welter of lower court decisions was not cohesive 60 years ago when Randolph Paul tried to encapsulate it,[21] and is less so now (except to the extent the economic substance doctrine has coalesced as a positive rule of law in the lower courts); (3) the passage of time and the gradual diminution of the Court's involvement in tax issues has dimmed knowledge of many of its earlier rulings (aside from a handful that achieved super status, such as Gregory, and even those take on a gloss that is not their holding); and (4) founding an interpretive approach on the Supreme Court's tax jurisprudence is an attainable middle ground between purely theoretical approaches to statutes, and purely empirical studies, which are not abundant in the tax law.[22] The excellent empirical studies of Supreme Court tax cases by Professor Nancy Staudt, et al, that have been done largely are consistent with the approaches discussed herein, as discussed in Ch. III.C.2 below.[23] The only group of Supreme Court federal tax opinions that is intentionally not examined in this book is the constitutional decisions, covered in Cummings, The Supreme Court, Federal Taxation, and the Constitution (2013).

---

[16] *See, e.g.*, Bankman, *The Economic Substance Doctrine*, 74 S. Cal. L. Rev. 5 (2000) (starting with the existence of the doctrine as a given).

[17] *See, e.g.*, Cunningham & Repetti, *Textualism and Tax Shelters*, 24 Va. Tax Rev. 1 (2004) (focusing on the partnership anti-abuse rule).

[18] *See, e.g.*, Donahue, *The Rule of* Sheldon v. Commissioner: *Is it an Economically Efficient Evolution of the Sham Transaction Doctrine?*, 13 Va. Tax Rev. 165 (1992).

[19] *See, e.g.*, McMahon, *Beyond a GAAR: Retrofitting the Code to Rein in 21st Century Tax Shelters*, 98 Tax Notes (TA) 1721 (Mar. 23, 2003) (arguing not only that there is no right to tax planning, but also that it is not a societal value).

[20] Staudt et al., *Judging Statutes: Interpretive Regimes*, 38 Loy. L.A. L. Rev. 1909 (2005). However, Blank & Staudt, *Corporate Shams*, *supra* note 4, at 1642, does focus on the Supreme Court's handling of corporate tax shelters and finds some evidence for corporations tending to win when the literally followed the statute.

[21] Paul, Studies I.

[22] *See* Staudt, *Empirical Taxation*, 13 Wash. U. J.L. & Pol'y 1 (2003). Another example of a useful empirical study is Shores, *Textualism and Intentionalism in Tax Litigation*, 61 Tax Law. 53 (2007) (finding that the Tax Court is more likely to ignore the words of the Code to reach the "correct" result than are courts of appeal).

[23] Staudt et al., *Judging Statutes*, *supra* note 20, at 1909; Blank & Staudt, *Corporate Shams*, *supra* note 4, at 1642 (statistical analysis of Supreme Court's corporate shelter decisions).

I.A.3. *The Problem of Code Application*

The need for clear understanding of the federal tax law is great because the impact of the Code on all persons is tremendous: virtually everyone pays or is subject to paying federal taxes, and the government relies on taxes for its life blood. But rules and methods for Code application are in disarray because:

- Statutory and administrative tax law tends to be made, or at least influenced, by tax experts, who too frequently are not in close contact with other branches of the law, and thus tend to view tax law as isolated, self sufficient, and not in need of fertilization by general legal learning;[24]
- The voluminous controlling interpretations of the law makes synthesis difficult;
- Interpretation of the Code is not a common subject of study;[25]
- The tax law is notoriously complex;
- The tax law has not adequately worked out the relationship between application of general law principles to tax issues and tax-specific rules;[26] and
- These factors tend to impel the Service, and then the lower courts, to default to broadly applicable tax-specific doctrines (such as the ESD) that do not require full understanding and application of the nuances of the sections at issue.

Put another way, the Code suffers from its own "popularity:" it is a means to widely differing ends for its users, which is all of us, and its use cannot be avoided. It is a means to tax reduction in a multitude of ways for taxpayers, and a means to indispensable revenue raising for the government; in addition it has become a means to implement a variety of social programs, unfortunately including the Affordable Care Act. Its unavoidable ubiquity and built-in conflicts distinguish the Code from other bodies of statutory law, such as the criminal law or the federal bankruptcy Code, which individuals encounter only episodically, and which most can avoid. Therefore, application of the Code is a subject of the highest economic and social importance.

The Code's popularity has resulted in a huge volume of disputes between government and taxpayers producing a similarly huge volume of precedents. Many interpretational disputes result from (1) the absence of authoritative policies on Code interpretation and application, (2) the hodge podge of judge made policies on Code application that go in and out of favor, and (3) the withering of more traditional processes in favor of tax specific doctrines. The lower federal courts, urged on by a vitally interested partisan, the Service,

---

[24] PAUL, STUDIES I, at 66.

[25] Barker, *Statutory Interpretation, Comparative Law, and Economic Theory: Discovering the Grund of Income Taxation*, 40 SAN DIEGO L. REV. 821, 825 (2003).

[26] *See* Reiling, *Developing a Law of Income Taxation*, 32 TAXES (CCH) 546 (1954) (author was Assistant Chief Counsel of the Service; he observed that at least as of 1954 the tax law had not been logically organized in terms of those two types of rules).

have attempted to supply such authoritative interpretive policies by creating particularly the ESD. The meaning and scope of the ESD and the other doctrines generally have been uncertain, except in one sense: they always favor the government. They function as a sort of general anti-abuse rule (GAAR), but not enacted by Congress (even as to the partly codified ESD).[27]

The government seems to find the resulting *in terrorem* effect more beneficial to the fisc than clearer rules around which taxpayers might maneuver.[28] Taxpayers generally have deplored the uncertainty of the doctrines, but embrace some of the other judge made policies and have opposed the codification of broad anti-abuse rules.[29] In encouraging the lower courts to create particularly the ESD, the Service has violated its own policies: "The proper method for conveying the positions of the Office and the policies of the Service is through published guidance. In contrast, litigation should be used as an enforcement tool to advance and defend established positions, not as a vehicle for making policy."[30]

Examples of the Code's interpretive uncertainties that result from the judge made doctrines and from failing to apply more standard legal methods include:

- Retention of outmoded policies: a hotly contested 2007 D. C. Circuit Court of Appeals opinion[31] cited a 1917 Supreme Court opinion[32] for the policy that ambiguous revenue raising sections should be construed in favor of the taxpayer, despite the fact that the Supreme Court long ago abandoned that authority;[33]
- Statement of Supreme Court "rules" that do not exist: a Tax Court judge in a frequently cited "tax shelter" opinion[34] relied upon *Gregory*[35] as creating a "business purpose" requirement for apparently all tax-favorable

---

[27] For discussion of GAAR, generally, see West, *Antiabuse Rules and Policy: Coherence or Tower of Babel?*, 118 TAX NOTES (TA) 513 (Jan. 28, 2008). *See also* Libin, *Congress Should Address Tax Avoidance Head-On: The Internal Revenue Code Needs a GAAR*, 30 VA. TAX REV. 339 (2010-2011) (not recognizing the ESD codification as a GAAR).

[28] *See* OFFICE OF MGMT. & BUDGET, EXECUTIVE OFFICE OF THE PRESIDENT, STATEMENT OF ADMINISTRATION POLICY, FOOD AND ENERGY SECURITY ACT OF 2007, H.R. 2419, *available at* 2007 TAX NOTES TODAY 216-41 (Nov. 6, 2007).

[29] *See, e.g.,* N. Y. State Bar Assn. Section of Taxation, *Comments on the Administration's Corporate Tax Shelter Proposals*, 83 TAX NOTES (TA) 879 (May 10, 1999) (rejecting nonspecific anti-abuse statute "super 269"); *infra* Ch. V.F (codification of the economic substance doctrine).

[30] I.R.M. 31.1.1.1.3(1).

[31] Murphy v. Internal Revenue Service, 493 F.3d 170 (D.C. Cir. 2007), *reh. denied*, 100 A.F.T.R. 2d 6049, *cert. denied*, 128 S. Ct. 2050 (2008).

[32] Gould v. Gould, 245 U.S. 151 (1917).

[33] *See infra* Ch. II.B.2(c)(4).

[34] ACM P'ship v. Commissioner, 1997 T.C.M. (RIA) 97,115, *aff'd*, 157 F.3d 231 (3d Cir. 1998).

[35] Gregory v. Helvering, 293 U.S. 465 (1935).

transactions,[36] even though *Gregory* did no more than interpret the words "pursuant to a plan of reorganization";[37]

- A section that the Congress intended and the Treasury embraced as an actual but limited anti-abuse rule, section 269, which has been gutted by the courts and ignored by the Service and Treasury;[38] and
- The repeated statement that ". . . the doctrine of 'substance over form' recognizes that the substance of a transaction, rather than its form, governs for tax purposes,"[39] when, in fact, sometimes it does and sometimes it doesn't.[40]

As a result of these and many, many, more legal cross currents, proposals were made between 1999 and 2010 to codify the ESD, as discussed in Ch. V.F. The question of the authority of the ESD has become more prominent since the 1980s when the Service began to assert tax specific doctrines generally and the ESD in particular in virtually all cases it considered to be tax shelters, and thereafter when the lower federal courts began to agree and to treat the doctrines as transitioning from fact finding methods in cluster areas to ever more rigid, but no less uncertain, rules of positive law.[41]

The most fundamental of the causes of the problems of Code application seems to derive from the failure to adequately work out the relationship between the general law rules' application to tax issues and the special tax rules. The general law rules mostly derive from the laws of the 50 states. This causes an inherent potential lack of uniformity in the federal tax law. In addition, there are express or implied statutory meanings in the Code that find no analogs or even sound guides in state law characterizations (income being the chief one). Therefore the creation of tax specific rules has been inevitable, but chaotic.[42] At one end of the spectrum is the development by the Supreme Court of a genuine general principle of Code application, the assignment of income doctrine, as well as other cluster rules discussed in Ch. VI.F; at the other end is the application by the lower federal courts of the ESD, which they use to override a wide variety of forms chosen by taxpayers.

Finally, Justice Robert H. Jackson pointed out a special cause of the peculiar British-American difficulty with tax administration. He explained that continental legal systems had worked out a way to treat administrative law

---

[36] *See* Cavanaugh, *Order in Multiplicity: Aristotle on Text, Context and the Rule of Law*, 79 N.C. L. Rev. 577, 602 n. 77 (2000) (which attributes such a general doctrine to *Gregory* without citation or a second thought).

[37] *See infra* Ch. V.F.2 (roots of economic substance doctrine); *infra* Ch III.C.3.a(1) (*Gregory*).

[38] *See infra* Ch. IV.A.

[39] *See, e.g.*, BB&T Corp. v. United States, 523 F.3d 461 (4th Cir. 2008).

[40] *See infra* Ch. VI.E.1.

[41] *See* Gideon, *Mrs. Gregory's Grandchildren: Judicial Restrictions of Tax Shelters*, 5 Va. Tax Rev. 825-26 (1986) (decrying the uncertainty of the judicial doctrines and stating that the uncertainty might have been tolerable earlier, but not now that they had become so widespread).

[42] *See generally* Reiling, *supra* note 26, at 546-58 (July 1954).

as different from private disputes. In contrast, the only way a taxpayer could initially contest a federal tax was to sue the tax collector for acting outside the law. Though this method was changed, "the earlier method of thinking has colored our whole development of administrative law."[43] Put another way, resolving federal income tax issues in the United States is inherently an adversarial and not an administrative process.

I.A.4. *Imbalance: The Service Versus the Taxpayer*

The federal tax laws have enjoyed a century long movement, unevenly but inexorably, against the taxpayer and in favor of the government. The judge made doctrines discussed in this book arose to combat "tax shelters" and provide flexibility in the tax law in only one direction: against taxpayers. Important aspects of the trend include the following:

- Taxpayers have lost the 19th century presumption that taxes are to be strictly construed against the government, which has been replaced by a broad definition of income and pro-government presumptions as to deductions, nonrecognition, and allowances.[44]
- The principles of equity are not employed in favor of taxpayers; indeed no actor in the system is authorized to do equity for taxpayers.[45]
- Although taxpayers beat back the *Dobson* rule[46] so that the Tax Court does not have near total control over fact finding in its cases, that taxpayer victory has been mostly neutralized by the tax specific doctrines, which sometimes operate like factual presumptions for the government.
- Taxpayers are subject to the presumption of correctness of the Commissioner's determination and the burden of proof is on the taxpayer to prove its case.[47]
- The courts show substantial deference to federal agency regulations in general and Treasury regulations in particular.[48]
- Taxpayers must clearly prove any waiver of procedural requirements by the Service.[49]
- Penalties have become progressively heavier, and are now aimed also at tax advisors.[50]

---

[43] JACKSON, THE SUPREME COURT IN THE AMERICAN SYSTEM OF GOVERNMENT 47 (Harper 1963) (1955).

[44] *See infra* Ch. II.B.2(c)(4).

[45] *See infra* Ch. V.E.1.f.

[46] The *Dobson* case applied a fairly clear statute to remove factual findings made by the Board of Tax Appeals from appellate review. *See infra* Ch.VI.E.3.a.

[47] *See infra* Ch. VI.E.4.

[48] *See infra* Ch. VI.D.

[49] Angelus Milling Co. v. Commissioner, 325 U.S. 293 (1945). *But see* Tucker v. Alexander, 275 U.S. 228 (1927) (procedures for refunds should not be "trap for the unwary").

[50] BITTKER & LOKKEN, at 114.2.

- Congress has created and increased requirements that taxpayers notify the Service of questionable positions.[51]
- The Service will not rule on a transaction lacking a bona fide business purpose or having a principal purpose of tax reduction.[52]
- Financial accounting standards combined with requirements to report uncertain tax positions to the Service have come to impose almost as much constraint on tax reduction activity by reporting companies as the tax laws themselves.[53]
- Many statutory changes have effected broad scale as well as targeted tax benefit disallowance rules, such as the repeal of the *General Utilities* Doctrine in 1986,[54] enactment of the at risk and passive loss rules of sections 465 and 469, and the 2004 enactment of section 409A curtailing flexibility in deferred compensation.
- However, in the area of forum selection, taxpayers have suffered the least erosion of their rights, enjoying maximum flexibility in the choice of three trial court venues, with their varying routes of appeal;[55] but taxpayers have never had a constitutional right to a prepayment remedy;[56] and all courts seem to be tending to rule against "tax shelters."

These changes and rules weigh heavily against taxpayers, leaving to the taxpayer the principal advantages of choice of form, choice of forum, and self reporting (and minimal audit coverage, subject to self-identification of questionable positions).

I.A.5. *Methodology and a Caution*

This book mostly ignores lower court opinions (except in discussing the ESD), and cites most of the Supreme Court tax decisions since 1913, the bulk of which date from the first half of the 20th century. The choice of Supreme Court over lower court decisions is motivated both by supremacy and triage: focus on the Court's authoritativeness trumps a futile attempt at completeness that will not reveal coherence. It turns out that the Supreme Court's tax opinions do support a coherence that can inform the broader case law. However, this book mostly ignores Supreme Court decisions on constitutionality of federal taxes, except for the unavoidable *Eisner v. Macomber*, because of their peculiar and limited impact on broader matters of Code interpretation.[57]

---

[51] Bittker & Lokken, at 111.1A.

[52] Rev. Proc. 2016-3, 2016-1 I.R.B. 126, § 3.02(2).

[53] *See, e.g.*, Wells, *New Schedule UTP: Uncertain Tax Positions in the Age of Transparency*, 63 Baylor L. Rev. 392 (2011).

[54] Bittker & Eustice, at 8.20.

[55] The United States Tax Court, United States District Courts, and The United States Claims Court, appealable variously to the Circuit Courts of Appeal and the Court of Appeals for the Federal Circuit.

[56] Phillips v. Commissioner, 283 U.S. 589 (1931) (shareholders of liquidated corporation can be subject to summary collection procedures).

[57] *See* Cummings, Constitution.

Admittedly the interpretational styles of the Court have changed over its history, beginning with a creative or "grand" style employed by Chief Justice Marshall, moving to a more formal precedential style by the end of the 19th century, and moving back toward creativity in the first part of the 20th century,[58] with more current emphasis on formality and text. Since style per se is not a ground for distinguishing an opinion, emphasis on all of the Supreme Court precedent under the tax laws is justifiable on several grounds:

- The Court is proud of its own decisions, and will follow them to a near fault.[59]
- Absent a fairly clear reversal, "old" Supreme Court decisions remain good law, despite frequently being ignored or just forgotten.
- Very few of the current problems of tax law application are of a new variety.

This book also cites many "old" articles and tax books, generally for the purpose of gaining contemporaneous understanding of past tax events. Many brilliant students of the tax law, including Randolph Paul, Louis Eisenstein, Erwin Griswold, Boris Bittker, Stanley Surrey, William Plumb (holding the list to the deceased), have studied the matters discussed here, and made recommendations, or at least recorded ideas, that are useful today, but also tend to be ignored or forgotten. Tax practitioners seem to like to reinvent wheels and ignore what went before.

Because this is also a reference book, it assumes that the law, and how it is employed, actually matter in deciding legal cases and in applying the tax law apart from litigation. There are many contrary or contrasting academic viewpoints, summarized in Ch. I.B.1. below, which espouse theoretical approaches to the tax law that this book eschews. Like Randolph Paul's works,[60] this book attempts to address what the law is. Even "critical legal studies" proponents agree that law places some constraints on judges.[61] Moreover, close observers will agree that within the government there is widespread and honest fealty to the law and congressional purpose, and that responsible tax advisors do

---

[58] *See* Llewellyn, *Remarks on the Theory of Appellate Decisions*, 3 VAND. L. REV. 395, 396 (1950) (tracing how Marshall relied on principle over precedent, referred to as the Grand Style; then in the period of 1880-1910 the Formal Style depended more on precedent; thereafter the Grand Style began to creep back in).

[59] *See* Brudney & Ditslear, *The Warp and Woof of Statutory Interpretation: Comparing Supreme Court Approaches in Tax Law and Workplace Law,* 58 DUKE L.J. 1231, 1253 (2009) (survey showing 81.6% reliance on Supreme Court precedent in tax cases, substantially greater than any other measured ground, including text); *see also* United States v. Hatter, 532 U.S. 557, 567 (2001) (only the Supreme Court can overrule its own prior decisions). *See* Chapter III.C.4.d. However, stare decisis does not apply to interpretational methods. Foster, *Should Courts Give Stare Decisis Effect to Statutory Interpretation Methodology?* 96 GEO. L. REV. 1863 (2008).

[60] PAUL, STUDIES I; STUDIES II; and STUDIES III.

[61] Cross, *Political Science and the New Legal Realism: A Case of Unfortunate Interdisciplinary Ignorance*, 92 NW. U. L. REV. 251, 271 (1997).

attempt to know the law. Therefore, trying to discern what the tax law is must be important.

Finally, this book relies on close attention to what courts, and specifically the Supreme Court, say and do in their written opinions, with emphasis on their holdings as contrasted with their dictum. Many of the key points of this book are based on accurate readings of Supreme Court precedents, which are frequently at odds with the gloss created by hindsight.

I.B. Statutory Interpretation and Construction in the United States

This book is based on the view that tax frequently is cut off from the general law. That is true of the much more widely discussed issues of statutory interpretation. Outside of tax, this subject has enjoyed great attention in the academic press, and to some extent in the general press, due to beliefs that underlying political, social and economic forces are at work in schools of statutory interpretation.

I.B.1. *The Ideologies of Statutory Interpretation*

Statutory interpretation, like all of the law, mediates between multiple competing forces in society. Those seeking stability generally want the law interpreted literally; those seeking change generally attempt to interpret law based on its purpose, although sometimes the roles are reversed.[62] The tension is ancient. The Bible suggests that the ox may be pulled from the ditch on the Sabbath, despite a general prohibition against work on that day.[63] Justinian forbade the writing of commentaries on the Corpus Juris because he thought they would unsettle the law.[64] However:

> The object which he [Justinian] aimed to accomplish was neither attainable nor desirable. To enforce any system of law it is necessary to find out what the system is, to ascertain its meaning, to interpret and expound it. Ambiguities of language are unavoidable, even in the most carefully constructed documents. Even if the language is unambiguous in itself, its application to new circumstances and conditions will involve uncertainties and queries.[65]

Wise observers reject over emphasis on the words of the statute:

> Under this argument, interpreters should generally try to interpret statutory ambiguities in the most numbskulled way possible because that is more

---

[62] For example, King v. Burwell, 135 S. Ct. 2480 (2015), ruled that the subsidies in the Affordable Care Act are not limited to insurance bought on state exchanges, even though the statute seems to say that. The opponents of the law wanted one sort of stability (no federally subsidized insurance) and the proponents wanted another.

[63] *Exodus* 20:8-11.

[64] Hadley, Introduction to Roman Law 20 (New York, Appleton 1893).

[65] *Id.; see also* Barker, *supra* note 25, at 870-73 (discussing similarity of Roman law purposivism).

likely to deviate from legislative preferences and provoke textual specification.[66]

Generally taxpayers are expected to comply with the law's text; that leaves the government to more frequently rely on purpose in tax cases. This has tended to produce a role reversal in the judiciary, leading even conservative judges, like Justice George Sutherland who led the Court's opposition to New Deal legislation, to adopt purposive interpretations of the Code in favor of the government, as in his unanimous opinion for the Court in *Gregory v. Helvering*. But before examining the Court's principles of Code interpretation, it is useful to understand the broader context of statutory interpretation in the United States.

I.B.1.a. *Purposivism and Textualism and Tax*

Many legal academics have shown that the federal courts' styles of statutory interpretation have changed over time, as outlined below, fluctuating between emphasis on text ("textualism") and emphasis on considerations beyond text (generally referred to as "purposivism," but also by other terms). Tax practitioners tend to be ignorant of those changes,[67] but need to understand the outlines of the academic debates to avoid being dismissed as mere practitioners (an odd status, given the fact that no one is more interested in the subject matter than a practitioner of the subject).

The core Supreme Court tax opinions of the late 1930's and 1940's fit squarely into the then dominant view of the federal courts as collaborators with Congress in carrying out Congress' purpose behind the tax laws (purposivism). That view waned after 1960, about the same time the tax specific doctrines began to come into vogue in the lower federal courts' tax opinions, using citations to the Supreme Court opinions of the 1930's and 1940's. This flowering of the tax specific doctrines is somewhat counter to the rise of emphasis on a statute's text rather than its purposes (textualism) in the courts after 1960, and is best explained by the shift of the Tax Court from textualism toward purposivism just as the rest of the law was moving in the other direction. The appellate courts took their cues from the Tax Court, at least in

---

[66] Elhauge, *Preference-Eliciting Statutory Default Rules*, 102 Colum. L. Rev. 2162, 2275-76 (2002).

[67] Cummings, *The Debate You Never Heard Of*, 2008 Tax Notes Today 166-24 (Aug., 26, 2008).

the area of "tax shelters," with a strong assist from Judge Learned Hand in his earlier Second Circuit tax opinions.

I.B.1.b. *Interpretational Shifts over Time*

Academics view the general jurisprudence of law in the United States as having undergone a four phase maturing process over the last 150 years,[68] going from (1) the traditional school of formalism or doctrinalism that focused on relatively immutable legal principles and centered around the Harvard Law School of the late 1800's, to (2) the "legal realists" at Yale and Columbia in the 1920's and 1930's, who asserted that law was not rules but was what the judges do,[69] to (3) the Hart and Sacks school of "legal process,"[70] which attempted to reinvigorate doctrinalism by purifying the processes by which law was announced, to (4) the more recent "critical legal studies" school, which focused on those social forces and power centers and interest groups that affect what the law is.[71] Perhaps a fifth phase is "new legal realism," which would apply more rigorous interdisciplinary tools to legal realism,[72] or legal

[68] *See* Calabresi, *An Introduction to Legal Thought: Four Approaches to Law and the Allocation of Body Parts*, 55 STAN. L. REV. 2113 (2003). Judge Calebresi describes the four approaches to law that have dominated the last century: (1) doctrinalism or formalism (Langdell/Harvard school), (2) functionalist or interdisciplinary, (3) legal process, (4) law and status or critical legal studies.

[69] *See* Green, *Legal Realism as Theory of Law*, 46 WM. & MARY L. REV. 1915 (2005). The article observes that H.L.A. Hart made legal realism unfashionable by observing that the law must be more than just decisions; judges have to decide on some basis, which ultimately is guided by the law. This observation has to be true, and a rereading of JEROME FRANK'S LAW AND THE MODERN MIND (Brentano's 1930) will convince the reader that the legal realists went too far.

[70] Feldman, *The Transformation of an Academic Discipline: Law Professors in the Past and Future (or Toy Story Too)*, 54 J. LEGAL EDUC. 471, 485 (2004) (Observed the shift from realism to emphasis on "legal process" in the writings of Hart and Sacks. He explains this as an attempt to bolster the traditional view by invoking reasoned analysis to prevent courts from being viewed as making arbitrary decisions, as the realists might imply.). But the Legal Process school may have come too late to impact the decline of purposivism and rise of textualism. *See* POPKIN, at 147-49.

[71] Feldman, *supra* note 70, at 487 (observing that critical legal studies tends to hark back to the realists, but differs from the realists in looking for interest groups and power centers that had their way with real life legal interpretation).

[72] Macauley, *New versus Old Legal Realism: Things Ain't What they Used to Be*, 2005 WIS. L. REV. 365. This article describes the progression from "traditional legal scholarship that focused on the logic of doctrine" and was reflected in the great Harvard written textbooks and Langdell type courses of the early part of the 20th century (p. 369), to the legal realism school that developed mostly at Yale and Columbia in the '20's and '30's and basically observed that judges "make law" in the sense of bringing to their decisions views and information not found in the record and the formal law, to the "new legal realism" that basically attempts to put empirical analysis at the service of legal realism and let the chips fall where the may in terns of left versus right tilt, that critical legal studies might discern.

pragmatism.[73] These lists overlooked the "grand style" exemplified by Chief Justice's Marshall's seminal writings.[74]

Professor Popkin (a tax professor) has ably charted in another way the shifts in courts' approaches to statutory interpretation.[75] He shows that the courts in the 1800s generally addressed statutory issues in the context of the dominance of the common law; statutes ordinarily were not viewed as creating systems of laws so much as remedies for defects in the common law.[76] The courts' view of statutes shifted roughly during the period 1900-1960 because (1) the dominance of the common law was waning,[77] (2) statutes were becoming more numerous and important to the industrialized society, (3) legislatures were viewed as more competent to enact needed laws in general, (4) the New Deal Congresses in particular were viewed positively, and (5) the federal courts in effect wanted to collaborate with Congress in carrying out its purposes.[78] After 1960 faith in legislation is thought to have waned, due perhaps to a distrust of the political process.[79] This shift is one explanation for the relative increase in judges claiming to be textualists rather than purposivists;[80] textualism actually reflects pessimism about judging as well as about legislation.[81]

I.B.1.c. *The Current Debates and Emphasis on Textualism*

There are many views of how courts work and decide cases today. For example, social scientists can show that judicial attitudes are far more likely to determine legal outcomes than legal precedents.[82] There is a view that doctrines and maxims cited by court, including particularly the Supreme Court, are just covers for decisions already made on other grounds.[83] Indeed, the faith of most lawyers in the motive force of their arguments has been called a "mass delusion."[84] Most academic discussions of statutory interpretation tend to start from premises that are largely alien to practicing lawyers (formalism or

---

[73] POSNER, at 230-65.

[74] *See* Llewellyn, *supra* note 58, at 396 (1950) (tracing how Marshall relied on principle over precedent, referred to as the Grand Style; then in the period of 1880-1910 the Formal Style depended more on precedent; thereafter the Grand Style began to creep back in).

[75] POPKIN.

[76] *Id.* at 67, 112.

[77] *Id.* at 126 (citing an important statement by Roscoe Pound in 1912 that the strict construction of statutes as in derogation of the common law was no longer appropriate).

[78] *Id.* at 115-49.

[79] *Id.* at 174.

[80] *Id.* at Part III and Ch. 5.

[81] *Id.* at 153; *see also id.* at 172 (stating that modern textualists are more concerned with limiting judging than deferring to the legislature); *id.* at 247 (summarizing the trends from common law to purposive interpretation to modern textualists who may think they have little to do as judged).

[82] *See* Cross, *New Legal Realism*, *supra* note 61, at 251.

[83] Martineau, *Craft and Technique, Not Canons and Grand Theories: A Neo-Realist View of Statutory Construction*, 62 GEO. WASH. L. REV. 1, 37 (1993).

[84] Cross, *New Legal Realism, supra* note 61, at 254.

utilitarianism, etc.). There are schools even more unusual.[85] There is a school of thought that assumes that in the hard cases the courts have to resort to the judge's own best judgment, sometimes more charitably called pragmatism.[86] One noted academic has stated that if you don't analyze tax law on a welfarist/ efficiency basis (which this book does not) you will be marginalized.[87]

In response to the increasingly strict or legalist construction of statutes exhibited by the Supreme Court, the academic community has taken a great interest in statutory interpretation.[88] Profs. Sunstein and Vermeule have catalogued the state of the debate as ricocheting among three poles: reliance on text, reliance on legislative purpose as informing text, and license to fill gaps in text (or even to deviate from text) without regard to legislative purpose, based on other values.[89] The academic literature places the Supreme Court squarely in the strict construction/ purpose camp by the late 19th century.[90] Sunstein and Vermeule explain that currently courts are seen as in fact pursuing a "new textualism,"[91] while Eskridge and Frickey advocate a dynamic interpretation of statutes to update them to modern meanings and needs, rejecting formalistic reading of words original meanings and emphasis on

[85] *See, e.g.,* McCaffery, *Tax's Empire*, 85 Geo. L.J. 70 (1996) (using as a model Ronald Dworkin's work).

[86] *See, e.g.,* Cross, *Statutory Interpretive Methodologies*, 81 Notre Dame L. Rev. 1971, 1977 (2007). Dworkin styles his approach to statutory interpretation as "integrity" in Law's Empire (Harvard 1986).

[87] Bankman, *The Business Purpose Doctrine and the Sociology of Tax*, 54 SMU L. Rev. 149, 157 (2001).

[88] For a review of the academic literature, *see* Smith, *The Deliberative Stylings of Leading Tax Scholars*, 61 Tax Law. 1 (2007); Smith, *Formulaically Expressing 21st Century Supreme Court Tax Jurisprudence*, 8 Hous. Bus. & Tax J. 37 (2007).

[89] Sunstein & Vermeule, *Interpretation and Institutions*, 101 Mich. L. Rev. 885, 899-913 (2003). For other such surveys see Aleinikoff, *Updating Statutory Interpretation*, 87 Mich. L. Rev. 20 (1988). He states that Blackstone favored a so-called common law approach to statutory interpretation, which shared with the common law the characteristic of flexibility, based on seeking the lawmaker's actual or presumed purposes ("purposivism") and avoiding absurd results; but in the "hard cases" Blackstone chose to hew to formalistic law if the only other option was to "do equity" on some policy grounds divorced from the statute's words and the legislative intent. His contemporary, Bentham, espoused a more formal and utilitarian approach, with greater emphasis on codification and, where that is lacking, judicial interpretive power unrestrained by concepts like purposivism. *See also* Manning, *Textualism and the Equity of the Statute*, 101 Colum. L. Rev. 1, 7, 25 (2001) (ascribing belief in the equity of the statute to Blackstone); Cavanaugh, *supra* note 36, at 577 (also cataloguing the interpretive schools in the tax area).

[90] Manning, *supra* note 89 at 103-04. This article examines another concept, the equity of the statute. It argues that that concept is yet another judicial strain that did not survive in the United States, whose courts focused more on the intent and purpose of Congress. Manning found that focus operative in the late 19th century, but it did not mean that the Court was not focused on text.

[91] *See, e.g.,* Solimine & Walker, *The Next Word: Congressional Response to Supreme Court Statutory Decisions*, 65 Temp. L. Rev. 425, 431 (1992).

original intent, which they call practical reasoning.[92] Professor Popkin calls the current trend "pragmatic."[93]

Judge Posner takes a different view. He endorses more emphasis on the practical consequences of decisions, starting with active reimagination of what the original enactors would have done with the current case (like Blackstone),[94] but when that fails, moves on to relatively unbounded judicial rule making based on the desirability of results (like Hart). He justifies this freedom in part by the failure of Congress to legislate clearly. However, one must acknowledge that it is hard to know which is the cause and which is the effect: Congress does not legislate clearly so judges must step in, or Congress knows that judges will step in and so do not legislate clearly?

Academics long ago began to denigrate the role of the law itself in judicial decision making. That role is called "legalism," which may be viewed either aspirationally (as in the view that judges should follow the law, which academics refer to as a "normative" theory), or descriptively, as in the view that judges do follow the law (which academics refer to as a "positive" theory).[95] Judge Posner says of the legalist theory:

> Legalists acknowledge that their methods cannot close the deal every time. That is an understatement. . . . Yet the existence of a solid legalist core in judicial decision making even at the highest levels must not be overlooked. . . . The percentage [36% from 1995-2005] of the [Supreme] Court's decisions that are unanimous might seem to place an upper bound on legalism in the Court.[96]

Posner describes as fruitless the search for "legalist meta-rules" as a response to ambiguity in the law; he cites as an example the "rule" that the constitution must be strictly construed.[97] He decries such rules because they must be posited, they cannot be deduced. They represent policy choices, "and policy choices so unsatisfactory that as a result there are no consistent legalists . . . in the judiciary, as distinct from the academy, where [referring to the academy] reality does not constrain imagination."[98] Posner goes so far as to denigrate the very process by which administrators are forced to interpret the law (although addressing the parallel process applied by judges):

---

[92] Eskridge & Frickey, *Statutory Interpretation as Practical Reasoning*, 42 STAN. L. REV. 321, 321 (1990).

[93] POPKIN, at 153.

[94] But pinning down Blackstone's interpretive style is difficult. *See id.* at 19-22 (pointing out that he clearly put text ahead of "equity").

[95] POSNER, at 41 (Although Judge Posner is not an academic, he is an acute student of the academic thinking on judging, as reflected in his latest book, which discusses eight different ways of explaining why judges rule as they do, in addition to the law: attitudinal, strategic, sociological, psychological, economic, organizational, and pragmatic. (*Id.* at 19)).

[96] *Id.* at 47-50.

[97] *Id.* at 47-8.

[98] *Id.* at 48.

> . . . Interpretation is a natural, intuitive human activity. It is not rule-bound, logical or step-by-step. It is possible to *impose* a rule . . . but [t]he procedure is spurious. It might make sense if legislators or the drafters of constitutions were committed to the canons of construction, but they are not, . . . and if in addition the legalist judge-interpreter felt bound only by substantively neutral canons . . . as distinct from substantive canons. . . .[99]

In effect, Posner opposes not only meta-rules but the very process of trying to decide cases in an orderly fashion using accepted methods of fact finding and statutory interpretation and construction. In contrast, this book assumes that a step by step process is at least useful in reminding us of all available steps.

Sunstein and Vermeule believe that most of the foregoing approaches err in failing to take account of institutional needs, for example by failing to plan for second best alternatives. They come down on the side of formalism, which they define as sticking close to the surface meaning of the texts, where possible, generally avoiding purposive readings, and placing great emphasis on the institutional need to promote clarity in the law.[100] They posit that due to their institutional expertise administrative agencies may be given broader range to make law than courts.[101] On the other hand Professor Barker has written a very insightful article that reaches many of the same conclusions as this book, but concludes that interpretation of the Code must be expansive because in 1913 Congress and the People decided they wanted an expansive income tax.[102] This assumes an overarching interpretational rule, which this book shows (perhaps unfortunately) does not exist.

Thus, the grand choices laid out by academics currently appear to be formalism and textualism, purposivism, and some amalgam leaning toward formalism but striving to make the law clear with an eye to institutional needs and capabilities. An example of extreme purposivism is the Uniform Commercial Code, which contains important statements of its own purposes to be followed by all users.[103]

There is a huge disconnect between these academic debates and the conduct of the real users of judicial opinions, including principally the public and other government employees such as the Service.[104] Busy judges are going

---

[99] *Id.* at 193.

[100] Sunstein & Vermeule, *supra* note 89, at 921.

[101] *Id.* at 928.

[102] Barker, *supra* note 25, at 873-80.

[103] *See* McDonnell, *Purposive Interpretation of the Uniform Commercial Code: Some Implications for Jurisprudence*, 126 U. PA. L. REV. 795, 797-98 (1978). Even by 1978 the author was able to say that the purposive effort had failed to the significant extent that some courts would not embrace it, but remained positive on the purposive approach. *See infra* Ch.VI.B.1.d.

[104] Other federal judges, of course, are also a constituent user group, but a very small one on a relative basis. There are only about 800 Article III judges, and 1200 including senior status judges. *See* POSNER, at 60.

to do what judges do, without too much analysis of the processes that they intuitively apply. Thus, when they apply the tax specific doctrines they may be doing no more than applying some law school rule they long ago learned, such as the canon that a literal interpretation will not be adopted if the result would be an absurdity so gross as to shock the moral sense, which shock presumably derives from a sense of how the Congress' purpose would be subverted by the literal reading.[105]

I.B.2. *Contrast Interpretation of U.S. Nontax Statutes*

Different types of statutes enjoy different interpretational approaches.[106] In contrast with the Code, some other statutory regimes enjoy some overarching interpretive presumptions or rules, which either have been written into them or reflect a long tradition extending back to the common law. The tax law has come to apply a broad interpretation of income and strict construction of deductions, but there is no general direction on interpretive issues either in the Code or in Treasury regulations.[107]

Sometimes statutory regimes apply certain interpretive presumptions for reasons of public policy and legislative intent: most importantly, public policy requires that penal statutes be strictly construed against the government; legislative intent requires that statutes remedying defects in the common law be liberally construed to carry out the legislative purpose; statutes that affect commercial transactions reflect a concern with the intention of the parties. The Supreme Court has construed various parts of the federal Bankruptcy Code to maximize the coverage of the bankrupt estate and of the bankruptcy discharge, based on Congress' intent.[108] As a result, even federal tax issues decided by a Bankruptcy Court tend to go in the taxpayer's favor more frequently than when decided outside the bankruptcy process.

In contrast to the approach to taxes, an important anti-government presumption founded on Congress' purpose applies in the construction of the Sherman Antitrust Act of 1890. The statute declares illegal *every* contract in restraint of trade and *every* attempt to monopolize any part of interstate commerce. The government sought to break up such a contract and attempt to which Standard Oil and others were parties. The trial court agreed, as did the

---

[105] Murtagh, *The Role of the Courts in the Interpretation of the Internal Revenue Code*, 24 TAX LAW. 523, 524 (1970) (not referring to the doctrines).

[106] *See, e.g.*, Oei, *Context Matters: The Recharacterization of Leases in Bankruptcy and Tax Law*, 82 AM. BANKR. L.J. 635, 656 (2008).

[107] I.R.C. § 7806. "Construction of Title" is the closest provision in the Code to this proposal and it only identifies some interpretational doctrines *not* to use (no inference from Code arrangement, classification, titles). See further discussion *infra* Ch. VI.B.1.a. The Bankruptcy Code, Title 11 of the U.S. Code, also contains no rules of construction.

[108] *See, e.g.*, Kokoszka v. Belford, 417 U.S. 642 (1974) (construe property of the estate generously); Callaghan v. Reconstruction Fin. Corp., 297 U.S. 464 (1936) (strict allowance of trustee's commissions); Local Loan Co. v. Hunt, 292 U.S. 234 (1934) (precluding creditor from access to debtor's funds outside bankruptcy); Williams v. U.S. Fid. & Guar. Co., 236 U.S. 549 (1915) (discharge generously construed).

Supreme Court in *Standard Oil.*[109] But the Supreme Court took the opportunity to construe the Sherman Act to apply only to "unreasonable" restraints of trade.[110] This decision was widely criticized, but defended on the basis of Congress' purpose to adopt the common law tradition.[111] Nevertheless, just as the application of "substance over form" is episodic in the tax law, "rule of reason" is episodic in the federal law generally.[112]

As another example, the courts early adopted a nuanced approach to application of the usury statutes, which bear an important resemblance to taxing statutes. The courts construed the usury statutes strictly because they principally imposed penalties.[113] But in identifying the contract and the interest, the courts employed the liberal rules of equity to find a loan that the parties tried to obscure, as discussed in Ch. V.E.1.c., below.

Contract law has always looked to the intent of the parties. The Uniform Commercial Code[114] section 1-103 states: "The Uniform Commercial Code must be liberally construed and applied to promote its underlying purposes and policies, which are: (1) to simplify, clarify, and modernize the law governing commercial transactions; (2) to permit the continued expansion of commercial practices through custom, usage, and agreement of the parties; and (3) to make uniform the law among the various jurisdictions." But in

---

[109] The Standard Oil Co. v. United States, 221 U.S. 1 (1911); *see also* Atiyah & Summers, at 77 (citing this decision as a prime example of the American courts' tendency to take a hard and fast rule and turn it into a flexible rule as applied).

[110] The Court reasoned that the English common law enforced a similar rule where the restraint was unreasonable, thus implying a wrongful purpose; that some courts in this country had followed that view; that Congress wrote the Sherman Act in light of the context of the times and those judicial interpretations; that Congress must have contemplated the exercise of judicial discretion and restrain in enforcing the Act, because it used such broad terms (every contract), which would have been imprudent given the impossibility of forseeing the new forms contracts and monopoly attempts might take; therefore, Congress contemplated and intended the standard of reason. *See Standard Oil,* 221 U.S. at 1.

[111] Taft, The Anti-Trust Act and the Supreme Court, 114-15 (Harper 1914).

[112] *Cf.* Chicago, Burlington & Quincy Ry. Co. v. United States, 220 U.S. 559 (1911) (refusing to read a negligence requirement into the federal Safety Appliance Act making railroads liable for not having certain equipment meeting specific standards).

[113] Lake Benton First Nat. Bank v. Watt, 184 U.S. 151 (1902) (stating that federal usury statute was penal); Webb, Treatise on the Law of Usury 230 (St. Louis, The F. H. Thomas Law Book Co. 1899) (discussing rule of liberal construction to avoid finding usury); On Usury, 1 Al. L.J. 431, 433 (1870).

[114] *See generally* Breen, *Statutory Interpretation and the Lessons of Llewellyn,* 33 Loy. L.A. L. Rev. 263 (1999). Breen describes how Llewellyn wrote tools into the first drafts of the U.C.C. for interpreting the contract but not the statute, for which he proposed a "four corners" approach. He did not want resort to legislative history because he *did* want the statute to be flexible, and not bound to its original intent. The author argues for contextualism in interpreting statutes.

practice the UCC has had to back away from reliance on standards and to add formalities and more specific rules.[115]

The Sales chapter of the UCC was famously built upon principles of fair dealing in interpretation. This can be traced back to the principle of *bona fidei* (obligations of good faith) that the Roman Corpus Juris applied to most bilateral contracts:

> [In contrast to delict obligations, which were strictly enforced, the reciprocal and consensual contracts]. . . were bona fidei (obligations of good faith) . . . And these services and duties were often of such a nature that they could not be distinctly forseen or explicitly provided for in the contract. They must depend in part on custom, in part on tacit understandings, above all on the obvious requirements of fair and honorable dealings, that is on bona fides. This bona fides, this subjection to equity and reason, was an actual element in such contracts. . . .[116]

This brief review of other statutory regimes suggests that (1) codes or groups of statutes can have interpretive guides, which are usually (2) built on the well understood fundamental roles of the statutes, and (3) have some legislative imprimatur or long acceptance. As shown below, the revenue Code both has no well understood role and no clear interpretive doctrines.

I.B.3. *Contrast Other Countries*

American courts generally and historically have fallen on the substantive end of the substantive versus textual spectrum along which courts may interpret statutes. That is, United States courts exercise more interpretive discretion than our closest legal brethren in British courts, as well as the courts of many other western countries; and the Supreme Court has not heavily relied on British case law in tax.[117] Perhaps the American difference explains why the U.S. tax system has so far resisted adoption of a general anti-abuse rule (GAAR), such as many other countries' tax Codes have adopted.[118] See discussion of U.K. GAAR below.

Internationally the form versus substance dichotomy describes contrasting methods of statutory construction that tend to be true throughout a nation's legal system: the rules based, formal, literal approach of a formal system of

---

[115] Litowitz, Perspectives on the U.C.C. (Carolina Academic Press 2001); Maggs, *Karl Llewellyn's Fading Imprint on the Jurisprudence of the Uniform Commercial Code* 71 U. Colo. L. Rev. 541, 559-64 (2000).

[116] Hadley, *supra* note 64, at 255-56.

[117] *See, e.g.*, Merchant's Loan & Trust Co. v. Smietanka, 255 U.S. 509 (1921) (finding that the British income tax statutes are so different that they are quite without value in construing the tax statutes).

[118] *See* Edgar, *Building a Better GAAR,* 27 Va. Tax Rev. 833 (2008). The Treasury has suggested that the absence of a GAAR in the U.S. is attributable to the greater willingness of the U.S. courts to create judicial doctrines. *Treasury White Paper on Corporate Tax Shelters, supra* note 14, at sec. VIB. Some other countries do have such general rules. *See* Int'l Fiscal Assoc., Form and Substance in Tax Law, Vol. LXXXVIIa, 50 (Kluwer 2002).

law versus the search for reasons of substance underlying a statute where lower "content formality" and "rank formality" are accorded the statute.[119]

British courts historically have tended to read statutes in a more formalistic manner,[120] while American courts historically have tended to rely more heavily on substantive reasoning. These tendencies have been explained as logical reactions to the broader political contexts in which the two court systems have operated:

- In Britain, courts have more reason to expect that an "unfair" result of a formal reading of a statute will receive fuller attention as a matter of law reform in Parliament,[121] as assisted by interested constituencies.
- In America, that expectation is less, for a variety of reasons, which promotes the desirability of solving the problem in the courts.[122]
- It is easier for Parliament to act than for Congress to act.[123]

Thus, American judges tend to be willing to consider evidence of statutory purpose in deciding whether the words are unclear in the first place.[124] Perhaps another reason for this tendency is that American statutes tend to be incomplete upon enactment, due to the larger array of forces brought to bear on their enactment.[125] In contrast, British courts' emphasis on plain meaning is supported by these more granular considerations:

- Greater confidence that proficient drafting will invest the statute with the legislative purpose;
- Greater confidence in the ability of the legislature to remedy an unsatisfactory application of statute;
- Greater reliance by British lawyers on plain meaning as properly effecting sensible interpretation;
- Greater concern with the right of the citizen to rely on the statute;
- Less belief that the courts should override the legislature; and

---

119 *See generally* ATIYAH & SUMMERS, at 20. *See also* Cunningham & Repetti, *supra* note 17, at 23 (discussing Atiyah and Summers' observations).

120 Barker, *supra* note 25, at 828-30 (2003); *see Treasury White Paper on Corporate Tax Shelters*, *supra* note 14. This includes not relying on legislative history. *See* Commissioner v. Acker, 361 U.S. 87 (1959) (Frankfurter, J., dissenting).

121 Burgess, *Form without Substance? A Comment on Tax Avoidance and its Influence on Interpretation of Tax Statutes*, 1982 STATUTE L. REV. 87, 88 (1982) ("The traditional British approach to the problem of tax avoidance is to attack it legislatively. . .").

122 ATIYAH AND SUMMERS, at 29-30, 37, 100-01; *see* Gunn, *Some Observations on the Interpretation of the Internal Revenue Code*, 63 TAXES (CCH) 28 (1985) (reminding the tax bar to avoid wooden interpretations, in contrast with British approach).

123 Elhauge, *supra* note 66, at 2223.

124 ATIYAH AND SUMMERS, at 102 (citing as an example the dissents in United States v. Locke, 471 U.S. 84 (1985)).

125 *Id.* at 307 (*citing* POSNER, THE FEDERAL COURTS: CRISIS AND REFORM 19 (Harv. U. Press 1985)).

- The additional and unnecessary expense of determining the meaning of statutes beyond their face.[126]

Political scientists explain this difference as one of many indications that Americans distrust their government, as written deep in the Constitutional fabric through checks and balances, division of power and the like.[127] Such a view would explain the relative lack of formalism in American statutory construction as dictated by the nature of the country's traditions and institutions.[128] De Tocqueville attributed the substantial political power of American judges to their power to apply the Constitution to invalidate laws, contrasting both the French and the British systems.[129] Barker attributes the difference between the British and American approaches to a combination of factors related in part to the timing of the adoption of the income tax and the populist aspect of that movement.[130]

There also will be a linkage between a country's judicial view of agency regulations and its view of statutes: the more formal authority given to statutes the more controlling authority given to regulations and vice versa. Thus, British courts tended to impose a heavy burden on efforts to upend a regulation, whereas American courts historically asserted greater control over the regulations.[131]

But the American rule of flexibility is not solely due to substantive construction of formal rules. There are probably more rules in America that are inherently flexible, thus helping to acculturate the courts to substantive reasoning.[132] In the early 20th century, Roscoe Pound observed that American judges tended to treat statutes as general guides, a view that had wide observance.[133] Atiyah and Summers noted that John Adams, a distinguished lawyer before being president, argued against strict interpretation of statutes on the basis of a higher law of "God and Nature."[134]

In a movement associated with Justice Holmes, by the end of the 19th century law was viewed as separated from morals and religion, and more a matter of controlling statutes, no doubt aided by the more formalistic legal education then provided, and the needs of a growing economy for firm rules.[135]

---

[126] *Id.* at 104-05.

[127] *Id.* at 40.

[128] *Id.* at 41.

[129] De Tocqueville, Democracy in America Ch. 6 (Harvey C. Mansfield & Delba Winthrop, eds., Univ. Chicago Press 2000) (1835, 1840).

[130] Barker, *supra* note 25, at 832.

[131] Atiyah & Summers, at 61. However, Atiyah and Summers, writing just two and a half years after the *Chevron* opinion (discussed *infra* Ch. VI.D.), missed it, and cited the Davis treatise for the prevalent and appropriate substitution of judicial for administrative judgment in America in the 1980's.

[132] *Id.* at 75-6.

[133] *Id.* at 88 (quoting Pound, *The Scope and Purpose of Sociological Jurisprudence*, 25 Harv. L. Rev. 489, 515 (1912)).

[134] *Id.* at 234.

[135] *Id.* at 246-47.

But at the same time Holmes ushered in the intense recognition that law is what judges do,[136] which turned into legal realism.[137] Of course realism is profoundly at odds with formalism.[138] Atiyah and Summers explain that formalism was tempered in America by the views that law was an instrument of social improvement and must be practically applicable (utilitarian).[139] Unfortunately, the liberation of American law from formalism by realism and utilitarianism left it without any coherent theory of substantive law to replace formal rules.[140]

The Duke of Westminster's Case and the British GAAR. CIR v. Duke of Westminster, [1936] A.C. 1 (H.L.) is the British decision that is commonly cited for British tax literalism, and described as the classic British example of the success of a factual sham.[141] As such it is the British equivalent of the *Isham* (1873) opinion.[142]

Unfortunately such "common knowledge" is not so clear. The Duke's case was simply a fact finding case in which a divided court found the facts in a fairly ordinary way. The Duke could not deduct wages paid but could deduct annuities paid and had to withhold tax on the annuities. Thus, he helped himself to a deduction by reformatting his wage payments as annuity payments. He won because the servants were *entitled to the annuities whether they worked or not.* This appears to be a substantive and not just a cosmetic difference.

Subsequently in 1982 the *Ramsay* decision applied what was viewed as a more purposive approach to tax statutory interpretation,[143] by effectively reversing a strict construction of taxing provisions. Thus, the U.K. courts shifted towards a purposive reading of taxing statutes in favor of the tax collector about 50 years later than did the Supreme Court of the United States.[144]

Great Britain adopted a GAAR in 2013 as the result of a study concluded in 2011.[145] The study identified the shift to the *Ramsay* approach to statutory interpretation as one of three ways the law had addressed tax avoidance, but the study wholly failed to identify common law fact finding as another way.[146] Perhaps a reason why the Study did not list fact finding as a method of

---

[136] Holmes, *The Path of the Law*, 10 HARV. L. REV. 457, 461 (1897).

[137] *See* FRANK, LAW AND THE MODERN MIND (Brentano's 1930); POPKIN, at 144-47 (stating that the realists were supporters of collaborative purposivism by judges).

[138] ATIYAH & SUMMERS, at 255.

[139] *Id.* at 256.

[140] *Id.* at 262-63 (also noting that the most recent movement, critical legal studies, has not produced any constructive theory).

[141] *See, e.g.*, Sheppard, *China Tries a GAAR*, 123 TAX NOTES INT'L (TA) 523 (May 4, 2009).

[142] See Ch. II.B.2.a(2).

[143] Ramsay v. IRC [1982] AC 300.

[144] *See* Ch. II.B.

[145] *See* GAAR Study by Graham Aaronson QC (Nov. 11, 2011).

[146] Other ways were (1) specific statutory changes, and (2) required disclosures.

combating tax avoidance was that the courts had rejected application of step transaction analysis in tax cases.[147]

The concern with the ability of statutory interpretation to cope with tax avoidance seems to have been exacerbated by a 2011 ruling finding no way to disallow a loss claimed by a U.K. taxpayer; the loss derived from basis obtained by virtue of gain recognized by a foreign person who was not subject to U.K. tax.[148] The transaction was similar to one identified as a "listed transaction" by the Service in 2001.[149] The Study concluded that tightening of the substantive law would be inadequate or impossible, and did not discuss the possibility of regulations other than to note that regulatory efforts up to that point had caused more confusion than they helped.

The Study said an overarching principle was to limit the GAAR to schemes "which are widely regarded as intolerable," without even a hint of embarrassment at using a know-it-when-I-see-it approach. It said the GAAR would not be a rule of statutory interpretation, but rather an additional positive rule of law laid on top of the substantive rule that the taxpayer presumably satisfied,[150] which is the way the U.S. economic substance doctrine has turned out. The Study recommended identifying the questionable transactions by asking whether they were "abnormal."[151] It recommended against trying to apply the intent of Parliament, and instead to ask if the tax benefit achieved was a reasonable response to the choices offered by the statute. This, however, is an obfuscation of looking to Parliament's intent, which the Study said was contrary to normal British statutory interpretation that focused on the words of the statute.[152] The Study recommended against special penalties attached to assertion of the GAAR because that would encourage the revenue officials to use it as a sword rather than a shield,[153] contrary to the approach followed with the adoption of section 7701(o).

The GAAR adopted in 2013 generally follows the Study's proposal. At its heart is the definition of an abusive tax arrangement: obtaining a tax advantage was one of the main purposes of the arrangement and the arrangement was not a "reasonable course of action in relation to" the tax provisions,[154] as evidenced by "abnormal" steps and exploiting shortcomings in the statute. All three examples are based on divergence of the tax result from the economic results (gains or losses that were not economic and credits for taxes not paid).

The U.K. GAAR was motivated by a legal climate that differed substantially from the U.S. tax enforcement climate. Evidently U.K. law had been much less successful in finding factual shams, and much slower to purposively

---

[147] Study Sec. 5.6, citing Craven v. White [1989] AC 398.
[148] Mayes v. HMRC [2011] EWCA Civ 407.
[149] Notice 2001-45, 2001-2 CB 129
[150] Study Sec. 5.4.
[151] Study Sec. 5.15.
[152] Study Sec. 5.21.
[153] Study Sec. 5.48.
[154] Finance Act 2013, Chapter 29, Part 5, sec. 206 et seq.

interpret the taxing statutes. In what looks like a rush to catch up, the U.K. GAAR creates a very vague rule that depends on administrative discretion.

Ch. II. Issues of Statutory Application Unique to the Internal Revenue Code

Chapter I argued that tax should not be divorced from the more general law. But one must deal with the fact that it has been, and as a result has spawned the tax specific doctrines that seem peculiar to the interpretation of the Code. Such doctrines do not appear, at least by name, to nearly as great an extent in the case law applying other federal statutes. That absence suggests that the tax specific doctrines are hot house plants, which grew in the special environment of the tax law. This chapter aims to explore the tax environment and the peculiar reasons for special rules and what they are and should be.

II.A. Confusion About the Role of Taxation

An important reason for the growth of the tax specific doctrines is that the Code does not state a policy explaining the role of taxation in the federal system and there is no general agreement as to any such policy. The conflicting views of taxation are illustrated by the tension between the statement that there is not even a patriotic duty to increase one's taxes,[155] and the fact that the Code routinely exacts substantial penalties for even innocent understatements (in contrast, for example, with breaches of contract, for which punitive damages are unavailable),[156] and can impose jail time on recalcitrant taxpayers. The view most likely to obtain consensus support is the pragmatic one that revenue collections must be protected so the government can oper-

---

[155] United States v. Carlton, 512 U.S. 26 (1994) (O'Connor, J., concurring) (quoting Helvering v. Gregory, 69 F.2d 809, 810 (2d Cir. 1934), *aff'd*, 293 U.S. 465 (1935)).

[156] Perillo, Corbin on Contracts 59.2 (Matthew Bender).

ate.[157] The absence of other generally accepted policy likely results from the following:

- A variety of political, historical, and practical influences tend to prejudice United States taxpayers against taxation in general.[158] The principal influence is the role of the income tax in initiating a profound change in the relationship of people to government in generally, which is viewed in profoundly different ways by different interest groups.[159]
- Different types of taxes in Britain and the United States over the centuries have elicited different types of judicial interpretive presumptions, which have tended to be cited indiscriminately, without regard to source.
- The era of the New Deal and the Second World War marked a profound shift in the needs of the federal government and hence the needs for taxation, as well as deference to the federal government in matters of property regulation (of which taxes can be viewed as one example), as reflected in pro-government Supreme Court opinions.
- Subsequent lower court opinions cited those Supreme Court opinions to support tax specific doctrines, which form a judge made set of statements about the role of taxation in America, favoring the government in interpretation and fact finding.
- In contrast, some other federal codes, such as the Bankruptcy Code, employ a narrower and easier to pursue purpose (to maximize value for creditors).[160]

The absence of any generally understood or agreed upon (or congressionally mandated) role of federal taxation in the United States is a fundamental, if elusive, reason for the difficulties of Code interpretation, construction and application that this book addresses. For one example, the author has heard a very senior and knowledgeable Treasury official state publicly that taxes are impositions on the people that should not be collected unless they are stated very clearly and unambiguously, which sounds very much like *Merriam,* which the Supreme Court long ago rejected as discussed in Ch. II.B.2.c(4), below.[161] That view might be appropriate, and certainly the system could live with it if it were adopted, but there is no such view in the modern opinions of the Supreme Court. Rather the Court applies a balanced approach to taxa-

---

[157] *See, e.g.,* California Bankers Assn. v. Shultz, 416 U.S. 21 (1974) (emphasizing the long-standing importance of self-assessment).

[158] *See* Einhorn, *Tax Aversion and the Legacy of Slavery,* 2006 Tax Notes Today 113-29 (June 13, 2006); Rabushka, Taxation in Colonial America (2008); Sneed, *The Rule of Good Law and Federal Taxation,* 2 B.C. Indus. & Commercial L. Rev., 203, 204 (1960).

[159] *See* Friedman, A History of American Law 494-97 (1973); Mehrotra, *Edwin R.A. Seligman and the Beginnings of the U.S. Income Tax,* 109 Tax Notes (TA) 933 (Nov. 14, 2005) (telling the story of the struggle of the progressive economists and others for income taxation).

[160] Segal v. Rochelle, Jr., 382 U.S. 375 (1966) (an important case deciding that a bankrupt's loss carryback tax refund rights were property of the bankrupt estate).

[161] United States v. Merriam, 263 U.S. 179 (1923), *abrogated by* White v. United States, 305 U.S. 281 (1938).

tion, essaying to determine and carry out the purposes of Congress by a variety of methods including equitable fact finding tools that can look through form to substance, using step transaction theory in addition to identifying frauds.

From the Boston Tea Party to the Republican "tea parties" and other tax protestors of the 21st century, there has been ambivalence about the role of taxation in the United States. It is not surprising that this ambivalence has contributed to confusion about interpreting taxing statutes. In the early years, the government enforced taxes predominantly by seeking criminal penalties; but criminal penalties are much less likely today, because the emphasis is on collection, and with civil penalties and interest. The early approach aided in viewing taxes as burdens and penalties, and so to be strictly construed against the government. It probably did not help that early tax collectors might be individuals in various parts of the country who were contract agents to collect taxes, and that the federal government did not provide nearly as many services and benefits to individuals as it has since the New Deal. Similarly, tax statutes could not be entitled to a liberal construction because they were remedial of shortcomings in the common law; they were unknown to the common law.

But practical fiscal need has compelled the aggressive enforcement of taxes and at least rendered anti-government presumptions inconvenient if not wrong. The absence of a clear dividing line for this shift of view contributed to the confusion that still surrounds the role of taxation and the presumptions about its collection. A careful review of the history of interpretation of American tax law will indicate how this shift occurred.

II.B. The Evolution of Interpretive Presumptions

II.B.1. *Summary*

The confusion about the role of taxation in the United States is both reflected by and partly attributable to the changes that have occurred in interpretive presumptions over time.[162] The major stages in that history are as follows:

- Article 1, sec. 8 of the Constitution authorizes taxes, duties, impost and excises, and the Supreme Court has treated all of these as taxes.[163]
- The predominant early federal taxes were customs duties, and to a lesser extent stamp taxes and other excises, which generally were strictly construed against the government for reasons peculiar to those types of levies.

[162] *See generally* Likhovski, *The Lady and the Duke,* Helvering v. Gregory *and the History of Tax Avoidance Adjudication,* 25 Cardozo L. Rev. 953, 977-82 (2004) (this article refers to the Second Circuit opinion in its title).

[163] *See* Chas. C. Steward Mach. Co. v. Davis, 301 U.S. 548 (1937); Pollock v. Farmers' Loan & Trust Co., 157 U.S. 429, *modified,* 158 U.S. 601 (1895). However, it also has recognized that imposts and duties are narrower than the term taxes. United States v. IBM, 517 U.S. 843 (1996).

- In the early income tax period it was thought that an even handed regime would apply, neither construing the tax to cover intended subjects that were missed by its words or to exempt unintended subjects that were caught.
- However, during the period of intensive Supreme Court tax rulings in the late 1930's and 1940's, which amounted to almost a rewriting of the revenue laws, the Court applied various interpretive and fact finding methods that appeared to disadvantage taxpayers who attempted to reduce their taxes.
- Lower courts subsequently expanded these techniques into tax specific doctrines favoring the tax collector.
- Meanwhile strict construction of exemptions and allowances and broad interpretation of income added generally to an anti-taxpayer tilt in the application of the federal tax laws.

The interpretive presumptions, which now mostly run against the taxpayer, are part of a broader overall regime of mostly anti-taxpayer tilts in the tax law identified in Ch. I.A.4., above: increasingly heavy penalties, increased requirements that taxpayer identify questionable positions on their returns, increased limitations on tax advisors, absence of access to equity in the tax system for the taxpayer, burden of proof on the taxpayer, and presumption of correctness of the Commissioner's assessments. In the taxpayer's favor are the reviewability of factual determinations made by the Tax Court, the great flexibility in the choice of three trial court venues, with their varying routes of appeal, self reporting (and minimal audit coverage, subject to requirements to identify certain questionable positions), and ability to choose the form of transactions.

II.B.2. *History of Interpretive Presumptions About Taxes*

II.B.2.a. *Before the Income Tax Period*

II.B.2.a(1) *Overview*

Strict construction of taxing statutes against the state prevailed before the income tax period. That approach originated in British law viewing stamp taxes as "burdens" on the people and commerce, which became extended to customs duties thought to share the same character. Taxes were tolerated, but grudgingly, in the 19th century also because taxation was ratcheted up only in response to episodic national disasters (like the Civil War).[164]

It was natural later to apply the same presumptions to general internal taxes like the income tax, but the presumptions did not fit. Instead, as discussed in the next Chapter, the Supreme Court eventually construed the core term "income" broadly, which led the way to removal of any strict construction doctrine and to the application of the opposite strict construction of deduc-

[164] Barker, *supra* note 25, at 827.

tions and exemptions. The tax specific doctrines generally and the ESD in particular may be an extension of this reversal, an overreaction needed to counter the early strict construction against the government.

Even so expert an observer as Robert H. Jackson did not distinguish how different presumptions might apply to different types of taxes. In 1935 Jackson, then General Counsel of the Bureau of Internal Revenue, characterized the opinion of the Supreme Court in a stamp tax case, *Isham*,[165] as a choice for law rather than "equity" in applying the tax laws, which "has given comfort to every tax trickster since."[166] Others observed, however, that the rule of *Isham* was improperly spread from its stamp tax origin to apply to the income tax.[167] The end of *Isham* can be found in *Gregory*,[168] (discussed in Ch. III.C.3.a(1) below in detail), where the Court reduced it to standing for the doctrine that the taxpayer is allowed to intentionally decrease his taxes by legal means.

II.B.2.a(2) *Taxes as Burdens: Strict Construction of Stamp Taxes and the* Isham *Case*

Isham became a standard cite for the view that the form of the transaction controls its tax treatment.[169] It involved criminal enforcement of a Civil War stamp tax that was not paid on a note because it was not in form the note of a corporation (even though the facts showed that the corporation had its officers issue their own notes on behalf of the corporation for the purpose of evading the stamp tax). It occurred at a time when usury laws were in disrepute, at least in commercial transactions.[170] The Court said it was unnecessary to decide if the drawer was in fact acting as an agent for the corporation. "Whatever upon its face it purports to be, that it is for the purpose of ascertaining the stamp duty." The opinion admitted that the form of the note might be a device and even a fraud upon the revenue, but "if the device is carried out by the means of legal forms, it is subject to no legal censure."[171]

Isham never was proper authority for a strictly formalistic approach to tax liability generally because:

- It was a criminal case and thus the taxpayer benefited generally from the doctrine of lenity (discussed below);
- It depended on British law that was peculiar to stamp taxes;

---

[165] United States v. Isham, 84 U.S. 496 (1873).

[166] Jackson, *Equity in the Administration of Federal Taxes,* 13 TAX MAG. 641, 642 (Nov. 1935). To like effect was the observation of Rudick, *The Problem of Personal Income Tax Avoidance*, 7 LAW AND CONTEMP. PROBS. 243, 246 (1940).

[167] *See* Buck, *Income Tax Evasion and Avoidance: Some General Considerations*, 25 GEO. L.J. 863, 868-69 (1937) (analyzing subsequent Supreme Court decisions that took different courses).

[168] Gregory v. Helvering, 293 U.S. 465 (1935).

[169] *Isham*, 84 U.S. at 496.

[170] FRIEDMAN, *supra* note 159, at 476.

[171] United States v. Isham, 84 U.S. 496, 506 (1873).

- Stamp taxes were generally disliked and were viewed in America as penal and thus subject to the rule of strict construction of penal statutes;[172] and
- Applicability of the stamp tax had the unreasonable side effect of preventing enforcement of contracts or notes on which the stamp tax was not paid.

The Supreme Court in *Isham* explicitly relied upon the British doctrine[173] that taxes were to be strictly construed, referring to stamp taxes in particular.[174] The doctrine, which had early taken root in American courts, was based generally on the understanding that the stamp tax was a burden on commerce, and specifically on its potential to invalidate an unstamped document, making it unenforceable at law; also stamp taxes generally were disliked in the States.[175] A more raw explanation of the anti-tax view in *Isham* and similar cases is that the Supreme Court after the Civil War has been called "a court for the gilded age," populated by railroad lawyers and very protective of property interests.[176]

Perhaps the dislike of stamp taxes also related to their fundamental character as "indirect" taxes, in contrast with "direct" taxes such as property, inheritance and (for some purposes) income taxes. While indirect taxes were originally an improvement over direct regressive taxes such as the poll tax, they were thought to have been designed by the monarch to disguise the imposition of the tax in the form of a fee for a government service.[177] The United States had a stamp tax from 1797 until 1812, and not again until 1862, when it was adopted apologetically due to the bad odor in which stamp taxes were held as a result of the experience of the colonies with Britain.[178] Exemptions from the stamp tax were said to be for the protection of commerce and should be

---

[172] *See* Parsons, The Law of Contracts 287 (Boston, Little Brown 1864). But the strict construction of penal statutes waned. *See* Hall, *Strict or Liberal Construction of Penal Statutes*, 48 Harv. L. Rev. 748 (1935).

[173] *See also* Treat v. White, 181 U.S. 264 (1901).

[174] Burgess, *supra* note 121, at 90 ("A subject is to be taxed only upon clear words, not on the intendment or the equity of an Act.").

[175] *See* Gurr v. Scudds, (1855) 156 Eng. Rep. 798 (Exch.) (this was the cite in *Isham*, where Judge Pollock said stamp tax exemption for contracts for sales of goods should be construed in favor of taxpayers, without citation); Sadler v. Johnson, (1847) 153 Eng. Rep. 1403 (Exch.) (exemptions from the stamp law are for the protection of commerce and should be liberally construed); Harris v. Burch, (1842) 152 Eng. Rep. 249 (Exch.) (stamp act to be strictly construed); Conroy v. Warren, 3 Johns. Cas. 259 (N.Y. 1802) (concerning a similar federal stamp tax as in *Isham* and stating that the act ought not to be construed to extend beyond its clear meaning, without citation). *But cf.* Goldberg, *The Supreme Court and the Federal Income Tax Since Pearl Harbor: A Study in Trends of Decision*, 33 Iowa L. Rev. 22, 42-3 (1947) (viewing the steps taken by the check writer in *Isham* as having business significance and thus qualifying for respect under the tax law).

[176] Burns, Packing the Court ch. 6 (Penguin Press 2009).

[177] Seligman, Essays in Taxation 1-18 (Macmillan Co. 1921).

[178] Harrar, *Federal Stamp Taxes on Deeds*, 20 Taxes (CCH) 594, 595 (1942).

liberally construed.[179] The Parsons treatise, which predated *Isham*, observed that stamp taxes could be avoided by purposefully reducing the amount of an instrument to fall below the threshold for application.[180]

Probably the fact that *Isham* involved the criminal enforcement of the stamp tax weighed most heavily in favor of its strict construction as a penal statute. The government could obtain a conviction only by proving that the defendant intended to avoid the stamp tax.[181] It was pretty clear that such intent existed in *Isham*, but the taxpayer nevertheless escaped conviction.

A contemporaneous treatise on taxation did not ascribe huge significance to *Isham*.[182] Nevertheless, the opinion subsequently obtained a high profile, no doubt due to the desire of taxpayers and their advisors to cite it for their protection. *Isham* became a handy all purpose cite for construction of all taxing statutes in favor of exemption for taxpayers; even the government cited it for this view.[183] But one writer proved in 1937 that the Supreme Court had not intended *Isham* to state a principle applicable to taxation generally, as shown by contemporaneous Supreme Court cases.[184]

Eventually in 1947 the *General Motors* opinion curtailed *Isham* even in the stamp tax arena, by reversing the district court, which had relied on *Isham* to rule that corporate debt denominated as "notes" were not securities and thus not subject to the stamp tax.[185] The Second Circuit opinion did not cite *Isham*. *General Motors* later was called a landmark decision and *Isham* was distinguished as an earlier case emphasizing form in stamp taxes.[186] Also taxpayers would forbear citing *Isham* when they wanted the courts to apply legislative intent in their favor, rather than the strict words of the statute.[187]

II.B.2.a(3) *Taxes as Burdens: Customs Precedents and* Wigglesworth

Customs duties were also strictly construed against the government. Customs were much more important than the episodic stamp taxes as a revenue source

---

[179] *Sadler*, 153 Eng. Rep. at 1403 (exemptions from the stamp law are for the protection of commerce and should be liberally construed).

[180] Parsons, *supra* note 172, at 288.

[181] Burroughs, Treatise on the Law of Taxation 698-99 (New York, Baker, Voorhis & Co. 1877).

[182] *Id.*

[183] *See* March 20, 1900 opinion from Assistant General Counsel to Secretary of the Treasury, 17 Banking L.J. 276, 280 (1900).

[184] Buck, *supra* note 167, at 868-70 (also discusses the efforts of the Service to combat *Isham*, which he concluded reached fruition in *Gregory*).

[185] Gen. Motors Acceptance Corp. v. Higgins, 60 F. Supp. 979 (S.D.N.Y. 1945), *reversed by* 161 F.2d 593 (2d Cir.) (GM's attorney was Mr. Smith of *Smith v. Higgins*, discussed *infra*); *see also* Lederer v. Fid. Trust Co., 267 U.S. 17 (1925) (Holmes agreed with taxpayer for purposes of argument that *Isham* applied, but found the face of the instrument to be a corporate security under any rule.).

[186] Kronemyer, *The Stamp Tax Controversy and Commercial Bank Term Loans*, 32 Taxes (CCH) 831, 834 (1954).

[187] *See, e.g.*, Provost v. United States, 269 U.S. 443 (1926) (the argument of Charles Evans Hughes, which failed to cite *Isham* for the taxpayers).

during the entire period up to the brief Civil War income tax, and from the post-Civil War period to the 1909 and 1913 income taxes.[188] Customs are "external" revenue taxes, as contrasted with "internal" revenue taxes, and were indirect as contrasted with the constitutionally circumscribed direct taxes. Indeed the internal revenue laws (now the Code) are internal by contrast with external customs and duties.[189] Nevertheless, cases tended to lump together customs with other taxes for purposes of analysis, which contributed to the confusion of interpretational presumptions. Customs were collected by the relatively easy method of seizing the goods on which they were levied.[190] Customs were levied not only for revenue but also to protect local industries, called a protective tariff.[191]

Justice Story is responsible for statements of a strict constructionist view of customs duties, and a generous reading of their exemptions. First in 1838,[192] and then in 1842 in the much cited *Wigglesworth* opinion,[193] he stated without citation the theories that customs were burdens, and were not remedial and so should be strictly construed against the government. Thereafter the Supreme Court's customs opinions tended to cite one or the other of the

---

[188] Taxes in the United States mostly consisted only of customs duties, and yielded to "internal taxes" only three times up to and including the Civil War tax acts. *See The Internal Revenue System*, 2 Am. L. Rev. 240 et seq. (1868). First, there were various excises and a stamp tax at times from 1791 to 1802. *See* Hylton v. United States, 3 U.S. 171 (1796). Then there was a similar system from 1813 to 1818. Then in 1861 a broad revenue system was begun, with revenue collectors having broad discretion that sometimes led to abuse. 2 Am. L. Rev. at 246. The stamp tax generally made unstamped documents void, which was "repugnant" to the general law and was utilized reluctantly. *Id.* at 256.

[189] *See* Talbert, *Relief Provisions and Treasury Procedure on Appeal, in* Haig et al., The Federal Income Tax 254 (Columbia Univ. Press 1921).

[190] Burroughs, *supra* note 181, at 512.

[191] Futrell, History of American Customs Jurisprudence, Chs. 2-4 (1941).

[192] Adams v. Bancroft, 1 F. Cas. 84 (1838).

[193] United States v. Wigglesworth, 28 F. Cas. 595 (1842):

> In the first place, it is, as I conceive, a general rule in the interpretation of all statutes, levying taxes or duties upon subjects or citizens, not to extend their provisions, by implication, beyond the clear import of the language used, or to enlarge their operation so as to embrace matters, not specifically pointed out, although standing upon a close analogy. In every case, therefore, of doubt, such statutes are construed most strongly against the government, and in favor of the subjects or citizens, because burdens are not to be imposed, nor presumed to be imposed, beyond what the statutes expressly and clearly import. Revenue statutes are in no just sense either remedial laws or laws founded upon any permanent public policy, and, therefore, are not to be liberally construed.

See Burroughs, *supra* note 181, at 544 (observing that the *Wigglesworth* presumption applied only after all other indicia of congressional intent was exhausted); Elmes, A Treatise on the Law of Customs, 26 (Boston, Little Brown 1887). *See also* Bittker, *Pervasive Judicial Doctrines in the Construction of the Internal Revenue Code*, 21 How. L.J. 693 (1978) (attributing the early strict construction against the government to *Wigglesworth*, and also stating that the practice has been largely abandoned).

Story opinions for strict construction, mixing in cites to *Isham* and other stamp tax cases.[194]

The remedial statute categorization is not a familiar one today. In the 19th century, statutes were thought to be either remedial of a defect in the common law, declaratory of the common law, or penal.[195] Penal statutes were strictly construed, but remedial statutes were to be liberally construed to carry out the legislature's purpose.[196] They were also said to be *pro bono publico*.[197] Remedial statutes were thought to be outside the common law and in the nature of equity, and so in order to cure the problem the legislature intended to remedy, remedial statutes can be applied beyond their strict literal meaning.[198] There also was a concept of strictly construing a statute thought to be in derogation of the common law.[199] In England, taxing statutes were neither penal nor for the public good nor remedial, so taxes were viewed as burdens on the public that must be clear to be due.[200]

But Story did not seem to go as far as the English in finding taxes burdens to be strictly construed. An even earlier opinion by Story strongly suggests that he did not have such a negative view of customs duties. In 1832, Justice Story in the *Breed* opinion stated that tariff and revenue acts are neither penal (which would require strict construction) nor are they remedial (which would require liberal construction).[201] Rather, Story said they are to be construed according to their true import and meaning of their terms, as was usual in the search for legislative intent. He stated that the Court would not strain to tax

---

[194] *See* Hartranft v. Wiegmann, 121 U.S. 609 (1887) (stating that doubts should be resolved against a customs tax) (citing Powers v. Barney, 19 F. Cas. 1234 (1863) (no. 11,361) (customs case, no citation)); United States v. Isham, 84 U.S. 496, 504 (1873); Gurr v. Scudds, (1855) 156 Eng. Rep. 798 (Exch.); *Adams*, 1 F. Cas. at 84 (customs decision by Story, customs are a burden, no cite); Am. Net & Twine Co. v. Worthington, 141 U.S. 468 (1891) (citing both stamp and customs cases).

[195] *See* WEBB, *supra* note 113, at 257; BLACKSTONE, COMMENTARIES ON THE LAWS OF ENGLAND 86 (Oxford 1765); DWARRIS, GENERAL TREATISE ON STATUTES AND THEIR RULES OF CONSTRUCTION, 58-9 (Philadelphia, J.S. Littell 1835).

[196] POPKIN, at 18-9 (a remedial statute would be extended; a statute in derogation of the common law would be limited to its text). But even a remedial tax provision (payment of tax on refunds) was not construed to relieve the taxpayer of strict compliance with the conditions for relief. Maas & Waldstein Co. v. United States, 283 U.S. 583 (1931) (a letter was not a protest).

[197] DWARRIS, *supra* note 195, at 60.

[198] *Id.*

[199] *See* Pasquantino v. United States, 544 U.S. 349 (2005) (recognizing the possible continued validity of the derogation doctrine, but finding it inapplicable where a statute speaks specifically to the issue at hand); Stone, *The Common Law in the United States*, 50 HARV. L. REV. 4, 18 (1936) ("We need to be reminded, too, that in the construction of statutes establishing administrative agencies and defining their powers there is little scope for the ancient shibboleth that a statute in derogation of the common law must be strictly construed,. . .").

[200] Stone, *supra* note 199, at 76.

[201] United States v. Breed, 24 F. Cas. 1222 (D. Mass. 1832) (No. 14638).

or strain to avoid taxing based on a belief that the case was within or without the policy of the tax.[202]

There was a contrary line of opinions on customs duties. After the Civil War several Supreme Court decisions (mostly by Justice Swayne) labeled customs duties and their enforcement rules as remedial,[203] or at least not penal and to be liberally construed.[204] In *Hodson*,[205] the Court said that whatever is implied in a statute is as much a part of it as whatever is expressed,[206] and that revenue statutes are not penal and not to be strictly construed but rather are remedial and are to be liberally construed to carry out their purposes.[207] This line of cases may be explained as addressing penalty provisions within the customs statutes,[208] or provisions to prevent fraud on the revenue.[209] Also there are other rules of interpretation peculiar to tariffs, including that if words used therein to designate particular kinds or classes of goods have a well-known signification in our trade and commerce, different from their ordinary meaning among the people, the commercial meaning is to prevail, unless Congress has clearly manifested a contrary intention; and that it is only when no commercial meaning is called for or proved, that the common meaning of the words is to be adopted.[210]

---

[202] *See also* Erhardt v. Schroeder, 155 U.S. 124 (1894) (remanding for a jury trial and stating that importer had burden of proving that imported tobacco was in a class to be taxed at a lower rate).

[203] Stockwell v. United States, 80 U.S. (13 Wall) 531 (1871).

[204] Smythe v. Fiske, 90 U.S. 374 (1874).

[205] United States v. Hodson, 77 U.S. (23 Wall) 395 (1870).

[206] *Id.* (citing United States v. Babbit, 66 U.S. (1 Black) 55 (1862), which was not a tax case and merely cited general law on statutory construction).

[207] *Id.* (citing *Cliquot's Champagne*, 70 U.S. (3. Wall) 114 (1866)). This opinion went on to explain that revenue laws, as remedial, are intended to prevent fraud and suppress public wrong and promote the public good, thus they should be interpreted to carry out the congressional purpose, citing Taylor v. United States, 44 U.S. (3 How) 197 (1845), in which Justice Story agreed with the lower court's observation that revenue laws were not to be analogized to penal laws, although they may impose penalties, but implied they were like remedial laws that prevent fraud, suppress public wrong, or effect a public good and so should be construed to carry out that purpose. The citation is to BLACKSTONE I COMMENTARIES 88 (1803), which does say remedial statutes are to be liberally construed to achieve their purpose, but does not discuss taxes. The case involved forfeiture of imports on which duties were not paid by fraud. Justice Story's brief statement is not clear and it seems that the later cases read too much into it.

[208] *See* Helvering v. Mitchell, 303 U.S. 391 (1938) (discussing double jeopardy).

[209] United States v. Stowell, 133 U.S. 1, 12 (1890) (statutes to prevent fraud on the revenue are enacted for the public good, and although they are penal, are not to be construed strictly like penal laws but are to be construed fairly and reasonably to carry out the intent of the legislature); United States v. Ryan, 284 U.S. 167 (1931) (this is the last opinion to use the fraud on the revenue principle).

[210] United States v. Stone & Downer Co., 274 U.S. 225 (1927).

II.B.2.a(4) *Taxes Not Penal*

Taxes are not penalties and so are not subject to any interpretive doctrines applicable to penalties. A tax is an enforced contribution to the costs of government; a penalty is a punishment for an unlawful act.[211]

Penalties traditionally have been applied under a "rule of lenity"[212] that is applied to the interpretation of criminal statutes.[213] Chief Justice Marshall announced what came to be called the rule of lenity as follows:

> The rule that penal laws are to be construed strictly, is perhaps not much less old than construction itself. It is founded on the tenderness of the law for the rights of individuals; and on the plain principle that the power of punishment is vested in the legislative, not in the judicial department. It is the legislature, not the Court, which is to define a crime, and ordain its punishment.[214]

The rule of lenity in criminal statutory interpretation has been recognized as a general principle in criminal tax cases, which also has waned as emphasis on text has increased.[215] Its view that citizens can plan to avoid violating stat-

---

[211] *See* United States v. Reorganized CF&I Fabricators, 518 U.S. 213 (1996) (deciding that a 100% tax penalty for underfunding a pension plan was a penalty and not a tax for bankruptcy purposes); *see also* United States v. Carlton, 512 U.S. 26 (1994) (taxes are not a promise, a penalty or a liability assumed by contract) (citing Welch v. Henry, 305 U.S. 134 (1938)).

[212] *See* United States v. Santos, 553 U.S. 507 (2008). Elhauge has made an elegant argument that two canons appropriately apply in the tax law: tax levying rules are interpreted under the rule of lenity. Elhauge, *supra* note 66, at 2208.

[213] United States v. Wiltberger, 18 U.S. (5 Wheat.) 76 (1820). John Yoo has studied Justice Marshall's plan for rationalizing the interpretation of statutes. Yoo, *Marshall's Plan: The Early Supreme Court and Statutory Interpretation*, 101 Yale L. Rev. 1607 (1992); *see also* Dwarris, *supra* note 195, at 68. Blackstone, 1 Commentaries, *supra* note 195, at 88 traces the rule of lenity back to Roman law concerning slavery; *cf.* Freund, *Interpretation of Statutes*, 65 U. Pa. L. Rev. 207, 214, 219 (1916) (lumping revenue statutes with penal statutes as strictly construed).

[214] *Wiltberger*, 18 U.S. at 76. The opinion went on to give a detailed analysis of legislative purpose:

> It is said, that notwithstanding this rule, the intention of the law maker must govern in the construction of penal, as well as other statutes. This is true. But this is not a new independent rule which subverts the old. It is a modification of the ancient maxim, and amounts to this, that though penal laws are to be construed strictly, they are not to be construed so strictly as to defeat the obvious intention of the legislature.

Id. at 95-6.

[215] E.g., Kawashima v. Holder, 132 S. Ct. 1166 (2012). *See* Johnson, *Easterday and the Inability to Pay Defense for Tax Crimes*, 124 Tax Notes (TA) 787, 795 (Aug. 24, 2009) (discussing the waxing and waning of the rule of lenity); Price, *The Rule of Lenity as a Rule of Structure*, 72 Fordham L. Rev. 885, 889, 899 (2003).

utes making particular acts criminal is still the law.[216] Sometimes the Court implies lenity without invoking the rule.[217]

However, strict construction akin to the rule of lenity does apply to taxes that are penal such as the accumulated earnings tax,[218] and estimated tax penalties.[219] In addition, the Court has directly applied the rule of lenity to an ambiguous tax statute in a civil setting whose violation could lead to a criminal sanction.[220]

II.B.2.b. *At the Beginning of the Income Tax Period: Congress' Purpose and Balanced Interpretation*

By the time of the adoption of the income tax in 1913 there was a recognition that a balanced approach to interpretation of taxing laws should be the norm.[221] Observers thought that taxes should be applied not according to their spirit but according to their terms: they should not be extended to cases Congress intended to tax but did not,[222] but taxpayers who Congress did not intend to tax should not be relieved of the tax if they were described in the statute.[223] As late as 1936 it was thought that the courts applied substance over form in favor of taxpayers "with absolute impartiality."[224] In a 1938 decision

---

[216] *See* Ratzlaf v. United States, 510 U.S. 135 (1994). Defendant knew that he had to report cash payments in excess of $10,000 and structured a $100,000 payment into multiple payments to avoid the duty. He did not know that the structuring itself was a crime. The court ruled that the government had to prove the defendant knew structuring was a crime. The general rule that people are expected to rely upon is that you can structure your way out of a violation, even if the structure is purely formal. *Id.* (citing United States v. Isham, 84 U.S. 496 (1873)). The court also referred to the common practice of making a $10,000 gift on December 31 and another on January 1 and avoiding the duty to report as a gift.

[217] United States v. Carroll, 345 U.S. 457 (1953).

[218] Ivan Allen Co. v. United States, 422 U.S. 617, 627 (1975).

[219] Commissioner v. Acker, 361 U.S. 87 (1959); *see also* Yu Cong Eng v. Trinidad, 271 U.S. 500 (1926) (applying the rule of lenity to a Phillipine tax accounting rule having penal consequences).

[220] United States v. Thompson/Center Arms Co., 504 U.S. 505, 518 & n. 10 (1992) (manufacturing a fire arm); *see also* Dean & Solan, *Tax Shelters and the Code: Navigating Between Text and Intent*, 26 Va. Tax Rev. 879, 891-92 (2007) (observing that to the extent the criminal laws are used to enforce the civil tax there could be a broader collision between the rule of lenity and the deference accorded Treasury positions); Hickman, *Of Lenity, Chevron and* KPMG, 26 Va. Tax Rev. 905, 909 (2007).

[221] *See* Bittker & Lokken, at 4.3.1 n. 3 (noting 1886 treatise commending a balanced approach).

[222] Frost, A Treatise on the Federal Income Tax Law 2-4 (Matthew Bender 1913) (citing several sources). In a telephone excise tax case, the court stated that it would not extend the tax beyond the words of the statute even though Congress may have intended it. N. Y. Tel. Co. v. Treat, 130 Fed. 340 (2d Cir. 1904).

[223] *See also* Braunstein v. Commissioner, 374 U.S. 65 (1963) (holding that Congress could have reasonably written a mechanical, and sometimes over inclusive, definition of collapsible corporation, which caught a case where there was no effort to convert ordinary income to capital gains).

[224] Layman, *Some Suggestions for Reducing Income Tax Liability*, 14 Taxes (CCH) 575, 576 (1936).

regarding the exemption from the income tax for inheritances, Chief Justice Hughes made no distinction between the plenary power of Congress under the Constitution to both tax income and grant exemptions.[225] But at least one prescient observer predicted that the national need for revenue would impel a liberal construction of the income tax in favor of the government.[226]

The balanced approach had a good historical base to recommend it. Chief Justice Marshall applied a balanced approach relying on the intent of Congress in a prominent early excise tax case, *Pennington v. Coxe*.[227] Similarly in 1868 a review of internal revenue taxes stated "The Federal Courts have always construed the revenue laws liberally and in accordance with the usages of trade."[228] One justification for a balanced approach in an income tax is that many provisions do not inevitably benefit either the government or the taxpayers.[229] Another general justification is that taxes are not based on common law and therefore may contain more apparently arbitrary decisions made by Congress than in cases of statutes codifying the common law.[230]

But it is not surprising that the precedents for strict construction that had been applied to customs duties (and stamp act taxes) tended to be applied to the income tax, because customs and stamp taxes were the only taxes with which the federal government had any experience. Even the 1913 income tax was section 2 of the tariff bill entitled "An Act to Reduce Tariff Duties and to Provide Revenue for the Government and for other Purposes."[231] Statements about interpretation of tax laws by the Supreme Court in the early years of

225 Lyeth v. Hoey, 305 U.S. 188 (1938).

226 WHITE, THE FEDERAL INCOME TAX LAW 31 (Banks Law Pub. 1913).

227 Pennington v. Coxe, 6 U.S. (2 Cranch) 33 (1804). The question was whether tax that appeared to fall on sugar refining was due rather only upon shipment and not refining, contrary to the literal words of the statute. Taxpayer's counsel argued that the tax was like a penal statute that should be strictly construed. Justice Marshall did not refer to any maxim, but rather looked to the intent of the Congress and the purpose of the statute to construe it somewhat contrary to its literal reading to apply only upon shipment. This is consistent with Story's statements in *United States v. Breed*. *See* Crane, Pennington v. Coxe, *A Glimpse of the Federal Government at the End of the Federalist Era*, 23 VA. TAX REV. 417 (2003); POPKIN, at 73 (opining generally that Justice Marshall's views of statutory interpretation have "limited" significance currently).

228 *The Internal Revenue System*, *supra* note 188, at 253.

229 *See* Burnet v. Guggenheim, 288 U.S. 280, 286 (1933) ("The construction that is liberal to one taxpayer may be illiberal to others.").

230 Crane, *supra* note 227, at 466.

231 *See* FROST, *supra* note 222, at 2.

the income tax were inconsistent.[232] Although *Wigglesworth* cites persisted into the income tax period as an accepted canon of tax law construction,[233] a perusal of cites to it in the Lawyer's Edition of the Supreme Court Reports indicates that it appears considerably more often in taxpayers' briefs than in the Court's opinions.[234] As discussed in Ch. II.B.2.c(4), below, the Supreme Court specifically adopted the balanced approach in *White,* while also requiring the taxpayer to prove clear entitlement to a deduction.[235]

Perhaps in contrast with prior strict construction, the income tax was thought to reflect a presumption *for* taxation in its construction.[236] Others have observed that the adoption of the income tax coincided roughly with the beginning of the third major era of statutory construction in the United States: the grand liberal style was observed by the Court in the early years, which was replaced by a formalistic style in the late 1800's, which gave way to a more liberal style in the early 1900's.[237]

II.B.2.c. *During the Income Tax Period*

Although some careful observers still evaluate the federal tax system as pursuing a balanced approach, neither leaning for or against taxpayers,[238] there is scant room left for a balanced interpretation when taxpayers must first deal with (a) a broad interpretation of income, (b) strict construction of exemptions, allowances, deductions, nonrecognition and credits, and (c) total absence of provision for equity to be accorded to taxpayers by the Service or the courts.

---

232 The state of the law on the eve of the income tax is fairly well stated in *Eidman v. Martinez*, 184 U.S. 578 (1902), which undertook to summarize the prevailing presumptions in tax cases and did so by first relying on English cases, including stamp act cases, for the proposition that the statute was construed strictly against the state and exemptions were construed liberally in favor of the taxpayer, then recognizing the possibility of a different presumption in cases of "general" taxes, and then stating a strict construction rule for customs taxes, including a cite to United States v. Wigglesworth, 28 F. Cas. 595 (1842) (No. 44). The case at issue involved the inheritance tax. For the customs tax rule, *Eidman* cited Hartranft v. Wiegmann, 121 U.S. 609 (1887) (stating that doubts should be resolved against a customs tax and citing *Isham*). Also from *Eidman* the Court drew another statement of a presumption against extending the applicability of a tax. *See* Reinecke v. Gardner, 277 U.S. 239 (1928).

233 Black, A Treatise on Federal Taxes § 61 (Vernon Law Book Co. 1917) ("Rule of Strict Construction").

234 *See, e.g.,* McFeely v. Commissioner, 296 U.S. 102 (1935) (one of the last statements of the pro-taxpayer doctrine).

235 White v. United States, 305 U.S. 281 (1938).

236 *See* United States v. Guggenheim Exploration Co., 238 F. 231 (S.D.N.Y. 1917); *see also* Secretary of the Treasury, Notes on the Revenue Act of 1918 10 (1919) (citing *Guggenheim* as the only statement of principles of statutory construction of the income tax).

237 *See* Likhovski, *supra* note 162, at 977-82.

238 *See* Bittker & Lokken, at 4.3.1.

By 1927 Justice Holmes would say that taxes are the price of civilization,[239] a far cry from the burden view of taxes in the 19th century. The Supreme Court has always acted to protect the government's power of taxation and its importance to the nation.[240] Even the conservative Justice Sutherland said in the important 1934 decision of *Stockholms Enskilda Bank* that:

> The general object of this act is to put money into the federal treasury; and there is manifest in the reach of its many provisions an intention on the part of Congress to bring about a generous attainment of that object by imposing a tax upon pretty much every sort of income subject to the federal power.[241]

To the extent the Supreme Court may appear to have leaned more in favor of the government in the income tax period, that likely has been due to (1) the extensive role the Court was forced to play in the early years of defining fundamental aspects of the tax base and of tax accounting, which almost necessarily were pro-government, (2) the fact that the income tax increasingly became a mass tax on which the growing government more heavily depended,[242] (3) the broad definition of income the Court came to supply,[243] and (4) the now forgotten fact that the adoption of an income tax was "the opening wedge for a major transformation of American society."[244]

II.B.2.c(1) *Rejection of Pro-Taxpayer Bias*

The Supreme Court and commentators have long recognized that the tilt toward taxpayers in construing the federal tax statutes did not long survive the enactment of the income tax;[245] and a mirroring anti-taxpayer tilt in construing deductions and allowances was discovered.[246] The demise was consistent with (1) the questionable nature of the application to the U.S. in general

---

239 Compania General de Tabacos v. Collector, 275 U.S. 87, 100 (1927) (Holmes, J., dissenting).

240 *See* McCulloch v. Maryland, 17 U.S. 316 (1819) (stating that the prompt collection of the revenue and its faithful application is one of the most vital duties of government; for that reason, the taxpayer's means of disputing taxes are tightly circumscribed and interpreted); *see also* Cheatham v. United States, 92 U.S. 85 (1876) ("All governments, in all times, have found it necessary to adopt stringent measures for the collection of taxes, and to be rigid in the enforcement of them. . ." by employees of a revenue system apart from the judiciary) (citing, Nichols v. United States, 74 U.S. 122 (1868)).

241 Helvering v. Stockholms Enskilda Bank, 293 U.S. 84 (1934) (also stating but refusing to apply the pro-taxpayer presumption) (quoted in Commissioner v. Wodehouse, 337 U.S. 369, 378 (1949)).

242 *See* Paul, Prosperity, at Ch. 3.

243 *See infra* Ch. II.B.2.c(3).

244 Friedman, *supra* note 159, at 497.

245 *Cf.* Elhauge, *supra* note 66, at 2206-08 (Elhauge has assumed and applauded a pro-taxpayer canon while arguing that some such canons reflect a view on substantive law that should be resolved by the political process; he argues that canons are appropriate only when used to elicit a response from the legislature.).

246 *See* Bittker & Lokken, at 4.3.1.

and to the income tax in particular of the strict construction approach to the dissimilar British stamp taxes, as discussed above, (2) the great breadth accorded to taxing statutes generally as a matter of constitutional power,[247] (3) the Court's refusal to extend to the revenue laws the presumption of strict construction of the 16th Amendment itself (which was based on its posture as an exception to the Constitution's general prohibition against unapportioned direct taxes[248]), and (4) the eventual replacement of the statutory definition of income used in *Eisner v. Macomber*[249] based on sources with a definition based on accessions to wealth, from whatever source derived.[250]

Unfortunately, casual but usually well-informed observers miss the change. The *Sutherland Statutes and Statutory Construction* treatise still states that "courts have settled the rule that tax laws are strictly construed against the state and in favor of the taxpayer. Where there is reasonable doubt about the meaning of a revenue statute, that doubt is resolved in favor of those taxed."[251] Although the state court opinions cited for this statement may support it, the Supreme Court decisions cited do not.[252]

The broad definition of income and a strict interpretation of deductions also reflects more practical influences, including:

- Deductions tend to be easier to identify, and hence to limit, than are provisions that increase tax liability;
- The liberal construction of "income," the pivotal ambiguity in the income tax,[253] makes it harder to apply pro-taxpayer presumptions to other tax imposing parts of the statute;
- The taxing laws implicitly aspire to 100% collection, in contrast to the criminal laws role as a deterrent against criminal activity that will always exist;
- Taxpayers generally have the burden of proving their deductions and credits when contesting the Service;[254] and

---

[247] *See* Flint v. Stone Tracy Co., 220 U.S. 107 (1911) (upholding the power to levy an excise tax on the income of corporations under the broad constitutional power to tax, limited only by uniformity, which was not violated by taxing only corporations).

[248] Eisner v. Macomber, 252 U.S. 189 (1920) (stating that the 16th Amendment should not be extended by "loose construction"). However, the pro-taxpayer tilt continued in the customs cases. *See, e.g.*, Anhydrides & Chemical, Inc. v. United States, 130 F.3d 1481, 1485 (Fed. Cir. 1997) (citing United States v. Wigglesworth, 28 F. Cas. 595 (1842) (No. 44)).

[249] Eisner v. Macomber, 252 U.S. 189 (1920) (from labor or capital).

[250] *See* Commissioner v. Glenshaw Glass Co., 348 U.S. 426, 430 (1955).

[251] 3A Sutherland Statutory Construction 66:1 (7th ed.).

[252] The most recent citation is Morrissey v. Commissioner, 296 U.S. 344 (1935), which does not contain such a statement. The next cite does contain the point, but bases it on older discredited opinions. Old Colony R. Co. v. Commissioner, 284 U.S. 552 (1932). The Supreme Court has never cited *Old Colony* for this point and reached the opposite conclusion in White v. United States, 305 U.S. 281 (1938).

[253] *Id.*

[254] *See* Ch. VI.E.4 *infra*.

- Last but not least, the multitude of taxpayers who may take inconsistent positions are always pitted against a single opponent, the Service, whose views on the law can be more consistent and receive some degree of deference.[255]

When the Supreme Court addressed the prototypically ambiguous term "income" under the 16th Amendment and the Revenue Act in 1917 in *Gould*,[256] it cited *Wigglesworth* in support of excluding alimony received from taxation. But that principle of statutory construction did not last long;[257] Paul called it "moribund" in 1940.[258] Perhaps the last strong defense of

---

[255] *See* Ch. VI.D. *infra*; Hickman, *supra* note 220, at 909.

[256] Gould v. Gould, 245 U.S. 151 (1917). This was an appeal of a divorce action from the New York courts, which had decided whether the $3,000 a month payments from husband to wife would be taxable as federal income. The Supreme Court said it would not, citing the maxim that:

> In the interpretation of statutes levying taxes it is the established rule not to extend their provisions, by implication, beyond the clear import of the language used, or to enlarge their operations so as to embrace matters not specifically pointed out. In case of doubt they are construed most strongly against the government, and in favor of the citizen. (internal citations omitted).

The Court basically looked at the list following "shall include" in the statutory definition of income and did not think that alimony was of the same nature as interest and compensation, etc. The Court relied on *Gould* in *Old Colony R.R. Co. v. Commissioner*, 284 U.S. 552 (1932), and in *Hassett v. Welch*, 303 U.S. 303 (1938). Some suggest that the *Gould* concept lives and rests on the subsequently discovered theory that a statute is like a contract of adhesion, to which the taxpayers have no say in its drafting and therefore it should be construed in their favor. *See* Raby and Raby, *Substance v. Form: The Taxpayer Catch 22*, 2005 Tax Notes Today 221-41 (Nov. 17, 2005).

[257] *See* Vasquez & Lowy, *Interpreting Tax Statutes: When Are Statutory Presumptions Justified*, 4 Hous. Bus. & Tax L.J. 389, 395 (2004) (*Gould* lasted about 15 years).

[258] Paul, Studies III, at 244; *see also* Blatt, *The History of Statutory Interpretation: A Study of Form and Substance*, Cardozo L. Rev. 799, 823-26 (1985) (suggesting the change occurred two decades earlier); Bank & Stark, Business Tax Stories 27-88 (Foundation Press 2005) (tracing the decline of the taxpayer-favorable view during the 1920's and 1930's); Goldberg, *supra* note 175, at 25 (*Gould* yielded in favor of judicial legislation); Likhovski, *supra* note 162, at 102-04; Rudick, *supra* note 166, at 265 (quoting the similar phrase in *U.S. v. Merriam*, 263 U.S. 179 (1923), and stating that it had now been discarded).

Wigglesworth and *Gould* was in 1923 in *Merriam*,[259] which clearly restated the logical view that because generally there is no equitable escape from a clear taxing statute, it was only fair that some leniency be accorded taxpayers when the statute is not clear. But *Merriam* revealed its outmoded status by having to reach back to British law for support.

Nevertheless, *Merriam* cites continue to appear,[260] as do cites to other similar strict construction against the government statements of Justice Sutherland, who was the last strong proponent of that view.[261] He dissented from Holmes' opinion in *Irwin v. Gavit*,[262] in which Holmes relied on *Macomber* and the "whole text" to rule that the income beneficiary of a testamentary trust had received taxable income and not excludable property acquired by inher-

---

[259] *Merriam*, 263 U.S. at 179 (Sutherland, J., for unanimous Court). The decision was an extreme case of form controlling substance. A.G. Vanderbilt left specific bequests of cash to five relatives whom he also named as his executors. His will directed that the bequests would be in lieu of any compensation as executor or trustee. The issue was whether the bequests were gross income. The court held not because the bequests were independent of the service; that is, the heirs were to be paid in any event. The court stated:

> On behalf of the government it is urged that taxation is a practical matter and concerns itself with the substance of the thing upon which the tax is imposed rather than with legal forms or expressions. But in statutes levying taxes the literal meaning of the words employed is most important for such statutes are not to be extended by implication beyond the clear import of the language used. If the words are doubtful, the doubt must be resolved against the government and in favor of the taxpayer. The rule is stated by Lord Cairns in Partington v. Attorney General, L. R. 4 H L. 100, 122: 'I am not at all sure that in a case of this kind—a fiscal case—form is not amply sufficient; because, as I understand the principle of all fiscal legislation, it is this: If the person sought to be taxed comes within the letter of the law, he must be taxed, however great the hardship may appear to the judicial mind to be. On the other hand, if the crown, seeking to recover the tax, cannot bring the subject within the letter of the law, the subject is free, however apparently within the spirit of the law the case might otherwise appear to be. In other words, if there be admissible in any statute what is called an equitable construction, certainly such a construction is not admissible in a taxing statute, where you can simply adhere to the words of the statute.' (internal citations omitted).

[260] *See* UDI, Inc. v. United States, 532 U.S. 822, 839 (2001) (Thomas, J., concurring).

[261] *See* United States v. Galletti, 541 U.S. 114 (2004) (partner's liability is secondary) (citing United States v. Updike, 281 U.S. 489 (1930) (Sutherland, J.)) (citing Bowers v. New York & Albany Lighterage Co., 273 U.S. 346 (1927) (Butler, J.)).

[262] 268 U.S. 161 (1925).

itance,[263] uttering some of his most memorable phrases.[264] Justice Holmes stated that the pro-taxpayer policy was no reason to create or exaggerate a doubt. In dissent, Justice Sutherland also relied on the plain words of the statute and his own opinion in *Merriam*.[265]

Justice Cardozo relied on a presumption that is exactly the opposite of that of *Gould* in 1932: "Expediency [meaning the practical necessity to collect revenue] may tip the scales when arguments are nicely balanced."[266] Cardozo was right, but his view has not been enshrined as an interpretive doctrine. In 1933, Cardozo deflected the pro-taxpayer presumption in *Burnet v. Guggenheim* by noting that the construction of a statute that is pro-taxpayer in one case may be pro-government in another case.[267]

The *White* opinion in 1938 most clearly marks the Supreme Court's rejection of the taxpayer's argument for the strict construction doctrine, stating that it was the business of courts to resolve doubts correctly and not based

---

[263] Holmes cited *Macomber* for Congress' intent to tax to the fullest extent possible. At that time the predecessor of current section 102(b)(1) was the extent of the gift exclusion and it did not exclude income from gift property. Holmes reasoned that this meant that the owner of a life estate would be taxed on the income from the life estate; and the income beneficiary of a trust was in the same position as the life tenant. Holmes built on *Macomber's* ignoring of a severance in finding absence of income to find income even without severance. Perhaps more important, "the money was income in the hands of the trustee, and we know of nothing in the law that prevented its being paid and received as income by the donee." POPKIN, at 128-29 (viewing *Gavit* as straightforward interpretation rather than an overly purposive approach).

[264]

> Neither are we troubled by the question where to draw the line. That is the question in pretty much everything worth arguing in the law. . . . Day and night, youth and age are only types. But the distinction between the cases put of a gift from the corpus of the estate payable in installments and the present seems to us not hard to draw, assuming that the gift supposed would not be income. . . . It is said that the tax laws should be construed favorably for the taxpayers. But that is not a reason for creating a doubt or for exaggerating one when it is no greater than we can bring ourselves to feel in this case.

Irwin, 268 U.S. at 168.

[265]

> By the plain terms of the Revenue Act of 1913, the value of property acquired by gift, bequest, devise, or descent is not to be included in net income. Only the income derived from such property is subject to the tax. The question, as it seems to me, is really a very simple one. Money, of course, is property. The money here sought to be taxed as income was paid to respondent under the express provisions of a will. It was a gift by will—a bequest. . . It, therefore, fell within the precise letter of the statute; and, under well settled principles, judicial inquiry may go no further. The taxpayer is entitled to the rigor of the law. There is no latitude in a taxing statute; you must adhere to the very words.

United States v. Merriam, 263 U.S. 179 (1923).

[266] Woolford Realty Co. v. Rose, 286 U.S. 319 (1932).

[267] Burnet v. Guggenheim, 288 U.S. 280, 286 (1933).

on presumptions.[268] *White* actually invoked and stated the new interpretive doctrine that the taxpayer must clearly show the grounds for a deduction; this presumption continues to be cited by the courts.[269]

The need for interpretations of ambiguous taxing provisions without the thumb on the scales of *Wigglesworth* and *Gould* grew rapidly after the enactment of The Revenue Acts of 1913 and its biannual updates, which were brief on instructions. The Acts did not define income except by example and the concept of realization of income had to be worked out in the courts. Therefore, what might have initially looked like mechanical accounting issues turned out to be a morass of confusion, which the Treasury could not quell.[270] Within ten years it became apparent that a special tax court was needed due to the large number of taxpayer appeals from audits (and it was established in 1924). But in the meantime, the Revenue Acts had to be interpreted and applied and the Supreme Court took up the challenge by accepting and deciding a proportionately large volume of tax cases.

A reduced role for a pro-taxpayer presumption in interpretations may continue as to a limited number of provisions specifically designed to provide procedural relief to taxpayers.[271]

II.B.2.c(2) *The Containment of* Isham

The use of *Isham*[272] (Ch. II.B.2.a(2)) as authority for a formal construction of the income tax waned fairly quickly. *Isham* had much in common with the broader view in the common law (as contrasted with equity) that form generally controls legal outcomes because the law has provided the forms (such as the corporate form) themselves.[273] Although sporadic cites to *Isham* con-

---

[268] White v. United States, 305 U.S. 281 (1938). The strictness doctrine had begun to give way earlier. *Helvering v. Stockholms Enskilda Bank*, 293 U.S. 84 (1934), written by Sutherland, recited the often stated doctrine of strictness but explained several reasons it should not apply, amounting to the Court's conclusion that it could construe the meaning the Congress intended, at least to give expansive meaning to the term income. *See* Helvering v. Inter-Mountain Life Ins. Co., 294 U.S. 686 (1935) (recited the doctrine but did not apply it); Burnet v. Guggenheim, 288 U.S. 280, 286 (1933) (" . . . there are many facits to such a maxim."); *see also* INDOPCO, Inc. v. Commissioner, 503 U.S. 79, 84 (1992); Interstate Transit Lines v. Commissioner, 319 U.S. 590, 593 (1943); Deputy v. Du Pont, 308 U.S. 488, 493 (1940); New Colonial Ice Co. v. Helvering, 292 U.S. 435, 440 (1934); Woolford Realty Co. v. Rose, 286 U.S. 319, 326 (1932); Griswold, *An Argument Against the Doctrine that Deductions Should Be Narrowly Construed as a Matter of Legislative Grace*, 56 HARV. L. REV. 1142, 1143 (1942) (identifying *White* as the end of the strictness doctrine).

[269] *See infra* Ch. II.B.2.c(4).

[270] Confusion started even before the 1913 Act, when disputes arose between the accounting profession and the Attorney General over the use of the accrual method of accounting. *See* HAIG ET AL., *supra* note 189, at 30-4.

[271] *See, e.g.*, Bonwit Teller & Co. v. United States, 283 U.S. 258 (1931).

[272] United States v. Isham, 84 U.S. 496 (1873).

[273] *See, e.g.*, Jenkins v. Moyse, 254 N.Y. 319 (1930) (holding that an individual could incorporate his house in order to be able to borrow at a higher rate of interest through the corporation).

tinued to appear, the Supreme Court has ceased to cite it except in decisions involving the same stamp taxes.[274] The last Supreme Court tax opinion to cite *Isham* (aside from a criminal or stamp tax case) was *Gregory*, which effectively neutered it by faint praise (taxpayer can avoid tax "by means which the law permits").[275] There the Court gently transmuted *Isham* into a cite for one of *Gregory's* twin doctrines, that taxpayers have the legal right to arrange their affairs to produce the least tax. But that doctrine had a different pedigree,[276] as discussed below.

II.B.2.c(3) Eisner v. Macomber: *Substance and Form*

Any study of Supreme Court tax opinions must address in detail *Eisner v. Macomber*, the Supreme Court's seminal opinion on the 1913 act, even though it fits uncomfortably with evidence of the Court's movement away from a pro-taxpayer bias.[277] *Macomber* ruled that additional shares received by shareholders in a pro rata dividend of common stock with respect to common stock could not be taxable income to the shareholders under the 16th Amendment, even though Congress specifically made them taxable in the Revenue Act of 1916. The key points about *Eisner v. Macomber* include the following:

- It was a case of constitutional interpretation and so does not necessarily control Code interpretation.[278]
- *Macomber's* rule has been described as the now discarded source based definition of income: if the benefit does not come from labor or property owned, it cannot be income.[279]

---

[274] *See, e.g.*, United States v. Leslie Salt Co., 350 U.S. 383 (1956) (applying the same principle to a stamp tax almost 100 years later). Similarly, Justice Brandeis rejected as irrelevant the argument that the stamp tax at issue in *Isham* would not have applied if the taxpayer had used another form. Founders Gen. Corp. v. Hoey, 300 U.S. 268 (1937) (limiting *Isham* to the need for certainty in levying a stamp tax).

[275] Gregory v. Helvering, 293 U.S. 465, 469 (1935).

[276] The second case cited was *Superior Oil Co. v. Mississippi*, 280 U.S. 390 (1930), which depended on *Bullen v. Wisconsin*, 240 U.S. 625 (1916) which held that an intention to evade the tax law is not a problem so long as the taxpayer only goes close to but does not cross over the line drawn by the law.

[277] Eisner v. Macomber, 252 U.S. 189 (1920). *See generally* Kornhauser, *The Story of* Macomber*: The Continuing Legacy of Realization, in* TAX STORIES 53-96 (CARON, ed., Foundation Press 2003). Earlier attempts to define income had been unsatisfactory. *See* Gray v. Darlington, 82 U.S. 63 (1872) (finding the increase in value of a bond not to be income but to be an increase in capital; the opinion was influenced by an emphasis on the income having been earned in a single year).

[278] Wales, *Legislative Aspects of Ten Years of Federal Income Tax Opinions of the Supreme Court*, 4 TAX L. REV. 73, 77 (1949). Wales has shown that the Court was creating the common law of an income tax in the sense of a philosophy rather than interpreting a statute. He concluded that well over half of the Court's federal tax decisions from 1937 to 1948 were in this category, as contrasted with cases of more pure statutory interpretation.

[279] Barker, *supra* note 25, at 835.

- *Macomber* also was a case of fact finding in which the Court allowed the taxpayer to win by articulating and relying both on substance over form (a stock dividend did not really give the shareholder any new wealth) and form over substance (the corporation's income was not legally the shareholder's income, despite receipt of a stock dividend).
- The opinion's use of substance over form in the taxpayer's favor was not unusual in the Court's early income tax opinions,[280] but soon faded.
- The earliest Supreme Court opinions on the 1913 act that cited substance over form ideas were addressing the diffuse issue of what was income and whether it was earned before or after 1913, as contrasted with some narrow statutory rule, which shows that the substance idea was and should have been viewed as a cluster rule related to the general meaning of income.[281]
- The opinion was not an expansive reading of the income concept, and so was the antithesis of the pro-government view of income inclusion that the Court later adopted, as reflected in *Glenshaw Glass*.[282]

Gregory v. Helvering, the Supreme Court's next opinion that has attained similar prominence, did not cite *Macomber*, even though it had been viewed as a substance over form ruling, and *Gregory* has come to be viewed as a substance over form case; rather *Gregory* marked the Court's shift away from a constitutional focus to a focus on the statute, and to grappling with tax avoidance; that is, *Gregory* ruled against the taxpayer by construing the statute.

Eisner v. Macomber's opinions, both majority and dissent, in hindsight seem flawed in reasoning, but its creation of the realization requirement served a useful function in filling in a large gap in the income tax,[283] thus showing that it is not so important what the Court says as what it does.

Macomber was viewed by business interests as a victory of limited government over expansive government: the stock market rose significantly when word of the decision arrived because corporations were accustomed to

---

[280] *See, e.g.,* Helvering v. F. & R. Lazarus & Co., 308 U.S. 252 (1939); Helvering v. Tex-Penn Oil Co., 300 U.S. 481 (1937); S. Pac. Co. v. Lowe, 247 U.S. 330 (1918); Lynch v. Turrish, 247 U.S. 221 (1918) (the form of a corporate liquidation after 1913 could not mask the substance of the increase in value of the corporation as having occurred before 1913); Pollock v. Farmers' Loan & Trust Co., 157 U.S. 429, *modified,* 158 U.S. 601 (1895) (found the income tax to indirectly tax the property that produced the income); Brushaber v. Union Pacific R. Co., 240 U.S. 1 (1916) (explaining *Pollock* and that 16th Amendment made form govern).

[281] In addition to *Macomber,* see *Lynch*, 247 U.S. at 221; *Lowe*, 247 U.S. at 330. *See* further discussion *infra* Ch. VI.E.1.b(1).

[282] Commissioner v. Glenshaw Glass Co., 348 U.S. 426 (1955); *see* Bittker & Lokken, at 5.1; G.C.M. 37,354 (Dec. 21, 1977) (explains how *Glenshaw* replaced the *Macomber* income test).

[283] Bittker & Lokken, at 5.2.

enhancing their aggregate share capital values by stock dividends, much like the current use of spin-offs.[284] *Macomber's* reasoning was viewed as a thoughtful analysis of income and the timing of its taxation as an economic matter,[285] but today the reasoning is suspect due in part to the broader definition of income adopted in later cases. The public's view may have been right and the earlier praise for reasoning inaccurate, because *Macomber* actually was rooted in form over substance policy: the income of the corporation that was capitalized into the stock dividend was not the income of the shareholders because the Court respected the formal separation of shareholder and corporation; the paper certificates did not effect a movement of the corporation's income to the shareholders.

The five-to-four opinion written by Justice Pitney introduced many terms commonly used in later tax opinions:

- Because the 16th Amendment was an exception to the rule against unapportioned direct taxes, it should be *strictly construed.*
- Constitutionally speaking, income is a matter of *truth and substance* and not of form.
- Income is analogous to the *fruit from the tree* of capital.[286]
- Therefore, a dividend in form is not necessarily income in substance if it does not share the character of fruit.
- Shareholders did not economically gain from the stock dividend, which did not share the fruit-like characteristic of a *severance* from capital.[287]
- The fact that the corporation previously had earnings does not translate into shareholder income upon the stock dividend because "we

---

284 Warren, *Taxability of Stock Dividends as Income*, 33 Harv. L. Rev. 885, 886 (1920) (Warren observed that stock dividends frequently did result in an increase in the aggregate share value of the corporation, which is contrary to the theory of the *Macomber* opinion).

285 *See,* Surrey, *Supreme Court and the Federal Income Tax: Some Implication of the Recent Decisions*, 35 Ill. L. Rev. 779, 801 (1941) (stating that later income tax definition cases never matched the rigor of this decision, and the definition of income was rapidly expanded); Wales, *supra* note 278, at 75 (stating that the gross income cases illustrate the common law of taxation, and that the Court best has provided the philosophy of the definition of income and has related the substance of transactions to the purpose of the law; beyond that it should not have to decide minute points).

286 This diversion of the law of income to be based on capital likely was related to the many issues that arose concerning the 1913 cut off date for nontaxable pre-1913 income and taxable post-1913 income items, which generated the original fruit and tree distinction based on the choate nature of capital. *See* United States v. Safety Car Heating & Lighting Co., 297 U.S. 88 (1936).

287 This view may have been encouraged by a brief filed by the prominent scholar E.R.A. Seligman, *reprinted* in 9 Am. Econ. Rev. No. 3, at 517 (1919).

must treat the corporation as a substantial entity separate from the stockholders."[288]

- For the same reason, an increase in corporate value through earnings is not income to the shareholders, whether reflected in a stock dividend or not.
- Usually the market price of stock adjusts down in proportion as the number of shares is increased by a stock dividend (which may have been an erroneous assumption).
- The stock dividend is different from the shareholder's receipt of a cash dividend and exercise of an option to trade it for more stock.

Thus, *Eisner v. Macomber* looks like a substance over form ruling (no income in substance),[289] but it depended on the formal separation of the corporate entity from its shareholder. That is, the Court rejected an economic concept of the substance of what is income (increased value enjoyed by the shareholders) and adopted a legal concept, based on the respect the general law and the tax law accorded the legal separation of the shareholder from the corporation's assets and earnings.[290] Probably the decision was also motivated by the intensely practical but unstated fact that the stock dividend did not provide cash with which to pay the tax (absent sale of stock, which *would* change the shareholder's interest in the corporation).[291]

Justice Pitney did not cite his opinion in an earlier income tax case, *Southern Pacific*,[292] but used the same words "truth and substance" that he had used in that opinion (also to rule for the taxpayer in finding a corporate subsidiary to have been the agent of its shareholder, a view that the Service and courts will no longer follow). This pro-taxpayer usage of "truth and substance" did not last, save in the episodic cases like *F.& R. Lazarus* and cluster areas like debt, discussed below.

The government staked its whole case against taxpayer Macomber on the argument that Congress had the power under the 16th Amendment to tax undivided profits to the shareholders when earned by the corporation (which Pitney ruled it did not), and therefore surely it had power to tax the distribution of certificates representing those undivided profits, even though it chose at the time not to tax the undivided profits themselves.[293] The Court's rejec-

---

[288] *Cf.* Clark, Eisner v. Macomber *and Some Income Tax Problems*, 29 YALE L.J. 735, 744 (1920) (arguing that as a constitutional matter Congress could choose to tax shareholders on corporate income; but that once it chose to tax them separately, it should not at the same time treat them as a collection of individuals in order to increase taxable income).

[289] *Id.* at 841("the Supreme Court's analysis relied on its view of substance.").

[290] *Cf. id.* at 842 ("The Court . . . was not particularly interested in economic concepts of income . . . [but rather concluded] . . . that the concept of income in the statute and the Constitution was a legal concept, and not an economic or accounting concept . . .").

[291] *See Id.* at 736.

[292] S. Pac. Co. v. Lowe, 247 U.S. 330 (1918).

[293] Brief for the United States, Eisner v. Macomber 252 U.S. 189 (1920) (No. 914), *available at* http://www.law.uc.edu/taxstories/#two.

tion of this argument further proves the fundamentally form over substance grounding of the decision.

The government did not pursue a less expansive argument that was buried in its brief, stating that the reclassification of the corporation's surplus to capital, which had attended a stock dividend, "prevents the board of directors from thereafter treating them (the undivided profits) as anything but capital. . . "[294] This overlooked, now or never, argument had substantial appeal if its facts were correct, as discussed further below.

Holmes dissented even though he had written in *Towne v. Eisner*[295] that a stock dividend could not be taxed under the 1913 Revenue Act. His dissent reflected his own expansive view of Congress' power and stated that the 16th Amendment encompassed income as normally understood, which could include stock dividends. Brandeis dissented (and Holmes did not join his dissent). Analysis of his lengthy dissent is worthwhile because of (a) his great knowledge of the subject matter, and yet (b) the apparent error of his analysis.

Brandeis relied primarily on an alternate transaction analysis: that the market equated a pro rata stock dividend with a cash distribution coupled with an attractive offer to use the cash to buy more stock (as if the shareholder had a choice between two alternatives);[296] the taxpayer conceded the cash plus stock purchase would be taxable to the extent the stock was taken.[297] Then Brandeis explained how a corporation could make other taxable distributions, and could find no difference between, for example, distributing to common shareholders bonds or preferred stock as opposed to more common stock. Brandeis relied heavily on state trust law, although it seems inappo-

---

[294] *Id.* at 15-6.

[295] Towne v. Eisner, 245 U.S. 418 (1918).

[296]

> It thus appears that among financiers and investors the distribution of the stock, by whichever method effected, is called a stock dividend; that the two methods by which accumulated profits are legally retained for corporate purposes and at the same time distributed as dividends are recognized by them to be equivalents; and that the financial results to the corporation and to the stockholders of the two methods are substantially the same—unless a difference results from the application of the federal Income Tax Law. . . . If such a different result can flow merely from the difference in the method pursued, it must be because Congress is without power to tax as income of the stockholder either the stock received under the latter method or the proceeds of its sale.

Eisner v. Macomber, 252 U.S. 189, 199 (1920) (Brandeis, J., dissenting).

[297] This is the case that Pitney distinguished as involving a real choice, but Brandeis viewed it as a distinction without a difference; many later commentators have failed to see Brandeis' claim of identity. *See* Clark, *Eisner v. Macomber*, *supra* note 288, at 737 (stating that the difference is a real one, between realized and unrealized gains); Warren, *Taxability of Stock Dividends*, *supra* note 284, at 891-94.

site.[298] He also relied on the then prevalent view that treasury stock was real outstanding stock (which is not the approach of the Code today).[299] Finally, Brandeis implied that he agreed with the government's suggestion that the stock dividend was accompanied by capitalization of earnings and profits, which removed those earnings and profits from being thereafter possibly distributed as taxable dividends.[300]

---

[298] Green v. Bissell, 79 Conn. 547 (1907) (holding a stock dividend of recently repurchased treasury stock to be income for trust accounting purposes). In that case, the issue was one of defining income for trust purposes. The trust held about ¼ of the stock of a corporation that had redeemed some shares from another shareholder. The corporation distributed those shares pro rata. The opinion stated that a true stock dividend did not change the proportionate interest of the trust. However, this case was different because the stock distributed was outstanding in the hands of the corporation as treasury stock. Thus when its ownership was moved from the treasury to the shareholders their relative interests increased. And since the financial mechanics of the capitalization of surplus into capital occurred at the same time, the increase in proportionate interest constituted a distribution of the surplus.

[299] Nevertheless, the same result could be reached under current section 305 if the redemption was coupled with the dividend so as to represent the receipt of cash *treated as a section 301 distribution* by the redeemed shareholder and an increase in proportionate interest by the remaining shareholders. Brandeis did not think that change of proportionate interest had any bearing on the issue, by analogizing to the effects of a cash dividend, which long has been recognized to not give the shareholder anything he did not have before. In taking this position, Brandeis rejected the importance of segregating the dividend in the shareholder's hands. He said a new share of stock segregates value just as much as a bond would. (But this relies too much on a surprising commonality of stock and debt.) *Macomber*, 252 U.S. at 199 (Brandeis, J., dissenting). *See* Del Cotto & Wolf, *The Proportionate Interest Test of Section 305 and the Supreme Court*, 27 Tax L. Rev. 49 (1971-1972).

[300] Whether or not this was the correct view of the law then is unclear. Relatively contemporaneous commentators did not think that book surplus was prima facie the same as earnings or profits for tax purposes, but most of the questions surrounded ignoring book revaluations on the upside, not book decreases. *See* Holmes, Federal Taxes 790 (6th Ed. 1925). But Justice Holmes strongly implied in *Towne v. Eisner* that book capital and income tax capital, *i.e.* non earnings or profits, were the same: "we cannot doubt that the dividend was capital as well for the purposes of the Income Tax Law as for distribution between tenant for life and remainderman. What was said by this Court upon the latter question is equally true for the former." Towne v. Eisner, 245 U.S. 418 (1918); *see also* Doyle v. Mitchell Bros. Co., 247 U.S. 179 (1918) (treating book revaluations that were not actually written down in the accounting books as controlling for corporate income tax purposes). A contemporaneous observer stated: "Thus the surplus was capitalized. A fund out of which dividends might have been paid to the stockholders at the discretion of the directors became part of the corporate capital, and so a part of funds out of which dividends might never be paid." Warren, *Taxability of Stock Dividends*, *supra* note 284, at 885.

The Court's approach in *Macomber* bears similarities to its approach nine years earlier in *The Standard Oil* opinion.[301] Chief Justice White, who had authored The *Standard Oil* opinion, was in the majority in *Macomber*. The earlier opinion ruled that the Sherman Act did not forbid every contract in restraint of trade, even though it said that, but only unreasonable restraints of trade. White reasoned that by using such a sweeping term Congress must have intended the courts to exercise discretion to apply the term in the way it had been applied at the common law. *Macomber* took an analogous approach, similarly weakening the government's hand, and ushered in a new level of fluidity (some would call uncertainty) to the tax law.[302] But, as noted, the fluidity that favored taxpayers later transmuted into an expansive reading in favor of inclusion.

There ensued after *Macomber* a decade or more of vacillation between such purportedly economic readings and more technical but certain readings of the Revenue Acts, mostly revolving around the core definition of income, and when it was realized and recognized. The Supreme Court began to shorthand *Macomber* as the "substance over form" case.[303] The vacillation included a seeming retreat to form in both *Phellis*[304] and *Rockefeller*,[305] which ruled taxable transactions in which one corporation was divided or reincorporated (but

---

It later was resolved that earnings and profits were not reduced by a nontaxable stock dividend. *See* Helvering v. Griffiths, 318 U.S. 371 (1943) (which refused to overturn *Macomber* and stated that nontaxed stock dividends had not reduced earnings and profits); *see also* Act Oct. 3, 1917, c. 63, § 1211, 40 Stat. 338 (limiting stock dividends to decreasing pre-1913 earnings and profits); Revenue Act of 1916, 39 Stat. 756 (as amended by Act Feb. 24, 1919, c. 18, § 201(b), 40 Stat. 1059) (adding for the first time to the definition of dividend the statement that earnings and profits must have been previously "distributed" in order to be currently unavailable to support a dividend, presumably referring to distributions for tax purposes and not reclassifications for state law purposes; *cf.* Walker v. Hopkins, 12 F.2d 262 (5th Cir. 1926) (involving a 1918 dividend and assuming that prior stock dividends did not reduce earnings and profits)).

[301] Standard Oil Co. v. United States, 221 U. S. 1 (1911).

[302] Mehrotra, *The Story of the Corporate Reorganization Provisions, in* BUSINESS TAX STORIES 61 (BANK & STARK, eds., Foundation Press 2005).

[303] "In determining what constitutes income substance rather than form is to be given controlling weight." Bowers v. Kerbaugh-Empire Co., 271 U.S. 170 (1926) (citing *Macomber*, 252 U.S. at 189).

[304] United States v. Phellis, 257 U.S. 156 (1921). E.I. Du Pont effectively split off all of its operating business in a new corporation and remained in existence but inactive. It distributed shares of the new corporation pro rata to its shareholders. The Court of Claims thought the case was controlled by *Macomber* because the shareholders had no more after than before the distribution. The Supreme Court reversed because the shareholders got a severed exchangeable interest, which was in form and substance a dividend and income. *Id.*

[305] Rockefeller v. United States, 257 U.S. 176 (1921). Oil and gas corporations spun off their pipelines for business and state tax savings reasons, pro rata to shareholders. Even though the Court realized that the distribution did not produce any increase in wealth to the shareholders as a group, it was a partial realization of their stock interest because it allowed them to exchange their interest in a portion of the corporate assets. Therefore, it was income in substance, effect and form. *Id.*

not acquired), because the shareholders received a severed interest in a different asset. Arthur A. Ballantine observed at the time that the Supreme Court had been willing to investigate whether nominal income was real income in the stock dividend cases (*Macomber*), but in the *Phellis* and *Rockefeller* cases rejected such arguments and showed that the general rule is that the law is applied as written.[306]

The matter became a dispute between Holmes and Brandeis and the rest of the Court as *Cullinan v. Walker*[307] ruled in a similar case for the government, but *Weiss v. Stearn*[308] followed *Eisner* and rejected *Phellis* and *Rockefeller*, and then *Marr*[309] (involving the 1916 statute) ruled for the government. Again, observers viewed cases like *Weiss* as turning away from certainty.[310] But *Marr* confused the issue even more, and the Chief Counsel wrote in 1982 that "Attempts to steer a path among these decisions proved to be exceedingly difficult."[311] These cases involved what we now view as either reincorporations that are tax free under section 368(a)(1)(F) or corporate divisions that can be tax free and are heavily regulated by section 355. Therefore, there is little to be learned today from the period of vacillation from *Phellis* to *Marr*, particularly

---

306 Ballantine, *Nine Years of Income Tax,* N.Y. TIMES, Feb. 12, 1922, at Special Features 91.

307 Cullinan v. Walker, 262 U.S. 134 (1923). A corporation split up into two corporations, which became subsidiaries of a new holding company. The shareholders got the stock of the holding company and bonds of the subsidiaries and the old corporation liquidated. The shareholder claimed he received no income, relying on *Macomber.* The Bureau claimed he did, relying on *Phellis* and *Rockefeller*. Brandeis agreed with the Bureau both because the holding company stock was different from the old corporation's stock (form) and because the liquidation could have been done in several other ways that obviously would have been taxable (his *Macomber* dissent theory). *Id.*

308 Weiss v. Stearn, 265 U.S. 242 (1924). Holmes and Brandeis dissented. The facts were basically an early "private equity" deal in which the shareholders of the old corporation put there stock into a holding company and Eastman, Dillon & Co. put in $7.5M and got half of the holding company's stock and the old shareholders got the other half and the $7.5M. The Court ruled that they were taxable only on the cash. The Court distinguished *Phellis* and *Rockefeller* on account of the separation of less than all of the old corporation's assets. The opinion emphasized that the Court was regarding matters of substance and not mere form. *See* Mehrotra, *supra* note 302, at 71 (calling *Weiss v. Stearn* a power shift on the court).

309 Marr v. United States, 268 U.S. 536 (1925). General Motors reincorporated from New Jersey into Delaware and Marr was a shareholder who exchanged old stock for new stock. Marr relied on *Macomber* and *Weiss.* Brandeis wrote that the case was more like *Phellis, Rockefeller* and *Cullinan* because the Delaware stock was "different." *Id.*

310 Note, *Recent Supreme Court Decisions Confuse Application of Tax Law,* 2 NAT'L INCOME TAX MAG. 201 (1924) (reviewed *Weiss v. Stearn* and *United States v. Biddle-Supplee Hardware Co.*, 265 U.S. 189 (1924) and viewed them as turning away from a practice of applying the law based on the legal consequences of transactions in favor of reliance on "actual benefit" when that differed from the legal consequences. It noted the lack of standard for such rule.).

311 G.C.M. 38,838 (Apr. 19, 1982).

since the Supreme Court's decision in *Cottage Savings*, which was the subject of the Chief Counsel's reexamination of the *Marr* history.[312]

Eventually, the Court relegated *Macomber* to a minor role and adopted an expansive definition of income as reflected in *Glenshaw Glass*.[313] Nevertheless, *Macomber's* substance over form terminology stuck, to be used almost uniformly against the taxpayer in interpreting the Code. However, the Supreme Court did not, in *Macomber* or later, impose a substance over form rule generally on the finding of facts under the Code, as contrasted with finding facts for tax purposes in all of the ways common law courts find facts.

II.B.2.c(4) *Strict Construction of Exemptions, Deductions, Exclusions, Nonrecognition, Credits, and Other Allowances*

The Supreme Court ultimately adopted a principle of strict construction of those Code rules that allow a taxpayer to reduce its gross income in computing taxable income or otherwise reduce the taxes owed: exemptions, deductions, exclusions, nonrecognition, credits and other allowances. This principle acts as a comfortable, if not inevitable, partner with the expansive definition of income that the Court also adopted, largely as a matter of constitutional interpretation. The Court's tax opinions at first applied such strict construction,[314] and then announced it, as shown below. Strict construction can serve the same function as the tax specific doctrines (like the economic substance doctrine), for example in converting apparent capital gain on non-interest bearing notes into ordinary income, without resort to a substance over form theory.[315] However, strict construction of deductions, etc., is confusing because it flows from a variety of sources in the law.

Exemptions and exclusions. The earliest strictness doctrine related to exemption and exclusion from tax, because they can occur in any taxing system,

---

312 Cottage Savings Assn. v. Commissioner, 499 U.S. 554 (1991) (ruled that swapping economically identical pools of mortgages resulted in loss recognition, and explaining that a reincorporation in the same state was the same corporation, but in a different state was not). *See infra* Ch. V.F.8.

313 Commissioner v. Glenshaw Glass Co., 348 U.S. 426 (1955). *See, e.g.*, Commissioner v. Jacobson, 336 U.S. 28, 49 (1949); *see generally* BITTKER & LOKKEN, at 5.1.

314 *See, e.g.*, Deputy v. Du Pont, 308 U.S. 488 (1940). The case involved a deduction for dividends paid to the lender of stock in a short sale. The Court held the payments were not deductible as ordinary and necessary business expenses because they were not made in the taxpayer's business, but rather the business of his corporation (to whose employees he had sold the borrowed stock), and that in any event they were not ordinary as to him, and also were not interest because there was no indebtedness. The opinion did not actually speak of strictness of construction but that a clear provision for a deduction is required, rather than an equitable deduction. *Id.* at 492 (citing New Colonial Ice Co. v. Helvering, 292 U.S. 435 (1934) (holding that what would today be called a reorganization under section 368(a)(1)(D) did not constitute the new corporation as "the taxpayer" so as to be able to deduct the prior losses of the old corporation. This can be viewed as a strict construction of "taxpayer" because the transferee certainly did have many characteristics of the transferor corporation.)).

315 United States v. Midland-Ross Corp., 381 U.S. 54 (1965) (citing Commissioner v. Gillette Motor Transport, Inc., 364 U.S. 130 (1960)).

whereas deductions are more peculiar to an income tax. The strict construction of complete exemption of an item from tax,[316] and exemption of taxpayers,[317] seem to have relied on the fundamental concept that "taxes are the sole means by which sovereignties can maintain their existence . . .,"[318] and that "the whole community is interested in retaining it [the power to tax] undiminished; that community has a right to insist that its abandonment ought not to be presumed in a case to which the deliberate purpose of the state to abandon it does not appear."[319] Exclusions share the same strictness as exemptions,[320] and are more common to an income tax. A variation of the presumption is that when the law has been consistently interpreted not to exempt a type of income, a change in the law must clearly express an intent to change that approach.[321] Another variation is that when Congress enacts a tax exemption, it ordinarily does so explicitly.[322] The strict construction of exemptions can support granting *Chevron* deference to a regulation imposing the tax.[323]

There also was a related doctrine that a taxpayer claiming a "privilege" from the government of not paying a tax had to prove it clearly in the statute and

---

[316] *See, e.g.*, United States v. Stewart, 311 U.S. 60 (1940) (bond interest exemption did not include gains); Heiner v. Colonial Trust Co., 275 U.S. 232 (1927) (holding that exemptions are never lightly inferred; taxpayer was lessee of oil property from American Indians and claimed income from such property was exempt). The strict construction of exemptions continues. *See* Bingler v. Johnson, 394 U.S. 741 (1969) (scholarships).

[317] *See* Squire v. Capoeman, 351 U.S. 1 (1956) (exemptions of American Indians should be "clearly expressed"). This principle is in tension with a principle that ambiguous statutes are to be liberally construed in favor of American Indians. Chickasaw Nation v. United States, 534 U.S. 84 (2001) (no exemption from federal gaming tax).

[318] Bank of Commerce v. Tennessee, 161 U.S. 134 (1896) (involving a claimed exemption from a state tax); *see also* Yazoo and M. V. R. Co. v. Adams, 180 U.S. 1 (1901) (state property tax exemptions strictly construed); Sw. R.R. Co. v. Wright, 116 U.S. 231 (1886) (also state tax).

[319] The Del. R.R. Tax, 85 U.S. 206 (1874); Providence Bank v. Billings, 29 U.S. 514 (1830) (Chief Justice Marshall rejecting a state bank's claim that the state had impaired the obligation of its charter contract by taxing it); Proprietors of Charles River Bridge v. Proprietors of Warren Bridge, 36 U.S. 420 (1837) (applying *Billings* principle to exclusive right to operate bridge). *See also* United States v. Wells Fargo Bank, 485 U.S. 351 (1988) ("well settled principle that exemptions from taxation are not to be implied; they must be unambiguously proved"). *But see* Helvering v. Bliss, 293 U.S. 144 (1934) (stating that exemptions and reduced rates were liberalizations and should not be narrowly construed). This was probably a misapplication of that principle from the criminal law. *See* Bishop, Commentaries on the Law of Statutory Crimes § 226 (Boston, Little Brown, 1883).

[320] Commissioner v. Schleier, 515 U.S. 323 (1995); *see also* Helvering v. Canfield, 291 U.S. 163 (1934) (refusing to lightly assume a congressional purpose to exclude dividend income as from pre-1913 corporate earnings where the 1913 surplus had in fact been shrunk by subsequent corporate losses).

[321] Commissioner v. Wodehouse, 337 U.S. 369, 377 (1949).

[322] Chickasaw Nation v. United States, 534 U.S. 84, 90 (2001).

[323] *See* Mayo Found. for Med. Educ. & Research v. United States, 562 U.S. 44 (2011) (exemption of students who work in the hospital).

the statute would be construed in favor of the government.[324] Contracts of tax exemption, which is a rare bird found sometimes at the state level, also are to be read narrowly and strictly.[325]

But the strict construction of exclusions and exemptions of types of income has another source in Code jurisprudence: the broad construction of income.[326] The Court states that exemptions from income are specifically stated and should be construed with restraint in light of the same policy that broadly taxes income.[327]

Deductions. Before a presumption of strict construction of deductions could arise in the income tax, the courts had to resolve the constitutional status of deductions: whether netting is required by the constitutional concept of income.[328] Finally in 1934 the Supreme Court stated: "Unquestionably Congress has power to condition, limit or deny deductions from gross income in order to arrive at the net that it chooses to tax."[329]

Deductions (and allowances, which refers to the allowance of deductions, as in section 161) also came to be described as strictly construed.[330] Dean Griswold analyzed this development in 1942 and found that the statement was of very recent origin, specifically 1934;[331] to the extent it had earlier roots it related to the taxpayer's burden of proof;[332] and it made no more sense to strictly construe deductions than to strictly construe taxing statutes.

---

[324] Cornell v. Coyne, 192 U.S. 418 (1904) (the exemption claimed was under the Constitution). But the citations were copied in whole from *Hannibal and S. J. R. Co. v. Mo. River Packet Co.*, 125 U.S. 260 (1888) and all involved grants of licenses to erect bridges and the like by the government.

[325] Atl. Coastline R.R. Co. v. Phillips, 332 U.S. 168 (1947).

[326] Helvering v. Am. Dental Co., 318 U.S. 322 (1943) (exemption); Commissioner v. Glenshaw Glass Co., 348 U.S. 426 (1955) (broad construction of income).

[327] *See, e.g.*, Commissioner v. Schleier, 515 U.S. 323 (1995); Commissioner v. Jacobson, 336 U.S. 28, 49 (1949) (exclusions strictly construed in parallel with broadly defining income); *cf.* Murtagh, *supra* note 105, at 528 (opining based on lower court opinions that the doctrine was honored more in the breach).

[328] *See generally* Gray, *The Federal Taxing Power and the Income Tax*, 26 MINN. L. REV. 421 (1941).

[329] Helvering v. Independent Life Ins. Co., 292 U.S. 371, 381 (1934); *see also* New Colonial Ice Co. v. Helvering, 292 U.S. 435 (1934) (to same effect, decided a week later). *See* CUMMINGS, CONSTITUTION, at 395.

[330] *See, e.g.*, INDOPCO, Inc. v. Commissioner, 503 U.S. 79 (1992) (matter of grace).

[331] Griswold, *An Argument Against the Doctrine*, *supra* note 268, at 1143 (1942) (citing New Colonial Ice Co. v. Helvering, 292 U.S. 435, 440 (1934) (allowance of deduction for loss)); *see also* Deputy v. Du Pont, 308 U.S. 488, 493 (1940); White v. United States, 305 U.S. 281, 292 (1938); Helvering v. Inter-Mountain Life Ins. Co., 294 U.S. 686 (1935) (insurance company deduction for reserves); Woolford Realty Co. v. Rose, 286 U.S. 319 (1932) (involving a consolidated return group that sought to deduct pre-affiliation NOL of member from group income; the Court stated that seeking to use losses of prior year against current income required taxpayer to point to a specific allowance or fail, based on the annual accounting principle).

[332] Griswold, *An Argument Against the Doctrine*, *supra* note 268, at 1144 (citing Burnet v. Houston, 283 U.S. 223, 237 (1931)).

Despite Dean Griswold's arguments, the strict construction of deductions has continued.[333] The Court calls deductions matters of "legislative grace."[334] Capital gains preferences also are strictly construed, even though they may not involve deductions or allowances but preferential rates; the Court has said the definition of capital asset should be strictly or narrowly construed (but may have limited that to income-like property).[335] However, there is contrary dicta in earlier cases as to preferential treatment of capital gains in relation to computation of charitable contribution deductions: some opinions state a presumption of liberality as to the deduction for charitable contributions, which may not attach solely to the capital gains definitions.[336] And sometimes without citing the strictness canon, the Court also has gone out of its way to erect other barriers to deductions,[337] but not always.[338]

The structure of the Code itself fosters a strict construction of deductions, both through a series of ordering rules and direct limitations:

---

[333] *See INDOPCO*, 503 U.S. at 84; Commissioner v. Nat'l Alfalfa Dehydrating & Milling Co., 417 U.S. 134 (1974); Equitable Life Assur. Society v. Commissioner, 321 U.S. 560 (1944) (interest deduction); Interstate Transit Lines v. Commissioner, 319 U.S. 590, 593 (1943) (Held that a parent could not take a section 162 deduction for the operating deficit of its subsidiary, which it had formed and contracted with to carry on its business in a state where the parent could not legally be licensed. The Court in effect construed the statutory phrase "in carrying on any trade or business" to refer to the trade or business carried on by the subsidiary and gave no thought to the possibility that the trade or business of the parent might suffice*But cf.* Gitlitz v. Commissioner, 531 U.S. 206 (2001) (involving taxpayer reliance on both deductions and exclusions and in which the Court evidenced no interest in interpreting an ambiguous provision in favor of the government, because it found its meaning plain in the taxpayer's favor).

[334] Knight v. Commissioner, 552 U.S. 181 (2008); *Nat'l Alfalfa*, 417 U.S. at 134 (refusing to broadly construe the interest deduction); *New Colonial Ice*, 292 U.S. at 440; Deputy v. Du Pont, 308 U.S. 488 (1940) (also stating that allowance of deductions does not turn on "equitable considerations"); Helvering v. Bankline Oil Co., 303 U.S. 362 (1938). Evidently the first use of the term appeared in Bloch v. Commissioner, 16 B.T.A. 425, 430 (1929).

[335] Arkansas Best Corp. v. Commissioner, 485 U.S. 212, 220 (1988) (citing the principle but limiting it to property that represents the right to income); *see also* Massey Motors, Inc. v. United States, 364 U.S. 92 (1960) (In which the Court ruled for the government on a very contentious issue of method of computing depreciation under an ambiguous statutory term in part because the taxpayer's method converted "inflated amounts" into capital gain, contrary to Congress' intent; the intent could not have been as to the depreciation method, but rather must have been as to the capital gains preference.); Commissioner v. Gillette Motor Transport, Inc., 364 U.S. 130 (1960); Commissioner v. Brown, 380 U.S. 563, 570 (1965) (citing Corn Products Refining Co. v. Commissioner, 350 U.S. 46, 52 (1955) (which seems to have originated the statement, without clear underlying citation)).

[336] United States v. Pleasants, 305 U.S. 357 (1939); Helvering v. Bliss, 293 U.S. 144 (1934). Both cases involved the charitable deduction as determined in relation to capital gains preferences and so the statements about capital gains were dictum.

[337] *See, e.g.*, Libson Shops v. Koehler, 353 U.S. 382 (1957) (creating a "continuity of business" requirement for NOL carryovers to avoid a "windfall").

[338] Despite the government's argument for strict construction of deductions and deferral, the *Gitlitz* opinion ruled for the taxpayer and did not discuss the principle. 1999 U.S. Briefs 1295 (Lexis); Gitlitz v. Commissioner, 531 U.S. 206 (2001).

- Section 61 states what the Supreme Court has construed to be a very broad definition of income "except as otherwise provided in this subtitle."
- Section 63(a) limits deductions in computing taxable income to those "allowed by this chapter."
- Sections 64 and 65 effectively default all gain and loss to ordinary status, except for defined cases.
- Section 161 limits deductions to those specifically allowed.[339]
- Section 211 states and limits certain additional deductions for individuals.
- Section 261 precludes a group of specific deductions of a very broad nature.
- Regulation section 1.269-2 assumes Congress intends a strict construction of allowances and deductions.

Such strictness can result in a small change of facts producing a big tax result, and so appear to be arbitrary, to which arguments the Court generally responds that the taxpayer should address Congress.[340]

But the strict construction of deductions can bend to a finding of Congress' purpose to extend a deduction's availability in construing an ambiguous provision,[341] and does not extend to denying a properly interpreted deduction even when the result looks like a windfall or double deduction. Justice Douglas stated in a case of the latter type:

> But the rule that general equitable considerations do not control the measure of deductions or tax benefits cuts both ways. It is as applicable to the Government as to the taxpayer. Congress may be strict or lavish in its allowance of deductions or tax benefits. The formula it writes may be arbitrary and harsh in its applications. But where the benefit claimed by the taxpayer is fairly within the statutory language and the construction sought is in har-

---

[339] Brown v. Helvering, 291 U.S. 193 (1934). *Cf.* Ericksen, *The Common Law of Federal Taxation*, 7 U. FLA. L. REV. 178, 183 (1954) (making the observation that that the pro-taxpayer presumptions gave way due to the combined pressure of the broad definition of income and the strict construction of deductions, and attributing the directive for strict construction to Congress).

[340] Commissioner v. Kowalski, 434 U.S. 77 (1977) ("Arguments of equity have little force in construing the boundaries of exclusions and deductions from income many of which, to be administrable, must be arbitrary."); White v. United States, 305 U.S. 281 (1938) (a small liquidating distribution produces a capital loss, whereas no distribution can produce an ordinary loss); *cf.* United States v. Gilmore, 372 U.S. 39 (1963) (Court reluctant to interpret the law to create an arbitrary distinction without any rational basis).

[341] *See* Helvering v. Morgan's, Inc., 293 U.S. 121 (1934) (ruling that carryover of NOLs for two years should mean two full years and not two short years created upon the entry of the taxpayer into a consolidated group; ruling allowed by the ambiguity of the statutory definition of taxable year as meaning calendar year and including short years). The current section 441(b) curiously contains the same ambiguity, but Regulation section 1.441-1(b) undertakes to rectify it. *See infra* Ch. VI.F.9 (discussing liberality accorded to application of oil depletion allowance).

mony with the statute as an organic whole, the benefits will not be withheld from the taxpayer though they represent an unexpected windfall.[342]

Nonrecognition and deferral. The Supreme Court also has recognized the strict treatment of nonrecognition and income deferral rules,[343] which now is reflected in a regulation that presumably relied on the case law. Regulation section 1.1002-1[344] (numbered for a section that no longer exists because it was combined with section 1001) requires strict construction of nonrecognition rules:

- It applies to nonrecognition of both gains and losses, thus *not* acting as a one way rule.
- It recites and is based on the normal strict treatment of "other exceptions from a rule of taxation of general and uniform application," thus recognizing the strict construction of exemptions discussed above.
- It doubly limits nonrecognition rules: both to their words and to their "underlying assumptions and purposes of the exception" from the general rule of recognition, thus showing that Treasury can write a purpose based regulation when it chooses.
- It seems to impose a business purpose requirement for nonrecognition treatment.

---

[342] Lewyt Corp. v. Commissioner, 349 U.S. 237 (1955) (arriving at the pro-taxpayer interpretation of the statute required some effort); *see also* Helvering v. Gowran, 302 U.S. 238 (1937) (Congress' exclusion of income upon the receipt of a stock dividend went beyond that required by *Eisner v. Macomber*, but is clear and controlling despite the fact that Congress may have erroneously understood that case's meaning). However, Justice Douglas came out the exactly opposite way by rejecting general equitable considerations in United States v. Olympic Radio & Television, Inc., 349 U.S. 232 (1955) (companion to *Lewyt*).

[343] United States v. Centennial Savings Bank FSB, 499 U.S. 573, 583 (1991); *see also* Paulsen v. Commissioner, 469 U.S. 131 (1985) (stating that unlike the interpretation of the securities laws, there is no similar liberality in construing the reorganization rules requiring the Court to stretch to find that an interest in a corporation was a security qualifying for tax free receipt).

[344] Reg. § 1.1002-1(b):

> Strict construction of exceptions from general rule. The exceptions from the general rule requiring the recognition of all gains and losses, like other exceptions from a rule of taxation of general and uniform application, are strictly construed and do not extend either beyond the words or the underlying assumptions and purposes of the exception. Nonrecognition is accorded by the Code only if the exchange is one which satisfies both (1) the specific description in the Code of an excepted exchange, and (2) the underlying purpose for which such exchange is excepted from the general rule. The exchange must be germane to, and a necessary incident of, the investment or enterprise in hand. The relationship of the exchange to the venture or enterprise is always material, and the surrounding facts and circumstances must be shown. As elsewhere, the taxpayer claiming the benefit of the exception must show himself within the exception.

See also Prop. Reg. § 1.1001-6 (2009) (which continues unchanged parts of the current regulation).

- The taxpayer has the burden of proving entitlement to nonrecognition.
- It characterizes nonrecognition rules as applying to exchanges where differences are more formal than substantial, but in practice that is not true. The corner grocery store's stock may be exchanged tax free for stock of Wal-Mart in a merger, but the change is more than formal.
- The "underlying assumption of these exceptions is that the new property is substantially a continuation of the old investment still unliquidated; and, in the case of reorganizations, that the new enterprise, the new corporate structure, and the new property are substantially continuations of the old still unliquidated."[345]

This often overlooked regulation is surprising in its boldness, when contrasted with the Service's employment of the judge made doctrines (such as the economic substance doctrine) without benefit of regulations, and the failure of the Treasury to write a regulation embodying the judge made doctrines. The "germane" and "necessary incident" requirements could call into question taxpayer choices in structuring nonrecognition exchanges; and yet the Service has clearly allowed taxpayers to make alterations in transactions to move them under nonrecognition rules, with rare exceptions.[346] Indeed the Supreme Court allowed the taxpayer's bookkeeping rather than its contract to control the finding of a reorganization in *Tex-Penn Oil Co.*, discussed in Ch. VI.E.3.b. below. However, the Court made clear that failure to qualify for one nonrecognition benefit does not preclude another.[347]

Strict construction of exceptions generally. There is a less used interpretive principle that reads exceptions to general rules narrowly for the purpose of promoting the general rule as the presumed primary aim of Congress. The application of this principle does not depend on whether the party claiming the exception is receiving a tax benefit or a tax detriment. The Court applied it in *Clark* to help the taxpayer avoid the higher tax on dividends and to enjoy the preference for capital gains; it relied on a decision refusing to extend an exemption to the Fair Labor Standards Act to chain stores, which seems

---

[345] Regulations governing reorganization specifically require business purpose and contain other uncodified requirements. Reg. § 1.368-1,-2.

[346] One such exception is making a subsidiary solvent in an effort to liquidate it under section 332. Rev. Rul. 1968-602, 1968-2 C.B. 135.

[347] Helvering v. Cement Investors, Inc., 316 U.S. 527 (1942) (an early application of the later rediscovered principle that a failed reorganization can qualify for section 351 nonrecognition).

to involve a considerably more important general purpose of Congress than allowing capital gains.[348]

Other miscellaneous categories. Statutes of limitations on assessment are strictly construed in favor of the government,[349] but statutes of limitations for filing refund claims are strictly construed against the taxpayer.[350] Procedural requirements of tax refund claims against the government are strictly construed,[351] taxpayers must clearly prove any waiver of procedural requirements by the Service,[352] and refund suits are subject to equitable defenses favoring the government.[353] Waivers of sovereign immunity are strictly construed.[354] The government's tax priority in bankruptcy is accorded some liberality to carry out Congress' purpose.[355] The Supreme Court has given no indication of construing anti-abuse rules in favor of the government.[356] But in certain instances the Code gives to the Service such extensive discretion to reduce tax liability that the Supreme Court has declared it unreviewable, except for fraud.[357]

Conclusion. One empirical study concluded that the strict construction doctrines, while recited by the Supreme Court, have not actually figured

---

[348] Commissioner v. Clark, 489 U.S. 726 (1989) ("In construing provisions such as § 356, in which a general statement of policy is qualified by an exception, we usually read the exception narrowly in order to preserve the primary operation of the provision. *See* Phillips, Inc. v. Walling, 324 U.S. 490, 493 (1945) ("To extend an exemption to other than those plainly and unmistakably within its terms and spirit is to abuse the interpretative process and to frustrate the announced will of the people. Given that Congress has enacted a general rule that treats boot as capital gain, we should not eviscerate that legislative judgment through an expansive reading of a somewhat ambiguous exception.")

[349] Badaracco v. Commissioner, 464 U.S. 386 (1984); Bufferd v. Commissioner, 506 U.S. 523 (1993).

[350] Kavanagh v. Noble, 332 U.S. 535 (1947).

[351] Webre Steib Co. v. Commissioner, 324 U.S. 164 (1945).

[352] Angelus Milling Co. v. Commissioner, 325 U.S. 293 (1945). However, the Court has found implicit waiver of a procedural defense by the government. Tucker v. Alexander, 275 U.S. 228 (1927) (procedures for refunds should not be "trap for the unwary").

[353] Stone v. White, 301 U.S. 532 (1937).

[354] Ford Motor Co. v. United States, 134 S. Ct. 510 (2013); United States v. Nordic Vill. Inc., 503 U.S. 30 (1992).

[355] United States v. Marxen, 307 U.S. 200 (1939); Bruning v. United States, 376 U.S. 358 (1964) (Congress was more concerned with protecting revenue than with the bankrupt's fresh start.).

[356] The principal anti-abuse rule in the Code is section 482. *See* Commissioner v. First Sec. Bank, 405 U.S. 394 (1972) (ruling section 482 inapplicable because it would have assigned income to a taxpayer that could not legally have earned it); United States v. Bayse, 410 U.S. 441, 454 n. 13 (1973) (limiting the significance of the nonapplication in *First Security*). As discussed in Ch. III.C.3.b. *infra*, the Court's opinion in *McWilliams* can be viewed as a purposive application of an ambiguous anti-abuse section in the government's favor, but it appears to be an exception to which the Court has not returned.

[357] Heiner v. Diamond Alkali Co., 288 U.S. 502 (1933); Williamsport Wire Rope Co. v. United States, 277 U.S. 551 (1928) (ruling that the Commissioner had the power, after determining "true net income" as normally done, to reduce a corporation's excess profits tax liability so as to match the proportion of tax to net income of other similar corporations).

heavily in the Supreme Court's tax decisions.[358] Others suggest the reason for apparent lack of influence of these doctrines is that the Court applies them only when it can find no extrinsic evidence whatsoever of Congress' intent, which is the rare case.[359] One writer argues that they can serve the reasonable function of discommoding only interest groups that are more likely to be able to lobby Congress to clarify the allowances.[360]

Usually the taxpayer seeks the exclusion, deduction, nonrecognition, and the government opposes it.[361] Therefore, strict interpretation of such provisions is almost always a government argument. Properly applied, the strict construction doctrines can explain much of the tax specific doctrines discussed in Ch. V.

II.C. Intentional Tax Reduction: General Principles

A major issue of statutory application that is unique to the Code is dealing with intentional tax reduction. Chapters IV. and V. address the reactions of Congress, the Treasury, the Service and the courts to intentional tax reduction. This subchapter examines the root of the problem: the Code as written is best able to deal with taxpayers and their transactions as they occur in their natural state (that is, as they occur without reference to the tax laws).

The Code generally is written and designed to be a template to which events in the natural state can be fitted for purposes of determining their tax treatment. But taxpayers frequently plan events for tax effect, and the Service is suspicious of many such events, which leads the Service to two inevitable and appropriate reactions: (1) strict interpretation of the law that otherwise would benefit the taxpayer, and (2) suspicion of the facts asserted by taxpayers.

Facts based on the forms or labels of transactions are subject to revision through (1) application of state law methods of identifying facts that are important to tax determinations (as the mortgage in *F & R Lazarus*, for

---

358 Staudt et al., *Judging Statutes*, *supra* note 20, at 1956.

359 Murtagh, *supra* note 105, at 527.

360 Elhauge, *supra* note 66, at 2208. Evidence that Congress does respond to court decisions on tax with which it disagrees was found by Solimine & Walker, *supra* note 91, at 445 (between 1969 and 1988 Congress legislated to overrule Supreme Court decisions almost twice as often as would be statistically predicted by the proportion of tax cases to all statutory construction cases considered by the Supreme Court in that period. *See also* Shaviro, *Beyond Public Choice and Public Interest: A Study of the Legislative Process as Illustrated by Tax Legislation in the 1980s*, 139 U. PA. L. REV., 1, 55 (1990) (attributing the heightened congressional interest to interest group activity); Boyle, *The Rehnquist Court: Nineteen Years of Tax Decisions*, 25 VA. TAX REV. 451 (2005) (finding a high percentage of tax laws addressed by the Court to have been changed by Congress by or shortly after the Court's decision); Christiansen & Eskridge, *Congressional Overrides of Supreme Court Statutory Interpretation Decisions, 1967-2011*, 92 TEX. L. REV. 1317 (2013-2014). For a response in favor of the government see *Gitlitz v. Commissioner*, 531 U.S. 206 (2001), reversed by amendment of Code section 108(d)(7) in 2002.

361 The roles can be reversed, for example, when a taxpayer wants to avoid a loss nonrecognition rule, or reorganization/reincorporation treatment under *General Utilities* era law, *See* BITTKER & EUSTICE, at 12.64.

example), and (2) federal tax law fact finding methods (as in assignment of income cases, for example), which inevitably must exist because state law never wholly controls federal taxation. These special factual considerations in the federal tax law have developed in cluster areas, as discussed in Ch. VI.F.

However, as discussed in Ch. V.F. below, the lower federal courts have gone beyond fact finding and legal interpretation to create a rule of positive law that erects an additional set of requirements for the enjoyment of potentially all tax benefits (the economic substance doctrine, now partly codified in section 7701(o)). This has been the most dramatic response to the failure of the assumption that the tax law can be applied to facts in their natural state.

II.C.1. *The Natural State*

Edmond N. Cahn cogently argued in 1942 that the tax law generally can be expected to operate properly on transactions and events found in their natural states, not having been modified or fashioned due to considerations of the tax law.[362] He asserted that once the "tax motive" is introduced, taxation requires new techniques: "It can no longer classify exclusively in terms of the civil transactions of men; it must classify also in terms of itself, its own body of law, its revenue and its social aims."[363] He believed that tax planning undermines the implicit assurance of an accurate fit between events in their natural state and the prescribed tax law treatments.

It is fruitless to wish for a natural state in the income tax. Some other taxing systems may be more impervious to avoidance (a head tax being most impervious), but none is immune. Congress has made several attempts to have tax outcomes turn on the taxpayer's motive, but such efforts generally have failed to produce the desired effects: the classic example is section 269, as discussed in Ch. IV.A. below.

In 1938 Randolph Paul studied the tax avoidance case law and reached a conclusion that is still valid today: interest in the taxpayer's motive by the courts and the Service is inevitable, but does little more than create a healthy skepticism of the taxpayer's facts and legal arguments. He thought that taxpayers were less prejudiced than they claimed by the resulting uncertainty, particularly given their sole control over evidence of their own motives.[364]

Evidence of such skepticism is on clear display in the 21st century, in the treatment by the Service and the courts of the wave of tax shelter cases, in which lower federal courts have generally applied the economic substance doctrine as an uncodified GAAR. Instead they might have treated the more prominent shelters as clusters that merited particular methods of fact finding as discussed in Ch. VI.F.

---

362 Cahn, *Taxation: Some Reflections on the Quest of Substance*, 30 Geo. L. Rev. 587 (1942).

363 *Id.* at 597.

364 Paul, Studies II, at 300-04.

II.C.2. *Taxpayer Purpose*

II.C.2.a. *Permitted Intentional Tax Reduction: The Neutrality Doctrine*

It was not cases like *Isham*,[365] but rather a broader tolerance of approaching a line drawn by Congress that caused the Court to recognize taxpayers' right to intentionally reduce tax liabilities.[366] Also the Court has at times rejected interpretations of the Code that would focus on motive rather than objective evidence, as a matter of administrability.[367] Thus, despite the administrative and judicial distrust generated by evidence of taxpayer planning, there persists in the Supreme Court's opinions and other well regarded opinions a neutrality doctrine standing for the principle that taxpayers' tax reduction motives are not improper and do not necessarily preclude the desired tax outcome.[368] The Supreme Court stated in a state tax case:

> As to the astuteness of taxpayers in ordering their affairs so as to minimize taxes, we have said that "the very meaning of a line in the law is that you intentionally may go as close to it as you can if you do not pass it." *Superior Oil Co.* v. *Mississippi*, 280 U.S. 390, 395-96. This is so because "nobody owes any public duty to pay more than the law demands: taxes are enforced exactions, not voluntary contributions." Learned Hand, C. J., dissenting in *Commissioner* v. *Newman*, 159 F.2d 848, 851.[369]

A variety of Supreme Court tax decisions in the post-*Isham* era rule in favor of taxpayers who obviously fashioned their facts to produce a desired tax result, without spelling out the neutrality doctrine. Examples include:

---

[365] United States v. Isham, 84 U.S. 496 (1873) (discussed *supra* Ch. II.B.2.a(2)).

[366] See *Superior Oil Co. v. Mississippi*, 280 U.S. 390 (1930), which depended on *Bullen v. Wisconsin*, 240 U.S. 625 (1916) (intention to evade the tax law is not a problem so long as the taxpayer only goes close to but does not cross over the line drawn by the law, according to Justice Holmes).

[367] *See, e.g.*, Hernandez v. Commissioner, 490 U.S. 680 (1989) (*quid pro quo* received from Church of Scientology).

[368] Gregory v. Helvering, 293 U.S. 465 (1935) ("the motive of the taxpayer thereby to escape payment of a tax will not alter the result"); United States v. Consumer Life Ins. Co., 430 U.S. 725, 739 (1977) (even a "major motive" to reduce taxes would not vitiate an otherwise substantial transaction); *see also* Knetsch v. United States, 364 U.S. 361, 365 (1960) ("We put aside a finding by the District Court that Knetsch's only motive 'in purchasing these 10 bonds was an attempt to secure an interest deduction.'"). Judge Learned Hand stated "there is nothing sinister in so arranging one's affairs as to keep taxes as low as possible." Commissioner v. Newman, 159 F.2d 848, 850-51 (2d Cir. 1947). *See generally* Bittker & Lokken, at 4.3.2; Chirelstein, *Learned Hand's Contribution to the Law of Tax Avoidance*, 77 Yale L.J. 440 (1968); Cummings, *Quote Learned but Cite Gus*, 142 Tax Notes (TA) 993 (March 3, 2014).

[369] Atlantic Coastline R.R. Co. v. Phillips, 332 U.S. 168, 172-73 (1947). The opinion went on to emphasize that the state also could sail as close to the exemption line as possible: "This is an old canon of judicial construction. The policy on which it rests antedates the charter before us, and it forms the setting in which the exemption is to be read." *Id.* at 173 (internal citations omitted).

- *Cumberland Public Service Co.*;[370]
- *General Utilities*;[371] and
- *Cottage Savings*.[372]

The doctrine of neutrality is based on the facts that Congress did intend many tax allowances to be wholly elective by form,[373] and the Code, like all statutes, is necessarily dependent on form in the first instance, and on self reporting based on form. The neutrality doctrine also is a necessary adjunct to the fundamental values found in clear taxing laws that are equally applicable to all.[374] The neutrality doctrine's validity, or at least existence, is further supported by:

- Congress' typical approach to an abuse of a tax law through corrective legislation (for example section 465), which suggests that intent to reduce tax must be met with a rule;
- A long history of limitations in the income tax statutes on specific instances of tax planning,[375] which suggests that other planning is untouched; and
- Various examples of moving away from intent based rules to objective rules; for example, when consolidated filing was first made optional, the Commissioner had the power to require consolidation for the purpose of making an accurate distribution of tax items among the affiliated corporations, to prevent "improper manipulation" and "arbitrary shifting."[376] These standards proved too elusive and the power eventually was eliminated (adoption of consolidated filing became elective in what became section 1502 et seq., and the discretionary power of the Secretary moved into the predecessor of section 482). A similar experience occurred with section 367(a), which for a time required the Commissioner to evaluate each outbound transfer for bad purpose.

---

[370] United States v. Cumberland Pub. Serv. Co., 338 U.S. 451 (1950) (discussed *infra* Ch. VI.F.2.e).

[371] General Util. & Op. Co. v. Helvering, 296 U.S. 200 (1935).

[372] Cottage Savings Assn. v. Commissioner, 499 U.S. 554 (1991).

[373] *See, e.g.*, Rev. Rul. 1976-363, 1976-2 C.B. 90 (S corporation); Rev. Rul. 1970-238, 1970-1 C.B. 61 (Western Hemisphere trading corporation); *accord*, Lederman, *W(h)ither Economic Substance?*, 95 Iowa L. Rev. 389, 397 (2010) (arguing that the taxpayer's intent to reduce taxes is irrelevant because in many instances Congress intended to induce just such taxpayer behavior). *See generally* Bittker & Eustice, at 14.41[2][c].

[374] Smith, An Inquiry into the Nature and Causes of the Wealth of Nations V.I.2 (London, Straman & Cadeli 1776).

[375] *See, e.g.*, Meyer v. Commissioner, 383 F.2d 883 (8th Cir. 1967) (quoting several sections of the 1938 Bankruptcy Act denying exemption if the plan had for one of its principal purposes the evasion of any income tax); Revenue Act of 1913, § II(A)(2), ch. 3, 38 stat. 114, (added to the taxable income of individual his undistributed share of gains and profits of all corporations formed or fraudulently availed of for the purpose of preventing the taxation thereof through the medium of accumulating income); H.R. 3321, 63d Cong. (1913) ("being a mere holding company or accumulating earnings beyond the reasonable needs of the business shall be prima facie evidence of fraudulent purpose").

[376] Revenue Act of 1921, § 240(d), ch. 136, 42 Stat. 227.

However, when a court recites the neutrality doctrine it generally is signaling that the doctrine will not be applied in the case at hand, which reveals its weakness as a determinant of the outcome.[377] Also, there is a view amongst some commentators that tax planning is inherently evil, which view seems to be directly at odds with the Supreme Court's neutrality doctrine.[378]

So in summary, the neutrality doctrine allows taxpayers to plan into Congressionally authorized tax savings statuses, but there is confusion about the identification of such statuses, which is discussed further in Ch. V.F.7.b.

II.C.2.b. *Intentional Tax Reduction That Leads to Denial of Desired Tax Benefits*

The most debated issue in federal taxation is the location of the line between permitted intentional tax reduction and the tax reduction efforts that can lead to denial of desired tax benefits, if audited and observed and pursued by the Service. The ability of taxpayers to hope that their efforts will go undiscovered (the so-called audit lottery) has been eroded by various reporting and disclosure requirement.[379] The area is so confused that only the following points can be made with some confidence:

- Even though the cases that fall on the wrong side of the line always involve intentional tax reduction planning, the explanations for why they fail do not always depend primarily or even necessarily on taxpayer intent, and logically cannot.[380]
- The methodologies used in court opinions to rule against a taxpayer vary widely, and include not only the economic substance doctrine but also statutory interpretation, finding an absence of facts needed for the tax benefit, ignoring an entity, and applying presumptions such as strict construction.
- Several of the most important types of tax reduction activities form cluster areas around which rules have coalesced to support particular fact finding methods (see Ch. VI.F.).
- Neither Congress nor the Treasury has attempted to write any general rule in the Code or regulations to identify defective tax planning (other than the partial codification of the ESD in 2010).

---

[377] *See* Rice, *Judicial Techniques in Combating Tax Avoidance*, 51 MICH. L. REV. 1021, *passim* (1953).

[378] *See, e.g.*, Rosenberg, *Tax Avoidance and Income Measurement*, 87 MICH. L. REV. 365, 441-42 (1988) (summarizing his thesis that the tax specific doctrines are ex post justifications for punishing tax avoidance; article did not identify the economic substance doctrine); Schizer, *Frictions as a Constraint on Tax Planning*, 101 COLUM. L. REV. 1312, 1319 (2001); Weisbach, *Ten Truths about Tax Shelters*, 55 TAX L. REV. 215, 222-25 (2002).

[379] BITTKER & LOKKEN, at 111.1A. Also Reg. § 10.37 states that written advice on tax cannot take into account the fact that the taxpayer's return might not be audited.

[380] *See* Reiling, *supra* note 26, at 567 (observing that because tax reduction is a permitted motive it cannot be the determinant of the cases that fail; rather he looked for a "balance" producing uniformity of taxation across similar cases).

- However, the reporting and disclosure rules and the doctrines form a powerful combination to force many transactions that the Service thinks are suspect to the attention of the Service and support their defeat.

The intentional tax reductions that tend to be treated as improper generally involve a small but critically important group of issues and transactions: (1) deductions and losses; (2) transactions with tax indifferent persons; (3) related party transactions; (4) many forms of partnership creation, contributions to partnership, distributions from partnerships and allocations; and (5) income shifting (which can overlap other categories). As discussed in Ch. VI.F., these (and others) can be viewed as cluster areas in which rules have grown up and are properly applicable to the clusters. In 1940, Randolph Paul predicted that "some rule more definite than the broad generalization that substance, and not form, controls will eventually develop from the cases."[381] Unfortunately, there also developed the ESD, not a fact finding method but a positive requirement of law, discussed in Ch. V.F.

These five categories are reflected in Code sections and regulations that impose several rules that apply to "tax shelters," "reportable transactions," and "listed transactions," as identified by the Treasury and Service.[382] These rules require taxpayers to bring such transactions that affect their returns to the attention of the Service, require tax advisors to identify some of those transactions and employ a higher standard for giving legal opinions,[383] and impose more onerous interest and penalty rules on taxpayers found to have engaged in such transactions.[384] The definitions of reportable transactions are based on the nature of the transaction and on ancillary facts thought to be indicative of tax avoidance.[385] In addition, corporations must report "uncertain tax positions" as to which financial reserves exist.[386]The Service cumulates reportable listed transactions in Notices,[387] the most recent of which describes the following transactions by type: (1) acceleration of real deductions, (2) increased amounts of real deductions, (3) shifting income to tax indifferent persons while deductions or losses are claimed by U.S. taxpayers, (4) mischaracterization of amounts in order to produce losses, (5) creating losses through where no loss was sustained, (6) improper interpretation of favorable categories, (7) shifting income to tax indifferent parties or parties that misuse deductions, (8) other mischaracterized transactions with related parties, and (9) violating the intent of ERISA.

---

[381] Paul, Studies III, at 130.

[382] *See generally* Bittker & Lokken, at 111.1A. In addition, Regulation section 1.6011-4(b)(6) requires reporting of "transactions of interest."

[383] Bittker & Lokken, at 110.2.6.

[384] *Id.* at 114.1, 114.4.

[385] Reg. § 1.6011-4.

[386] Form 1120, Schedule UTP.

[387] Notice 2009-59, 2009-31 I.R.B. 1.

II.D. Compare Interpretation of State Tax Statutes

The main difference between state and federal tax interpretational maxims is that the federal courts long ago abandoned the 19th century view that a taxing statute should be construed in favor of the taxpayer, but many states hold onto it while construing exemptions strictly against the taxpayer as under the Code.[388]

The Supreme Court and most commentators recognized that the tilt toward taxpayers in construing the federal tax statutes did not long survive the enactment of the income tax;[389] and a mirroring anti-taxpayer tilt in construing deductions and allowances was discovered.[390] At least since 1954 writers have observed the divergence between the tendency of the federal courts to construe income broadly and deductions narrowly, and the tendency of state courts to say that they construe taxing statutes strictly against the government and in favor of the taxpayer.[391] The pro-taxpayer presumption has persisted in some states likely for two reasons: (1) the contrasting change was brought about in federal cases by the United States Supreme Court in cases involving only the federal taxes, and (2) busy state judges tended to resort to standard reference works, which up into the late 20th century continued to state generally a taxpayer favorable construction maxim for taxation. Once that is picked up in a state's tax opinions, it is hard to turn around.

Nevertheless, the issues addressed in this book generally are relevant to state tax laws.[392] The principal factors motivating other divergences between state and federal taxing statutes are (1) the lack of need in the states to produce uniformity of taxation in multiple jurisdictions having nonuniform local laws (in that regard the states are more akin to England, which did not have to accommodate its income tax to multiple states[393]), (2) the lack of need in the states to accommodate to the 16th Amendment, and (3) the much

---

388 *See, e.g.,* Director v. Medical Underwriters, 115 Haw. 180 (2007); Scott & Scott v. City of Mt. Brook, 844 So. 2d 577 (Ala. S. Ct. 2003); McLane S., Inc. v. Bridges, 84 So. 3d 479 (S. Ct. La. 2012); Michigan Bell Tel. Co. v. Dep't of Treasury, 518 N.W.2d 808 (Mich. 1994) (authority to impose tax must be clearly stated); Moore Leasing, Inc. v. Director, 869 S.W.2d 760 (Mo. 1994); Appeal of Genesis Health Clubs, 210 P.3d 663 (Kan. Ct. App. 2009); J.W. Hobbs Corp. v. Revenue Division, 268 Mich. App. 38 (Mich. Ct. App. 2005) (discussing Standard of Review and stating pro-taxpayer presumption and also stating that exemptions are construed against the taxpayer); Revenue Cabinet v. O'Daniel, 2001 KY App LEXIS 1145 (Ky. Ct. App. Nov. 9, 2001), *aff'd*, 153 S.W. 3d 815 (Ky. 2005) (lower court stated the presumption in favor of the taxpayer and higher court in effect applied it without stating it); Centric-Jones Co. v. Town of Marana, 937 P.2d 654 (Ariz. Ct. App. 1996); City of Phoenix v. Santa Anita Dev. Corp., 141 Ariz. 179 (Ariz. Ct. App. 1984).

389 *See, e.g.,* White v. United States, 305 U.S. 281 (1938); *infra* Ch. II.B.2.b.

390 *See* Bittker & Lokken, at 4.3.1; *infra* Ch. II.B.2.c.

391 *See* Ericksen, *supra* note 339, at 182-83.

392 *See generally* Glickman and Calhoun, *The "States" of the Federal Common Law Tax Doctrines*, 61 Tax Law. 1181 (2008).

393 *See* Reiling, *supra* note 26, at 565-67.

greater prevalence of other constitutional issues in state tax cases (uniformity, Commerce Clause, due process).

Despite the relative quiescence of the Supreme Court in addressing state tax interpretations as contrasted with constitutional issues, one of the more famous quotations about intentional tax reduction by Mr. Justice Holmes appears in *Bullen,* a state tax case:

> We do not speak of evasion, because, when the law draws a line, a case is on one side of it or the other, and if on the safe side is none the worse legally that a party has availed himself to the full of what the law permits. When an act is condemned as an evasion, what is meant is that it is on the wrong side of the line indicated by the policy if not by the mere letter of the law.[394]

[394] Bullen v. Wisconsin, 240 U.S. 625 (1916). Despite the statement, the decision held that a grantor in trust who had retained the power of control in effect held the fee, which could be taxed by the Wisconsin inheritance tax upon his death. *Id.* Another famous state tax decision with a similar statement is Brown v. Maryland, 25 U.S. 419 (1827) ("The power, and the restriction on it, though quite distinguishable when they do not approach each other, may yet, like the intervening colours between white and black, approach so nearly as to perplex the understanding, as colours perplex the vision in marking the distinction between them. Yet the distinction exists, and must be marked as the cases arise. Till they do arise, it might be premature to state any rule as being universal in its application.").

Ch. III. The Supreme Court and Federal Tax Laws

III.A. Restating the Rules of Application of the Code Through Focus on Supreme Court Opinions

The most authoritative and substantial body of principles for the application of the Code is the tax opinions of the Supreme Court of the United States. It created many core concepts of the income tax (income and its realization, assignment of income, the treatment of debt and basis) and of the estate and gift taxes, and has informed the meaning of numerous statutory provisions and regulations in well over 900 opinions.[395] All of those opinions impact the application of the tax laws:interpretation, construction and fact finding. Such a mass of precedent suggests the need for restatement, which Randolph Paul[396] undertook in one area in his 1937 study entitled Restatement of the Law of Tax Avoidance.[397] The restatement approach borrowed from the view of Cardozo, that:

> Of all these causes [of uncertainty in the law] the weightiest, I fancy, is the multiplication of decisions. . . . An avalanche of decisions by tribunals great and small is producing a situation where citation of precedent is tending to

---

[395] For a compilation of Supreme Court quotations on taxation, see JACKSON, THE WISDOM OF THE SUPREME COURT 433 et seq. (1962).

[396] Paul is perhaps best recognized today as the founder of Paul, Weiss, Rifkind, Wharton and Garrison LLP. The Supreme Court has cited Paul's various writings at least 14 times.

[397] PAUL, STUDIES I. For another more limited analysis of Supreme Court tax decisions, see Staudt et al., *Judging Statutes*, *supra* note 20, at 1959 (determining that over the history of the Supreme Court's federal tax cases the Court has cited policy rationales in 46% of the cases and the largest single group concerned a policy of tax avoidance concerns).

> count for less, and appeal to an informing principle is tending to count for more. . . . We shall be caught in the tentacles of the web, unless some superintending mind imparts the secret of the structure, lifting us to a height where the unity of the circle will be visible as it lies below. The perplexity of the judge becomes the scholar's opportunity.[398]

Paul's Restatement did not limit his sources to Supreme Court tax opinions, but rather had the energy and ability to survey most of the lower federal courts' decisions over the then 24 year life of the income tax, a feat now impossible (at least for this author). This Chapter shows how it is possible to see some of the "secrets of the structure" of the federal tax laws by focusing on the Supreme Court's opinions, particularly in tax avoidance cases. That focus is dictated not only by the impossibility of reconciling the vast tax case law of the lower federal courts, but also by the need to refocus on the most authoritative sources of law. Before World War II, the most knowledgeable commentators were bemoaning both the multiple sources of coordinate authority in federal taxation and the huge mass thereof.[399] As stated above, this book does not attempt to rationalize or even to survey all federal court tax decisions, even limited to issues of interpretation, as did Paul, because it can't be done. Even if attempted, no path can be pricked through the web; or if a path could be pricked, ultimately what would be its relevance if contrary to the views of the Supreme Court's opinions?[400]

Paul exercised a wisdom and confidence in his own abilities of analysis rarely seen today, by calling some decisions "sports,"[401] meaning they were too rebellious for classification. Just as Paul did not discern the economic substance doctrine or any judicial doctrines in 1937 from a survey of all federal tax decisions (he did write about step transactions, but as a fact finding process, not as a positive rule of law), Chapter V below does not discern the currently presumed ESD in all Supreme Court tax decisions. In his 157-page, 503-footnoted review of the status of the law of tax avoidance, Paul reached these modest conclusions, which remain valid today:

- It is critically important to the correct decision of tax cases to properly identify whether the outcome is principally dependent on issues of fact or issues of law.[402]
- *Gregory v. Helvering* was a case of statutory construction, seeking the meaning of the words: "in pursuance of a plan of reorganization."[403]

---

398 Cardozo, The Growth of the Law 5-6 (Yale 1924).

399 Paul, Studies II, at 2 n. 2; Jackson, *Equity in the Administration of Federal Taxes*, *supra* note 166, at 641.

400 Unfortunately, litigants and prospective litigants cannot ignore the views of their "local" circuits, or the Court of Federal Appeals or the Claims Court, or of the Tax Court (if they don't want to pay for privileges of litigation).

401 Paul, Studies II, at 252.

402 Paul, Studies I, at 130.

403 *Id.* at 143.

- The best examples of fact cases are those involving related party transactions, such as *Higgins v. Smith*.[404]
- The principal issue in the fact cases is likely to be whether the taxpayer intended to abide by what he had done, meaning accepting the necessary real life consequences of the papered transaction.[405]
- Courts will be motivated to closely scrutinize the facts by evidence of the taxpayer's tax avoidance motive, but will not for that reason reject the normal consequences of a transaction that has really occurred.[406]
- Courts will tend to construe a statute against a person who has intentionally tried to avoid taxes.[407]
- The resulting uncertainty of facts and law creates pitfalls for the unwary, is probably unavoidable and even beneficial to some extent, but the time may come when the harm done is greater than the good; then the policy of vagueness will cause the government to "do then the harm that good men do."[408]

Professor Rice essayed a similarly well footnoted survey of the case law in 1953,[409] and pushed Paul's analysis farther by concluding that the effort to encapsulate all purpose rules should be abandoned in favor of tracking the evolving conclusions reached by courts in a limited number of specific problem areas. This book pursues that recommendation by identifying the special treatment of cluster areas in Chapter VI.E.

Review of the Supreme Court's tax opinions will show the following:

- The Supreme Court plays a huge role in the federal tax system, but its opinions need to be better understood and placed in context of the times.
- In applying the Code the Court places greatest emphasis on the words of the statute and on congressional purpose.
- The period of the New Deal Court marked a pivotal turning point that produced many of the Supreme Court opinions that are heavily relied on (and sometimes over read) to this day.
- However, the Supreme Court did not thereby create the positive rule of law now called the economic substance doctrine.

---

[404] *Id.* at 150. *See also* Helvering v. Clifford, 309 U.S. 331 (1940) (referencing the Paul article and stating that special scrutiny applies to related party transactions).

[405] *Id.* at 137.

[406] *Id.* at 152; *see also* Paul, Studies II, at 271-76 (evidence of taxpayer's motive will inevitably be used to interpret equivocal conduct).

[407] Paul, Studies I, at 153.

[408] *Id.* at 157.

[409] Rice, *supra* note 377, at 1021.

III.B. Role of the Supreme Court in Federal Tax Cases

III.B.1. *Historical Role*

The Supreme Court properly and inevitably has played a substantial role in the establishment, interpretation and construction of the federal tax law.[410] As a result, its methods of interpretation and construction and fact finding necessarily have informed what the lower courts do in tax cases.[411] However, the role of the Supreme Court in generally fashioning the federal tax law over time has not been adequately appreciated and studied recently,[412] although what it does in specific cases and areas and specific terms or periods have been well studied.[413] This lack of appreciation is likely to increase as the Court's federal tax case load drops to near zero.

---

[410] *See* Dailey, Sporadic Omnipotence: The Supreme Court and the Federal Income Tax, S-2 (BNA 1990) ("on balance the Court's contribution to the development of a coherent body of substantive income tax law has been substantial and will reward thoughtful attention."). This source contains a particularly useful review and categorization of all Supreme Court civil income tax decisions up to 1990.

[411] However, stare decisis does not apply to interpretational methods. Foster, *Should Courts Give Stare Decisis Effect to Statutory Interpretation Methodology?*, 96 Geo. L. J. 1863 (2008).

[412] A prominent exception is the work of Professors Lee Epstein, Nancy Staudt, and Peter Wiedenbeck. *See* Epstein et al., *Judging Statutes: Thoughts on Statutory Interpretation and Notes for a Project on the Internal Revenue Code,* 13 Wash. U. J. L & Pol'y 305 (2003); Staudt et al., *Judging Statutes: supra* note 20, at 1909; Staudt et al., *The Ideological Component of Judging in the Taxation Context,* 84 Wash. U. L. Rev. 1797 (2006); Staudt et al., *Judicial Decisions as Legislation: Congressional Oversight of Supreme Court Tax Cases*, 82 N.Y.U. L. Rev. 1340 (2007); Blank & Staudt, *Corporate Shams, supra* note 4, at 1641.

[413] For principal examples, see ABA Section of Taxation, *Proposal for a Procedure for Developing Better Responses to Problems Created by Complex Supreme Court Tax Opinions*, 47 Tax Law. 789, 790 (1994) ("The implications of [many of the Supreme Court] opinions in different factual settings may be so important as to require the attention of the most senior tax policy officials of the executive branch."); Axelrod and Blank, *The Supreme Court, Consolidated Returns, and the 10 Year Carryback,* 2001 Tax Notes Today 43-121 (March 5, 2001); Blum, *Dissenting Opinions by Supreme Court Justices in Federal Income Tax Controversies*, 82 Mich. L. Rev. 431 (1983) (advises against detailed dissents in cases involving narrow issues); Blum, *The Role of the Supreme Court in Federal Income Tax Controversies—Hillsboro National Bank and Bliss Dairy, Inc.*, 61 Taxes 363 (1983) (dislikes analysis of two particular decisions; sees unwarranted policy determinations passed off as technical matters); Brudney & Ditslear, *supra* note 59, at 1231; Zelenak, *Court and the Code: A Response to the Warp and Woof of Statutory Interpretation*, 58 Duke L.J. 1783 (2009); Hanes, *The Supreme Court, Accounting, and the Tax Accrual of True Income*, 28 Wash. & Lee L. Rev. 1, 74 (1971) (the definitive article on Supreme Court and Tax Accounting, it concludes that the accrual rules are illogical and that results from an initial incoherence in the statute and necessary intervention by the Court beyond its expertise and episodic intervention by Congress to benefit certain business interests: "Basically the responsibility for raising revenue is legislative and executive rather than judicial."); Staudt, *Agenda Setting in Supreme Court Tax Cases: Lessons from the Blackmun Papers*, 52 Buff. L. Rev. 889, 894 (2004) (noting that the justices nearly always consider the impact of the lower court decision on the fisc in deciding to grant cert.); Staudt et al., *Judicial Decisions as Legislation*, *supra* note 412, at 1351 (concluding that the Code was the most litigated of all statutes and rules during the Rehnquist Court Era 1986-2002); Sutherland, *Recent Federal Tax Decisions of the Supreme* Court, 19 Ark. L. Rev. 247, 252 (1965) (discussing Braunstein v. Commissioner,

The federal tax laws have been the federal statutes most litigated in the Supreme Court throughout most of the history of the Court.[414] The decisions of the Supreme Court in tax cases are of parallel weight with the Code, and revenue agents are required to follow Supreme Court interpretations of the law.[415] In contrast, the decisions of the United States Tax Court are accorded no special deference on appeal,[416] despite it being a specialty court. During the decades of the Supreme Court's heaviest load of tax cases, commentators sometimes referred to a "tax wreath" worn by Brandeis and Jackson and Blackmun,[417] and perhaps Black,[418] and Douglas.[419]

The Supreme Court is second only to Congress in creating the federal income tax law. Its closest competitor, the Treasury, is a distant third. The Court's early tax caseload was heavy, as it worked out the uncertainties in the relatively brief biannual revenue laws that exploded in terms of revenue production to fund the First World War, and became a mass tax to fund the Second World War.[420] In creating tax law, the Court did not always reach the "right" answer, but usually could be credited with satisfying Justice Brandeis' view that it is ". . . more important that the applicable rule of law be settled, than that it be settled right."[421]

---

374 U.S. 65 (1963), the article states: "While the Supreme Court may have from time to time resorted to ad hoc decisions bordering on legislation to prevent tax avoidance, it maintains a thoroughly proper judicial attitude when the result is to impose a tax in accordance with statutory language, even when the transaction may not be at all within the spirit of the statute."); Wales, *supra* note 278, at 75; Wolfman, *The Supreme Court in the Lyon's Den: A Failure of Judicial Process*, 66 Cornell L. Rev. 1075 (1981) (on average the Supreme Court has heard fewer than four civil federal tax cases a year for the past decade); Wood, *Supreme Court Jurisprudence of Tax Fairness*, 36 Seton Hall L. Rev. 421 (2006) (Discusses the role of fairness in statutory construction).

414 Epstein et al., The Supreme Court Compendium (1996 CQ Press); Epstein et al., *Judging Statutes*, *supra* note 412, at 309.

415 I.R.M. 4.10.7.2.9.8.

416 *See* I.R.C. § 7482(a)(1) (courts of appeal review decision of Tax Court as of any lower federal court sitting without a jury).

417 *See* Stark, *The Unfilled Tax Legacy of Justice Robert H. Jackson*, 54 Tax L. Rev. 171, 214 (2001). As to Blackmun, *see* Green, *Justice Blackmun's Federal Tax Jurisprudence*, 26 Hastings Const. L. Q. 109 (1999); Brudney & Ditslear, *supra* note 59, at 1270 et seq.; Resolution in Tribute to Harry A. Blackmun, 1999 J. Sup. Ct. U.S. 241, 254 (1999-2000) (large number of tax opinions indicated he was "in the dog house with the Chief"). Other contenders include Butler, Roberts, Stone, Douglas, Marshall, and Souter, at least based on numbers of tax opinions. *See* Cohen, *Thurgood Marshall: Tax Lawyer*, 80 Geo. L.J. 2011 (1992).

418 *See generally* Paul, *Justice Black and Federal Taxation*, 65 Yale L.J. 495 (1956).

419 *See* Wolfman et al., *Behavior of Justice Douglas in Federal Tax Cases*, 122 U. Pa. L. Rev. 235, 365 (1973); Katz, *The William O. Douglas Tax Factor: Where Did the Spin Stop and Who Was He Looking out For*, 3 Charlotte L. Rev. 133, 216 (2011-2012).

420 *See* Frankfurter & Landis, *The Business of the Supreme Court at October 1930 Term*, 45 Harv. L. Rev. 271, 297 (1932) (tax caseload "since 1913 has enormously increased"; listed 30 tax cases on certiorari, mostly accepted due to conflicts in the circuits, with as many as 16 appellate court cases being involved in one issue).

421 Burnet v. Coronado Oil and Gas Co., 285 U.S. 393 (1932) (Brandeis, J., dissenting), *overruled by* Helvering v. Mountain Producers Corp., 303 U.S. 376 (1938).

The most important areas in which the Court has contributed to the tax law,[422] aside from the initial rulings of constitutionality, include (1) the meaning of income itself, particularly the timing of its reporting,[423] with the thrust of its decisions being to expand the scope of income taxation to the maximum extent possible;[424] (2) corporate reorganizations;[425] (3) ownership of property and income,[426] including particularly the assignment of income doctrine; and (4) the tax liabilities of married persons.[427] Indeed, the activism of the Supreme Court with respect to the income tax likely spurred a greater role for the courts and lawyers in general with the income tax, as contrasted with it being administered by accountants and bureaucrats.[428]

The scope of the new income tax and the constitutional amendment that authorized it were in the news from the start, and the 1920 decision in *Eisner v. Macomber* was closely followed by stock market participants. This level of general interest was repeated in the 1930s when the Supreme Court began to curb literal interpretations of the tax laws, making news not limited to the tax world.[429] Recognition of the importance of the Court's role in tax cases is reflected in the multiple early studies thereof. Charles L. B. Lowndes began an annual review of Supreme Court tax cases with the 1936 term in which he chronicled the large number of precedents overturned, and the "govern-

---

[422] For one numerical count of decisions in particular areas, *see* DAILEY, *supra* note 410. To 1990 the Supreme Court decided 76 cases concerning permissible deductions, 75 cases defining what is income, 50 cases on timing, 44 cases identifying the taxpayer, 34 on reorganizations and other corporate transactions, 24 on capital versus ordinary, 24 on determining basis or tax cost, 12 on substance over form.

[423] *See, e.g.*, Hort v. Commissioner, 313 U.S. 28 (1941); North American Oil Consolidated v. Burnet, 286 U.S. 417 (1932) (claim of right doctrine); Burnet v. Sanford & Brooks Co., 282 U.S. 359 (1931) (Sixteenth Amendment adopted to enable the government to raise revenue and no other known method of doing that except on a periodical basis, thus establishing the taxable year concept). *See generally* BITTKER & LOKKEN, at 5.1, 5.2.

[424] *See, e.g.*, Commissioner v. Glenshaw Glass Co., 348 U.S. 426 (1955); Commissioner v. LoBue, 351 U.S. 243 (1956) (stock options given to employees have to be compensatory; there is no third category of noncompensatory "gifts" from employers).

[425] *See generally* BITTKER & EUSTICE, at 12.03.

[426] *See generally* BITTKER & LOKKEN, at 75.1, 75.2.

[427] *See generally id.* at 76.1. Obergefell v. Hodges, 135 S. Ct. 2584 (2015).

[428] *See* Crane, Pollock, Macomber, *and the Role of the Federal Courts in the Development of the Income Tax in the United States*, 75 LAW AND CONTEMP. PROBLEMS 1 (Winter 2010).

[429] *See, e.g.*, Nelson, *Avoidance of Tax Upheld by Courts, No Fundamental Change Seen in Judicial Attitude on Lawful Escape*, N.Y. TIMES, July 28, 1935, at F1 (reporting that the Court of Appeals in *Chisolm v. Commissioner*, 79 F.2d 14 (2d Cir.), distinguishes *Gregory* so as to remove much of the existing apprehension that there had been a change in judicial attitude toward the sufficiency of a technical compliance with the tax laws as a means of reducing taxes); *Tax Field Widened by Supreme Court*, N.Y. TIMES, Mar. 8, 1938 at 1 (reporting that Helvering v. Mountain Producers Corp., 303 U.S. 376 (1938) overruled Burnet v. Coronado Oil and Gas, and held that the gas could be taxed even though leased from state).

ment minded" tenor of the outcomes.[430] Lowndes was joined by other academic and practice observers who also saw the burgeoning Supreme Court tax caseload and the similarity of the struggles over tax interpretation to struggles over interpretations of the New Deal legislation.[431] In 1941, Stanley Surrey wrote that federal tax cases constituted the largest group of cases on the Supreme Court's docket by subject matter.[432] Looking back from 1960, Lowndes observed that the Court had made 524 income tax decisions, 75 estate tax, 19 gift tax; the vast majority involve only construction.[433]

But the concerns of the Court shifted by the 1960's.[434] Shapiro said in 1963 that the Supreme Court and tax is "Hardly an unnatural combination,

---

[430] Lowndes, *The Tax Burden of the Supreme Court 1935 Term*, 5 FORDHAM L. REV. 426, 451 (1936) (noting that last term the Court decided over 60 tax cases including cert denials, etc.); Lowndes, *The Supreme Court on Taxation: 1936 Term*, 86 U. PA. L. REV. 1 (1937); Lowndes, *Taxation and the Supreme Court : 1937 Term*, 87 U. PA. L. REV. 1 (1938); Lowndes, *Tax Decisions of the Supreme Court 1938 Term*, 88 U. PA. L. REV. 1, 34 (1939) ("Landmarks did tumble like tenpins" which author attributed to changed court personnel; "Taxation is the critical domestic problem of the day."); Lowndes, *Tax Decision of the Supreme Court 1940 Term*, 90 U. PA. L. REV. 1 (1941) (Two-thirds of the decisions in the 1940 term involved federal taxes, stating that the court was "Government minded" and that taxpayer chances of prevailing about ten percent.

> Transposed to the pre-Roosevelt era, the tax cases decided by the Court at the last term are starkly incredible. Viewed against the more immediate background of contemporary legal history, they become the verriest commonplaces.

Id. at 156).

[431] *See* Bergman, *The Trend of Supreme Court Tax Decisions*, 15 ST. JOHN'S L. REV. 203 (1940) (observed a fundamental change in the philosophy behind Supreme Court state tax decisions, and wondered if it was personnel or the economic demands on the country); Cogger, *Tax Avoidance versus Tax Evasion*, 15 TAX MAG. 518 (1937); Magill, *The Supreme Court on Federal Taxation 1939-1940*, 8 U. CHI. L. REV. 1 (1940) (tax cases by far the largest group); Traynor, *Tax Decisions of the Supreme Court, 1937 Term*, 33 ILL. L. REV. 371 (1938) (stating that nearly one-third of written opinions in the 1937 term were on taxes, making up by far the largest single group).

[432] Surrey, *Supreme Court and the Federal Income Tax*, *supra* note 285, at 779.

[433] Lowndes, *Federal Taxation and the Supreme Court*, 1960 SUP. CT. REV. 222-24.

[434] *Cf.* Barker, *supra* note 25, at 850 (identifying the period 1930-1956 as marking the shift to purposivist interpretation).

but nevertheless one rarely made."[435] Wolfman said in 1981 that on average the Supreme Court had heard fewer than 4 civil federal tax cases a year for the past decade.[436] The trend continued downward from there. The bulk of the total number of Supreme Court opinions on the Code were issued before 1950, and 1935 was the high water mark.[437] Nevertheless, the tax case load of the Court remained statistically substantial both quantitatively and proportionately during the Burger and Rehnquist Courts.[438]

It is common knowledge that the Court does not grant its writ of certiorari merely to correct error,[439] although it has played that role in the past. Because it long since ceased to be a court of error correction,[440] and because most federal tax cases do not involve constitutional issues, when it reviews them it is correcting error usually to resolve a conflict in the circuits. Moreover, the increasingly heavy federal court case load of the last 50 years has shrunk drastically the percentage of cases reviewed, forcing the Court even more not to correct errors but to lay down broad guidance (although the Court's own case load has declined generally).[441] The shifting role of the Court seems part of a larger shift from being a resolver of disputes in the judicial context to functioning as a rule maker and legislature for other courts.[442] The volume of tax decisions in the first half of the 20th century presumably predates this shift of

---

[435] Shapiro, *The Warren Court and Federal Tax Policy*, 36 S. Cal. L. Rev. 208 (1963). This article observed that the Warren Court's approach to taxes was gingerly and modest, desiring to avoid over-involvement in complex tax matters. As a consequence the Court tended to reduce the case materials to the simplest form. The Court also avoided establishing legal standards to justify case by case decisions, rather stressing facts over law. For example, *Knetsch* depended on the facts and refused to confirm or deny the appellate court's rule that the total absence of nontax purpose itself voided the interest deduction. He observed that if the Court had consistently pursued a course of deciding tax cases on substantive grounds it would show itself to be activist and would affect the conduct of taxpayers. But instead he found that the Court entered the field only episodically and by focusing on facts and creating no policy it shifted the burden to the lower courts. The article viewed the Warren Court as unwilling to lead or even play. He thought the Court tended to have a distaste for avoidance like the Service, but less so. Consequently it followed the easiest course of deferring to the Service. *Id.* at 223. Shapiro recommended a more active policy making role for the Supreme Court in tax cases.

[436] Wolfman, *The Supreme Court in the Lyon's Den*, *supra* note 413, at 1075.

[437] Staudt et al, *Judging Statutes*, *supra* note 20, at 1927; Epstein et al., *Judging Statutes*, *supra* note 412, at 325.

[438] Epstein et al., *Judging Statutes*, *supra* note 412, at 310; Moran & Schneider, *The Elephant and the Four Blind Men: The Burger Court and Its Federal Tax Decisions*, 13 How. L.J. 841, 866-67 (1996); Solimine & Walker, *supra* note 91, at 445 (from 1969 to 1988, of the Court's decisions involving statutory interpretation, tax cases comprised 4.9%; economic regulation at 25.5%, and civil rights at 21.9% were the largest groups, two areas that were considerably less important before the New Deal (as to economic regulation) and before the 1960's (as to civil rights)). *See* Boyle, *The Rehnquist Court: Nineteen Years of Tax Decisions*, 25 Va. Tax Rev. 451 (2005).

[439] Sup. Ct. Rule 10.

[440] Atiyah & Summers, at 294-95.

[441] *See* Posner, at 269-72.

[442] Bhagwat, *Separate But Equal: The Supreme Court, the Lower Federal Courts, and the Nature of the Judicial Branch*, 80 B.U. L. Rev. 967, 968 (2000).

focus, but also likely reflects the huge importance the Court then attributed to the issue of taxation.

The relative rarity of recent high profile Supreme Court tax decisions has contributed to a current lack of appreciation of the role of the Court in tax cases, and to a longer standing suspicion of the Court's intervention. Even Justice Jackson stated: ". . . I still think the Tax Court is a more competent and steady influence toward a systematic body of tax law than our sporadic omnipotence in a field beset with invisible boomerangs."[443] As far back as 1936 a careful observer of the Court's tax cases stated: "The unhappiest expression in the lawyer's vocabulary from the point of view of clear and realistic thinking is the Supreme Court. There are nine justices, but there is no objective reality apart from them, no collective mind which dictates their opinions."[444]

Such views likely have increased even as the Court's tax docket has become relatively lighter because the Court's tax decisions now appear even more episodically to swoop in to upset someone's settled expectations.[445] Also the Justices may have become less conversant with the tax law than they once were (when the law was shorter and the tax case load larger), which partly may explain the deference to regulations and textual readings of the Code. The tax wreath formerly worn by such luminaries as Brandeis may have become a less admirable badge as the assignment to write the tax decisions came to be viewed as having drawn the short straw.

In addition to the dwindling tax case load handled by the Court, its tax opinions are more likely to be unanimous. For example, the four federal tax decisions of the 2013 term were all unanimous. The two of the three decisions of the 2012 term that were not constitutional cases were unanimous. But all four decisions of the 2011 term had dissents (one being the Affordable Care Act decision). Observers of the Court have noted a trend toward unanimity generally. In tax, it could indicate a waning interest in the subject or an effort to obtain consensus. The muddled analyses in some recent unanimous tax decisions suggests that the latter may be true.[446]

The view that Supreme Court tax opinions are unprincipled and dangerous to the health of the law also may prove the contention that ". . . too much intellectual inbreeding [in the federal tax law] often transforms minor variations into fundamental alterations."[447] Such intellectual inbreeding tends to

---

443 Arrowsmith v. Commissioner, 344 U.S. 6, 12 (1952) (Jackson, J. dissenting). For a review of all 339 federal tax decisions of the Supreme Court to 1989, *see* DAILEY, *supra* note 410.

444 Lowndes, *1935 Term*, *supra* note 430, at 451; *see also* Cohen, INDOPCO *and* Arkansas Best—*Or Why Tax Advisors Cringe When Tax Cases Go to the Supreme Court*, Outline B, 1994 Southern Federal Tax Institute.

445 *See* CARON, TAX STORIES 136 (2003).

446 *See* Cummings, *The Supreme Court's 2013 Term in Tax*, 145 TAX NOTES (TA) 65 (Oct. 6, 2014).

447 Surrey, *Supreme Court and the Federal Income Tax*, *supra* note 285, at 779.

occur not only in the Treasury, but among practitioner "tax experts" and in the Tax Court. When the thinking resulting from such inbreeding comes before a general jurisdiction court such as the Supreme Court, it often receives rough treatment.[448]

Although this book supports paying considerably more attention to what the Supreme Court has done in tax cases, it cautions against a tendency to rely on dictum in Supreme Court opinions to expand the amount of "law" created by the Court.[449] The Court also has warned against this, stating "it is a maxim, not to be disregarded, that general expressions, in every opinion, are to be taken in connection with the case in which those expressions are used."[450] Lawyers should not disregard the critical distinction that accords binding legal status only to those statements that relate to the specific issue that occasioned the litigation giving rise to a majority opinion of the Supreme Court: the specific holding and its directly related reasoning.[451] This is discussed further in the next Chapter.

Two scholars who made statistical analyses of Supreme Court decisions in corporate tax shelter cases found a correlation between increased national defense spending and rulings against the corporate taxpayers.[452] However, the likelihood of the Court seeking to pump up tax collections for that particular element of the annual deficits seems improbable.

III.B.2. *Systemic Roles*

The Supreme Court's tax opinions play three primary roles and one minor episodic role within the federal tax system. First, they play a key role in rela-

---

[448] *See, e.g.*, Shores, *Textualism and Intentionalism*, *supra* note 22, at 53 (finding that the Tax Court is more likely to ignore the words of the Code to reach the "correct" result than are courts of appeal). For examples of the rough treatment by the Supreme Court, see *Cottage Savings Assn. v. Commissioner*, 499 U.S. 554 (1991), and *Gitlitz v. Commissioner*, 531 U.S. 206 (2001). *See also* Cummings, *The Supreme Court's 2014 Term in Tax*, 148 Tax Notes (TA) 1005 (Aug. 31, 2015); Cummings, *The Supreme Court's 2015 Term in Tax*, 152 Tax Notes (TA) 979 (August 15, 2016).

[449] *See* Maltz, *The Function of Supreme Court Opinions*, 37 Hous. L. Rev. 1395, 1418 (2000).

[450] Zenith Radio Corp. v. United States, 437 U.S. 443 (1978) (referring to one of its prior opinions in a tariff case).

[451] *See* Maltz, *supra* note 449, at 1418. *See* Cohens v. Virginia, 19 U.S. 264 (1821) (recognizing that the Court may state principles broader than needed to decide the case, without adequately investigating the possible effect on other cases). The repetition of dictum does not turn it into holding. DOR v. Kurth Ranch, 511 U.S. 767 (1994).

[452] *See* Blank & Staudt, *Corporate Shams*, *supra* note 4, at 1642, 1694.

tion to Congress, which regularly takes into account the Court's tax decisions and frequently confirms them (and sometimes overrides them).[453]

Second, lower federal courts and others attempt to drain every drop of meaning out of the Court's opinions. Practitioners and judges "are prone to cull quotations from the Supreme Court's decisions in much the same manner as theatrical producers choose phrases from reviews of dramatic critics for their newspaper advertisements."[454] Even Justice Scalia cautioned against such overreading.[455] Many examples of over reading (of *Gregory, Knetsch, Frank Lyon*, for examples) will be discussed herein.[456] More generally it has been observed that now the lower federal circuit courts appear to be following the Supreme Court's shift toward "plain meaning."[457] Of course, insofar as statutory interpretation is concerned, a close observance of the Supreme Court's methods is entirely warranted: that is the point of this book. The Court decides the hardest cases, and statutory construction is what the Supreme Court does. As Justice Cardozo stated:

> [The New York Court of Appeals] is a great common law court; its problems are lawyers' problems. But the Supreme Court is occupied chiefly with statutory construction—which no man can make interesting—and with politics.[458]

So, for example, lower courts should take notice that the Court is most likely to use interpretational default rules in deciding hard tax cases.[459]

The preclusive effect on lower federal of decisions of the Supreme Court rests on the doctrine of stare decisis, as well as the constitutional supremacy of the Supreme Court relative to other federal courts.[460] The Court itself has more flexibility as to its prior decisions and can ignore, reject, claim to distinguish, or change a decision that it finds to be unsound in principle

---

453 Staudt et al., *Judicial Decisions as Legislation*, *supra* note 412, at 1340; *see also* Paul, *Justice Black and Federal Taxation*, *supra* note 418, at 516 n. 118 (listing 13 Supreme Court tax decisions that Congress had responded to by changing the Code). An analysis of the Rehnquist Court found that nineteen of 26 decisions to review tax cases were based on a conflict in the circuits. F. Ladson Boyle, *The Rehnquist Court: Nineteen Years of Tax Decisions*, 25 VA. TAX REV. 451, 456 (2005).

454 Surrey, *Supreme Court and the Federal Income Tax*, *supra* note 285, at 813.

455 Commissioner v. Bollinger, 485 U.S. 340 (1988) ("we decline to parse the text of *National Carbide* as though that were itself the governing statute.").

456 *See* Blank & Staudt, *Corporate Shams*, *supra* note 4, at 1642, 1698-1699 (statistical analysis shows that the Supreme Court's "old" tax abuse decisions never go out of style).

457 Shores, *Textualism and Intentionalism*, *supra* note 22, at 62-3.

458 JACKSON, FULL FAITH AND CREDIT 2 (1945).

459 *See* Elhauge, *supra* note 66, at 2031 (asserting that the Supreme Court is most likely to invoke statutory interpretation default rules because it decides the most difficult cases).

460 MOORE'S FEDERAL PRACTICE 134.01[1]. This preclusive effect derives from the fact that the United States has a common law legal system rather than a civil code based system. Moore & Oglebay, *The Supreme Court, Stare Decisis and the Law of the Case*, 21 TEX. L. REV. 514, 515 (1942).

or unworkable in practice.[461] The Court's flexibility is at its greatest in cases of constitutional interpretation, due to the very limited ways in which the Constitution otherwise can be changed.[462]

"The doctrine of stare decisis extends to the holdings of prior decisions, but it does not extend to mere dicta (e.g., statements that were unnecessary to the result in a prior decision)."[463] Therefore, other courts must at a minimum reach a result consistent with the result reached by the Supreme Court.[464] When a majority of the Justices constituting the Court agree to one opinion, the holding stated in the opinion is entitled to stare decisis effect.[465] The holding is the determination of an issue of law, not of fact or of mixed law and fact.[466]

Holding is in contrast to dictum;[467] although alternative grounds supporting a result are part of the holding, dictum can be identified by asking if it could be deleted without impairing the basis of the court's decision.[468] When there is no opinion of the Court on an issue but concurrence in the result, the narrowest ground of concurrence is the holding of the Court.[469] Sometimes the reasoning of a decision is distinguished from both the holding and the result; generally the reasoning need not be followed.[470] However, the rule of law selected, created, or identified by the Court to be applied to the facts to reach the result necessarily is the holding, else stare decisis would have no use in future cases.[471]

One of the great errors in the lower courts' readings of their own and Supreme Court opinions is that they induce generic rules from sporadic forays where only the forays are important.[472] This may serve some positive functions of giving the lower courts and the Service more "law" to work with, and thus limiting their discretion, but it must be balanced against the Court's own

---

[461] Moore's Federal Practice at 134.02[1][b].

[462] *See* Agostini v. Felton, 521 U.S. 203, 235 (1997) (stare decisis "is at its weakest when we interpret the Constitution because our interpretation can be altered only by constitutional amendment or by overruling our prior decisions").

[463] Moore's Federal Practice at 134.01[1].

[464] *Op. cit.* at 134.03[1].

[465] *Op. cit.* at 134.04[1], 134.03[2].

[466] *Op. cit.* at 134.04[2].

[467] *Id.*

[468] *Id.*

[469] *Id.*

[470] *Op. cit.* at 134.03[3]. *See* Knowlton v. Moore, 178 U.S. 41 (1900) (refusing to follow or infer reasoning as to direct taxes in the *Pollock* opinion, based on whether the tax could be passed on to another, because that was not the ground of the decision).

[471] *See* Moore & Oglebay, *supra* note 460 at 516-517 ("Thus, if a court adjudges, in litigation between A and B, that the applicable rule of law is 'X-Y,' this rule is the law of the case for the A-B litigation, but the court also establishes 'X-Y' as the rule of law to be applied by it, and all courts owing obedience to it, in all subsequent litigation between any and all parties where such a rule is relevant and properly applicable.").

[472] One such effort to synthesize Supreme Court authority in this area is Grewal, *Economic Substance and the Supreme Court*, 2007 Tax Notes Today 176-52 (Sept. 10, 2007).

refusal to accord dictum the power of laws.[473] The inability of others to be similarly clear eyed about Supreme Court's dictum has led to many decades of confusion in a variety of areas, not the least of which is the alleged Supreme Court underpinning of the economic substance doctrine, as discussed elsewhere herein.[474]

The third systemic role of Supreme Court tax decision is that the Court is prone to cite and rely upon itself first.[475] This is true no matter how old its prior decision may be.[476] Such continuity of decision implicitly engenders substantial reliance on those decisions by taxpayers, which the Court acknowledges.[477]

The Court's tax opinions have not only embodied principles of statutory interpretation, but have also interpreted important factual requirements into Code rules (such as the requirement of business purpose for reorganizations) and have shown how common law fact finding should apply in tax cases (*Higgins v. Smith, F. & R. Lazarus*).

The minor episodic role of the Supreme Court's tax opinions is to correct error. Despite the fact that the Supreme Court does not issue the writ of certiorari to correct error, sometimes it is the only actor in the government that can cut a Gordian knot. When this occurs, it marks a failure for the tax system, though perhaps a victory for the Court.[478] Justice Douglas complained about this systemic failure to resolve the problem through regulations or statutory changes.[479] In addition, the Court sometimes asserts procedural rules, such as precluding the Commissioner from asserting a ground it either waived or failed to preserve previously.[480]

---

473 Maltz, *supra* note 449, at 1420.

474 For examples of other misadventures, see *Commissioner v. Munter*, 331 U.S 210 (1947) (implies that a corporate distribution that the shareholder treats as basis recovery cannot reduce E&P, but this is not the law); *Commissioner v. Estate of Bedford*, 325 U.S. 283 (1945) (implying that all boot in reorganizations should be treated as dividends, but affirming a Tax Court decision that said no such thing and simply taxed boot in a recapitalization based on the similarity of its effect to a dividend).

475 *See, e.g.,* United States v. Dalm, 494 U.S. 596 (1991) (starting and ending with "our" decision in Bull v. United States, 295 U.S. 247 (1935)); United States v. Wells Fargo Bank, 485 U.S. 351 (1988) (citing first its opinions from 1900 and 1920 for the view that a general exemption of property refers only to direct taxation like income taxation and not to indirect excises like the estate tax, and applying that view in the face of contrary evidence of legislative intent).

476 The *Home Concrete* decision essentially reaffirmed a 1958 ruling. United States v. Home Concrete & Supply, LLC, 132 S. Ct. 1836 (2012); The Colony, Inc. v. Commissioner, 357 U.S. 28 (1958).

477 *See, e.g.,* United States v. Byrum, 408 U.S. 125 (1972) (discussing that reliance and affirming a 1929 decision 53 years later).

478 An example is United States v. Quality Stores, Inc., 134 S. Ct. 1395 (2014),

479 United States v. Generes, 405 U.S. 93 (1972) (dissent).

480 E.g., Helvering v. Wood, 309 U.S. 344 (1940).

III.B.3. *Getting to the Court*

The Supreme Court cannot interpret a federal tax statute unless it first wants to review a lower court ruling, and it chooses to hear tax cases almost exclusively because there is a conflict in the circuits, although other reasons may also exist.[481] A case coming up to resolve a circuit conflict may not be the most exciting for the Court. According to Justice Stewart, the only cases on which Chief Justice Warren would not firmly state his position were tax cases that were before the Court due to a conflict in the circuits, to which he would say, "Look, our duty is to resolve this conflict. I'm not a tax lawyer. I'll go whichever way you want to go on this, just go with the majority and get this conflict resolved … I just have no view on this one."[482]

Recent history has shown a substantial increase in amicus briefs, not only on the merits but also urging the Court to hear cases. Organizations like the Chamber of Commerce of the United States maintain large legal departments dedicated to such litigation. The Court has heard at least one federal tax case in recent years that lacked a circuit split but involved a Chamber of Commerce amicus brief, which used a tax case to pursue a constitutional issue of interest to it.[483]

III.C. Historical Development of the Supreme Court's Tax Jurisprudence

III.C.1. *Summary*

The Supreme Court's tax jurisprudence shifted fundamentally in the 1930's and 1940's, reflecting the Depression and the New Deal Court's tolerance for greater governmental powers. Ch. II.B. above shows that the Supreme Court originally tended to interpret federal tax laws strictly for reasons having nothing to do with the income tax. However, the government's need for revenue rose, the income tax was adopted, and taxes increased, leading to increased tax avoidance efforts. These changes occurred in two stages:[484] first with the adoption of the income tax, and second with the steady conversion of the

---

[481] An analysis of the Rehnquist Court found that nineteen of 26 decisions to review tax cases were based on a conflict in the circuits. F. Ladson Boyle, The Rehnquist Court: Nineteen Years of Tax Decisions, 25 VA. TAX REV. 451, 456 (2005).

[482] Quoted in SCHWARTZ, SUPER CHIEF: EARL WARREN AND HIS SUPREME COURT, A JUDICIAL BIOGRAPHY 143 (1983).

[483] Ford Motor Co. v. United States, 134 S. Ct. 510 (2013) (sovereign immunity issue).

[484] As to the utility of historical analysis in law, see Bank & Stark, *An Evolutionary Perspective on the History of U.S. Business Taxation*, *in* BUSINESS TAX STORIES, *supra* note 258, at 3 (disagreeing with Charles Clark that greater historical detail in studying the tax law might obfuscate the explanatory effort); *see also* Thorndike, 2008 TAX NOTES TODAY 247-50 (Dec. 23, 2008) (reviewing KABUSHKA, TAXATION IN COLONIAL AMERICA (2008)) (identifying sparse list of recent in depth historical analyses of tax); EDLING, A REVOLUTION IN FAVOR OF GOVERNMENT (2003); JOHNSON, RIGHTEOUS ANGER AT THE WICKED STATES (2005); EINHORN, AMERICAN SLAVERY, AMERICAN FREEDOM (2006); Mehrotra, *Envisioning the Modern American Fiscal State: Progressive-Era Economists and the Intellectual Foundations of the U.S. Income Tax*, 52 UCLA L. REV. 6, 1793-866 (2005).

income tax from a class tax to a mass tax (occurring in two steps attending the First and Second World Wars).[485] The revenue needs implicitly made lenient interpretations of the tax laws inconvenient at a minimum, and more likely a luxury that the country could no longer afford. For example, in 1940 Justice Reed said:

> Each tax, according to a legislative plan, raises funds to carry on government. The purpose here is to tax earnings and profits less expenses and losses. If one or the other factor in any calculation is unreal, it distorts the liability of the particular taxpayer to the detriment or advantage of the entire taxpaying group.[486]

It is not by accident that this statement appeared in the period of the late 1930's through the 1940's when Supreme Court tax cases reached their peak, and public outrage about wealthy tax avoiders was high.[487] The writer, Justice Reed, had been President Roosevelt's Solicitor General. But the propriety of collecting all of the revenue to which the government was entitled predated the New Deal and was not limited to the Democratic Justices. For example, Justice Sutherland, one of the Four Horsemen who struck down New Deal legislation, authored the seminal anti-tax planning *Gregory v. Helvering*.[488] And in 1931, the Court began a huge shift of law to restrict the scope of the exemption for governmental instrumentalities, stating:

The limitation of this principle to its appropriate applications is also important to the successful working of our governmental system. The power to tax is no less essential than the power to borrow money, and, in preserving the latter, it is not necessary to cripple the former by extending the constitutional exemption from taxation to those subjects which fall within the general application of non-discriminatory laws, and where no direct burden is laid upon the governmental instrumentality, and there is only a remote, if any, influence upon the exercise of the functions of government.[489]In the income tax period, of necessity the Supreme Court first addressed the constitutionality of the income tax act and the meaning of the term "income." *Eisner v. Macomber*,[490] decided in 1920, adopted a flexible, as contrasted with expansive, interpretation of the revenue act in defining "income," and when it should be taxed. The flexible interpretation favored the taxpayer by looking

---

[485] *See* Bittker & Lokken, at 1.1.

[486] Higgins v. Smith, 308 U.S. 473 (1940).

[487] *See* Likhovski, *supra* note 162, at 1004-07; Bank, *Tax, Corporate Governance and Norms*, 61 Wash. & Lee L. Rev. 1159, 1176 (2004).

[488] *See* Ch. III.C.3.a(1).

[489] Willcutts v. Bunn, 282 U.S. 216, 225 (1931); *see also* Burnet v. Coronado Oil & Gas, 285 U.S. 393 (1932) (allowing governmental exemption to an oil lessee), *overruled by* Helvering v. Mountain Producers Corp., 303 U.S. 376 (1938). But it took decades for *South Carolina v. Baker*, 485 U.S. 505, 517 (1988) to find a racially discriminatory charity not exempt.

[490] Eisner v. Macomber, 252 U.S. 189 (1920); *see infra* Ch. II.B.2.c(3). *See generally* Kornhauser, *supra* note 277, at Ch. 2.

to the "economic substance" of a stock dividend to reject taxation based on a literal reading of the law that clearly intended to tax stock dividends.

This pro-taxpayer resort to substance and interpretive flexibility was not to last, however. Eventually, the Court supplanted *Macomber* with an expansive definition of gross income in *Glenshaw Glass*,[491] and generally strove to make the federal tax system work by not acceding to overly technical taxpayer arguments.[492] In 1940, the Court began the shift from *Macomber* by focusing on the "flow of economic benefits" in a different way in *Higgins v. Smith*, to let stand a jury finding that the sole shareholder of a corporation had not sold stock to his corporation and so had not recognized a loss.[493] The Court stated that the jury could have properly disregarded the formal sale because the shareholder controlled the corporation, among other reasons, which actually made *Smith* a forerunner of *Moline Properties, Inc.*, which tried to define when a corporation would be respected as a separate entity.[494] The Court did not purport to interpret the statute at issue to require a business purpose. But the opinion in *Higgins v. Smith* contains broad language that seems to permit ignoring all transactions between related parties not having a business purpose. Such an approach almost always operates against the taxpayer because generally taxpayers are not allowed to disavow their chosen forms.[495]

But the Court has never applied the dictum in *Higgins* to disregard a controlled corporation simply because it was controlled, and instead began in 1943 in *Moline Properties, Inc.* to work out the tax implications of the corporate form, and to establish the low threshold (not met in *Higgins v. Smith*) for when a corporation will be regarded for tax purposes as a separate entity.

This Chapter will show that *Gregory v. Helvering* is a boundary decision that boldly construed a major requirement into the reorganization statute,[496] but that *Higgins v. Smith*, and a similarly far reaching decision in *McWilliams* are "sports," except as carefully limited to a disregard of fraudulent conduct on the facts in *Smith* and an exceptionally purposive reading of the statute in *McWilliams*. The path through the Supreme Court precedents is tangled, however, due to shifts in doctrine over time. For that reason the following analysis distinguishes between authorities involving ambiguous and unambiguous sections of the law and focuses on certain talismanic cases called here "boundary decisions."

Finally, this Chapter addresses the second and inevitable minor shift in the Court's federal tax jurisprudence, which seems to move back toward a literal

---

[491] Commissioner v. Glenshaw Glass Co., 348 U.S. 426, 431 (1955).

[492] *See, e.g.*, United States v. Quality Stores, Inc., 134 S. Ct. 1395 (2014), discussed in Cummings, *Negative Implications and Code Interpretation*, 143 Tax Notes (TA) 931 (May 26, 2014).

[493] Higgins v. Smith, 308 U.S. 473 (1940). Subsequently, Congress enacted section 267 to address the problem of related party loss transactions.

[494] Moline Prop., Inc. v. Commissioner, 319 U.S. 436 (1943).

[495] *See infra* Ch. VI.E.1.e(4).

[496] Gregory v. Helvering, 293 U.S. 465 (1935).

reading of the Code. In fact, any such movement mostly is the inevitable result of a maturing of the statutes: in the early years of the income tax the Court was compelled to make much law and do so by discerning the policies on which the much smaller income tax (and the estate and gift taxes) statutes were based. But over almost 100 years the statute has grown in length and detail, much of it incorporating or at least reflecting policies discerned by the Court in its earlier decisions, which inevitably makes it more likely that the Court will find the Code to have a plain meaning that will remain undisturbed by interpretation.

III.C.2. *Empirical Studies*

Empirical studies have contributed to the understanding of Supreme Court tax decisions and the results cited in the studies are consistent with those observed in this book. An empirical study by Professor Staudt, et al.[497] of the 922 distinct federal tax cases decided by the Supreme Court from 1912 to 2000 revealed the following:

- The Court cited textual canons of construction in 39.46% of the cases,[498] with a dramatic shift to more textual emphasis occurring in the mid to late 1970's.[499]
- The adoption of "technical meaning" and "plain meaning," in that order, were by far the most commonly cited canons, with *expressio unius* and reliance on the whole act among the more prominent of the lesser canons.[500]
- The Court cited evidence concerning the legislative process much more frequently than it cited textual canons, most importantly the various components of legislative history including but not limited to committee reports (48.9%), related statutes (44.7%), coordination and consistency with other laws (about 20%).[501]
- The Court's reliance on legislative materials increased over time, peaking in the 1960-1990 period, and then declined to around 50% of the cases.[502] As of 2005 the Court generally depended on the text but "checks its work" by resort to legislative history.[503] The result has been that in 69% of the tax cases since 1912 the Court explicitly deferred to Congress by following either the text or the legislative history and inferred intent of Congress.[504]

---

[497] Staudt et al., *Judging Statutes*, *supra* note 20, at 1927. See other studies cited in Ch. III.B.1.

[498] *Id.* at 1935.

[499] *Id.* at 1936.

[500] *Id.* at 1935.

[501] *Id.* at 1940-42.

[502] *Id* at 1945.

[503] *Id.* at 1946.

[504] *Id.*

- Textual evidence dominated legislative evidence up to the 1940's, which marked a shift toward legislative evidence that continued into the 1970's and then shifted back toward textual dominance.[505]
- At the beginning of the 21st century the Court rarely relied exclusively on either textual or legislative evidence and cannot be said to have embraced the view that once the Court ascertains the statute's plain meaning it will not resort to legislative evidence.[506]
- In 21% of its cases the Court cited Treasury regulations, and this source was far and away the leading source of administrative guidance on which it relied.[507] Up to the 1990's the Court's reliance on administrative guidance increased gradually.[508]
- The Court has cited its own precedents in 35% of the cases and in 1/3 of those has relied on precedent alone, but the tendency has declined dramatically since the early period;[509]and now it rarely relies solely on "judicially selected policy norms."[510]
- The Court has not cited judge made rules with any regularity, with the most common being the presumption against irrationality and injustice (9%).[511]
- The Court has relied on other policy rationales relatively infrequently: tax avoidance concerns (14%), horizontal equity (12-13%), administrative ease (9%), revenue (6%).[512]
- Considering the Court's reliance on combinations of its own or legislative or administrative guidance, it was far more likely to rely on its own precedents plus legislative materials (32.69%), judicial precedents alone (23.92%), all three branches (16.65%), legislative only (13.93%), administrative only (1.51%).[513]
- Over time the Court's reliance on legislative, judicial and executive precedent has increased generally, suggesting a greater need to justify its tax decisions,[514] with the ranking of reliance currently being legislative in preference to judicial/textual in preference to administrative.[515]

In 2009 other researchers used and updated the Staudt databases to compare Supreme Court majority opinions in tax and workplace law and found:[516]

---

505 *Id* at 1945-46.
506 *Id* at 1946.
507 *Id* at 1941.
508 *Id.* at 1952.
509 *Id.* at 1955.
510 *Id.* at 1960.
511 *Id.* at 1957.
512 *Id.* at 1959.
513 *Id.* at 1961-64.
514 *Id.* at 1965.
515 *Id.* at 1935.
516 Brudney & Ditslear, *supra* note 59, at 1253-56.

- Reliance on text in two-thirds of the opinions, slightly more than for workplace law cases;
- A high 81.6% reliance on the Court's own precedents;
- Significantly greater reliance on legislative history and language canons and somewhat more reliance on substance canons than in workplace law cases;
- Significantly less reliance on legislative purpose relative to workplace law cases; and
- From the Burger to the Rehnquist/Roberts Courts they observe a shift to more reliance on text and less reliance on legislative history.

These observations are consistent with the history recounted below and the conclusions that the Court obviously looks to the text because the Code is a relatively fulsome statute, that it primarily tries to interpret the Code where necessary according to the will of Congress and will readily look outside the text of the Code provision at issue to legislative history, and that the Court does not rely on judge made doctrines other than its own precedents. However, while the Supreme Court has shifted more towards reliance on text, some of the lower courts have remained more antitextual, largely because of their willingness to apply the doctrines that they have created, particularly the economic substance doctrine.[517]

III.C.3. *Boundary Decisions*

The following two subchapters discuss in detail three selected tax opinions of the Supreme Court in the fluid period of 1935-1949. Two of them are inarguably pivotal: *Higgins v. Smith* and *Gregory v. Helvering*; they are two of the four opinions cited in Regulation section 1.269-2(b), the regulation that gives the most attention to Supreme Court tax avoidance principles. The third, *McWilliams*, is selected as an example of a case of relatively extreme liberal statutory construction in the government's favor. Together they illustrate how the Court shifted toward applying and construing the tax laws in the government's favor in the critical years of 1935-1949. However, the three decisions are not "typical." Two of them, *Higgins* and *McWilliams*, are boundary decisions that arguably go farther than the Court has since, unless their meaning is carefully related to existing law, as explained in the discussions in this book. Of course *Gregory* can hardly be called typical due to its foundational importance.

III.C.3.a. *The Court Deals with Unambiguous Sections*

Sections of the Code that appear superficially to be unambiguous necessarily have played the greatest role in the Court's use of nonliteral approaches, or what can appear to be nonliteral approaches, to the application of the tax laws. The nonliteral approaches can be the interpretation of a major

[517] *See* Madison, *supra* note 15, at 700.

additional limitation into the apparently clear section on the basis of rather modest statutory language (*Gregory*). Fact finding cases frequently are misidentified as cases of nonliteral interpretation of the law (*Higgins v. Smith*, which sometimes is viewed as a special rule of law for transactions between sole shareholders and their corporations). See also Ch. VI.B.1.c.

III.C.3.a(1) Gregory v. Helvering: *Law*

Gregory v. Helvering,[518] is said to be "all things to all men,"[519] and it created "one of the most protean judicial doctrines in the tax law" (business purpose, though limited to reorganizations).[520] The Treasury identifies it as the origin of both the substance over form doctrine (which is an inaccurate reading) and the business purpose doctrine (also inaccurate),[521] and hence of the core of the tax specific doctrines. But in reality, *Gregory* was a case of statutory construction in which the Supreme Court construed a normal course of business requirement into the statutory words "in pursuance of a plan of reorganization." *Gregory* did not create an all purpose requirement for "business purpose" for enjoyment of all allowances and deductions, much less all tax "benefits" (as asserted in the economic substance doctrine).[522] No Supreme Court decision says it did,[523] although later Supreme Court opinions recognized that the transitory corporation Mrs. Gregory's plan employed could be ignored for tax purposes (and called a sham) because it had no business or corporate purpose, under the later announced rule of *Moline Properties, Inc.*[524]

Although it seems odd today, at the time of *Gregory* the reorganization statute was thought to be unambiguous. However, that view overlooked the critical point, seized on by the Supreme Court opinion in *Gregory*, that "reorganization" was not fully defined by the mechanical forms of reorganizations

---

518 Gregory v. Helvering, 293 U.S. 465 (1935). The articles on *Gregory* are legion. *See, e.g.*, Gideon, *supra* note 41 at 825; Cavanaugh, *supra* note 36, at 610 (which, like this article, takes *Gregory* as a template for a broader approach to statutory interpretation); *cf.* Cummings, *Core-Dependent Homonyms and Gregory v. Helvering,* 123 TAX NOTES (TA) 495 (Apr. 27, 2009) (criticizing Cavanaugh's thesis).

519 PAUL, STUDIES III, at 126.

520 Clark, *Morphogenesis of Subchapter C,* 87 YALE L.J. 90, 122 (1977).

521 *Treasury White Paper on Corporate Tax Shelters, supra* note 14.

522 Summers, *A Critique of the Business Purpose Doctrine*, 41 OR. L. REV. 38, 40 (1961) (identifying as one of the least accurate formulations of the doctrine the statement that "to reduce taxes, a taxpayer must always show that he intended his transactions to serve a nontax purpose").

523 *Higgins v. Smith* 308 U.S. 473 (1940) (comes close, but is explained below).

524 Moline Properties, Inc. v. Commissioner, 319 U.S. 436 (1943); *see infra* Ch. VI.F.3.b.; *see* Miller, *Federal Courts as Makers of Income Tax Law*, 6 TAX L. REV. 151, 161 (1951) (citing *Gregory* as a chief example of lower courts turning what should have been a dummy corporation decision into a new principle of law). The Court made this connection of *Moline* to *Gregory* in *Nelson v. Adams, USA, Inc.*, 529 U.S. 460, 471 (2000) and *Nat. Carbide Corp. v. Commissioner*, 336 U.S. 422 (1949). But even in 1935 the Court called *Gregory* a sham transaction case. Helvering v. Minnesota Tea Co., 296 U.S. 378, 385 (1935).

described in the statute.[525] The taxpayer contended the statute was unambiguous, and both the taxpayer and amicus in *Gregory* (the amicus was quite worried about uncertainty, if motive were to govern taxation of reorganizations) relied on *Isham*.[526] The taxpayer argued that if *Isham* were the law then the Court of Appeals must have construed the statute rather than found against her on the basis of her intent. And of course that is exactly what the Supreme Court held to have occurred, citing *Isham* for the last time in a civil tax Supreme Court opinion that did not involve the stamp tax at issue in *Isham*. In effect, the Supreme Court did not treat *Gregory v. Helvering* as an *Isham* case, but rather as a *Macomber* case,[527] involving a provision that it treated as ambiguous.

Contemporaneous commentators agreed that *Gregory* was a case of statutory construction. J.S. Seidman, a preeminent student and on-the-scene observer of the history and development of the federal tax laws, reported contemporaneously on the *Gregory* case.[528] He said tax experts thought that if the case went against the taxpayer it would be the death knell of tax minimization, and evidence of tax savings motive would render nugatory efforts to reduce taxes.[529] However, even though the decision went against the taxpayer, Seidman found it not to have those consequences; it had "a rather limited and restricted niche." Seidman thought that the Court simply construed the statute's phrase "in pursuance of a plan of reorganization" and found none on the facts required for a reorganization.

[525] *Cf.* Cavanaugh, *supra* note 36, at 577 (arguing that "reorganization" is a "core dependent homonym" and attempting to explain *Gregory* on that basis).

[526] Brief for the Petitioner, Gregory v. Helvering, 293 U.S. 465 (1935) (No. 127), 1934 WL 60333; Brief Amici Curiae, *Gregory*, 293 U.S. at 465, 1934 WL 60143. For discussion of *Isham*, *see supra* Ch. II.B.2.a(2).

[527] *See supra* Ch. II.B.2.c(3).

[528] Seidman, *The Gregory Reorganization Case*, 13 Tax Mag. 130 (1935).

[529] This was the import of the New York Times article on the opinion. Nelson, *Federal Victory in Tax Case*, N.Y. Times, Jan. 13, 1935 at 9 ("In all events, such a practice will probably do more to contribute to uncertainty to judicial interpretations than one of applied rigidity.").

The equally eminent observer, Randolph Paul, agreed.[530] Reorganization experts Baar and Morris agreed.[531] Even Learned Hand agreed.[532] Boris Bittker agreed.[533] A later dissenting view thought the statutory construction explanation was merely a cover for naked judicial power.[534] *Gregory* did "jolt" the tax bar in the area of corporate reorganizations, which had been thought to be unusually form driven, based on the statute being literally applied.[535] Unfortunately, in later decades, most commentators who did not think as deeply or have as much information have viewed *Gregory* as changing the entire universe of tax law interpretation to the substance model.[536]

It is critically important to recall that *Gregory* involved a real business transaction: the sale of stock to an unrelated buyer. It did not, for example, involve the reporting of an unsustained or artificial loss. Therefore, the taxpayer thought she fell within the doctrine allowing a real transaction to be accomplished in the most tax efficient way (the neutrality doctrine, discussed in Ch. II.C.2.a.), through use of a corporate reorganization. The taxpayer, however, did not attach sufficient important to the transitory nature of the corporation used to carry the asset to be sold out of the corporation that the taxpayer claimed to have been reorganized.

---

[530] Paul, Restatement of Tax Avoidance, 125 (1937); Paul, Studies III, at 126-27 ("in reality the case does not go so far as to wholesale indict tax avoidance; it involved a point of law, of statutory construction, in which the Court read the statute as requiring the reorganization to have a relation to the business reorganized").

[531] Baar and Morris, Hidden Traps in Corporate Reorganizations, 199 (Foundation Press 1935).

[532] Nat'l Investors Corp. v. Hoey, 144 F.2d 466 (2d Cir. 1944) (likening the reading of a business purpose requirement into "corporation" to what Gregory did for "reorganizations). On Thursday, December 13, 1951, Justice Robert H. Jackson spoke at the New York County Lawyers' Association's annual dinner, held at the Waldorf-Astoria Hotel in Manhattan. The Association and its 1,000 guests that evening honored senior federal Circuit Judges (and cousins) Learned Hand (age 79, and a judge since 1909) and August Noble Hand (age 82 and a judge since 1914). To close the program, Justice Jackson delivered a "benediction" speech that included a now-famous line: "If I were to write a prescription for becoming the perfect district judge, it would be always to quote Learned and always to follow Gus." *See* Cummings, *Quote Learned but Cite Gus*, 142 Tax Notes (TA) 993 (Mar. 3, 2014).

[533] Bittker, *Pervasive Judicial Doctrines in the Construction of the Internal Revenue Code*, 21 How. L.J. 693, 706-707, 714 (1978).

[534] Rice, *supra* note 377, at 1043.

[535] *See* Reiling, *supra* note 26, at 560 (the narrow view was "surprisingly jolted"); *see also* Miller, *Federal Courts as Makers of Income Tax Law*, *supra* note 524, at 152-53 (explaining how no one knew of the condition the Court imposed until it imposed it).

[536] *See, e.g.*, Nelson, *Substance Vital in Income Tax Suit, Technical Observance of All Legal Forms Insufficient if Evasion is Purpose—Common Law Expanding*, N.Y. Times, Aug. 4, 1945, at Bus. & Fin. 62 (attributing to *Gregory* a change requiring more than technical compliance, which he said was expanded by *Court Holding Co.* decision; "Definite expansion of the common law in its application to income taxes."); Friederich, *Substance versus Form in the Interpretation of the Internal Revenue Code*, U. of Ill. L. Forum 816, 817 (1967) ("After *Gregory* mere compliance with statutory form was an insufficient basis for assessing the tax consequences of a particular transaction."). *But cf.* Lederman, *W(h)ither Economic Substance?*, *supra* note 373, at 393 (agreeing that *Gregory* was a case of statutory construction).

Facts. Mrs. Gregory owned United Mortgage Corporation which owned stock in Monitor; United organized Averill Corporation and transferred Monitor shares to it. United distributed Averill stock to Mrs. Gregory. Averill quickly liquidated, distributing the Monitor stock to Mrs. Gregory (which would have been the only taxable event in the transactions as planned, producing a capital gain to Mrs. Gregory), who immediately sold it with no additional gain. United was the corporation that should have been "reorganized" to qualify the distribution for nonrecognition treatment under what is now section 355, but it was not; it merely disposed of an investment asset. Thus, the distribution could not be "in pursuance of a plan of reorganization."

Supreme Court's Analysis. The Supreme Court opinion did not disregard the transitory Averill Corporation because it never conducted any business (it existed less than a day). That would be the better analysis under the cluster rule of *Moline Properties, Inc.*, to be stated eight years later—a connection the Court later made.[537] Instead, the Supreme Court accepted the facts that the creation and dissolution of the transitory corporation actually occurred, and focused on the meaning of the controlling statutory term "in pursuance of a plan of reorganization." The Court's view that some real rearrangement of business, as opposed to investment assets, was required was not novel. In 1921 testimony in Congress, A.W. Gregg, the author of the reorganization section, said that reorganization exchanges were not to be taxed "in order that ordinary business transactions will not be prevented on account of the provisions of the tax law,"[538] which was quoted in a congressional report and quoted in the government's brief in *Gregory*.[539] Compared with this definition, it was clear that United was not trying to reorganize a corporation, but to sell stock on the market for the benefit of Mrs. Gregory. Furthermore, Justice McReynolds had stated in an earlier reorganization opinion, *Weiss v. Stearn*, that "… upon the transfer of its entire property and business for the purpose of reorganization and future conduct …" a reorganization could occur.[540]

There are several other factors supporting the view that the Supreme Court treated *Gregory* as a case of statutory interpretation, in addition to the words of the opinion. First, Justice Sutherland wrote the opinion. He was one of the conservative Justices who uniformly opposed New Deal legislation, opposed

---

[537] Nelson v. Adams, USA, Inc., 529 U.S. 460, 471 (2000) (identifying *Gregory* as a sham corporation case because of lack of business or corporate purpose). However, it is both inaccurate and leads to missing the real point of *Gregory* to assert that the Court disregarded the transitory corporation. This unfortunate gloss seems to be fixed in some Justices' minds, perhaps from their law school days. *See* Abramski v. United States, 134 S. Ct. 2259 (2014).

[538] *Treasury Expert Explains Tax Bill*, N.Y. Times, Jan. 5, 1924, at 1 (quoting A.W. Gregg, Statement of the Changes in the Revenue Act of 1921).

[539] Brief for the Respondent, Gregory v. Helvering 293 U.S. 465 (1935) (No. 127), 1934 WL 60141, at 6.

[540] Weiss v. Stearn, 265 U.S. 242 (1924).

the exercise of power by the federal government, and stated that judges could only apply the law as written.[541]

Second, in the context of the times, the affirmation that tax free reorganizations were appropriate for "normal business readjustments" could be viewed as a pro-business position that both coincided with the contentions of corporate America and served to preserve the nonrecognition rule by showing it should be properly limited. In 1933 and 1934, there were serious proposals to repeal the reorganization allowances entirely.[542] Instead, in 1934 Congress amended the reorganization definition in section 112 by replacing the ambiguous parenthetical that had encompassed what are now the Types B and C reorganizations with more exact descriptions of those types of reorganization.[543] No doubt the Justices were aware of this and so even business oriented Justices would have an interest in preserving the true function of the nonrecognition rules.

Third, the only cases the Supreme Court's opinion cited were for the proposition that taxpayers are allowed to plan to reduce their taxes, which hardly suggests that the Court was creating an anti-abuse rule. Fourth, the first argument made by the amicus brief, which was signed by such luminaries as Whitney North Seymour, was that the Second Circuit had erroneously relied on the Supreme Court's opinion in *Pinellas*,[544] which they distinguished as a case of statutory interpretation: what was the meaning of "securities." They argued "no violence is done to the statutory language by that decision."[545] Presumably the Court wished to show that it was doing no violence to the statutory language by its decision in *Gregory*.

Seidman agreed that the *Gregory* opinion established that motive (meaning taxpayer purpose) is important in reorganizations, but only because the statute makes it so, as construed: "That is a far cry from saying that hereafter tax motives are to be regarded as putrefying a transaction. Motives become immaterial where the statute ignores them or does not condition tax consequences upon them."[546] He observed that the ruling can be pro-taxpayer where losses are concerned. Others read *Gregory* the same way.[547]

---

[541] MASON, THE SUPREME COURT FROM TAFT TO WARREN 138-40 (1958); Ferguson, *The Legacy of Louis Eisenstein*, 32 TAX L. REV. 7, 17 (1966) (identifying Sutherland as a "patron saint" of the letter of the tax law).

[542] S. COMM. OF HOUSE WAYS AND MEANS PREVENTION OF TAX AVOIDANCE, PRELIMINARY REPORT, 73d Cong. 8 (Comm. Print 1933). *See* Bank, *supra* note 487, at 1177-86.

[543] *See* Bank, *supra* note 487, at 1177-86.

[544] Pinellas Ice and Cold Storage Co. v. Commissioner, 287 U.S. 462 (1933).

[545] Brief Amici Curiae, Gregory v. Helvering, 293 U.S. 465 (1935) (No. 127), 1934 WL 60143.

[546] Seidman, *supra* note 528, at 130.

[547] *See* Brady, *A Challenge to the Right of Legitimate Tax Savings*, 13 TAX MAG. 571 (1935); *see also* Rudick, *supra* note 166, at 255 (the court "interpolated" the business purpose requirement into the statute).

Most of the later broader reading of *Gregory* is based on Learned Hand's opinion in the Second Circuit.[548] The Supreme Court did not adopt Hand's opinion.[549] Nevertheless, Judge Hand's words frequently are cited as authoritative, as for example this statement in another Second Circuit opinion: "The doctrine of *Gregory v. Helvering* . . . means that in construing words of a tax statute which describes commercial or industrial transactions we are to understand them to refer to transactions entered upon for commercial or industrial purposes and not to include transactions entered upon for no other motive but to escape taxation."[550] Hence one origin of the economic substance doctrine.

Gregory predated by five years the Court's other major construction in 1940 in *Le Tulle* of an uncodified requirement into the reorganization statute: the creation of the continuity of interest doctrine.[551] That construction is more radical than the one in *Gregory* because it was not based on common usage but perhaps on the fact that the Court wanted to enforce the fundamental tax concept that a reorganization was accorded nonrecognition because it was different from a sale.[552] The continuity requirement was forecast in 1933 by *Pinellas,*[553] but *Le Tulle* announced a requirement of "proprietary interest," or at least that the need for such an interest was not satisfied by

---

[548] *See, e.g.,* Chirelstein, *supra* note 368, at 450-51; Isenbergh, *Musings on Form and Substance in Taxation*, 49 U. Chi. L. Rev. 859 (ignoring the Supreme Court opinion and categorizing the "reorganization" as a Code created term rather than one reflecting common understanding, as the Supreme Court found); Likhovski, *supra* note 162, at 953; Steinberg, *Form, Substance and Directionality in Subchapter C*, 52 Tax Law. 457 (1999).

[549] *Cf.* Madison, *supra* note 15, at 721-22 (claiming that the Court adopted Hand's opinion; it is "more eloquent.").

[550] Commissioner v. Transp. Trading and Terminal Corp., 176 F.2d 570, 572 (2d Cir. 1949). *See generally* Bittker & Lokken, at 4.3.4.

[551] LeTulle v. Scofield, 308 U.S. 415 (1940). It was not until *Le Tulle* that the Court took the leap to say that even though the act provided that an exchange for security debt met its requirement, there was a further requirement of an ownership interest continuity. The profound effect of *Gregory* and its status as a statutory construction decision is evidenced by the statement in *Le Tulle* that the reorganization section "is not to be read literally." *See* Bittker & Eustice, at 12.21[2][a].

[552] David S. Miller aptly concluded that ". . . for the first time, the Supreme Court implied that the continuity of interest doctrine might be regarded as a requirement wholly independent of the statutory language." Miller, *The Devolution and Eventual Extinction of the Continuity of Interest Doctrine*, 97 Tax Notes Today 189-40 (Sept. 25, 1997).

[553] Pinellas Ice & Cold Storage Co. v. Commissioner, 287 U.S. 462 (1933). The Court appeared to have construed a continuity requirement into the definition of reorganization but actually held only that short term notes were not the "stock or securities" that must be exchanged in order for a reorganization to qualify for tax-free treatment. The Court probably relied on the fact that the asset transfer at issue was supposed to be analogous to a merger and mergers were commonly understood to involve a continuation of shareholders. *See* Cummings, *Core-Dependent Homonyms, supra* note 518, at 495. Shortly after the Court decided *Gregory v. Helvering,* it cited *Pinellas* rather than *Gregory* for the view that common understanding of a reorganization did not include a transaction in which the target shareholders did indirectly receive the acquirer's stock, but in an odd way. Bus & Transport Sec. Corp. v. Helvering, 296 U.S. 391 (1935).

the receipt of long term (secured) debt, which the statute indicated was sufficient. Previously proprietary interest had not been a commonly used term and when it had been used, referred to voting control.[554] *Le Tulle* reversed six courts of appeal and the Court of Claims, which viewed a real interest in the affairs of the business to be provided by bonds secured on the transferred business assets.[555]

Without denying that the Court purported to interpret or construe the statute in *Gregory*, some view the effort as an unreasonable reach beyond the words of the statute.[556] However, that argument also is based on an extensive analysis of legislative history.[557] Therefore it is ultimately consistent with the view expressed here that the Supreme Court attempted to carry out the purposes of Congress with some degree of respect for the words of the statute.

Gregory and *Le Tulle* established corporate reorganizations as an important area for cluster rules on the construction of the reorganization statute, a statute that had been thought to be unambiguous. They show that the Supreme Court will fill gaps in the revenue laws by construing terms that the Court finds to be implicit in common understanding, and hence the Congress' intent, for the provision. They do not stand for any generalized anti-abuse or pro-government reading, much less the economic substance doctrine.

III.C.3.a(2) Higgins v. Smith*: Facts*

Higgins v. Smith involved ambiguous facts and a clear statute.[558] It was viewed as the first example of a turning of the Court toward judicial legislation in the tax area to meet the need for revenue.[559] The key points about this case are as follows:

- It is a fraud case, although the jury refunded the fraud penalty and the government did not appeal that verdict.[560]
- It can be viewed as an application of the cluster rule of *Moline Properties, Inc.* to determine whether a shareholder's dealings with his corporation will be respected according to form (". . . so long as that purpose is the

---

[554] *See* Bickford's, Inc. v. Helvering, 98 F.2d 568 (2d Cir. 1938). Conversely, other contemporaneous usage treated proprietary interest as indicative of legal ownership. *See* In re National Pub. Serv., Corp. 18 F. Supp. 293 (S.D.N.Y. 1936).

[555] *See, e.g.*, Commissioner v. Tyng, 106 F.2d 55 (2d Cir. 1939), *rev'd*, 308 U.S. 527 (1940); Nash, *What Law of Taxation?* 9 Fordham L. Rev. 165, 192 (1940) (distinguishing *Tyng* and *Le Tulle* from cases like *Gregory* and stating that they were bona fide transactions relying on commonly understood meaning of the statute).

[556] Coverdale, *Text as Limit: A Plea for a Decent Respect for the Tax Code*, 71 Tul. L. Rev. 1501, 1532-33 (1997).

[557] *Id.* at 1533-38.

[558] Higgins v. Smith, 308 U.S. 473 (1940). When the shoe was on the other foot and the corporation sold the asset to the shareholder, it had to recognize the gain. Burnet v. Commonwealth Improvement Co., 287 U.S. 415 (1932). For additional analysis of *Higgins v. Smith, see infra* Ch. VI.F.3.b(2).

[559] Goldberg, *supra* note 175, at 28.

[560] *See* Smith v. Higgins, 102 F.2d 456 (2d Cir. 1939).

equivalent of business activity or is followed by the carrying on of business by the corporation, the corporation remains a separate taxable entity."),[561] even though it was decided two-and-a-half years before that rule was announced.

- The *Moline* rule is a distinct cluster rule worked out by the Supreme Court in *National Carbide* and *Bollinger* for corporate entities (see Ch. VI.F.3.b. below).
- However, the *Smith* opinion contains some of the broadest dictum appearing in any Supreme Court opinion that has been cited in support of various doctrines.[562]
- Properly read, *Smith* does not create or rely on a tax specific doctrine (aside from a preview of *Moline*).

Facts. The taxpayer, John Thomas Smith, was the General Counsel of General Motors. In 1926, he set up what can be called a desk drawer corporation that he wholly owned, which would enjoy a lower rate of tax on income from various stocks he transferred to it. When losses came in vogue in 1929, he also used the corporation to facilitate his recognition of losses by purportedly selling stocks to it, without losing control of the stock sold.[563] Smith litigated the same issues for different years in the Board of Tax Appeals and the federal district court (the latter led to the opinion discussed here). Both the Supreme Court (in *Moline Properties, Inc.*) and the Second Circuit (in Smith's appeal from the Board of Tax Appeals) thought that Smith's corporation did not earn the income ascribed to it and thus did not operate at all as a separate entity, which is the crux of the Court's ruling. The various decisions in taxpayer Smith's cases were as follows:

- On March 6, 1939, the Second Circuit (including Learned Hand, who had thwarted Mrs. Gregory's tax reduction efforts 5 years earlier) reversed a jury verdict that denied Smith a loss on a sale of stock to his corporation for 1932.[564]

---

561 Moline Properties, Inc. v. Commissioner, 319 U.S. 436 (1943); *see infra* Ch. VI.F.3.b.

562 For example:

> On the other hand, the Government may not be required to acquiesce in the taxpayer's election of that form for doing business which is most advantageous to him. The Government may look at actualities and upon determination that the form employed for doing business or carrying out the challenged tax event is unreal or a sham may sustain or disregard the effect of the fiction as best serves the purposes of the tax statute. To hold otherwise would permit the schemes of taxpayers to supersede legislation in the determination of the time and manner of taxation. It is command of income and its benefits which marks the real owner of property.

Higgins, 308 U.S. at 477.

563 Smith v. Commissioner, 40 B.T.A. 387 (1939).

564 *Smith v. Higgins*, 102 F.2d at 456. The corporation paid by offsetting a debt Smith owed the corporation; the corporation retained the shares.

- On August 15, 1939, the Board of Tax Appeals ruled the same way as the Second Circuit had on similar issues for earlier years of Smith, also rejecting government claims that the income of the corporation with respect to stock it bought should be taxed to Smith.[565]
- On January 8, 1940, the Supreme Court reversed the Second Circuit as to Smith's stock sale loss in the decision at issue here.
- On August 9, 1940, the Board vacated its prior decision in the other case and entered judgment for the government on the stock loss based on the Supreme Court's recent ruling, *but refused to disregard the corporate entity for purposes of attributing its income generally to Smith.*[566]
- On June 1, 1943, the Supreme Court released its opinion in *Moline Properties, Inc.*, which cited *Higgins v. Smith* as an example of the rare exception to the general (new) rule that corporations that carried on any business would be respected, in contrast with the Smith corporation that was a "sham or unreal. . . bald and mischievous fiction."
- On June 9, 1943, the Second Circuit reversed as to the income inclusion in the appeal from the Board of Tax Appeals case, citing *Moline* and thus totally disregarding the corporation.[567]

In the appeal from the Board of Tax Appeals, Judge Augustus Hand summarized the facts that made the corporation unreal; they amount to the shareholder not treating it as real, or rather not allowing it to conduct the business that the shareholder actually conducted:

> He retained as much practical control over the corporate assets of Innisfail as though they were his own. The directors, other than himself, were his friends and he was both the president of the company and its sole stockholder. *He kept its securities with his own and his wife's in his safe deposit boxes. No notes were issued for advances made by himself or Innisfail to one another and no interest was charged by either on balances.* He could and did operate Innisfail to his great advantage in respect to saving of taxes. . . . there was no substantial business reason for the creation or continued existence of Innisfail since its only, or at least, its main object was to furnish the owner of all its stock with a means of diminishing his taxes. It not only conducted no business enterprise but had no justification for existence even as a holding company. *It ordinarily left its securities in Smith's name and possession, and*

[565] Smith v. Commissioner, 40 B.T.A. 387 (1939).

[566] Smith v. Commissioner, 42 B.T.A. 505 (1940).

[567] Commissioner v. Smith,136 F.2d 556 (2d Cir. 1943). The Second Circuit also called the corporation a "personal agency." It directed a "consolidation" of the two incomes. It made no mention of the possibility of applying Revenue Acts section 45 (current section 482) or section 104 (accumulated earnings tax), either of which would have seemed applicable. It rejected the Board's distinction between losses and dividends as "illusory" in light of the complete lack of business purpose or business conduct by the corporation and ordered the Commissioner to "consolidate" the income of the corporation with the shareholder.

most of its dealings with him merely took the form of book entries.[568] (emphasis added)

Although Hand mentioned control, control cannot be the talisman because it always exists in closely held corporations. Similarly, formation of a corporation for purposes of saving its shareholder taxes cannot be the talisman because that has been commonly allowed.[569] Rather, the shareholder's failure to treat the corporation as a separate entity, to rent for it a safe deposit box, to give it notes for debts, to set up its own bank account rather than using book entries, and most importantly to transfer assets into its name, present difficult hurdles for a shareholder to overcome when he has the burden of proof and is held to his form.[570] In other words, Mr. Smith conducted the alleged corporate business in the form of a proprietorship, and the Court held him to *that* form.

Higgins v. Smith is one of several important decisions the Supreme Court announced in 1940, which was a pivotal year because it reflected the complete New Deal Court for the first time, and because interest in taxes and tax cheats had been at a high point for several years due to revelations of tax avoidance.[571] The *Smith* decision has been cited many times, usually for the wrong reasons. Superficially, the case might appear to stand for some special prohibition on tax advantaged dealings with wholly owned corporations, or on loss recognition on a sale to such a corporation, or a special rule for dealings between a single shareholder and his corporation. In hindsight, it might appear to be an early example of a the ESD. It is none of these.

The Supreme Court decided the case, as did the jury it affirmed, on the basis of an important cluster rule that disregards a corporation that exists in legal form when it does not reach a low threshold for entity treatment (see Ch. VI.F.3.b.); there was a business being conducted (investing in stocks), but the corporation did not conduct it. This understanding of the holding is supported by three linkages listed below of *Higgins* with *Moline Properties, Inc.*,[572] the seminal decision on the corporate entity treatment, decided two-

---

[568] *Id.*

[569] *See* BITTKER & LOKKEN, at 85.3.1.

[570] *See, e.g.*, Roubik v. Commissioner, 53 T.C. 365 (1969) ("Nor do we think that the corporation was ever, as a practical matter, given the right to direct any of its "employees" in their professional activities."); *see infra* Ch. VI.F.3.

[571] PAUL, PROSPERITY, at 58 (Congress' Joint Committee on Tax Evasion and Avoidance met in 1937, when J.P. Morgan stated "If the government does not know how to collect its taxes, a man is a fool to pay them."); *cf.* Barker, *supra* note 25, at 821, 855 (also identifying 1940 as "an important turning point at which the Court openly rejected the fetters of past precedents in interpreting tax statutes").

[572] Moline Properties, Inc. v. Commissioner, 319 U.S. 436 (1943).

and-a-half years later by the Supreme Court (in addition to the further link that Justice Reed wrote both opinions):[573]

- *Higgins* is the example that *Moline* cites of the rare corporation that cannot clear the low threshold for being respected as an entity because it has no actual or intended business activity. *Moline* also cites *Gregory*, but incorrectly because the Court did not disregard the corporation's existence in *Gregory* (although it might have, under the *Moline* standard).
- The Second Circuit in Mr. Smith's parallel Tax Court case on appeal agreed that the corporation should be disregarded on that basis, after obviously waiting for the *Moline* decision.[574]

National Carbide treated *Higgins v. Smith* as an example of a *Moline* unreal corporation.[575] The Supreme Court also later characterized *Higgins* as an "alter ego" situation.[576]

So understood, *Higgins v. Smith* is not nearly as remarkable as its broad language might suggest, but it is important for two other reasons. The Supreme Court later referred to it as a case of sham, implying that the use of the corporation was fraudulent;[577] also the Service asserted the civil fraud penalty but the jury did not impose it. Also, the case establishes a benchmark for when a one shareholder corporation that exists entirely on paper does and does not carry on business separate from the shareholder (see further discussion in Ch. VI.F.3.b.).

Higgins v. Smith's significance is reduced by its procedural posture. The Court simply let stand a jury verdict that the nominal business activities of

---

[573] Justice Stanley Reed wrote both *Moline Properties* (1943) and *Higgins* (1940) and cited *Higgins* in *Moline* as an example of a sham corporation that did not carry on a business. He also cited *Gregory*, which was decided before Reed was Solicitor General or on the Court, as involving a sham corporation. Perhaps in hindsight that was an alternate ground for *Gregory*, but we know from the analysis above that the Court did not reject the reality of Averill and that *Gregory* was a statutory construction case based on "reorganization" and not "association." Therefore, *Higgins v. Smith* was Reed's best example of what he had viewed as a disregardable corporation.

[574] Commissioner v. Smith, 136 F.2d 556 (2d Cir.) (issued on June 9, 1943). *Moline* was issued June 1, 1943.

[575] National Carbide Corp. v. Commissioner, 336 U.S. 422 (1949) ("sham or unreal," but also referring to *Gregory v. Helvering* in same category, evidently lifting the idea from *Helvering v. Minnesota Tea Co.*, 296 U.S. 378 (1935), where it was improperly applied because *Gregory* did not find the transitory corporation to be a sham, although it might have).

[576] G.M. Leasing Corp. v. United States, 429 U.S. 338, 351 (1977).

[577] Moline Properties, Inc. v. Commissioner, 319 U.S. at 436 (bald and mischevious fiction); *see infra* Ch. VI.E.1.e(2).

the corporation were actually those of its shareholder.[578] The case might have gone off on the law peculiar to loss allowance (loss must be "sustained" to be deducted under section 165),[579] if the trial court had so charged, but it did not. Alternately, the case could have rested on whether the corporation was Smith's agent, but evidently the Service did not pursue that argument due to the high threshold the Service wanted to erect for agency status when the taxpayer wanted it (as adopted in 1949 in *National Carbide*[580]) and the fact that the Court emphatically respected separate treatment of shareholder and corporation in *Eisner v. Macomber*.[581]

If the broad dictum in *Smith* is read to go farther,[582] the case is a sport, not to be followed. Four circuits had ruled for taxpayers on similar facts; none for the government, as Justice Roberts pointed out in the dissent. Roberts also said that "the Solicitor General considered the law so well settled that he refused to apply for certiorari in the *Eldridge*[583] case, although the Treasury recommended such action."[584] That Solicitor General was the author of the *Higgins* opinion, Justice Stanley Reed, and the *Eldridge* case was one of the

---

578

> The trial court gave an instruction, which this Court approved, that the jury were to find whether the sales by Smith to the corporation, out of which grew the asserted loss, were actual transfers of property out of Smith into something that existed separate and apart from him, or to be regarded as simply a transfer by Smith's left hand "being his individual hand, into his right hand, being his corporate hand, so that in truth and fact there was no transfer at all." The jury took the latter view and brought in a verdict for the Collector. This Court not only said there was sufficient evidence to sustain the verdict. The opinion goes further and adds that "this domination and control is so obvious in a wholly owned corporation as to require a peremptory instruction that no loss in the statutory sense could occur upon a sale by a taxpayer to such an entity.

Brief for Petitioner, *Moline Properties*, 319 U.S. at 436 (No. 660), 1943 WL 71819.

579 *See* Surrey, *Supreme Court and the Federal Income Tax, supra* note 285, at 801 (stating such a view).

580 *Nat'l Carbide Corp.*, 336 U.S. at 438 n. 20 (observing that while Smith's corporation might have been his agent, it could not have been because it was not recognized as a separate entity).

581 Eisner v. Macomber, 252 U.S. 189 (1920).

582

> If, on the other hand, the *Gregory* case is viewed as a precedent for the disregard of a transfer of assets without a business purpose but solely to reduce tax liability, it gives support to the natural conclusion that transactions, which do not vary control or change the flow of economic benefits, are to be dismissed from consideration. There is no illusion about the payment of a tax exaction. Each tax, according to a legislative plan, raises funds to carry on government. The purpose here is to tax earnings and profits less expenses and losses. If one or the other factor in any calculation is unreal, it distorts the liability of the particular taxpayer to the detriment or advantage of the entire taxpaying group.

Higgins v. Smith, 308 U.S. 473 (1940).

583 Commissioner v. Eldridge, 79 F.2d 629 (9th Cir. 1935).

584 *Higgins*, 308 U.S. at 486, n. 12 (Roberts, J., dissenting).

lower court decisions for the taxpayer on this issue. Professor Chirelstein has described how *Smith* troubled Learned Hand, who viewed it as "extremely puzzling" and "as having expressed a broader view of the *Gregory* decision than he himself had intended."[585]

Three other Supreme Court decisions that were contemporaneous with *Smith* further evidence the narrowness and the factual nature of its holding.

1. *Smith* is contrary to the Court's general view applied in *Interstate Transit Lines*[586] that a sole shareholder and its corporation are separate entities.
2. *Helvering v. Johnson,* argued at the same time as *Smith,* came out the other way on a four-to-four *per curiam* affirmance leaving the Court of Appeals decision for the taxpayer intact.[587] The difference between the two cases seemed to be that the taxpayer's wife was also a shareholder of the corporation to which he sold stock at a loss.[588]
3. A case often cited as paired with *Smith* (as for example in Regulation section 1.269-2), but actually much more straightforward in its reasoning, is *Griffiths.*[589] It addressed the timing of a sale, and ruled that it occurred in the hands of the shareholder and not the corporation to which the shareholder attempted to shift the sale.[590] Thus, *Griffiths* is simply a *Court Holding* assignment of income case, another cluster case discussed below, and not at all like *Smith.*[591]

---

[585] Chirelstein, *supra* note 368, at 450-51 (noting that others found its rationale was "difficult to isolate . . .").

[586] *Interstate Transit Lines v. Commissioner*, 319 U.S. 590, 593 (1943), also written by Justice Reed, held that a parent could not take a section 162 deduction for the operating deficit of its subsidiary, which it had formed and contracted with to carry on its business in a state where the parent could not legally be licensed. The Court in effect construed the statutory phrase "in carrying on any trade or business" to refer to the trade or business carried on by the subsidiary and gave no thought to the possibility that the trade or business of the parent might suffice. Thus, in effect, the Court thought Congress would not have intended such result. Reed made a *cf.* cite to *Smith* in analyzing the possibility, which he granted could be the case that the subsidiary operated as agent for the taxpayer, at least as to the interstate part of its business, which the taxpayer could have conducted. This shows that he viewed *Smith* as involving a corporation that operated its sole shareholder's business. Justice Jackson wrote a cogent dissent arguing that just as a business can deduct the cost of legal services that it cannot supply because it is not a licensed attorney so it should also be allowed to deduct the loss of its California business.

[587] Helvering v. Johnson, 308 U.S. 523 (1939).

[588] Moreover, this is consistent with the result in the case against Andrew Mellon, who was charged with civil tax fraud for essentially the same sort of sales at a loss to his family's banking and other corporations; he won presumably in part because he was not the sole shareholder of the buyers. Mellon v. Commissioner, 36 B.T.A. 977 (1937).

[589] Griffiths v. Helvering, 308 U.S. 355 (1939).

[590] In *Griffiths*, an individual attempted to shift to his controlled corporation a tort recovery. The Supreme Court cited *Lucas v. Earl* and indicated it was deciding on assignment of income grounds. The Board found as a fact: "This petitioner had sold and transferred his stock and the claim against Lay before the settlement with Lay had reached the stage where it had any income tax significance." The Court of Appeals reversed, and the Supreme Court affirmed. *Id.*

[591] *See infra* Ch. VI.F.2.d.

The Supreme Court has no subsequent record of viewing *Smith* or *Griffiths* as standing for a general doctrine. Rather, it has cited *Smith* for two points: for the point that a sale by one person cannot be converted into a sale by another,[592] and the Commissioner may disregard a corporation that is "a sham or unreal,"[593] meaning it does not have the minimally required level of business activity of its own to be regarded as an entity for tax purposes under the *Moline Properties, Inc.* standard.

However, some contemporaneous commentators gave the 1940 string of anti-avoidance decisions considerable prominence in creating a larger zone of uncertainty.[594] This no doubt suited the government, which wanted *Higgins v. Smith* construed as an all purpose doctrine that a transaction producing a loss or exemption must have been entered into for a purpose other than tax avoidance.[595] Commentators clearly saw *Smith* as rejecting reliance purely on the form of a corporate entity, but not supplying a clear rule for how much more was required. Indeed, these reactions forecast how cases like *Smith* could be misread as support for an economic substance doctrine:

> There is more than an indication in the decisions of the present term that the Court is itself willing to supply deficiencies in the statute [citing *Higgins v. Smith*] . . . It may come to pass that a legislature eager to rid itself of the laborious task of attempting to write an air-tight taxing statute will abandon the job to the courts, contenting itself with a simple declaration of policy that it wishes to tax incomes of certain individuals at certain rates. . . . the real difficulty . . . is lack of assurance as to what legal consequences are apt to follow a proposed course of action involving tax matters. If one can-

[592] Commissioner v. Court Holding Co., 324 U.S. 331 (1945).

[593] National Carbide Corp. v. Commissioner, 336 U.S. 422 (1949); Moline Properties, Inc. v. Commissioner, 319 U.S. 436 (1943).

[594] *See* Case, *Disregard of Corporate Entity in Federal Taxation: The Modern Approach*, 30 Va. L. Rev. 398, 414 (1944) (reading *Higgins* and *Griffiths* as standing for ability of the government to ignore corporations available for tax avoidance purposes); Harrar, *The Function of the Entity in Federal Income Taxation: Recent Developments*, 25 Minn. L. Rev. 189, 200 (1941) (Higgins will "mean all things to all men"); Levitt, *Disregarding the Corporate Entity in Tax Cases*, 22 Taxes (CCH) 457, 464 (1944) (surveying the various authorities and listing eight possible scenarios on which validly existing corporations might have their transactions disregarded, and concluding that it came down to "anti-social stockholder ends"); Rudick, *supra* note 166, at 260-63.

[595] *See* Nash, *supra* note 555, at 187 (noting that the predecessor of section 267, which would have prevented the loss allowance at issue, had been adopted six years earlier, thus long since closing the loophole).

not obtain this assurance from a reading of the statute, the only remaining source of a beforehand answer is the Treasury.[596]

[*Higgins v. Smith*] creates a dangerously bureaucratic precedent in its clear implication that 'the government may sustain or disregard the effect of the (corporate) fiction as best serves the purposes of the tax statute.' Such a conclusion is fully repudiated by Mr. Justice Holmes' observation that "If it is a fiction, it is a fiction created by law with intent that it should be acted on as if true."[597]

Higgins v. Smith is a remarkable challenge to the capacities of intelligent tax administration. . . . The case for continued uncertainty is frequently pitched on the thought that precise delineations of principle simply advise the chronic avoider how to escape tax, and that uncertainty is a necessity if not a virtue. This argument is a ghost which should be laid once and for all.[598]

. . . the usually accepted division of labor between a legislature and a court would suggest that [the result in *Smith*] . . . should have been reached, as it later was, by statute rather than by decision. . . . The Court ought not to feel that it has the burden of supplying statutory omissions in the few individual cases that come before it eight or ten years after the event."[599]

Stanley Surrey foresaw the untoward consequences of an opinion like *Smith*:

While . . . the approach being developed by the . . . *Higgins* type cases is justifiable, that approach demands a high degree of technical competence. One Supreme Court decision commences a pattern which must be filled in by hundreds of lower court decisions and administrative rulings. The

---

596 *Id.* at 190-93; *see also* Goldberg, *supra* note 175, at 25, 29 (". . . the rule of *Gould v. Gould* . . . seems to have yielded in favor of judicial legislation . . . [so] judges must and do legislate" and the issue is whether they legislate differently in tax cases. As early as 1940 the trend was detected by Justice Roberts in his dissents in *Smith* and in *Clifford*: "A judgment by the high court becomes a mandate for all others." The article notes a shift from guarded statements to broad generalizations. "To say that taxation depends on substance rather than form is well enough when added to a more particularized reason based on the statute but otherwise it itself exalts form over substance, yielding to tags tickets and slogans. The *Dobson* rule left to the tax court all matters that were not clear cut issues of law."); Paul, Studies III, at 207 n. 155 (identifying *Smith* as the more radical step among radical tax opinions).

597 Dean, *Decadence of the Corporate Device*, 15 Temp. L. Q. 65, 86-7 (1941).

598 Eisenstein, *Some Iconoclastic Reflections on Tax Administration*, 58 Harv. L. Rev. 477, 497-503 (1945). However, in another article he thought that the concern about confusing Supreme Court decisions was overblown. Eisenstein, *The Clifford Regulations and the Heavenly City of Legislative Intent*, 2 Tax L. Rev. 327, 388 (1947) (Describes the heavenly city that existed before the Supreme Court began to legislate when the personnel changed, evidently in late 1930's. He does not agree; but he acknowledged the change.); Eisenstein, *Estate Taxes and the Higher Learning of the Supreme Court*, 3 Tax L. Rev. 395, 431 (1948) (spoke of the renovated and reconstructed Supreme court, which saw few if any limits on the power to tax transmission of property).

599 Magill, *supra* note 431, at 10.

> intent of the Supreme Court is as vital in the tax field as is the intent of the Congress. If the developing lines of the pattern are not clearly indicated, much costly litigation will ensue. Thoughts must be phrased with caution and an eye to their use in other situations. Lawyers and judges are prone to cull quotations from the Supreme Court's decisions in much the same manner as theatrical producers choose phrases from the reviews of dramatic critics for their newspaper advertisements . . . Nor should the Court's energies be dissipated on the trivia of income tax litigation.[600]

In more recent years, the Supreme Court in *Cottage Savings*[601] distinguished *Higgins v. Smith* because it was the only case the government cited. This is a telling rejection; evidently the Service wanted to rely on this most bold source of judicial power statements, but the Court wanted to rely on the facts of legal ownership to determine tax outcomes.

In conclusion, never after *Higgins v. Smith* has the Supreme Court so cavalierly ignored a corporation in a tax case (including *Moline Properties, Inc.*). Properly viewed, *Smith* is either the example of the corporation that did not conduct business that failed the *Moline* test, or a case rested on the corporation serving as agent of its shareholder. *See* Ch. VI.F.3.b. for further discussion of the separateness of corporations.

III.C.3.b. *The Court Deals with an Ambiguous Section:* McWilliams v. Commissioner

McWilliams is like *Macomber* in that it purported to interpret an ambiguous section; it is like *Smith* in being the Court's second major apparent reach too far in the government's favor, though requiring an interpretive rather than a factual explanation. The key points about *McWilliams*[602] are as follows:

- It is a case of statutory construction focusing on the words: "no deduction shall in any case be allowed in respect of losses from sales or exchanges of property, directly or indirectly . . . between members of a family, . . ."[603]
- The Court construed "indirectly" to include a sale that literally was not of the same property "between" the family members.
- The Court was motivated by perceived congressional purpose and an apparent sense that it was up to the Court to prevent massive tax avoidance that would be very damaging to the fisc.

---

600 Surrey, *Supreme Court and the Federal Income Tax*, *supra* note 285, at 813. Surrey also observed that in the *Higgins* and *Clifford* decisions the Court did not make fine distinctions of law but rather looked to the realities and rejected the taxpayer's transaction that had no purpose but tax avoidance, stating: ". . .such an attitude if continued will have a profound effect upon our tax structure." *Id.* at 803-04.

601 Cottage Savings Assn. v. Commissioner, 499 U.S. 554 (1991).

602 McWilliams v. Commissioner, 331 U.S. 694 (1947); *see* Feld, *When Fungible Portfolio Assets Meet: A Problem of Tax Recognition*, 44 Tax Law. 409, 439 (1990) (calling *McWilliams* "celebrated," without cite).

603 Goldberg, *supra* note 175, at 45 (identifying the case as one of statutory construction).

- The Court did not employ a doctrine, but rather employed an extreme purposive statutory construction that the Court likely would not pursue today.

Facts. Husband and wife filed separate returns and had their own bank accounts and stock accounts. On various occasions in 1940 and 1941 husband directed that stock owned by himself, his wife or mother, be sold on the market and an identical number of shares be bought at the same time on the market for one of the other persons. Each paired purchase and sale was at the same price, although the taxpayer did not require that. Husband expected the loss sales would avoid the loss disallowance rule of section 267, which was applicable to related party sales; there was then no "wash sale" rule. The Service disagreed.

It did not claim that the proceeds of the sales were used to make the simultaneous purchases, or that there was any shifting of funds related to the transactions, or that one person was the agent of another person. Thus, the facts were much cleaner than in *Higgins v. Smith*. Nevertheless, the Supreme Court sustained a reversal of the Tax Court, which had found separate sales and purchases to have occurred with the market, not the family members. The Supreme Court reasoned that the term "directly or indirectly" in the statute encompassed these transactions, despite the fact that the relative did not buy the shares that the seller husband sold. The decision clearly was a reach because the several cases cited by the government for an expansive application of section 267 had all involved strawmen or some intermingling of funds.[604]

Decision's Significance. One might explain *McWilliams* as standing for strict construction of an anti-abuse rule (section 267) against the taxpayer, but the Court has never said that and has acted otherwise in relation to the analogous section 482 in its one case considering that section.[605] If not so viewed, *McWilliams* can seem to be a sport, a bridge too far, to which the Supreme Court has not returned. It is best understood as a purposive reading of the Code, albeit based on slim statutory basis. The lower courts and the Service have not been inclined to extend it beyond its facts of purely simultaneous

---

[604] Brief for the Respondent, McWilliams v. Commissioner, 331 U.S. 694 (1947) (No. 945), 1947 WL 44077.

[605] *See* Commissioner v. First Sec. Bank, 405 U.S. 394 (1972) (Commissioner cannot allocate income to a taxpayer that could not legally have earned it). However, the Court downplayed the significance of *First Security in United States v. Bayse*, 410 U.S. 441, 453 n. 13 (1973), citing it for a "peculiar" circumstance where the assignment of income doctrine could not be applied because the taxpayer could not legally have earned, and thus assigned, the income.

transactions ordered by one person.[606] The Service has never cited it in a letter ruling interpreting section 267. However, *McWilliams* did plant the concept that "indirectly" means something more than a transaction conducted through a third party serving as agent or strawman.[607]

McWilliams should be limited to agency situations (which it likely was not). It was wrong in effectively attributing ownership of stock from a relative because it is well understood that attribution rules apply only where specifically stated, and not otherwise.[608] Therefore, stock owned indirectly by the husband either means anything a court wants it to mean or it means indirect ownership as commonly understood, which is ownership by an agent.

Unfortunately, the Court did not go into any such analysis. Rather it depended on the view that the stock bought and sold were "fungibles." The opinion viewed the failure to consider fungibles as the same stock as "crippling" the statute and leaving a loophole as large as the one Congress sought to close. This is a quaint view of loopholes by today's standards: the seller really did sustain a loss and another taxpayer bought stock with his own money, hardly crippling to the Treasury.[609]

What happened in *McWilliams* looks a lot like what happened in *Cottage Savings,* which came out the other way 50 years later.[610] It is hard to square *McWilliams* with *Cottage Savings,* except by saying that the mortgage pools exchanged in *Cottage Savings* were more different than identical shares, which is true enough, but is a formal rather than a substantive difference. Moreover, the Court has not before or since viewed market stock as fungible for tax purposes,[611] except in relation to stock lending transactions; the Treasury clearly

---

[606] *See* United States v. Norton, 250 F.2d 902 (5th Cir. 1958) (son sold 800 shares and mother bought 800 shares 28 days later at different price; said "control" broken by 28 days); G.C.M. 34,706 (Dec. 3, 1971) (refused to extend McWilliams to treat estate as representing the beneficiaries; stated that "indirectly" generally refers to interposition of third person and purported to see that theory carried out in *McWilliams*). For an example of a third party conduit sale, see Estate of Estroff v. Commissioner, 1983 T.C.M. (RIA) 1983-666.

[607] *See, e.g.,* Miller v. Commissioner, 510 F.2d 230 (9th Cir. 1975) (suggesting that in the context of section 1239 it might mean sales and purchases involving unrelated counterparties, citing *McWilliams).*

[608] The Code contains a variety of attribution rules and none of them is generally applicable; rather they only apply where the Code explicitly adopts them. The primary example is section 318, which is made applicable in section 302. For example, section 318(a)(1)(A) attributes the stock owned "directly or indirectly" by a husband to a wife. There "indirectly" cannot refer to stock owned by the husband by attribution, because another rule covers that situation. For a cogent explanation why "directly or indirectly" does not imply an attribution rule see G.C.M. 35,481 (Sept. 19, 1973).

[609] Furthermore, the paucity of following case law involving facts like those in *McWilliams* suggests that it was not as big a problem as the Court thought it to be.

[610] Cottage Savings Assn. v. Commissioner, 499 U.S. 554 (1991) (taxpayer allowed to deduct loss upon swapping identical mortgages with unrelated party).

[611] *See, e.g.,* Snyder v. Commissioner, 295 U.S. 134 (1935) (stock held in margin account could be identified for purposes of first in first out rule); Provost v. United States, 269 U.S. 443 (1926) (ruling that the stamp tax applied to all four transfers of stock in a stock lending and short sale transactions, because all of the shares were different sales).

does not.[612] The better explanation is that *McWilliams* reflects a purposive application of an anti-abuse rule (section 267), whereas *Cottage Savings* did not cross any anti-abuse rule because it was not a transaction between related parties.

III.C.4. *Explanations for the Supreme Court's Fundamental Shift*

Ch. II.B. shows that the Supreme Court spent its first hundred years mostly reading taxing statutes in favor of taxpayers and frequently failing to use the fact finding power to look through forms to substance in order to tax. Indeed in 1895 the Court used substance over form in the taxpayer's favor to find the second federal income tax to be a direct tax on property that violated the constitution because not apportioned among the states.[613] But by the early 1930's the Court had moved toward a broader conception of the taxing power, both in reading taxing statutes broadly and in looking through form to substance in fact finding, as illustrated by the three boundary decisions discussed above. Even the conservative Justice Sutherland would say in the important 1934 decision of *Stockholms Enskilda Bank* that "The general object of this act is to put money into the federal treasury; and there is manifest in the reach of its many provisions an intention on the part of Congress to bring about a generous attainment of that object by imposing a tax upon pretty much every sort of income subject to the federal power."[614]

The Court applied substance in its seminal interpretation of the constitutional concept of the 1913 income tax law in the taxpayer's favor in *Eisner v. Macomber*,[615] but it later shifted to interpret income quite broadly as a matter of law. *Higgins* and *McWilliams* are the farthest reaches of the Court's pro-government interpretations and fact finding, coming in 1940 and 1947. Ch. V.E.1 will show how the Court and lower courts employed equitable principles and fact finding, sometimes properly (as in *F. & R. Lazarus*) and sometimes spuriously in favor of the government. What brought about these shifts?

They depended on the needs of the country stemming from Depression and the New Deal, on the shifts in the Court's jurisprudence, and on the core assignment of income doctrine.

---

612 *See* Bittker & Eustice, at 12.44[3][c] (first in first out rule).

613 Pollock v. Farmers' Loan & Trust Co., 157 U.S. 429, 581, *modified,* 158 U.S. 601 (1895) (viewed a tax on the income from property as a tax on the property itself).

614 Helvering v. Stockholms Enskilda Bank, 293 U.S. 84 (1934).

615 *See supra* Ch. II.B.2.c(3).

III.C.4.a. *The Political Explanation: the Depression and the New Deal*

The New Deal brought a huge expansion of the power and scope of the federal government in general, and to tax in particular.[616] Justice Jackson said:

> It was not until the famous decision holding the Social Security Act constitutional that this controversy over the federal power to tax and spend for the general welfare was settled, and settled in favor of the existence of that power in the Federal Government.[617]

The Roosevelt Supreme Court faced tax cheats in the Depression era when rates mounted,[618] and the need for revenue increased due to the Second World War. The Court was tough on perceived tax cheats, protective of the fisc, and respectful of the federal administrators,[619] who were probably more aggressive than they had been in the easy days before the market crash.[620] The Congress and its legislation had acquired a more positive image.[621] These factors supported the Court's broadening of the income definition, abandoning pro-taxpayer presumptions, applying anti-taxpayer presumptions as to deductions,[622] adopting nonliteral interpretations of the Code,[623] and deferring to the views of the Service and the Tax Court.[624] (The latter suffered a blow in the con-

---

[616] *See, e.g.,* remarks of Robert H. Jackson at 1939 American Bar Association meeting, linking the Supreme Court's revision of its approach to taxation to similar changes as to the due process and commerce clauses. He particularly noted the Court's overruling, in *Graves v. New York*, 306 U.S. 466 (1939), of *Collector v. Day*, 78 U.S. 113 (1870) (Civil War income tax could not apply to state judges). N.Y. Times July 11, 1939 at 1. *But cf.* Richards, *The Supreme Court Justice and Boring Cases*, 4 Green Bag 2d 401, 405 (2001) (suggesting that the reason for the admitted surge in tax cases in 1941 was the enactment of the 1939 Code).

[617] Jackson, The Supreme Court, *supra* note 43, at 67.

[618] Paul, Prosperity, at 278-79 (up to 75% in 1936).

[619] Surrey, *Supreme Court and the Federal Income Tax*, *supra* note 285, at 810 (observing that the *in terrorem* effects of the Supreme Court decisions of 1935-1940 were not insignificant); Marcosson, *Stare Decisis in the Tax Law*, 20 Taxes (CCH) 137 (1942) (decrying the increasing willingness of courts to overturn precedent in the aid of tax collection).

[620] Jackson, *Changes in Treasury Tax Policy*, 12 Tax Mag. 342, 343 (1934).

[621] Popkin, at 131.

[622] Helvering v. Independent Life Ins. Co., 292 U.S. 371, 381 (1934) (deductions were not required); New Colonial Ice Co. v. Helvering, 292 U.S. 435 (1934) (to same effect, decided a week later); *see* Gray, *supra* note 328, at 460 (identifies 1934 and these opinions as marking a decided shift to viewing Congress' power to deny deductions as absolute).

[623] Paul, Prosperity, at 395 (stating that the literal interpretations that would be completely unrealistic in normal times would be "almost fantastic" in that time of "dizzying economic and social change"); *see* Popkin, at 201 (observing that the increasing importance of revenue in the modern state undermined the strict construction canon).

[624] *See* Hellerstein, *Federal Tax Policy During the Roosevelt Era*, 5 Law. Guild Rev. 160, 164 (1945) (describing the Roosevelt emphasis on combating tax avoidance, and stating:

> New Judges on the bench approached tax cases with a skepticism for such devices and some of the older Judges were likewise affected by the temper of the administration. Out of this era have come a whole series of revolutionary tax decisions, which bear the mark of the thinking and philosophy of Roosevelt and his followers.

The article cited *Higgins v. Smith* as the first fruit of this change in the Supreme Court.).

gressional override of the *Dobson* decision as to fact finding in the Tax Court, discussed in Ch. VI.E.3.a. below.)

Therefore, although all cases cannot be neatly fitted into the scheme, the New Deal Court and its successors that were aware of the dark days of the Depression, up to the Rehnquist era, can be viewed as the major architects of the modern interpretation of the Code.[625] The New Deal Court was largely responsible for the pro-government shift in tax decisions,[626] in which the Court was perceived to have taken over Congress' role in loophole closing.[627]

Justice Reed, who wrote *Higgins v. Smith*, was viewed as "a strong federal-government man, upholding its laws and the orders of its administrative agencies, whether directed against wealth or against the personal freedom of citizens; . . ."[628] Few Supreme Court opinions of the era failed to enforce taxation.[629] The abandonment of both the *Isham* formal approach to facts in tax cases and the *Wigglesworth* presumption in favor of the taxpayer explains the rise of "flexible" reading of apparently certain tax statutes. These trends all flowed from the Roosevelt Court.[630]

The 1939 Term (1939-1940) was called the "great divide" when the Roosevelt majority first coalesced; a divide between the supremacy of the rights of the individual and the subjection of the individual to governmental supremacy.[631] Although the Roosevelt Court was not fully in place until 1939,[632] the earliest turning of the Court under the pressure of the New Deal

---

[625] *See* Staudt et al., *Judging Statutes, supra* note 20, at 1966 (positing that the Warren Court relied more on legislative materials because it was compatible with them but that the Republican dominated Court began in the 1990's to show declining respect for administrative (Clinton era) guidance, and current trend to textualism also reflects Republican domination of the bench).

[626] *Contra* Clark, *The Morphogenesis of Subchapter C, supra* note 520, at 92-3 (arguing that the development of the corporate tax law was controlled by elements built into it from the start rather than events).

[627] Wales, *supra* note 278, at 80.

[628] Rodell, Nine Men 268 (Random House 1955).

[629] One that did fail was *Helvering v. Griffiths*, 318 U.S. 371 (1943), which refused to overturn *Macomber* and stated that untaxed stock dividends had not reduced earnings and profits. *See* Stark, *supra* note 417, at 198-99, 214 (stating that Roosevelt advisor Tommy Corcoran wanted *Macomber* eliminated because it had placed a constitutional limit on taxing stock dividends; also stating that this was a widespread New Deal view; Jackson took over Brandeis tax wreath, but Jackson did not overrule *Macomber* because he knew the practical problems of taxing such stock dividends).

[630] *See* Nash, *supra* note 555, at 167-69, 174-75; *see also Id.* at 193 n. 140 (quoting an article by Wendell Wilkie, "The Court Is Now His," and an AICPA proposal calling for more certainty in the tax law in 1940).

[631] Moore et al., *The Supreme Court 1939 Term: Public Law*, 27 Va. L. Rev. 253, 326 (1940). It is interesting and perhaps unfortunate that the principal investigators of the Supreme Court's tax opinions to date selected 1940 as the beginning point for their study and concluded that they could find no liberal-conservative patterns generally in tax cases, but did in corporate tax cases. Staudt et al., *Judging Statutes, supra* note 20, at 1909.

[632] Rodell, *supra* note 628, at 264.

occurred in 1937.[633] Academic and practice observers saw the burgeoning Supreme Court tax caseload and the similarity of the struggles over tax interpretation to struggles over interpretations of the New Deal legislation.[634] The paradigm shift in tax cases started even before the New Deal Court was fully in place. *Stockholms Enskilda* has been identified as marking the shift from literal interpretation in 1934.[635]

One case that cannot be fitted neatly into the historical analysis is the 1935 *Gregory* decision (discussed in detail above), which should be viewed in the context of cases that surrounded and preceded it, not the later cases, but it still unsettled taxpayer expectations. It was written by the conservative Justice George Sutherland. The same day the Court announced *Gregory* it announced *Panama Refining*,[636] which ordered a permanent injunction against an exercise of executive authority under the NIRA and was a precursor of the infamous anti-New Deal decision in *Schechter Poultry*.[637] Thus, *Gregory* preceded and was not a Roosevelt Court decision. Nevertheless, as Likhovski[638] concluded, it could have been influenced by the political context of the Depression times, combined with a growing anti-avoidance view fanned by the Roosevelt administration.[639] Also, as discussed in Ch. III.C.3.a.1., the reading of a business purpose requirement into the reorganization section may have been a pro-business move having the effect of preserving the basic nonrecognition rule, which had been under attack as a haven for tax avoidance.

The role of the 16th Amendment as a governor on the Revenue Acts had loomed large up to the 1930's (e.g., *Eisner v. Macomber*). In addition, congressional efforts to install an anti-abuse rule in the estate tax suffered a due process clause rebuke in *Heiner v. Donnan* in 1932.[640] However, the constitutional limits on the meaning of income were thought to have been a target of

---

633 *Id.* at 248.

634 Bergman, *supra* note 431, at 203 (observed in a review of state tax cases a fundamental change in the philosophy behind tax decisions, and wondered if it was personnel or the economic demands on the country); Traynor, *supra* note 431, at 371 (stating that nearly one-third of written opinions in the 1937 term were on taxes, making up by far the largest single group); Magill, *supra* note 431, at 1 (tax cases by far the largest group); *see also* Cogger, *Tax Avoidance versus Tax Evasion,* 15 TAX MAG. 518 (1937).

635 Barker, *supra* note 25, at 852.

636 Panama Refining Co. v. Ryan, 293 U.S. 388 (1935).

637 A.L.A. Schechter Poultry Corp. v. United States, 295 U.S. 495 (1935) (decided five months after *Panama*).

638 Likhovski, *supra* note 162, at 958-59 (asserting that such historical and sociological analyses of tax cases are lacking; but contending that generally public arousal against tax evaders influenced the *Gregory* decision particularly).

639 Roosevelt approved the civil fraud proceeding against Andrew Mellon, which was tried in the Tax Court for six months by Robert H. Jackson and which Mellon won. Mellon v. Commissioner, 36 B.T.A. 977 (1937). The facts were quite similar to *Higgins v. Smith. See generally* CANNADINE, MELLON (2008).

640 Heiner v. Donnan, 285 U.S. 312 (1932) (Stone and Brandeis dissented to the ruling that Congress could not constitutionally tax all gifts within two years before death as transfers at death).

the Roosevelt Administration,[641] and the issue was largely put to rest by the *Bruun* decision in 1940.[642]

One of Roosevelt's responses to the Depression was to address the need for increased revenue, which obviously could come only from the more prosperous ranks of society. To that end he directed a complete study of taxation in 1934, which led to various tax increases (for example, the end of the 100% dividends received deduction) and to a 1937 congressional investigation of tax evasion or avoidance.[643] Secretary of the Interior Harold Ickes stated: "The fundamental political issue today [July 27, 1936] is taxation."[644]

Roosevelt lost the vote on his 1937 Court packing plan but won the war. While the struggle was going on the Court upheld the constitutionality of the Wagner Act and Social Security; by 1940, Roosevelt had installed Reed, Frankfurter, Douglas, Jackson and Murphy.[645] ". . .[T]here was a general impression that the mental attitude of the Court toward problems of constitutional interpretation was much affected by his [Roosevelt's] persistent criticism."[646] That is, politics affected the Court.[647]

While the courts played an activist role in taxation through the 1940's,[648]after the Second World War the tax role of the Supreme Court sub-

---

[641] *See* Stark, *supra* note 417, at 198-99 (Tommy Corcoran wanted *Eisner v. Macomber* eliminated because it had placed a constitutional limit on taxing stock dividends); Lowndes, *A Day in the Supreme Court with the Federal Estate Tax*, 22 VA. L. REV. 261 (1936) (viewed *Helvering v. City Bank Farmers Trust Co.*, 296 U.S. 85 (1935) as clear rejection of most constitutional objections to the estate tax, brought about by F.D.R. appointees.) *See Dividend in Stock Remains Tax Free*, N.Y. TIMES, Mar. 2, 1943, at Bus. & Fin. 27 (explaining how the Government had set up a $9.60 assessment to try to overturn *Macomber*, only to be rebuffed by a former administration member, Justice Jackson).

[642] Surrey, *Supreme Court and the Federal Income Tax*, *supra* note 285, at 883-84 (stating that *Helvering v. Bruun,* 309 U.S. 461 (1940) settled the constitutional question when it held that a landlord realized income when the tenant forfeited his building to the landlord at the end of the lease term).

[643] JACKSON, THAT MAN 126-33 (Oxford Univ. Press 2003). As to the heightened concern with tax evaders generally in the 1930's, see Likhovski, *supra* note 162, at 1004-07; Bank, *supra* note 487, at 1176.

[644] ICKES, THE SECRET DIARY OF HAROLD L. ICKES 652 (Simon & Shuster 1953).

[645] GUNTHER, ROOSEVELT IN RETROSPECT 296-97 (Harper & Bros. 1950).

[646] PEPPER, PHILADELPHIA LAWYER 250 (Lippincott 1944); *cf.* Epstein et al., *Judging Statutes, supra* note 412, at 315-16 (surmising that the state of the economy figures into the Supreme Court's calculus when making decisions that may affect the economy, as tax decisions may).

[647] *See, e.g.,* RODELL, *supra* note 628 (arguing generally that substantially all of the major Supreme Court decisions have been politically motivated, mostly for the purpose of protecting property rights).

[648] PAUL, PROSPERITY, at Ch. 44. Paul observed that the federal courts handle a large number of tax cases, both in absolute and relative numbers. He thought the administration had mostly abdicated interpretation of the laws to the courts. He recorded that many said that the courts were too hard on tax avoidance, by "judicial legislation." Paul rejected the complaints because modern times require flexibility in the law, particularly when the object of the flexibility is to thwart tax avoidance. His objection was that the courts should not be doing this in most cases; the Treasury should do it. "The choice is between the present unsatisfactory method of litigation and more administrative finality." *Id.* at 398.

sided for a variety of reasons, including the enactment the 1954 Code; the growth of administrative rule making; the rising importance of social issues that attracted the attention of the country; and increasing prosperity, which made taxation less objectionable if not loved. The rise of social issues reflected the New Deal Court's general view that the rights of property interests might be held subservient to federal legislation, while laws affecting individual rights would face a "narrower scope for the operation of the presumption of constitutionality."[649] More recently the "Reagan Revolution" hit the Court and technical constructions have achieved a revival, largely for political rather than economic reasons.[650]

This brief history suggests that the Court's general rejection of technical interpretations of the tax laws beginning in the 1930's is attributable to the intertwining of two disparate themes: (1) a need to fill in the gaps in a sparse taxing statute (which began in cases like *Macomber*), and (2) a need to collect revenue in an era when many forces were driving the Court to a more activist role (*Smith* and *McWilliams*). The needs did not, however, culminate in the Court adopting a full scale doctrine of nontechnical interpretation, probably because the Court found that too demanding; each case just cannot be another *Eisner v. Macomber* that pushes the analysis back to supposed first principles; there must be an administrable set of rules, which the Court's workmanlike opinions of the era produced, with the exceptions of a few "boundary" opinion like *Smith* and *McWilliams*.

Although the Court has created a number of interpretational doctrines and doctrines filling out the concept of a net income tax (see Chapter VI.A.) it has not created general anti-taxpayer doctrines (except possibly for a bias against tax avoidance[651]). Rather, it has createdcluster rules, as discussed in Ch. VI.F. In any event, the Court's interpretations could not be uniformly pro-government, because as Cardozo pointed out in *Guggenheim*,[652] the interpretation that was pro-taxpayer in one case was pro-government in another case and so laying down rules required a balancing.[653]

---

[649] United States v. Carolene Prod., 304 U.S. 144 38. n. 4 (1938); *see* BURNS, PACKING THE COURT 166 (2009).

[650] *See, e.g.*, Fallon, *The Conservative Paths of the Rehnquist Court's Federalism Decisions*, 69 U. CHI. L. REV. 429 (2002).

[651] *See* PAUL, STUDIES I, at 61 (an inevitable bias for courts).

[652] Burnet v. Guggenheim, 288 U.S. 280 (1933). The pre New Deal Court may have had this in mind when it created the "open transaction" doctrine in the famous case of *Burnet v. Logan*, 283 U.S. 404 (1931). While agreeing that the taxpayer's sale consideration could not be valued, the Court postponed loss recognition as well as income inclusion.

[653] Tarleau, *Recent Supreme Court Decisions and the Interpretation of the Income Tax Law*, 18 TAX MAG. 293 (1940); Bittker, *Pervasive Judicial Doctrines in the Construction of the Internal Revenue Code*, 21 HOW. L.J. 693, 694 (1978).

III.C.4.b. *The Jurisprudential Explanation*

Coincident with the Depression and the response to the government's efforts to address it in the New Deal, the Supreme Court was returning to the more liberal style of decision making that had marked its earliest days, but had been interrupted by a formal period in the late 1800s. This shift affected tax jurisprudence too.[654] Ch. III.B. provides an overview of the Supreme Court's interpretational trends. That discussion leads to the second explanation of the Supreme Court's shifting views of taxes in the 1940s discussed here: its pivotal tax opinions of the 1940s reflect a jurisprudence of activism in protection of the fisc because revenue needs precluded a strict construction of taxing statutes,[655] a general rejection of formalism, an effort to enforce the purposes of Congress, and a willingness to apply equitable fact finding methods to do so.[656]

The Court's jurisprudence has continued to evolve in the 21st century. The New Deal Court's interest in supporting the power of the executive branch has transmuted into a supposedly heightened standard of deference to administrative interpretations (although the reality is less clear).[657]

Finally, to the extent the Court's shifts involved moving away from its own prior limitations on the power to tax (as in the movement from *Macomber* to *Glenshaw Glass*), the Court knew it had to do the heavy lifting, because the Congress could not change the constitution or the constitutional interpretations that the Court had made; only the Court could do that by reading the tax laws more purposively.[658]

III.C.4.c. *The Fact Cluster Explanation: Assignment of Income and Agency*

The assignment of income doctrine explains many of the New Deal era pro-government tax decisions, even though it was not always their stated ground. As discussed in Ch. VI.F.2.d. below, the assignment of income doctrine is the tax law's primary cluster rule, it operates almost exclusively in the related party arena, and it is tax specific (although derived from conceptions of agency). It had to be developed to prevent evasion of a progressive income tax, the utilization of one person's favorable tax attributes by another, and the avoidance of one person's unfavorable tax attributes.[659] Its development was the "central issue" of the period in which the Supreme Court was shifting to a purposive from a literalist view of tax.[660]

---

[654] As to tax jurisprudence generally, see Sneed, *supra* note 158, at 205-06.

[655] *See* Popkin, at 201.

[656] Goldberg, *supra* note 175, at 29 (identifying the post-Pearl Harbor years as marking an acceleration of judicial legislation; the Court ceased trying to mark the limits of its decisions in order to avoid giving evaders aid and assistance).

[657] *See* discussion of *Chevron infra* Ch. VI.D.

[658] *Cf.* Barker, *supra* note 25, at 853.

[659] Bittker & Lokken, at 75.1.

[660] *See* Barker, *supra* note 25, at 855.

The Supreme Court in the three boundary decisions discussed above did not rely directly on the assignment of income doctrine, but each case involved an assignment of income or property for the purpose of tax avoidance, and in each case the taxpayer utilized an agent:

- Most obviously, Mrs. Gregory wanted to recognize her corporation's income on the stock sale, while avoiding the double taxation of the income that would occur if the corporation sold the stock and distributed the after tax proceeds.
- Mr. Smith used his corporation to be the assignee of his income when the investments were profitable and to be the assignee of his property when they produced losses that he wanted to recognize while his alter ego kept the property; that assignment of income was on the Court's mind is evidenced by the opinion's first cite supporting the disregard of the taxpayer's form: *Lucas v. Earl*, the seminal assignment of income opinion.
- *McWilliams*, like *Smith*, refused to allow the taxpayer to assign loss property to a relative while enjoying a tax loss.

Assignment of income is at the root of another major branch of the Supreme Court's tax jurisprudence: the confusing partnership decisions, *Tower* and *Culbertson*.[661] The latter also applies the basic rule that state law does not control federal tax law, stating that the gift of the partnership for state purposes might be respected for tax purposes.

III.C.4.d. *Stare Decisis and the Supreme Court*

The preceding discussion of the greatest shift in the Supreme Court's view of federal taxation raises the question of the role of the doctrine of stare decisis in the Supreme Court's willingness to change or follow its own prior rulings.[662] The principle justification for stare decisis is reliance.[663] Naturally the Court is more willing to overturn longstanding precedent, when the precedent is not its own, as occurred in *Fink*,[664]and *Higgins v. Smith*.[665] But the Court has overruled itself in federal tax cases, directly or indirectly, in:

- Moving from the pro-taxpayer presumptions of the 1800s to the pro-government presumptions of the 1900s;[666]

---

[661] Commissioner v. Culbertson, 337 U.S. 733 (1949) (citing and backing away from *Tower*).

[662] For an early analysis, see Marcosson, *supra* note 619, at 137.

[663] United States v. Mason, 412 U.S. 391, 395 (1973) (stating that people in their everyday affairs should be able to rely on the Court's decisions and should not be penalized for doing so); *see also* United States v. IBM, 517 U.S. 843 (1996) (declining to overrule an earlier decision on grounds not argued by the parties).

[664] Commissioner v. Fink, 483 U.S. 89, 101 (1987) (Stevens, J., dissenting).

[665] Higgins v. Smith, 308 U.S. 473 (1940); *see infra* Ch. III.C.3.a(2); Paul, Studies III, at 458-59 ("numerous Board and circuit court decisions" relied on by the taxpayer).

[666] *See infra* Ch. II.B.2.

- Moving from the definition of income requiring that it come from either the source of labor or the source of capital (reflected in *Eisner v. Macomber*) to an accession to wealth, from whatever source derived (*Glenshaw Glass*);[667]
- Moving from easily viewing a subsidiary as the agent of its shareholder (*Southern Pacific*) to requiring a special proof to create such agency;[668]
- Rejecting the *Corn Products* doctrine;[669]
- *Helvering v. Hallock,* which overruled two earlier decisions;[670]
- *Estate of Church*, which continued the overruling in the same estate tax area that *Hallock* addressed by directly overruled *May v. Heiner* and included in a grantor's estate a gift in trust with a remote possibility of reversion and retention of a life estate, after substantial discussions of stare decisis and the reenactment doctrine in the majority and dissenting opinions;[671]
- *James*, which overruled *Wilcox* in finding illegally obtained income to be taxable;[672] and
- Repudiating the intergovernmental tax immunity doctrine applied in *Coronado Oil & Gas.*[673]

The best citation for the Supreme Court when it wants to overrule its earlier decisions is Justice Brandeis' dissent protesting the Court's holding onto precedent in *Coronado*. He stated:

---

[667] Eisner v. Macomber, 252 U.S. 189 (1920) ("Income may be defined as the gain derived from capital, from labor, or from both combined . . ."); Commissioner v. Glenshaw Glass Co., 348 U.S. 426, 431 (1955) (rejecting the dictum the Court used in *Eisner v. Macomber* by saying: "In that context . . . the definition [of income] served a useful purpose. But it was not intended to provide a touchstone to all future gross income questions.").

[668] S. Pac. Co. v. Lowe, 247 U.S. 330 (1918); *see infra* Ch. VI.F.3.b.

[669] Corn Prod. Refining Co. v. Commissioner, 350 U.S. 46, 52 (1955) ("the capital-asset provision of section 117 must not be so broadly applied as to defeat rather than further the purposes of Congress.") The Court retreated from the perception of the meaning of its earlier decision in *Arkansas Best Corp. v. Commissioner*, 485 U.S. 212 (1988). *See also* Stefan F. Tucker, *The Warren Court: Its Impact on the Capital vs. Ordinary Concept Under the Internal Revenue Code*, 17 KAN. L. REV. 53 (1968).

[670] Helvering v. Hallock, 309 U.S. 106 (1940), *overruling* Helvering v. St. Louis Union Trust Co., 296 U.S. 39 (1935), and Becker v. St. Louis Union Trust Co., 296 U.S. 48 (1935). The issue was whether the decedent's retention of a possibility of a reverter in a trust should require the inclusion of the property in decedent's estate; *Hallock* ruled that it should. *See* PAUL, STUDIES III, at 456 *et seq.* (discussing stare decicis in this case).

[671] Commissioner v. Estate of Church, 335 U.S. 632 (1949); May v. Heiner, 281 U.S. 238 (1930). Additional dissenting opinions of Reed and Frankfurter appear in *Spiegel's Estate v. Commissioner,* 335 U.S. 632 (1949) (Appendix B to Frankfurter's dissent is entitled "Opinions During the Past Decade Resting Upon the Rule That the Reenactment of a Statute Carries Gloss of Construction Placed Upon It by This Court.").

[672] James v. United States, 366 U.S. 213 (1961) (embezzled income taxable; reversing Commissioner v. Wilcox, 327 U.S. 404 (1946)).

[673] Burnet v. Coronado Oil, 285 U.S. 393 (1932); rejection explained in *State of South Carolina v. Baker*, 485 U.S. 505 (1988). *See* CUMMINGS, CONSTITUTION, at Ch. II.C.

> Stare decisis is not, like the rule of res judicata, a universal inexorable command. "The rule of stare decisis, though one tending to consistency and uniformity of decision, is not inflexible. Whether it shall be followed or departed from is a question entirely within the discretion of the court, which is again called upon to consider a question once decided." . . . Stare decisis is usually the wise policy, because in most matters it is more important that the applicable rule of law be settled than that it be settled right. . . . This is commonly true even where the error is a matter of serious concern, provided correction can be had by legislation. But in cases involving the Federal Constitution, where correction through legislative action is practically impossible, this court has often overruled its earlier decisions. The court bows to the lessons of experience and the force of better reasoning, recognizing that the process of trial and error, so fruitful in the physical sciences, is appropriate also in the judicial function. . . . Recently, it overruled several leading cases, when it concluded that the states should not have been permitted to exercise powers of taxation which it had theretofore repeatedly sanctioned. In cases involving the Federal Constitution the position of this court is unlike that of the highest court of England, where the policy of stare decisis was formulated and is strictly applied to all classes of cases. Parliament is free to correct any judicial error; and the remedy may be promptly invoked.[674]

On the other hand, the Court is proud of its own prior rulings in tax and tends to follow them, whether termed stare decisis or not.[675] Stare decisis generally is also discussed in Chapter III.B.1.

III.C.5. *Twenty-First Century Supreme Court Tax Jurisprudence*

In comparison to the fundamental shift in Supreme Court tax jurisprudence that occurred in the New Deal era, a later shift is the relatively minor and inevitable shift toward letting the Code stand on its own two feet now that it has had nearly 100 years of modification and expansion at the hands of Congress and the Treasury in regulations. Thus, Supreme Court tax opinions of the 21st century can seem to be more literal in their interpretive methods. In addition, the federal tax opinions have dwindled in number, reaching zero in the 2014 term. The Supreme Court's 21st century opinions on Title 26 are as follows (with indication of who won—T or G—who wrote the majority opinion, and the general nature of the issue):

1. *Baral*[676] (G; Thomas; procedural issue): Estimated taxes are "paid" on the original due date of the return and not when the Service later assessed the tax or the taxpayer later filed the return, based on a plain reading

---

[674] Burnet v. Coronado Oil, 285 U.S. 393, 406 (1932) (Brandeis, J., dissenting).

[675] *E.g.*, United States v. Home Concrete & Supply, LLC, 132 S. Ct. 1836 (2012) (asserting stare decisis); United States v. Davila, 133 S. Ct. 2139 (2013) (not referring to stare decisis); United States v. Quality Stores, Inc., 134 S. Ct. 1395 (2014) (referring to decision in *Mayo* and *Nierotko*).

[676] Baral v. United States, 528 U.S. 431 (2000).

of Section 6513(b), plus analysis of the entire scheme of tax payments, filings and assessments.

2. *United Dominion Industries, Inc.*[677] (T; Souter; substantive issue): The Court held the Treasury to its regulation, which denies the existence of separate net operating losses for consolidated group members. The Court was not moved by various arguments that the result did not make sense under the general structure of the tax law, and so the opinion can be viewed as a literalist ruling in the context of carefully crafted legislative regulations.
3. *Gitlitz*[678] (T; Thomas; substantive issue): The Court adopted a literal reading of subchapter S and rejected government arguments that were mostly based on the absurdity of the result, without any legislative history or other secondary indication that Congress intended anything other than what it wrote. See Ch. VI.B.1.c.
4. *Cleveland Indians*[679] (G; Ginsburg; procedural issue): The Court deferred to the Service's interpretation that the tax rate applicable to withholding on back pay was the rate of the later year of payment, even though back pay was not specifically addressed in the statute, and was treated for other purposes as if it related to the year in which it should have been paid.
5. *Chickasaw Nation*[680] (G; Bryer; substantive issue): The Court construed an internally inconsistent and therefore ambiguous provision not to exempt gambling on American Indian reservations from tax, based on legislative history and the course of the enactment process.[681]
6. *Young*[682] (G; Scalia; procedural issue): Court applied principle of equitable tolling of statutes of limitations in favor of the Service to bring the due date of bankrupts' return within three years of the filing of a second bankruptcy petition and thus render the tax liability nondischargeable.
7. *Fior D'Italia*[683] (G; Breyer; procedural issue): Service could properly estimate waiters' tips for purposes of FICA withholding by extrapolating from credit card tips, based on the breadth of the Service's power to determine proper methods of accounting.
8. *Craft*[684] (G; O'Connor; collection issue): The Court ruled that the federal tax lien could attach to the property that was the spouse's interest in entireties property despite the fact that state law did not allow creditors of

---

677 United Dominion Industries, Inc. v. United States, 532 U.S. 822 (2001). Litigation arose because the Joint Committee on Taxation opposed a refund the Service had been willing to allow.

678 Gitlitz v. Commissioner, 531 U.S. 206 (2001).

679 United States v. Cleveland Indians Baseball Co., 532 U.S. 200 (2001).

680 Chickasaw Nation v. United States, 534 U.S. 84 (2001).

681 But *Comptroller of the Treasury of Md. v. Wynne*, 135 S. Ct. 1787 (2015), a state tax decision, turned away from the power of a state to tax its own residents; the opinions discussed *Chickasaw*.

682 Young v. United States, 535 U.S. 43 (2002).

683 United States v. Fior D'Italia, Inc., 536 U.S. 238 (2002).

684 United States v. Craft, 535 U.S. 274 (2002).

one spouse to execute upon entireties property, relying on the traditionally expansive meaning of property for federal tax collection purposes.

9. *Boeing Co.*[685] (G; Stevens; substantive issue): The Court gave deference to Treasury regulations attributing costs for purposes of measuring income from export sales.
10. *Galletti* [686] (G; Thomas; procedural issue): The Court ruled that the Service's assessment of tax against a partnership applied to the partners and that they did not have to be separately assessed, based on general reasoning about the structure and function of assessments.
11. *Ballard* [687] (T; Ginsburg; procedural issue): The Court ruled that the Tax Court had failed to follow its own rules by treating the reports written by special trial judges as drafts, which the Tax Court judge could rework in collaboration with the trial judge. Rather, the Court read the rule to require a more formal acceptance or rejection of the trial judge report. The Tax Court's rule at issue was at least ambiguous and it seems that the Court's ruling was motivated by the secrecy applied to the report in a case finding fraud.
12. *Pasquantino* [688] (G; Thomas; procedural/criminal issue): Court enforced the literal terms of the wire fraud statute where the defrauded party was the foreign government defrauded of its taxes, despite the "revenue rule" that normally precludes the collection of another country's taxes.
13. *Banks* [689] (G; Kennedy; substantive issue): The Court applied historic assignment of income rules developed by the Court to find that the attorney's fee portion of a tort recovery was income to the injured plaintiff.
14. *Hinck* [690] (G; Roberts; procedural issue): The Court ruled that the Tax Court had exclusive jurisdiction to consider the Service's refusal to abate interest, despite the fact that the statute did not say the jurisdiction was exclusive, relying on the backdrop of history and the view that a detailed provision must have been intended to supplant more general remedies.
15. *EC Term of Years Trust* [691] (G; Souter; procedural/collection issue): Similar in reasoning to *Hinck*: ruled that a third party could oppose a levy only through the specific mechanism provided in the Code and not through a suit for refund.
16. *Knight* [692] (G; Roberts; substantive issue): The Court interpreted "would not" as not customarily done, and applied the canon that exceptions to a general rule should be narrowly construed.

---

[685] Boeing Co. v. United States, 537 U.S. 437 (2003).
[686] United States v. Galletti, 541 U.S. 114 (2004).
[687] Ballard v. Commissioner, 544 U.S. 40 (2005).
[688] Pasquantino v. United States, 544 U.S. 349 (2005).
[689] Commissioner v. Banks, 543 U.S. 426 (2005).
[690] Hinck v. United States, 550 U.S. 501 (2007).
[691] EC Term of Years Trust v. United States, 550 U.S. 429 (2007).
[692] Knight v. Commissioner, 552 U.S. 181 (2008).

17. *Boulware* [693] (T; Souter; substantive/criminal issue): Assuming but not finding that the alleged income at issue was received by the criminal defendant with respect to stock he held in his corporation from which he diverted the funds, the Court ruled that the absence of corporate earnings and profits precluded treatment of the funds as dividends.
18. *Clintwood Elkhorn* [694] (G; Roberts; procedural issue): Similar to *Hinck* and *EC Term*, except the statute the Court enforced against the taxpayer more clearly purported to be the exclusive remedy for recovering taxes paid but not due.
19. *Mayo* [695] (G; Roberts; substantive issue): Gave *Chevron* deference to regulation, treating persons who are both full-time students and full-time employees as employees for FICA purposes. Commonly viewed as ending "tax exceptionalism."[696]
20. *NFIB v. Sebelius* [697] (G; Roberts; constitutional and procedural issues): Upheld the health insurance tax against constitutional claims and held that the Anti-Injunction Act did not preclude jurisdiction, in a feat of interpretational jujitsu.
21. *Home Concrete* [698] (T; Breyer; procedural issue): Held that the taxpayer's overstatement of the basis of property sold, resulting in a substantial understatement of gain, was not an omission from gross income, and so the three-year and not the six-year statute of limitations applied to the Service's assessment, meaning the assessment came too late.
22. *Hall* [699] (G; Sotomayor; procedural bankruptcy issue): Held that the tax arising from a sale of his farm during Chapter 12 bankruptcy was not a liability incurred by the estate and, therefore, could not be included in the plan or discharged by the bankruptcy court.
23. *Kawashima* [700] (G; Thomas; criminal case): Held that two resident aliens could be deported for willfully filing false tax returns in which the government's loss exceeded $10,000.
24. *PPL* [701] (T; Thomas; substantive issue): Held unanimously that a foreign tax with an algebraic interrelationship to the foreign corporation's book net gain or "true net income" was an income tax and, therefore, creditable against the U.S. income tax, even though the foreign tax appeared to be a property tax.

---

693 Boulware v. United States, 552 U.S. 421 (2008).

694 United States v. Clintwood Elkhorn Mining Co., 553 U.S. 1 (2008).

695 Mayo Found. for Med. Educ. & Research v. United States, 562 U.S. 44 (2011).

696 Hoffer & Walker, *The Death of Tax Court Exceptionalism*, 99 Minn. L. Rev. 221 (2014-2015).

697 Nat'l Fed'n of Indep. Bus. v. Sebelius, 132 S. Ct. 2566 (2012).

698 United States v. Home Concrete & Supply LLC, 132 S. Ct. 1836 (2012).

699 Hall v. United States, 132 S. Ct. 1882 (2012).

700 Kawashima v. Holder, 132 S. Ct. 1166 (2012).

701 PPL Corp. v. Commissioner, 133 S. Ct. 1897 (2013).

25. *Davila* [702] (G; Ginsburg; criminal case): Rejected the vacatur of a tax identity thief's criminal conspiracy conviction.
26. *Windsor* [703] (T; Kennedy; constitutional issue): Held section 3 of DOMA unconstitutional, thus allowing the plaintiff to recover estate taxes that were refundable because her same-sex marriage to the decedent was respected by the decedent's state of residence and her inheritance was therefore subject to the marital deduction.
27. *Woods* [704] (G; Scalia; procedural issue): Held that (1) the trial court had jurisdiction in a TEFRA partnership audit proceeding to impose the 40% valuation/basis misstatement penalty (on the partners), and (2) the penalty applies to a basis misstatement without regard to whether it was the result of a legal or factual error.
28. *Ford* [705] (T; per curiam; procedural issue): Remanded for reconsideration of taxpayer's argument that it should receive interest on deposit that it converted to a payment that was later refunded, before a 2004 change in the law.
29. *Clarke* [706] (G; Kagan; procedural issue): Held that circuit had incorrectly ruled on right of taxpayer to cross examine the agent, but in the process stated some principles that could generally harm the IRS.
30. *Quality Stores* [707] (G; Kennedy; substantive): Employed numerous interpretive principles to turn back a group of FICA tax refund claims filed by many bankrupt corporations.

These 30 decisions divide 22 for the government and 8 for the taxpayers. Two involved constitutional issues. Two were criminal cases. Sixteen involved procedural or collection issues. Only one, *Banks*, could be said to be in the style of the Court's early decisions resting on general principles of the tax law, and it broke no new ground. However, *Clarke* employed numerous interpretational tools, also reminiscent of earlier times. Most of the decisions rested on statutory interpretation, and the Court was willing to interpret the statutes, including at least one, *Knight*, in which the interpretation was by no means obvious.

From this record of the 21st century decisions one may conclude that the grand issues of the tax law have greatly diminished in number, probably because they have been settled, that mundane procedural and collection issues predominate and the Court is not particularly interested in them, and that the Court necessarily decides more cases based on the statute because

[702] United States v. Davila, 133 S. Ct. 2139 (2013).

[703] United States v. Windsor, 133 S. Ct. 2675 (2013).

[704] United States v. Woods, 134 S. Ct. 557 (2013).

[705] Ford Motor Co. v. United States, 134 S. Ct. 510 (2013).

[706] United States v. Clarke, 134 S. Ct. 2361(2014). *See* Cummings, *Summons Enforcement and the Supreme Court*, 144 Tax Notes (TA) 835 (Aug. 18, 2014).

[707] United States v. Quality Stores Inc., 134 S. Ct. 1395 (2014). *See* Cummings, *Negative Implications and Code Interpretation*, 143 Tax Notes (TA) 931 (May 26, 2014).

more cases involve specific provisions, but remains amenable to all types of interpretive methods.

III.D. Contrast Role of the Lower Federal Courts

Sometimes, despite the availability of a Supreme Court decision on point, the tax opinions of lower federal courts tend to be the most cited because most practitioner and government arguments tend to start with the most recent opinion on the issue written by the most relevant lower federal court (the circuit court that will hear the appeal, or the district court itself). This is natural and logical, but does not foster a cohesive nationwide development of the tax law because it reflects a hard eyed approach to winning the current argument. Yet, even the most seasoned litigator must admit that Supreme Court dictum "on point" should have the power to trump an opinion of the local circuit.

While the Tax Court has moved to the "left" in terms of being activist on behalf of the government, the other lower federal courts have moved to the "right" in terms of applying the Code literally, with the major exception being their creation of the economic substance doctrine. Understanding these trends helps put some of their decisions in perspective.

III.D.1. *Evolution of the Tax Court*

The relationship of the Tax Court to the Supreme Court has been an uneasy one because the Tax Court has had a different perspective and has experienced its own interpretive shifts over time. The Board of Tax Appeals (whose name was changed to the United States Tax Court in 1942) began its life as a relatively literalist court, populated by tax technicians.[708] Professor Shores identified the first phase as the period of the Board's landmark decisions between 1928-1942 when it generally ruled on the basis of text and was frequently reversed on the basis of congressional intent.[709]The Supreme Court led it to a more expansive view of its powers, and then the Tax Court went beyond the Supreme Court in helping to create tax specific doctrines, principally the economic substance doctrine (see Ch. V.F.).

As prime examples of the first and second shifts, the Supreme Court effectively reversed the Board of Tax Appeals to rule for the government in all three of the "tax shelter" boundary cases discussed above: *Gregory v. Helvering*,

---

[708] For example J.S.Y. Ivins was an original member of the Board of Tax Appeals, and later founded Ivins Phillips and Barker, a leading tax advisory and litigation firm. For the definitive history of the Tax Court see the series of articles by Dubroff at 40 Alb. L. Rev. 7, 53, 253 (1975), 41 Alb. L. Rev. 1, 639 (1977), 42 Alb. L. Rev. 161, 191 (1978), and 42 Alb. L. Rev. 353 (1978). Part II of Dubroff's articles recounts at 40 Alb. L. Rev. 87-112 that all of the original Board members were lawyers, and many were former Bureau employees. However, the early Board decided a sufficient number of cases for, or partly for, taxpayers to prevent any serious charges of government bias. See also Part III, 40 Alb. L. Rev. at 290-91. As to the constitutional status of the Tax Court, see Cummings, Constitution, at 591.

[709] Shores, *Textualism and Intentionalism*, *supra* note 22, at 62-3.

McWilliams, and *Higgins v. Smith*.[710] Another example of the Board's early literal interpretations of the law, this time in favor of the government, was its ruling that a transaction did not fit the strict definition of reorganization in *Minnesota Tea*,[711] which the Supreme Court reversed, like the three boundary cases. Similarly in *Owens* the Board very logically ruled that a nonbusiness taxpayer could deduct its cost for property lost in a casualty because the taxpayer had not been allowed to deduct depreciation in prior years; the Supreme Court reversed, shifting the focus from an accounting like treatment of basis to focus on what the taxpayer actually lost, ruling that the taxpayer could only deduct the basis as it would have been adjusted downward if depreciation had been allowed.[712] A literal approach probably was dictated to some extent by the Board's early huge case load and the high respect accorded it by the courts of appeal.[713]

Before the creation of the Board, a committee within the Bureau of Internal Revenue conducted its own appeals of its own audit decisions. Early on observers noted that the Bureau was likely to become more strict in its application of the revenue laws after the creation of the Board of Tax Appeals, because the Bureau would let the Board solve the doubtful cases.[714] If the Bureau did become more strict, it is also possible that such strictness tended to become the default result in the Board, which immediately was deluged with a huge number of appeals. Also, in the early days the Bureau rarely introduced evidence in Board cases; for that reason the Board placed an unusually heavy burden on the taxpayer to carry its burden of proof.[715]

But empirical analysis shows that the Tax Court now is far more likely than the federal courts of general jurisdiction to rule purposively, and to do so usually against the taxpayer.[716] This trend followed rather than preceded the

---

[710] The *Smith* case actually appealed to the Supreme Court was a jury verdict for the government, reversed by the Court of Appeals. But Smith had brought a parallel case in the Board of Tax Appeals, which he initially won.

[711] , 28 B.T.A. 591 (1933). The Board went off on a "little frolic of its own" to deny reorganization treatment by a wooden reading of the statute, even though the Bureau had not contested that the transaction was a reorganization. Hendricks, *The Minnesota Tea Case*, 11 Tax Mag. 291, 320 (1933). The Supreme Court reversed. Helvering v. Minnesota Tea Co., 296 U.S. 378 (1935).

[712] Helvering v. Owens, 305 U.S. 468 (1939).

[713] Dubroff, The United States Tax Court: An Historical Analysis, Part II 73, 74 n. 113 (1979) (filed cases in 1926 were 12,867); Reiling, *Shall We Simplify and Preserve the Federal Income Tax?* 13 Tax Mag. 3, 4 (1935) ("the income tax law is what the Board determines it to be . . . the future of the income tax depends upon the Board"; in the first ten years it received 80,000 appeals).

[714] Brewster, *Some Observations Relating to the Board of Tax Appeals*, 3 Nat. Income Tax Mag. 251, 253 (1925); Jackson, *Changes in Treasury Tax Policy*, *supra* note 620, at 343 (confirming that this did occur).

[715] McClure, *Practice Before the United States Board of Tax Appeals*, 6 Nat. Income Tax Mag. 92 (1928).

[716] Shores, *Textualism and Intentionalism*, *supra* note 22, at 62-3.

Supreme Court's shift in the New Deal era.[717] Yet to the extent the Courts of Appeal are willing to accept a purposive reading, they have the model set for them by the Tax Court. They seem to have followed that model most forcefully in the area of the economic substance doctrine, as discussed in Ch. V.F.

Some academic writers have characterized this relatively activist stance of the Tax Court as a violation of the Administrative Procedure Act, a failure to give deference to the Service and Treasury.[718] Whether or not that is a correct analysis, it supports the point here: the Tax Court in recent decades has been relatively more willing to construe the Code.

III.D.2. *Tyranny of the Lower Courts*

A book about the Supreme Court's federal tax jurisprudence cannot ignore the fact that a single lower court tax opinion has the disturbing ability to paralyze later development of the law by the government and other courts, if the government chooses not to appeal or cannot have the decision reviewed. That is, in practice, it can have the effect of a Supreme Court decision. Moreover, that lower court judge may believe he is acting in accordance with the Supreme Court when he is claiming only a tenuous reliance on dictum. Thus, to a significant degree, the lower federal courts can tyrannize the tax law.

Of course the lower federal courts also properly exercise a necessary and powerful role in writing cluster rules for application of the federal tax laws, particularly as the involvement of the Supreme Court in federal tax cases (and the size of its case load in general) declines. For example, the Board of Tax Appeals was responsible for the tax benefit rule.[719] But their activist role is less beneficial when the lower courts create general positive rules of law, as they have in the case of the economic substance doctrine; the Memorandum Decision in *ACM* is the second major turning point in the creation of that doctrine (after *Rice's Toyota*).[720] Indeed, the ESD is wholly a construct of the lower federal courts,[721] notwithstanding Supreme Court decisions, such as

717 Paul, Studies III, at 380 ("For gossamer distinctions intervene based upon the intricacies of . . . legalistic niceties which have lost favor more with the Supreme Court than the Board," citing Helvering v. Hallock, 309 U.S. 106 (1940).).

718 Hoffer & Walker, *The Death of Tax Court Exceptionalism*, 99 Minn. L. Rev. 221 (2014-2015).

719 *See* Plumb, *The Tax Benefit Rule Today*, 57 Harv. L. Rev. 129, 133 (1943) (initially the Bureau of Internal Revenue agreed that recovered deductions were not income if the deductions produced no tax benefit, but quickly reversed field, whereupon the Board established the doctrine, as approved in *Dobson v. Commissioner*, 320 U.S. 489 (1943), and adopted by Congress in section 116 of the Revenue Act of 1942, now I.R.C. § 111).

720 *See infra* Ch. V.F.2.

721 For an early analysis, see Donahue, *supra* note 18, at 168 (attributing to Learned Hand the standard gloss on *Gregory v. Helvering*).

Frank Lyon[722] and *Knetsch*,[723] which do not state such doctrine, as explained below.[724]

Even more troubling is the tendency of the Service and the Treasury to buckle in the face of a single adverse opinion on a Treasury Regulation in the lower federal courts, as occurred with *Rite Aid*.[725] Robert N. Miller (of Miller & Chevalier) observed this curious trend in 1951 and explained how it occurred:

> The commonest way by which a judge-made tax rule becomes gradually established is interesting and a little surprising. Such a change is not normally initiated by a decision of the Supreme Court, but by a number of decisions of inferior courts which seize on language that had been used rather casually in some opinion of the Supreme Court. Very often the Supreme Court opinion . . . was one in which a decision for the government could properly be reached without establishing the so-called "principle" attributed to the opinion.[726]

For examples of powerful, unreversed, lower court rulings that have led to much strife and turmoil in the tax law, see:

- *Ashland Oil/Kimbell-Diamond*[727] (the "*Kimbell-Diamond* doctrine");[728]
- *General Utilities*[729] (the "*General Utilities* doctrine");[730]
- *Spalding Bakeries*[731] (the gloss on subsidiary liquidations);[732]
- *Rite Aid*, which forced an amendment to section 1502 in 2004 and a multi year rewrite of consolidated return regulations;[733] and
- *Helmer*, which like *Kimbell-Diamond* was a government victory that taxpayers turned into a tax avoidance tool.[734]

---

[722] Frank Lyon Co. v. United States, 435 U.S. 561 (1978).

[723] Knetsch v. United States, 364 U.S. 361 (1960).

[724] *See infra* Chs. V.F.2., VI.F.2.c., VI.E.1.e(2)(c).

[725] Rite Aid Corp. v. United States, 255 F.3d 1357 (Fed. Cir. 2001); *see* Reg. § 1.1502-36; T.D. 9424, 2008-44 I.R.B. 1012.

[726] Miller, *Federal Courts as Makers of Income Tax Law*, *supra* note 524, at 161 (citing *Gregory* as a chief example).

[727] Commissioner v. Ashland Oil & Ref. Co., 99 F.2d 588 (6th Cir. 1938); Kimbell-Diamond Milling Co. v. Commissioner, 187 F.2d 718 (5th Cir.).

[728] Bittker & Eustice, at 10.41.

[729] Gen. Util. & Op. Co. v. Helvering, 296 U.S. 200 (1935) (due to failure to raise the issue at the proper time, the Supreme Court did not really consider the core issue of the case).

[730] Bittker & Eustice, at 8.20.

[731] Commissioner v. Spaulding Bakeries, Inc., 252 F.2d 693 (2d Cir. 1958).

[732] *See* Cummings, *New Prop. Regs. Change Rules for Transactions Where Property or Stock Lacks Net Value,* 103 J. Tax'n. 14 (2005).

[733] Rite Aid Corp. v. United States, 255 F.3d 1357 (Fed. Cir. 2001); *see* Reg. § 1.1502-36; T.D. 9424, 2008-44 I.R.B. 1012.

[734] Helmer v. Commissioner, 1975 T.C.M. (RIA) 1975-160.

But observers confident in their tax judgment know that some lower court opinions are plain wrong.[735] The same can be said of Supreme Court opinions, but at least they are universally binding and final (until Congress acts). Moreover, the Service need not fear having to reverse years of prior rulings if and when a court disagrees with it because Section 7805(b)(8) gives the Secretary authority to deny retroactive effect to even Supreme Court tax rulings.[736]

> Justice Cardozo said, "The output of a multitude of minds must be expected to contain its proportion of vagaries."[737] It is such decisions that largely stymie efforts to prick a logical path through the lower court authorities. Although litigants cannot ignore them, someone must call them out if they are ever to be corrected or modified. Even Supreme Court tax opinions are of limited scope,[738] and that should be even more true of lower courts' opinions. Professor Lowndes, a student of Supreme Court tax decisions, said in 1937: Oddly enough, when the Supreme Court decides a case it decides a case. It does not fix the pattern of future judicial conduct through the ages."[739]

Similarly, Dean Griswold, citing Dean Pound, decried in discussing a Supreme Court tax opinion "the many places where a statement has been made which seems perfectly sound in the light of the case then before the court, but which turns out to have been too broad when further cases arise involving different facts."[740] Justice Scalia said in *Bollinger*:

> In any case, we decline to parse the text of *National Carbide* as though that were itself the governing statute.[741]

Practitioners have the right if not the duty to seize onto any favorable authority in support of their clients' positions: that is merely the exercise of the required warm zeal in diligently representing a client.[742] But the lower

---

[735] As to the value of lower court decisions, see FRANK, LAW AND THE MODERN MIND, CH XIII (Tudor 1936), which presents Frank's example of "Judge Brilliant" who decides against Mr. Evasion in a tax evasion case and writes an opinion with a new rule proclaimed, which Judge Conformity may thereafter follow in the case of Rex v. Humpty Dumpty. Similarly, Randolph Paul exercised a wisdom rarely seen today by declining to categorize some cases because he viewed them as "sports." PAUL, STUDIES II, at 252.

[736] *See* Cent. Laborer's Pension Fund v. Heinz, 541 U.S. 739 (2004).

[737] CARDOZO, *supra* note 398, at 5.

[738] *See, e.g.*, Helvering v. Or. Mut. Life Ins. Co., 311 U.S. 267 (1940) (rejecting a regulation that Treasury wrote in reliance on earlier Supreme Court decisions by finding that Treasury did not understand the limited basis of the prior decisions).

[739] Lowndes, *1936 Term*, *supra* note 430, at 170, 172 ("legal doctrines are verbal devices that try to reflect considerations, which vary in importance from justice to justice. This is why there is lack of stability and certainty and it is a better state of affairs than mechanical legalisms.").

[740] Griswold, *Securities and Continuity of Interest*, 58 HARV. L. REV. 705, 709 (1945).

[741] Commissioner v. Bollinger, 485 U.S. 340 (1988).

[742] *See* MODEL RULES OF PROF'L CONDUCT, R. 1.3, 3.1 and Comments thereto (2008).

courts often miscite general statements in Supreme Court opinions (*Gregory v. Helvering* is a common example) in support of creations of their own.

Government lawyers will do the same when the decisions go their way, but any single adverse opinion written by one judge of the Tax Court, one federal district judge, one claims court judge, one appellate panel, is often likely to govern the Service absent a high level and difficult decision to fight an issue in multiple courts. And this is despite the Service's stated rule that none but the Supreme Court's interpretations of the Code bind them.[743] Indeed, the Supreme Court has made it clear that lower courts can err in their interpretation of the Code and that the Service properly can nonacquiesce in those rulings, and can even reverse an acquiescence retroactively;[744] section 7805(b)(8) makes clear that this power was not changed by the 1996 Taxpayer Bill of Rights amendments to that section.

Nevertheless, there are practical systemic reasons for the power of even a single, erroneous, court decision to determine the law, which include the following:

- Federal courts normally can't duck issues; they can't just say they don't know, because they have the power to resolve all cases and controversies that come before them, subject to jurisdictional limits; and so in every instance must decide the issues before them.[745]
- The *Golsen* rule binds the Tax Court to the appellate decisions in the circuit to which the case is appealable.[746]
- If a court announces that a section has only one allowable meaning (and so is unambiguous as properly interpreted), then the Treasury can change the result by issuing regulations only by disagreeing with the decision on ambiguity. [747] *Chevron* deference extends to allowing an agency's legislative regulation to overturn judicial precedents,[748] but not after the

---

[743] I.R.M. 4.10.7.2.9.8. The Manual directs agents to settle cases in circuits with adverse case law until different case law can be developed in other circuits. I.R.M. 31.1.1.1(3).

[744] Dixon v. United States, 381 U.S. 68 (1965).

[745] U.S. Const., Art. III, § 2. Some argue that at the extreme of ambiguity a statute should be given no effect, but this is seldom possible. *See* Elhauge, *supra* note 66, at 2263 et seq. When the 11th Circuit declined to engage in the "Sisyphean" task of finding discrimination in a state tax case, the Court rebuked it, stating that such work "is a Sisyphean task that the statute imposes." Alabama Dept. of Revenue v. CSX, 135 S. Ct. 1136 (2015).

[746] Golsen v. Commissioner, 54 T.C. 742 (1970), *aff'd*, 445 F.2d 985 (10th Cir.).

[747] *See* Smith, *Brand X and Omissions from Gross Income*, 126 Tax Notes (TA) 665 (Feb. 1, 2010) (showing that the administrative interpretation cannot overturn a court finding that the statute unambiguously had only one meaning, based on all traditional tools of statutory construction, including legislative histories); *see infra* Ch. VI.D.

[748] Nat'l Cable & Telecomm. Assn. v. Brand X Internet Services, 545 U.S. 967; *see* Daniel J. Gifford, *Emerging Outlines of a Revised Chevron Doctrine,* 59 Admin. L. Rev. 783, 828-32 (2007); Smith, *Brand X, supra* note 747, at 665 (showing that the administrative interpretation cannot overturn a court finding that the statute unambiguously had only one meaning, based on all traditional tools of statutory construction, including legislative histories).

Supreme Court has established a statute's meaning by announcing its interpretation.[749]

- The nationwide jurisdiction of the Claims Court, and the fact that all appeals from it flow to the Court of Appeals for the Federal Circuit, means that those courts have near final power over statutory interpretation in the cases that come before them, which can include any cases in which the taxpayer has paid or is willing to pay the tax to dispute it. And the Tax Court will follow its own prior decisions, absent contrary controlling circuit rules.
- The Supreme Court no longer sees itself as a court for correcting error and has a much reduced case load in general; even though a conflict in circuit opinions is the most common ground for issuing its writ of certiorari,[750] achieving such a split in the circuits presents an arduous challenge for the Service (including combating claims of collateral estoppel).[751]
- Section 7430 can authorize recovery of fees and expenses by a winning taxpayer based on, among other reasons, whether the Service has lost in other circuits on the same issue.[752]
- The Service will not issue a private letter ruling in the face of any court decision adverse to the government as to which the question of following the decision or litigating further has not yet been resolved.[753]

Granted the Service can attempt to maneuver around conflicting circuits by picking the ones it will follow and agreeing to the others only in their

---

[749] United States v. Home Concrete & Supply, LLC, 132 S. Ct. 1836 (2012) (plurality opinion, joined as to this point by Justice Scalia). *See* Cummings, *Tax Decisions of the Supreme Court's 2011 Term*, 137 Tax Notes (TA) 93 (Oct. 1, 2012).

[750] The exceptions are rare, one being Ford Motor Co. v. United States, 134 S. Ct. 510 (2013), in which the political overtones of the interests of the amicus United States Chamber of Commerce in the sovereign immunity issue may have motivated at least four justices to hear the case. *See* Cummings, *A Chamber of Commerce Victory*, 144 Tax Notes (TA) 1201 (Sept. 8, 2014).

[751] *See* Divine v. Commissioner, 500 F.2d 1041, 1049 (2d Cir. 1974) (explaining why it was rejecting the taxpayer's attempt to collaterally estop the Service form arguing against the view adopted by another circuit, for reasons including the fact that such a decision would inhibit the ability of the Service to reach the Supreme Court, stating:

> In federal tax cases disputed questions of law are satisfactorily resolved only by U.S. Supreme Court decisions, for the Commissioner of the Internal Revenue Service has on many occasions taken the position, as he has in this litigation, that a Court of Appeals decision with which he disagrees has no binding effect on the Service's policies in other circuits. The uncertainty which may result is exacerbated by the fact that the decisions of a U.S. Court of Appeals are not habitually reviewed by the Supreme Court.").

[752] *See* Kafka & Cavanaugh, Litigation of Federal Civil Tax Controversies 23.03[10][e](Warren, Gorham & Lamont).

[753] Rev. Proc. 2016-3, at § 3.02(3), 2016-1 I.R.B. 126.

circuits.[754] But the process hamstrings the Service and subjects it to assertions of discrimination among taxpayers, while taxpayers have near full freedom of choice, limited only by their ability to pay the tax in order to sue in the Claims Court, and their domiciles (or not pay and petition the Tax Court).

The approach of lower court judges in tax cases probably has not changed much from those expressed with unusual candor by Judge Orie L. Phillips (Tenth Circuit), who in 1935 described the basic questions he brought to tax appeals:

> Is the taxpayer standing on a technical or arbitrary rule to escape a just tax? Is the government insisting on a like rule to exact an unjust tax? . . . we want to know the substance of the transactions involved and not their mere forms. . . . we should not permit hard cases to make bad law.[755]

Various considerations may encourage the government to acquiesce (formally or informally) in erroneous lower courts decisions: (1) a motive to avoid decision making, to avoid discretion exercising, to avoid statutory interpretation when any court appears to have done that job for them; (2) the depressing realization that the process of appeal is long and arduous; (3) the fact that *Chevron* deference (discussed in Ch. VI.D. below) to a new administrative interpretation may be weakened by the fact of prior contrary court decisions.[756]

Nevertheless, on occasion the Service does stand on principle and reject the tyranny of the lower courts. Justice Jackson stated in upholding a regulation that several lower courts had rejected: "Despite these adverse decisions, however, the Commissioner persisted in applying the regulation. The question was never reviewed here."[757] The Internal Revenue Service Manual indicates that agents will not be bound as to other taxpayers by an adverse Tax Court

---

[754] *See, e.g.*, Commissioner v. Lester, 366 U.S. 299 (1961). For general discussion of the Service's acquiescence program and observance of controlling circuit opinion in the circuit, see Rogovin & Korb, *Four Rs Revisited: Regulations, Rulings, Reliance and Retroactivity in the 21st Century—The View from Within*, 46 Duq. L. Rev. 323, 366-67 (2008), discussing the rule of Golsen v. Commissioner, 54 T.C. 742 (1970), *aff'd*, 445 F.2d 985 (10th Cir.).

[755] Phillips, *What Does a Circuit Judge Look for in a Tax Appeal?* 13 Taxes (CCH) 523 (1935).

[756] Although generally *Brand X* recognized a power in the regulator to reject a court's interpretation. Nat'l Cable & Telecomm. Assn. v. Brand X Internet Services, 545 U.S. 967 (2005).

[757] Commissioner v. Wheeler, 324 U.S. 542, 545-46 (1945).

decision unless the Service has filed a formal acquiescence.[758] But when a court agrees with the Service in what turns out to be an unfortunate choice for the Service, the Service usually feels stuck with the result.[759]

In conclusion, the multiplicity of tax litigation forums gives taxpayers maximum flexibility in all directions and tends to hamstring the Service and Treasury.[760] But when the lower courts generate a pro-government doctrine like the ESD their tyranny is embraced by the Service. For possible solutions see Ch. VII.

---

[758] I.R.M. 4.10.7.2.9.8, 32.2.3.5.1.2.3.2. The Supreme Court did not think acquiescence bound the Service absent other evidence of "settled administrative practice." Higgins v. Commissioner, 312 U.S. 212 (1941); *see also* Rogovin & Korb, *supra* note 754, at 363-69 (explaining that acquiescence does not adopt the theory of the court, that the Service can non-acquiesce in a decision of a court of appeals in its own circuit and that taxpayers should not plan transactions based on acquiescences). *But see* Dixon v. United States, 381 U.S. 68 (1965) (carefully parsing when the Service has acquiesced in a court's reasoning); *see also* Estreicher & Revesz, *Nonacquiescence by Federal Administrative Agencies,* 98 YALE L. REV. 679 (1989) (arguing that even intra-circuit nonacquiescence can be appropriate).The playing field potentially was changed in 2002 with the adoption of 28 U.S.C. 530D, which requires the Attorney General to inform the Congress of any DOJ decision to disregard the decision of any court that is binding in its jurisdiction relative to the interpretation or construction of any statute, regulation, rule, program, policy or other law within the agency's jurisdiction. In theory, this could apply to a decision of the Tax Division, but the DOJ has never reported such a tax case to Congress (as of 2015).

[759] The classic example being Kimbell-Diamond Milling Co. v. Commissioner, 14 T.C. 74 (1950), *aff'd,* 187 F.2d 718 (5th Cir. 1951). A recent example is *Helmer*, 1975 T.C.M. (RIA) 1975 at 160, the reasoning of which the Service felt obliged to follow until changed by regulations, as explained in Notice of Proposed Rule Making 68 Fed. Reg. 37,434 (June 24, 2003), finalized by T.D. 9207, 70 Fed. Reg. 30,334 (June 1, 2005). *See generally* Rogovin & Korb, *supra* note 754, at 363-69.

[760] *See generally* Greenaway, *Choice of Forum in Federal Civil Tax Litigation*, 62 TAX LAW. 311 (2009).

Ch. IV. Reactions of Congress and Treasury to Intentional Tax Reduction

This chapter focuses on Congress and the Treasury and their reactions to tax planning they find inappropriate. This is a proper subject in a book on the Supreme Court, because only when Congress and the Treasury fail in this effort does the Court need to step in and create doctrines or interpret the Code to carry out Congress' purposes. Therefore, the Court's tax doctrines, and the lower courts' efforts to create doctrines, discussed later, are informed by these rules made by Congress and Treasury. This chapter makes the following points:

- Congress has supplied several targeted anti-abuse rules in the Code.
- They are not unlimited presumptions or rules like the ESD, but they approximate the ESD in circumscribed areas.
- The statutory rules have not been particularly successful, and also have not been well tended by the Treasury and the Congress (it is unclear which is the cause and which is the effect).
- Lower courts show a tendency to reject or avoid an apparently applicable targeted Code or regulatory anti-abuse rule, while at the same time being willing to apply a lower court made doctrine such as the ESD.
- One could infer that Congress relies on the courts' tendency to create and apply their own doctrines, but Congress did not signal this until the "codification" of the economic substance doctrine in 2010, discussed in Ch. V.F.
- These points also suggest an unfortunate preference for vague rules over specific rules, thus relying substantially on the *in terrorem* effect of uncertainty of doctrines.
- A close examination of the history of section 269 is instructive, because it is the closest approximation to the ESD in the Code.

- Treasury frequently has chosen not to write broad anti-avoidance rules in regulations, while presumably championing the Service' assertion of broad anti-avoidance rules in litigation, without benefit of regulations.

IV.A. The Code's Primary Anti-Abuse Rule: Section 269

Section 269 is the closest approximation to the economic substance doctrine now in the Code,[761] and it has failed in that role due to (1) relentless attack by taxpayers, (2) puny defense by the courts, and (3) virtual abandonment by the Treasury and the Service.[762] As an example of the latter, the Treasury has not issued any new regulations under the section since 1991,[763] and the core regulation dates from 1962,[764] despite the dramatic change in the types of corporate tax avoidance transactions compared with the ones described in the original regulations. A Treasury initiative to amend the regulation in 1999 was abandoned.[765] Even the Supreme Court has encouraged the Service to utilize section 269 (in a case where it did not), stating:

> . . . the Government may, as always, address tax-motivated behavior under Internal Revenue Code §269, which gives the Secretary ample authority to "disallow [any] deduction, credit or other allowance" that results from a transaction "the principal purpose [of] which . . . is evasion or avoidance of Federal income tax."[766]

These facts do not mean that statutory anti-abuse rules are useless, but rather that they require careful attention in their creation and careful tending. Treasury should have adopted regulations adapting section 269 to current issues,[767] and the Service should more vigorously assert it and should encourage the courts to utilize it.[768] Absent such steps the courts and the Service

---

[761] Section 269 has been the focus of prior efforts to create a super, or enhanced, anti-abuse rule built on the section 269 approach. *See* Bittker & Eustice, at 14.41[6]. *See also* Libin, *Congress Should Address Tax Avoidance Head-On: The Internal Revenue Code Needs a GAAR*, 30 Va. Tax Rev. 339 (2010-2011) (recognizing that section 269 is a mini-GAAR).

[762] *See* Fuller, *Business Purpose, Sham Transactions and the Relation of Private Law to the Law of Taxation*, 37 Tul. L. Rev. 355, 392 (1963) (little asserted at first, but "recently" before 1963 had been litigated with some success but also with some losses).

[763] T.D. 8388, 1992-1 C.B. 137.

[764] Reg. § 1.269-2; T.D. 6595, 1962-1 C.B. 43.

[765] *See* N.Y.S.B.A., *Comments on the Administration's Corporate Tax Shelter Proposals*, 83 Tax Notes (TA) 879 Section V (May 10, 1999) (criticizing proposed amendments to section 269).

[766] United Dominion Industries, Inc. v. United States, 532 U.S. 822, 838 (2001). *See also* United States v. Consumer Life Ins. Co., 430 U.S. 725 (1977) (observing that the Service could have but did not assert section 269).

[767] The current regulations are concerned with shelters like creating multiple corporations to obtain multiple runs up the corporate tax rate schedules, hardly a huge problem today. Reg. § 1.269-3(b)(2).

[768] The Service has cited section 269 in a few listed transactions Notices. *See* Notice 2004-20, 2004-11 I.R.B. 608.

will continue to default to judicial doctrines,[769] which is a curious example of undermining Congress' purpose in two ways at the same time: both ignoring rules that Congress did write, like section 269, and applying rules Congress did not write.

IV.A.1. *Section 269 as Expanded by Its Regulations*

Section 269 authorizes the Secretary to exercise broad discretion on audit to disallow deductions, credits and other allowances and take other actions if one of two types of acquisitions occurs and "the principal purpose" for the acquisition was the "evasion or avoidance of Federal income tax by securing the benefit of a deduction, credit or other allowance which such person or corporation would not otherwise enjoy." The two types of acquisitions are (1) acquisition of control (50% vote or value) of a corporation by any person, and (2) acquisitions of property by a corporation from another corporation with a carryover basis when a common control exception does not apply. While limited, this section potentially describes a wide swath of cases.

Thus, the hallmarks of section 269 are as follows:

- It potentially applies only to a defined set of acquisitions involving corporations;
  - The acquisitions must involve acquisition either (1) of control of a corporation, or (2) by a corporation of carryover basis assets from an uncontrolled corporation.
- It protects against abuse of deductions, credits, exemption, exclusions and other allowances, and "anything which diminishes tax liability;"[770]
  - If "the principal purpose" for the acquisition was securing the benefit ofthe deduction, credit or allowance that the person or corporation

---

[769] *See, e.g.*, Black & Decker Corp. v. United States, 436 F.3d 431 (4th Cir. 2006) (rejecting application of section 357(b)); Coltec Indus., Inc. v. United States, 454 F.3d 1340 (Fed. Cir. 2006) (similar); Tribune Co. v. Commissioner, 125 T.C. 110 (2005) (examining economic substance of corporate tax avoidance transaction and declining to consider section 269); Long Term Capital Holdings v. United States, 330 F. Supp. 2d 122 (D. Conn. 2004) (noting that legal opinions failed to discuss section 269, but ruling against taxpayers based on economic substance), *aff'd*, 150 Fed. Appx. 40 (2d Cir. 2005) (did not refer to section 269); BNY Mellon Corp., 140 T.C. 15 (2013) (ruling against taxpayer but declining to apply section 269). *See generally* Cummings, *The New Normal: Economic Substance Doctrine First*, 126 TAX NOTES (TA) 521 (Jan. 25, 2010).

[770] Reg. § 1.269-1(a) (expands "allowances" with this phrase, which could apply to income deferral and not just deductions).

would not otherwise enjoy.[771]

Section 269 along with section 482, and section 446,[772] are unusual grants of authority to the Secretary to apply discretion, not in writing regulations (as is more common, as in section 1502), but in auditing. Perhaps as a resultTreasury did not write extensive regulations applying section 269 (though it has for section 482). Therefore, revenue agents are left with little specific guidance in applying a rule that substantially deviates from the Code. This places revenue agents in somewhat unknown territory once they assert section 269, because they have no discretion to compromise the issue.[773]

Congress enacted section 269's predecessor in 1943.[774] The Supreme Court found it inapplicable in an early test because the trial court had not even considered it and so made no finding on principal purpose;[775] the Tax Court is said to have emasculated it.[776] A significant rewrite occurred in 1954, but it retained the principal purpose standard, which then was said to render its ineffectiveness manifest,[777] with its successful application seeming in 1955 to

---

[771] "The principal purpose" generally means more important than any other. *Compare* Regulation section 1.269-3(a) (stating: "If the purpose to evade or avoid Federal income tax exceeds in importance any other purpose, it is the principal purpose") *and* Commissioner v. Indianapolis Power & Light Co., 493 U.S. 203 (1990) (addressing whether a deposit was security or a payment and did not adopt the Tax Court's test of the principal purpose but rather looked at the rights and obligations of the parties at the time of the deposits).
The Supreme Court most prominently addressed the word "principal" in the Code (in connection with the principal place of business) by emphasizing its relative nature Commissioner v. Soliman, 506 U.S. 168 (1993). In contrast, "primarily" means of first importance. *Malat v. Riddell*, 383 U.S. 569 (1966) addressed the capital asset definition for inventory: "primarily for sale to customers" and ruled that "primarily" means "of first importance or principally" and not simply "substantial."

United States v. Donruss Co., 393 U.S. 297 (1969) interpreted "formed or availed of for the purposes of avoiding the income tax." The Court specifically refused to attach any significance to the use of the article "the" or to the fact that it was changed from "a." Accordingly the Court ruled that it meant "one of the purposes" based on an overall reading of congressional intent. The opinion stated that rarely is there one motive or even one dominant motive for corporate decisions. *Id. See* Cummings, *How Much Is Enough or Too Much?*, 150 TAX NOTES (TA) 1025 (Feb. 29, 2016).

[772] *See* Thor Power Tool Co. v. Commissioner, 439 U.S. 522 (1979).

[773] *See* SALTZMAN & BOOK, at 15.07[1].

[774] The Revenue Act of 1943 added to the 1939 Code section 129. H.R. 3687, 78th Cong. (1943).

[775] Libson Shops v. Koehler, 353 U.S. 382 (1957) (ruling that the losses of 16 merged corporations could not be used by the surviving corporation because it was not the same business that generated the losses; the opinion created a third suspect category after the two statutory ones of "evasion" and "avoidance": "windfall."). *See generally* BITTKER & EUSTICE, at 14.02.

[776] Rice, *supra* note 377, at 582. *See, e.g.*, Shaw Constr. Co. v. Commissioner, 35 T.C. 1102, 1114 (1961), *aff'd*, 323 F.2d 316 (9th Cir. 1963), *acq.* (declined to apply sections 269 and 482 after finding *Moline* to have been flunked).

[777] Rice, *supra* note 377, at 581.

be extremely remote in any carefully planned transaction (articulating some business purposes was thought to be easy enough).[778]

Nevertheless, Treasury finalized a set of general regulations in 1962 that asserted an optimistic view of its ability to combat tax avoidance in the corporate area. Commentators remained skeptical primarily because of the multiple hurdles the words of the statute erected, the most difficult of which is the "doubly subjective tests": (1) the agent or judge's view of what constitutes tax avoidance, and (2) the taxpayer's state of mind in relation to that tax avoidance.[779] Nevertheless, in earlier days, section 269 did receive some fair readings supporting the Service.[780]

The regulations essay breadth in several ways.[781] But the core definition in the regulation appears to ask whether Congress intended the particular result a taxpayer is claiming, by reference to Congress' purpose:

> Characteristic of such circumstances are those in which the effect of the deduction, credit, or other allowance would be to distort the liability of the taxpayer when the essential nature of the transaction or situation is examined in light of the basic purpose or plan which the deduction, credit or other allowance was designed by the Congress to effectuate.[782]

---

[778] *Id.* at 600-01.

[779] Watts, *Acquisitions Made to Avoid Taxes: Section 269*, 34 TAX L. REV. 539, 567 (1978). *But see* Eustice, *Tax Problems Arising from Transactions Between Affiliated or Controlled Corporations*, 23 TAX L. REV. 451, 457 (1968) (categorizing the section as "truly formidable" in combating multiple incorporations and listing failed attempts to enforce it).

[780] *See, e.g.*, Borge v. Commissioner, 405 F.2d 673 (2d Cir. 1968). Indeed, at least six Circuits have addressed the issue whether the marrying of post-acquisition losses with post-acquisition income can be prevented under section 269, with only two refusing (Herculite Protective Fabrics Corp. v. Commissioner, 387 F.2d 475 (3d Cir. 1968); Zanesville Inv. Co. v. Commissioner, 335 F.2d 507 (6th Cir. 1964)), and four agreeing, at least that application of section 269 was possible (Hall Paving Co. v. United States, 471 F.2d 261 (5th Cir. 1973); *Borge*, 405 F.2d at 673; Luke v. Commissioner, 351 F.2d 568 (7th Cir. 1965); R.P. Collins & Co. v. United States, 303 F.2d 142 (1st Cir. 1962)). Both *Herculite* and *Zanesville* relied mostly on the broad view that there was no distortion of income because Congress in various ways (including the consolidated return rules) has indicated a willingness for corporations to offset ongoing income and losses.

[781] First, Regulation section 1.269-2(a)(2) states that the acquired corporation can be the beneficiary of the proscribed deduction. Second, it also defines the principal purpose as the most important purpose, but not necessarily a more than 50% purpose or a purpose without which the acquisition would not have occurred. This second rule implies that section 269 picks up where Regulation section 1.1002-1(b) stops; that is, there could be enough of a business purpose to have motivated the deal under normal circumstances (and thus Regulation section 1.1002-1(b) does not apply); but the principal purpose still could be tax avoidance, to which section 269 can apply. Third, Regulation section 1.269-3 describes several examples whereby income can be brought into conjunction with loss, involving previously related or unrelated corporations.

[782] Reg. § 1.269-2(b).

The regulation furthers confusion by stating that it describes a single "principle" reflected in *Gregory*,[783] *Griffiths*,[784] *Higgins*[785] and *Spreckels*,[786] which include two of the boundary decisions discussed earlier. The legislative reports on the enactment of the predecessor of section 269 cited *Higgins* most prominently of all.[787] "Distortion" does not seem to add to the definition: it is just another way of saying that the allowance looks wrong when the transaction enjoying it does not have the essential nature that Congress intended to benefit.

The meaning of the regulation is made somewhat clearer only through the following sentence describing three situations, which is followed by the citation of the four cases:

> The distortion may be evidenced, for example, by the fact that the transaction was not undertaken for reasons germane to the conduct of the business of the taxpayer, by the unreal nature of the transaction such as its sham character, or by the unreal or unreasonable relation which the deduction, credit, or other allowance bears to the transaction.

The three questionable situations do not describe cases to which the courts applied a single "principle." Rather, they describe (1) two cases turning on statutory construction, (2) a *Moline Properties* sham corporation case, and (3) a case where a deal as papered was unreal when compared with what the parties actually did.

Fairly clearly the lack of business reasons cases referred to are *Gregory v. Helvering* and *Spreckels*. Ch. III.C.3.a(1) above shows how *Gregory* construed a business purpose requirement into the reorganization statute, and gave no indication of creating a global principle. The legal issue decided in *Spreckels* was whether the consolidated return statute and regulations required a business purpose to consolidate an inactive loss corporation (they did). Also fairly clearly the principal sham case was *Higgins v. Smith*; the Supreme Court itself later called the corporation used there a sham, as discussed in Ch. III.C.3.a(2) above. The "unreal or unreasonable relation" language is the most obscure until one examines the facts of *Griffiths* and learns that the taxpayer arranged a purported installment sale for $100,000 of stock worth less than $10,000 to his controlled corporation, which allegedly resold the stock again for much more than it was worth, to the person who had agreed to pay $100,000 to Mr. Griffiths to settle his fraud claim, who otherwise would have rescinded the prior fraudulent sale for $100,000, as to which Mr. Griffiths had already

---

783 Gregory v. Helvering, 293 U.S. 465 (1935).

784 Griffiths v. Helvering, 308 U.S. 355 (1939).

785 Higgins v. Smith, 308 U.S. 473 (1940).

786 J.D. & A.B. Spreckles Co. v. Commissioner, 41 B.T.A. 370 (1940) (construing the consolidated return statute and regulations to require a business purpose for consolidation and finding none to exist; the group acquired a loss corporation solely to use its losses).

787 Seidman, Seidman's Legislative History of Federal Income and Excess Profits Tax Laws 1953-1939, Vol. 1, 1971-74 (Prentice Hall 1954).

claimed a $92,000 tax loss! That reflects an unreasonable relation of the purported facts to the real facts, and approaches fraud.

Thus, when unpacked the seemingly expansive regulation simply, but importantly, relies on what the courts, mostly the Supreme Court had done in finding facts (usually fraud) and statutory interpretation (using a purposive and not literalist approach).

IV.A.2. *Taxpayer Defenses to Section 269*

Taxpayers have contested with considerable success the application of section 269 in every possible way. For examples: (1) the taxpayer may want to aggregate non-tax-avoidance purposes so as to weigh more than the tax avoidance purpose;[788] (2) the taxpayer may contend that the larger transaction has business purposes that count even though the particular step that directly facilitated the allowance might not;[789] (3) taxpayers where possible will utilize an asset basis carryover transaction so as to avail themselves of the common control exception;[790] (4) taxpayers can claim they would have "oth-

---

[788] Although Regulation section 1.269-3(a)(2) does say "any other purpose," it is reasonable to interpret "other purpose" to be business purpose as an aggregate type (to be contrasted with tax avoidance purposes). Bobsee Corp. v. United States, 411 F.2d 231, 239 (5th Cir. 1969). The Service has rejected the view that there are only two grouped purposes to be considered and contended that a "40%" tax avoidance purpose is sufficient, but the Claims Court also disagreed. U.S. Shelter Corp. v. United States, 13 Cl. Ct. 606 (1987).

[789] This is a contentious point that pits the maxim allowing the taxpayer to select the most tax efficient route to a business end (*see supra* Ch. II.C.2.a.) against the view that some such selections are beyond the pale. *Gregory v. Helvering*, discussed above, certainly is relevant to this question because it is cited in the section 269 regulations and it both stated the right of taxpayers to choose the more tax efficient route and found the route chosen to be beyond the pale because there was no reorganization of an actual business. This holding does not stand for a requirement of business purpose for each step of a transaction that has an overall business purpose. For further discussion of the courts' choices to focus on the whole transaction or parts of it, see *infra* Ch. V.F.7.c(2) discussing the economic substance doctrine.

[790] The logic and purpose of this exception have never been entirely clear. It apparently was meant to exclude transfers between commonly controlled corporations, which were thought to be adequately covered by the predecessor of section 482. *See* Barnard, *Acquisitions for Tax Benefit,* 34 CAL. L. REV. 36, 109-10 (1946); *see also* Chase, *An Analysis of Section 129 of the Internal Revenue Code*, 30 CORNELL L. Q. 421(1945).

erwise enjoyed"[791] the allowance despite the control or asset acquisition and therefore section 269 cannot apply;[792] taxpayers will intentionally utilize an

---

[791] This requirement should not bear the weight placed on it by taxpayers. The Senate Report discussed the adoption of the term and does not show that the Senate believed or intended its addition of "otherwise enjoy" was central. S. Rep. No. 627, (1943), 1944 C.B. 973 et seq. The Senate amendment limited in several ways the House bill, which would have applied to any property acquisition; the Senate limited it to apply only to a corporation to corporation carryover basis property acquisition, and proposed to define control as "more than 50%" (a definition that did not make its way into the final act); it also eliminated the words "availed of" in connection with acquisition being made or availed of for the avoidance purposes; most importantly, it increased the amount of tax avoidance required from "one of the principal purposes" to the principal purpose "that outranks, or exceeds in importance, any other one purpose." *Id.* at 1016-17. In the context of these changes to the House Bill, the Senate Report stated that the House version "creates a realm of uncertainty in connection with any acquisition which might result in any reduction of tax liability or be availed of in reduction of tax liability by any person or persons." *Id.* at 994. But in the detailed explanation of its changes, the Senate Report had nothing to say about the "otherwise enjoy" change. In contrast, it emphasized the increase in the level of tax avoidance purpose required and it explained that more than a 50% acquisition should be required because "such acquisitions are clearly those in which the opportunities for distortion and perversion are largest, both in method and result." *Id.* at 1016.

The most detailed contemporary analysis of the legislation contained no specific discussion of the "otherwise enjoy" phrase, in contrast to specific discussions of other provisions, and that analysis states that "The Finance Committee in its report did not clearly articulate the reasons for the changes it made." Ruddick, *Acquisitions to Avoid Income or Excess Profits Tax: Section 129 of the Internal Revenue Code*, 58 Harv. L. Rev. 196, 203 (1944).

[792] An example is an allowance that could have been obtained from acquired assets without a carryover basis. The issue is whether the allowance has to stem from the acquisition or from the acquisition with a carryover basis in order for section 269 to apply. The legislative history supports the first reading, stating:

> Section 129, under your committee's amendment, as under the House bill, recognizes that any attempt to encompass tax evasion and avoidance problems by a specific description of the tax avoidance schemes will catch within its net both intended transactions and those not intended and will fail to catch both those intended to be caught and not intended. Furthermore, the specific description tends to center attention upon the form and technical character of the scheme, and to let the substance of the tax avoidance escape. To determine what transactions constitute the condemned evasion or avoidance, section 129 must be read in its context and background.

S. Rep. No. 627. *See generally* Cohen et al., *The Internal Revenue Code of 1954: Carry-overs and the Accumulated Earnings Tax*, 10 Tax L. Rev. 277, 294 (1955).

Cases bearing on this issue do not yield a clear reading. They include Scroll, Inc. v. Commissioner, 447 F.2d 612 (5th Cir. 1971); Vulcan Materials Co. v. United States, 446 F.2d 690 (5th Cir. 1971); F.C. Publication Liquidating Corp. v. Commissioner, 304 F.2d 779 (2d Cir. 1962); James Realty Co. v. United States, 280 F.2d 394 (8th Cir. 1960); *cf.* Cromwell Corp. v. Commissioner, 43 T.C. 313 (1964), *acq.*, 1965-2 C.B. 4 (the court properly found business purpose for the direct and indirect acquisitions of corporate control at issue); Coastal Oil Storage Co. v. Commissioner, 25 T.C. 1304, *aff'd in part and rev'd in part,* 242 F.2d 396 (4th Cir. 1957) (the broad language in the Tax Court opinion is contrary to a later opinion in *Army Times Sales Co. v. Commissioner*, 35 T.C. 688 (1961), and is contradicted by *Thomas E. Snyder Co. v. Commissioner*, 34 T.C. 400, 406 (1960), *aff'd*, 288 F.2d 36 (7th Cir.), and *J.T. Slocomb Co. v. Commissioner*, 334 F.2d 269 (2d Cir. 1964)); Commodores Point Terminal

existing owned corporation to avoid acquisition of control of a corporation. However, Regulation section 1.269-3(b) Example shows that the carryover basis nature of the transaction need not have been the exclusive route to the tax benefit.[793]

IV.A.3. *The Relation of Section 269 to the Economic Substance Doctrine*

Without regard to whether it overstates the cases on which it relies or makes a single principle out of three, Regulation section 1.269-2(b) interprets the statute to require enforcement of Congress' basic purpose or plan for the allowance claimed by the taxpayer.[794] It asserts that only in light of that purpose can a utilization of the allowance be found to be "distortive," which

---

Corp. v. Commissioner, 11 T.C. 411 (1948), *acq.* 1949-1 CB 1 (the argument that this decision requires the tax benefit to depend on the acquisition of at least 50% of the stock in the transaction would render ineffective a substantial body of authority); Briarcliff Candy Co. v. Commissioner, 1987 T.C.M. (RIA) 1987-487; G.C.M. 39,472 (Aug. 2, 1985) (misreading *Cromwell*).

[793] Not to the contrary is the statement in the example:

> The acquisition occurs at a time when the parent would not succeed to the net operating loss carryovers of the subsidiary if the subsidiary were liquidated, and the profits of business Y [the contributed property] are sufficient to offset a substantial portion of the net operating loss carryovers attributable to business X [the sub's business] (see further example (3) of §1.269-6).

The example, and its companion example in Regulation section 1.269-6, appear to involve a unique scenario as explained in Cohen et al., *The Internal Revenue Code of 1954*, *supra* note 792, at 277, discussing *Kimbell-Diamond Milling Co. v. Commissioner*, 14 T.C. 74 (1950), *aff'd*, 187 F.2d 718 (5th Cir. 1951). The particular alternate transaction that the example excludes is one to which section 269 could also have applied but for failing another requirement: a liquidation under section 332 could have been subject to section 269(a)(2) but for the fact that the transferee corporation was in control of the transferor corporation. Thus section 269 by its terms specifically excludes such a transaction from its coverage, making it more than just an alternate transaction to which section 269 could not have applied because there was no carryover basis; section 269 could not have applied because of a very specific exception that presumably was aimed at saving clearly nonabusive transactions from the reach of the statute. That approach is not applicable to unavailable alternative transaction that would similarly be distortive.

Furthermore, the example was added by the 1962 regulations to illustrate the subsequently repealed section 269(c). In any event, the example does not say that section 269 applies; it says that the described facts are ordinarily indicative of the principal purpose of tax avoidance or evasion. In this context, the example implies that if the liquidation route that was clearly nonabusive and permitted by the statute (as discussed above) had been available, then the bad principal purpose would not be indicated. Finally, the final regulation adopted in 1962 did not contain the following sentence that was in the proposed regulation: "The principal purpose actuating the acquisition must have been to secure the benefit which such person or persons or corporation would not otherwise enjoy." F. R. 12,705 (Dec. 9, 1960). The deletion was due to the failure of the sentence to require tax avoidance.

[794] *See, e.g.*, Silvano Achiro v. Commissioner, 77 T.C. 881 (1981) holding that incorporations for the principal purpose of enjoying benefits such as the then more favorable corporate retirement plan accruals were not subject to section 269 because Congress intended the benefits to be enjoyed). *cf.* Hariton, *Kafka and the Tax Shelter*, 57 TAX L. REV. 1 (2003).

describes the state of falling outside Congress' purpose for the allowance, rather than some undefined independent standard. The regulation states three nonexclusive *evidences* of distortion: nonbusiness purpose, sham (which appears to mean sham in fact or fraud), and lack of reasonable relation of the allowance to the transaction (which also amounts to fraud).

Thus, the regulation is based on the premise that Congress' plan in writing an allowance *never* grants the allowance to a taxpayer with respect to a transaction that lacks a suitably important business motivation or is a factual sham. Subject to defining what these conditions mean in practice, this regulation effectively states the economic substance doctrine, for the circumscribed types of corporate transactions. Therefore, in applying the economic substance doctrine apart from section 269 the lower federal courts in effect have chosen to disregard the limiting conditions stated by section 269 of control or asset acquisition and allowances, and to apply the purpose test unrestrained.

The significance of these observations cannot be overstated:

- *The section 269 regulations confirm that Congress intends stricter application of the portions of the Code that grant deductions, credits and allowances; but, on the other hand,*
- *They do not authorize disallowance based on the violation of Congress' purposes or plan alone—they also require the triggering transaction, either acquisition of control of a corporation or acquisition of assets in a carryover basis transaction.*

The ESD stands this approach on its head: it does not purport to rely on or be limited to traditional protection of allowances, nor does it focus on Congress' purposes in connection with a particular allowance or require any particular form of transaction; but it treats the satisfaction of the court made rule as paramount.

At this point a Supreme Court decision will be required to limit the economic substance doctrine on the grounds that it is precluded by section 269, but the argument should not be ignored. Section 269 well could have been recognized as displacing court made rules in the corporate area, and its limitation to certain corporate transactions raises a valid question about the application of similar doctrines outside the corporate area (despite section 7701(o), which does not say when the ESD applies). The same can be said for related party transactions and section 482 (which provides broad anti-abuse discretion as to related party transactions), and as to partnership transactions and Regulation section 1.701-2(a). If just these three rules had been better applied by the Service and received by the courts, the ESD might never have been invented.

A general principle applies in other areas of the law that where Congress has acted to create a remedy or a scheme of proceeding the courts will not create another.[795] A somewhat related doctrine holds that usually the codification of a part of a common law rule does not preclude the continued application of the uncodified portion, assuming it is not inconsistent with the codification.[796] Similarly, Congress' provision of one remedy has been held not to necessarily preclude another.[797] But nonpreclusion rests on the view that "long established and familiar principles" in the common law should not be thrown out without rather clear congressional direction.[798] Such direction may be inferred from the fact that the statute speaks directly to the case addressed by the common law rule.[799] Thus, the issues are how directly must Congress speak to the common law issue[800] and how entrenched must be the common law rule, and is there any common law rule here at all?

Congress wrote the predecessor of section 269 in 1943 when the principal case on which the ESD is thought to be based (*Gregory v. Helvering*) was only eight years old. Granting the fact that "common law" has come to refer to court made law in generally, one would have a hard time finding the coalescing of such common law in the federal tax area by 1943. Therefore, section 269 should be viewed as stating the law rather than partly embodying a court-made doctrine.

Section 269 speaks to the issue of intentional tax avoidance with sufficient specificity, and the common law rules of the income tax were sufficiently nubile in 1943, to support the view that section 269 restates and contains any such rules, leaving no room for a more expansive common law doctrine, at least in the corporate area. The ESD amounts to a de facto expansion of section 269 to circumvent the parameters Congress set and instead to treat the taxpayer's purpose as sufficient to deny a tax allowance (and other favorable outcomes not involving allowances).

Nevertheless, section 269 does not disturb the application of traditional common law principles such as the law of agency and the general power of equity to, for example, disregard a corporation interposed for a fraudulent purpose or a purpose contrary to the intent of Congress. See Ch. III.C.3.a(2).

---

795 *See* Schweiker v. Chilicky, 487 U.S. 412, 424 (1988) (ruling that remedies provided by statute precluded the *Bivens* remedy).

796 *See* United States v. Texas, 507 U.S. 529, 534 (1993).

797 *See* Exxon Shipping Co. v. Baker, 128 S. Ct. 2605 (2008).

798 *See* United States v. Texas, 507 U.S. at 534.

799 *See* Pasquantino v. United States, 544 U.S. 349, 359 (2005).

800 *See* United States v. Bestfoods, 524 U.S. 51, 63 (1998) (failure of CERCLA law to speak to the matter of parent liability for subsidiary torts at all evidences no intent to abrogate common law doctrine of piercing the corporate veil).

IV.B. Section 482

Section 482 is the principal guardian of the Code from abuse by related party transactions,[801] a cluster area as discussed in Ch. VI.E.1.e(3). It shares section 269's feature of authorizing the Secretary to act upon audit on the basis of broad anti-avoidance policies, but differs in two important ways. First, it primarily addresses non-arm's-length dealings between related businesses, or at least was so construed through most of its history, which dates back to 1934 in the origin of most of its current form.[802] It generally was understood to attack income shifting among entities as such, and was not much enforced up to adoption in 1966 of an extensive set of regulations.[803]

Second, unlike its treatment of section 269, the Treasury has issued massive regulations under section 482. The likely reason for the more substantial regulations is that the international applications of section 482 have overtaken the domestic corporate applications;[804] indeed section 482 is not limited to corporate transactions (although it is limited to businesses).

Section 482 authorizes the Secretary to reallocate income or deductions among two or more related businesses as necessary to prevent evasion of taxes or to clearly reflect income; but it does not specifically authorize regulations, in contrast with section 1502, which is similarly brief.[805] Needless to say this is a bare bones and extremely broad grant of authority. However, from three elements of the section one must infer that it mainly aims at locating income, as otherwise defined (see section 61) and as otherwise timed (see section 446), in the return of one of the two or more taxpayers: (1) the requirement that two businesses be involved, (2) the requirement that they be commonly controlled or otherwise related, and (3) the reference to clear reflection of income, which takes on an assignment of income quality in an area of multiple related taxpayers.[806] The regulations adopt such an understanding, by opening with a statement of the "arm's length standard,"[807] which attempts to correct mispricing, and hence assignment of income or deduction, between related taxpayers.

---

[801] *See generally* Bittker & Eustice, at 13.20. Congress enacted the predecessor of section 482 in 1928 when it repealed the provision that allowed the Secretary to forced consolidation, that had been enacted in 1917. The Service issued regulations in 1935 setting out the arm's length standard. *See* Avi-Yonah, *The Rise and Fall of the Arm's Length Standard,* 15 Va. Tax Rev. 89, 95-6 (1995). The Court has referred to sections 269 and 482 as a set. United States v. Vogel Fertilizer Co., 455 U.S. 16 (1982)(aimed at multiple incorporations, no longer much of a problem).

[802] *See* Lent, *New Importance for Section 482 of the Internal Revenue Code,* 7 Wm & Mary L. Rev. 345-49 (1966).

[803] *Id.*

[804] Even though the Associate Chief Counsel (Corporate) and Associate Chief Counsel (International) have joint authority over section 482, the Chief Counsel has given International effective ultimate authority over its interpretation.

[805] This approach also is used in section 269A.

[806] *See infra* Ch. VI.F.2.d.

[807] Reg. § 1.482-1(b).

Although section 482 has been more successful than section 269, there is a strong view that "transfer pricing," as its application to international transactions is called, ultimately cannot be adequately policed.[808]

IV.C. Section 701

In theory the anti-abuse rules that are specific to partnerships, when combined with section 269 in the corporate area, plus section 482 in the related business area, could form a nearly universal, albeit fragmented, anti-abuse regime for business income taxation. However, they have not, both for reasons peculiar to each section and the absence of understanding that they form a regime.

Thus, like the section 269 regulations, the partnership anti-abuse regulation, Regulation section 1.701-2 adopted in 1994, has been relatively unsuccessful so far, but for different reasons.[809] Its use got off to a slow start, but by 2011 a writer observed that the Service had asserted it many times, but only a handful of court opinions had interpreted it, that other anti-abuse doctrines such as the ESD had surpassed it, and that it should be repealed.[810] The limited role is partly due to the requirement that agents apply it only with the approval of the National Office,[811] and also to the apparent unwillingness of the Service to have its validity tested in court, leading to relying on multiple grounds.[812]

In the regulation the Treasury grasped the nettle and required bona fides and business purposes for partnerships. The Supreme Court has required a business purpose for the formation of a partnership, also a cluster area.[813] In contrast, there is no such general regulation as to corporations, because sec-

---

[808] Reuven Avi-Yonah, *The Rise and Fall of Arm's Length: A Study in the Evolution of U.S. International Taxation*, 15 VA. TAX REV. 89, 112 (1995-1996).

[809] T.D. 8588, 1995-1 C.B. 109. The regulation met with, and continues to meet with, massive resistance and dislike. *See* MCKEE, NELSON & WHITMIRE, FEDERAL TAXATION OF PARTNERSHIPS AND PARTNERS, at 1.05[1][a] (calling it ". . . a stunning departure from existing law. First, the rule creates a separate standard for applying Subchapter K based on the existence of a tax reduction motive. In the absence of statutory direction to the contrary, the U.S. Supreme Court has repeatedly stated that the tax motivation of taxpayers does not alter what would otherwise be the result of the application of the tax law."); *see also* Schlueter, *The Partnership Anti-Abuse Rule: A Chronological Perspective*, 6 J. PASSTHROUGH ENTITIES 37, 38 (2003). *But see*, Cunningham & Repetti, *supra* note 17, at 23 (strongly supporting the regulations). *See also* Reg. §1.704-4(f), 1.752-2(j).

[810] Sowell, *The Partnership Anti-Abuse Rules: Where Have We Been and Where are We Going*, 89 TAXES 69, 104 (2011).

[811] Announcement 94-87, 1994-27 I.R.B. 124. But blanket approval has been given in several specified areas; *see, e.g.*, Notice 2004-31, 2004-1 C.B. 830.

[812] *E.g.*, Russian Recovery Fund Ltd. v. United States, 122 Fed. Cl. 600 (2016) (IRS relied in part on regulation but court ruled on sham partnership); Jade Trading LLC v. United States, 80 Fed. Cl. 11 (2007), *aff'd*, 2010 U.S. App. LEXIS 5901 (Fed. Cir. Mar. 23, 2010) (FPAA relied on the regulation but the court did not discuss it).

[813] Commissioner v. Culbertson, 337 U.S. 733 (1949) (the purpose of carrying on a business).

tion 11 imposes a separate tax on the corporate entity, and particularly after *General Utilities* repeal, anyone wanting to volunteer into the two-tier tax regime should be able to do so.[814]

The regulation construes subchapter K to imply three rules:

1. The partnership must be bona fide and each partnership transaction (or series of related transactions) must be entered into for a substantial business purpose.
2. The form of each partnership transaction must be respected under substance over form principles.
3. The tax consequences under subchapter K to each partner of partnership operations and of transactions between the partner and the partnership must accurately reflect the partners' economic agreement and clearly reflect the partner's income, except to the extent that a provision of subchapter K that is intended to promote administrative convenience or other policy objectives causes tax results that deviate from that requirement. In determining whether a transaction clearly reflects the partners' income, the principles of sections 446(b) and 482 apply.[815]

The regulation evolves from the logical view that Congress intended to accord partnership benefits (principally freedom from partnership level taxation) only to partners who operate a bona fide business in a bona fide partnership; this has roots in the common law of partnerships. Secondarily, it imposes the reasonably objective requirement that the tax consequences follow the economics of the partnership. But it goes farther afield when it requires that the partner's income "clearly reflect income" despite compliance with the law, except as a different result is clearly contemplated by the statute; the statute contemplates broad reallocation of tax items to partners, the root of both the attraction and threat of partnerships in tax. It invokes general concepts of bona fides[816] and substance over form. It makes clear that choosing the partnership model for tax reasons is not contrary to clear reflection of income so long as a bona fide partnership operates a real business. It states an independent "abuse of entity rule" that empowers the Commissioner to treat partners as co-owners rather than partners in order to "carry out the

---

[814] But the Service has argued vehemently that there is a business purpose requirement for the creation of a corporation, citing proudly a thin stream of authority. *See* Caruth v. United States, 688 F. Supp. 1129 (N.D. Tex. 1987), *aff'd on other grounds,* 865 F.2d 644 (5th Cir. 1989); Rev. Proc. 1983-59, 1983-2 C.B. 575 (ruling guidelines under section 351, which did require an explanation of the business reasons for the transaction).

[815] T.D. 8588, 1995-1 C.B. 109.

[816] The regulation's requirement of a bona fide partnership appears not to refer to traditional sham transaction analysis but rather to incorporate excessive tax avoidance purposes into the finding of bona fides of the partnership entity itself. *See* Reg. § 1.701-2(d) (Example 7). This has been criticized as an effort to reverse a battle the Service lost long ago in the Culbertson case. *See* McKee, Nelson & Whitmire, at 1.05[4][a].

purposes" of any part of the Code or regulations;[817] and it states that the regulation does not preclude the application of any other doctrine.[818]

Experience suggests that to be successful, such a regulation (1) must be based on a specific statutory authorization (like, or more specific than, section 482, discussed above), which it lacks, (2) should not rely so heavily on taxpayer purpose (which it does), (3) should not rely so heavily on undefined knowledge of the intent of Congress contrary to the words of the statute (which it does), and (4) should not utilize a standard such as "clear reflection of income" to define income, as contrasted with defining which of multiple businesses owns income or when income is recognized,[819] or whether fraudulent practices have caused the underlying facts from which income is determined to be misstated.[820]

The regulation's fundamental fault is succinctly stated as follows:

> Thus, under the statutory interpretation scheme adduced by the abuse-of-Subchapter-K rule, the literal and unambiguous language of the statute is presumptively *not* governing where the statutorily prescribed result fails to satisfy a proper-reflection-of-income test that finds no expression in either the words of Subchapter K or its legislative history. Such a rule of statutory construction is unprecedented.[821]

These criticisms of the section 701 regulation do not mean that uncodified doctrines are superior; rather they apply doubly to court made doctrines.

IV.D. Loss Limitations

If the limits on the losses that are in the Code had been developed and adequately enforced, probably the majority of so-called tax shelters would be impossible; but, like the foregoing anti-abuse rules, these limits have been underutilized. Like expenses, losses are potential deductions, but, unlike expenses, losses usually are not paired with offsetting related income in the current period; that is, they reflect the excess of expense deductions or depreciation over the income from an activity or investment, either on an annual basis (net operating losses) or when the activity or investment comes to an end. Therefore, losses generally are used to offset income from the same or

---

[817] Reg. § 1.701-2(e). The Supreme Court has identified such a grant of authority as for "legislative" regulations. *See infra* Ch. VI.D.5.

[818] Reg. § 1.701-2(i).

[819] Clear reflection of income appears most prominently in section 446. However, its regulations do not attempt to promote it into a para-definition of income. Rather methods of accounting in general and the clear reflection of income requirement in particular are recognized as matters of timing the recognition of income and deduction and not of defining them. *See* United States v. Fior D'Italia, Inc., 536 U.S. 238 (2002) (limited to one corner of the income tax).

[820] *See, e.g.,* United States v. Hughes Properties, Inc., 476 U.S. 593, 605 (1986) (stating that if the Service determined that a taxpayer manipulated its slot machines so as to not properly reflect income, section 446(b) could be applied).

[821] McKee, Nelson & Whitmire, at 1.05[1][a].

other activities or investments in a later period (NOLs) or to offset income from unrelated activities. Such uses make losses especially desirable, particularly if they can be obtained in a way that does not reflect real economic loss, or as much economic loss as the tax loss, or at least not economic loss to the taxpayer who will benefit from use of the loss.

The malleability of losses to reduce tax (1) on a variety of incomes of different activities and investments, (2) in different years, and perhaps (3) of different taxpayers, with (4) different tax rates, and (5) income taxed in different ways (ordinary income versus capital gains), has led to a wide variety of loss limitations in the Code.[822] Primary examples include:

- The basic requirement of "entered into for profit" for loss deductions on transactions in section 165(c)(2);[823] also this section requires that the loss be "sustained" to be deductible, which if enforced could have solved most of the problem cases;[824]
- The passive loss rules of section 465;[825]
- The "at risk" loss rules of section 469;[826]
- The severe limitations on deduction of capital losses in section 1211;
- The limits on recognition of losses incurred in dealings with related persons, as in section 267;
- The corporate net operating loss limitations of section 382;[827]
- The consolidated return unified loss rule;[828]
- The hobby loss rule for individuals; and
- The wash sale rule of section 1091 and straddle rules of section 1256 and 1092.

For individuals and partnerships and S corporations, section 183, referred to as the hobby loss rule, would appear to cover most of the ground of the ESD.[829] The section targets "activities not engaged in for profit," which is exactly that group of cases that the ESD essays to catch. But in contrast with the ESD, the level of profitability required is an honest and actual objective to make a profit, rather than objective criteria.[830] Section 183 basically operates in conjunction with section 162 and 212; activities that are not trades

---

[822] *See* Cummings, *Discontinuities in Corporate Recognition of Loss*, 44 TAX LAW. 39 (1990).

[823] *See* Yosha v. Commissioner, 861 F.2d 494 (7th Cir. 1988) (the first appellate opinion to use the term "economic substance doctrine," which correctly observed that the matter was controlled by the profit requirement of section 165; ruled that an alleged straddle was not a straddle because contractual terms foreclosed the possibility of risk).

[824] See Ch. VI.F.5.

[825] BITTKER & LOKKEN, at 28.1.

[826] *Id.*

[827] BITTKER & EUSTICE, at 14.42-.47.

[828] Reg. § 1.1502-36.

[829] *See generally* BITTKER & LOKKEN, at 22.5.

[830] *Id.* at 22.5.2; *see* Rev. Rul. 1970-300, 1970-2 C.B. 112 (ruling that section 183 did not apply to limit the losses derived from government financed housing projects for which the rents were limited, because Congress intended to encourage the projects).

or businesses and are not investments for profit are not engaged in for profit. The individual subject to section 183 can deduct expenses not in excess of the income from the activity.

Bittker & Lokken have observed that if section 183 did not exclude C corporations from its reach it might have provided the ground for very analogous reasoning in *ACM Partnership* and other tax shelter cases.[831] However, evidently the shortcoming of section 183 is the perception that its enforcement relies principally on absence of the taxpayer's subjective intent to make a profit, which intent is easy for the taxpayer to allege and hard to disprove.[832]

IV.E. Other Targeted Anti-Abuse Rules

Anti-avoidance rules have been part of the U.S. taxing statutes from the start.[833] In addition to the rules discussed above, there is a variety of other targeted anti-abuse rules based on taxpayer motive.[834] The list below could be substantially longer, but the point is that Congress knows how to write targeted, objective, anti-abuse rules, which tend to render "off-Code" court made rules unnecessary, or at least questionable. The Code and regulations also contain a small number of generally applicable rules based on "substance," including:

- Regulation section 1.165-1(b) ("Substance and not mere form shall govern in determining a deductible loss.");
- Regulation section 1.351-1(b)(1) (recharacterizing a non-economic exchange of property without reference to a doctrine);
- Regulation section 1.338-1(c)(anti-abuse rule for section 338 elections);

---

[831] Bittker & Lokken, at 22.5.6.

[832] *See* Rose v. Commissioner, 88 T.C. 386 (1987) *aff'd,* 868 F.2d 851 (6th Cir. 1989) (stating that section 183 depended on lack of subjective intent to profit, and due to its shortcoming attempted to create a special rule for "generic tax shelters" that combined subjective and objective prongs; the appellate court affirmed, but declined to adopt the generic tax shelter approach).

[833] *See, e.g.*, United States v. 67 Packages of Dry Goods, 58 U.S. 85 (1855) (1799 statute addressed attempt to avoid customs duties by causing shipping documents to show undervalued goods "with a design to evade the duties").

[834] *See, e.g.*, I.R.C. §§ 302(c)(2)(B)(ii) (principal purpose of tax avoidance precludes a safe harbor), 306(b)(4)(B) (absence of principal purpose of tax avoidance will excuse taxpayer from anti-abuse rule), 355(a)(1)(D)(ii)(distributing corporation can retain stock of controlled corporation if not for purposes of tax avoidance), 357(b) (corporation's assumption of shareholder's liability will be treated as boot if for purpose of tax avoidance), 382(l)(1)(A) (disregarding efforts to increase value of loss corporation if for tax avoidance purposes), 453(e)(7) (allowing taxpayer to prove out of acceleration of installment sale gain if not for tax avoidance), 1551 (disallowance of multiple corporate rate treatment if formed for tax avoidance purpose). Section 131(a) of Pub. L. No. 98-369, 98 Stat. 494 (1984) removed a requirement in section 367(a) that the taxpayer establish that an exchange was not in pursuance of a plan having as one of its principal purposes the avoidance of federal income taxes in order to have a foreign corporation treated as a corporation in certain tax deferred exchanges. The rule originated as section 112(k) of the 1932 Revenue Act.

- Section 446(b) (allowing the Secretary to determine that taxpayer's method of accounting does not clearly reflect income)[835]—Treasury views sections 446 and 7701(l) as analogous to sections 269 and 482;[836]
- Regulation section 1.451-1(a) (constructive receipt doctrine);
- Regulation section 1.752-2(j) (assessing economic risk of loss in identifying obligations);
- Regulation section 1.1002-1(c) (describes nonrecognition provisions as those involving exchanges where the differences in the property are more "formal than substantial.");
- Regulation section 1.1275-2(g) (original issue discount anti-abuse rule);
- Regulation section 1.1502-13(h)(1) (intercompany transaction anti-abuse rule); and
- Section 7701(l) (authorizing regulations on conduit financing for "recharacterizations appropriate to prevent avoidance of any taxes").[837]

And it was unnecessary for Congress to write into the statute anti-abuse rules that the Supreme Court clearly created, with the most prominent example being the assignment of income doctrine.

Another larger set of anti-abuse rules is not based on taxpayer motive and does not require ad hoc determinations of substance, but rather undertakes to define objectively cases that should not receive beneficial treatment, including:

- The wash sale rule, section 1091;[838]
- Section 367;
- The subpart F rules and other regimes addressing inappropriate holding offshore of passive income and related deemed abuses;
- The unrelated business income rules applicable to exempt entities;
- The accumulated earnings and personal holding company taxes and the former collapsible corporations earnings tax; and
- The alternate minimum tax.

The Supreme Court explained in *Braunstein*[839] that Congress could rightly conclude that an over-inclusive objective rule was better than a motive based

---

[835] Brown v. Helvering, 291 U.S. 193 (1934) (the accounting method applied by the taxpayer is never conclusive).

[836] *Treasury White Paper on Corporate Tax Shelters*, *supra* note 14, at Sec. V; *see also* United States v. Hughes Properties, Inc., 476 U.S. 593 (1986) (stating that if the Service determined that a taxpayer manipulated its slot machines so as to not properly reflect income, section 446(b) could be applied).

[837] Reg. § 1.7701(l)-1.

[838] *See* Du Pont v. Commissioner, 118 F.2d 544 (3d Cir. 1941) (containing a succinct review of how Congress cuts the Gordian knot with a rule like section 1091, on occasion).

[839] Braunstein v. Commissioner, 374 U.S. 65 (1963); *cf.* Helvering v. Hammel, 311 U.S. 504 (1941) (declining to construe into the capital loss limitation rule an exception for involuntary sales, even though Congress may have been concerned with the taxpayer's ability to voluntarily recognize capital losses).

rule aimed at the exact loophole at issue (collapsible corporations); the objective rule would avoid difficult ad hoc fact finding.

IV.F. Conclusion

The foregoing review suggests as to Congress' and Treasury's efforts to combat tax avoidance that:

- Where specific Code authorization for regulations exists (section 269) the Treasury has not kept the regulations up to date or has not adequately defended the regulations;
- Where the Treasury has written regulations in the vitally important related party area (section 482), it has developed tunnel vision by focusing the regulations on international transactions and transfer pricing, largely for the purpose of facilitating negotiated compliance by multinationals that often turns out to function as tax avoidance;
- In other areas it has not issued needed regulations at all;[840]
- In some areas it needs perhaps more specific congressional directions (section 701); but
- It knows how to find the "substance" of a transaction without resort to a doctrine (section 7872; Regulation section 1.351-1); and
- It has written a regulation that approximates a doctrine in the large cluster area of nonrecognition rules, without the benefit of a specific grant of regulatory authority (Reg. section 1.1001-2), presumably based on Supreme Court precedent.

On the legislative side, certainly some high profile anti-abuse rules like section 269 have largely failed of their purpose in part because of their subjective elements, but objective rules largely have succeeded.

This is a long history of missed regulatory opportunities, for which the Service and courts now try to substitute doctrines, inappropriately and unnecessarily, as shown below. Better that the Service litigate less in uncertain law areas, and the Treasury promulgate regulations more, with notice and hearing, as recommended below in Ch. VII.A., and Congress write objective rules as it has in many cases.

[840] The Treasury is fairly far behind statutory changes in its regulation writing. For example, the investment company definition in section 351(g) was amended in 1997, but Regulation section 1.351-1(c) remains unchanged; Regulation 15a.453-1(c) remains unchanged after its misuse by the taxpayer in ACM P'ship, 1997 T.C.M. (RIA) 1997-115, *aff'd,* 157 F.3d 231 (3d Cir. 1998).

Ch. V. Enforcement Responses to Intentional Tax Reduction, Including the Economic Substance Doctrine

V.A. The Problem of Intentional Tax Reduction

Several responses to intentional tax reduction have developed at the enforcement level, either because Congress and the Treasury have not been up to the task, or because the tools they have provided have not been properly used, or because the lower federal courts have been complicit in these developments (or all three). Although lower courts and the Service tend to attribute all of these responses to Supreme Court opinions, in many cases the attribution is incorrect. This chapter will show the following:

- The Service is responsible for pushing the courts to create and apply allegedly tax specific doctrines of uncertain scope to combat what the Service perceives as improper intentional tax reduction activities.
- To the extent this has led to the creation of a positive rule of law in the form of the economic substance doctrine (ESD), the Service has violated its own policy against making law through litigation,[841] and in fact has promoted the most significant positive rule of law ever created by courts in the federal tax law.
- The ESD lacks authority in Supreme Court decisions, in the Code (despite section 7701(o)), or in Treasury regulations, except to the extent it reflects standard methods of fact finding and statutory interpretation that are found in many Supreme Court opinions.

[841] I.R.M. 31.1.1.1.3(1).

- The uncertainty of the scope of the ESD is an inherent part of its charm for the Service, which relies on its *in terrorem* effect.
- The tax specific doctrines are best explained as a combination of standard statutory interpretation and construction plus common law and equitable fact finding, which sometimes are carried to extremes (such as a presumed universal requirement of business purpose), and sometimes are promoted into a true positive rule of law in the case of the ESD.
- The role of equitable and common law fact finding is key to the fact finding roots of the tax specific doctrines, but has been completely overlooked.
- In addition to the statutes and regulations discussed in the preceding Section, there do exist general principles for the application of the tax law, which do have the imprimatur of the Supreme Court, and which can go a long way toward the goals of the tax specific doctrines.

Taxpayers' efforts to reduce their taxes have driven the reliance of the Service and the lower courts on what they treat as tax specific doctrines, despite the absence of (1) any general canon of liberal construction of the Code in favor of the government (as shown in Ch. II.B.2.b.), (2) effective enforcement of the statutory and regulatory anti-avoidance rules on the books (as shown in Ch. IV.), and (3) any proof of congressional intent allowing off Code rules to usurp the written Code (prior to the codification of the ESD).

This state of affairs developed in the last third of the 20th century and the ESD coalesced into a "doctrine" by the early 21st century. Randolph Paul published his Restatement of the Law of Tax Avoidance in 1937 and did not discern the ESD or a general requirement for business purpose, even though he discussed *Gregory v. Helvering*, which was then two years old. He reviewed methods of Code interpretation and fact finding in tax disputes during the first 20 plus years of the income tax (and estate tax), including particularly step transactions. His preface stated conclusions with respect to tax avoidance that are still true today, including: (1) economic crisis puts pressure on taxpayers, who respond with efforts to reduce their tax liabilities, (2) courts "legislate" in opposition, and (3) the resulting welter of case law cannot be fit into a "fixed body of academic principles," but (4) is best studied in terms of "what variable courts do in fact."[842]

As in 1937, the set of federal tax decisions that address intentional tax avoidance is large relative to the total of all tax disputes, and occupies a disproportionate volume of the interpretive cases, and so has a disproportionate effect on all questions of Code interpretation and tax fact finding. What has changed is that the even larger welter of case law has begun to self identify its own body of doctrines thought to be specific to taxation, be they theoretical or pragmatic in origin, including most prominently the ESD, in contrast

[842] PAUL, STUDIES I, at iii-viii.

with Paul's approach of inducing trends in the law from cases in certain areas, called here clusters.

The tax specific doctrines ostensibly are made necessary by the third of three categories of transactions into which all transactions having tax effects may be placed: (1) transactions that happen without participants giving any thought to how they will be taxed, or at least to altering them in light of taxation; (2) transactions that may or may not be pursued based on how they are taxed (for example, many real estate transactions depend for their profitability on the tax effects of depreciation and interest deductions), and that may be fashioned to conform to the presumed requirements of the desired tax result, which frequently is elective by form; and (3) transactions that occur for the principal purpose of producing a tax effect, which most commonly are deductions, losses, credits or income shifting (in rare cases the goal can be income generation, when the taxpayer has expiring losses, etc.). See Ch. II.C., above.

Even though category (2) cases also usually involve deductions and losses, the Service usually will respect a taxpayer's choice to accomplish a goal motivated by profit making or nontax personal concerns in the way that incurs the least tax liability, including transactions that can be profitable only because of the way they are taxed (for example, through accelerated depreciation, credits, reduced rates, etc.).[843] Conversely, as to category (3) the Service seeks to have taxpayers call them to the Service's attention (through listed transactions, enforced by penalties),[844] and frequently will deny the tax result claimed. Inevitably, it is hard to obtain agreement between taxpayers and the Service about which cases are in category (2) and which are in category (3).[845] Even so astute a jurist as Oliver Wendell Holmes could only refer to a line on one side of which the taxpayer was safe.[846]

Strangely enough, the seminal cite for most tax specific doctrines, the *Gregory* case, involved a transaction in the second category.[847] Indubitably Mrs. Gregory wanted her corporation to sell some stock it owned, and that sale in fact occurred at the end of the steps; it was a bona fide business transaction. A way was found to effect the sale with the least tax to the related group of taxpayers—or at least Mrs. Gregory hoped for that result. The confusion

[843] *See* Bittker & Lokken, at 4.3.2.

[844] Reg. § 1.6011-4(b) (reportable transactions list only §165 loss generators as reportable based on the tax effect); Notice 2009-59, 2009-31 I.R.B. (cumulating listed transactions that are reportable).

[845] *See, e.g.,* Basic, Inc. v. United States, 549 F.2d 740 (Ct. Cl. 1977) (The parent planned to sell a two-tier chain of subsidiaries, S-1 and S-2. The parent first had S-1 pay a dividend in kind of its S-2 stock, and then it sold the stock of both subsidiaries to the buyer; the dividend of S-2 stock was ignored as a transitory step without business purpose. The parent's capital gain was increased by the amount of the S-2 dividend.).

[846] Bullen v. Wisconsin, 240 U. S. 625 (1916); *see also* Irwin v. Gavit, 268 U. S. 161, 168 (stating that he was not troubled by the need to draw a line because"That is the question in pretty much everything worth arguing in the law.").

[847] Gregory v. Helvering, 293 U.S. 465 (1935).

of doctrine and authority that has resulted from citing *Gregory* to support both the ESD and a general requirement of business purpose across all Code section involving deductions and allowances, shows that careful attention should be paid to the particulars of case law, which is attempted below.

The Service and lower courts act as if the Code were subject to an over-arching rule that taxpayers cannot plan to obtain a tax benefit if the benefit flows from a transaction that lacks a business purpose that passes muster and a profit potential.[848] The Treasury and others commonly announce that all transactions must have business purposes in order to be respected for tax purposes.[849] This Chapter addresses how this state of affairs has arisen, given the absence of any such preamble in the Code or regulations (even section 7701(o) does not apply to the estate, excise and other taxes); and further, why there is no such preamble in either the Code or the Regulations. It disagrees with the view of many that the tax specific doctrines are appropriate correctives to formalism,[850] at least to the extent the doctrines go beyond normal fact finding and purposive statutory interpretations.

V.B. The Tax Specific Doctrines

There is a range of tax specific doctrines, meaning labeled principles in aid of judicial decision making (and Service decision making, based on the case law), which federal courts in federal tax cases commonly cite to support conclusions that may be either (a) contrary to the law and facts as normally determined, or (b) consistent with the law and facts as normally determined, but employ tax specific labels. As to the second group of cases, federal courts apply many of these principles in other areas of law, without using the tax labels: for example, the *step transaction doctrine* seldom appears outside federal tax law by that label, yet it reflects a common law method of fact finding. For another example, a technical breach of duty that did not cause the damage is not actionable as a tort, or at least will not produce a recovery for the damages, because *substance rather than form* controls the determination of causal relation; but the tort law does not generally purport to apply a substance over form doctrine. And perhaps the most ubiquitous divergence of tax doctrines from the common law is that the Service and courts persist in ignoring the possibility that a third party acted as the agent of the taxpayer.[851]

The tax specific doctrines are confusing for many reasons.[852] One reason is indicated above: sometimes they reflect normal legal methods but use tax specific labels, and other times they reflect rules that are truly unique to federal tax cases (*assignment of income doctrine*, and *economic substance doctrine*

[848] *See infra* Ch. V.F.4.

[849] *Treasury White Paper on Corporate Tax Shelters*, *supra* note 14, at 127-12.

[850] *See, e.g.*, Weisbach, *Formalism in the Tax Law*, 66 U. Chi. L. Rev. 860 (1999); Cunningham & Repetti, *supra* note 17, at 1.

[851] *E.g.*, Webber v. Commissioner, 144 T.C. No. 17 (2015) (the investor control doctrine).

[852] *See* Jellum, Codifying and Miscodifying Judicial Anti-Abuse Doctrines, 33 Va. Tax Rev. 579 (2014) (for a summary of doctrines).

as a positive rule of law*)*. Another reason for confusion is that in addition to fact finding methodologies, the tax specific doctrines sometimes reflect interpretations of law (and in the case of the *economic substance doctrine,* a positive rule of law*)*. The Supreme Court in *Gregory* interpreted the reorganization statute to contain a *business purpose* requirement, but the positive rule of law known as the *economic substance doctrine* purports to impose a business purpose requirement as a precondition to all tax benefits. This suggests another reason for confusion about the tax specific doctrines: a tendency to overstate. For example, Treasury regulations (adopted in 2003) show how easily the tax specific doctrines have come to be assumed: ". . . statute and legislative history, treaties, administrative guidance, and judicial decisions that establish principles of general application in the tax law (e.g., Gregory v. Helvering, 293 U.S. 465 (1935))."[853] *Gregory* established no rule of general application, as demonstrated in Ch. III.C.3.a.(1). A final reason for confusion is a tendency to conflate all three of fact finding and interpretive doctrines and positive rules. For example: "[T]ransactions are to be taken at face value for tax purposes only if they are imbued with a 'business purpose or reflect economic reality' . . ."[854] That brief summary by the most astute current commentators identifies the strains within the tax specific doctrines:

- Judicial and administrative skepticism is triggered by a perception of tax avoidance purposes rather than *business purposes*, despite the facts that the Supreme Court has stated repeatedly that tax avoidance efforts are at worst a neutral factor,[855] and that legal efficacy usually suffices to identify the facts of a business transaction.
- Courts and the Service frequently insist that *economic reality* (sometimes called *economic substance*) match up with tax treatment, despite the fact that core elements of the Code are inherently at odds with economic reality and instead depend on legal efficacy (the key example being the treatment of the corporation as a person and taxpayer separate from its shareholders).
- The Service requires taxpayers to report on the basis of form but routinely attempts to reject the control of form over the tax treatment in deference to substance (*substance over form).*

Because of the divergent natures and roles of the tax specific doctrines, it is necessary to peel them apart with deliberation. The doctrines fit together properly like this:

---

[853] Reg. § 301.6111-2(b)(4)(i).

[854] Bittker & Lokken, at 4.3.1. The Treasury has lumped two other "judicial doctrines" with the two stated in the text, but they are actually fact finding tools as opposed to interpretive doctrines, and are discussed as such in Ch. VI.E. *infra. See Treasury White Paper on Corporate Tax Shelters, supra* note 14, at 127-12. For other Service statements of the judicial doctrines, see Rev. Rul. 2002-69, 2002-2 C.B. 760; Rev. Rul. 2000-12, 2000-1 C.B. 744; Rev. Rul. 1999-14, 1999-1 C.B. 835; Notice 2005-13, 2005-1 C.B. 630.

[855] *See supra* Ch. II.C.2.a.

- *What happened?* The common law and equity courts have always known how to find facts without resort to tax specific doctrines. Because fact finding can be difficult, courts sometimes develop rules of thumb for repeating situations, called here cluster rules to help make fact finding easier in similar cases (for cluster rules see Ch. VI.F.). But courts don't need cluster rules to distinguish the *substance* of a thing from the *form* in which it appears, and to make the substance control the legal result when the law so requires, which it does in most cases where the facts must fit a term of common usage (such as loan, ownership, lease). Courts of equity understand that form is suspect because in most cases some party has caused the facts to take the form used in order to achieve a result favorable to that party.[856]
- One non-tax-specific fact finding method used to identify substance is the *step transaction* method, by which a final step is linked with a beginning step when the integrated sequence of steps is sufficiently certain. In tax cases, that is commonly labeled as the *step transaction doctrine.*
- Another non-tax-specific fact finding method used to identify substance in financial and business transactions (and hence tax cases) is to assess the *economic impact or substance* of transactions that might be different from their forms; this is natural because economics is the standard by which business and financial transactions are measured by the participants. The progenitor of this concept, *Eisner v. Macomber*,[857] applied the concept in the taxpayer's favor to look through a corporate form in a way that would not be done today. For another example, in *Knetsch* the Supreme Court determined that the taxpayer did not borrow money and so could not pay deductible interest, because in *economic substance* the taxpayer did not get the fruits of a loan. The *potential to make a profit* from borrowing money and using the loan proceeds to make an investment may be a fact that bears on whether there was a loan at all, as in *Knetsch*. But tax cases tend to label this approach as the *economic substance doctrine.*
- Another non-tax-specific fact that has a proper role in many tax cases is *business purpose*, not because the Code requires it, but because it is an additional indicator of the substance of events (whether Mr. Smith's corporation in *Higgins v. Smith* had any business activity or purpose other than to buy his stock so he could claim losses, informed the conclusion that it did not exist as a separate entity[858]). But tax cases tend to label this approach as the *business purpose doctrine,* which has the tendency to imply a positive requirement of law in all cases.
- A particularly confusing term used in tax fact finding is the *sham transaction* or entity. It commonly is used to describe a court's discovery that the taxpayer has attempted to use a factual disguise to obscure the nature of

[856] *See infra* Ch. V.E.
[857] Eisner v. Macomber, 252 U.S. 189 (1920); *see supra* Ch. II.B.2.c(3).
[858] *See supra* Ch. III.C.3.a(2).

its transaction. It arose first in connection with, and is most commonly applied to, corporations that do not actually engage in business transactions and transactions with such *sham corporations*. Rather than labels, special clarity is needed in this area because corporations are inherently artificial structures, which the law has chosen to regard as real.[859]

- The Service has promoted such traditional fact finding methods to the status of tax specific doctrines (including the *step transaction doctrine*, the *economic substance doctrine*, the *sham transaction doctrine*, and the *business purpose doctrine*), either with the purpose or effect of making them appear knowable only to the tax intelligentsia, and making them appear other than the common law or equity processes that they reflect.
- *What is the law?* The courts also know how to interpret statutes. The tendency of courts to apply more or less purposive readings of statutes waxes and wanes with the decades, but at bottom the courts remain tethered to the words of statutes. For example, the Supreme Court construed a *business purpose* requirement into the reorganization provisions in *Gregory v. Helvering*, based on the words "in pursuance of a plan of reorganization."[860] No interpretation is needed to find a *business purpose* (or at least profit making purpose) requirement for several other key tax benefits because they are stated in the Code (for examples, the section 162 deduction, the section 165 loss, the section 269 benefit disallowance rules). Beyond these cases of interpretation of specific provisions and stated requirements in the Code, there is no overall requirement of *business purpose*.[861]
- But the Service and the lower federal courts have come to impute a *business purpose* requirement into all tax benefits, without the benefit of statutory or Supreme Court authority.
- More troubling, they have conflated that imputed *business purpose* (or *profit making* purpose) requirement with both normal fact finding methods (*economic substance*) and sometimes tax specific fact finding methods to create an overarching positive rule of law for the Code, the *economic substance doctrine*.[862] And sometimes the ascertainment of *economic substance* goes beyond normal fact finding into the category of eyeballing a

---

[859] *See* Cummings, *The Sham Transaction Doctrine*, 145 TAX NOTES (TA) 1239 (Dec. 15, 2014).

[860] *See supra* Ch. III.C.3.a(1).

[861] *See generally* Rice, *supra* note 377, at 1041-46 (identifying at that time only reorganization cases and corporate entity recognition cases as authority for business purpose requirements, although there were many lower court authorities). *See also* Cummings, *Reorganization Business Purpose*, 136 TAX NOTES (TA) 1069 (Aug. 27, 2012) (showing that even where a regulation requires a business purpose, in practice everyone assumes a purpose to exist in most cases).

[862] *See generally* BITTKER & LOKKEN, at 4.3.4A; Ch. V.F., *infra*.

transaction and concluding that it sort of looks like something else and so must be taxed as something else.[863]

V.C. Critique of the Tax Specific Doctrines

The Service and the courts commonly cite and rely on the tax specific doctrines in general, and the ESD in particular, and so criticizing them is of limited utility, but for two facts: (1) some courts still will emphasize the tax law as written, and (2) the Supreme Court has yet to speak on the flowering of doctrine that has occurred through miscitation of its opinions. These exceptions render useful a thorough understanding of the limits of the doctrines.

V.C.1. *Summary*

The tax specific doctrines occupy a space between the finding of pure or evidentiary facts and the interpretation of the Code.[864] As such they have influenced both the finding of legal facts (lease, contract, loan) and the finding of the law, in practice.[865] To the extent they stray beyond aids in fact finding and state positive rules of law (the business purpose doctrine and the ESD), or are conceived to be peculiar to tax (step transaction doctrine) their principal faults are:

- Fostering in the reader an embarrassment of not understanding the greater truth that the writer (usually a judge) employing a tax specific doctrine must have, when too often the truth is that there is no "impalpable essence which is beyond our mental grasp";[866]
- Failure to observe how the federal tax law has developed over its existence;
- Miscitation of the Supreme Court decisions on which they commonly rely, including most importantly *Gregory v. Helvering*;
- Inconsistency with other Supreme Court authority, such as *Cottage Savings*,[867] and *Clay Brown*;[868]
- Theoretical uncertainty;
- Practical uncertainty, vagueness, confusion, and complexity;
- Unfairness due to the episodic nature of their application;
- The resulting inability to hold the Treasury accountable for rule making; and perhaps most important,

---

[863] *See, e.g.*, Schering-Plough Corp. v. United States, 651 F. Supp. 2d 219 (D. N.J. 2009), aff'd, 652 F.3d 475 (3d Cir. 2011) (sale of receive leg of interest rate swap to related party treated as loan from buyer to seller even though seller paid third party one set of payments that differed materially from payments made to buyer).

[864] *See* INT'L FISCAL ASSOC., FORM AND SUBSTANCE IN TAX LAW, *supra* note 118, at 28-9.

[865] *Id.*

[866] Eisenstein, *Book Review*, 20 TAX L. REV. 215, 228 (1966) (the observation related to the "business purpose doctrine," which has been extrapolated from *Gregory v. Helvering*).

[867] Cottage Savings Assn. v. Commissioner, 499 U.S. 554 (1991).

[868] Commissioner v. Brown, 380 U.S. 563 (1965).

- Withering of the law of fact finding and legal interpretation and construction.

First, the Supreme Court has created only a few broad scale doctrines, though it has created many more cluster rules to address specific situations. In the important *Culbertson*[869] decision, the Supreme Court rejected government efforts to completely ignore the state law creation of a partnership among family members for tax reduction motives, although it left the law unclear.[870] In the equally important *Clifford*[871] decision, the Supreme Court said it did not have to apply the most important of its doctrines—the assignment of income doctrine—where the taxpayer tried to shift his own income away by declaring himself a trustee for family members; instead, the Court simply found as a fact that he continued to own the property.[872] When the Supreme Court faced a classic situation in *McWilliams*,[873] in which it might have said substance controlled form, it instead applied a one-off solution based on statutory construction of the wash sale rule, proving once again that when the Supreme Court decides one case it decides that case and not others.[874]

Second, the doctrines as usually cited in lower court opinions are not supported by the single Supreme Court opinion on which they most commonly rely, *Gregory v. Helvering*, as discussed more fully in Ch. III.C.3.a(1).

Third, the principal tax specific doctrine of the lower courts, the ESD, is inconsistent with an important Supreme Court precedent, *Cottage Savings*,[875] in which the Supreme Court rejected the core theory of the ESD by respecting an exchange to recognize losses, which had no business purpose and lacked

---

[869] Commissioner v. Culbertson, 337 U.S. 733 (1949).

[870] *See* McKee, Nelson & Whitmire, at 3.02[2].

[871] Helvering v. Clifford, 309 U.S. 331 (1940).

[872] *See* Bittker & Lokken, at 80.1.1; *see infra* Ch. VI.F.2.

[873] McWilliams v. Commissioner, 331 U.S. 694 (1947) (discussed *supra* in Ch. III.C.3.b.).

[874] *See* Commissioner v. Bollinger, 485 U.S. 340 (1988) (Scalia refusing to parse a prior Supreme Court opinion as if it were the governing statute); Lowndes, *1936 Term, supra* note 430, at 170 (1937) (observing that when the Supreme Court decides a case it decides a case).

[875] Cottage Savings Assn. v. Commissioner, 499 U.S. 554 (1991). The Federal Home Loan Bank Board adopted a rule allowing savings and loans to swap substantially identical mortgage pools, or participations in such pools, for the purpose of generating tax losses and hence tax savings, but without having to book a loss for financial reporting purposes. The Court agreed with a Treasury regulation stating that a disposition of property occurred only when the property received in exchange was materially different, but the Court rejected the argument that materiality was a matter of economics rather than legal entitlements that differ in kind or extent. *See* Evans, *The Realization Doctrine after Cottage Savings,* 70 Taxes (CCH) 12 (Dec. 1992) ("The Court properly refused to be enticed into analyzing the economics of the transaction. . .").

economic substance, because it actually occurred in legal effect.[876] *Cottage Savings* made clear, as did *Culbertson*, that the taxpayer can have a business purpose in pursuing a transaction that does not change economic reality but does change legal reality, and thus obtain congruence with the Code requirement. Indeed the absence of a business purpose for voluntary loss recognition is probably the reason for the panoply of Code limitations on loss recognition and allowance;[877] but if those rules can be avoided, voluntarily recognized loss is allowed.

Fourth, the doctrines are uncertain, thus violating two of Adam Smith's four maxims of taxation: equal treatment and certainty.[878] This general statement is applicable:

> If a valid statute could be disregarded by a judge whenever he felt that it led to a result which he would not have reached in the absence of the statute, then a statute would cease to be a formal reason for deciding a case in the sense in which we are using the term. It would even cease to be a formal reason for making a decision if the substantive reasons enshrined in the statute were simply treated as additional arguments to be considered along with all the other reasons of substance bearing on the case, with the reasons so enshrined having no primacy over other reasons.[879]

The desirability of certainty in the tax law is a firm starting premise.[880] The reasons include the facts that a complex and large nation must have relatively formal tax rules:

- To provide answers to the questions of the numerous users of the law,
- To facilitate administration of the law by relatively minor officials who cannot be expected to exercise discretion on a regular basis,
- To limit the possibilities of corruption within the government that can be fostered by the ability to exercise too much discretion, and
- To avoid the appearance of preferential treatment of persons to which the formal rules are not applied due to considerations of substance.[881]

Fifth, the doctrines have contributed to new confusions and disputes in the application of the tax laws.[882] Because they elevate the relevance of taxpayer

---

[876] *See Cottage Savings*, 499 U.S. at 568. (Blackmun, J., dissenting); Madison, *supra* note 15, at 701 (observing that the lower courts had relied on substance over form in the case and the Supreme Court sidestepped the issue). Some have complained that by selling a 90% participation in the mortgages the taxpayer did not really dispose of property, but the Tax Court found that a disposition occurred in fact. Cottage Savings Assn. v. Commissioner, 90 T.C. 372 (1988).

[877] *See* Cummings, *Discontinuities in Corporate Recognition of Loss*, *supra* note 822, at 39.

[878] Smith, Wealth of Nations, *supra* note 374, at Book V, Ch. 1, Part 2.

[879] Atiyah & Summers, at 8-9.

[880] *See, e.g.*, Rice, *supra* note 377, at 1023.

[881] Atiyah & Summers, at 74.

[882] *See Treasury White Paper on Corporate Tax Shelters*, *supra* note 14, at 127-12 (acknowledging that the doctrines increase uncertainty and arguing that this "cuts both ways").

intent and purpose, they have encouraged the Service to seek discovery of documentation in the hands of the taxpayers and their advisors showing that the taxpayers were uncertain about the viability of their tax plans and had little if any business purposes. This has led to a huge outburst of litigation over the attorney-client privilege, the accountant-client privilege, the attorney work product doctrine and Federal Rule 26(b)(3).[883]

Indeed, the conflicting formulations of the ESD inevitably caused confusion and disagreement over whether the taxpayer, once tarred with the brush of evil purpose, must show both business purpose and economic reality/substance, or one or the other, until "clarified" by legislation in 2010.[884]

Sixth, the doctrines apply only upon audit, and only when the Service detects a problematic transaction. As a result, *while taxpayers are allowed to plan their transactions with tax reduction purposes, they also are required to follow the written rules and generally are not allowed to ignore the form of their transactions in favor of some substance that taxpayers might ascribe to their transactions.*[885] Therefore, taxpayers have to report their transactions according to their forms, even if planned to save taxes, and such planned results can be denied only if (1) the Service audits, (2) the Service discovers the issue, (3) the agent bases an adjustment on the issue, and (4) the Service is ultimately upheld if the taxpayer disagrees. The results of this process will necessarily be discriminatory (except as ameliorated by "listed transaction" reporting requirements).

Seventh, the Service' use of the doctrines frees the Treasury from the need to issue rules with notice and hearing, as discussed below under Deference to Regulations.

Finally, the doctrines have supplanted more traditional legal principles,[886] thus contributing to a withering of their knowledge among the enforcers and their utility in the courts, discussed in great detail below. This is not a new problem, but since the advent of the ESD has been an accelerating problem.[887]

---

883 *See, e.g.,* United States v. Textron, Inc., 553 F.3d 87 (1st Cir. 2009), *withdrawn for rehearing*, 560 F.3d 513 (1st Cir. 2009).

884 Experienced practitioners have admitted to the author that they could not keep the prior disjunctive vs. conjunctive or two-prong vs. one-prong "tests" of the ESD straight.

885 *See* Blatt, *Lost on a One Way Street: The Taxpayer's Ability to Disavow Form*, 70 OR. L. REV. 381 (1991). For exceptions, see *infra* Ch. VI.E.1.e(4). But a study of cases suggests that the street is not so one-way as commonly thought. Schneider, *Use of Judicial Doctrines in Federal Tax Cases Decided by Trial Courts 1993-2006: A Quantitative Analysis*, 57 CLEV. ST. L. REV. 35 (2009).

886 *See* Yin, *The Problem of Corporate Tax Shelters: Uncertain Dimensions, Unwise Approaches*, 55 TAX L. REV. 405, 420-21 (2002) (arguing that in the "tax shelter" cases discussed, the government should have relied on statutory tools rather than the economic substance doctrine).

887 *See* Cummings, *When Is a "Doctrine" Just the Law? - "Investor Control" of Life Insurance*, 148 TAX NOTES (TA) 1539 (Sept. 28, 2015).

V.C.2. *Lack of Authority*

V.C.2.a. *Congress and Treasury*

Proponents of the tax specific doctrines do not ascribe near enough importance to the absence from both the Code[888] and the Treasury regulations of anything approaching them. The federal income tax is over 100 years old and the Treasury's regulations are close behind in age. We know that problems of interpretation and construction, tax evasion and avoidance based on literal readings of the Code, are of long standing, reaching back before the income tax. If Treasury thought that all transactions require a business purpose, for example, one would expect to see Regulation section 1.1 so stating. There is no such statement. As discussed in Ch. IV. above, there are targeted anti-abuse sections such as section 269, but their very existence augurs against tax specific doctrines, not for them. Robert N. Miller observed these same shortcomings in 1951 in relation to Learned Hand's efforts to create the business purpose doctrine.[889]

Therefore, the absence of guidance from either Congress or Treasury can mean one of two things: (1) they do not support the doctrines, or (2) they are content to allow the courts to perform a role that is peculiar to American courts,[890] of exercising more flexibility in solving statutory problems.[891] The latter may be closer to the truth, but is speculative and provides no logical basis of authority of the doctrines. The enactment of section 7701(o) is consistent with (2).

V.C.2.b. *Supreme Court*

The Supreme Court has not created or applied the ESD, as discussed further below. The Supreme Court has not created a Code preamble that substance always controls form or that business purpose is always required of a transaction to achieve its desired tax result. It is not that the Court cannot "make law,"[892] but rather that it has not done so in these ways; moreover, when the Supreme Court has pushed the boundaries of the statute or identified particular ways to find particular facts (who sold the property—*Cumberland/Court*

---

[888] *Cf.* The Coal Industry Retiree Health Benefits Act of 1992, 26 U.S.C. §§ 9701-9722 (1992), which enacted § 9722, entitled Sham transactions: "If a principal purpose of any transaction is to evade or avoid liability under this chapter [the chapter concerning coal industry pensions], this chapter shall be applied (and such liability shall be imposed) without regard to such transaction."

[889] Miller, *Federal Courts as Makers of Income Tax Law*, *supra* note 524, at 160 (Miller was the founder of Miller & Chevalier).

[890] English courts historically have tended to read statutes in a more formalistic manner. *See* Ch. I.B.3.

[891] Atiyah & Summers, at 29-30, 37, 100-01. *See* Gunn, *supra* note 122, at 28 (reminding the tax bar to avoid wooden interpretations, in contrast with British approach).

[892] *See* Eisenstein, *The* Clifford *Regulations*, *supra* note 598, at 388 ("Judicial legislation may be hateful to many of us, but we should try to get used to the activity until courts are finally abolished.").

Holding Co.—who borrowed the money—*Frank Lyon*) it generally has the wisdom to act interstitially.[893]

Instead, the Court has at times construed requirements such as business purpose into a limited number of ambiguous sections, and has at times applied generally applicable fact finding techniques (including the equitable doctrine that substance should control form, described below, and the linking together of related steps) to determine whether the thing that occurred was the thing the tax statute describes. The lower courts and the Treasury have tended to extrapolate from these standard decisional techniques a generally applicable Code preamble that can override the words of the Code. Even taxpayers have wearied of trying to correct them. The result has been much unnecessary confusion in the enforcement of the tax laws.[894]

There is no general Supreme Court theory on the application of the Code, either in the minds of the justices,[895] or on the pages of the reports. The Supreme Court has not fixed a roving preamble to the Code. Taxpayers and their advisors long have believed this, while having practical sense enough to behave as does Justice Holmes' "bad man" who wants only to know what the courts will do.[896] See, for examples, the discussions of *Gregory* in Ch. III.C.3.a(1); of *Knetsch* in Ch. VI.E.1.e(2)(c); and of *Frank Lyon* in Ch. VI.F.2.c.

---

[893]

> I recognize without hesitation that judges do and must legislate, but they can do so only interstitially; they are confined from molar to molecular motions. A common-law judge could not say I think the doctrine of consideration a bit of historical nonsense and shall not enforce it in my court. No more could a judge exercising the limited jurisdiction of admiralty say I think well of the common-law rules of master and servant and propose to introduce them here en bloc. Certainly he could not in that way enlarge the exclusive jurisdiction of the District Courts and cut down the power of the States.

S. Pac. Co. v. Jensen, 244 U.S. 205, 221 (1916) (Holmes, J., dissenting).

[894] Randolph Paul described essentially the same level of confusion in 1937 in RESTATEMENT OF TAX AVOIDANCE, *supra* note 530, at 73 et seq.

[895] *See* Lowndes, *1935 Term*, *supra* note 430, at 451 (noting that last term the Court decided over 60 tax cases including cert. denials, etc., and stating "The unhappiest expression in the lawyer's vocabulary from the point of view of clear and realistic thinking is the 'Supreme Court.' There are nine justices, but there is no objective reality apart from them, no collective mind which dictates their opinions."); *Id.* at 170-72 ("Oddly enough, when the Supreme Court decides a case it decides a case. It does not fix the pattern of future judicial conduct through the ages. . . . legal doctrines are verbal devices that try to reflect considerations, which vary in importance from justice to justice. This is why there is lack of stability and certainty and it is a better state of affairs than mechanical legalisms.").

[896]

> If you want to know the law and nothing else, you must look at it as a bad man, who cares only for the material consequences which such knowledge enables him to predict, not as a good one, who finds his reasons for conduct, whether inside the law or outside of it, in the vaguer sanctions of conscience.

Holmes, *The Path of the Law*, *supra* note 136, at 993.

V.C.2.c. *The Common Law of Tax?*

The tax specific doctrines frequently are identified as the common law of tax.[897] In one sense, common law is any court-made substantive rule, including a court's construction of a nonstatutory requirement into a statute; evidently that is the sense in which section 7701(o)(5)(A) uses the term. But that is not the original sense of the common law: there is a difference between the slow and incremental process by which the English common law developed certain principles and entire rule schemes (tort law, for example), and how a particular court construed a statute last week (which some call tax common law).

Undoubtedly federal courts can create common law in the sense of judge made law in the area of federal tax, because federal tax is an area within their direct and exclusive jurisdiction. For example, on the same day *Erie v. Tompkins* was decided Justice Brandeis said: [interstate water rights are a] "question of federal common law."[898] Thus, the federal courts retain the power to create federal common law in areas particularly affecting federal interests.[899] However there is an issue of the degree of law creation: at what point does normal judicial discretion preempt Congress? The tension between exercising discretion and preempting Congress was reflected in Justice Brandeis' opinion in *Erie v. Tompkins*, which rejected the role of the federal courts in creating a federal common law in diversity cases.[900] As the Supreme Court later stated: ". . . in [*Erie v. Tompkins*] . . . we denied the existence of any federal 'general' common law . . . which largely withdrew to havens of specialty, some of them defined by express congressional authorization to devise a body of law directly (listing four examples, none of which was tax). . . ."[901] However, Justice Brandeis' reasoning in *Erie* is also applicable to the preemption of Congress that occurs when lower federal courts create an economic substance doctrine: it is improper for a court to extend itself to become the prime branch of government.[902]

Commentators began referring to the common law of tax at least as early as 1949, mostly in reference to the Supreme Court's development of doctrines

---

[897] *See generally* Cummings, *Nationwide Uniformity and the Common Law of Federal Taxation*, 66 Tax Law. 1 (Fall 2012).

[898] Hinderlider v. La Plata River Co., 304 U.S. 92, 110 (1938).

[899] *See* Chemerinsky, Federal Jurisdiction 365-66 (Aspen Publishers 5th ed. 2007).

[900] Erie R.R. Co. v. Tompkins, 304 U.S. 64 (1938).

[901] Sosa v. Alvarez-Machain, 542 U.S. 692 (2004). *See generally* Field, *Sources of Law: The Scope of Federal Common Law*, 99 Harv. L. Rev. 881 (1985).

[902] Urofsky, Louis D. Brandeis—A Life 746 (2009). Federal common law is a popular topic for law professors, who generally are clear eyed enough to see that it exists, despite protests that it should not from other quarters. *See, e.g.*, Nelson, *The Legitimacy of (Some) Federal Common Law*, 101 Va. L. Rev. 8 (2015) (not discussing any tax common law).

such as the assignment of income doctrine.[903] But it has been an uncertain type of law; an Assistant Chief Counsel stated in 1954 that there was no "generally recognized, well defined law of income taxation," due to a failure to recognize the differences and different roles played by general law rules and tax specific rules.[904] However, more recently the term "common law" has become entwined with the tax specific doctrines in a way that might seem to validate them through association; it does not.[905] The difference between the earlier use of the common law concept in tax and the current one is illustrated surprisingly well by a 2008 change in the Internal Revenue Manual. The I.R.M. now states that the common law of tax refers to law created by courts,[906] suggested above to be a spurious definition. However, from 1998-2008 the I.R.M. contained a quite different definition:

> Common law comprises the body of principles and rules of action relating to government and security of persons and property which derive their authority solely from usage and custom or from judgments and decrees of courts recognizing, affirming, and enforcing such usage and custom.[907]

The earlier version correctly emphasized the primary authenticating role of usage and custom, as contrasted with the ability of a court to announce a common law rule.

The term common law appears generally and in relation to tax in the following ways:

- It properly refers to that body of law providing remedies both civil and criminal that was created by judges, without benefit of statute, in the English courts.[908] Although such remedies do not encompass taxation, many of the nonstatutory definitions developed by the common law are

---

[903] Brown, *The Growing "Common Law" of Taxation*, 34 S. CAL. L. REV. 235 (1961) (describing the assignment of income doctrine as the prime example of the common law of tax); Wales, *supra* note 278, at 75, 80 (stating that the gross income cases illustrate the common law of taxation, and that the Supreme Court best has provided the philosophy of the definition of income and has related the substance of transactions to the purpose of the law; beyond that it should not have to decide minute points); Ericksen, *supra* note 339, at 178.

[904] *See* Reiling, *supra* note 26, at 546.

[905] The Treasury views the economic substance doctrine as common law. *Treasury White Paper on Corporate Tax Shelters*, *supra* note 14, at Appendix C. The 2007-2010 proposals to codify the economic substance doctrine referred to it and other doctrines as common law, as does section 7701(o). *See infra* Ch. V.F. Also lower courts have referred to classic anti-abuse doctrines of substance over form, sham transaction, step transaction and the business purpose rule are sometimes called the common law. *See, e.g.*, Fink v. Commissioner, 789 F.2d 427, 432 (6th Cir. 1986), *rev'd*, 483 U.S. 89 (1987).

[906] I.R.M. 9.1.3.2.2. ("The common law is the body of law that develops and derives through judicial decisions, rather than from legislative enactments."). Also the struggle of the courts to deal with a single problematic Code provisions can be referred to as a type of common law of interpretation.). See for example the courts' responses to difficulties in the application of §357(c)(3), described in S. REP. No. 1263, 95th Cong. (1978).

[907] I.R.M. 9.1.3.2.2 (1998).

[908] *See generally* HOLMES, THE COMMON LAW (Howe ed. 1963).

used in applying tax laws (for examples, partnership, master and servant, employees,[909] gifts, charity).[910]

- The Court sometimes takes a shortcut to state the terms of a common law rule by citing the Restatements.[911] This provides a sort of nationwide uniformity, but not a uniformity attributable to creating a unique federal rule.[912]
- It is properly extended to those statutes that codified the common law,[913] with the best examples being the criminal law, the Commercial Codes, and more analogous to the tax law, the Sherman Antitrust Act.[914] Because these statutes could not totally encompass the common law they codified, the courts found it necessary to construe the statutes to contain common law modifications. For example, the Supreme Court construed "unreasonable" into the Sherman Act,[915] because Congress "expected the courts to give shape to the [Sherman Act's] broad mandate by drawing on common-law tradition."[916] Another classic example is *Riggs v. Palmer*, holding that a murderer could not inherit from the victim, despite his legal rights.[917]
- The term might be used to refer to the application of equitable principles to determine facts (such as the ownership of property) or a fact finding method having roots in the common law and equity (such as the equity of redemption of a mortgagor) in applying a statute that does not codify the common law (such as a taxing statute) as discussed in Ch. V.E. below.
- By analogy the common law label is used to describe a limited number of other judge made rules that interpret statutes that were not based on

---

[909] *See* Rev. Proc. 2009-3, 2009-1 I.R.B. 107, sec. 3.02(7) (referring to common law employer-employee relationship).

[910] Bob Jones Univ. v. United States, 461 U.S. 574 (1983).

[911] Commissioner v. Banks, 543 U.S. 426 (2005).

[912] *See* Kolstad v. ADA, 527 U.S. 526 (1999); Burlington Indus. v. Ellerth, 524 U.S. 742 (1998).

[913] *Cf.* Badaracco v. Commissioner, 464 U.S. 386 (1984) (referring to the "common law" background of the extended statute of limitations in tax audits where the taxpayer had engaged in fraudulent concealment).

[914] The Supreme Court referred to the Sherman Act as a common law statute. Leegin Creative Leather Prod., Inc. v. PSKS, Inc., 551 U.S. 877, 899 (2007); *see also* Nat'l Soc. of Prof'l Engineers v. U.S., 435 U.S. 679, 687 (1978) (stating that the Sherman Act "cannot mean what it says. . . ").

[915] *See* The Standard Oil Co. v. United States, 221 U.S. 1 (1911). The Court reasoned that the English common law enforced a similar rule where the restraint was unreasonable, thus implying a wrongful purpose; that some courts in this country had followed that view; that Congress wrote the Sherman Act in light of the context of the times and those judicial interpretations; that Congress must have contemplated the exercise of judicial discretion and restrain in enforcing the Act, because it used such broad terms (every contract), which would have been imprudent given the impossibility of forseeing the new forms contracts and monopoly attempts might take; therefore, Congress contemplated and intended the standard of reason.

[916] State Oil Co. v. Kahn, 522 U.S. 3 (1997).

[917] Riggs v. Palmer, 115 N.Y. 506 (1889).

the common law, in ways that are not based on the common law but on the inherent characteristics of the law at issue. In the case of an income tax system, the best examples are the assignment of income doctrine and the doctrine of constructive receipt, which have been clearly established by the Supreme Court.[918] These doctrines mostly conflict with the actual common law.[919] They share with the foregoing uses of common law the possibility of inferring legislative intent.[920]

- Similarly tax common law can result from the principle that state law characterizations do not necessarily control federal tax outcome because there are 50 states and to turn over all tax results to state law control would seriously undercut the uniformity of taxation that is desired in the U.S.[921] IRS arguments for nationwide uniformity, free of dependence on state laws, are usually based on *Clearfield Trust.*[922] However, that decision opted for a national rule only because the alternative was a state rule that the United States could never satisfy. In fact, the Court generally supports default to state law and rejects calls for nationwide uniform tax procedures where the Code intends to rely on state law.[923]
- A discrete use of the term occurred when the Supreme Court referred to the common law "revenue rule" holding that the United States will not enforce the revenue laws of another nation.[924]

The defining characteristics of the common law tradition were described by Cardozo:

> The very strength of our common law, its cautious advance and retreat a few steps at a time is turned into a weakness unless bearings are taken at

[918] *See infra* Ch. VI.F.2.d.; Bittker & Lokken, at 75.2, 75.9. A less global but fairly well known usage of the term "common law" to refer to a substantive income tax law rule outside the anti-abuse area is the former stock-for-debt exception to discharge of indebtedness income, which was finally ended by the 1993 adoption of Section 108(e)(8). *See, e.g.,* Silverman & Keyes, *Restructuring Corporate Debt,* 19 J. Corp. Tax 2 (1992). This usage actually referred to statutory construction in Capento Sec. v. Commissioner, 47 B.T.A. 691 (1942), *aff'd,* 140 F.2d 382 (1st Cir. 1944).

[919] *See* Buck, *supra* note 167, at 111 n. 15, 125 (treatment of trust income and other assignment of income cases disregard common law ownership); *Id.* at 268 (partnerships were creations of the common law but tax law does not follow common law principles).

[920] *See* Wales, *supra* note 278, at 75 (stating that the gross income cases illustrate the common law of taxation, and that the court best has provided the philosophy of the definition of income and has related the substance of transactions to the purpose of the law; beyond that it should not have to decide minute points).

[921] *See* Reiling, *supra* note 26, at 564-65. *See infra* Ch. VI.E.2 as to "tax facts."

[922] Clearfield Trust Co. v. United States, 318 U.S. 363 (1943).

[923] *See* Cummings, *Nationwide Uniformity and the Common Law of Federal Taxation*, 66 Tax Law. 1 (Fall 2012). *E.g.*, Billings v. United States, 232 U.S. 261 (1914) (taxes and refunds bear interest under federal equitable principles even though that is generally not the common law in states).

[924] Pasquantino v. United States, 544 U.S. 349 (2005). This opinion seems to view a common law rule as any "well established" judicial doctrine. For the revenue rule, see Bittker & Lokken, at 65.4.7.

> frequent intervals, so that we may know the relation of the step to the movement as a whole. . . . We shall be caught in the tentacles of the web, unless some superintending mind imparts the secret of the structure, lifting us to a height where the unity of the circle will be visible as it lies below. The perplexity of the judge becomes the scholar's opportunity.[925]

In contrast to the common law method of accreting separate solutions to discrete problems, the ESD, for example, applies one solution to multiple dissimilar problems, and frequently is applied where a targeted statute could have been applied.[926] For another difference, the tax specific doctrines result from the active pursuit of one view by the same party in multiple cases: the Chief Counsel or the Justice Department.

The common law of tax is more properly viewed as tax specific applications of statutory interpretation and construction in cluster areas. This view may seem contrary to distinguished commentators' description of the concept of "federal common law" that refers to "federal rules of decision whose content cannot be traced by traditional methods of interpretation to federal statutory or constitutional commands . . . ,"[927] but is not when one identifies proper subcategories of tax common law: those applying equitable fact finding principles and rules based on the inherent nature of an income tax and statutory interpretation.

The United States Code, of which the Internal Revenue Code is a small part, does not contain anything like the tax specific doctrines, and refers only

---

925 CARDOZO, *supra* note 398, at 6; *see also* DERSHOWITZ, THE GENESIS OF JUSTICE 212 (Warner Books 2000).

926 Judge Henry Friendly stated in reversing the Tax Court in Rubin v. Commissioner, 429 F.2d 650 (2d Cir. 1970):

> Confronted with this welter of doctrines and statutory provisions, the Tax Court fell back on what Professor Brown has called *The Growing "Common Law" of Taxation*, 34 So. Cal. L. Rev. 235 (1961), and the general provisions of § 61 of the Internal Revenue Code. Specifically it relied on Lucas v. Earl, *supra*, 281 U.S. 111, for the rule that 'income is taxed to the true earner thereof,' . . . .We believe the Tax Court erred in its approach to the problem. Resort to 'common law' doctrines of taxation and the broad sweep of § 61 may occasionally be useful in connection with 'transactions heavily freighted with tax motives' which cannot be satisfactorily handled in other ways, . . . , but they have no place where, as here, there is a statutory provision adequate to deal with the problem presented. Section 482 of the Code allows the Commissioner to 'distribute, apportion, or allocate gross income, deductions, credits or allowances' between or among 'two or more organizations, trades or businesses . . . owned or controlled directly or indirectly by the same interests' if he determines that such action is 'necessary in order to prevent evasion of taxes or clearly to reflect the income of any of such organizations, trades, or businesses.'

On remand the Tax Court applied section 482 in a reviewed decision, without dissent. 56 T.C. 1155, *aff'd per curiam*, 460 F.2d 1216 (2d Cir. 1972).

927 FALLON ET AL., HART AND WESCHLER'S, THE FEDERAL COURTS AND THE FEDERAL SYSTEM, 756-57 (4th ed. 1996); *see* Wallis v. Pan Am. Petroleum Corp., 384 U.S. 63, 68 (1966) (declining to establish federal common law in place of state common law, but when there is such, it begins with the federal statute).

sparsely to common law and then in its traditional meaning. The Internal Revenue Code refers to the common law only in three places that are not instructive,[928] plus the spurious usage in section 7701(o) enacted in 2010. "Common law doctrines" appears in the Treasury Regulations under two Code sections, dating only from 1995 and 1996.[929] Treasury appears to have referred to common law only in connection with the cited regulations,[930] or relatively recently in connection with anti-abuse provisions.[931] However, many regulations related to employment refer to common law employees, and a few to other common law concepts such as trusts, partnerships, agents, gifts; and a few of those appropriately distinguish common law concepts from tax concepts, where a difference exists.[932]

In sum, the tax specific doctrines in general and the ESD in particular share nothing with the process of the evolution of the common law, except for judicial origin. They did not create causes of action where none existed. They did not develop over long period of time. They were not synthesized from numerous finding. They were not deduced, rather they were induced, and in the case of the economic substance doctrine were induced from faulty premises and faulty readings of Supreme Court cases. The Supreme Court has not referred to a tax common law.[933]

V.C.3. *Perceived Advantage of the Tax Specific Doctrines: Uncertainty*

Ch. V.C.1. above stated the case for certainty in a tax law, but that case long has been opposed by an almost equally authoritative case for uncertainty, which now embraces the tax specific doctrines. Champions of the tax specific doctrines brush aside the charge of uncertainty by viewing them as a second best solution (instead of greater specificity) to a major problem of intentional tax reduction.[934] Such views often are based on (1) a general dislike of intentional tax reduction, and (2) a bland assumption that the doctrines have rock

---

[928] I.R.C. §§ 62, 3121, 7525.

[929] Reg. § 1.168(i)-2(f); Reg. § 1.1502-13(h)(2) (Intercompany transaction anti-abuse rules refer to "common law doctrines or other authorities that might apply to recast a transaction or to otherwise affect the tax treatment of a transaction. Thus, in addition to adjustments under this paragraph (h), the Commissioner can, for example, apply the rules of section 269 or Regulation section 1.701-2 to disallow a deduction or to recast a transaction."); Reg. § 1.168(h)-1(d) (". . . common law or other doctrines that may apply to recharacterize or alter the effects of the transactions. . . .").

[930] T.D. 8667, 1996-1 C.B. 22 (issuing regulations under section 168).

[931] T.D. 8590, 1995-1 C.B. 15 (adopting regulations under § 246); Prop. Reg. § 409A, 70 Fed. Reg. 57,984 (2005) (regulations under section 409A, general reference to common law tax doctrines).

[932] See, for example, Reg §25.2512-8, which states that common law gifts are included in but do not define taxable gifts.

[933] It has referred to a common law jurisdiction to tax. *See* Japan Lines Ltd. v. County of Los Angeles, 441 U.S. 434 (1979).

[934] *See, e.g.,* Gergen, *The Common Knowledge of Tax Abuse*, 54 SMU L. Rev. 131 (2001).

solid authority, which (3) fails to discern the many streams flowing together in the tax specific doctrines.[935]

Not only is some level of uncertainty inevitable in any law, but it also is desirable in any law. Uncertainty goes hand in hand with flexibility, and flexibility in the interpretation of the law is essential to its being able to accommodate to reality.[936] Indeed the law itself grows through uncertainty.[937] The doctrines are a type of flexibility that has been stimulated in part by the ever increasing apparent certainty, or at least length and detail, of the Code.[938]

But the ESD in particular cannot logically claim the high ground of providing flexibility of interpretation to the extent it states a positive rule of law that applies episodically, without benefit of Congress or even the Treasury saying when. The doctrines generally function to undo the Code certainty in a one way direction, against the taxpayer who has relied on an apparently certain Code rules.[939] Therefore, their principal function is not flexibility but uncertainty itself; presumably the government believes it benefits from the *in terrorem* effects of uncertainty.[940] Nevertheless, the inherent characteristic of such doctrines that depend on a nonliteral interpretation of the Code, as Randolph Paul observed, is that you never know when they will apply, which ultimately can create more problems than they solve.[941] Therefore the upshot of the combination of a relatively detailed statute[942] with relatively vague doctrines is a heads-I-win-tails-you-lose situation for the government.

Taxpayers probably are less prejudiced than they may claim to be by the resulting uncertainty because taxpayers enjoy (1) the ability to fashion their transactions (and if necessary, to evince the proper motives) to minimize tax

---

[935] *Id.* at 133 ("these standards are well established," conflating *Gregory* and the section 701 regulations).

[936] Paul, Prosperity, at 395. Paul observed that the federal courts handle a large number of tax cases, both in absolute and relative numbers; that the administration has mostly abdicated interpretation of the laws to the courts; that the courts are seen as too hard on tax avoidance, by "judicial legislation." Paul rejected the complaints because modern times require flexibility in the law, particularly when the object of the flexibility is to thwart tax avoidance. His objection was that the courts should not be doing this in most case; the Treasury should do it. "The choice is between the present unsatisfactory method of litigation and more administrative finality." *Id.* at 398.

[937] *See* Paul, Studies III, at 210 ("Uncertainty is not weakness; it helps to make the tax law strong and useful.").

[938] *See* Clark, *The Morphogenesis of Subchapter C, supra* note 520, at 92 (making such argument specifically in regard to the corporate income tax).

[939] *See* McMahon, *Beyond a GAAR, supra* note 19, at 1736 (listing advantages of tax uncertainty).

[940] *Cf.* Surrey, *Supreme Court and the Federal Income Tax, supra* note 285, at 810 (observing that the *in terrorem* effects of the Supreme Court decisions of 1935-1940 were not insignificant).

[941] *See* Paul, Studies I, at 265 ("The trouble with dependence on free or liberal statutory interpretation of a taxing statute, is that no one can be sure when it will be employed.").

[942] *See, e.g.,* Gregory v. Commissioner, 27 B.T.A. 223, 225 (1932) ("A statute so meticulously drafted must be interpreted as a literal expression of the taxing policy, and leaves only the small interstices for judicial consideration.").

liability,[943] and (2) the ability to argue that the law means what it literally says. However, this is true only of taxpayers who are well informed and able to control their tax environment. The great mass of taxpayers is disadvantaged by the woodenness of the standard application of the tax laws. These taxpayers would benefit from less ability to control tax outcomes by choice of form and more substantive construction of rules in their favor by the granting of equitable relief to taxpayers (for example a failure to file on time might be waivable if the taxpayer made its best effort to file on time),[944] which is just the opposite of the current regime.

In practice the most important, if unspoken and illogical, reason for the doctrines' uncertainty is that the "bad person" who tries to evade tax has no right to claim being upset and the "good person" will not fall into a trap for the unwary. This is a peculiar ground for a governmental policy. It assumes the result by assuming who is a "bad person."

> [T]he resulting uncertainty of facts and law creates pitfalls for the unwary, is probably unavoidable and even beneficial to some extent, but the time may come when the harm done is greater than the good and then the policy of vagueness will cause the government to "do then the harm that good men do."[945]

Or put another way:

> . . . although uncertainty to a degree is unavoidable, it scarcely follows that the greater the uncertainty the better the tax system. Tax principles are created for intelligent application in the concrete world of affairs; and a type of administration which leaves a principle hanging in mid air, with the courts pulling it down at odd moments, is a sorry contribution to such application. The case for continued uncertainty is frequently pitched on the thought that precise delineations of principle simply advise the chronic avoider how to escape tax, and that uncertainty is a necessity if not a virtue. This argument is a ghost which should be laid once and for all.[946]

V.D. Practical Origins of the Tax Specific Doctrines

V.D.1. *Inherent Strains in the Tax Law*

Inherent features of the Code and of its application over time have helped to bring its interpretation to the current state of confusion, including the various tax specific doctrines. These include the following:

- The drafters of the 1954 Code, mostly in the Senate, were said to have left sufficient flexibility in the law to require substantial applications

[943] Paul, Studies II, at 293, 300-04.

[944] Atiyah & Summers, at 73-4.

[945] Paul, Studies I, at 156-57; Paul, Studies III, at 211-12 ("There is such a thing as firing a shot gun into a crowd, and at some point the harm of uncertainty becomes greater than the good of tax avoidance prevention.").

[946] Eisenstein, *Some Iconoclastic Reflections*, *supra* note 598, at 497-503.

of judicial judgment, and thereby preclude literalism in the tax law, at least so long as raising revenue remained very important (which means forever).[947] For example, the Senate rejected a House proposal for more detailed rules for spinoffs because it valued the flexibility of a vaguer statute.[948]

- The Code implicitly assumes that it will function as a tax template to which events must be matched as they arise in their "natural state" without regard to tax; this assumption inevitably misses its mark;[949] events are commonly fashioned to fit the most favorable Code results, and the Code generally ignores that fashioning.[950]
- The Code sometimes overtly provides choices by selection of form, most importantly respecting the form of the corporation.
- In a few, but important, cases the Code specifically addresses and attempts to penalize transaction planning.[951]
- Such conflicting signals are not unique in the federal statutory law, but rather show that statutes inevitably encompass cases never thought of by Congress, and miss cases Congress may wish it had thought of,[952] which results normally are allowed to stand.
- But the lower federal courts, mostly responding to the assertions of the Service, have not allowed all such results to stand, with little discernable consistency.

V.D.2. *Predilections of Courts and Administrator*

Just as "bad money drives out good,"[953] easy law drives out hard law. The Chief Counsel, and the Justice Department when litigating for the Service, have asked courts to apply various tax specific doctrines, most importantly the ESD, in pursuing taxpayers perceived to be law breakers. The lower federal courts generally have cooperated, and even encouraged the process,[954] for reasons perhaps including:

---

[947] Bittker, *Tax Policy Aspects of the Code*, 1954 ANN. SURV. AM. L., 151, 158 (1954).

[948] S. REP. No. 1622 at 41-2 (1954) (". . . such certainty is not to be achieved at the expense of the legislative flexibility necessary to provide a statutory pattern which will tax, in an equitable manner, the myriad business transactions with which this area of law is concerned. [Therefore we reject rules that] . . . would make it difficult for necessary business transactions to be carried out with a minimum of interference from the tax laws.").

[949] *See supra* Ch. II.C.1.

[950] This is true if for no other reason than that the Code depends on voluntary enforcement by taxpayers who do not have the right to disregard their own forms. *See infra* Ch. VI.E.1.e.4.

[951] *See, e.g.*, I.R.C. §§ 357(b), 269, 482.

[952] *See* Woolford Realty Co. v. Rose, 286 U.S. 319 (1932) (". . . in a system of taxation so intricate and vast as ours there are many other loopholes unsuspected by the framers of the statute, many other devices whereby burdens can be lowered.").

[953] Gresham's Law, named after Sir Thomas Gresham (1519-1579). *See* BLACK'S LAW DICTIONARY 722 (8th ed. 2004).

[954] *See* Schneider, *supra* note 885, at 35 (showing that from 1993-2006 the courts were more likely to raise the doctrines than the government).

- A collective memory loss of the tools of the general law and a feeling of speciality leading to the view that the tax law must develop its own unique rules to deal with issues of statutory construction and fact finding;[955]
- The relative ease of analysis provided by the ESD;
- The assumption that the Service knows what the tax law is;
- The fact that the courts operate in the broad American traditions of common law rule making and purposive construction of statutes, whereby the Congress legislates with the knowledge of that common law tradition and view of statutory construction;[956]
- The possible systemic reason that the tax law is just too hard to apply as written;
- The implicit appeal of the doctrines to institutional needs of the lower federal courts by charging them with substantial discretion and relieving them of figuring out what the Code actually means;
- The explicit appeal to the revenue needs of the government; and
- The relieving of Congress of writing greater specificity into the statute and relieving of the Service and Treasury of having to involve Congress in these issues.[957]

The resulting symbiotic relationship between the Service' desire for the doctrines and the lower courts' cooperation have contributed to a systemic failure to supply rules in the Code itself or in Treasury regulations and traditional fact finding that could reach the same results. The ESD in particular has tended to swallow the more standard processes for the application of the Code, as discussed in Ch. V.F.

Robert N. Miller observed this tendency of the courts to remake tax law in another context in a 1951 article, where he stated:

> When one of these divergencies [of a Code rule from tax theory] is noticed by a judge who is not in touch with the vital governmental problems of maintaining a great flow of revenue and who feels that, on the facts of the case at bar, the text of the law operates illogically or otherwise produces too small a tax, he not infrequently refuses to believe that Congress could have intended the law to apply as it was enacted, and he proceeds to create a new rule, on the ground that it must have been intended by Congress in the first place.[958]

---

[955] *See* Paul, Studies I, at 66 (decrying the failure to observe anti-avoidance tools used in other areas of the law).

[956] *See supra* Ch. I.B.

[957] *See* Surrey, *Complexity and the Internal Revenue Code: The Problem of the Management of Tax Detail*, 34 Law & Contemp. Probs. 673 (1969).

[958] Miller, *Federal Courts as Makers of Income Tax Law*, *supra* note 524, at 151.

V.D.3. *Tax Shelters*

What came to be called "tax shelters" have always been the motivator of tax specific doctrines in the courts.[959] Randolph Paul concluded in 1937 that the outpouring of case law and judicial legislation on tax avoidance derived directly from the impact of the Depression on both taxpayers and the government.[960] Tax shelters next appeared most forcefully in the 1960's through 1980's, know as "retail" shelters in that they were devices to generate deductions for many individuals, for example accelerated losses from various pseudo businesses and investments, including the most mundane real estate investments,[961] enjoying accelerated depreciation and investment tax credits (first enacted in 1962). The Congress further encouraged the process in 1981 by making the treatment of many investments better than expensing,[962] and then reversed course and addressed these deduction generators successfully by broadly applicable objective rules (for example the passive activity loss rules of section 469), which were said to attack the symptoms rather than the cause.[963]

But the repeal of the *General Utilities* doctrine and other corporate base broadening by the 1986 Tax Reform Act subjected corporations to new pressures to avoid the previously avoidable tax on built in gain.[964] When added to the economic pressures of the 1990's, these conditions spawned a new wave of corporate tax shelters of greater sophistication, which relied on literal interpretations of the Code.[965] Similarly individuals cashing out of capital investments in the boom years at the end of the 1990's were ready targets for acconunting firms' plans for loss generators. In response, the Service relied more on the doctrines.

The difficulties of attacking tax shelters with judicial doctrines was described by Professor Rice in 1953, and the analysis is still accurate:

> There is no problem today more fundamental in federal tax law than the rationale (or lack of it) that underlies the conduct of the courts in striking

---

[959] The term was first used in connection with relatively benign tax planning: tax exempt bonds. *Testimony of Robert H. Jackson on Roosevelt's 1935 tax proposals*, N.Y. TIMES (Aug. 7, 1935); 28 BULL. NAT'L TAX ASS'N 140 (1942-1943). It appeared in a headnote, but not in the opinion in a 1949 family partnership case. Snyder v. Smith, 50-1 U.S. Tax Cas. (CCH) P9138.

[960] PAUL, STUDIES I, at Preface.

[961] *See* GRAETZ, THE DECLINE [AND FALL?] OF THE INCOME TAX, Ch. 3 *et seq.* (Norton 1997); STEUERLE, THE TAX DECADE 50 (Urban Instit. Press 1991).

[962] Cunningham and Schenk, *Taxing the House that Jack Built,* 43 TAX L. REV. 447, 463 at n. 61 (1988). Expensing of investment means first year write off for tax purposes, which means that the taxpayer will not be taxed on any income in that year to the extent of the cost of a new investment (absent passive loss rules, etc.); the 1981 regime allowed accelerated depreciation plus tax credits, which in combination produced even greater tax savings than expensing alone.

[963] *Treasury White Paper on Corporate Tax Shelters*, *supra* note 14, at sec. VI.

[964] *Id.* at sec. III.A.1.

[965] *See* Cunningham & Repetti, *supra* note 17, at 2, 62; Dean & Solan, *supra* note 220, at 879.

down tax avoidance devices and refusing to recognize business arrangements which meet statutory requirements for tax saving but exude an odor piscatorial.[966]

V.D.4. *Creation of Policy Through Litigation*

By encouraging the courts to apply the doctrines, particularly the ESD, the Service has violates its own policies against making policy through litigation. The Internal Revenue Manual states:

> The proper method for conveying the positions of the Office and the policies of the Service is through published guidance. In contrast, litigation should be used as an enforcement tool to advance and defend established positions, not as a vehicle for making policy.[967]

This policy may be peculiar to the Internal Revenue Service among federal agencies (no similar Justice Dept. doctrine seems to exist), but failure to observe such a policy has been recognized as a problem at other agencies.[968] Moreover, such tax luminaries and litigators as Randolph Paul, Erwin Griswold, Louis Eisenstein, and Robert H. Jackson all thought tax was too much litigated.[969] Stanley Surrey decried the creation of "law" in court decisions of the 1940s.[970] Robert N. Miller noted the corrosive effect of compliant courts on tax officials who would put off seeking a law change in hopes that a case with sympathetic facts would find a sympathetic judge; in addition, the new "law" will always be retroactive, without any thought to the wisdom or propriety of general retroactivity.[971]

Martin D. Ginsburg in 1984 stated his famous maxim about the Commissioner's club turning into a large green snake to bite the Commissioner on the hind parts, with the club being wielded primarily in the multifarious venues of tax litigation.[972] Of course the same problem of turning a rule against the Commissioner in unanticipated ways can occur with a ruling or regulation, but not nearly as easily, for two reasons. First, the Treasury and the Service devote a huge amount of attention to regulations, and revenue rulings, at the highest level, for the very reason of trying to anticipate the unan-

---

[966] *See* Rice, *supra* note 377, at 1021.

[967] I.R.M. 31.1.1.1.3.1.

[968] *See* Karmel, *Creating Law at the Securities and Exchange Commission,* 61 LAW & CONTEMP. PROBS. 33 (1998) (agreeing that the SEC can create law and policy through its enforcement actions and questioning the wisdom of that approach).

[969] PAUL, PROSPERITY, at 397-98 (speaking for himself and Griswold); Jackson, *Equity in the Administration of Federal Taxes, supra* note 166, at 641; Eisenstein, *Some Iconoclastic Reflections, supra* note 598, at 487-89.

[970] Surrey, *Supreme Court and the Federal Income Tax, supra* note 285, at 810 ("The crucial question is whether it is sound tax administration to rely upon judicial ingenuity to protect the revenues in accord with underlying principles until the legislative ingenuity has an opportunity to function.").

[971] Miller, *Federal Courts as Makers of Income Tax Law, supra* note 524, at 162, 164.

[972] Ginsburg, *Making Tax Law Through the Judicial Process,* 70 A.B.A. J. 74, 76 (1984).

ticipated; indeed sometimes they are nearly paralyzed by such efforts. Second, it is far easier for the Treasury or the Service to revoke or amend published guidance than it is to ignore an adverse court opinion, even a mere Tax Court memorandum opinion that is supposed to have no precedential authority.[973]

Alternatively, the Treasury and the Service could (1) issue published guidance on the specific matter in one of many forms available to them, (2) seek amendments to the Code, or (3) adopt regulations embodying the doctrines, as was finally done in the partnership area in Regulation section 1.701-2. Indeed, Paul remarked upon the lack of any such policy guidance in the Code in 1938,[974] and the situation has not improved.

The huge volume of published guidance outstanding on the Code belies the great care and difficulty exercised in its issuance. Part of that comes from knowledge of the many interrelationships in the tax law and the desire to maintain maximum consistency. Part of it comes from fear of whipsaw or unintended consequences in taxpayers' favor. The Treasury and the Service are even more fearful of judicial interpretation of the Code.[975] That is probably another reason why they would prefer to have a court adopt a doctrine as a reason to rule for the Service than to construe the statute. For further discussion of the Service's efforts to make law through litigation, see Ch. VII.A.

V.E. Legal Roots of the Tax Specific Doctrines

The tax specific doctrines (principally substance over form, business purpose, step transaction doctrine, economic substance and economic substance doctrine) sprang from deep common law and equity roots of (1) fact finding, and (2) statutory interpretation, each of which sought out remedies for wrongs to individuals based on the realities rather than the forms of events. And yet, the tax law has never acknowledged the debt to these two sources or the curious way in which concepts designed to aid individuals came to aid the government. On the fact side they reflect equitable methods of fact finding to ensure that substance and not form guides the courts in common law disputes. On the law side they reflect the loss of any presumption favoring taxpayers as discussed in Ch. II.B. above, and the treatment of tax statutes as if they were remedying the needs of the government, as discussed below.

The following discussion will show how traditional fact finding methods and liberal interpretational methods, both originating in efforts to aid individuals obtain needed remedies, have been transposed into anti-avoidance tools to the benefit of government.

---

[973] Kafka & Cavanaugh, *supra* note 752, at 2.06[3]. An example of a memorandum opinion that has generated a huge number of tax shelters and finally had to be disclaimed by the Treasury in Reg. § 1.752-1 is *Helmer v. Commissioner*, 1975 T.C.M. (RIA) 1975-160.

[974] Paul, Studies II, at Preface v-vi.

[975] Hence certiorari was not sought in *Rite Aid Corp. v. U.S.*, 255 F.3d 1357 (Fed. Cir. 2001).

V.E.1. *The Curious Role of Equity in Fact Finding and in the Tax Law*

V.E.1.a. *Summary*

Equity principles bear a startling, but largely unacknowledged,[976] resemblance to the doctrines that reflect fact finding, principally in the core principle that the equity courts provide remedies based on the substance of events not their forms. This resemblance is curious for at least two reasons: (1) equity was created to provide remedies that the law courts would not provide to the people,[977] in the nature of the King's grace; in contrast the doctrines, particularly the ESD, now are used to provide revenues to the King; and (2) the tax law does not afford equity to taxpayers, both because it normally prevents them from rejecting the forms they choose for their transactions,[978] and because it does not afford them grace in matters of tax compliance; rather taxpayers normally must comply with the letter of the tax laws ("turn square corners" in Justice Holmes' words).[979] However, the role of the courts of equity and their jurisprudence has faded from memory due to the long ago elimination of the distinction between law and equity courts in most jurisdictions (but not until 1938 in the federal district courts).

The explanation for the transformation and importation of equity into the tax law appears to lie in history and in the practical needs of the revenue system. The Supreme Court first applied the substance over form concept to the income tax of 1913 as part of its struggle to inform the central but undefined concept of income;[980] it did so rather naturally because it applied the concept in a pro-taxpayer way in *Macomber*[981] and *Southern Pacific*.[982] Then the Court specifically applied the equitable principle of the mortgagor's equity of redemption in taxpayer's favor in *F. & R. Lazarus*.[983] But the period of 1930-

---

[976] The development of some such chancery powers in the tax area was forecast by Cahn, *Federal Taxation and Private Law*, 44 COLUM. L. REV. 669, 693 (1944) (but he cautioned that elasticity is not the sole end of law); *accord*, Fuller, *Business Purpose*, *supra* note 762, at 367 (noting that equity and other legal methods could ferret out "simulations").

[977] *See* POSNER, at 83-4.

[978] *See* Blatt, *Lost on a One Way Street*, *supra* note 885, at 381. For exceptions, see *infra* Ch. VI.E.1.e(4). But a recent study of cases suggests that the street may not be so one-way as commonly thought. Schneider, *supra* note 885, at 35.

[979] Rock Is., Ark. & La. R.R. Co. v. United States, 254 U.S. 141, 143 (1920). *E.g.*, United States v. Felt & Tarrant Mfg. Co., 283 U.S. 269 (1931) (Court cannot dispense with requirement that taxpayer file a proper claim for refund, even if it was certain to be rejected); Rand v. United States, 249 U.S. 503 (1919) (similar); Lucas v. Pilliod Lumber Co., 281 U.S. 245 (1930) (accurate but unsigned return was not a return).

[980] The Court used substance over form to defeat the income tax of 1894 by finding that a tax on income from property was in substance a tax on the property. Pollock v. Farmers' Loan & Trust Co., 157 U.S. 429, 581, modified, 158 U.S. 601 (1895).

[981] Eisner v. Macomber, 252 U.S. 189 (1920) (ruled that the stock dividend in form was not income).

[982] S. Pac. Co. v. Lowe, 247 U.S. 330 (1918) (ruled that the subsidiary had earned income on behalf of the parent).

[983] Helvering v. F. & R. Lazarus & Co., 308 U.S. 252 (1939).

1950 brought a huge need for revenue and a public dislike of tax avoiders. Hence the courts began to apply the equitable principles to find tax liability in the government's favor, severing the link with traditional notions of equity for the people and retaining only the equitable methods of fact finding.

Equitable principles properly apply in two different ways in the government's favor in tax cases. First, when the tax law depends on the characterization of the legal rights and duties of the taxpayer, principles of equity that would apply to establish those rights and duties also apply to inform the facts that determine the tax characterization. The classic example is indebtedness and interest thereon and the terms of contracts generally. Second, the government appears to have come to stand in the position of a wronged or defrauded third party in relation to the taxpayer's business dealings, whom equity will free from limitations like the parol evidence rule in order to be able to get at the truth of those dealings.

V.E.1.b. *Brief History of the Development of Equity*

Equity developed in England as an anodyne to law; courts of equity developed equitable rights and remedies, which are still recognized and applied by the unified courts to right wrongs not provided for at the common law. The Supreme Court has continued to rely on the substance over form maxim of equity outside the tax law, usually in the context of a federal court providing an equitable remedy.[984]

The substance over form maxim of equity developed to relieve persons from the "arbitrary . . . peculiarly rigid . . . almost barbarous" strictures of the forms required by the common law, such as the requirement of seals.[985] For example the common law refused to protect the maker of a sealed obligation from a collection action simply based on proof of payment; rather the maker had to produce the original obligation or another sealed instrument proving payment. In contrast, equity courts looked to the reality of payment rather than the form of the seal and would protect the debtor based on proof of the substance of the real relation of the parties.[986]

The most important application of this maxim has been the recognition of constructive rights in property.[987]

> It is by disregarding these forms and looking at the real relations involved in the acts of the parties, at the real substance and intent of the transaction, that the court of chancery has built up its magnificent structure of equitable property, estates and proprietary interest.[988]

---

[984] *See, e.g.,* Young v. Higbee Co., 324 U.S. 204 (1945) (bankruptcy court had equitable powers to order an accounting).

[985] Pomeroy, at § 379.

[986] *Id.* at § 70.

[987] *Id.* at § 380.

[988] *Id.*

That maxim helped to carry out another maxim of equity that treats as done that which in good conscience ought to be done.[989] Equity always tries to get at the "real relations of the parties."[990] However, equity always recognized a limit where "some positive and mandatory rule of law" provided otherwise.[991] In contrast to equity, the common law was rooted in conformance to forms.[992]

Another example that relates more closely to the tax law is the treatment of uses or trusts by equity. The use or trust developed in England as a way for a landowner to defraud his feudal superior by conveying his land to another (who for some reason was not subject to a feudal obligation; such transferees must have been the original tax indifferent parties!), for the use of the original owner.[993] Similarly, friars who could not own property conveyed their property to the borough for their use, with instructions to deed it to their heirs after their death.[994] The common law did not recognize the rights of the *cestue que trust*,[995] but the equity courts did.[996] Thus, the law looked only to the legal title while the courts of equity would look behind the legal title to recognize the rights of the beneficial user.

But equity evidently would not apply its principle to enforce the lord's feudal rights. In what may be one of the first anti-abuse tax statutes,[997] Parliament enacted the Statute of Uses in 1535, at the King's urging, to convert certain equitable estates into legal ownership, and thus restore the feudal obligations to the King.[998] Notice that equity had acted to secure the ownership rights of the *cestue que trust*, not to protect the feudal rights of the King; the King's interests had to be protected by statute.

Even more closely related to taxation is the equitable doctrine of consideration as applied to trusts. Equity used this doctrine to overcome the control of the form of title in determining ownership of property. Equity reasoned that he who supplies the consideration in a transaction involving the acquisition of property will be the owner, and that good and valuable consideration must exist for the doctrine to apply, except in family situations where "love

---

989 *Id.* at Vol. 1, p. 41.

990 *Id.*

991 *Id.* at Vol. 1, p. 42.

992 *Id.*

993 *Id.* at § 978.

994 MAITLAND, EQUITY—TWO COURSES OF LECTURES, LECTURE III "USES AND TRUSTS" (Cambridge 1929).

995 POMEROY, at § 979.

996 *Id.* at § 980. Maitland explained that the equity of uses straddled the categories of ownership and contract, which reflected the great legal divide between *in rem* and *in personam* rights. The courts of equity began to recognize and enforce the *in rem* rights of the *cestue que trust* as owner, but did so on the basis of *in personam* reasoning that was used in cases of contract, without saying so. MAITLAND, *supra* note 994.

997 *See* POPKIN, at 16.

998 POMEROY, at § 983; Holdwsorth, *Political Causes which Shaped the Statute of Uses*, 26 HARV. L. REV. 108 (1912).

and affection" sufficed. Thus, if A conveys fee title to B without consideration (other than a Seal) and B is not a family member, equity will enforce a resulting or constructive trust to treat A as the owner of the property because B did not pay any consideration.[999] Similarly, if A pays consideration to B for property and directs it to be titled in the name of C and C pays nothing and is not a family member, a constructive trust can arise that will treat A as the owner because A provided the consideration.[1000] This sounds like Regulation section 1.351-1(b)(2) Example (1) (the father and son capitalizing a corporation and receiving amounts of stock that were not in proportion to the value they had contributed to the corporation); and *Deputy v. Du Pont* (shareholder's payment to corporation's creditor not deductible because not paid upon shareholder's debt; may be contribution to capital).[1001]

Thus, courts of equity developed methods of finding the real relations between parties and applying those facts both for the purpose of creating primary rights and for the purpose of providing remedies different from the rights and remedies at common law where more formal considerations controlled.[1002] The rights recognized all had to do with property rights, whether deriving from contract or otherwise, and could be either contrary to legal rights or could create a right where the law had a gap.[1003] For example, equity created the primary right of freedom from having to pay a sealed debt a second time, whereas the law would have required it.[1004] As the powers of the courts of law and equity coalesced, the equitable methods of both creating primary rights and providing remedies were assimilated into the law.[1005] However, principles of equity permeated the common law even before the two were consolidated.[1006]

In the processes both of creating and applying the primary equitable rights and the equitable remedies, the courts of equity utilized an array of principles and doctrines generally developing in equity.[1007] Pomeroy listed the principles of equity that are so important as to form the maxims of equity as follows: (1) equity regards that as done which ought to be done, (2) equity looks to the intent rather than to the form,[1008] (3) he who seeks equity must do equity, (4) he who comes into equity must come with clean hands, (4) equality is equity, (5) where there are equal equities, the first in time shall prevail, (6) where there is equal equity the law must prevail, (7) equity aids the vigilant, not

---

[999] Pomeroy, at § 981.

[1000] *Id.*

[1001] Deputy v. Du Pont, 308 U.S. 488 (1940).

[1002] Pomeroy, at § 97.

[1003] *Id.* at §§ 98-101.

[1004] *Id.* at § 102.

[1005] *Id.* at § 70.

[1006] *Id.* at §§ 40, 65.

[1007] *Id.* at § 150.

[1008] *See, e.g.*, Craig v. Leslie, 16 U.S. 563, 577 (1818); Pomeroy, at § 378, p. 40 et seq. (equity looks to the intent rather than to the form, sometimes referred to as "equity regards substance rather than form").

those who slumber on their rights, (8) equity imputes an intention to fulfill an obligation, (9) equity will not suffer a wrong without a remedy, (10) equity follows the law, and (11) where one of two innocent parties must suffer, he through whose agency the loss occurred must bear it.[1009]

In the United States the importation of the rules of equity into the Bankruptcy Code has been a cornerstone feature of that body of law. The Supreme Court stated in *Pepper v. Litton* that bankruptcy courts are essentially courts of equity and they apply the principles and rules of equity jurisprudence, which will be invoked to the end that "fraud will not prevail, that substance will not give way to form, that technical considerations will not prevent substantial justice from being done."[1010]

Equity also was responsible for the movement of the law of trials toward procedural flexibility in the 20th century, but that did not much influence the tax law. The English common law pleadings, which fused procedure and substantive law, were rigid and not much changed by the Field Code, which also avoided judicial discretion and flexibility.[1011] But the Federal Rules of Civil Procedure largely adopted the discretion and flexibility that was the hallmark of English equity practice; in fact they largely adopted the Rules of Equity as applied in the federal courts as procedural rules.[1012]

V.E.1.c. *The Example of Usury and Equitable Fact Finding*

Randolph Paul analogized tax law to the usury laws: both statutes engender avoidance efforts.[1013] He observed that the courts generally allow parties to plan around the usury laws, *i.e*, to avoid them by business structuring (such as organizing a corporation to borrow).[1014] This is analogous to the general principle that taxpayers are allowed to use legitimate means to reduce their taxes (see Ch. II.C.2.a.). But, like the tax law, the usury laws employ standard fact finding methods to discern usury.[1015]

Usury was forbidden by statutes that usually could be enforced by the criminal law or by defense of the debtor or suit of the debtor. The debtor could plead the defense in the law courts and could proceed as plaintiff in either the law or equity courts, with the law courts applying equitable principles.[1016]

[1009] POMEROY, at § 363.

[1010] Pepper v. Litton, 308 U.S. 295, 304-05 (1939).

[1011] Subrin, *How Equity Conquered Common Law: The Federal Rules of Civil Procedure in Historical Perspective*, 135 U. PA. L. REV. 909, 931-35 (1987).

[1012] *Id.* at 922.

[1013] PAUL, STUDIES I, at 67. As to usury generally in United States law, see FRIEDMAN, *supra* note 159, at 474-76 (observing that the popularity of usury laws waxed and waned depending on the needs of the borrowers).

[1014] *Id.; see, e.g.*, Seeman v. Philadelphia Whse. Co., 274 U.S. 403 (1927) (lender could stipulate that usury law of state of payment controlled).

[1015] *See also* Bittker, *Pervasive Judicial Doctrines in the Construction of the Internal Revenue Code*, 21 HOW. L.J. 693, 705 (1978) (likewise analogized the early search for substance in usury cases).

[1016] COMYN, TREATISE ON THE LAW OF USURY 79-83 (Littell, 1834).

Both the law and the equity courts applied various fact finding techniques to discern usury in a variety of situations including: purported sales of goods for a deferred price, stock loans, the payment by the debtor of something other than formal interest (an example being forcing the debtor to rent property at an exorbitant rate), fees, compounding,[1017] and sale leasebacks (which could be proved to be disguised loans by parol evidence of the parties).[1018]

Where the usury was not obvious on the face of the contract, the intent of both parties had to be found to support a finding of usury.[1019] The statutes on usury assumed that the parties would try to hide the nature of their transaction and so employed application of all legal techniques to find it out.[1020] Commentators recognized that fact finding in usury applied the equitable principles.[1021] The questions of whether a loan existed and whether usurious interest was charged are questions of fact to be determined from all of the facts and circumstances by the jury.[1022]

The usury jurisprudence shows that the liberal fact finding methods in usury cases stemmed from the remedial character of the statute, which character tax laws originally did not share.[1023] However, the Code has come to be interpreted and applied in ways quite similar to those used in applying usury laws. Evidently the tax laws have come to be viewed as remedial in favor of the government and the courts presume the intent of Congress to collect needed taxes through the application of equitable methods of fact finding.

V.E.1.d. *Parol Evidence*

Tax treatment normally is determined by the taxpayer's legal rights, which are often established by contracts. But the rules of evidence generally prevent a contracting party from using parol evidence to disprove his written contract. Conversely, when taxation is dependent on the nature of the transaction for federal tax purposes (which usually is not controlled by state law determinations), then parol evidence can be admissible even though the taxpayer might be precluded from introducing such evidence to vary its contract.[1024]

1017 *Id.* at 39-61.

1018 WEBB, *supra* note 113, at 27-9, 490.

1019 Bank of United States v. Waggener, 34 U.S. 378 (1835).

1020 WEBB, *supra* note 113, at 228; *see* President, Directors & Company of the Bank of the United States v. Owens, 27 U.S. 527 (1829) (holding that the Bank had violated its own charter by charging more than six percent interest through the mechanism of taking Owen's note in exchange for notes of a third party, which had a significantly lower value than their face amounts. The Court stated that it did not matter whether the Bank intended or even knew that it was charging usury in effect.).

1021 WEBB, *supra* note 113, at 227.

1022 PROFFATT, TREATISE ON TRIAL BY JURY 354-55 (Whitney, 1877).

1023 WEBB, *supra* note 113, at 257-59.

1024 BITTKER & LOKKEN, at 4.4.5 (also discussing generally the lack of impact of the parol evidence rule on the government's ability to restructure transactions for tax purposes); *see also* JONI LARSON, A PRACTITIONER'S GUIDE TO TAX EVIDENCE: A PRIMER ON THE FEDERAL RULES OF EVIDENCE AS APPLIED BY THE TAX COURT (ABA 2013).

Apparently independent of equity, the common law allowed parol evidence to prove facts contrary to written instruments in cases very similar to tax cases. The preclusion of parol evidence traditionally operated only between the parties to the writing. Where a third party is defrauded or otherwise harmed by a writing, the third party is allowed to offer parol evidence to vary the facts stated in the writing:

> Therefore, a lord may be admitted to prove by witnesses, in opposition to a contract of sale, that an estate was sold for a larger price than that which is expressed in the act, with a view to diminishing the dues to which he is entitled; vice versa, a relative may prove than an estate was sold for a less considerable price than that which is expressed in the act in fraud of his right of retrait. And many other instances of these frauds might be adduced.[1025]

Substitute the Service for the lord and this sentence applies perfectly to tax disputes.

In his 1938 work on Step Transactions Randolph Paul stated that lawyers forget, if they ever knew, that the parol evidence rule only applies between the parties to the contract.

> The rule has no application where the controversy is not between the parties to an instrument but involves the government,—a third party not signatory to the written contract. In such cases it is permissible, where the meaning of a contract is sufficiently ambiguous to give trouble, to offer extraneous evidence to show the circumstances surrounding the parties when the contract was made.[1026]

Even more to the point is the footnote to that statement:

> Unquestionably the parol evidence rule has no application where the issue in dispute is a right of the *third party*, rather than what are the obligations of the parties to the contract. The right of the government in asserting a tax liability, to vary by parol evidence the terms of a written contract is analogous to the law of fraudulent conveyances, much of which turns upon the right of creditors to attack instruments which purport to be absolute conveyances as between the parties.[1027]

V.E.1.e. *Equity as a Remedy for the Government*

The tax specific doctrines are applied by the lower federal courts as if the government were the party entitled to equity, which is a curious role reversal. The foregoing discussion describes equitable methods of finding facts and establishing the rights and duties of a taxpayer vis a vis other persons (for example, is the person a debtor, an owner, a creditor ?) that are relevant also

---

[1025] POTHIER, TREATISE ON THE LAW OF OBLIGATIONS OR CONTRACTS 453-54 (1826).

[1026] PAUL, STUDIES II, at 216.

[1027] *Id.*, at 216 n. 66. For an application of the Supreme Court's use of parol and other evidence to contradict a contract in the taxpayer's favor, see Helvering v. Tex-Penn Oil Co., 300 U.S. 481 (1937).

for the application of tax rules. It suggests a completely different way in which equity principles seem to be employed in the tax specific doctrines: they place the government in the posture of a defrauded or wronged third party.[1028] The parallel with equity is flawed, not only because equity was not created for the benefit of the King but because the core occasions of the need for equity are mistake, accident and fraud.[1029]

Surely not all "tax planning" with which the government disagrees is the result of fraud, much less accident or mistake. Nevertheless, the cross fertilization of equity and tax has occurred. Fraud for the purpose of equity was never limited to the boldest varieties. Fraud may be either active misrepresentation or concealment of the truth with intent to mislead, or constructive fraud, covering an array of less egregious wrongdoings.[1030] Within the category of constructive frauds are transactions that are not fraudulent as between the parties but can be fraudulent as to third parties, with the primary example being conveyances for inadequate consideration in fraud of creditors.[1031] The similarity with the doctrines is made even greater by the key required element of intent in cases of fraud.

Nevertheless, the importation of equity into the tax law remains curious because equity was created to correct a violation of a legal right held by persons,[1032] not governments. The exclusion of the government as a recipient of equity is so elemental that it is not directly discussed in Pomeroy, but flows from the fact that the original grantor of equity, was the King's own Chancellor, who was not likely to be petitioned by the King himself.[1033]

In effect, the courts using the doctrines have plucked the maxim that substance controls form out of equity and applied it in tax cases.[1034] At first, this application favored taxpayers (*Pollock v. Farmers' Loan & Trust Co., Eisner v. Macomber, F. & R. Lazarus*), but ultimately it has become a mostly one way doctrine applied in favor of the government against taxpayers. This is obviously a perversion of the equitable maxim, especially when none of the other equitable principles are commonly applied to relieve taxpayers of the harshness of the tax laws, as discussed in the next Section.

Another sense in which the Court applies equity for the government is in the rare cases of a two way "equitable" rule like the tax benefit rule, where the failure to include income would be an "inequitable windfall" to the tax-

---

1028 *See also* I.R.C. § 7403, which allows the appointment of a receiver with equitable powers to enforce a lien on behalf of the Service.

1029 POMEROY, at § 822.

1030 *Id.* at §§ 872-974.

1031 *Id.* at §§ 966-970.

1032 *Id.* at § 185.

1033 *Id.* at § 33. The granting of equity by the King was often referred to as an act of grace. However, equitable remedies, as opposed to rights, can be pursued by the government. *See, e.g.*, Ash Sheep Co. v. United States, 252 U.S. 159 (1920) (injunction).

1034 Kneeland v. Am. Loan and Trust Co., 138 U.S. 509 (1891) (stating in a nontax case that "equity regards the substance and not the form").

payer.[1035] Similarly, the Court in *James* thought that equity demanded an embezzler be taxed on the fruits of his crime.[1036]

V.E.1.f. *No Equity for Taxpayers*

V.E.1.f(1) *General Rule*

As between the government and the taxpayer, the courts do not apply the principle of equity "that which should have been done will be treated as done"; nor do the courts generally apply the other principles of equity in taxpayers' favor, including the substance over form maxim, except as discussed in the next section.[1037] Equity always tended to protect persons from penalties and forfeitures; equity usually held that time of performance was immaterial; equity would find substantial compliance with requirements to be sufficient.[1038] Such equity in favor of the taxpayer is essentially missing from the federal tax laws, except for a narrow substantial compliance doctrine discussed below.

An early reason for the absence of equity for taxpayers was that many if not most tax disputes that were not criminal proceedings arose as suits of taxpayers in equity to restrain the collection of a tax. The Supreme Court refused to aid taxpayers who engaged in rather straightforward efforts to avoid a tax: for example, the Court refused to aid Mitchell avoid a Kansas tax on bank accounts when he had obtained a payout of his account in cash which he held for three days including the day for levying of the tax on bank accounts; the Court viewed the taxpayer as not having clean hands because he was trying to avoid his proportionate share of the tax.[1039] When statutes later prevented taxpayers from enjoining both state and federal taxes in federal courts, direct resort to the maxims of equity as a ground for decision in tax cases was lost, and the forcing of all taxpayer cases into the law courts might have contributed to a rise of taxpayer reliance on form.

As to the absence of equity for taxpayers, Robert H. Jackson pointed out that it was rooted in the early view that the tax laws were to be technically applied as written to the taxpayer's advantage.[1040] Where the same rule was

---

[1035] *See* Hillsboro National Bank v. Commissioner, 460 U.S. 370, 403 (1983) (Brennan, J., dissenting).

[1036] *See* Barker, *supra* note 25, at 858 (discussing James v. United States, 366 U.S. 213 (1961)).

[1037] *But see* Schneider, *supra* note 885 (empirical study showing that taxpayers argue for equity and sometimes obtain substance over form results, which probably are explained by the fact finding exceptions discussed herein).

[1038] Pomeroy, at § 72.

[1039] Mitchell v. Board of Commissioners, 91 U.S. 206 (1876); *cf.* Shotwell v. Moore, 129 U.S. 590 (1889) (same result on same facts in a case at law where the state law included an averaging rule).

[1040] Jackson, *Equity in the Administration of Federal Taxes*, *supra* note 166, at 642; *see also* Lewyt Corp. v. Commissioner, 349 U.S. 237, 240 (1955) (lack of equity cuts both ways, meaning that taxpayers can obtain a tax windfall if they qualify literally).

applied to the taxpayers' disadvantage they were precluded from complaining. But as shown above, the rule of strict construction against the government has waned and yet equity for taxpayers still is absent; for examples:

- The Commissioner is "without dispensing power."[1041]
- Even as early as an interpretation of the Corporation Tax Act of 1909 the Court admitted but was unwilling to apply the "equitable consideration" that a mine owner should be allowed a deduction for depletion;[1042]
- *J.E. Riley* refused the "equitable" consideration pressed by the taxpayer that it had missed an election because it did not know about it: "That may be the basis for an appeal to Congress in amelioration of the strictness of that section. But it is no ground for relief by the courts from the rigors of the statutory choice which Congress has provided."[1043] The Court reasoned that the tax administrator should not be invested with that sort of discretion and the courts did not have the power; the only resort was to Congress.
- *Midland Insurance* stated that "Where the legal effect of a transaction fits the plain letter of the statute, the tax is held payable, unless there is clearly revealed in the Act itself or in its history a definite intention to exclude such transactions from the operation of its applicable language."[1044] It is noteworthy that the statement admitted "its history," if clear, can vary the words of the statute.
- *Electric Storage* refused to extend the equitable recoupment allowed by *Bull* (discussed below) in cases that "tempt the equity-minded judge to seek for ways of relief in individual cases."[1045]

1041 Meaning he could not dispense with the requirement for filing a new return if the statute required it. Zellerbach Paper Co. v. Helvering, 293 U.S. 172, 178 (1934).

1042 Von Baumbach v. Sargent Land Co., 242 U.S. 503 (1917).

1043 J.E. Riley Inv. Co. v. Commissioner, 311 U.S. 55 (1940). The strictness of the *Riley* decision was softened in the lower courts for a period, but the courts have returned to strictness. Levin, *The Substantial Compliance Doctrine in Tax Law: Equity v. Efficiency*, 40 UCLA L. Rev. 1587 (1993); Chouest, Note, *Dot All I's and Cross All T's: Estate of Tamulis v. Commissioner and the Narrowing of the Substantial Compliance Doctrine to the Technical Compliance Doctrine*, 62 Tax Law. 259 (2008); *see also* Foster v. United States, 303 U.S. 118 (1938) (to make concession for the equity of shareholders); Pac. Nat'l Co. v. Welch, 304 U.S. 191 (1938) (too late to claim installment method).

1044 Helvering v. Midland Mutual Life Ins. Co., 300 U.S. 216 (1937); *see also* Commissioner v. Nat'l Alfalfa Dehydrating & Milling Co., 417 U.S. 134, 149 (1974) (taxpayer must accept the consequences of his choice of form whether contemplated or not); Boulware v. United States, 552 U.S. 421 (2008) (partly because the taxpayer normally can choose its facts, it is stuck with the tax consequences of those facts).

1045 Rothensies v. Elec. Storage Battery Co., 329 U.S. 296 (1946).

- The view of *Gould*,[1046] that because there was no equity for taxpayers when the statute is clear, there should be some leniency when the statute is not clear, has been discredited. Justice Holmes said: "Men must turn square corners when they deal with the Government."[1047]
- The doctrine of election, generally ascribed to *Pacific National Co. v. Welch*: having missed a favorable election, the taxpayer cannot amend his return to claim it.[1048] Actually, the doctrine of election is an equitable rule of procedure that has been applied to give equity to the government.[1049] The citations in *Pacific* reveal that the doctrine of election originated entirely in the lower courts, principally the Board of Tax Appeals, and almost entirely involved the installment method.[1050]
- The Supreme Court has expressed sympathy for the fact that the "government has millions of taxpayers to monitor, and our system of self-assessment in the initial calculation of a tax simply cannot work on any basis other than one of strict filing standards."[1051]
- The Service uses broad information gathering powers to establish the tax owing;[1052] constitutional protections against information gathering by the Service give way until the taxpayer has been referred to the Justice Department for prosecution.[1053]

1046 Gould v. Gould, 245 U.S. 151 (1917); *see also* Boehm v. Commissioner, 326 U.S. 287 (1945) (hapless taxpayer missed the right year to deduct the loss and got no help from the Court); Burnet v. Thompson Oil & Gas Co., 283 U.S. 301 (1931) (erroneous failure to take adequate depletion deductions in earlier years cannot be made up later, and basis must be reduced as if proper deductions were claimed); United States v. Merriam, 263 U.S. 179, 188 (1923) (no equitable construction of taxing statutes, which are applied as written, meaning they are not intended to be extended beyond their literal terms).

1047 Rock Is., Ark. & La. R.R. Co. v. United States, 254 U.S. 141, 143 (1920) (the government assessed additional tax, which the taxpayer requested to be abated and the government refused; the taxpayer then paid the tax and sued for refund, without appealing for refund to the government; the statute required such an appeal for refund post-payment; the Court rejected the taxpayer's contention that such a second appeal was meaningless).

1048 Pac. Nat'l Co. v. Welch, 304 U.S. 191 (1938) (known as establishing the "doctrine of elections," but not using that term); *see also* United States v. Kaplan, 304 U.S. 195 (1938) (same). For some purposes relief can be obtained under Regulation section 301.9100-3. *See generally* Helvey and Stetson, *The Doctrine of Election*, 62 TAX LAW. 335 (2009) (criticizing the doctrine of election; discussing C.C.N. 2002-27, announcing change in litigating position on one application of doctrine of election). *But see* C.C.A. 201009013 (Mar. 5, 2010) (relying on *Pacific National* and the doctrine of election).

1049 For example, the oldest refund case cited in *Pacific National* denied the taxpayer's effort to change its installment method election, stating that an action to recover an alleged overpayment of taxes is governed by equitable principles and it would be in equitable to allow the taxpayer to so reduce its tax liability. Marks v. United States, 18 F. Supp. 911 (S.D.N.Y. 1937).

1050 *See* Lee v. Commissioner, 6 B.T.A. 135 (1927).

1051 United States v. Boyle, 469 U.S. 241, 245 (1985).

1052 United States v. Arthur Young & Co., 465 U.S. 805 (1984) (restrictions on the summons power should be avoided).

1053 *See* United States v. La Salle Nat'l Bank, 437 U.S. 298 (1978).

- The government as a tax collector is not subject to the equitable doctrine of marshalling of assets, which normally requires a creditor with two properties from which a lien can be satisfied to first deplete the property against which another creditor of the taxpayer does not have a lien.[1054]
- The requirement that administrative remedies be properly exhausted by the taxpayer before suit applies inflexibly.[1055]
- There is no "equitable tolling" of the statute of limitations for senility, alcoholism, etc.[1056]
- There is no equitable exception to the preclusion of suits to enjoin federal taxes.[1057]
- The doctrine of equitable estoppel does not bar the correction of a mistake of law by the Commissioner.[1058]
- The Court reversed a ruling that the taxpayer fell within the "spirit" of beneficial regulations providing an election because the taxpayer never filed in compliance with the regulation.[1059]
- Equitable considerations in a particular case should not divert the annual accounting principles from the normal rules of cash and accrual accounting (whether favoring the taxpayer or the government).[1060]
- The Court rejected arguments about the inequities of the claim of right doctrine.[1061]
- Statutory construction could not avoid even an "unfair burden" of lack of basis step up on death for surviving joint tenant.[1062]
- The Court has recognized the principle that "Courts of equity may, and frequently do, go much farther both to give and withhold relief in furtherance of the public interest than they are accustomed to go when only private interests are involved."[1063]
- The tax collector is not required by equity to join all who might be jointly and severally liable as transferees for the taxpayer corporation's taxes, but can proceed against and collect all of the tax from one of them.[1064]

[1054] Meyer v. United States, 375 U.S. 233 (1963).

[1055] United States v. Clintwood Elkhorn Mining Co., 553 U.S. 1 (2008).

[1056] United States v. Brockamp, 519 U.S. 347 (1997). *But see* I.R.C. § 6511(h); Bittker & Lokken, at 112.5.3; *cf.* Young v. United States, 535 U.S. 43 (2002) (Court applied equitable tolling against bankrupt to allow priority to tax lien).

[1057] Dodge v. Osborn, 240 U.S. 118 (1916).

[1058] Auto Club of Michigan v. Commissioner, 353 U.S. 180 (1957).

[1059] Burnet v. Sanford & Brooks Co., 282 U.S. 359 (1931).

[1060] Security Flour Mills Co. v. Commissioner, 321 U.S. 281, 286 (1944).

[1061] Healy v. Commissioner, 345 U.S. 278 (1953). *See also* United States v. Lewis, 340 U.S. 590 (1951) (while opening a prior year might be equitable for this taxpayer, for others the year would be barred by the three year statute of limitations).

[1062] Lang v. Commissioner, 289 U.S. 109 (1933).

[1063] United States v. First Nat'l City Bank, 379 U.S. 378, 383 (1965).

[1064] Phillips v. Commissioner, 283 U.S. 589 (1931).

- Constitutional protections play a very circumscribed role in shielding the taxpayer from the tax collector.[1065]

Put another way, the courts do not sit as courts of equity where the rights of taxpayers are concerned. In fact, the Supreme Court has made an interesting juxtaposition of equity versus legislative grace in stating that deductions are not matters of equity but legislative grace.[1066]

The narrow exceptions that have explicitly applied equitable principles in taxpayers' favor are listed here:

- The Court in *Bull* decided that a taxpayer can seek recoupment of a related, and inconsistent, but now time barred tax claim relating to the same transaction for which the Service now seeks additional taxes.[1067] *Bull* not only applied the equitable principle that a defendant can offset a barred claim against the plaintiff's recovery, but ingeniously adapted it to tax by reasoning that the taxpayer could assert the offset in its own suit for refund because taxpayers generally must pay first and dispute later.[1068]
- Justice Holmes indicated that it might be possible to relieve the taxpayer of the duty to do a useless thing.[1069]
- Another remnant of equity for taxpayers in the tax law may be seen in the concept of "substantial compliance," which usually is allowed only by statute or regulation.[1070]
- A more specific "substantial compliance doctrine" has been applied to taxpayer elections, but is rarely applied now; the doctrine allows a technically defective election to be honored if the taxpayer has a good excuse,

---

1065 *See, e.g.,* United States v. Sullivan, 274 U.S. 259 (1927) (Justice Holmes said that to allow a bootlegger to file no return at all because to do so might reveal his illegal income would improperly allow him to "draw a conjurer's circle around the whole matter."). *See generally* CUMMINGS, CONSTITUTION.

1066 Commissioner v. Nat'l Alfalfa Dehydrating & Milling Co., 417 U.S. 134, 149 (1974); Knight v. Commissioner, 552 U.S. 181 (2008).

1067 Bull v. United States, 295 U.S. 247 (1935); *see* BITTKER & LOKKEN, at 113.10; United States v. Dalm, 494 U.S. 596 (1990) (refusing to extend the doctrine and contrasting Stone v. White, 301 U.S. 532 (1937) (the origin of equitable recoupment, which discusses the equitable nature of the refund suit, citing United States v. MacDaniel, 32 U.S. 1 (1833) (which refers to the equitable right of the claimant))).

1068 The *Bull* opinion contained this very strong statement: "The United States, we have held, cannot, as against the claim of an innocent party, hold his money which has gone into its treasury by means of the fraud of its agent. United States v. State Bank, 96 U.S. 30 (1878). While here the money was taken through mistake without any element of fraud, the unjust retention is immoral and amounts in law to a fraud on the taxpayer's rights. What was said in the *State Bank* case applies with equal force to this situation."

1069 Rock Is., Ark. & La. R.R. Co. v. United States, 254 U.S. 141, 143 (1920) (taxpayer's protest of the assessment after payment was not useless in light of its earlier protest of the assessment because the government might have changed its mind).

1070 *See, e.g.,* Reg. § 1.275-5T(c)(2)(v) (substantiation); substantial compliance with the requirement to file a "return"; BITTKER & LOKKEN, at 111.1.8, "Deficient, Skeleton and Tentative Returns."

other than a legal justification, to an unimportant or confusing requirement.[1071]

- In a decision allowing a wife to sue to dispute her husband's taxes, the Court was motivated in part by the absence of any other remedy, which is an equitable consideration.[1072]
- Some opinions that purport to accord taxpayers equity, in fact apply general rules of statutory construction to ambiguous statutes and sometimes extend to taxpayers general principles that have grown up around a particular subject.[1073]
- The Court has referred to the tax benefit rule, which may apply to taxpayers' advantage or disadvantage, as "transactional equity."[1074]
- And Congress should not lightly be assumed to have foreclosed a federal court from exercising its traditional equitable discretion.[1075]

In sum, we now have a curious regime that both establishes many rigid rules to which taxpayers must conform, provides virtually no grace for slight and meaningless errors, and applies anti-taxpayer doctrines (substance over form) that stem from the rules of equity.

V.E.1.f(2) *Exceptions:* Helvering v. F. & R. Lazarus

The clearest example of the Supreme Court's application of equitable fact finding methods in favor of a taxpayer is *F. & R. Lazarus.*[1076] Its approach continues to be applied generally to identify things and events defined in the Code, sometimes in favor of taxpayers, more frequently against taxpayers under the rubric of a doctrine.

This case involved an unambiguous statute and facts that become ambiguous only through the application of well recognized equitable principles applied to determine ownership of property. *Lazarus* is important because the ambiguous *Frank Lyon*[1077] decision heavily relied upon it (or on distinguishing it), and because it illustrates how the Supreme Court relied on standard fact finding methods rather than a tax specific doctrine. *Lazarus* also

---

[1071] Levin, *The Substantial Compliance Doctrine, supra* note 1043, at 1587; Chouest, *supra* note 1043, at 259.

[1072] United States v. Williams, 514 U.S. 527 (1995).

[1073] *See, e.g.,* Commissioner v. Gordon, 382 F.2d 499 (2d Cir. 1967)

> . . . these cases properly stand for the proposition that in determining tax results, the courts do not merely look to the literal language of the statute but also view the business transaction as a whole in conjunction with the underlying purpose of the taxing statute. We are not aware of any rule of law that preserves such a salutary tenet of construction for the exclusive benefit of the Commissioner.

[1074] *See* Hillsboro National Bank v. Commissioner, 460 U.S. 370 (1983) (exclusionary and inclusionary).

[1075] United States v. Rodgers, 461 U.S. 677, 708 (1983).

[1076] Helvering v. F. & R. Lazarus & Co., 308 U.S. 252 (1939); *see also infra* Ch. VI.F.2.c(3) discussing the lease cluster rule.

[1077] Frank Lyon Co. v. United States, 435 U.S. 561 (1978); *see infra* Ch. VI.F.2.c.

shows how Justice Black imported equitable fact finding into the tax law by questionable reasoning, where it has remained without proper recognition since; at least Black acknowledged the need for the connection with equity. Unfortunately *Lazarus* provided a basis on which later courts could cite the opinion's "substance and realities" language without grasping the equitable rule being applied.

Facts and Ruling. Lazarus & Co. (part of Federated Stores, which became Macy's) wanted to depreciate its store that it had sold to a lender and leased back with an option to purchase. The Court first delinked the issue from one of title ownership by observing that the right to a deduction for depreciation depended on who made the investment, which was a tax concept (although there might be an analogous state law concept). Next the Court found the taxpayer made the investment because it had the equity of redemption under state law. That is, at equity the taxpayer could reclaim the property once it had paid off the "rental." The Court affirmed the Board of Tax Appeals,[1078] which had relied on the power of a court of equity to prevent a lender from fraudulently claiming that the deed he received was absolute; in examining the facts a court of equity could receive parol evidence to contradict sale documents signed by the borrower. The Supreme Court stated:

> We think the Board justifiably concluded from its findings that the transaction between the taxpayer and the trustee bank, in written form a transfer of ownership with a lease back, was actually a loan secured by the property involved. General recognition has been given the "established doctrine that a court of equity will treat a deed, absolute in form, as a mortgage, when it is executed as security for a loan of money." [cites to equity cases omitted] In the field of taxation, administrators of the laws and the courts are concerned with substance and realities, and formal written documents are not rigidly binding. Congress has specifically emphasized the equitable nature of proceedings before the Board of Tax Appeals by requiring the Board to act "in accordance with the rules of evidence applicable in courts of equity of the District of Columbia." 26 U.S.C. § 611, 26 U.S.C.A. § 611.

The opinion also cited another depreciation case, which recited the statute that then referred to the ownership status of one having a duty to capital-

[1078] F. &. R. Lazarus & Co. v. Commissioner, 32 B.T.A. 633 (1935). The Board cited *Southard v. Russell*, 57 U.S. 547 (1854), which applied the equitable remedy of treating a deed absolute on its face as a loan and security, based on facts such as the inadequacy of the consideration, and citing *Conway's Executors v. Alexander*, 11 U.S. 218 (1812) (Chief Justice Marshall considering, without citations, the possibility that a sale was a mortgage for which the equity of redemption should be allowed, but not finding facts necessary to so rule). Southard explained that for the "buyer" to assert that his deed was absolute when it was intended to be a mortgage deed is a fraud in equity, and equity will relieve the "seller" from the fraud, and the seller will not be bound by the document he had to sign stating that it was a sale.

ize and a right to depreciation as an "equity."[1079] In addition to this statutory reference to equity, the Court could rely on a second indication from Congress that it should look to equity: Congress had authorized the trial court to receive evidence as a court of equity, which meant that it could hear parol and other evidence to vary the form of a contract.

Analysis of Court's Reasoning. Did this mean that the Board was a court of equity? That the equity evidence rules operated only in favor of the taxpayer? That there was a well recognized set of equity evidence rules that were being incorporated? That the D.C. courts had some special evidence rules? No to all questions. There has been a considerable amount of litigation over whether the Tax Court has jurisdiction to grant equitable remedies (for examples, recoupment, estoppel, innocent spouse relief) and the conclusion has been generally no because it is an Article I and not Article III court.[1080]

Evidently Congress did not intend to do anything other than to authorize the generally looser rules of evidence used in non-jury chancery proceedings, as contrasted with common law jury trials, because the Board, like the chancery courts, did not use juries. But Justice Black's statement in *Lazarus* inferred from the reference to equity evidence an authorization for the Board to make factual determinations like a court of equity would make, despite the fact that the Board was not deciding equity causes of action between two private parties.

The reference to equity evidence was added by the Revenue Act of 1926. Rep. Mills explained:

> Why not adopt the rules of evidence prevailing in the United States courts? We then found that Congress had said that the rules in the United States courts should be laid down by the Supreme Court of the United States. But the Supreme Court of the United States has said that the rules in equity cases should be governed by the same determining factors as at common law. We then looked up what the rules of evidence were in the United States district courts at common law, and discovered that they applied the rules of the particular state in which they were located.[1081]

Apparently Rep. Mills likened the District of Columbia to a state. The court of equity of the District of Columbia was the equity court of what them was called the D.C. Supreme Court, which had all of the powers of U.S.

[1079] Duffy v. Central R. Co. of N.J., 268 U.S. 55 (1925) (ruling that amounts paid for property were not deductible as rentals but were capital expenditures. At that time the section allowing deduction for rentals described them as payments with respect to property in which the payor had no "equity." This now is section 162(a)(3).).

[1080] Commissioner v. McCoy, 484 U.S. 3, 7 (1987*); see generally* Lederman, *Equity and the Article I Court: Is the Tax Court's Exercise of Equitable Powers Constitutional?* 5 Fla. Tax Rev. 5 (2001).

[1081] Seidman's Legislative Histories of Revenue Acts 1938-1861, 652-53 (1938). The 1924 Act had not specified rules of evidence.

District Courts, and not any special rules.[1082] In general, the rules of evidence at common law trials prevailed in equity.[1083] Wigmore's 1934 supplement[1084] recounted the adoption of the rule of evidence for the Board of Tax Appeals and stated that the common law of equity evidence generally applied and could be cited to the Board.[1085]

There really was not a body of equity evidence rules as much as of equitable remedies that required or allowed relaxed fact finding methods. The most important differences between law and equity were (1) use of written rather than oral testimony (at least in England), (2) allowance of discovery in equity, which meant that a party opponent could not refuse to testify or disclose his proof, and (3) rules such as allowing parol evidence to reform a deed.[1086]

At the time of the 1926 Act there was interest in and confusion about the necessity for administrative tribunals to follow common law jury trial evidence rules; Wigmore thought it should not be necessary.[1087] The evidence rules for jury trials were thought to be complex rules of limitation that were not appropriate to a judge sitting in equity or an administrative agency otherwise finding facts without a jury.[1088] Wigmore reviewed rules for administrative and tribunals other than traditional courts and found a variety of rules but in no case did he describe the rules as equity evidence.[1089]

Contemporaneous commentators did not perceive the requirement of equity evidence to mean anything other than (1) to impose legal limits on admissible evidence as in a court, in contrast with looser rules applied in administrative bodies, and (2) to select the looser rules of evidence allowed

---

[1082] 31 Statutes at Large 1199-1202. The equity court's practice was under the "established course of equity" and any rules established by the D.C. Supreme Court. *Id.* Sec. 85, ch. 854.

[1083] Wigmore, Treatise on the Anglo-American System of Evidence § 4 (Little Brown, 1923). Law and equity were supposed to have been merged in many jurisdictions by this time, but that had not necessarily occurred in practice. *See* Clark, *Union of Law and Equity*, 25 Colum. L. Rev. 1 (1925).

[1084] Wigmore, *supra* note 1083, at § 4(c) (Supp. 1934).

[1085] *Id.* at 6. He stated that between 1924 and 1926 the Board had been applying rules of evidence that more or less would apply in equity proceedings. Wigmore thought that the 1926 change would narrow rather than broaden the scope of admissible evidence. Wigmore pointed out that evidentiary matters such as valuation would be more common in the Board, and cases bore that out. *See* Garden City Feeder Co. v. Commissioner, 75 F.2d 804 (8th Cir. 1935) (stating that the D.C. courts had adopted the Supreme Court Equity Rules, which the Court had adopted in 1912); Andrews v. Commissioner, 38 F.2d 55 (2d Cir. 1930) (stating that the D.C. courts thought evidence of sales more reliable than expert reports). For the Rules of Procedure for the Court of Equity of the Untied States, *see* 75 Cent. L.J. 385 (1912). Those equity rules appear to have been a forerunner of the Federal Rules of Civil Procedure. Like those later rules, the Equity Rules did not touch upon evidence, other than to require it to be given orally or in writing (historically, equity courts had not heard oral evidence), and for excluded evidence to be preserved for review on appeal (Rule 46).

[1086] Wigmore, *supra* note 1083, at § 4(c) (Supp. 1934).

[1087] *Id.* at § 4(b).

[1088] *Id.*

[1089] *Id.*

in non-jury matters as contrasted with a common law jury trial.[1090] In 1928, a former special attorney with the Board wrote an analysis of the meaning of the use of equity evidence rules by the Board, which was then in Board Rule 39.[1091] He concluded that it only was meant to differentiate the looser standard applied by English and Maryland courts of equity from the stricter standards imposed in jury trials, supposedly to prevent confusion of the jury; the article gave no indication that substantive evidence rules (as for example how to prove a deed was a mortgage) were intended. He stated that the standard of competence of evidence was the same at law and at equity (which would seem to address questions like parol evidence), and that the difference was the strictness by which possibly immaterial and irrelevant evidence was admitted. Other commentators stated specifically that the Board did not have equity powers.[1092]

But in 1926 Gilmer Korner, Chairman of the Board, gave a speech in which he stated that "By the statute we are placed on the basis of a court of equity. In the old days the Chancellor was called the keeper of the King's conscience, and I hope that no one will feel that in keeping our conscience we have a sinecure. We do really try to do it. We try to administer these rules and treat everybody alike in the administration of them."[1093] Thus, Korner limited equity to the principle of equal treatment.

Conclusion. Therefore when Justice Black observed the equitable nature of the proceedings in the Board of Tax Appeals in 1939, he extended the meaning of the statute, albeit in a natural and obvious way. Neither of the parties had even mentioned the equity evidence rule in their briefs.[1094] The government did not dispute that a deed in form could be proved to be a mortgage, but disputed that the evidence presented was sufficient to overcome the form and other evidence supporting its treatment as a deed and lease. Justice Black's statement meant that the statute did more than permit a loosening of jury evidence rules; it meant that the equitable approach of treating things

---

1090 *See* Dubroff, *Creation of the Board of Tax Appeals*, 40 Alb. L. Rev. 53, 103 (1975); Hammond, *The United States Board of Tax Appeals*, 11 Marq. L. Rev. 1, 9 (1926); Hopkins, *The United States Board of Tax Appeals*, 12 A.B.A. 466, 468 (1926); Kahn, *The Status of the United States Board of Tax Appeals as a Judicial Body*, 7 Nat. Inc. Tax Mag. 135, 136 (1929); Korner, *United States Board of Tax Appeals*, 11 A.B.A., 642, 643 (1925); Sebree, *The United States Board of Tax Appeals*, 7 Temp. L. Q. 428, 441 (1932); Siefkin, *Procedural Methods of the Board of Tax Appeals*, 6 Nat. Inc. Tax Mag. 334, 337 (1928); Silbert, *The Board of Tax Appeals and Finality*, 15 Tax Mag. 335, 337 (1937).

1091 Stevens, *Legal Evidence Before the Board of Tax Appeals*, 6 Nat. Inc. Tax Mag. 459 (1928).

1092 McClure, *Practice Before the United States Board of Tax Appeals*, 6 Nat. Inc. Tax Mag. 92, 95 (1928); *see also* Jackson, *Equity in the Administration of Federal Taxes, supra* note 166, at 643 ("No one is given, and none will assume, power to do equity.").

1093 Proceedings of Dinner Given in Honor of the Board of Tax Appeals, 4 Nat. Inc. Tax Mag. 233, 243 (1926).

1094 Brief for the Petitioner, Helvering v. F. & R. Lazarus & Co., 308 U.S. 252 (1939) (No. 56), 1939 WL 48791; Brief for Respondent, *F. & R. Lazarus*, 308 U.S. at 252, (No. 56), 1939 WL 48659.

other than according to their form applied because such treatment necessarily depended on evidence.

Whether recognized or not, the extension of equitable fact finding methods into the Board of Tax Appeals was inevitable because equity is not really a matter of evidence but of two grand divisions: (1) the recognition of equitable estates in property, and (2) equitable remedies and remedial rights.[1095] *Lazarus* was both about equitable estates in property and the equitable remedy the taxpayer might have obtained in state court. The Court asked whether the taxpayer could have gone to a court of equity and obtained the equity of redemption of the property it wanted to depreciate.

In 1954 the reference to equitable evidence in the Tax Court was replaced in section 7453 by a general reference to rules of evidence of the U.S. District Court of the District of Columbia, without the recognition of any significance in the change.[1096] The District Courts have the same equitable powers, and hence evidentiary rules in equity cases, as the D.C. courts had previously. Therefore there is no reason to view Justice Black's formulation in *Lazarus* as having been changed in 1954: the Tax Court can find facts as if it were a court of equity being asked to do equity between the parties to a transaction, rather than between the taxpayer and the Service.

Thus, *Lazarus* shows that references to substance over form and economic substance in tax cases can very comfortably be viewed as proper applications of an equity court's fact finding, and hence evidentiary, techniques. They are applied most commonly to find which person owns or has certain interests in property or income, which usually overlaps with finding whether courts of equity would enforce rights and remedies and property interests contrary to the form of transactions. Thus, the Tax Court does not function as a court of equity, according equity to any party, but puts itself in the place of a court of equity in deciding what rights parties would have. This is not a tax specific process; it is an equitable process. The same analysis should apply to District Court and Claims Court tax cases. But to the extent the doctrines have gone farther and treated the government at times as a party in need of equity, that is an entirely different and questionable use of equity, not supported by *F. & R. Lazarus.*

The Supreme Court also has implicitly employed equitable principles of property ownership, with[1097] or without[1098] referring to equity. But the Court does not always allow equitable principles of ownership to trump tax doc-

---

[1095] Pomeroy, at Vol. 2, § 360.

[1096] 1954 U.S.S.C.A.N., Vol. 3, 4581 and 5263. *See generally* Larson, Tax Evidence, *supra* note 1024, (a thorough compilation, but not addressing any of the issues raised here).

[1097] *See, e.g.,* Helvering v. Cement Investors, Inc., 316 U.S. 527 (1942) (bankrupt corporation's creditors acquired equitable interest in corporate assets, which they could exchange for stock and securities without gain recognition under Section 351).

[1098] *See, e.g.,* Helvering v. Gambrill, 313 U.S. 11 (1941) (ruling that an heir's holding period begins upon the death of the decedent even though his interest does not ripen into possession until distribution by a trustee).

trine: for example, even though a shareholder who is also an employee may be treated as a trustee in equity to return excessive compensation to the corporation, he can hold the funds under a claim of right and be taxed upon its receipt.[1099]

V.E.2. *Flexible Statutory Interpretation*

V.E.2.a. *General*

The second root of the tax specific doctrines in the tax opinions of the lower federal courts is the tradition in American courts of relatively liberal interpretation of statutes generally, as discussed in Ch. I.B. Indeed, what is simply an exercise of statutory construction is often presented as a tax specific doctrine (*Gregory v. Helvering* being so cast, in hindsight).[1100] Even the English courts sometimes interpreted the laws according to "the equity of the statute."[1101] Pomeroy pointed out that this was a spurious meaning of equity sometimes applied "when the provisions of a statute being perfectly clear, do not in terms embrace a case which, in the opinion of the judge, would have been embraced if the legislator had carried out his general design."[1102]

Flexibly interpreting the tax laws in favor of the Treasury usually is based on the presumed or found purposes of Congress, including the general purpose to raise money. Even the conservative Justice Sutherland (who wrote *Gregory v. Helvering)* said about the revenue laws:

> The general object of this act is to put money into the federal treasury; and there is manifest in the reach of its many provisions an intention on the part of Congress to bring about a generous attainment of that object by imposing a tax upon pretty much every sort of income subject to the federal power.[1103]

V.E.2.b. *Purposivism, Textualism, and the Tax Specific Doctrines*

The current state of the tax law reflects the facts that (1) most tax advisors would like to apply the Code under the formalist approach of the late 1800s up to the time of *Gregory v. Helvering* (1935); (2) but the realists would observe that courts do not in fact apply the Code that way, for a variety of reasons that now include reference to the doctrines; and (3) critical legal studies theory might say that individualism (read limits on government, Republicans, big business) favors rigid knowable rules, while more altruistic concern for the

---

[1099] Healy v. Commissioner, 345 U.S. 278 (1953).

[1100] *See, e.g.,* Stobie Creek Investments, LLC v. United States, 82 Fed. Cl. 636 (2008) ("In evaluating a transaction's economic reality, the Supreme Court and the Federal Circuit, along with other courts of appeals, look for a business purpose, beyond reducing taxes, to support a transaction; a transaction without a business purpose lacks economic reality and must be disregarded.").

[1101] Popkin, at 11; Barker, *supra* note 25, at 869-70 (discussing the equity of the statute in the tax context).

[1102] Pomeroy, at §45 (called "the equity of the statute").

[1103] Helvering v. Stockholms Enskilda Bank, 293 U.S. 84 (1934).

public interest favors more flexible standards that would limit the mechanistic provision of tax benefits.[1104]

The doctrines occupy an uneasy position in the current era when the Supreme Court's views on statutory interpretation have tended toward (1) less discretion for judges[1105] and (2) more discretion for the administration.[1106] Although they appear to reflect judicial law making, in fact they reflect deference to the party that always espouses application of a doctrine, the Service.[1107] But acceptance of the new regime is not universal: confusion about the validity particularly of the ESD is exemplified by the logical if unique Court of Claims opinion in *Coltec*, which stated that it would be a violation of the separation of powers to apply a judicial doctrine to the tax Code.[1108] Some say that is a "commonly held belief by certain, more conservative-leaning judges."[1109]

Gitlitz[1110] is an example of the Supreme Court declining to exercise discretion and deferring to the Service in a case of statutory construction, showing "strict" construction and eschewing judicial doctrines (unless you view literalism as a doctrine), or more standard canons of statutory construction.[1111] The author, Justice Thomas, is thought to be in the camp of politically conservative strict constructions on the Court. Chief Justice Roberts perhaps unwittingly identified a likely practical explanation for the trend in Supreme Court interpretation: the Court has had few if any justices in recent years who were not previously judges of lower courts. Such lower court judges are less likely to have been active political figures on the national scene (as were, for examples, Brandeis, Black, Douglas, Fortas, Goldberg, Warren, Stone,

---

1104 *Cf.* Kennedy, *Form and Substance in Private Law Adjudication*, 89 HARV. L. REV. 1685 (1976) (describing private law in this way).

1105 *See* Merrill, *Chief Justice Rehnquist, Pluralist Theory, and the Interpretation of Statutes*, 25 RUTGERS L.J. 621, 624 (1994) (Rehnquist would not adopt a dynamic method of interpretation, but distinguishing him from a textualist like Scalia); Schacter, *Metademocracy: The Changing Structure of Legitimacy in Statutory Interpretation,* 108 HARV. L. REV. 593, 617 (1995) (deference to regulations can be read to mean that judicial resolution of ambiguity is illegitimate policy making); Solan, *Learning Our Limits: The Decline of Textualism in Statutory Cases,* 1997 WIS. L. REV. 235, 263-64 (current Court employs a modified textualism); Sunstein, *Interpreting Statutes in the Regulatory State*, 103 HARV. L. REV. 405, 430, 448 (pointing out Scalia's favoring both executive power and deference to agencies).

1106 *See infra* Ch. VI.D.

1107 *See, e.g.,* Glassman, *"It's Not a Lie if You Believe It": Tax Shelters and the Economic Substance Doctrine,* 58 FLA. L. REV. 665, 670 (2006).

1108 Coltec Indus., Inc. v. United States, 62 Fed. Cl. 716 (2004), *vacated and remanded,* 454 F.3d 1340 (Fed Cir. 2006).

1109 Parillo, *Codification of Economic Substance Doctrine Could Be on Obama Tax Agenda,* 2008 TAX NOTES TODAY 219-5 (Nov. 12, 2008) (quoting Joshua D. Odintz, tax counsel to the Senate Finance Committee Democratic majority).

1110 Gitlitz v. Commissioner, 531 U.S. 206 (2001). For another example, see *United States v. Brockamp*, 519 U.S. 347 (1997) (no equitable tolling).

1111 *See* Cummings, *BB&T versus Gitlitz,* 119 TAX NOTES (TA) 863 (May 26, 2008); Cunningham & Repetti, *supra* note 17, at 17-9 (arguing that the Court should have consulted legislative history in order to determine ambiguity).

Reed, Jackson) who may tend to be more motivated to expand the judicial reach.[1112]

Gitlitz, combined with the lower court decisions applying the ESD, all suggest that (1) any current trend toward literalism in tax is a refuge for judges who are insecure about their feel for the federal tax laws, but (2) any acceptance of countervailing soft doctrines tends to build on itself so that once those applications reach a critical mass (which they did around the turn of the 21st century) the same judges that are relatively unschooled in federal tax are willing to go with that flow, particularly when instructed by the presumably more informed judges, found primarily in the Tax Court.[1113]

As described above under Evolution of the Tax Court (Ch. III.D.1.), the Board of Tax Appeals started out as a conservative body, hewing strictly to the words of the Revenue Laws. The purposivism of the 1930's and 1940's is easy enough to see in the Supreme Court's construction into the reorganization statute of the business purpose, continuity of interest and business continuity requirements.[1114] Yet the ESD arose in the lower federal courts after 1960 and can be traced mostly to a handful of repeatedly cited decisions like *Goodstein* in 1959,[1115] *Goldstein* in 1964,[1116] and *Rice's Toyota*[1117] in 1985.

All three of these appellate decisions affirmed Tax Court rulings, but tended to broaden the grounds of the Tax Court's decision. For example, the Tax Court mostly hewed to relatively traditional tax analysis of debt and equity, as shown in *Estate of Franklin* in 1975,[1118] and *Pleasant Summit* in 1987.[1119] But when the Supreme Court addressed a similar fact pattern in 1978 in ruling for the taxpayer in *Frank Lyon*,[1120] it wrote an opinion that has been read to set loose or confirm a variety of doctrines. Thereafter the Tax Court adapted some of the dictum in *Frank Lyon* to go beyond the more circumscribed grounds it had used in *Estate of Franklin* and to "sham" an entire transaction in 1983 in *Rice's Toyota*. This tendency reached a high point in the high pro-

---

1112 Liptak, *Judging a Court with Ex-Judges Only*, N.Y. Times, Feb. 17, 2009, at A14 (Roberts observed that since 1972 "the method of analysis and argument shifted to the more solid grounds of legal arguments. What are the texts of the statutes involved? What precedents control?" That move, he said, has resulted in "a more legal perspective and less of a policy perspective.").

1113 *See generally* Shores, *Textualism and Intentionalism, supra* note 22, at 53.

1114 *See generally* Bittker & Eustice, at 12.61.

1115 Goodstein v. Commissioner, 267 F.2d 127 (1st Cir. 1959) (affirming the Tax Court).

1116 Goldstein v. Commissioner, 44 T.C. 284 (1965), *aff'd*, 364 F.2d 734 (2d Cir. 1966).

1117 Rice's Toyota World v. Commissioner, 752 F.2d 89 (4th Cir. 1985), *aff'g in part and rev'g in part*, 81 T.C. 184 (1983) (where the Tax Court declined to restrict itself to determining the existence of a depreciable ownership interest and felt compelled to sham the entire transaction, citing Frank Lyon).

1118 Estate of Franklin, 64 T.C. 752 (1975), *aff'd*, 544 F.2d 1045 (9th Cir. 1976).

1119 Pleasant Summit Land Corp. v. Commissioner, 1987 T.C.M. (RIA) 1987-469, *aff'd*, 863 F.2d 263 (3d Cir. 1988).

1120 Frank Lyon Co. v. United States, 435 U.S. 561 (1978) (affirming the District Court, reversing the Court of Appeals).

file "tax shelter" opinion of the Tax Court in *ACM Partnership.*[1121] Similarly *Knetsch* in 1960 has been viewed in hindsight as implying a tax specific doctrine rather than being a standard fact finding case.[1122]

Without regard to the reasoning the Tax Court used, why did the Tax Court flip from strict construction of the early Revenue Acts to purposivism in the so-called textualist period after 1960? That it now follows purposivism has been proved by Professor Shores in a study showing a huge disparity in the Tax Court's willingness to rule against the words of the Code, usually in favor of the government, and the appellate courts' refusal to do the same.[1123]

The explanations probably include the following: (1) the Tax Court *understands* the purpose behind the Code much better than the general jurisdiction judges, (2) the "tax shelter" period from 1960-2000 (and particularly the era of the mass marketed individual tax shelters from 1975-1986[1124]) drew forth a sympathetic protection of the taxing system from the judges most familiar with it, (3) the Tax Court was bound in many cases to follow, and chose to follow, the Second Circuit opinions of Learned Hand, who was thought to embody the purposive approach,[1125] and (4) judges who believe that they are experts in the field are more willing to adapt the statute to the changing needs of the Treasury.[1126] As a result of such factors the judicial doctrines have arisen in recent decades in part through statutory construction.

V.F. Codification of the Economic Substance Doctrine

As a small part of the budget reconciliation act and the adoption of the Affordable Care Act in 2010, Congress addressed the economic substance doctrine by adopting section 7701(o). It defines the standard taxpayers must meet to avoid application of the ESD if "relevant" to the tax benefits the taxpayer claims, and a related section imposes no fault penalties of 20 or 40%, applicable to transactions after March 30, 2010.[1127] The ESD is by far the most significant of the tax specific doctrines discussed in this book, not only because of the partial codification but also because the ESD purports to be a positive rule of law: not merely a fact finding method, or a method of statutory interpretation, or a cluster rule (see Ch. VI.F.), but rather a gener-

---

1121 ACM P'ship v. Commissioner, 1997 T.C.M. (RIA) 1997-115, *aff'd,* 157 F.3d 231 (3d Cir. 1998.

1122 Knetsch v. United States, 364 U.S. 361 (1960).

1123 Shores, *Textualism and Intentionalism, supra* note 22, at 62-3.

1124 For description of the shelters of this period, see Yin, *Getting Serious about Corporate Tax Shelters: Taking a Lesson from History*, 54 SMU L. Rev. 209-15 (2001).

1125 Popkin, at 134-35. *See* Cummings, *Quote Learned but Cite Gus*, 142 Tax Notes (TA) 993 (March 3, 2014).

1126 Popkin, at 238.

1127 H.R. 4872, 111th Cong. (2010) (signed by President Obama on March 30, 2010, making certain adjustments to the Patient Protection and Affordable Care Act, Pub. L. 111-148, 111th Cong. (2010)).

ally applicable precondition for all income tax benefits (subject to undefined exceptions).

"Codifying economic substance doctrine" was the first listed (but not largest) revenue raiser in President Obama's 2010 Budget.[1128] Increasingly similar versions of codification had appeared in many bills in earlier years, finally emerging in near final form in Senator Baucus' substitute for H.R. 4213 in early 2010. The heart of the provisionis the following, now in section 7701(o)(5)(A):

> The term 'economic substance doctrine' means the common law doctrine under which tax benefits under subtitle A with respect to a transaction are not allowable if the transaction does not have economic substance or lacks a business purpose.[1129]

The operative rule of section 7701(o)(1) states that if the ESD is "relevant" to a transaction the transaction shall be treated as "having economic substance" only if it changes in a meaningful way the taxpayer's economic position and the taxpayer has a substantial purpose for entering into the transaction apart from federal income tax effects.

These two core elements (commonly called "prongs") of the codified test reflect two different usages of the term "economic substance," each of which is different from the more common meaning referring to common law fact finding based on what happened economically (e.g., did the nominal borrower really get any money?).[1130] First, section 7701(o)(5)(A) treats "economic substance" as equivalent to the meaningful economic position change prong of the test. But second, section 7701(o)(1) treats "having economic substance" as equivalent to satisfying both prongs of the test. Using the term within the statute in two different ways, when combined with the confusion resulting from turning the economic substance fact finding method (see Ch. VI.E.1.b(3)) into a positive rule of law, are likely to seriously impede the clarifying goal of this statute.

[1128] Department of Treasury, General Explanations of the Administration's Fiscal Year 2010 Revenue Proposals, May 2009, at 25 (hereinafter "Administration Proposal").

[1129] *Cf.* "Joint Comm. on Tax'n, Technical Explanation of the Revenue Provisions of the "Reconciliation Act of 2010," As Amended, in Combination with the "Patient Protection and Affordable Care Act," JCX-18-10, fn. 353 (March 21, 2010) (hereinafter "Reconciliation Act Explanation") ("Thus the definition includes any doctrine that denies tax benefits for lack of economic substance, for lack of business purpose, or for lack of both.") This paraphrase is an overstatement to the extent it encompasses all disallowances on account of lack of business purpose, because that would include the denial of reorganization treatment on account of lack of business purpose; but in such cases the tax benefit is denied because the taxpayer fails to conform with the requirements of the statute as interpreted by the Supreme Court and by regulations, not because it fails the economic substance doctrine, which was not created until decades after the earliest such Supreme Court rulings. Similarly it is an overstatement to any extent "economic substance" is read to mean that the transaction did not actually occur as papered, which is properly viewed as common law fact finding, as occurred in *Helvering v. F. & R. Lazarus & Co.*, 308 U.S. 252 (1939).

[1130] *See infra* Ch. VI.E.1.

The most extensive discussion of the ESD generally appears in the 2009 Joint Committee on Taxation Staff Description of the Administration's Budget Proposals, which drew from various bills introduced in 2007 and is consistent with the enacted legislation.[1131] The Description and subsequent JCT explanations of the bill as enacted, and an earlier House report, state the following important general points about the ESD:

- It is wholly court generated.
- It applies the Code nonliterally only in favor of the government in cases of "tax-motivated transactions."[1132]
- It serves an "important role in the administration of the tax system."[1133]
- It applies even though "the purported activity actually occurred," and therefore the ESD is not an exercise in finding shams or frauds or facts to be other than they appear.[1134]
- It represents a "less predictable interpretive element" to the otherwise objective law.[1135]

Therefore, the Joint Committee confirms the role of the ESD as a substantive rule of law—an uncodified general anti-abuse rule (referred to in other countries that have codified such a rule as a GAAR)—rather than a

---

1131 STAFF OF THE JOINT COMM. ON TAX'N, DESCRIPTION OF REVENUE PROVISIONS CONTAINED IN THE PRESIDENT'S FISCAL YEAR 2010 BUDGET PROPOSAL, PART II: BUSINESS TAX PROVISIONS, 34-71, JCS-3-09 (Comm. Print 2009) (hereinafter "DESCRIPTION OF F.Y. 2010 BUDGET"); *see also* STAFF OF THE JOINT COMM. ON TAX'N, TECHNICAL EXPLANATION OF THE REVENUE PROVISIONS CONTAINED IN H.R. 3962, JCX-47-09, 80 et seq. (2009) (hereinafter "EXPLANATION OF H.R. 3962") (which is considerably shorter than the Description of F.Y. 2010 Budget, but essentially the same where they overlap); STAFF OF THE JOINT COMM. ON TAX'N, TECHNICAL EXPLANATION OF THE REVENUE PROVISIONS CONTAINED IN THE "AMERICAN WORKERS, STATE AND BUSINESS RELIEF ACT OF 2010," JCX-11-10 at 179 *et seq.* (2010) (hereinafter "TECHNICAL EXPLANATION"); RECONCILIATION ACT EXPLANATION 142-56 The House Report accompanying the Reconciliation Bill contains an earlier version of the section. H.R. REP. No. 111-443 (*see bill* sections 452 and 453) (2010). Attached to that Report was the House Ways and Means Committee Report 111-299 (October 15, 2009). The Treasury first cited No. 111-299 in Notice 2014-58, 2014-44 I.R.B. 746, as if it were controlling legislative history.

Other early commentary includes Lederman, *W(h)ither Economic Substance?, supra* note 373, at 389; Jackel, *For Better or Worse: Codification of Economic Substance*, 103 TAX NOTES (TA) 1069 (May 24, 2004); Jackel, *Farming for Economic Substance: Codification Fails to Bear Fruit*, 119 TAX NOTES (TA) 59 (Apr. 7, 2008); *Treasury White Paper on Corporate Tax Shelters, supra* note 14, at Appendix C; McMahon, *Beyond a GAAR, supra* note 19, at 1735; Keinan, *The Economic Substance Doctrine,* 508 TAX MGMT. PORT. (BNA), at Ch. VIII; Cummings, *The Obama Administration and "Codifying the Economic Substance Doctrine,"* 41 DAILY TAX REP. (BNA), Mar. 5, 2009, at J-1; Chirlestein & Zelenak, *Tax Shelters and the Search for a Silver Bullet*, 105 COLUM. L. REV. 1939 (2005) (generally opposing codification).

1132 RECONCILIATION ACT EXPLANATION, *supra* note 1129, at 142.

1133 *Id.*

1134 *Id.* at 143.

1135 This language in DESCRIPTION OF F.Y. 2010 BUDGET, *supra* note 1131, at 34, was toned down to "can be see at odds with an objective rules based system of taxation" in the RECONCILIATION ACT EXPLANATION, *supra* note 1129, at 142.

method or methods of Code interpretations and fact finding. Indeed the JCT Description specifically states that the economic substance doctrine applies in parallel with statutory interpretation and fact finding.[1136]

V.F.1. *The Path of Codification*

Congress finally enacted the partial codification of the economic substance doctrine as a $4.5 billion revenue raiser[1137] inserted into the Health Care and Education Reconciliation Act of 2010.[1138] The enactment ultimately resulted from a combination of influences: (1) the proposal carried a $4.5 billion revenue estimate (over 10 years) and so was used to bring down the cost of the historic health care bill, to which it was attached in the last days; (2) earlier, at least, some taxpayer groups wanted more certainty about the ESD test, which the section supplies to some extent; (3) the ESD was viewed as part of cracking down on abusive taxpayers; and (4) the idea of ESD codification had become somewhat of a political football, first being in favor during the last days of the Clinton administration, then out of favor during the Bush administration, then back in favor as Senator Obama co-sponsored one of the earlier codification bills in 2007, and finally it was enacted during the Obama administration, after having been included in the President's 2010 Budget proposal.

The idea of codifying the economic substance doctrine has progressed in this fashion:[1139]

- On February 1, 1999, Treasury proposed to amend section 269: (1) to authorize the Service to exercise discretion on audit to deny certain tax benefits, being the same list of benefits already covered by section 269 ("deduction, credit or other allowance") plus "exclusion," and (2) to define the appropriate cases as those involving either insignificant pre-tax profit relative to tax benefits or "improper" elimination or reduction of tax on economic income.[1140]
- On April 27, 1999, the American Bar Association Section of Taxation disagreed with amending section 269 and recommended instead codify-

---

1136 Description of F.Y. 2010 Budget, *supra* note 1131, at 35.

1137 The Joint Committee projected the codification and the penalties to raise $4.5 billion over the period 2010-2019. Joint Comm. on Tax'n, Estimated Revenue Effects of the Amendment in the Nature of a Substitute to H.R. 4872, the "Reconciliation Act of 2010," as Amended, in combination with the Revenue Effects of H.R. 3590, JCX-17-10 (Mar. 20, 2010).

1138 Section 1409 of H.R. 4872, 111th Congress (2010) (signed by President Obama on March 30, 2010).

1139 *See generally* Keinan, *The Economic Substance Doctrine, supra* note 1131 , at Ch. VIII; *see also* Korb, *Schemes, Shelters and Abusive Transactions*, 2000 Tax Notes Today 29-61 (Feb. 11, 2005) (for an inside overview of the Service's view of actions against tax shelters and view of codification).

1140 Staff of the Joint Comm. on Tax'n, *General Explanations of the Administration's Revenue Proposals*, 1999 Tax Notes Today 21-36 (Feb. 1, 1999).

ing the ESD to the extent of requiring either substantial net economic benefits or business purpose (at least in situations like section 355 where business purpose is allowed to suffice).[1141]

- On June 17, 1999, Rep. Doggett introduced H.R. 2255, which did not amend section 269 and left the ESD to operate in parallel as a court made rule, but adopted a separate rule disallowing any deduction, loss or credit unless the taxpayer's economic position was meaningfully affected and pre-tax profit was substantial, with special presumptions against (1) borrowings and financial transactions where the economics diverged from the tax reporting, (2) losses not reported for book purposes, and (3) non-economic allocations to tax indifferent persons. The rule would be applied to an overall transaction and also to each separate step, and it attempted to carve out the *Cottage Savings* type of transaction by not applying to losses economically built in before the transaction at issue.[1142]
- In July 1999, the Treasury's White Paper on corporate tax shelters recommended codifying the ESD by creating a positive rule rather than authorizing audit action like section 269, and essentially adopted the Doggett bill.[1143]
- The Joint Committee's 1999 analysis of tax shelters did not recommend a positive rule of law like that proposed in the Doggett bill, but analyzed it extensively.[1144]
- On February 2, 2000, the final Clinton Budget Proposals for FY 2001 effectively adopted the Doggett bill, and would have authorized regulations.[1145]
- Shortly thereafter the New York State Bar Tax Section opposed codifying a positive rule of law.[1146]
- On April 9, 2003, the Senate passed S. 476, the CARE Act, which contained a "clarification" of the ESD that had the features of (1) supplying a definition of economic substance, (2) requiring both a business purpose and a meaningful economic impact, (3) containing a special presumption against income and basis shifting transactions with tax indifferent parties, and (4) attempted to protect lessors of tangible property. But the Act did not specify to which transactions the test would apply.
- On May 11, 2004, the Senate passed S. 1637, which contained a clarification of the ESD that would apply only when a court determined

---

1141 Testimony of Stefan F. Tucker, 1999 Tax Notes Today 84-141 (Apr. 27, 1999).

1142 The Abusive Tax Shelter Shutdown Act of 1999, H.R. 2255, 106th Cong. (1999).

1143 *Treasury White Paper on Corporate Tax Shelters*, *supra* note 14.

1144 Staff Of The Joint Comm. On Tax'n, Appendix II: Description And Analysis Of Present Law Tax Rules And Recent Proposals Relating To Corporate Tax Shelters, JCX-82-99 (Nov. 10, 1999).

1145 Dep't of the Treasury, *General Explanation Of The Administration's FY 2001 Revenue Proposals*, 2000 Tax Notes Today 26-8 (Feb. 7, 2000).

1146 *See* Hariton & Scarborough, *Report on Treasury's Proposal to Codify the Economic Substance Doctrine*, 2000 Tax Notes Today 157-41 (Aug. 14, 2000).

that the ESD should apply and defined economic substance in terms of meaningful economic effect and substantial nontax business purpose; it contained the special rules for transactions with tax indifferent parties, for lessors and authorized regulations.[1147]

- On November 17, 2005, after years of reports of the Bush Administration's lack of support for ESD codification, the White House issued a press release opposing it.[1148]
- On February 17, 2007, Senator Obama cosponsored S. 681, which was essentially the same as the 2004 bill.
- On September 18, 2007, candidate Obama promised to "firmly institutionalize the economic substance doctrine."[1149]
- On October 25, 2007, the Finance Committee reported out S. 2242, which contained the clarification proposal, but without the particularized rules for tax indifferent parties and lessors.[1150] S. Rep. 110-206 contained a list of tax benefits not intended to be affected: debt v. equity; foreign versus domestic corporation; corporate reorganizations; dealing with a related party at arms length; and leasing. On the same day H. R. 3970 was introduced in the House with essentially the same language except it was not limited to court application of the ESD; see also H. R. 2419, which the Senate adopted on December 14, 2007, and which included a codification proposal that was deleted before final enactment of the bill. These bills contained mandatory penalties.
- In 2009, H.R. 3962, The Affordable Health Care for America Act, was passed by the House on November 7 and contained as sec. 562 the codification of the ESD.
- In 2010, The Hiring Incentives to Restore Employment Act (HIRE) contained a revised version of the ESD proposal. It appeared in the Baucus Senate substitute to H.R. 4213, known informally as the "extenders bill." Finally, it appeared in Substitute H.R. 4872, which was passed by the House on March 21, 2010, as the Health Care and Education Reconciliation Act of 2010,[1151] approved by the Senate on March 25 and reconfirmed by the House on March 25 and signed by President Obama on March 30, 2010.

1147 On November 11, 2005, the Senate passed S. 2020 with essentially the same provisions. On September 15, 2006, the Senate Finance Committee reported out S. 1321 with essentially the same provisions.

1148 OMB, *Statement of Administration Policy*, 2005 Tax Notes Today 223-75 (Nov. 17, 2005).

1149 Tax Analysts Document No. 2007-21285.

1150 This version referred to a "transaction (or series of transactions)."

1151 The Report accompanying the reconciliation act was H.R. Rep. 111-443, to which H.R. Rep. 111-299 was attached. The latter was the 2009 House Ways and Means Committee Report that accompanied an earlier version of the bill. *See* John Cannan, *A Legislative History of the Affordable Care Act*, 105 Law Libr. J. 131 (2013).

V.F.2. *Origins of the Economic Substance Doctrine as a Positive Rule of Law*

V.F.2.a. *The Progression*

The ESD is applied as a positive court made rule of law that denies federal income tax benefits that otherwise would be allowed; it is neither a method of fact finding nor of statutory interpretation. Rather it reflects the construction into the entire Code of a general anti-abuse rule. It claims roots in both fact finding and statutory interpretation.

As a positive rule of law the ESD has no proper origin in Supreme Court opinions or in the Code (section 7701(o) just modified a rule Congress neither made or adopted). Its announcement derives entirely from lower federal court opinions, and quite recent ones, principally *Rice's Toyota* (1985),[1152] and *ACM* (1997),[1153] with *Coltec* (2006) serving as its capstone.[1154] The ESD was first identified by that term in a 1988 trial court opinion.[1155] Before the term was used, the ESD coalesced as what should have been limited to a fact finding methodology in leveraged lease cases in *Rice's Toyota* in 1985,[1156] which has been generally recognized as the turning point for the ESD.[1157] *Rice's* appellate opinion did not use the term "doctrine," and the Tax Court opinion in that case referred to a "sham transaction doctrine," which generally is distinguished from the ESD: sham transactions don't actually occur; the ESD can deny tax effect to transactions that did occur.[1158]

After a few losses in the first decade of the 21st century, the ESD has picked up steam as it became more and more accepted as not the last resort of the Service or the lower federal courts, but their first resort.[1159] Arguably the most prominent affirmance of the ESD appeared in the opinion of the Federal

---

1152 Rice's Toyota World v. Commissioner, 752 F.2d 89 (4th Cir. 1985).

1153 ACM P'ship v. Commissioner, 1997 T.C.M. (RIA) 1997-115, *aff'd*, 157 F.3d 231 (3d Cir. 1998).

1154 Coltec Indus., Inc. v. United States, 454 F.3d 1340 (Fed. Cir. 2006).

1155 Georgia Cedar Corp. v. Commissioner, 1988 T.C.M. (RIA) 1988-213; *see also* Yosha v. Commissioner, 861 F.2d 494 (7th Cir. 1988).

1156 *Rice's Toyota*, at 89. The Service issued ruling guidelines for leveraged leases in Revenue Ruling 1975-21, 1975-1 C.B. 715. Taxpayers did not feel compelled to conform to the guidelines because the Supreme Court treated a leveraged lessor that did not exactly fit the guidelines as an owner and lessor in *Frank Lyon*, 435 U.S. 561 (1978). Thereafter, lower federal courts interpreted *Frank Lyon* as stating a two-part test for leveraged leases, which interpretation started with *Rice's Toyota World*. By 1991 an informed observer could state that the two-part test had been devised by the lower courts, based on *Frank Lyon*, to address leveraged leases by requiring the taxpayer to prove either a business purpose or "economic substance." Bates & Cooper, *Structured Tax Benefits in Leveraged Leasing*, J. TAX'N. (1991).

1157 *See* BITTKER & LOKKEN, at 4.3.4A (identifying the case as one of the "earlier cases articulating" the economic substance doctrine); MCKEE, NELSON & WHITMIRE, at 1.05[4][b][ii] (clearest articulation of sham transaction doctrine); Madison, *supra* note 15, at 727.

1158 JOINT COMMITTEE ON TAXATION, DESCRIPTION AND ANALYSIS OF PRESENT LAW TAX RULES AND RECENT PROPOSALS RELATING TO CORPORATE TAX SHELTERS, Appendix II sec. II. (A)(2)(b) and (c), JCX-82-99 (Nov. 10, 1999).

1159 *See* Cummings, *The New Normal, supra* note 769, at 521; Cummings, *Economic Substance Doctrine as Penalty*, 138 TAX NOTES (TA) 1465 (Mar. 25, 2013).

Circuit in *Coltec*, which identified it as having "roots" in Supreme Court decisions, but properly stopped short of attributing it to actual Supreme Court rulings.[1160]

The ESD frequently displaces (or confuses) other methods of reaching the same result, including (1) common law fact finding of economic substance (e.g., *Knetsch*[1161] and *Frank Lyon*), (2) statutory interpretation (e.g., *Gregory*[1162]), (3) other legal doctrines such as refusing to give basis for contingent debt (which *Rice's* could have done), and most importantly (4) Code sections and regulations that Congress and Treasury adopted to deal with tax avoidance in specific cluster areas, including sections 162(a), 165(c), 183, 212(2), 269,[1163] 357(b), 357(c), 482, and Regulation sections 1.165-1(b), 1.368-1, 1.701-2, and 1.1002-1.[1164]

The codified ESD is mostly comprised of its two prongs. This may sound too obvious, but it emphasizes the point that the startling role of the ESD—denying the results that normal law and fact finding allow—frequently takes a back seat to overemphasis on its two tests, which admittedly have real, if spuriously related, roots in the federal tax law. The "economic substance" (meaningful change in economic position) prong is rooted in the ability of the law generally, and the tax law in particular, to discern the true nature of facts, sometimes based on their "economic substance,"[1165] as in *Frank Lyon*. The "business purpose" or tax avoidance (substantial non-tax-avoidance purpose) prong, is rooted in *Gregory v. Helvering*, which interpreted a business purpose requirement into the reorganization provisions (not into the Code generally).[1166] Somehow a fact finding method and the interpretation of the

---

[1160] Coltec Indus., Inc. v. United States, 454 F.3d 1340 (Fed. Cir. 2006). The cited roots were in *Gregory* (*see infra* Ch. III.C.3.a(1)), *Court Holding* (*see infra* Ch. VI.F.2.e.), *Frank Lyon* (*see infra* Ch. VI.F.2.c.), and *Knetsch* (*see* Ch. VI.E.1.e(2)(C)). The cited discussions elsewhere in this book show that these were either cases of statutory construction (*Gregory*) or of normal fact finding. *Coltec* never said that the taxpayer's subsidiary did not assume the liability that resulted in the inflated stock basis; rather it said that the assumption did not have "economic substance" because it did not change anything vis-à-vis third parties because the taxpayer was not released from the liabilities. Therefore, *Coltec* is a classic example of the ESD: the court admitted the transaction occurred in fact and concluded that it met the standards of the Code for the benefit the taxpayer claimed, but denied the benefit because the taxpayer failed to prove its way out of the positive rule of law that the Federal Circuit had created: the ESD. Instead, the court might have found as a fact that no assumption occurred or that section 357 requires more than formal debt assumption of recourse debt from which the primary debtor is not released: it requires an actual intention and agreement as between those parties that the assumer have ultimate liability. Congress codified this view in section 357(d).

[1161] Knetsch v. United States, 364 U.S. 361 (1960).

[1162] Gregory v. Helvering, 293 U.S. 465 (1935).

[1163] *See supra* Ch. IV.A.3. and *infra* V.F.6. for specific discussions of relation of section 269 to the ESD.

[1164] *See generally supra* Ch. IV.

[1165] *See infra* Ch. VI.E.1.b(3).

[1166] *Supra* Ch. III.C.3.a(1).

reorganization section got combined into a bastardized positive rule of law that is different from either of its alleged parents.

Of course the economic substance prong does not perform the common law fact finding function, but rather sets a general standard that is not tailored to particular fact finding: whether there was a meaningful change in the taxpayer's economic position, even if the facts occurred as the taxpayer's form showed them to have occurred. Likewise, the tax avoidance prong does not, as did *Gregory*, even purport to interpret a particular Code provision to require a business purpose.

One particular Code section and its related regulation that have played a large part in the development of the ESD are section 165 and Regulation section 1.165-1(b), which provides:

> To be allowable as a deduction under section 165(a), a loss must be evidenced by closed and completed transactions, fixed by identifiable events, and . . . actually sustained during the taxable year. Only a bona fide loss is allowable. Substance and not mere form shall govern in determining a deductible loss.

Probably the majority of the cases to which the ESD has been applied have involved claimed section 165 losses. The regulation requires bona fides (which hardly requires a specific invocation[1167]), but more importantly states that substance and not form "shall govern." This is a remarkable statement for the Treasury to have made, and should have been accorded more weight than it has been given even by the Service). It says that form never governs when it comes to determining whether taxpayer "sustained" a loss (although it may govern the timing of loss recognition, as in *Cottage Savings*[1168]). Unfortunately, the regulation has been generally overlooked. In 1986, the Tax Court understood the significance of this regulation and cited it to deny losses on paired options in the "London options cases," an early marketed "tax shelter," in *Glass*.[1169] In contrast, in 2009 the Tax Court denied a loss based on similar paired options by proceeding directly to rely on the ESD.[1170]

Thus, the Service and the lower federal courts have transmuted at least three disparate elements—(1) the substance over form cluster approach to fact finding, and (2) the loss disallowance regulation that always defaults to substance where sustaining a loss is involved, and (3) the *Gregory* requirement of business purpose for reorganizations—into something very different: an all purpose positive rule that tax benefits generally will not be allowed when the taxpayer acted primarily for tax reduction purposes, regardless of qualifying

---

[1167] *Infra* Ch. VI.E.1.b(5).

[1168] Cottage Savings Assn. v. Commissioner, 499 U.S. 554 (1991).

[1169] Glass v. Commissioner, 87 T.C. 1087 (1986), *aff'd*, Bohrer v. Commissioner, 945 F.2d 344 (10th Cir. 1991).

[1170] Palm Canyon Invs. LLC v. Commissioner, 2009 T.C.M. (RIA) 2009-228; *see* Cummings, *The New Normal*, *supra* note 769.

under the law and facts: the ESD. The major steps in federal tax history that in hindsight led to the creation of the ESD include, sequentially:

- 1918: Supreme Court relied on substance over form in taxpayer's favor: *Southern Pacific Co. v. Lowe* (finding that a subsidiary's business and income was the parent's business and income).[1171]
- 1920: Supreme Court relied on both substance over form and form over substance in taxpayer's favor: *Eisner v. Macomber* (finding that a stock dividend changes nothing in terms of shareholders' wealth, but that the skin of the corporation maintains the separation of the corporate earnings from the shareholder until dividended in property other than stock).[1172]
- 1933: First federal court use of term "economic substance" (not economic substance doctrine) in reference to finding a fact in a tax case: *American Security & Trust Co. v. Tait.*[1173]
- 1945: First use of term "economic substance" by Supreme Court in a tax case: *Fernandez v. Wiener* (referred to practical realities, in addition to legal effects, of death of community property owner).[1174]
- 1960: Second use of term "economic substance" by Supreme Court in a tax case; but only quoted trial court's words: *Knetsch v. United States.*[1175] In the same year, two distinguished commentators, Professors Eustice and Lyon, observed that the Tax Court had just stepped back (in a reviewed opinion) from some broad language that seemed to deny tax benefits where economic profit was lacking, to allow tax benefits in a case where there was admittedly no economic benefit without the tax benefits and the taxpayer had entered the transaction for the purpose of saving taxes.[1176]
- 1961: Recognition of a "business purpose doctrine," which seems to have reflected Second Circuit Judge Learned Hand's formulations from *Gregory* and other opinions, which were picked up in the *Knetsch* opinion in 1960.[1177]
- 1968: First use of "economic substance" term by Supreme Court to support its own reasoning in a tax case (in taxpayer's favor): *Frank Lyon Co. v. Commissioner.*[1178]

1171 S. Pac. Co. v. Lowe, 247 U.S. 330 (1918); *see also supra* Ch. II.B.2.c(3).

1172 Eisner v. Macomber, 252 U.S. 189 (1920); *see supra* Ch. II.B.2.C.3; *see also* Goldberg, *supra* note 175, at 40 (identifies *Macomber* as an early example of substance over form in taxation).

1173 Am. Sec. & Trust Co. v. Tait, 5 F. Supp. 337 (D. Md. 1933).

1174 Fernandez v. Wiener, 326 U.S. 340 (1945).

1175 Knetsch v. United States, 364 U.S. 361 (1960).

1176 Eustice and Lyon, *Federal Income Taxation,* 1960 ANN. SURV. AM. L. 226, 231 (1960), referring to Stanton v. Commissioner, 34 T.C. 1 (1960).

1177 Summers, *A Critique of the Business Purpose Doctrine, supra* note 522, at 47 ("appreciably affect his beneficial interest . . . the future of this formulation is difficult to predict").

1178 Frank Lyon Co. v. Commissioner, 435 U.S. 561 (1978).

- 1975: First juxtaposition of "economic substance" and "tax shelter": *E. Keith Owens v. Commissioner.*[1179]
- 1976: First use of "economic substance" in connection with apparently marketed individual tax shelter: *Arnold L. Ginsburg v. Commissioner.*[1180]
- 1979: First reference to "economic substance test," which was test for respecting partnership allocations of losses: *Holladay v. Commissioner.*[1181]
- 1981: Professor Alvin Warren writes important article on the "economic profit doctrine."[1182] Also, the term "economic substance doctrine" first appeared in two articles, with references to *Knetsch* and *Rice's Toyota*, (which did not designate it a "doctrine").[1183]
- 1985: *Rice's Toyota* stated two-pronged test for allowing deductions, one of which was "economic substance."[1184]
- 1985: "Economic substance test" term was applied to the "realistic opportunity for economic profit" prong of the *Rice's* rule: *Estate of Thomas.*[1185]
- 1987: Tax Court develops a later discarded approach to individual tax shelters that contrasted "generic tax shelters" with "synthetic tax shelters": *Rose v. Commissioner.*[1186]
- 1988: First federal tax opinion referring to "economic substance doctrine": *Georgia Cedar Corp. v. Commissioner* (issue was existence of true debt; the Tax Court adopted the argument of the government that a cir-

---

[1179] Owens v. Commissioner, 64 T.C. 1 (1975) (taxpayer sold stock of corporation that held nothing but cash; Court held taxpayer received a dividend).

[1180] Ginsburg v. Commissioner, 1976 T.C.M. (RIA) 1976-199.

[1181] Holladay v. Commissioner, 72 T.C. 571 (1979), *aff'd*, 649 F.2d 1176 (5th Cir. 1981).

[1182] Warren, *The Requirement of Economic Profit in Tax Motivated Transactions*, 59 Taxes (CCH) 985 (1981).

[1183] Barella, *Tax Straddle Odyssey*, 63 Taxes (CCH) 609, 613 (1985) (referring to *Rice's Toyota*); Freeman, *Interest, Contingent Interest and Original Issue Discount*, 59 Taxes (CCH) 942, 955 (1981) (referring to *Knetsch*); Ruga, *Sale and Leasebacks as a Tax Shelter*, 1981 Utah L. Rev. 843, 852. But because the "doctrine" is commonly confused with fact finding based on economic substance, the doctrine is often said to be old. *See, e.g.*, Bankman, *The Economic Substance Doctrine*, *supra* note 16, at 11.

[1184] Rice's Toyota World, Inc. v. Commissioner, 752 F.2d 89 (4th Cir. 1985).

[1185] Estate of Thomas v. Commissioner, 84 T.C. 412 (1985).

[1186] Rose v. Commissioner, 88 T.C. 386 (1987) *reviewed*, *aff'd*, 868 F. 2d 851 (6th Cir. 1989).

cular flow resulted in no debt and thus no interest deduction).[1187] Also, first reference to "economic substance doctrine" in *Tax Notes*, in connection with *Georgia Cedar*.[1188] But a major article on the general subject of tax anti-abuse doctrines in 1988 did not identify the ESD.[1189]

- 1994: First federal district court tax opinion to refer to "economic substance doctrine": *Peerless Ind., Inc. v. United States*.[1190]
- 2000: Last reference to Tax Court's terminology for "generic tax shelter" in federal tax opinion: *Internal Revenue Service v. CM Holdings, Inc.*[1191]

The substantial majority of cases in which the ESD has been applied by name since the term was first used in 1988 involve one or more of these features: (1) partnerships and partnership allocations; (2) debt that is not respected; (3) losses or other deductions; and (4) tax indifferent counterparties.[1192] The Supreme Court had never used the term prior to a passing reference in 2013,[1193] has never stated it as a general "doctrine," and has never ruled against a taxpayer in a case that might even conceivably be viewed as involving the doctrine since *Knetsch*[1194] in 1960; indeed *Knetsch* and *Frank Lyon* (which ruled for the taxpayer based on its form) are commonly (improperly) cited as the "source" of the ESD in Supreme Court cases.[1195] The Court

---

[1187] Georgia Cedar Corp. v. Commissioner, 1988 T.C.M. (RIA) 1988-213; *see also* Yosha v. Commissioner, 861 F.2d 494 (7th Cir. 1988) (Posner, J.) (the first appellate opinion to use the term "economic substance doctrine," which correctly observed that the matter was controlled by the profit requirement of section 165. The Seventh Circuit implied that the ESD predated section 165:

> This provision [section 165] can be viewed as codifying the economic substance doctrine for loss deductions, thus placing it beyond the power of judicial reexamination—not that we are empowered to reexamine doctrines approved by the Supreme Court. A transaction not 'entered into for profit' is, at the least (a relevant qualification, as we shall see), a transaction that lacks economic substance. Its only rationale is tax avoidance.).

[1188] *Interest Deduction Denied Because Circuitous Transaction was Mere Transfer of Funds Between Commonly Controlled Firms,* 39 Tax Notes (TA) 970 (May 23, 1988).

[1189] *See* Rosenberg, *Tax Avoidance and Income Measurement, supra* note 378, at 385-89.

[1190] Peerless Indus., Inc. v. United States, 73 A.F.T.R. 2d 1242 (E.D. Pa. 1994), *aff'd*, 37 F.3d 1488 (3d Cir. 1994).

[1191] Internal Revenue Service v. CM Holdings, Inc., 254 B.R. 578 (D.C. Del. 2000), *aff'd*, 301 F.3d 96 (3d Cir. 2002).

[1192] Reconciliation Act Explanation, *supra* note 1129, at 146 (describes the tax indifferent party cases).

[1193] United States v. Woods, 134 S. Ct. 557 (2013) (footnote 1 referred to economic substance doctrine, and the text stated that the penalty applied to "all sham transactions").

[1194] Knetsch v. United States, 364 U.S. 361 (1960); *see also infra* Ch. VI.E.1.e(2)(c) (discussing *Knetsch*).

[1195] *See* Bankman, *The Economic Substance Doctine, supra* note 16, at 7-8 (identifying *Knetsch* and *Lyon* as the Supreme Court's statement of the doctrine); Keinan, *Is It Time for the Supreme Court to Voice Its Opinion on Economic Substance?,* 7 Hou. Bus. & Tax L. J. 93, 98 (2007) (likewise stating that *Knetesch* and *Frank Lyon Co.*, which ruled for the taxpayer, based on form, were the last comments by the Supreme Court on the subject).

passed up its best chance in early 2016 to review three corporate tax shelter cases decided against the taxpayers based on the ESD.The foregoing history shows that the ESD is of relatively recent origin as a recognized positive rule of law and has a questionable pedigree as such. This conclusion likely comes as a surprise to many readers due to the tendency of even the most respected authorities to assume the propriety and history of the ESD. For example, Professor Yin stated in 2002 that taxpayers have been on notice of the economic substance doctrine since *Gregory v. Helvering*, which he said explained why the Service chooses to use it instead of more targeted attacks;[1196] of course, as shown in Ch. III.C.3.a.1., *Gregory v. Helvering* is not a proper cite for the ESD, but rather is a case of statutory construction. The only sense in which the ESD is a doctrine of statutory construction would be to assume that courts construed into the entire Code its positive rule of law (which, in effect, they have).

For another example, Professor Bankman has written the most widely cited academic analysis of the ESD, which also opines that it is largely a doctrine of statutory construction.[1197] He properly observed that it is applied without regard to any "formal discussion of text, intent or purpose";[1198] he categorized it within the purposivist school of interpretation of statutes, but failed to wonder how such a huge piece of statutory construction came to be viewed as the global purpose of Congress; he appears to think that line of inquiry unnecessary due to the ESD's status as a "long-standing common law doctrine" that has achieved "substantive canon" status that Congress presumably has come to approve by its silence. He appears to share the implicit assumption of most ESD proponents: that the lower court judges employing it saw a truth that was hidden from the rest of us, as suggested by Bankman's explanation that the doctrine is "dizzyingly complex,"[1199] rather than just confused. Bankman correctly identified the more likely application of the doctrine to "loss generator" cases,[1200] but failed to observe how that could hold the key to its shortcoming of ignoring the perfectly serviceable Regulation section 1.165-2(b).

In contrast to Bankman's analysis, Professor Warren wrote one of the most perceptive analyses of this issue in 1981, at the leading edge of the explosion of economic substance focus by the Service.[1201] He correctly concluded that "the requirement of economic profit should not be applied to transactions involving provisions specifically enacted by Congress as incentives, and that, where applicable, the doctrine should require only that the pre-tax return be

[1196] Yin, *The Problem of Corporate Tax Shelters*, *supra* note 886, at 421 (he stated that taxpayers have been on notice of the economic substance attack since *Gregory*, but was clearly referring to the economic substance doctrine).

[1197] Bankman, *The Economic Substance Doctrine*, *supra* note 16, at 11.

[1198] *Id.*

[1199] *Id.* at 29.

[1200] *Id.* at 21.

[1201] Warren, *The Requirement of Economic Profit*, *supra* note 1182, at 985.

positive."[1202] Warren traced the development of the economic profit requirement from (1) the sham transaction, based on findings of fact that events said to occur did not occur (for example, the securities the taxpayer purportedly bought with the loan proceeds were immediately resold so that the lender was made whole), to (2) what he called "the central stage in the development of the requirement of economic profit," the *Knetsch* decision, as interpreted by the Second Circuit opinion in *Goldstein*.[1203]

The district court opinion in *Knetsch* used the term "economic substance" in finding as a fact that *Knetsch* did not intend to pay the principal of the debt, had no personal liability on the debt, and had no economic incentive to pay the principal of the debt, and therefore did not owe the debt;[1204] the Court of Appeals affirmed on the view that an indebtedness for interest deduction purposes requires the receipt of money or something of economic benefit, which the taxpayer did not receive from the insurance company lender;[1205] this is the fact finding that the Supreme Court affirmed.

Warren's analysis of *Knetsch* supports the view that the opinion did not authorize a positive rule of law:

> The Court stated that the question for determination was "whether what was done, apart from the tax motive, was the thing which the statute intended." . . . Those assertions suggest that . . . one way of describing the defect in the *Knetsch* transaction is that the activity which actually occurred differed from that reported. On that view the requirement that a transaction have economic substance for tax purposes is surely an uncontroversial application of the general principle of *Gregory* that the substance of a transaction will control over its formal structure. . . . A second version of the defect in the *Knetsch* transactions is that the conversion of a pretax loss . . . into an after tax gain will not be given effect for tax purposes even if the transaction is precisely what it purports to be. There is language in the Supreme Court opinion [to support this view].[1206]

However, Warren wrote that the Second Circuit in *Goldstein* in 1966 is primarily responsible for adopting the second view of *Knetsch* as establishing a doctrine other than just fact finding. Warren is correct about the pivotal role of *Goldstein*, but properly understood, *Goldstein* did the same thing the Supreme Court did in *Gregory*: it purported to construe a business purpose

---

[1202] *Id.* The amount of profit needed continues to be the focus of attention. *See* Luke, *Risk, Return and Objective Economic Substance*, 27 VA. TAX REV. 783 (2008).

[1203] Goldstein v. Commissioner, 44 T.C. 284 (1965), *aff'd*, 364 F.2d 734 (2d Cir. 1966) (which did not use the term economic substance and did not identify any doctrine except the doctrine of strict construction of deductions, on which it relied). Warren also identified application of the doctrine in ownership cases as a separate stage. *See* Hilton v. Commissioner, 74 T.C. 305 (1980), *aff'd*, 671 F.2d 316 (9th Cir.).

[1204] Knetsch v. United States, 2 A.F.T.R. 2d 6115 (S.D. Cal. 1958).

[1205] Knetsch v. United States, 272 F.2d 200 (9th Cir. 1959) (adopted the approach of Weller v. Commissioner, 270 F.2d 294 (3d Cir. 1959)).

[1206] Warren, *The Requirement of Economic Profit*, *supra* note 1182, at 986.

requirement into the interest deduction to carry out the intent of Congress to encourage purposive activities.

The ESD has gained ground as the lower courts largely have refused to do the heavy lifting of appropriate fact finding and statutory construction in the so-called "tax shelter" cases.[1207] In addition to citing each other, in a sort of self-fulfilling prophecy, many of their citations are to broad statements by Second Circuit Judge Learned Hand, who has been identified as the codifier of at least the business purpose branch of the ESD.[1208] However, reliance on Hand is overstated. In his last opinion on the subject in *Gilbert*, Hand dissented from the court's remand to the Tax Court, which had ruled that nominal debt owed the shareholders of a two shareholder corporation was not debt, and stated:

> . . . indeed, I am not clear as to what [the doctrine on which the majority relied] . . . is. To say that it is whether the transaction has "substantial economic reality," or "is in reality what it appears to be in form," or is a "sham" or a "masquerade," or "depends upon the substance of the transaction": all of these appear to me to leave the test undefined, because they do not state the facts that are to be determinative. I would therefore substitute this which seems to me to avoid that defect and at the same time state the doctrine adequately: "When the petitioners decided to make their advances in the form of debts, rather than of capital advances, did they suppose that the difference would appreciably affect their beneficial interests in the venture, other than taxwise?"[1209]

Judge Hand rejected a common statement of doctrines and rather addressed the cluster issue of debt and equity characterization of ambiguous instruments in the related party context. Limited to that cluster, he stated a reliance on a burden of proof approach that required the particular taxpayer to explain how there was any significance to be derived from the formal label he applied of "debt."[1210] This is a considerably more targeted approach of fact finding as contrasted with the economic substance doctrine in its present form. Moreover, it is indicative of the confusion in the area that the Joint Committee explanation of the codified ESD test identified a safe harbor for the very debt versus equity choice that Judge Hand found so troubling (see discussion of profit potential, below).

[1207] *See, e.g.,* Henry Samueli v. Commissioner, 132 T.C. No. 4 (2009) (analogizing the case to *Goodstein,* discussed above and thus avoided finding as a fact whether an indebtedness existed, even though the facts of the two cases diverged significantly). *See* Cummings, *Stock Lending and* Samueli, 125 Tax Notes (TA) 143 (Oct. 5, 2009).

[1208] *See* Cunningham & Repetti, *supra* note 17, at 21-2. *But see* Chirelstein, *supra* note 368, at 440 (chronicling Hand's efforts prior to *Rice's Toyota*). For a critique of Hand's tax jurisprudence, see Cummings, *Quote Learned but Cite Gus,* 142 Tax Notes (TA) 993 (March 3, 2014).

[1209] Gilbert v. Commissioner, 248 F.2d 399 (2d Cir. 1957) (Hand, J., dissenting).

[1210] *See* Chirelstein, *supra* note 368, at 459 et seq.

In contrast, more recent lower court tax decisions rely on the very same broad statements that Judge Hand found wanting. One such influential statement of this view appears in the trial court opinion in *ACM Partnership*, which was prominently cited in the legislative history of the ESD codification in 2010. It placed the focus on presumed congressional intent, rather than finding that a transaction did not in substance occur:

> The tax law, however, requires that the intended transactions have economic substance separate and distinct from economic benefit achieved solely by tax reduction. The doctrine of economic substance becomes applicable, and a judicial remedy is warranted, where a taxpayer seeks to claim tax benefits, unintended by Congress, by means of transactions that serve no economic purpose other than tax savings.[1211]

Earlier, the Fourth Circuit in *Rice's Toyota* seemed to rely on the musings of the Supreme Court in a factual cluster case (sale-lease-loan) *Frank Lyon*, that the Court decided in the taxpayer's favor on the basis of form.[1212] *Rice's Toyota World* stated: "To treat a transaction as a sham, the court must find that the taxpayer was motivated by no business purpose other than obtaining tax benefits in entering the transaction, and that the transaction has no economic substance because no reasonable possibility of a profit exists."[1213]

Rice's Toyota could have reached similar conclusions without reference to business purpose and economic substance through the following analysis (which was cited but rejected by the Tax Court in favor of the more sweeping approach adopted): (1) contingent purchase money debt cannot be added to basis of the purchased property;[1214] (2) normally nonrecourse purchase money debt is not viewed as contingent;[1215] (3) however, if the nonrecourse debt is demonstrably in excess of the value of the property, or for other reasons is not likely to be repaid, it will be treated as contingent in whole or in part;[1216] (4) therefore, the facts in *Rice's* case permitted the conclusion made by the Tax Court that the nonrecourse debt (which exceeded the value of the security by 50%) was contingent because it was too uncertain of payment to support either basis or interest deduction.[1217]

1211 ACM P'ship v. Commissioner, 1997 T.C.M. (RIA) 1997-115, *aff'd*, 157 F. 3d 231 (3d Cir. 1998), quoted in Reconciliation Act Explanation, *supra* note 1129, at 142.

1212 It also relied heavily on *Knetsch* and Goldstein v. Commissioner, 44 T.C. 284 (1965), *aff'd*, 364 F.2d 734 (2d Cir. 1966).

1213 Rice's Toyota World, Inc. v. Commissioner, 752 F.2d 89, 91 (4th Cir. 1985).

1214 Albany Car Wheel Co. v. Commissioner, 40 T.C. 831 (1963), *aff'd per curiam*, 333 F.2d 653 (2d Cir. 1964).

1215 Mayerson v. Commissioner, 47 T.C. 340 (1966).

1216 Estate of Franklin v. Commissioner, 544 F. 2d 1045, 1048-49 (9th Cir. 1976).

1217 The much smaller recourse note was in fact given as a fee and not as part of the purchase price, so it too does not enter into the basis of the property. However, the recourse note was genuine indebtedness, principally because it was recourse and there was no offsetting arrangement, so it will have to be paid and interest paid will be deductible. *Cf.* Gideon, *supra* note 41, at 839-46 (arguing that ownership rather than profit motive should have been at issue in *Rice's Toyota*).

Instead, the Fourth Circuit opinion in *Rice's* gets partial credit for spawning a confusing search for whether the "test" of the newly minted economic substance doctrine should be conjunctive (requiring the taxpayer to prove both economic substance and business purpose) or disjunctive (either one will prevent disregarding the form).[1218] This search played a large part in generating the proposals to codify the test. In fact, *Rice's* can be viewed as simply finding as a fact that the Toyota dealer did not acquire ownership of the computer for tax purposes, in contrast with *Lazarus*, which would wind up with the store through the equity of redemption, and *Frank Lyon*, which would wind up owning the bank building because the form of the sale-leaseback reasonably comported with the economics.

Goodstein,[1219]even though not a Supreme Court decision, along with *Rice's Toyota*, *Knetsch* and *Frank Lyon,* also is frequently cited prominently in support of the ESD. Like *Knetsch*, *Goodstein* is a standard fact finding case in the cluster area of debt characterization, as discussed in Ch. VI.F.6. Thus, the lower courts have promoted common fact finding techniques into a wholesale rejection of form based on a doctrine they created. But this did not just start after *Knetsch*.

As explained in Ch. II.B.2.C.3., substance over form has always been a common law fact finding technique first applied in the federal tax law to the supremely important, but supremely ambiguous term "income." First the courts cross fertilized this approach into other areas of tax fact finding and second they transmuted it into a positive rule of law (the ESD) rather than a fact finding method. An early enthusiastic statement of the fertilization of the fact finding approach appears in *Kimbell-Diamond*[1220] in which the Tax Court stated: "It is well settled that the incidence of taxation depends upon the substance of a transaction. *Commissioner v. Court Holding Co.*, 324 U. S. 331." Consequently it treated a stock purchase followed by a liquidation as a purchase of the assets of the liquidated corporation, which then suited the government because it prevented the carryover of a high asset basis. Ever after, taxpayers relied on the doctrine of *Kimbell-Diamond* to obtain a cost basis in such assets that was higher than would have been the transferred basis, leading to a long and intricate history of legislation, from section 334(b)(2) to section 338 in its original and its current versions.[1221]

Kimbell-Diamond is properly viewed as an example of a judge made cluster rule that could be used to advantage by both taxpayers and the Service,

---

[1218] *See* Klamath Strategic Inv. Fund, LLC v. United States, 472 F. Supp. 2d 885 (E.D. Texas 2007), *aff'd*, 568 F.3d 537 (5th Cir. 2009) (selecting conjunctive, with the majority of the circuit courts).

[1219] Goodstein v. Commissioner 30 T.C. 1178, *aff'd*, 267 F. 2d 127 (1st Cir. 1959).

[1220] Kimbell-Diamond Milling Co. v. Commissioner 14 T.C. 74 (1950), *aff'd*, 187 F. 2d 718 (5th Cir. 1951).

[1221] *See* BITTKER & EUSTICE, at 10.41.

although taxpayers were the more frequent users.[1222] In contrast, the ESD by its so-called "terms" applies only to deny tax benefits and functions not as a cluster rule of fact finding but as a positive rule of law.

V.F.2.b. *A Contract Law Comparison*

The ESD as a positive rule of law relates to the other tax specific doctrines that aim at finding facts in precisely the same way that quasi contracts relate to implied contracts. The common law had all sorts of ways of finding the facts of offer and acceptance, agreement and consent, and became very willing to imply a contract, for example, from the fact that the property owner knew the bricklayer was not building the wall there for his health.[1223]

However, the common law took a very different turn when it imputed a contract where there was no evidence of consent because it was the right thing to do. The law creates the duty for reasons of its own so as to give a remedy to the harmed party.[1224] By analogy the tax law creates a duty to pay tax where the facts would not support that, through the positive rule of law, the ESD.

V.F.3. *Codification Versus Regulations*

If the ESD is such a firm rule of the tax law, why has not the Treasury written it into a regulation? There are three possible answers: (1) Treasury understood that the ESD is not an interpretation of the Code for which it is authorized by section 7805 to write regulations (which is true, because it is a positive rule of law that is not reflected in the Code); (2) the ESD does not have the imprimatur of the Supreme Court, based on whose opinions the Treasury has written many positive rules of law into the regulations (which is also true); or (3) the Service has gotten along quite well, thank you, without too much clarification of the ESD. The last reason is the most likely, but the first two support the view expressed above that the ESD has no firm footing in the law (Supreme Court case law or Code).

If the Supreme Court had defined the economic substance doctrine, then the Treasury could have codified it in regulations as it has done for other Supreme Court doctrines: for example, in Regulation section 1.368-1 (which states several positive requirements for reorganization treatment that are wholly generated by the Supreme Court), Regulation section 1.1002-1(b) (which states a rule of strict construction for nonrecognition provisions generally that is wholly based in Supreme Court case law), and Regulation section 1.451-2 (which sets out rules for constructive receipt of income that originated in Supreme Court decisions such as *Corliss v. Bowers*[1225]).

1222 The Tax Court opinion relied on *Commissioner v. Ashland Oil Co.*, 99 F.2d 588, which was a taxpayer victory based on treating the purchase and liquidation of a corporation as a purchase of the corporation's assets, which became know as the *Kimbell-Diamond* Doctrine. Bittker & Eustice, at 10.41[1].

1223 *See, e.g.*, Cincinnati Gas Co. v. Western Co., 152 U.S. 160 (1894).

1224 *See, e.g.*, Louisiana v. New Orleans, 109 U.S. 285 (1883).

1225 Corliss v. Bowers, 281 U.S. 376 (1930).

V.F.4. *Overview of Codified Economic Substance Doctrine*

The signal features of section 7701(o), adopted in 2010, are these:

- It confirms the existence of a court made positive rule of law that can deny the allowance of income tax benefits to which taxpayers are entitled under the normal application of the law to the facts as normally found, while avoiding the key element of a general anti-abuse rule: when does it apply?[1226]
- It defines the necessary but not necessarily sufficient proof taxpayers must make (unless the burden of proof has been shifted to the Service) to avoid denial of any subtitle A tax benefits resulting from a transaction to which the Service applies the ESD, without imposing any statutory limit on when the government can properly apply the ESD.

Statements in the JCT Description of the 2010 Budget Proposals[1227] and other legislative history speak as if the following statement were a section of the Code (but it is not):

> The Economic Substance Doctrine: A taxpayer whose facts (as properly determined by use of all applicable substance over form methods of fact finding) otherwise satisfy the legal requirements (as properly interpreted) for a tax benefit (whether the benefit is generally viewed as a benefit to taxpayers, or is beneficial to the particular taxpayer only because of the particular facts of the case), shall be denied that tax benefit if (1) the Service denies the tax benefits in whole or part by asserting application of the ESD to the taxpayer's transaction that facilitated the tax benefits, (2) the taxpayer was motivated to carry out that transaction by a purpose to obtain that tax benefit, (3) the benefit was not intended by Congress, and (4) the taxpayer fails to prove satisfaction of the two prong codified economic substance doctrine test.

However, section 7701(o) makes no refence to enforcing the intent of Congress.

1226 Reconciliation Act Explanation, *supra* note 1129, at 153 ("the fact that a transaction meets the requirements for specific treatment under any provision of the Code is not determinative of whether a transaction or series of transactions of which it is a part has economic substance."). However, note 351 to this statement makes the curious statement of offering examples of cases that either did not meet Code requirements or have economic substance.

1227 Description of F.Y. 2010 Budget, *supra* note 1131, at 34-71; *see also* Technical Explanation, *supra* note 1131, at 80 *et seq*. (which is considerably shorter than the Description of the F.Y. 2010 Budget, but essentially the same where they overlap).

V.F.5. *Congress' Purpose for Codification and Potential Effect on Taxpayer Behavior*

The JCT 2010 Budget Proposals Description is the most forthcoming explanation of the legislation and explains several purposes for and effects of codifying the test portion of the ESD:[1228]

- It provides partial certainty to the ESD by resolving the lack of uniformity in applying its two tests (while leaving its applicability largely undefined).
- It increases the level of profit and business purpose required relative to tests used by some courts.
- It possibly will lead to greater Service success in enforcing the ESD due to overruling of courts that allow proof of one prong of the ESD test to prevent the doctrine's application.
- It does not change the "existing judicial framework" under which the applicability of the ESD is determined.
- It does not intend to modify the application or development of other interpretive rules or prevent the Service from proceeding on multiple grounds.[1229]
- It intends to change taxpayers' cost-benefit analysis and deter some aggressive taxpayer behavior.
- It does not aim to displace the common law ESD in cases to which the statute's test is inapplicable (such as individual nonbusiness/income producing activities).

The legislative history of the proposals is relatively silent about the extent to which the codification will change what courts have been doing, despite its indications that codification likely will have cautionary effects on taxpayers. On the one hand the courts' determination of the "relevance" of the ESD to the case is supposed to be unchanged. But on the other hand, at least in those courts that have allowed a taxpayer to prove its way out of an ESD assertion by the Service through one prong of the test, the codification will make that proof harder. Furthermore, to the extent the "substantial in relation" test is harder to satisfy than the reasonable profit expectation test applied by some courts in the past, courts will have to ratchet up their standards for taxpayer escape from the ESD. To the extent the profits test is "clarified," presumably it will tend to make "planning" by taxpayers easier, or at least less uncertain.

[1228] DESCRIPTION OF F.Y. 2010 BUDGET, *supra* note 1131, at 34-71.

[1229] However, the final version of the bill deleted a provision that had appeared earlier:

> Other common law doctrines not affected: Except as specifically provided in this subsection, the provisions of this subsection shall not be construed as altering or supplanting any other rule of law, and the requirements of this subsection shall be construed as being in addition to any such rule of law.

Section 452 of H.R. 4872, RECONCILIATION ACT OF 2010 (Reported to House).

Such aid to planning likely motivated the ABA Tax Section to propose codification in 1999, as cited above.

Much of the effect on the tax system of codification perhaps had already occurred by the time of enactment. The lower courts' use of the ESD has begun to crowd out use of the more lawyerly methods of legal interpretation and fact finding.[1230] Unfortunately codification is not focused on the deductions and losses that the Supreme Court has already targeted for strict construction,[1231] or tax benefits that the Code or regulations target as discussed below, or any particular benefits, but rather leaves undefined its application and the tax benefits with which it is concerned, thus failing to clarify the root causes of uncertainties about the doctrine's application.

V.F.6. *Comparison of Codified ESD with the Most Analogous Code Rules*

The ESD occupies an unusual position in comparison with five other rules that bear the most similarity to it:

1. Regulation section 1.165-1(b) provides that substance always "shall" control form in determining whether a taxpayer has sustained a loss.
2. Section 269 provides that if a taxpayer does certain objectively determinable acts with a subjective principal purpose of tax avoidance by obtaining deductions, etc., the Secretary can disallow the deductions, etc.[1232] The defined acts are (a) acquire control of a corporation, or (b) acquire the assets of a corporation (not already controlled) with a carryover basis.
3. Regulation section 1.1002-1(b) provides that a nonrecognition rule does not apply unless the transaction satisfies the words of the Code and underlying purpose of the nonrecognition provision.
4. As a subset of the nonrecognition rules, Regulation section 1.368-1 requires that corporate reorganizations be analyzed under the step transaction doctrine, that the reorganization be justified by business exigencies (codifying *Gregory*), the underlying purposes and assumptions of section 368 must be satisfied, there must be a bona fide execution of the acts contemplated by the plan of reorganization and a bona fide satisfaction of the Code description of the reorganization, there must not be an abrupt departure from normal reorganization procedure on which the imposition of tax is imminent, and the transaction must not be a mere device that puts on the form of reorganization, and must be motivated by a business or corporate purpose.

[1230] *See* Cummings, *The Obama Administration, supra* note 1131, at J-1; *see also* Cummings, *The New Normal, supra* note 769, at 521.

[1231] *See* Miller, *An Alternative to Codification of the Economic Substance Doctrine*, 123 Tax Notes (TA) 747 (May 11, 2009). For Supreme Court strict construction of deductions, exemptions and exclusions, see *supra* Ch. II.B.2.c(4).

[1232] Regulation section 1.269-2(b) clearly shows that Treasury thought that section codified several court rulings.

5. Regulation section 1.701-2 provides that the Commissioner can recast a transaction to satisfy the intent of subchapter K if a partnership is formed or availed of in connection with a transaction that is contrary to the intent of subchapter K, despite compliance with the literal words of the law.[1233] The relevant facts and circumstances focus on using the partnership to reduce tax liability; the regulation calls for a business purpose, but does not measure the substantiality of profit.

In contrast with these five rules, the ESD in effect provides that if a taxpayer's transaction satisfies the Code requirements for a tax benefit, and the transactions actually occurred as determined by normal fact finding, and presumably none of the five rules above applies, but the taxpayer fails to prove a certain level of profit potential and business purpose, the Service can deny the benefit if it finds the ESD "relevant," which in practice means it thinks Congress would not have intended that taxpayer to have that tax benefit from that transaction.

The only thing that the five rules have in common with the ESD is the authority of the Service to deny the literal application of the law. The ESD is by far the least circumscribed of the rules because (1) unlike section 269 it is not triggered by defined objectively determinable transactions; (2) unlike the other rules it is not limited to a particular type of tax benefit (deductions, losses, nonrecognition, partnership, corporate reorganization); (3) unlike the others it requires a measurably significant profit motive; (4) unlike Regulation section 1.1002-1(b) and Regulation section 1.368-1 it does not have decades of Supreme Court and other case authority defining the underlying purposes of the nonrecognition and reorganization rules; and (5) it presumably requires the Service to determine the intent of Congress on a case by case basis (to determine the doctrine's relevance), whereas Regulation sections 1.1002-1(b) and 1.368-1 and 1.165-1(b) presume that Congress intended nonrecognition and reorganization rules to be strictly construed, and the partnership regulation presumes the same for the utilization of partnerships.

To a far greater degree than any of the most analogous rules, the ESD relies on pre-tax profit as a determinant. Only the partnership regulation directly requires the Service to speculate about the purposes of a broad range of rules, but even that range is much smaller than the potential impact of the ESD.

V.F.7. *The Operation of a Codified Economic Substance Doctrine*

The following discussion addresses the statute and its legislative history without attempting to accumulate the lower court authorities that continue to be decided using the pre-codification ESD. To 2016 no court decisions address the doctrine's application to a post-effective date transaction.

[1233] *See* McKee, Nelson & Whitmire, at 1.05[4] (relationship of regulations to other doctrines).

V.F.7.a. *What Types of Taxpayers?*

The section 7701(o) two-pronged test potentially applies to all income taxpayers except for individual taxpayers whose transactions producing tax benefits are not related to a trade or business and are not activities for the production of income. These individuals were not excepted from the ESD as a common law rule, but are excluded from the section 7701(o) test. The two categories of profit making and business activities track the requirements for deductions in sections 162 and 212. Therefore, "production of income," as in section 212(1) obviously refers to gross and not net income. Presumably activities not engaged in for the production of gross income would include hobbies, family activities, estate planning, charitable contributions, and any other activities for which deductions would not be allowable under section 212.

Therefore, individuals engaged in activities for the production of gross income but not profit will be subject to both the ESD codified tests and the section 183 hobby loss rule, which applies to individuals and S corporations whose activities are not engaged in for profit. Section 183 does not require even a "reasonable expectation of profit," but the taxpayer must have a subjective objective of making a profit.[1234] The ESD imposes a much higher standard on the taxpayer than section 183. Indeed, the JCT Description states that not even "reasonable possibility of profit," which is too high a standard for section 183, is sufficient for the ESD,[1235] even though that was the standard applied in *Rice's Toyota*.[1236] Perhaps the Service will not attempt to apply the ESD to transactions to which section 183 has traditionally been applied (horse training, and the like), on the theory that these represent longstanding choices allowed by the Service and the courts.[1237]

The ESD without the section 7701(o) tests can apply to non-income-seeking activities of individuals. The 2009 Joint Committee Description specifically noted this possibility, although it does not appear in the final JCT explanation.[1238] If and when the uncodified ESD is applied to individuals to which the codified ESD cannot apply, then presumably that uncodified ESD could be a "similar rule of law" for purposes of invoking the ESD penalties.

The ESD literally applies at the level of the taxpayer that engaged in the transaction producing the disputed tax benefit; section 7701(o)(1)(B) refers to the taxpayer's motive for engaging in the transaction. In the case of transactions of partnerships and S corporations, this should mean that the ESD

1234 Reg. § 1.183-2(a).

1235 Description of F.Y. 2010 Budget, *supra* note 1131, at 45; Reconciliation Act Explanation, *supra* note 1129, at 145 (softening the reference).

1236 Rice's Toyota World, Inc. v. Commissioner, 752 F.2d 89, 91 (4th Cir. 1985).

1237 IRS CC 2012-008 establishes internal procedures for the application of the ESD.

1238 Description of F.Y. 2010 Budget, *supra* note 1131, at 52 ("To the extent a transaction is entered into by an individual in some other context, the specific codification in the Administration proposal would presumably not apply but the transaction could still be disregarded under the economic substance doctrine or some other common law doctrine.").

applies to the entity and that the entity must demonstrate the business purpose and the profit potential. This will be a confused area because many ESD cases have involved taxpayers utilizing partnerships to generate losses at the partnership level through basis allocations and the like. Within consolidated filing groups presumably the ESD should apply to each corporate member. However, it is likely that disputes will arise in these areas, and the law will not turn out to be this straightforward.

Another unexplored area is the impact on counterparties to a transaction as to which the ESD is applied to another transaction party. Because the ESD does not depend on the entire transaction being "shammed" as a matter of general fact finding, there is no necessary reason why the counterparty should not be able to report the transaction according to its form (if it is a U.S. taxpayer).

V.F.7.b. *When Does the Economic Substance Doctrine Apply?*

V.F.7.b(1) *Not to Intended Tax Benefits and Longstanding Choices*

Section 7701(o)(5)(A) states that the ESD applies to all "tax benefits" under subtitle A, and gives no indication that there might be exceptions. But section 7701(o)(5)(C) states that the determination of the doctrine's "relevance to a transaction" is not affected by the legislation, and section 7701(o)(1) includes the words "to which [the ESD] is relevant." These competing statements create uncertainty whether Congress is saying (a) that the ESD applies to all tax benefits, but there may be some other undefined ground for making the ESD irrelevant in a particular case on an ad hoc basis, or (b) that there is some general principle by which it can be determined, and Congress intends, that the ESD should not apply to a type of benefits, albeit not defined in the Code. The legislative history indicates that the latter meaning was intended, and goes a good deal farther than the statute. Even though the history tries hard to say that courts should continue to do what they have been doing, it is highly likely that such legislative history as there is will be accorded significant weight by whichever party to a tax dispute it best suits.

The legislative history states that there are "present law standards in determining when to utilize an economic substance analysis, and that the legislation is not intended to change that analysis."[1239] That, of course, is an overstatement if not a misstatement. The history describes two sorts of standards: Congress' intent and purpose in writing the particular benefit provision at issue, and longstanding court and Service practice in allowing basic transactional choices to be made principally for tax saving reasons. Although the discussion here distinguishes these two categories for purposes of analysis, obviously they overlap, because the longstanding choices for tax reduction are traditionally sanctioned tax shelters. Presumably the Service and courts would not have longstanding practices of allowing tax induced choices to

---

[1239] RECONCILIATION ACT EXPLANATION, *supra* note 1129, at 152.

taxpayers without assuming or finding that was Congress' intent or consistent with its purpose.

Congress' intent. To illustrate the centrality of Congress' intent the JCT explanation quotes from a Tax Court opinion:

> The tax law . . . requires that the intended transactions have economic substance separate and distinct from economic benefit achieved solely by tax reduction. The doctrine of economic substance becomes applicable, and a judicial remedy is warranted, where a taxpayer seeks to claim tax benefits, *unintended by Congress*, by means of transactions that serve no economic purpose other than tax savings.[1240] (emphasis not in original)

Determining Congressional intent in such instances is the core uncertainty of the ESD, with or without codification.[1241] Close behind is the uncertainty of whether the ESD really is intended to change the longstanding principle that a statute means what it says, even if what it says produces consequences not intended by Congress.[1242] The 2009 JCT Description and the Senate Report in 2009 state that "if the tax benefits are clearly consistent with all applicable provisions of the Code and the purposes of such provisions, it is not intended that such benefits be disallowed if the only reason for such disallowance is that the transaction fails the economic substance doctrine as defined in this provision."[1243] However, the JCT explanation of H.R. 4213 that passed the Senate in 2010 and the later JCT explanations dropped the qualifier "clearly," and state in a footnote that if the tax benefits are consistent with Congress' purpose or plan it is not intended that the benefits be disallowed.[1244]

The JCT explanation illustrates how Congressional intent can be determined in two ways. First, it draws an analogy between the ESD and section 269, specifically Regulation section 1.269-2, which attempts to describe the sorts of evasion to which section 269 could be applied as transactions producing "distortions" of tax liability when compared with the plan or purpose Congress intended to effectuate.[1245] Second, it cites as examples of Congressionally intended tax benefits the tax credits allowed in sections 42, 45, 45D, 47 and 48, and stated that they would not be disallowed if the tax-

---

[1240] *Id.*, at 142 (quoting ACM P'ship v. Commissioner, 1997 T.C.M. (RIA) 1997-115, *aff'd*, 157 F.3d 231 (3d Cir. 1998)).

[1241] For an example of Congress' intent overriding an analogous loss disallowance rule, see Rev. Rul. 1979-300, 1979-2 C.B. 112 (section 183 did not apply to government financed housing partnership that was expected to operate at a loss).

[1242] *See* Ch. VI.B.1.d.

[1243] DESCRIPTION OF F.Y. 2010 BUDGET, *supra* note 1131, at 44 (quoting S. REP. No. 110-206, at 92 (2007)).

[1244] TECHNICAL EXPLANATION, *supra* note 1131, at 189, n. 414; RECONCILIATION ACT EXPLANATION, *supra* note 1129, at n. 344 ("If the realization of the tax benefits of a transaction is consistent with the Congressional purpose or plan that the tax benefits were designed by Congress to effectuate, it is not intended that such tax benefits be disallowed.").

[1245] RECONCILIATION ACT EXPLANATION, *supra* note 1129, at n. 344; *see infra* Ch. IV.A.1.

payer in form and substance engaged in the transactions Congress intended to benefit.[1246] In the case of a section 47 rehabilitation credit, for example, this should mean the taxpayer will be allowed the credit if it actually invested in the rehabilitated building in form and substance, but would have made no money without the credit and rehabilitated the building solely to make the money allowed by the credit.

Not only is determining Congress' intent the core uncertainty of the codified ESD, it has been and will remain the principal bone of contention between taxpayers and the Service. Standing on the text of the Code and other published guidance, as they commonly do, taxpayers will argue that Congress' intent is reflected in the words of the statute. That is, there can be no intent of Congress that is in direct conflict with what it said. The Service should feel constrained in arguing against the literal meaning of the text of the Code by its own authorities such as Revenue Procedure 64-22 (agents should not adopt a strained construction in the belief that they are protecting the revenue),[1247] and the I.R.M. position that the Service should convey its positions through published guidance and not use litigation to make policy (as contrasted with defending established positions).[1248] If the Service has not previously announced in published guidance that it intends to hold a Code provision subject to the ESD, and there is no established caselaw doing so, and the taxpayer disagrees and pursues litigation, will the Service be violating the I.R.M. by trying to establish that position through litigation?

Longstanding choices. The JCT explanation identifies a second group of transactions and tax benefits to which the ESD is not relevant, not necessarily on the basis of Congress' intent and purpose in enacting a particular benefit provision, but on the basis of (1) "longstanding judicial and administrative practice" applied to (2) "basic business transactions" as to which (3) "the choice between meaningful economic alternatives is largely or entirely based on comparative tax advantages."[1249] The reference to "meaningful economic alternatives" is troubling. It may correctly describe the choice between debt and equity, which can be meaningful alternatives because in the one case the debtor can be made to repay the principal more readily than in the other case.

But it does not correctly characterize the other categories. For one example, Regulation section 1.1002-1(c) in effect states that the differences that occur in incorporations and corporate reorganizations are more formal than sub-

---

[1246] Reconciliation Act Explanation, *supra* note 1129, at n. 344. These types of tax benefits are analogous to the benefits accorded to low income housing projects that the government sponsored, as discussed in Revenue Ruling 1979-300, 1979-2 C.B. 112. Such credits usually benefit taxpayers in conjunction with depreciation, interest deductions, and other benefits. Arguably any transaction to which the listed credits are important should be protected from the ESD; at a minimum the credits should not count as federal tax benefits in the ESD test.

[1247] Rev. Proc. 1964-22, 1964-1 C.B. 689.

[1248] I.R.M. 31.1.1.1.3(1).

[1249] Reconciliation Act Explanation, *supra* note 1129, at 152.

stantial; and yet the longstanding exceptions include organizations and reorganizations. If the Joint Committee thinks the other three examples discussed below offer meaningful economic alternatives (which they frequently do not), then taxpayers should be appreciative and accept the term as not too limiting.

The explanation lists four "nonexclusive" examples of permitted taxpayer choices in this category, including:

- Choice to capitalize a "business enterprise" with debt or equity;
- U.S. person's choice to operate a foreign business in a domestic or foreign corporation (but the footnote indicates that questions still can be asked about whether the corporation is acting as agent for its shareholders, which reflects naivete about the role of agency in the tax law);
- Choice to enter into a corporate reorganization, presumably referring to section 368 (which has its own business purpose requirement in regulations) or organization under subchapter C, presumably referring to section 351 (which does not have a business purpose requirement in regulations);[1250] note that there is no safe harbor for entering into a partnership organization; and
- Choice to utilize a "related-party entity" in a transaction, so long as arm's-length/section 482 standards and "other applicable concepts" (which the footnote indicates refers to the *Moline Properties–National Carbide–Bollinger* standards for respecting corporations and use of corporations as agents by their shareholders, and section 7701(l) conduit regulations) are followed.[1251]

The JCT explanation specifically refused to bless leasing transactions, placing them under the facts and circumstances test, like all other types of transactions.[1252]

The debt versus equity and related party "safe harbors" are odd. Presumably it was thought that debt and equity already are subject to enough, albeit uncertain, controls; and perhaps someone recalled the abortive efforts to define debt and equity previously under section 385. But debt is the principal ingredient in many if not most "tax shelters." Debt figured in the early cattle feeding and master recording shelters (through overstated nonrecourse debt); it supported the tax deductions denied in *Rice's Toyota*; and it was cen-

---

[1250] Explanation of H.R. 3962, *supra* note 1131, at p. 90, made clear that corporate organizations under subchapter C as well as reorganizations are protected choices. This was repeated in Reconciliation Act Explanation, *supra* note 1129, at 152. Footnote 348 itself purports to explain the availability of the choice with the fact that the Chief Counsel will not issue a private letter ruling on a reorganization or a corporate organization unless there is a "significant issue." It also references *Gregory v. Helvering*, 293 U.S. 465 (1935) to show that there are limits.

[1251] Reconciliation Act Explanation, *supra* note 1129, at 153 and n. 349. It is unclear whether the choice of the term "related-party entity" was accidental or purposeful. There can be transactions with related party individuals as well as entities.

[1252] *Id.* at 153 & n. 350.

trally involved in *Knetsch*. Debt not only allows an interest deduction, but more importantly it allows the creation of basis (using the borrowed cash to buy property), without either current payment or current income inclusion, and sometimes without future payment; and basis leads to depreciation and loss.[1253] Therefore, it is important to understand that debt *vel non* is not protected but only the debt versus equity choice in capitalizing a "business enterprise."

Presumably "business enterprise" includes not only entities but also a sole proprietorship and an entity that is disregarded for tax purposes. However, the tax law traditionally has drawn a distinction between business and investment activities, and the word "enterprise" adds emphasis to the likelihood that financing of investments is not protected.

More puzzling is the "related-party entity" safe harbor. The partnership anti-abuse regulation lists related party transactions as a fact and circumstance to consider, and rightly so.[1254] State revenue departments know that holding related parties to arms length standards does not solve the problems of tax shelters involving moving assets and businesses outside of a taxing jurisdiction (which commonly occurs in federal taxation too, in the context of international transactions); and Congress knows this too, as evidenced by the 1986 amendment to section 482. Related parties have been involved in almost all of the principal "tax shelter" cases the government has won—*Gregory, Higgins v. Smith, McWilliams, Court Holding Company*—though not the main one it lost: *Cottage Savings*. Again, perhaps the idea is that related party transactions are already well enough policed, but if they get a pass from ESD application, that is quite favorable to taxpayers.

The reorganization and corporate organization safe harbor is puzzling for different reasons. It lumps together two categories of transactions and treats them as choices that can be made solely for tax avoidance purposes. These two categories have two things in common: (1) the Service will not issue "comfort rulings" on them (as referenced in the JCT explanation), and (2) they both depend on nonrecognition rules. These nonrecognition rules are subject to Regulation section 1.1002-1, which both states that Congress enacted them to make substance control over form and also states that such nonrecognition rules must be strictly construed. It is not clear why reliance on a nonrecognition rule makes the choice for corporate reorganization and organization a longstanding free choice for tax avoidance; the best explanation is that Congress intended the benefits to be electable by form. But they clearly are not electable solely by form because Regulation section 1.368-1(b) requires that a reorganization be entered into on account of "business exigencies," and imposes a variety of other anti-abuse requirements (in addition to those

---

[1253] *See* Cummings, *The Silent Policies of Conservation and Cloning of Tax Basis and Their Corporate Applications*, 48 Tax L. Rev. 113 (1992).

[1254] Reg. § 1.701-2(c)(4) ("Substantially all of the partners (measured by number or interests in the partnership) are related (directly or indirectly) to one another.").

imposed by Regulation section 1.1002-1(b)). Therefore another reason why the ESD should not apply to reorganizations is that they are already hemmed in by sufficient safeguards.

But that is not true of corporate organizations; there is no analog for section 351 to Regulation section 1.368-1 and the host of Supreme Court opinions limiting reorganizations. The Service routinely contends that a shareholder must have a business purpose to utilize section 351, but no regulation says that and it certainly is not a long standing rule of courts.[1255] Taxpayers who rely on the use of what are called "blocker" corporations to separate one person from another or from an activity will rely on the longstanding exception noted for corporate organization.

The four examples of longstanding recognized tax choices are said to be nonexclusive. But such a list bounced around the history of the various bills over several years and these were the only ones that survived. Taxpayers who cannot point to court rulings or at least private letter rulings that explicitly or implicitly approve transactional choices on more than an isolated basis likely will have to argue their tax benefit was within Congress' intent and purpose. So far the Service and the courts have not developed any new "longstanding" choices. However, there may be types of tax planning that do not even fall into the category of choices that need a safe harbor.

- For example, when a corporation is being sold the sellers usually want to sell stock and the buyers usually want to buy assets. The roles might be reversed if the corporation has high inside basis in its assets. Arguably the ESD cannot be relevant to such transactions because they are purely business transactions that have one step, which happens to be either a stock or an asset acquisition, depending on the pricing and the relative bargaining strength of the parties.
- Similarly, the choice to retain or dispose of property with a built in loss should be totally outside the ESD as a single step that is heavily restricted by Code rules on loss deductions, similar to the heavy restrictions on corporate reorganizations.[1256]
- Also, arguably there should be a different sort of safe harbor for intercompany transactions tax benefits that are clearly contemplated by the highly detailed consolidated return regulations under section 1502. Some case law has refused to look behind those rules, even when they

---

[1255] *See* Caruth v. United States, 688 F. Supp. 1129 (N.D. Tex. 1987), *aff'd on other grounds*, 865 F.2d 644 (5th Cir. 1989) (the Service's poster child for this view).

[1256] *Cf.* Cottage Savings Assn. v. Commissioner, 499 U.S. 554 (1991) (which involved an asset swap that had no economic substance, in that it did not meaningfully change the taxpayer's economic position).

do not work as the Treasury might have intended if it had foreseen the particular transaction at issue.[1257]

Facts and circumstances. Finally, transactions that have long been taxed on the basis of "all of the facts and circumstances" present a special problem for the application of the ESD as explained by the JCT. On the one hand, the JCT explanation identifies the most notorious such transaction—leasing—and specifically states that "leasing transactions, like all other types of transaction, will continue to be analyzed in light of all the facts and circumstances."[1258] This sentence cites in a footnote *Frank Lyon* and appears to distinguish leasing from the four transactions involving longstanding tax motivated choices. This suggests that even though the list of four was said to be non-exclusive, it may not be expandable to include particularly fact intensive transactions like leasing (and like *Frank Lyon*).

But walling off leasing transactions would lead to walling off transactions like those that were at issue in *Court Holding Co.*[1259] and *Cumberland Public Service Co.*[1260] As discussed elsewhere herein,[1261] in those cases the Supreme Court recognized that taxpayers had a choice of tax treatment for the sale of corporate property by arranging who negotiated the sale. That choice seems to be exactly the sort of "longstanding judicial practice" allowing choice between "meaningful economic alternatives" based "largely or entirely on comparative tax advantage" to which the JCT explanation said the ESD is not relevant. Why are leasing transactions any less so, other than the failure of the Supreme Court to leave us with such a neat factual test (*Frank Lyon* listed 27 factors)?

The most reasonable explanation is that the ESD is not relevant at all to fact intensive clusters like these, but instead the Service and the courts must properly ascertain the facts. The same could be said of related party transactions, which the JCT explanation notes are policed by section 482 and other means. At least taxpayers should contend for "facts and circumstances" exceptions to the ESD, which really boils down to reverting such cases back to fact finding cases, rather than cases controlled by this positive rule of law.

Impact on legal opinions. Legal opinions on the potential applicability of the ESD must address relevance and the "prongs," with the latter being somewhat more objective under section 7701(o), but not the former. Once the ESD is found "relevant" to the transaction and the tax benefit at issue, the taxpayer frequently will face a difficult task of proving out of the two-pronged statu-

---

[1257] Such an approach would be consistent with Woods Inv. Co. v. Commissioner, 85 T.C. 274 (1985), *acq.* 1986-2 C.B. 1; United Dominion Industries, Inc. v. United States, 532 U.S. 822, 839 (2001).

[1258] Reconciliation Act Explanation, *supra* note 1129, at 153 & n. 350 (citing Frank Lyon Co. v. United States, 435 U.S. 561 (1978).

[1259] Commissioner v. Court Holding Co., 324 U.S. 331 (1945).

[1260] United States v. Cumberland Pub. Serv. Co., 338 U.S. 451 (1950).

[1261] *Infra* Ch. VI.F.2.e.

tory test if either (a) the substantiality of the expected profit is doubtful, or (b) the scope of the transaction to which the ESD profits test is applied is narrow (a single step that is not profitable).[1262] When the benefit is disallowed by reason of the transaction failing the ESD test, the no fault penalties apply and a legal opinion cannot prevent or lessen those penalties (although proper disclosure of the transaction can avoid the 40% penalty). Therefore, legal opinions on the ESD will tend to have a cliff effect, *i.e.*, they principally will have to focus on relevance of the ESD and if they are wrong in opining that the ESD is not relevant, the taxpayer may well face not only the tax liability but the no fault penalties.

Opinions addressing the relevance issue will need to rely on two helpful elements of the statute and its legislative history, as discussed above and below: (1) the view that "similar rule of law" is to be narrowly construed for purposes of the penalty,[1263] and (2) the longstanding administrative practice exception that can make the ESD irrelevant, in addition to the Congressional intent exception.

V.F.7.b(2) *Relevance of Flunking the Section 7701(o) Tests*

Can a transaction be subject to the ESD simply by virtue of failing the codified tests? No. If the transaction fails the test it is not necessarily subject to the ESD: the legislative history shows the existence of a super test: whether the tax benefits are consistent with the words and purposes of the Code, in which case the ESD is not "relevant" and does not apply.[1264]

However, in practice there may be a powerful incentive for the Service to negatively view a transaction that the agent believes lacks both subjective and objective business purpose. Moreover, the consistent with the Code purposes test is not in the statute, but rather relies on legislative history and presumably also on earlier caselaw. It remains to be seen whether taxpayers can prevail when (1) the Service asserts the ESD for the practical reason that the agent determines the two prongs of the statutory test have been flunked, and (2) the taxpayer cannot prove out of the tests. These situations, should they arise, will put the "intent of Congress" standard to the test.

V.F.7.b(3) *Benefits Otherwise Allowed*

The explanations of the codification proposals describe the ESD as applicable to deny tax benefits that are otherwise available under the law and facts as normally determined.[1265] The JCT explanation states: "Also, the fact that a

---

[1262] See Notice 2014-58, 2014-44 I.R.B. 746, which leaves the scope of the transaction in total confusion, but likely means it is whatever part of the transaction the agent does not like. Clarifying Notice 2010-62, 2010-40 I.R.B. 411.

[1263] *See* Ch. V.F.7.d.

[1264] Description of F.Y. 2010 Budget, *supra* note 1131, at 44.

[1265] Technical Explanation, *supra* note 1131, at 190; Reconciliation Act Explanation, *supra* note 1129, at 153.

transaction meets the requirements for specific treatment under any provision of the Code is not determinative of whether a transaction or series of transactions of which it is a part has economic substance."[1266]

However, in practice courts show a tendency to apply the ESD first rather than last,[1267] and to reject what appear to be plausible interpretive and fact finding methods that might lead to the same result as the ESD.[1268] These tendencies exist despite the power and sometimes duty of the trial court, particularly the Tax Court to decide a case on the proper grounds rather than the grounds argued by the parties, including the Service.[1269]

V.F.7.c. *How Does Test Apply?*

V.F.7.c(1) *Burden of Proof*

Section 7701(o) does not mention burden of proof, but rather the burden falls on the taxpayer under the normal rules allocating burden of proof and presuming the correctness of assessments.[1270] Therefore, if the ESD dispute occurs in the Tax Court, the burden of disproving the ESD as a ground of the assessment is on the taxpayer, and shifts to the Service only if the Service raises the ESD as a "new matter" under Tax Court Rule 142(a)(1).[1271] In refund litigation the taxpayer apparently always has the burden of proof with respect to ESD, once the government has asserted it as a defense (or ground for assessment if the taxpayer sued for refund of an assessed tax).[1272] Absent assertion of the ESD as a ground for its position by the Service, the taxpayer neither should have to satisfy the test nor should the ESD penalty be applicable.[1273]

Neither the courts nor the codification proposals have indicated that the taxpayer's burden is merely one of going forward or making a *prima facie* case, or is different in any way from the normal burden of proof carried by

---

1266 Reconciliation Act Explanation, *supra* note 1129, at 153.

1267 *See, e.g.*, Country Pine LLC v. Commissioner, 2009 T.C.M. (RIA) 2009-251 (failed to analyze Service's legal arguments); Cummings, *The New Normal, supra* note 769, at 521.

1268 *See, e.g.*, Am. Elec. Power Co. v. United States, 326 F.3d 737, 741 (6th Cir. 2003) (rejected trial judge's "sham in fact" finding of fact, while applying the economic substance doctrine).

1269 Cummings, *The Tax Court's Duty to Apply the Properly Applicable Law*, 23 Daily Tax Rep. (BNA), Feb. 5, 2010, at J-1. *See also* Beghe, *Reflections on the Public and Private Practice of Tax Law*, 82 Taxes (CCH) 205, 206 (2004) (agreeing that it is appropriate to decide cases on grounds not argued by the parties).

1270 *See infra* Ch. VI.E.4.

1271 *See* Claymount Invs., Inc. v. Commissioner, 2005 T.C.M. (RIA) 2005-254 (the Service conceded that because it raised the ESD as a new matter in the case the Service had the burden of proof).

1272 *See, e.g.*, Jade Trading LLC v. United States, 80 Fed. Cl. 11 (2007), *aff'd.*, 2010 U.S. App. LEXIS 5901 (Fed. Cir. Mar. 23, 2010) (citing Coltec Indus., Inc. v. United States, 454 F.3d 1340 (Fed. Cir. 2006); Wells Fargo & Co. v. United States, 105 A.F.T.R. 2d 377 (Fed. Cl. 2010); Southgate Master Fund, LLC v. United States, 104 A.F.T.R. 2d 6053 (N.D. Tex. 2009).

1273 Description of F.Y. 2010 Budget, *supra* note 1131, at 47.

the taxpayer, as discussed in Ch. VI.E.4. Rather, the taxpayer has the ultimate burden of proving the facts that meet the two-pronged test, and if it fails, the ESD applies, unless a court finds the case is one to which the ESD does not apply at all, as a matter of law (*i.e.,* not "relevant"). The taxpayer cannot obtain a letter ruling on the ESD.[1274]

As discussed in Ch. VI.E.4., section 7491 can shift the burden of proof of factual issues to the Service if certain conditions of record keeping and audit cooperation are met;[1275] it applies only to entities with less than 500 employees and less than $7 million in net worth.[1276] Peculiarly enough, many "tax shelter" entities have little net worth and virtually no employees and might qualify for the burden shifting rule.[1277] However, courts have found creative ways to avoid the application of section 7491.[1278]

Before the controversy reaches court, or if it does not reach court at all, presumably the Service will give the taxpayer the opportunity to prove to the Service the satisfaction of the tests. The procedure for obtaining technical advice on the matter from the Chief Counsel's National Office might be used;[1279] factual disputes normally are addressed in IRS Appeals. In any event the taxpayer will have difficulty disproving the Service's assertion of the ESD to the Service because, as the Joint Committee has described it, the entire ESD "arguably is ultimately subjective."[1280]

Whether the ESD is an issue of fact or law is discussed in Chapter VI.E.3.c.

V.F.7.c(2) *Scope of the Transaction*

Identifying the transaction to which the statutory ESD test must be applied may turn out to be the most difficult issue to be faced by business taxpayers concerning the codified ESD. In contrast, marketed "tax shelters" that were used by many individual taxpayers in the past often had relatively little realistic profit potential (certainly not "substantial" in relation to the tax savings), regardless of how they were parsed. But business taxpayers commonly pursue undeniably potentially profitable (or at least business related) transactions

---

1274 2016-3, 2016-1 I.R.B. 126, sec. 3.02(1).

1275 *See* Long Term Capital Holdings v. United States, 330 F. Supp. 2d 122 (D. Conn. 2004), *aff'd,* 150 F. App'x 40 (2d Cir. 2005) (refusing to apply section 7491 on grounds of lack of audit cooperation); Nichols v. Commissioner, 79 F. App'x 282 (9th Cir. 2003) (same).

1276 Economic substance doctrine cases in which the court considered section 7491 included *Long Term Capital Holdings*, 330 F. Supp. 2d at 122 (rejecting section 7491 because taxpayer did not cooperated on audit); Palm Canyon Invs. LLC v. Commissioner, 2009 T.C.M. (RIA) 2009-288 (court discussed section 7491 but the taxpayer did not assert it); Country Pine Fin., LLC v. Commissioner, 2009 T.C.M. (RIA) 2009-251 (court considered applicability but taxpayer did not assert it).

1277 *See, e.g., Palm Canyon*, 2009 T.C.M. (RIA) 2009-228 (no employees and net worth less than $100,000).

1278 *See, e.g., Jade Trading*, 80 Fed. Cl. at 11 (ruling the profit potential prong of the ESD test to be a legal issue).

1279 Rev. Proc. 2016-2, 2016-1 I.R.B. 102.

1280 DESCRIPTION OF F.Y. 2010 BUDGET, *supra* note 1131, at 44.

(e.g., all merger and acquisition activities) that carefully utilize many steps purely for tax minimization purposes.

If the ESD is focused on one step in such a multi step business transaction, and if the taxpayer cannot justify that step under the two-pronged test, then the taxpayer's only escape will be to argue lack of "relevance" of the ESD to the step, which must be based either on (a) Congress' intent that the law should produce the result the taxpayer desires, or on (b) identifying the step as one of those longstanding choices recognized and allowed by the Service and the courts. If the menu of longstanding choices is viewed as being a short one (four nonexclusive examples are listed in the Joint Committee explanation), then the focus of analysis on Congress' intent as to isolated steps will be intense.

The ESD two-pronged test asks whether a taxpayer had a substantial nontax purpose for entering into "the transaction" and whether "the transaction" changes in a meaningful nontax way the taxpayer's economic position. Presumably "the transaction" is the one referred to in section 7701(o)(5)(A) with respect to which the taxpayer claims tax benefits under subtitle A. Section 7701(o)(5)(D) defines a transaction as including a series of transactions. The only reason to define a term in reference to itself in this fashion is to make sure that a step in a larger transaction can be viewed as the pertinent transaction. If that had not been the intent of the draftspersons, they could have made the meaning clearer (and different) by stating that a transaction includes a series of steps. By defining transaction as it does, section 7701(o), evidently intentionally, allows the possibility that its test can be applied to a step in a series of steps making up a larger transaction.

Indeed, the legislative history supports that view.[1281] Also, the Joint Committee explained the legislation as not affecting:

> . . . the court's ability to aggregate, disaggregate, or otherwise recharacterize a transaction when applying the doctrine. For example, the provision reiterates the present-law ability of the courts to bifurcate a transaction in which independent activities with non-tax objectives are combined with an unrelated item having only tax-avoidance objectives in order to disallow those tax-motivated benefits.[1282]

The Joint Committee footnoted this statement with a caselaw quote isolating the particular step that afforded the high basis and produced the tax benefit in a larger integrated transaction.[1283] Likewise, the four safe harbors for longstanding transactional choices recited by the legislative history describe

---

[1281] *See* Reconciliation Act Explanation, *supra* note 1129, at 153 (" . . . whether a transaction or series of transactions of which it is a part has economic substance.").

[1282] Explanation of H.R. 3962, *supra* note 1131, at 91; Reconciliation Act Explanation, *supra* note 1129, at 153.

[1283] Reconciliation Act Explanation, *supra* note 1129, at n. 352 (quoting Coltec Indus., Inc. v. United States, 454 F.3d 1340 (Fed. Cir. 2006), *vacating and remanding* 62 Fed. Cl. 716 (2004) (slip opinion at 123-24, 128)).

transactions that normally are a step in a larger integrated transaction: capitalizing a business with debt or equity; organizing a corporation; operating abroad in a branch or a foreign corporation; utilizing a related party.[1284] Because of these conflicting signals, it is very likely that the Service will assert, when it suits its needs (which may be often), that the ESD test must be satisfied by any isolated step of a multi step transaction.[1285]

Conversely, there are important reasons to interpret the section 7701(o) ESD tests as applying to the integrated series of transactions of which the tax benefit generating transaction is one step.

- First, section 7701(o)(5)(D) says that the series of transactions is a transaction, and the statute applies to transactions.
- Second, as discussed in Ch. II.C.2.a., the Supreme Court and other courts frequently have reaffirmed taxpayers' rights to arrange their transactions so as to produce the least tax liability. To access this right taxpayers necessarily must be able to choose specific steps to obtain certain tax benefits, even though the specific steps were not required to accomplish the larger business purpose.
- Moreover, the bedrock principle allowing tax planning is consistent with the fact of life that profit making transactions commonly involve offsetting benefits and burdens, most of which result from different steps or parts of the transactions.

For example, the Supreme Court has affirmed such tax planning in these important decisions:

- In *Cumberland Public Service Co.*, the corporate officers understood that the corporation could not sell the property if two tier taxation of gain were to be avoided.[1286] Therefore, they arranged for the corporation to distribute the property to the shareholders, who then negotiated to sell and did sell the property, according to the Court.
- In *General Utilities*, which was very much like *Cumberland*, the corporation distributed stock that someone wanted to buy, so that the corporation would not recognize the gain.[1287]
- In *Frank Lyon Co.*, the property owner sold its property to Frank Lyon and allowed Frank Lyon to build a building on the property and lease it back to the property owner.[1288] If the property owner had had to justify its initial sale of the property under the ESD test, it might have failed.

[1284] *Id.* at 152.

[1285] *See* Notice 2014-58, 2014-44 I.R.B. 746, clarifying Notice 2010-62, 2010-40 I.R.B. 411.

[1286] United States v. Cumberland Pub. Serv. Co., 338 U.S. 451 (1950).

[1287] General Utils. & Operating Co. v. Helvering, 296 U.S. 200 (1935).

[1288] Frank Lyon Co. v. United States, 435 U.S. 561 (1978).

- In *Cottage Savings*, the S&L's were encouraged to swap their interests in identical mortgage pools solely for the purpose of producing deductible losses.[1289]
- In *Brown*, the taxpayer was allowed to structure into a charitable deduction, while shifting the tax cost of a corporate liquidation to a charity (which did not pay tax) and keeping use of the donated property.[1290]
- In *Byrum*, the Court ruled that careful adherence to the gift/estate tax rules precluded inclusion in the estate based on substance.[1291]
- In *Consumer Life*, reinsurance contracts that kept premiums out of taxpayer's income were respected, despite the fairly insubstantial nature of the distinction created by the contract.[1292]

A broad definition of the transaction normally will be best for the taxpayer that is attempting to satisfy section 7701(o)(1).[1293] However, in many cases the Service tries to focus the ESD on an isolated step of a larger transaction, because taxpayers are less likely to be able to show a business purpose and profit potential for a particular steps in a multi step transaction; in addition, the selection of what appears to an auditor to be an unnecessary or unusual step is usually what triggers a deficiency assessment based on the ESD and supports arguments that Congress would not have intended such a result.

In fact the scope of the transaction at issue frequently has been in dispute in ESD cases.[1294] This usually comes up in the context of asking how broadly must one look to find profit in the transaction (but also can be relevant to analysis of whether a longstanding permitted choice exists or Congress intended the single step to produce the tax benefit claimed). Courts have applied the ESD to a single step in a larger transaction,[1295] but at least one court has refused "slicing and dicing."[1296] The important *ACM* decision refused to allow the taxpayer to rely on profit from a step the taxpayer claimed to be related

---

[1289] Cottage Savings Assn. v. Commissioner, 499 U.S. 554 (1991)

[1290] Commissioner v. Brown, 380 U.S. 563 (1965).

[1291] United States v. Byrum, 408 U.S. 125 (1972).

[1292] United States v. Consumer Life Ins. Co., 430 U.S. 725 (1977).

[1293] *See, e.g.*, ACM P'ship v. Commissioner, 1997 T.C.M. (RIA) 1997-115, *aff'd*, 157 F.3d 231 (3d Cir. 1998) (in which taxpayer claimed a variety of incidental economic benefits from its strategy to employ section 453 regulations to produce losses).

[1294] *See generally* Hariton, *The "Frame" Game: How Defining the Transaction Decides the Case*, 63 Tax Law. 1, 9 (2009) (stating that identifying the transaction is the battleground where the case is won or lost). For the willingness of the Supreme Court to finely separate the giving of property from the receiving of the same property in the estate tax context, see United States v. Burnison, 339 U.S. 87, 91 (1950) (finding constitutional California's law preventing devising realty to the United States government).

[1295] *See, e.g.*, Coltec Indus., Inc. v. United States, 454 F.3d 1340 (Fed. Cir. 2006).

[1296] Shell Petroleum, Inc. v. United States, 102 A.F.T.R. 2d 5085 (S.D. Tex. 2008).

to the questioned step because the court thought those profits did not "arise from" the questionable step.[1297]

Taxpayers should be particularly assisted in arguing for a broad scope of the transaction when the integrated transaction has some relation to their usual business activities. Indeed, the best cases for taxpayers are likely to be those in which the taxpayer was doing something in the course of its ordinary business, but in a way that produced a surprisingly beneficial tax result. For example, selection of the broader scope can be of more benefit to business taxpayers who find a tax saving method of doing what they were going to do anyway for business reasons;[1298] however, the benefit of the wider scope can be modest.[1299] Yet lack of an ordinary business connection should not be dispositive. Section 7701(o) does not make such a relationship determinative, likely because Congress realized that business taxpayers will always say they are in business to make money, however that might be accomplished. That is why the statute's tests speak in terms of economic profit. Therefore, taxpayers may encounter the most difficulty with integration in transactions like the Service's listed transactions in which individual taxpayers enter into various sorts of hedging or straddle transactions allegedly to make a profit, but practically to generate uneconomic losses.[1300]

V.F.7.c(3) *Economic Position Prong of the Test*

Section 7701(o)(1) states that a transaction shall be treated as "having economic substance" only if the transaction changes in a meaningful way the taxpayer's economic position, apart from federal (and related state) income tax effects (and satisfies the second prong of the test). This literally says that such proof is necessary but not sufficient to cause the transaction to pass the ESD test. However, no one has suggested that in practice such proof will not be sufficient.

[1297] ACM P'ship v. Commissioner, 157 F.3d 231 (3d Cir. 1998). Conversely, in *Salina Partnership LP v. Commissioner*, 80 T.C.M. (CCH) 686, 2000 T.C.M. (RIA) 2000-352, the court refused to stop the analysis with the early phantom income from an investment, where the later years of the same investment produced market rate returns (and also refreshed the investor's loss); the later returns clearly resulted from the investment that was at issue. *Cf.* Rev. Rul. 1980-284, 1980-2 C.B. 117 (denying section 351 treatment because of the character of an integrated transaction) (revoked by Rev. Rul. 1984-71, 1984-1 C.B. 106 (stating that being part of the larger acquisitive transaction did not taint the section 351 exchange)).

[1298] *See, e.g., Shell Petroleum, Inc.*, 102 A.F.T.R. 2d 2008-5085. Indeed, *Gregory v. Helvering*, 293 U.S. 465 (1935) is this type of case, but the Supreme Court did not rule for the government based on the ESD. But this has not worked out for most other taxpayers. *See* Cummings, *The Supreme Court's Economic Substance Doctrine Opinion*, 149 Tax Notes (TA) 1295 (Dec. 7, 2015) (discussing ESD losses by banks engaged in activities banks customarily do).

[1299] *See, e.g.,* Rev. Proc. 2002-67, 2002-2 C.B. 733 (describing settlement initiative for liability management company tax shelters; taxpayers involved did have legitimate need to manage their employee health care and other liabilities, but the issue was whether and why that need justified the loss generation transactions engaged in).

[1300] *See, e.g.,* Notice 2000-44, 2000-2 C.B. 255 (son of boss listed transactions).

The taxpayer can prove a meaningful change occurred by proving profit potential as described below, or some other substantial economic change. Where the taxpayer relies on profit potential to prove meaningful economic change, and no profit actually results, presumably the statute intends the meaningful position change prong has been satisfied.

The transaction at issue is the taxpayer's transaction, and the required meaningful position change is the taxpayer's position. What if the taxpayer who entered the transaction is an entity and the person whose economic position is changed is an owner, or affiliate, or a relative or a counterparty? The confusion that can arise in such cases is akin to that of identifying partnership items for purposes of applying the right procedures for adjustment; a partner's basis in the interest may not be a partnership item.[1301]

V.F.7.c(3)(a) *Profit Potential as Meaningful Change*

The "special rule" of section 7701(o)(2) for determining meaningful economic position change based on profit potential is likely to be the general rule. It does not state that proof of substantial profit potential will satisfy the prong but rather states that such proof will be taken into account in determining whether either prong is satisfied, if a threshold proof is made. The statutory threshold is proof that the present value of "reasonably expected pre-tax profits from the transaction" must be "substantial" in relation to "expected net [federal] tax benefits" arising from the transaction if it were respected. Section 7701(o)(3) provides that state or local income tax effects shall be treated as federal income tax effects if they are related to the federal effects.

Thus, the special rule focuses on a relationship of amounts and not an absolute dollar figure.[1302] The statute does not define "substantial," but the JCT explanation indicates that the term imports a higher threshold than the "reasonable possibility of profit" test that some courts had applied.[1303] Businesses commonly select discount rates to evaluate the profitability of potential undertakings, and it would seem that proof based on such rates actually used by the taxpayer in contemporaneous transactions would be appropriate. The more difficult issues are determining:

- What is the scope of the transaction whose profit potential and tax savings are measured (discussed in Ch. V.F.7.c(2));
- What is "reasonably expected," as to the pre-tax profits and what is "expected" as to the tax benefits (the section seems to anticipate that the taxpayer will have a firmer grasp on the expected tax benefits than on the profits);
- When one amount is "substantial in relation" to the other; and

---

[1301] *See, e.g.*, Petaluma FX Partners, LLC v. Commissioner, 131 T.C. 84 (2008), *aff'd in part and rev'd in part*, 591 F.3d 649 (D.C. Cir. 2010).

[1302] Reconciliation Act Explanation, *supra* note 1129, at 155 ("does not require or establish a minimum return").

[1303] *Id.* at 356.

- What amounts go into the netting.

Reasonably expected. By phrasing the "special rule" in terms of reasonable expectations, the section imposes a hypothetical analysis as of the date of the transaction, and does not require the actual results to bear out the expectations. In fact for some time most taxpayers who were entering into large but questionable transactions producing tax benefits have made profit projections before the transactions, some of which have been quite elaborate and supported by expert analysis. The "special rule" provides even more reason for that sort of preparatory planning, and allows it to be better informed. The taxpayer may face more difficulty if it both made no prior profit projection and entered into a transaction that was outside the normal course of its business or of its business decision making, as has been the case with some marketed "tax shelters."[1304]

Of course if the taxpayer made a pre-transaction profit projection and the actual profits fall short of that projection, the taxpayer will face an even heavier burden in practice, if not in theory, in trying to show the projection to have been reasonable. Conversely, if things turn out better than were, or could have been, reasonably expected, the taxpayer should get the benefit.

Netting. Section 7701(o)(2)(B) states that fees and other transactions expenses shall be taken into account as expenses in determining pre-tax profits. This rule was generated by the many "tax shelter" participants who are known to have paid substantial fees in the years prior to enactment to investment advisors and others with respect to transactions that could be said to have modest profit potential only by disregarding the fees.[1305]

The measuring of pre-tax profits also raises the issue of the treatment of foreign taxes as expenses or akin to federal taxes. Section 7701(o)(2)(B) states that the Secretary shall issue regulations requiring foreign taxes to be treated as expenses in determining pre-tax profits in "appropriate cases." This provision changed three times in the final days before enactment, from the Secretary "may issue" such regulations,[1306] to a mandatory expense rule in the statute that did not require regulations to be operative,[1307] to the final version. The Service believes the courts can still treat foreign taxes as expenses without regulations.[1308]

The statutory reference to "appropriate cases" likely will be read to require expense treatment for foreign taxes in at least some cases. The JCT explanation stated that there was no intention to restrict the power of the courts to

---

[1304] *Id.* at 354 (references problem when transaction not undertaken for reasons germane to the conduct of the business of the taxpayer).

[1305] *See, e.g.,* Long Term Capital Holdings v. United States, 330 F. Supp. 2d 122 (D. Conn. 2004), *aff'd,* 150 F. App'x. 40 (2d Cir. 2005) (expected profit of about $2 million and fees in excess of $4 million).

[1306] Section 421 of H.R. 4213 as passed by the Senate on March 10, 2010.

[1307] Reconciliation Act of 2010, H.R. 4872, 111th Cong., § 452 (as reported by House Mar. 17, 2010).

[1308] Notice 2010-62, 2010-40 I.R.B. 411.

consider the treatment of foreign taxes in particular cases, as under present law,[1309] but earlier the JCT expressed a strong view that foreign taxes incurred by a transaction should be viewed as expenses for purposes of determining the "U.S. tax motivation."[1310] The appellate courts in two high profile cases involving quick purchases and sales of ADRs disagreed.[1311]

Substantial. It appears that by using the term "substantial" Congress intended to send a message that it will not be enough for taxpayers to prove a reasonable (much less remote) possibility of some positive economic profit: thus, the substantiality standard is higher than both the hobby loss standard and the standard applied by some courts in assessing ESD claims before codification. The standard under section 183, the hobby loss rule, does not require even a "reasonable expectation of profit," but the taxpayer must have a subjective objective of making a profit.[1312] The JCT Description states that not even "reasonable possibility of profit," which is too high a standard for section 183, is high enough standard for the ESD.[1313]

The "special rule" applies in the taxpayer's favor only if the reasonably expected net pre-tax profits from the transaction are substantial in relation to the expected net tax benefits, on a present value basis. In analogous tests used at various places in the Code, a relationship of one to three has been viewed as indicating substantiality. If this were the standard for purposes of the "special rule," then reasonably expected pre-tax profits of $1 million would be substantial in relation to net tax benefits of $3 million. In making the comparison, it will be necessary to establish a time horizon that is relevant, which normally should extend until all reasonably expected profits and expected tax benefits are exhausted (or for whatever period a reasonable business person would use to make such an analysis). In other contexts, the Supreme Court views substantial as more than de minimis.[1314]

The partnership regulations utilize the "substantial" standard in several places and a one in three relationship has been suggested as substantial.[1315] The identification of a "substantial part" has come up in the definition of a

---

1309 Reconciliation Act Explanation, *supra* note 1129, at n. 357.

1310 Description of F.Y. 2010 Budget, *supra* note 1131, at 50.

1311 Compaq Computer Corp. v. Commissioner, 277 F. 3d 778 (5th Cir. 2001); IES Indus. Inc. v. United States, 253 F. 3d 350 (8th Cir. 2001). But the certiorari petitions that the Supreme Court rejected in 2016 treated the foreign taxes as expenses. Bank of New York Mellon Corp. v. Commissioner, 801 F.3d 104 (2d Cir. 2015) (consolidated case also involving American International Group); Salem Financial Inc. v. United States, 786 F.3d 932 (Fed. Cir. 2015).

1312 Reg. § 1.183-2(a).

1313 Description of F.Y. 2010 Budget, *supra* note 1131, at 45; Reconciliation Act Explanation, *supra* note 1129, at 145.

1314 *See* Cummings, *How Much Is Enough or Too Much?*, 150 Tax Notes (TA) 1025 (Feb. 29, 2016).

1315 Reg. § 1.701-2(a)(1) (the partnership anti-abuse rule, which requires a transaction be entered into for a substantial business purpose); Reg. § 1.704-1(b)(2)(iii)(a); *see* Reg. § 1.704-1(b)(5), Ex. 2 (22.5% is not substantial).

publicly supported charity, and Regulation section 1.170A-9(f) defines it as one third. The Chief Counsel has stated in the collapsible corporation context that construing a statutory phrase "substantial part" to mean more than one third would not be defensible as a matter of law.[1316] In another context, the Chief Counsel thought more than half was an appropriate measure for a substantial part, but his reasoning depended on precluding an alternate transaction by going over half, a consideration that is not applicable here.[1317] Regulation section 1.355-2(b)(1) in effect requires a "substantial part" business purpose for a spin-off. A large amount of lore, though little hard law, has been generated around the measurement of the section 355 business purpose. The general view is that the purpose does not have to be a more than 50% purpose or even the primary (most important) purpose; that a "but for" purpose will suffice. In other words, if purposes could be quantified, a one third purpose probably is a substantial part for section 355 purposes.[1318] Also, for continuity of business enterprise purposes a "significant" line of business is one in three.[1319]

State tax benefits. Section 7701(o)(3) treats state and local tax effects the same as the federal tax effects "if related."[1320] Otherwise, the savings of state or local taxes can be treated as a non-federal tax benefit (*i.e.*, part of pre-tax profit). This view is similar to Regulation section 1.355-2(b)(2), which states: "A purpose of reducing non Federal taxes is not a corporate business purpose if (i) the transaction will effect a reduction in both Federal and non Federal taxes because of similarities between Federal tax law and the tax law of the other jurisdiction and (ii) the reduction of Federal taxes is greater than or substantially coextensive with the reduction of non Federal taxes."

Section 7701(o)(3) reflects an assumption that many states piggyback on federal taxable income, and so in many cases there can be state tax savings of a lesser order resulting from the same transaction. However, corporations routinely engage in transactions primarily to reduce state taxes, with little or no effect on their federal tax liability. Arguably the ESD should not be relevant to such transactions at all; and if it were, significantly larger state income tax savings should not be viewed as related to the federal income tax savings (but rather the other way around).

1316 G.C.M. 34,410 (Jan. 22, 1971).

1317 *See* G.C.M. 34,903 (June 7, 1972) (concerning the proportion of member's business that it must conduct with a cooperative).

1318 *See* Rev. Rul. 2003-52, 2003-1 C.B. 960 (This ruling finds the "go their own ways" purpose to be "real," meaning that the Service believed it was not cooked up for ruling purposes, and "substantial." We can infer that this purpose was no more than an equal one-third of the total purposes. This suggests that a real purpose that is one of at least three equally weighted purposes will support a section 355 division, at least where the other two purposes are shareholder level purposes that are not aimed at saving federal taxes.).

1319 Reg. § 1.368-1(d)(5).

1320 Description of F.Y. 2010 Budget, *supra* note 1131, at 52.

V.F.7.c(3)(b) *Other Meaningful Change*

The section 7701(o)(2) caption indicates that it is the taxpayer's choice to rely on profit potential to prove meaningful economic position change occurred, or a nontax purpose existed, or both. If the taxpayer elects not to rely on profit potential, it faces a less structured path to satisfaction of the ESD test. The 2009 JCT Description recognized that the profit potential test "does not address many types of transactions that may not specify a readily calculable profit potential as their business purpose—for example, various types of financial transactions or corporate reorganizations."[1321] It also stated that it will be up to the taxpayer to choose whether to invoke the profits test to satisfy the statute or utilize some other kind of proof.

The quoted portion did not appear in the later JCT explanations. Perhaps the reason it was dropped is the realization that it implies that the ESD applies to corporate reorganizations despite the fact that another part of the JCT explanation states that the choice to engage in corporate reorganizations is one of those long standing elective choices taxpayers can make for tax purposes. In addition, a panoply of soft doctrine already applies to reorganizations, which are partly codified in Regulation sections 1.368-1 and 1.1002-1.

Also, how could a financial transaction not have a readily calculable profit potential? Certainly the term "financial transaction" would encompass hedging, straddles, and notional principal contracts. Perhaps the explanation refers to hedging related to inventory valuation, as in *Arkansas Best.*[1322]

V.F.7.c(4) *Business Purpose Prong of the Test*

Section 7701(o)(1) states that a transaction shall be treated as "having economic substance" only if the taxpayer has a substantial purpose (apart from Federal income tax effects, plus related state and local income tax effects) for entering into the transaction that facilitates the challenged tax benefits (and the transaction also satisfies the first prong of the test). Literally this means that such proof is necessary but not sufficient to cause the transaction to pass the ESD test.

The statute converts the requirement that the cases usually shorthand as "a business purpose" into a requirement that the taxpayer prove it has a substantial purpose apart from federal income tax effects for entering into the transaction. The 2009 JCT Description viewed the substantial non-federal tax purpose prong of the codification proposal as the "dominant issue." It viewed the requirement as having been "elevated" to "an absolute requirement."[1323] These statements did not appear in later JCT reports.

The substantial non-federal tax purpose will either be (a) to achieve a meaningful change in the taxpayer's economic position as proven by satisfying the

---

[1321] Description of F.Y. 2010 Budget, *supra* note 1131, at 45.

[1322] Arkansas Best Corp. v. Commissioner, 485 U.S. 212 (1988).

[1323] Description of F.Y. 2010 Budget, *supra* note 1131.

profit potential standard (in which case the two prongs are the same), or (b) that effect plus some other nontax purpose, or (c) solely some other nontax purposes, when the taxpayer does not rely on profit potential to prove the substantial change in its economic position.[1324] If the taxpayer relies on profit potential as its non-federal tax purpose, it must prove the present value of the reasonably expected net profit and net tax benefits using the same methodology as stated for the economic substance prong.

Financial accounting benefits. Section 7701(o)(4) provides that financial accounting benefits of reducing federal income taxes cannot be relied upon as a non-federal tax purpose under the substantial purpose prong of the ESD test. Concern about this type of justification for a tax motivated transaction can be traced back to the Joint Committee's Enron investigation. The Joint Committee learned that legal opinions provided to Enron in the late 1990's, with respect to fairly artificial transactions, treated as a suitable business purpose Enron's desire for a positive effect on its stock price from reporting higher financial accounting income as a result of projected future tax savings (*i.e.,* deferred tax benefits).[1325] Case law shows that Enron was not alone.[1326] If the taxpayer can show that the financial accounting benefit motivated the transaction and the accounting benefit was not dependent on a federal income tax reduction, then the purpose may count for purposes of the subjective prong.

Some cases suggest that if the putative "tax shelter" is more closely related to the taxpayer's core business it may be more easily shown to have a business purpose.[1327]

V.F.7.d. *Penalty Provisions*

The most important part of the 2010 codification was intended to be its in terrorem effect, which depends on the addition of the no fault penalties to be imposed on taxpayers that cannot avoid application of the economic substance doctrine. The key features of the penalty rules are as follows:

- Section 6662(b) has a sixth category for the strict liability 20% accuracy related penalty for the portion of the underpayment attributable to the

---

1324 *Cf.* Blank & Staudt, *Corporate Shams, supra* note 4, at 1642, 1706-1708 (concluding on the basis of statistical analysis of Supreme Court corporate tax rulings that business purpose was not that important the outcome, perhaps because the taxpayer could always claim some purpose).

1325 Description of F.Y. 2010 Budget, *supra* note 1131, at 49; Reconciliation Act Explanation, *supra* note 1129, at nn. 314, 355; *see* Staff of the Joint Comm. on Tax'n, Report of Investigation of Enron Corporation and Related Entities Regarding Federal Tax and Compensation Issues, and Policy Recommendations, Vol. I pp. 25-6, 109-81; Vol. II, Appendices A and B (2003).

1326 *See, e.g.,* Am. Elec. Power Co., Inc. v. United States, 136 F. Supp. 2d 762, 791-92 (S.D. Ohio 2001), *aff'd,* 326 F.3d 737 (6th Cir. 2003).

1327 *See, e.g.,* Shell Petroleum, Inc. v. United States, 102 A.F.T.R. 2d 5085 (S.D. Tex. 2008); Consol. Edison Co. v. United States, 104 A.F.T.R. 2d 6966 (Fed. Cl. 2009), reversed, 703 F.3d 1367 (Fed. Cir. 2013).

disallowance of tax benefits by reason of a transaction lacking economic substance as defined in section 7701(o) "or failing to meet the requirements of any similar rule of law."

- The penalty amount is 20% of the portion of the underpayment attributable to such a disallowance; the determination of the "portion" to which the penalty applies is a general issue under section 6662(a).
- The penalty is not imposed if the fraud penalty is imposed, as provided by the general terms of section 6662(b).
- The 20% will be increased to 40% if the portion of the underpayment is "attributable to one or more nondisclosed noneconomic substance transactions," as defined in new section 6662(i).
- The 40% penalty supersedes the section 6662A reportable transaction penalty under amended section 6662A(e)(2)(B).
- The 20% penalty also applies to "excessive amounts" of refunds denied on account of lack of economic substance or any similar rule of law under new section 6676(c).
- There is no way to escape or reduce these penalties other than (1) to reduce the underpayment to which the penalty is applied, (2) properly disclose the transaction to the Service, (3) limit the relevant underpayment "portion" or the "attributable to" amount, or (4) prevent the disallowance from being by reason of the ESD and similar rules of law.

Any similar rule of law. This is a unique term in the federal law. No other part of the United States Code uses the words "similar rule of law."[1328] In 2014, the Treasury Department opined that it means a rule or doctrine that applies the same factors and analysis that is required under section 7701(o) for an economic substance analysis, even if a different term or terms are used to describe the rule or doctrine (including the "sham transaction doctrine").[1329] The term "rule of law" obviously does not refer to statutes alone; section 7701(o)(5)(C) in earlier versions equated rule of law with common law doctrines.[1330] The normal usage of the term "rule of law," apart from referring to a constitutional ideal,[1331] is to refer to a requirement (including a

---

[1328] *Cf.* Nicol v. Ames, 173 U.S. 509 (1899) (a federal excise tax case, which interpreted "similar place" to a stock exchange to include a stock yard).

[1329] Notice 2014-58, 2014-44 I.R.B. 746. *See* Cummings, *The Sham Transaction Doctrine*, 145 Tax Notes (TA) 1239 (Dec. 15, 2014).

[1330] Reconciliation Act of 2010, H.R. 4872, 111th Cong., § 452 (as reported by House Mar. 17, 2010).

[1331] Citizens United v. FEC, 130 S.Ct. 876, 924 (2010).

binding evidentiary presumption) that must be obeyed,[1332] in contrast with either a rule of procedure (which also may have a binding effect) or a evidentiary presumption or inference that does not compel a result.[1333]

The JCT explanation states that this term refers to any doctrine by another name that has "similar factors and analysis" to the ESD[1334] Accordingly, a rule of law that is similar to the ESD would be a positive, substantive rule that denies tax benefits that would otherwise be allowed under the Code as normally interpreted and the facts as normally found. Of course there is no such similar rule of law; therefore section 6662(b)(6) can only refer to the ESD that a court has mislabeled. There may have been instances in which courts in effect have applied the ESD by another name, and this seems to be the "similar rule of law" to which the statute refers.

In contrast, more commonly courts have found the facts did not satisfy the requirements of the law or have interpreted the law to preclude the benefits claimed; such grounds of decision are not similar rules of law. Thus, for example, a similar rule of law was not applied in *Knetsch*, because there simply was no money borrowed in *Knetsch* as a matter of fact finding.[1335] For a different reason a similar rule of law was not applied in *Gregory*, because *Gregory* construed a requirement of business purpose into the reorganization statute.[1336] And no rule of law at all was applied in *Frank Lyon*, because it, like *Knetsch*, was a fact finding case, albeit in a very ambiguous area, but one that could be classified as allowing longstanding electivity by form, at least within certain parameters.[1337]

1332 Riegel v. Medtronic, Inc., 552 U.S. 312, 333 (2008) (Stevens, J., concurring); Virginia v. Black, 538 U.S. 343, 395 (2003) (Thomas, J., dissenting) (describing binding presumption as rule of law); United States v. Mead Corp., 533 U.S. 218, 257 (2001) (Scalia, J., dissenting) (stating that *Chevron* established a rule of law in light of which Congress legislated); Allentown Mack Sales and Service v. NLRB, 522 U.S. 359, 378 (1998) (counterfactual evidentiary presumption is a substantive rule of law); Michael H. v. Gerald D., 491 U.S. 110, 119 (1989) (a conclusive presumption is a substantive rule of law); Ashcraft v. Tennessee, 322 U.S. 143 (1944) (an irrebutable presumption is a rule of law); United States v. Am. Trucking Associations, Inc., 310 U.S. 534, 544 (1940).

1333 Horne v. Flores, 129 S. Ct. 2579, 2631 (2009) (a judicial attitude is not a rule of law); Maggio v. Zeitz, 333 U.S. 56 (1948) (a nonconclusive evidentiary presumption is not a rule of law).

1334 Reconciliation Act Explanation, *supra* note 1129, at n. 359. Some confusion might be created by the preceding footnote 353, which attempted to explain the new statutory definition of the ESD: "Thus the definition includes any doctrine that denies tax benefits for lack of economic substance, for lack of business purpose, or for lack of both." This is most reasonably read to distinguish between the disjunctive and the conjunctive test "doctrines" applied by various courts to deny a tax benefit to a taxpayer who otherwise complied with the law based on the facts as normally found, and not to imply that interpreting a business purpose requirement into the Code (as occurred in *Gregory v. Helvering*) converts all such reorganization cases into ESD cases; or that finding that the transaction required for the Code benefit did not actually occur (as in *Knetsch*) depends on the ESD, as contrasted with common law fact finding.

1335 *Infra* Ch. VI.E.1.e(2)(c).

1336 *Supra* Ch. III.C.3.a(1).

1337 *Infra* Ch. VI.F.2(c)(2).

When opinions cite the ESD as an alternate ground for decision, the uncertainty will not necessarily be of similar rule of law but whether the disallowance is "by reason of" the ESD, as discussed below. The tendencies of courts to confuse the grounds of decision will result in much confusion about "any similar rule of law." Taxpayers should resist any attempt to treat any fact finding method or inference as a similar rule of law, to treat any decision based on an interpretation of the statute as a similar rule of law, and to treat the so-called "business purpose doctrine" and "substance over form doctrine" or "sham transaction doctrine" as similar rules of law.[1338] The "business purpose doctrine" can be no more than an interpretation of a business purpose requirement into a particular Code section, as occurred in *Gregory v. Helvering*.[1339] The substance over form doctrine can be no more than the common law fact finding method.[1340] Both of these methods should apply *before* the ESD can come into play, because the ESD is supposed to apply only to tax benefits otherwise allowed by the law and facts as properly determined. Similarly, if a court refers to the "sham transaction doctrine," it should be saying that it found the transaction did not actually occur in fact.[1341] Again, that is not part of the ESD, nor is it similar to the ESD.

Which underpayments. Section 6662(b)(6) says the penalty applies to disallowance of claimed tax benefits "by reason of" a transaction lacking economic substance or failing a similar rule of law. Disallowance is usually used in the Code to refer to deductions that otherwise would be allowed. See section 261 and its title ("general rule for disallowance of deductions"). Therefore, tax benefits not dependent on deductions arguably are not covered (such as nonrecognition, income acceleration, deferral). However, the Service likely will disagree, pointing to section 7701(o)(5)(A), which refers to all tax benefits under subtitle A, which encompasses any tax item that has the effect of a benefit to the particular taxpayer.[1342]

The "by reason of" requirement is likely to be more difficult to apply. If the Service asserts the ESD and the penalty in the audit and deficiency assessment and ultimately prevails on that ground alone, then clearly the disallowance is by reason of the transaction failing the ESD test. However, the applicability of the penalty may be less clear if either (a) the Service does not assert the ESD ground and the penalty in the deficiency assessment, or (b) the ground of the ultimate determination is unclear, which can result from the Service's or the court's assertion of multiple grounds for decision.

1338 The IRS has announced such an attempt as to the sham transaction doctrine. Notice 2014-58, 2014-44 I.R.B. 746. *See* Cummings, *The Sham Transaction Doctrine*, 145 Tax Notes (TA) 1239 (Dec. 15, 2014).

1339 *Infra* Ch. VI.E.1.b(4).

1340 *Infra* Ch. VI.E.1.

1341 *Infra* Ch. VI.E.1.e(2).

1342 For example, sometimes taxpayers want to acquire a carryover basis and sometimes they want to acquire a cost basis, which was at issue in the *Kimbell-Diamond* line of cases. Bittker & Eustice, at 10.41.

It turns out that interpreting the phrase "by reason of" is not virgin territory in the federal law. The Supreme Court has had several occasions to interpret the term "by reason of" appearing in the federal statutes and the opinions show that at minimum there must be a "but for" relationship between the ESD and the loss. If the taxpayer could have lost on other grounds, then the "but for" relationship is lacking.

In connection with RICO claims,the Court stated that "by reason of" means not only a "but for" relationship but also "the proximate cause."[1343] The Court based this interpretation on prior interpretations of the Sherman Act and the Clayton Act.[1344] In interpreting the term "because of" in the ADEA, the Court equated it with "by reason of" and quoted and relied on a textbook statement that required a causal relationship; i.e., it would not have occurred without it.[1345] In the tax area, damages are received "on account of" personal injuries when received by reason of the personal injuries; the fact that they would not have been received but for the injury is not enough.[1346]

What if the Service does not assert the ESD as a ground for the assessment, or does not assert the ESD penalty under section 6662(b)(6) in the deficiency assessment, but then the matter goes to court and the court rules against the taxpayer on the basis of the ESD (because argued by government lawyers)?[1347] The statute literally says that the portion attributable to the ESD is subject to the penalty, but the general practice of the Service is to require itself to assess penalties, and even the substantial understatement penalty is not automatically assessed.[1348] Of course, unlike the other section 6662(a) penalties and the section 6662A reportable transaction penalty, the ESD penalty cannot be avoided by any reasonable cause exception. Therefore, should the issue arise the Service may contend that even an unassessed ESD penalty must be added to an ESD deficiency as ultimately determined.

Confusion will arise in the case decided on multiple grounds, and the case in which the agent asserts multiple grounds and the assessment stands for any reason. The legal question will be whether a "but for" test applies (no

---

1343 Hemi Group LLC v. City of New York, 559 U.S. 1 (2010), interpreting 18 U.S.C. section 1964(c), and citing Holmes v. SIPC, 503 U.S. 258 (1992).

1344 15 U.S.C. § 15; Holmes v. SIPC, 503 U.S. 258 (1992).

1345 Gross v. FBL Fin. Serv., 557 U.S. 167 (2009).

1346 O'Gilvie v. United States, 519 U.S. 79 (1996). In another tax case, the Supreme Court ruled that a bank did not receive income by reason of the discharge of indebtedness when it never had a legal duty to pay the amount; thus, even though the income had a but-for relationship to the event, the Court demanded to know all about what the event was. United States v. Centennial Savings Bank FSB, 499 U.S. 573 (1991).

1347 LB&I-4-0711-015 is a Directive that agents must follow in deciding whether to assert the ESD in support of an audit adjustment.

1348 I.R.M. 20.1.5.2(9) (if the tax must be assessed by deficiency the penalty must be assessed by deficiency); I.R.M. 20.1.5.8 ("may" be assessed; automatic only in W/I and SBSE); 20.1.5.8.2 (agent must explain when penalty not asserted); I.R.M. 20.1.5.13.4 (taxpayers are entitled to pre assessment appeals and statutory notice of deficiency procedures for reportable transactions penalties).

deficiency unless ESD applied), or an "on account of" test applies (and what that means in this context),[1349] or some other test applies.

No fault. The penalty is made "no fault" and mandatory by removal of the reasonable cause/good faith exceptions by sections 6664(c)(2) and (d)(2) (as to reportable transactions understatements).[1350] In contrast, accuracy related tax penalties generally can be relieved for showing of reasonable cause.[1351] Therefore, if the underpayment portion is "attributable to" disallowance under the ESD or similar rule of law, neither in house analysis nor outside legal opinions will prevent imposition of the penalties,[1352] nor can any other belief save the taxpayer from the penalty.

There is no possibility that two 20% penalties could be applied to the same underpayment.[1353] Section 6662(a) either applies once or it does not apply, and it can be made to apply once for several different reasons (negligence and substantial understatement; substantial understatement and ESD). If the section 6662 20% penalty could also be imposed on account of negligence or a substantial understatement, then it will not matter whether the penalty is "by reason of" the ESD violation because the 20% penalty can be applied on the other ground, but for two factors: (1) the penalty imposed on the other ground may be relieved by the reasonable cause exception, and (2) if the section 6662(a) 20% penalty is not attributable to the ESD then the 40% section 6662(i) penalty cannot apply.[1354] For these reasons the Service will have to assert the ESD as a ground for assessments based on substantial understatements if it wants to avoid the reasonable cause exception and avoid losing the 40% penalty; on the other hand, if the 40% penalty cannot be imposed because the taxpayer has made adequate disclosure, the Service might use its discretion not to assert the ESD.

Refund disputes. The 20% no fault penalty also applies to erroneous claims for excessive refunds under section 6676(c), which shall not be treated as having a reasonable basis if attributable to an ESD transaction. Section 6676 generally has a "reasonable basis" exception. But that exception will not apply to a claim for refund found to be attributable to a transaction described in section 6662(b)(6). The 40% penalty will not apply.

[1349] *Cf.* Rousey v. Jacoway, 544 U.S. 320 (2005) (ruled that IRA payments are received "on account of age"; stated that "on account of," "by reason of," and "because of" all have the same meaning, which is not "but for.").

[1350] DESCRIPTION OF F.Y. 2010 BUDGET, *supra* note 1131, at 48 (". . . intends to change the taxpayer's cost-benefit analysis and deter some aggressive taxpayer behavior.")

[1351] BITTKER & LOKKEN, at 114.4.7, 114.4.3 as to relief from the substantial understatement penalty. The 2009 Joint Committee discussion details existing penalty provisions. DESCRIPTION OF F.Y. 2010 BUDGET, *supra* note 1131, at 53-62, as does RECONCILIATION ACT EXPLANATION, *supra* note 1129.

[1352] RECONCILIATION ACT EXPLANATION, *supra* note 1129, at n. 360.

[1353] Reg. § 1.6662-2(c) (no stacking).

[1354] It is most logical to equate the determinination of "by reason of" in section 6662(b)(6) with "attributable to" in section 6662(i)(1) so that once it is determined that the lower penalty applies, then the higher penalty applies if no disclosure is made.

Of course if a taxpayer seeks refund of tax paid under a deficiency assessment, it is likely that the ESD penalty will already have been assessed and paid and section 6676 will not be relevant. But this new rule may substantially change the planning for taxpayers who anticipate a dispute with the Service and so do not claim the tax benefit of a transaction on their return but rather claim it by refund. In those cases, a loss can result in a 20% no fault penalty, but at least the 40% penalty will be escaped.

40% penalty. Under new section 6662(i), the 20% penalty is increased to 40% with respect to an underpayment attributable to a "nondisclosed noneconomic substance transaction." Because many of the underpayments to which the ESD might be applied will already be subject to the section 6662(a) 20% penalty on account of a substantial understatement, the principal functions of identifying the ground of the disallowance as the ESD will be to prevent the taxpayer from asserting the reasonable basis exceptions and to allow the penalty to be increased to 40% if the transaction was not properly disclosed.

The required disclosure is of the relevant facts affecting the tax treatment. This terminology is the same as that used in section 6664(d)(2)(A) with respect to reportable transactions. That section incorporates the regulations of section 6011, which provide a form for disclosure of (a) the expected tax treatment and all potential tax benefits, (b) any tax result protection, and (c) describe the transaction in sufficient detail for the Service to be able to understand the structure and identify the parties.[1355] An effective disclosure cannot be made after the first date the taxpayer is first contacted by the Secretary regarding the examination of the return.

Abatement. The statute contains no specific limitation on abatement of the penalty. Earlier bills did limit the Service to abating the penalty only proportionately to abatement of the tax,[1356] which should be possible in any event.

V.F.7.e. *Regulations*

The statute does not direct the Secretary to adopt regulations necessary or appropriate to carry out the purposes of section 7701(o). Earlier versions had contained such a specific grant of purpose based regulation authority, which is usually granted *Chevron* deference,[1357] but it did not appear in the final act. The legislative history invokes the normal section 7805(a) authority.[1358] This confirms that section 7701(o) is operative without regulations, and so delay in issuing any regulations will not prevent its application. It implies that any regulations issued would be interpretive and not legislative.[1359]

[1355] Reg. § 1.6011-4(d).

[1356] *Id.*

[1357] *See, e.g.,* Arnett v. Commissioner, 473 F. 3d 790 (7th Cir. 2007); *see infra* Ch. VI.D.5 and 6.a.

[1358] Reconciliation Act Explanation, *supra* note 1129, at 155, n. 358.

[1359] *But see infra* Ch. VI.D.5 and 6.a.

V.F.8. *Continuing Role of Prior Case Law*

One of the most important questions about the state of the law after the enactment of section 7701(o) is whether the Service and the courts will decide cases the same way as before the enactment. Setting aside the imponderable effects of the Congress legislating on this subject at all, and the fact that a no fault penalty now will follow the application of the ESD, the answer should be that cases will come out about the same way as they did before (or would have absent the statute change) on the issue of relevance of the ESD (which courts seldom have considered explicitly), subject to one major and two relatively minor differences:

- The major difference is likely to be a ratcheting up of the profit expectation standard the taxpayer must meet, based on the "substantial in relation to" language.
- The courts in any circuit that had adopted the so-called disjunctive test for applying the ESD must switch to the statute's conjunctive test, which in theory will make it harder for taxpayers to prevail in those circuits.
- The specification of other guides for the application of the prongs of the ESD test also may be more rigorous than the way some cases had applied the test ("present value," "reasonably expected").

Section 7701(o)(5)(C) states that the determination of whether the ESD is relevant shall be made in the same manner as if the subsection had never been enacted. Section 7701(o)(5)(D) of the version of H.R. 4872 reported in the House stated that except as otherwise provided in this subsection (of which there is none), no other rule of law shall be altered or supplanted by the subsection;[1360] it was dropped from the statute but a similar statement remained in the JCT explanation.[1361] Presumably these statements mean that, insofar as the ESD is concerned, the subsection governs all matters except the "whether relevant" issue, and peculiarly enough the very existence of the rule. The JCT explanation states that no inference is intended as to the proper application of the ESD under existing law, which evidently is intended to avoid upsetting pending cases.[1362]

Most if not all of the examples below appear to be imperiled under the ESD. The only way to square these cases with the ESD is to assert that the results the taxpayers obtained were not inconsistent with the intent of Congress or that they involve longstanding elective choices that are administratively allowed.

[1360] TECHNICAL EXPLANATION, *supra* note 1131, at 193 (including any Code, regulation or other guidance).

[1361] RECONCILIATION ACT EXPLANATION, *supra* note 1129, at 155.

[1362] *Id.*

- *Cottage Savings.*[1363] The taxpayer swapped interests in mortgage pools for interests in other mortgage pools that were economically identical;[1364] the taxpayer's regulator allowed it not to book the loss it had sustained on the original mortgage interests and encouraged it to engage in the swap for the sole reason of recognizing tax losses and saving taxes. To avoid reversing *Cottage Savings* a court would have to conclude that the codified ESD did not apply because Congress intended for taxpayers to enjoy recognition of losses actually sustained whenever they legally part with ownership of the loss property, regardless of the similarity of the property acquired in exchange; in effect, the Court so ruled in that decision.
- *Esmark.*[1365] The overall transaction had business purpose and economic effect, but arguably that was not also true of the steps by which Mobil purchased Esmark stock from the public, followed by the stock's redemption by Esmark in exchange for stock of its subsidiary, Vickers; these steps were not economically different from a sale of Vickers by Esmark.
- *Chamberlin.*[1366] The corporation had no business purpose to distribute preferred pro rata on common, with a plan for the preferred to be bought by a friendly insurance company. However, applying the codified ESD to this sort of case will present the difficult question of whose intent is relevant; after all the shareholders likely had no control over the issuance of the dividend and should not be faulted for selling the preferred stock. (Sections 305 and 306 changed the result of this decision).
- *Cumberland Public Service.*[1367] Same overall business purpose as in *Gregory v. Helvering*, but no business purpose for step of distributing assets before their sale, allegedly by shareholders; no economic impact of steps on either corporation or shareholders other than tax reduction.
- *Frank Lyon.*[1368] Likely little if any business purpose for Lyon's seller/lessee (the bank) not to have borrowed the money and built its own building; after all, banks are "where the money is." Alleged the lease was economically similar to that result; no economic savings but tax savings. The Supreme Court's opinion did observe that Frank Lyon was legally on the hook for the loan, but the risk must have been slight. The JCT explanation cites *Frank Lyon* in stating that there is no safe harbor for leasing and those transactions will remain subject to a facts and circumstances analysis.[1369]

[1363] Cottage Savings Assn. v. Commissioner, 499 U.S. 554 (1991).

[1364] *See* Hariton, *The "Frame" Game, supra* note 1294, at 39.

[1365] Esmark, Inc. v. Commissioner, 90 T.C. 171, *aff'd*, 886 F.2d 1318 (7th Cir. 1989).

[1366] Chamberlin v. Commissioner, 207 F.2d 462 (6th Cir. 1953).

[1367] United States v. Cumberland Pub. Serv. Co., 338 U.S. 451 (1950).

[1368] Frank Lyon Co. v. United States, 435 U.S. 561 (1978). The national banking laws may have prevented the bank from owning the building, which would be a business purpose to lease.

[1369] Reconciliation Act Explanation, *supra* note 1129, at 153, n. 350.

- *Clay Brown.*[1370] The taxpayer's sale to and leaseback of its business assets from an exempt organization had no business purpose and did not even shift the risk to the charity, but the Court upheld the sale.
- *Gitlitz.*[1371] Taxpayer allowed to deduct presumably real losses on account of phantom income providing basis. Is this protected from ESD simply because taxpayer and S corporation did not engage in any "transaction" that they could control in the year at issue? Should the timing of the discharge of indebtedness of the S corporation in that year have been questioned? Presumably the majority who wrote this opinion would say Congress showed what it intended by the way it wrote the statute.

1370 Commissioner v. Brown, 380 U.S. 563 (1965).

1371 Gitlitz v. Commissioner, 531 U.S. 206 (2001); see also United States v. Brockamp, 519 U.S. 347 (1997) (no equitable tolling).

Ch. VI. The Supreme Court's Tax Doctrines, Principles of Code Interpretation, Methods of Fact Finding, and Factual Cluster Rules

This Chapter restates how the Supreme Court has applied the federal tax laws, which can and should be a serviceable guide to all Code users.[1372] The restatement recommends the following as best practices:

- First determine what requirements the Code imposes, as informed by interpretation and construction and appropriate presumptions, and including as part of the positive law the substantive tax doctrines created by the Supreme Court; and second determine what facts are relevant, and then find those facts, using the full range of equitable fact finding methods, including particularly consideration of agency and fraud.
- Only after the decider applies these two steps could it possibly enter a zone in which generalized judge made doctrines might be applied. Instead of, or before, entering that zone, the decider should apply any processes that have evolved in the courts for limited clusters of cases, such as indebtedness, lease financings, assignment of income, etc., as described below.
- Apply the law to the facts as found using the described two-step process.

1372 *See* POSNER, at 210-12 (describing how legal academia has largely abandoned such projects in favor of pointing to new considerations, leaving to others the "tidying up, synthesis, analysis and critique" of judicial decisions; observing that:

> [T]hese are intellectually demanding tasks, requiring vast knowledge and the ability (not only brains, knowledge, and judgment, but also *Sitzfleisch)*, to organize dispersed, fragmentary, prolix and rebarbarative materials. Though these tasks lack the theoretical ambition of scholarship in more typical academic fields, they are vital to the legal system and of greater social value than much of today's esoteric interdisciplinary legal scholarship.).

- Categorizing law and fact is impossible at the margins, but is unavoidably necessary,[1373] in order to allow application of the appropriate groups of methods, principles and doctrines (summarized below) that have proven useful to cluster areas and generally. While the distinction is rudimentary, one need not be embarrassed to emphasize it in tax cases.[1374]

VI.A. The Supreme Court's Tax Doctrines

VI.A.1. *A Variety of Doctrines*

The Supreme Court has a tendency to label any of its interpretations as a doctrine.[1375] Without necessarily accepting all such self-identifications, the following are authentic substantive doctrines and principles of relatively general application to the federal tax laws that are either supported by Supreme Court decisions, or where regulations are cited, they almost always can be traced back to Supreme Court precedent. Succeeding chapters discuss interpretive doctrines.

The Court is aware of the force of its doctrines as "well settled interpretations" and so is resistant to changing them.[1376] But sometimes experience forces the Court to change them,[1377] or they have been misinterpreted,[1378] or never rose to the status of a doctrine.[1379]

- The "cardinal principle" of the income tax is that in interpreting the term "gross income" Congress intended to use the full measure of its taxing power in the income tax,[1380] with the result that inclusion of income is to be applied liberally in favor of the government.[1381]

[1373] *See* Landis, The Administrative Process 145-46 (Yale 1938) (acknowledging the difficulties of the distinction between law and fact, but stressing it cannot be avoided because to do so "leaves nothing upon which to base a philosophy as to the appropriate spheres of administrative and judicial activity.").

[1374] *See* Paul, Studies I, at 130. Paul emphasized the centrality of the distinction to proper application of the tax laws. But in the Introduction to Paul's book, Jerome Frank questioned the objectivity of facts and the ability of courts to find them, while admitting that reduction of confusion should not be rejected simply because obliteration of confusion was not possible. *Id.* at 3-4. Paul in the same work also asserted that mere fact and law were "primitive tools" that must be augmented in tax avoidance cases. *Id.* at 100.

[1375] *See, e.g.*, Commissioner v. Jacobson, 336 U.S. 28, 31-32 (1949) (labeling two). Some of these and others have been called "tax logic" by Professor Dodge. Dodge, The Logic of Tax: Federal Income Tax Theory and Policy (1989).

[1376] *See, e.g.*, United States v. Lewis, 340 U.S. 590 (1951).

[1377] Corn Prods. Refining Co. v. Commissioner, 350 U.S. 46 (1955) (substantially limited by Arkansas Best Corp. v. Commissioner, 485 U.S. 212 (1988)).

[1378] *See* INDOPCO, Inc. v. Commissioner, 503 U.S. 79 (1992); Commissioner v. Lincoln Savings & Loan Assoc., 403 U.S. 345 (1971).

[1379] Commissioner v. Groetzinger, 480 U.S. 23 (1987) (gambler was in a trade or business; rejected Frankfurter's gloss requiring selling goods or services as not achieving "the status of a Court holding").

[1380] Commissioner v. Kowalski, 434 U.S. 77 (1977).

[1381] *See supra* Ch. II.B.2.c(1).

- The Court has taken to identifying as the "first principle of income taxation" the assignment of income doctrine,[1382] which phrase it attributes to *Culbertson*;[1383]
- The constructive receipt doctrine.[1384]
- The cancellation of indebtedness doctrine.[1385]
- The taxpayer has the burden of proving that the tax it owes is not what the Service says it is.[1386]
- The taxpayer usually must report its income according to the form of its transaction except where specifically directed otherwise by the Service.[1387]
- Tax provisions should generally be read to incorporate domestic tax concepts absent a clear congressional intent to incorporate foreign tax concepts.[1388]
- There is a presumption against double taxation.[1389]
- The origin of the claim doctrine.[1390]
- The tax benefit rule.[1391]
- The claim of right doctrine.[1392]
- The relation back doctrine.[1393]
- The substitute for ordinary income doctrine.[1394]

[1382] *See supra* Ch. III.C.4.c., and VI.F.2.d.

[1383] Commissioner v. Banks, 543 U.S. 426 (2005).

[1384] Corliss v. Bowers, 281 U.S. 376 (1930).

[1385] Commissioner v. Tufts, 461 U.S. 300, 310 n. 11 (1983). Cancellation of indebtedness income is different from the amount realized on exchange of property for discharge of indebtedness, which was at issue in the case.

[1386] *See infra* Ch. VI.E.4.

[1387] An example of such a direction is Revenue Ruling 1955-540, 1955-2 C.B. 39 (leases v. sales of business personal property). *See* United States v. Davis, 397 U.S. 301 (1970) (taxpayer argued it could have chosen a different form and avoided tax; Court said not relevant); Moline Properties, Inc. v. Commissioner, 319 U.S. 436 (1943) (having chosen the corporate form, taxpayer must live with it); Higgins v. Smith, 308 U.S. 473 (1940) (taxpayer must report according to its form, but government is not bound).

[1388] United States v. Goodyear Tire & Rubber Co., 493 U.S. 132, 145 (1989) (citing Biddle v. Commissioner, 302 U.S. 573 (1938)).

[1389] *See* Maass v. Higgins, 312 U.S. 443 (1941); Colgate-Palmolive-Peet Co. v. United States, 320 U.S. 422 (1943). But it is not always to be avoided. *See* United States v. Hemme, 476 U.S. 558 (1986). *See also Goodyear Tire & Rubber Co.*, 493 U.S. at 132 (finding arguments of taxpayer and government in equipoise, but ruling for the government because the risk of double taxation was less than the risk of nontaxation).

[1390] Bittker & Lokken, at 20.5.2; Woodward v. Commissioner, 397 U.S. 572 (1970); United States v. Gilmore, 372 U.S. 39 (1963).

[1391] *See* Hillsboro National Bank v. Commissioner, 460 U.S. 370 (1983) (noting that Congress had given "implicit approval" to the rule made by lower courts by partly codifying it in section 111).

[1392] Bittker & Lokken, at 6.3; *see* Healy v. Commissioner, 345 U.S. 278 (1953) (observing that "claim of right" is a real property doctrine used in adverse possession cases, which has an analogous meaning in tax); United States v. Lewis, 340 U.S. 590 (1951).

[1393] Arrowsmith v. Commissioner, 344 U.S. 6 (1952).

[1394] United States v. Midland-Ross Corp., 381 U.S. 54 (1965).

- The general welfare exclusion.[1395]
- Congress recognizes that partnerships have mixed aggregate and entity characteristics for tax purposes.[1396]
- Similarly situated taxpayers should be treated similarly where possible, sometimes referred to as tax parity and sometimes as a principle of equality;[1397] and the law should be applied the same way in all parts of the country.[1398]
- The Code denies double deductions (as evidenced by requiring reduction of basis by not less than the allowable depreciation and depletion whether or not claimed in the proper year).[1399] However, "windfalls" may or may not be allowed.[1400]
- A taxpayer cannot purge its fraud.[1401]
- The need of the government to promptly secure its revenues is recognized by the Court as a principle on which collection remedies should be interpreted and applied.[1402]

[1395] Not yet articulated by the Supreme Court, but originating with the Service. *See* Notice 99-3, 1999-1 C.B. 271. *See also* I.R.C. § 139E, enacted in 2014.

[1396] Neuberger v. Commissioner, 311 U.S. 83 (1940).

[1397] *See* Commissioner v. Idaho Power Co., 418 U.S. 1 (1974) (citing maintenance of "tax parity"); Dixon v. United States, 381 U.S. 68, 77 n. 9 (1965) (equality); Colgate-Palmolive-Peet Co. v. United States, 320 U.S. 422 (1943) (presume Congress intended equal treatment).

[1398] Thomas v. Perkins, 301 U.S. 655, 659 n. 2 (1937).

[1399] *See* United States v. Skelly Oil Co., 394 U.S. 678 (1969); United States v. Hill, 506 U.S. 546 (1993); United States v. Ludey, 274 U.S 295 (1927); Charles Ilfeld Co. v. Hernandez, 292 U.S. 62 (1934); McLaughlin v. Pacific Lumber Co., 293 U.S. 351 (1934) (the Court had to apply the double deduction principle because the early consolidated return rules did not require reduction of stock basis for use of a subsidiary's losses); Crane v. Commissioner, 331 U.S. 1 (1947); United Dominion Industries, Inc. v. United States, 532 U.S. 822 (2001) (rejecting government argument based on double deduction, because not proved); Hillsboro National Bank v. Commissioner, 460 U.S. 370 (1983) (an untaxed basis step up can produce the result of a double deduction). *Cf.* Gitlitz v. Commissioner, 531 U.S. 206 (2001) (refusing to deny a double benefit in a Subchapter S context); Commissioner v. Estate of Hubert, 520 U.S. 93 (1997) (estate and income tax deductions are not double). *But see* Maryland Casualty Co. v. United States, 251 U.S. 342 (1920) (acknowledging that Congress created the possibility of a double deduction). Several decisions have involved the taxation of tax exempt interest received by insurance companies and whether the method provided a double deduction. *See* United States v. Atlas Life Ins. Co., 381 U.S. 233 (1965).

[1400] *See* Cory Corp. v. Sauber, 363 U.S. 709 (1960) (per curiam opinion indicating windfall should not be allowed to person withholding excise tax but not owing it); Gitlitz v. Commissioner, 531 U.S. 206 (2001) (ruling in favor of a potential "double windfall"); O'Gilvie v. United States, 519 U.S. 79 (1996) (possible windfall under ruling); United States v. Skelly Oil Co., 394 U.S. 678 (1969) (windfall was reason to rule against taxpayer).

[1401] Badaracco v. Commissioner, 464 U.S. 386 (1984) (supporting the plain meaning of "return" as the original return by reference to the general principle under the Code).

[1402] *See* United States v. Nat'l. Bank of Comm., 472 U.S. 713 (1985) (and cases cited therein).

- The doctrine (not limited to tax) that the federal government is equitably entitled to collect interest on taxes due, and the taxpayer has the same right as to refund, despite state law to the contrary.[1403]
- The Social Security Act and its taxing provisions in the Code are to be broadly construed to achieve Congress' purpose in attacking recognized evils in the national economy (and thus may be viewed as sharing in the broad construction of remedial laws).[1404]Summons enforcement is guided by the "*Powell* factors," four observations stated in dictum.[1405]

See the subsequent section VI.B.2.1 on Other Maxims and Canons for interpretive doctrines.

VI.A.2. *Avoidance of Constitutional Decisions*

Last but not least, the Court tries to construe tax laws to avoid questions of constitutionality[1406] It has applied the doctrine to resolve what might look like an irresolvable clash between two plausible interpretations; the Court stated that it is an "elementary rule of interpretation that where there are two possible constructions of a statute, one of which will give rise to grave doubt as to its constitutionality, and the other avoids such question, the latter will be adopted."[1407] But the *Bennett* opinion emphasized the importance of the two preconditions of the doctrine: (1)a real inability to interpret the statute, and (2) a real likelihood of a constitutional violation. Chief Justice Taft showed the malleability of the doctrine when he said he would not treat a statute as a "nose of wax" to avoid finding it unconstitutional.[1408] For discussion of the many possible grounds of constitutional violation, see Cummings, *The Supreme Court, Federal Taxation, and the Constitution* (2013).

Sometimes the Court does not state the doctrine but must have applied it. A series of decisions in the 1920's addressed the statutory limitation on "ascertaining the gain" from property dispositions, and later also the loss: the 1913 value of the property shall be the basis for determining the amount of

---

1403 Billings v. United States, 232 U.S. 261 (1914).

1404 United States v. Silk, 331 U.S. 704 (1947).

1405 United States v. Powell, 379 U.S. 48 (1964), modified by United States v. Clarke, 134 S. Ct. 2361 (2014).

1406 *See, e.g.,* St. Martin Ev. Luth. Church v. S.D., 451 U.S. 772 (1981) (construing FUTA tax not to apply to church run school); United States v. Christian Echoes Nat'l. Ministry, Inc. 404 U.S. 561 (1972) (per curiam) (rejecting jurisdiction because no part of the law was held unconstitutional because trial court carefully avoided such holding). According to Justice Harlan's dissent, the Court did not follow this rule in upholding the tax in Knowlton v. Moore, 178 U.S. 41 (1900).

1407 United States v. Bennett, 232 U.S. 299 (1914). This opinion also employed an inference about the meaning of a statute based on whether Congress normally taxed with extraterritorial effect, but did not give great weight to the inference. However, outside the tax area the Court has revived the presumption against extraterritoriality. *See* Morrison v. Nat'l Austl. Bank Ltd., 561 U.S. 247 (2010).

1408 Yu Cong Eng v. Trinidad, 271 U.S. 500 (1926) (his decision likely was informed by his personal knowledge of the Phillipines as its former Governor General).

such gain derived. The most straightforward interpretation would be that the basis of all property held on 1913 would be marked to market for later gain and loss purposes. But because the Solicitor General agreed, the Court interpreted this provision to be applicable only if a gain existed based on original cost, even though the revenue statute did not then define gain or basis in terms of original cost.[1409] This interpretation laid the foundation for an obvious follow-on conundrum: what if there was a gain based on original cost, but it was less than the gain based on 1913 value? The Court ruled that the smaller gain controlled, without any analysis.[1410]

VI.A.3. *Other Principles*

Sometimes the Court seems to just make up a rule where Congress failed to provide one, limited to a discrete area of "tax logic," yet not so broad as to be called a doctrine. For example, *Clark* ruled for the taxpayer that the dividend character of boot received in a reorganization should be determined as though stock had been issued instead and then redeemed.[1411]

But on the other hand, the Court has explained why it often is not desirable to state a tax doctrine. The *Duberstein* opinion thought the government's proposed test for a gift in the business context was merely an attempt to restate the case law.[1412] It considered carefully and declined to formulate a test for reasons including: it would go beyond the law as the Court had analyzed it for purposes of the case at hand, it would overstate an inference into a preclusive rule, it would force the fact finder into other complex fact problems, future fact finding should be left flexible, the statute indicates Congress' desire for full play of the facts and circumstances, and producing a less diverse set of results is not the controlling consideration. Nevertheless, *Duberstein* stands for a doctrine that service related payments are usually compensatory income even if they are not literally payment for services rendered.[1413]

Finally, in reviewing the Court's tax doctrines and lesser principles, it is somewhat astounding that the Court has not affirmatively based any of its tax decisions on the Haig-Simons definition of income.[1414] This is remarkable in light of the broad definition of income created by the Court and the focus of academic writing on Haig-Simons.[1415]

[1409] Goodrich v. Edwards, 255 U.S. 527 (1921).

[1410] Walsh v. Brewster, 255 U.S. 536 (1921); Heiner v. Tindle, 276 U.S. 582 (1928) (loss also limited to loss from acquisition).

[1411] Commissioner v. Clark, 489 U.S. 726 (1989).

[1412] Commissioner v. Duberstein, 363 U.S. 278 (1960) (treatment of gifts in business context; declined to create a special test; reviewed facts in context of existing case law).

[1413] Applied in United States v. Quality Stores, Inc., 134 S. Ct. 1395 (2014) (ruling payment for not working to be payment for working).

[1414] *Cf.* Hillsboro National Bank v. Commissioner, 460 U.S. 370, 404 n. 1 (1983) (which does contain a cf. cite to *Haig-Simons* in a concurrence); *see* Weiss v. Wiener, 279 U.S. 333, 335 (1929) ("The income tax laws do not profess to embody perfect economic theory.").

[1415] Bittker & Lokken, at 3.1.1.

VI.B. The Supreme Court's Principles of Code Interpretation

It is not possible to interpret the Code without focusing on both its words and Congress' will, whether called its purpose or intent, however that is determined. This approach has proponents both recent and early, with most of the disputes being around the degree of attention paid to evidence of purpose outside the four corners of the Code. Chief Justice Marshall early stated the Supreme Court's desire to carry out the will of Congress and the tools it would use to infer that will when the words of statutes left gaps; for example, in that case he applied substance over form and the canon that the several parts of a statute should be read as informing the meaning of each other.[1416]

General theories of statutory interpretation abound[1417] and have an ancient history.[1418] Codes are a particular type of integrated statutes, and for that reason are seen as "special," which is often said of the Internal Revenue Code.[1419] Any effort to rethink statutory interpretation is challenging because the subject is viewed by practitioners and the courts as too pedestrian for analysis

---

[1416] Talbot v. Seeman, 5 U.S. 1 (1801). In effect Marshall applied substance over form in deciding the claim of a salvager who had taken a German ship from the French navy, which had captured it. Talbot wanted a salvage fee paid by the Germans. First the Court had to decide whether the capture was legal. The law did not allow capture of a German vessel manned by the French, but the Court reasoned that such was within the "real intent of Congress," which a "fair construction of the acts" will show to be "obviously the sense of Congress." Summing up the justification for such construction, Marshall said:

> If by the laws of Congress on this subject, that body shall appear to have legislated upon a perfect conviction that the state of war in which this country was placed was such as to authorize recaptures generally from the enemy; if one part of the system shall be manifestly founded on this construction of the other part, it would have considerable weight in rendering certain what might before have been doubtful. . . . The court goes no further than to use the provisions in one of several acts forming a general system, as explanatory of the other parts of the same system; and this appears to be in obedience to the best established rules of exposition, and to be necessary to a sound construction of the law.

See also United States v. Fisher, 6 U.S. 358 (1805); Pennington v. Coxe, 6 U.S. 33 (1804).

[1417] *See* Terrell, *Statutory Epistemology: Mapping the Interpretation Debate*, 53 Emory L.J. 523, 528 (2004) (counting 14); *also* Ch. I.B. for introduction to statutory interpretation.

[1418] *See, e.g.*, Plucknett, Statutes and their Interpretation in the First Half of the Fourteenth Century (Cambridge 1922).

[1419] *See, e.g.*, Cavanaugh, *supra* note 36, at 610-11. Compare the unfortunate statement in the opinion of the Board of Tax Appeals in *Gregory v. Helvering* that was reversed by the Supreme Court: "[a] statute so meticulously drafted must be interpreted as a literal expression of the taxing policy, and leav[ing] only the small interstices for judicial consideration." 27 B.T.A. 223, 225 (1932).

or too well understood for change,[1420] and by academics as implicating deep political issues rather than lawyerly thinking on what to do in real cases.[1421]

Professor Elhauge neatly sidestepped the academic debates over various interpretive methods by adopting the premise that Congress' intent or purpose should govern and that *standard interpretational methods do actually promote that result.* This is consistent with the empirical research of Professor Staudt that when the statute is unclear the Court makes paramount the preferences of Congress: in 69% of the tax cases since 1912 the Court can be said to have explicitly deferred to Congress by following either the text or the legislative history and inferred intent of Congress.[1422]

Elhauge argues that when Congress' intent is not discernable courts will try to determine "enactable preferences," meaning what Congress is likely to do if asked. This policy can maximize political satisfaction,[1423] and may *elicit* rather than reflect the views of Congress; it tracks the preference of the current rather than the enacting Congress, at least when the court can identify some "official action" of the current government that reflects current preferences, an approach reflected in the *Chevron* doctrine (discussed in Ch. VI.D. below). Ch. III.B. shows the substantial role the Supreme Court has played in the interpretation and application of the Code; the discussion below builds on that proof. The methods described below are the Supreme Court's methods, mostly drawn from its federal tax opinions. These methods fill the gap between the interesting, but ultimately impractical, debates among academics about statutory construction, and the frequently inaccurate and incomplete "black letter law" on the subject collected by texts.[1424] The academic disputes over statutory interpretation are irrelevant to the tens of thousands of government employees, judges, practitioners and taxpayers who honestly try to know what the tax law is, because (1) those users of the law are and will remain largely oblivious to the debates, and (2) in most cases the academic commentators provide no practically useable tools, even if they were studied

---

[1420] *See* POSNER, at 215-16 ("For it is what it is, . . .").

[1421] For example, one of the standard textbooks, ESKRIDGE, FRICKEY & GARRETT, LEGISLATION AND STATUTORY INTERPRETATION (2d ed. 2006), devotes the first 210 pages to theories of representation, theories of the legislative process, etc., 38 pages to competing theories of statutory interpretation, and the last 142 pages to specific methodologies of statutory interpretation.

[1422] Staudt et al., *Judging Statutes, supra* note 20, at 1946 (with René Lindstädt & Ryan J. Vander Wielen).

[1423] ELHAUGE, STATUTORY DEFAULT RULES: HOW TO INTERPRET UNCLEAR LEGISLATION, Preface generally, and p. 5 (Harvard 2008). This book is a composite of Elhauge's articles *Preference-Estimating Statutory Default Rules*, 102 COLUM. L. REV. 2027 (Dec. 2002) and *Preference-Eliciting Statutory Default Rules*, 102 COLUM. L. REV. 2162, 2208 (2002).

[1424] *See, e.g.,* MERTENS LAW OF FEDERAL INCOME TAXATION Ch. 3 (Thomson 2009).

by Code users.[1425] Even books appearing to give practical information actually focus more on the jurisprudence of legislation, etc.[1426]

Lawyers may, however, be willing to follow the interpretational directives of the Supreme Court, particularly when it suits their clients' interests. But there has been no generally available statement of the Court's interpretational views in tax cases, because it is scattered within more than 1,000 tax opinions decided over the last century (and some before). As the Supreme Court said in *Soliman*:

> Justice Cardozo's observation that . . . 'Life in all its fullness must supply the answer to the riddle,' . . . must not deter us from deciding upon some rules for the fair and consistent interpretation of a statute. . . .[1427]

This chapter employs a distinction between the interpretation, as contrasted with the construction, of statutes because that distinction is useful in parsing the confusing authorities. Although the words interpretation and construction have long been used interchangeably, the distinction has has a history.[1428] The confusion in meaning is partly due to the fact that construction has been used as a broader term that encompassed interpretation.[1429] Interpretation was understood to be the "art of finding out the true sense of any form of words, that is: the sense which their author intended to convey, ..."[1430]

Example: A statute referring to a "bank" could refer to a river bank or to a financial institution;[1431] presumably a brief survey of the surrounding text will show which was meant.

Example: Justice Holmes interpreted the statute governing suits to recover taxes paid after protesting the tax to require that the protest be made after payment. He refused to construe into the statute an implied exception where the taxpayer had protested the assessment before payment because the second protest should not be a useless act.[1432]

Construction was understood to be the process applied in cases unforeseen by the author of rules, or when the rules are internally inconsistent, or otherwise require "the drawing of conclusions respecting subjects that lie

---

1425 For a particularly elusive but high profile work on statutory interpretation, *see* DWORKIN, LAW'S EMPIRE (Harvard 1986). For an exception relied on in this book, see ELHAUGE, STATUTORY DEFAULT RULES, *supra* note 1423.

1426 *See, e.g.*, ESKRIDGE, FRICKEY & GARRETT, *supra* note 1421.

1427 Commissioner v. Soliman, 506 U.S. 168, 178 (1993).

1428 . The distinction has been traced to the writings of Lieber in 1839. *See* POPKIN, at 68.

1429 United States v. Keitel, 211 U.S. 370 (1908).

1430 LIEBER, *supra* note 11, at 23.

1431 This is the classic example of a homonym, as examined in detail in Cavanaugh, *supra* note 36, at 662.

1432 Rock Is., Ark. & La. R.R. Co. v. United States, 254 U.S. 141, 143 (1920); *see supra* Ch.V.E.1. on equity.

beyond the direct expression of the text—conclusions that are within the spirit though not within the letter of the text."[1433]

Example: The Supreme Court's reading of a rule of reason into the Sherman Antitrust Act in *Standard Oil*[1434] was construction, but the Court's reading of a business purpose requirement into the meaning of "in pursuance of a plan of reorganization" was an interpretation of language "in pursuance of a plan of reorganization." See Ch. III.C.3.a.1. Thus, ambiguous statutes are interpreted and apparently unambiguous (but sometimes incoherent) statutes are construed.

This book treats the interpretive methods used in the Supreme Court's opinions, particularly in its tax opinions, as controlling for Code interpretation today. Admittedly, this is a novel concept that can be hard to apply for several reasons: (1) the Court has not set out to display a complete method of interpretation of the tax statutes; (2) it has used a broad range of interpretive methods; and (3) those methods have varied over time with judicial philosophies and Court personnel. However, none of these reasons precludes following an interpretive example from the Court in a sufficiently analogous situation, most importantly the cluster rules discussed in Ch. VI.F.[1435] The burden should be on the party that would reject Supreme Court interpretational precedent to explain why. Empirical studies have shown that the Court shows high regard for its own opinions.[1436]

Nevertheless, reliance on Supreme Court precedent must be informed by an understanding of the incremental growth of the tax law, which this book emphasizes.[1437] Hopefully readers are by now armed, for example, with the knowledge that *Isham* (see Ch. II.B.2.a(2)) is no longer good law and has not been for decades; *Higgins v. Smith* is not nearly so broad a precedent as it seems, as explained in Ch. III.C.3.a(2); and equitable principles of fact finding are commonly applied in the government's favor, but not the taxpayers' favor, as discussed in Ch. V.E.1.f.

Tax cases have occupied a far larger part of the Court's output than any other single area of the law, and dominated it in some decades.[1438] Therefore, it is both reasonable and possible to give primacy to the Court's methods. Only sparing reference will be made to lower court opinions.

VI.B.1. *Primacy of Text*

No one disputes that the text of the Code is the primary source of its meaning. Chief Justice Marshall said in an early tax case: "A law is the best expositor of

---

1433 Lieber, *supra* note 11, at 56 (quoted in United States v. Farenholt, 206 U.S. 226, 229-230 (1907)).

1434 The Standard Oil Company v. United States, 221 U.S. 1 (1911).

1435 *See generally* Foster, *Should Courts Give Stare Decisis Effect to Statutory Interpretation Methodology?*, 96 Geo. L. Rev. 1863 (2008).

1436 *See supra* Ch. III.C.2.

1437 *See supra* Ch. II.B. and III.B.

1438 *See supra* Ch. III.A. and B.

itself."[1439] Justice Holmes said that taxpayers must turn square corners when dealing with the government and refused to deviate from the text controlling refunds.[1440] Justice Robert H. Jackson said in a tax case that the rule of law requires primary attention to the face of the statutes.[1441] Justice Thurgood Marshall repeated in a tax case the familiar words that the starting point for statutory interpretation must be the words employed by Congress.[1442] It could not be otherwise.[1443]

Perhaps all portions of the United States Code governing relations between persons and the federal government share the "square corners" rule of Justice Holmes and benefit from an extra dose of textual primacy for that reason. But many would go farther and contend that Title 26 has even more textual primacy. The Service believes the "courts give great importance to the literal language of" the revenue laws.[1444] Yet Professor Shores' analysis suggests that those who know the Code best now honor its literal words the least.[1445] Text may only appear to have special primacy in areas like taxation where (1) the courts tend less to pursue social goods through interpretation, and (2) general jurisdiction courts are often not able to understand or feel confident in applying nontextual meanings to the words and phrases of tax (although they have become quite comfortable applying the economic substance doctrine without benefit of text).

The better analysis is that Title 26 does not have a greater claim to primacy of text than other statutes concerning government relations, except as affected by the facts that (1) there is more of it than any other U.S. Code component, (2) its many sections are more interrelated than most other Titles, and (3) its authors (or at least their assistants) have deep institutional continuity with the subject matter. The problem is made no easier by the unfortunate statement about the reorganization statute by the Board of Tax Appeals in *Gregory* (reversed by the Supreme Court): "[a] statute so meticulously drafted must be interpreted as a literal expression of the taxing policy, and leav[ing] only

---

1439 Pennington v. Coxe, 6 U.S. 33 (1804). For in depth analysis of case, *see* Crane, *supra* note 227, at 417.

1440 Rock Is., Ark. & La. R.R. Co. v. United States, 254 U.S. 141, 143 (1920).

1441 Schwegmann Bros. v. Calvert Distillers Corp., 341 U.S. 384, 396 (1951) (Justice Jackson preferred primary resort to the face of the statute, stating that some judges seek to make the interpretation fit the legislative history and not the text).

1442 United States v. Goodyear Tire and Rubber Co., 493 U.S. 132 (1989). *See also* United States v. Quality Stores, Inc., 134 S. Ct. 1395 (2014).

1443 *See generally* Coverdale, *Text as Limit, supra* note 556, at 1501.

1444 I.R.M. 4.10.7.2.1.1.

1445 Shores, *Textualism and Intentionalism, supra* note 22, at 53 (The Tax Court has ". . . identified tools indicating congressional intent, with related statutes and committee reports predominating. . .".).

the small interstices for judicial consideration."[1446] In hindsight informed by successive efforts to constrict the definition of a corporate reorganization, we see the early reorganization statute was wildly vague, but the planners of the transaction in *Gregory v. Helvering* thought the law was clear, as discussed in Ch. III.C.3.a(1). Although that quotation is antique, its sentiment is followed in many cases even today.

Early and lately the Supreme Court has shown extreme reliance on text of the Code, including the following examples:

- *Wells* came to the rather obvious conclusion that "in contemplation of death" is a motive not limited to the moments when death is imminent, but rather refers to what the donor was thinking about when he made the gift;[1447] this illustrates the fact that the Court's penchant for literalism is a position that is teed up by the penchant of either party to a tax dispute to argue for a non-literal meaning.
- *Griffiths* interpreted the 1936 amendment to the Code that a stock dividend was not taxable as a dividend "to the extent it does not constitute income . . . under the 16th amendment" by focusing on the fact that "does" identified the current state of the law and not one that might exist in the future.[1448]
- *Bliss* ruled that the gross amount of preferentially taxed capital gains was the base for the 15% of gross income cap on charitable deductions because capital gains were listed as part of net income.[1449]
- *Lester* read "specifically designated" child support to exclude inferred child support.[1450]
- *Gitlitz*[1451] is a recent example of Supreme Court Code interpretation, which might be termed "strict," but does not rely on any standard canons of statutory construction.[1452]
- *Knight* interpreted "would not have been incurred if the property" were held by an individual rather than a trust in section 67(e)(1) as not meaning "could not" because of the words used, and interpreted "would" as implying customary conduct.[1453]

[1446] Gregory v. Commissioner, 27 B.T.A. 223 (1932); *but cf.* Palermo v. United States, 360 U.S. 343 (1959) (Justice Frankfurter calling the Jenks Act similarly detailed and not requiring much interpretation). He also held the tax laws up as subject to less purposive reading than the antitrust laws in United States v. Hutcheson, 312 U.S. 219, 235 (1941).

[1447] United States v. Wells, 283 U.S. 102 (1931).

[1448] Helvering v. Griffiths, 318 U.S. 371 (1943).

[1449] Helvering v. Bliss, 293 U.S. 144 (1934) (this opinion also contains a presumption of liberality as to the charitable deduction). Similarly, but against the taxpayer, United States v. Foster Lumber Co., Inc., 429 U.S. 32 (1976) refused to construe the statute to increase a NOL carryover even though it was not "used" by the taxpayer to full benefit in a prior year. *Compare* cases cited *infra* in Ch. VI.C.2.

[1450] Commissioner v. Lester, 366 U.S. 299 (1961).

[1451] Gitlitz v. Commissioner, 531 U.S. 206 (2001).

[1452] *See* Cummings, *BB&T versus Gitlitz*, *supra* note 1028, at 863.

[1453] Knight v. Commissioner, 552 U.S. 181 (2008).

The degree of the primacy of the Code's text will always be unclear, however, because of the collision of at least two other influences: (1) the general tendencies of American judges to be willing to find an apparently unambiguous statute to be ambiguous, based on understanding of legislative purpose and to interpret ambiguous statutes broadly;[1454] and (2) the multiplicity of purposive inputs on the tax laws: indeed many commentators assert that the Code is more susceptible to contextual construction than the average statute because of its interrelatedness, its incremental growth, and its complexity.[1455] However, for normal operating purposes it is simple common sense to place the text first.

Of late scholars have been less receptive to what they call "textualism,"[1456] and even think that recently textualism has not been the norm in courts.[1457] But to the consternation of many academics,[1458] the Supreme Court is perceived to have swung back toward formalism in statutory interpretation.[1459] Staudt's analyses show that the swing in tax cases to textualism has been overstated.[1460] If there is such a renewed preference for formalism, it is properly

---

1454 *See supra* Ch. I.B.

1455 *See generally* Geier, *Commentary: Textualism and Tax Cases*, 66 TEMP. L. REV. 445 (1993); Livingston, *Congress, the Courts and the Code: Legislative History and the Interpretation of Tax Statutes,* 69 TEX. L. REV. 819 (1991); Zelenak, *Thinking about Nonliteral Interpretations of the Internal Revenue Code*, 64 N.C. L. REV. 623 (1986). For other thoughts on interpreting the Code, see Westin, *Dubious Interpretive Rules for Controlling Federal Taxing Statutes*, 17 WAKE FOREST L. REV. 1 (1981); McMahon, *Random Thoughts on Applying Judicial Doctrines to Interpret the Internal Revenue Code,* 54 SMU L. Rev. 195 (2001).

1456 Simply stated, textualism is the view that the words of the statute are the best evidence of the intent of the legislature. For a review of interpretive schools, *see* Cunningham & Repetti, *supra* note 17, at 7 et seq.; Madison, *supra* note 15, at 702 et seq.

1457 Madison, *supra* note 15; Neuborne, *Background Norms for Federal Statutory Interpretation*, 22 CONN. L. REV. 721 (1990) (stating that the dominant approach in federal courts in 1990 was not literalism but legislative intent or purpose); Cunningham & Repetti, *supra* note 17 at 14.

1458 *See generally* Eskridge & Frickey, *Statutory Interpretation as Practical Reasoning, supra* note 92, at 354; Reynolds, *A Practical Guide to Statutory Interpretation Today*, 94 W. VA. L. R. 927 (1992) (cataloguing the various approaches to interpretation); Cunningham et al., *Plain Meaning and Hard Cases*, 103 YALE L.J. 1561 (1994); Schauer, *Statutory Construction and the Coordinating Function of Plain Meaning*, 1990 SUP. CT. REV. 231 (1991); Randolph, *Dictionaries, Plain Meaning and Context in Statutory Interpretation*, 17 HARV. J.L. & PUB. POL'Y. 71 (1994).

1459 In addition to *Gitlitz*, cited in the text, compare *Corn Products Refining Co. v. Commissioner*, 350 U.S. 46 (1955) (adopting a broad definition of capital assets for reasons related to presumed congressional policy and prevention of tax avoidance), with *Arkansas Best Corp. v. Commissioner*, 485 U.S. 212 (1988) (restricting the reach of the *Corn Products* doctrine to inventory substitutes, in a closer reading of the statute).

1460 *See supra* Ch. III.C.2.

viewed as a preference for the rule of law,[1461] which cannot be wrong until it reaches the "numbskulled" extreme.[1462]

Finally, the Supreme Court will always approach the Internal Revenue Code with a preference for literal reading because, up to now, most Justices generally have not arrived at tax cases with a political preference for a desired outcome (as contrasted, for example, with campaign spending or abortion cases). Plus, they may not know a lot about the lore and policy of the particular rule to be applied and are not much interested in that. Therefore, the most literal reading offers them the most ready answers, can hardly be faulted, and has the advantage of stating the obvious.

However much the scholars dislike textualism, none of them rejects the primacy of the statute. Tax practitioners and the government probably are most comfortable when hewing to plain meaning, and this is justified:

> But for the Court to lessen its reliance on plain meaning would serve only to substitute for the community's contingent normative choices the equally contingent and equally normative choices of individual interpretation. . . . Plain language may provide some minimal mutual understanding that guards something that is shared in the face of unduly disparate political views and social experiences.[1463]

VI.B.1.a. *Code Rules*

To accord primacy to text one must first know and use the Code's own rules of procedure and application. The Code, like the rest of the U.S. Code and most state statutes, provides only a few, inconsequential, guides for its own

---

1461

> At the heart of the word "formalism," in many of its numerous uses, lies the concept of decisionmaking according to rule. Formalism is the way in which rules achieve their "ruleness" precisely by doing what is supposed to be the failing of formalism: screening off from a decisionmaker factors that a sensitive decisionmaker would otherwise take into account. Moreover, it appears that this screening off takes place largely through the force of the language in which rules are written. Thus the tasks performed by rules are tasks for which the primary tool is the specific linguistic formulation of a rule. As a result, insofar as formalism is frequently condemned as excessive reliance on the language of a rule, it is the very idea of decisionmaking by rule that is being condemned, either as a description of how decisionmaking can take place or as a prescription for how decisionmaking should take place.

Schauer, *Formalism*, 97 YALE L.J. 509, 510 (1988); *see also* POPKIN, at 173 (textualism follows from emphasis on certainty in the rule of law).

1462 Elhauge, *supra* note 66, at 2275-76.

1463 Schauer, *Statutory Construction*, *supra* note 1458, at 256; *see also* Eskridge & Frickey, *Statutory Interpretation as Practical Reasoning*, *supra* note 92, at 321 (suggesting a hierarchical but inclusive analytical approach, moving from text to specific and general legislative history to legislative purpose and history to evolution of the statute to current policy); *see* Farber, *The Inevitability of Practical Reason: Statutes, Formalism and the Rule of Law*, 45 VAND. L. REV. 533 (1992).

interpretation. The need for more such guides has been noted.[1464] In addition to certain definitions, section 7806 "Construction of Title" is the only specific guidance on construction in the Code.[1465] Its guidance is negative rather than positive by forbidding giving legal effect to:

- Cross references;[1466]
- Location or grouping;[1467]
- Tables of contents and "similar outline, analysis, or descriptive matter relating to the contents of this title"; and
- Sidenotes and ancillary tables in prints of the Act before enactment (referring to the "Act" that was the 1954 Code).

Courts have not frequently cited this section, and they often violate its prohibition even after citing it.[1468] This is a curious state of affairs: Congress does not want something considered as reflecting its intention, but the courts nevertheless consider it. Professor Elhauge's analysis provides a good explanation that satisfies both the needs of the Congress and of the courts: reliance on this prohibited evidence may not be used to find Congress' intent, but is the best available evidence of Congress' current preferences or can elicit Congress' preferences; in any event, it appropriately relieves the courts of making an unguided choice based on their own predilections.

The resistance to titles, etc., may lie in the suspicion that they are inserted by compilers or publishers who have nothing to do with the legislative process, as contrasted with titles placed there by Congress, or at least congressional staff (which now are their sources).[1469]

The prohibition of section 7806 is not consistent with the law generally. The Supreme Court has said both before and after the enactment of section 7806 in 1954 that titles cannot vary or restrict the text of the statute, but

---

[1464] *See* Elhauge, *supra* note 66, at 2033 (citing Rosenkranz, *Federal Rules of Statutory Interpretation*, 115 Harv. L. Rev. 2085 (2002); Ross, *Where Have You Gone Karl Llewellyn? Should Congress Turn its Lonely Eyes to You?* 5 Vand. L. Rev. 561, 566-72 (1992)).

[1465] Section 7806 derives from the Act of Feb. 10, 1939, ch. 2, § 6, 53 Stat. 1a, which provided a similar restriction in the interpretation of the 1939 Code. Since that Code was a compilation of prior laws, the codifiers' characterization of statutory effect was deemed an uncertain guide to congressional meaning. *See* United States v. Dixon, 347 U.S. 381, 385-86 (1954).

[1466] *See also* MacLaughlin v. Alliance Ins. Co. of Philadelphia, 286 U.S. 244 (1932).

[1467] United States v. Reorganized CF&I Fabricators of Utah, 518 U.S. 213 (location of payment under heading of excise taxes did not make it an excise tax). Nat'l Fed'n of Indep. Bus. v. Sebelius, 132 S. Ct. 2566 (2010), which decided that the penalty in the Affordable Care Act was not a tax for injunction purposes but was a tax for constitutional purposes, did not cite section 7806, but the dissent cited *Fabricators* as a reason not to treat the penalty as a tax.

[1468] *See* Murtagh, *supra* note 105, at 530 (citing cases going both ways on this point); Dwan, *Internal Revenue Code of 1954: Legislative and Administrative Techniques*, 39 Minn. L. Rev. 819, 821 (1955) (observing that the prohibition started in the 1939 Code because of the desire not to change existing law by codification, which desire was not operative in 1954).

[1469] *See* G.C.M. 36,731 (May 18, 1976) (citing a text referring to compilers and publishers and applying section 7806 to a Revenue Ruling (to which it clearly does not apply)).

can be used to interpret ambiguities.[1470] The important *Knowlton v. Moore* decision on an early inheritance tax relied on the section heading "whilst not conclusive."[1471] The lower courts commonly at least consider section headings and the like, or distinguish what they are doing from what is prohibited.[1472] The Chief Counsel in G.C.M. 35908 cited section 7806, but nevertheless stated: "the location and title of Code § 4940 are significant in understanding its relationship to the rest of the Code." But the conservative origin of resistance to interpretive aids is reflected in Justice Field's refusal to rely on a heading or Congress' purpose in an 1866 federal tax opinion.[1473]

Other statutory guides include the following:

- Section 7701 contains many definitions and cross references, including Section 7701(a)(17), which allows husband to mean wife and wife to mean husband. Section 7701(a) states that the definitions apply to Title 26 "where not otherwise distinctly expressed or manifestly incompatible with the intent thereof. . . ." The language dates at least to 1878, but the option to ignore the stated definitions has been little used.[1474]
- Section 7701(c) states that "includes and including" in definitions do not exclude other things otherwise within the meaning of the thing defined;[1475] the Supreme Court has offered its view on "including" as contrasted to "means."[1476]

[1470] United States v. Quality Stores, Inc., 134 S. Ct. 1395 (2014) (ignoring section 7806 and stating that titles could be useful, but ultimately relying on a complete investigation of the purpose of the statute); INS v. St. Cyr, 533 U.S. 289 (2001); Baral v. United States, 528 U.S. 431, 437 (2000) (citing the caption of a section to support the Court's interpretation); Brotherhood of R.R. Trainmen v. Baltimore & Ohio R. Co., 331 U.S. 519, 528-29 (1947); Maguire v. Commissioner, 313 U.S. 1 (1941); Cornell v. Coyne, 192 U.S. 418 (1904) (stamp tax case in which Court stated that title was to be referred to only in case of ambiguity); Knowlton v. Moore, 178 U.S. 41 (1900) (relying on section heading to avoid injury); U.S. v. Fisher, 6 U.S. 358 (1805) (admitting that the statute's title was due "a degree of notice" when the statute was amgibuous, but ultimately disagreeing with the title); *see also* Pennsylvania Dept. of Corrections v. Yeskey, 524 U.S. 206 (1998) (nontax case; title useful but cannot limit the plain meaning of the statute); *cf.* United States v. Dixon, 347 U.S. 381 (1954) (declined to allow section heading "forfeitures" to prevent violation of section from being a crime; quoted predecessor of section 7806).

[1471] Knowlton v. Moore, 178 U.S. 41 (1900) (see also opinions cited therein). In the same era the Court relied on a title to determine the purpose of a revenue and tax bill. Millard v. Roberts, 202 U.S. 429 (1906).

[1472] *See, e.g.,* Ralim S. El v. Commissioner, 144 T.C. No. 9 (2015); Rhone-Poulenc Surfactants and Specialties, L.P. v. Commissioner, 114 T.C. 533 n. 14 (2000).

[1473] Hadden v. Collector, 72 U.S. 107 (1866).

[1474] *See* Lafayette v. La. Power & Light Co., 435 U.S. 389 (1978), *citing* Ohio v. Helvering, 292 U.S. 360 (1934). Although it may have dropped out of the biannual revenue acts for a while. *See* 53 Stat. 469, sec. 3797.

[1475] Sims v. United States, 359 U.S. 108 (1959) (person includes a state, because not excluded).

[1476] Helvering v. Morgan's, Inc., 293 U.S. 121, 125 n. 1 (1934). As to lists that use neither "means" nor "including," see HCSC-Laundry v. United States, 450 U.S. 1 (1981) (laundries were not on the list and so were excluded).

- Section 7701(o)(1) says "see" other definitions in Title 1 of the U.S. Code and then subsection (2) says see section 7801(a), which says cross references using "see" are for convenience only.
- Section 7701(p) cross references relevant general interpretive rules in Title 1 of the U.S. Code (including the Dictionary Act).
- Section 7852(d)(1) places tax treaties on a par with the statute, meaning neither has primacy except based on time of adoption.[1477] A treaty will not be deemed to have been abrogated or modified by a later (usually tax) statute unless such purpose on the part of Congress has been clearly expressed.[1478] Treaties are interpreted like contracts, so the parties' course of conduct may control; treaty interpretation has a jurisprudence of its own.[1479]
- Title 1 of the U.S. Code, the Dictionary Act, contains the definitions for the meaning of any Act of Congress (which includes the Code) "unless the context indicates otherwise."[1480] It prescribes that the singular includes the plural,[1481] the plural includes the singular, the present includes the future, and company or association includes successors and assigns (in 1 U.S.C. 5). The latter directive is seldom considered in the Code and usually special rules in the Code and regulations direct treatment of successors. The Court relied on the Act in *Hobby Lobby* to find that a for- profit corporation is a person that can assert an infringement on the exercise of religion through a penal tax, and did not consider whether the context indicated otherwise.[1482] The Court struck down as unconstitutional an amendment to the Dictionary Act to define marriage in the *Windsor* estate tax decision.[1483]
- Numerous Code sections contain definitions that are limited to a Part or Subpart or Chapter or the section itself. For example, section 317(b) defines redemption of stock only for purposes of this part, which runs

---

[1477] *See* BITTKER & LOKKEN, at 65.4.1 (but this rule can be changed by a specific Code section).

[1478] Cook v. United States, 288 U.S. 102 (1933).

[1479] *See* O'Connor v. United States, 479 U.S. 27 (1986) (Justice Scalia relying on context first, text second, and absurdity third); Maximov v. United States, 373 U.S. 49 (1963) (U.S. trust could not claim exemption for foreign resident on ground that its beneficiaries were foreign; Court found no purpose for such result and treaty was clear to the contrary; refused to deviate so far from domestic tax concepts); United States v. Stuart, 489 U.S. 353 (1989) (rights granted under treaties should be liberally construed).

[1480] 1 U.S.C. §1. *See* Rowland v. California Men's Colony, 506 U.S. 194 (1993) (indicates otherwise requires less than an absurdity).

[1481] United States v. Fior D'Italia, Inc., 536 U.S. 238 (2002) (dissent thought that when FICA withholding statute employed definition that referred to a single employee's compensation, the employer had to sum the separate actual compensation amounts that were tips reported by the waiters, but majority relied on another part of the statute that spoke of plural wages).

[1482] Burwell v. Hobby Lobby Stores, Inc., 134 S. Ct. 2751 (2014).

[1483] United States v. Windsor, 133 S. Ct. 2675 (2013).

> from section 301 to section 318. Distributions described in the later part governing reorganizations are not redemptions.

Also section 7851(a)(1)(C) establishes certain effective dates. A useful summary of current interpretive methods is contained in the Uniform Statute and Rule Construction Act of 1995 and its Comments.[1484]

Entrenchment rules are a different sort of Code rule that can have interpretive effects.[1485] These are rules that purport to limit the ability of later congresses to make changes except in certain ways. When a later change is made in a different way, the doctrine of implied repeal may apply.

For a linguistic maxim in an unsuspected location, see Regulation section 1.368-2(h):

> As used in section 368, as well as in other provisions of the Internal Revenue Code, if the context so requires, the conjunction "or" denotes both the conjunctive and the disjunctive, and the singular includes the plural. For example, the provisions of the statute are complied with if "stock and securities" are received in exchange as well as if "stock or securities" are received.

VI.B.1.b. *Internal Revenue Service Methods*

The Internal Revenue Manual discusses researching tax law, and provides guidelines to Service employees for legal interpretation in issuing published guidance,[1486] in audits and disputes,[1487] and in writing private guidance.[1488] The Manual contains directions on the weighting of various authorities, but contains no directions on how to interpret the Code, other than that strained interpretations not be adopted.[1489] In the absence of regulations, an unconditional ruling on an apparently clear section will be issued only after congressional reports are examined to determine if there is an ambiguity (a somewhat surprising approach).[1490]

Analysis of the relative validity of legal interpretations comes up most frequently in the civil penalty area where the taxpayer may be able to avoid a penalty by reliance on the opinion of a tax advisor.[1491] The Service's publications provide very limited information on the reasonableness of interpretations relative to penalties, with the discussion mostly focusing on the relative

---

[1484] UNIFORM STATUTE AND RULE CONSTRUCTION ACT (1995).

[1485] *See* Grewal, *Legislative Entrenchment Rules in the Tax Law*, 62 ADMIN. L. REV. 1011 (Fall 2010). For example, section 446(e) says "except as otherwise expressly provided..."

[1486] I.R.M. 32.1.1, 32.2.1, 32.2.3.

[1487] I.R.M. 4.10.7.

[1488] I.R.M. 33.1.2.

[1489] I.R.M. 40.10.7 (do not adopt strained interpretations); Rev. Proc. 1964-22, 1964-1 C.B. 689 (same); *see also* I.R.M. 31.1.1.1(3) ("It is our responsibility to find the true meaning of the statutory provision and not to adopt a strained construction with the goal of maximizing revenue. We properly protect the revenue only when we ascertain and apply the true meaning of the statute."); 40.10.7.2 (same); 32.1.1.1 (same).

[1490] I.R.M. 1.2.16.1.2 (1960).

[1491] *See* SALTZMAN & BOOK, at 7B.04[3].

weighting of, and ability to rely or not for certain purposes on various sources of authority.[1492]

The Service views:

- The decisions of the Supreme Court, but not of any other court, as on a par with the Code;[1493]
- Regulations as binding on it, whether legislative or interpretive;[1494]
- Legislative regulations as having the force of law (but no longer so stated in IRM),[1495]
- Legislative regulations as receiving more weight in court;[1496] and
- Regulations as not subject to change by any published guidance other than a regulation.[1497]

VI.B.1.c. *Literalism; Form over Substance; Is There a Plain Meaning?*

The Supreme Court says further judicial inquiry into the meaning of an unambiguous statute is unnecessary "except in rare and exceptional circumstances."[1498] The Court says it resorts to other evidence of Congress' intent only when the statute has no plain meaning.[1499] It stated the black letter rule in the famous *Crane* tax case:

[1492] Reg. § 1.6694-2(b) (reasonable belief); Reg. § 1.6662-4(d) (substantial authority).

[1493] I.R.M. 4.10.7.2.9.8.

[1494] I.R.M. 4.10.7.2.3.4.

[1495] *See, e.g.*, A.O.D. 1980-179 (Dec. 12, 1980). However, the Manual's general discussion of regulations does not make this assertion. In addition, as pointed out in *Dixon v. United States*, 381 U.S. 68 (1965), the front of the Internal Revenue Bulletin used to contain the following warning:

> . . . rulings [including acquiescences] are for the information of taxpayers and their counsel as showing the trend of official opinion in . . . the Bureau of Internal Revenue; the rulings *other than Treasury Decisions* have none of the force or effect of Treasury Decisions and do not commit the Department to any interpretation of the law which has not been formally approved and promulgated by the Secretary of the Treasury.

(Emphasis added.) This subject is discussed more fully in Ch. VI.D.5. below.

[1496] I.R.M. 32.1.1.2.7; 32.1.1.4; 4.10.7.2.3.2.

[1497] I.R.M. 32.1.1.4 (No other form of published guidance can change a regulation but another regulation.).

[1498] United States v. Clintwood Elkhorn Mining Co., 553 U.S. 1 (2008); Freytag v. Commissioner, 501 U.S. 868 (1991); Crooks v. Harrelson, 282 U.S. 55 (1930). *See also* Connecticut Nat'l Bank v. Germain, 503 U.S. 249 (1992); Barnhill v. Johnson, 503 U.S. 393 (1992) ("appeals to legislative history are well-taken only to resolve 'statutory ambiguity'"); Estate of Cowart v. Nicklos Drilling Co., 505 U.S. 469 (1992); Demarest v. Manspeaker, 498 U.S. 184, 190 (1991); United States v. Ron Pair Enterprises, Inc., 489 U.S. 235, 242 (1989) ("rare cases"); Am. Tobacco Co. v. Patterson, 456 U.S. 63, 74-5 (1982) ("Going behind the plain language of a statute in search of a possibly contrary congressional intent is a 'step to be taken cautiously' even under the best of circumstances.").

[1499] *See* United States v. Stapf, 375 U.S. 118 (1963).

> It is fundamental that an unambiguous statute should be given effect according to its plain and obvious meaning, [citing cases]. This principle is as applicable to a revenue statute as it is to any other type of legislation.[1500]

But the finding of ambiguity in the statute is itself an ambiguous process.[1501] Justice Holmes stated:

> It is said that when the meaning of language is plain we are not to resort to evidence in order to raise doubts. That is rather an axiom of experience than a rule of law, and does not preclude consideration of persuasive evidence if it exists.[1502]

Chief Justice Roberts in effect paraphrased Holmes when he wrote in his second opinion upholding the Affordable Care Act against a claim based on clear statutory words that were inconsistent with Congress' purpose:

> The Court nevertheless must do its best, "bearing in mind the 'fundamental canon of statutory construction that the words of a statute must be read in their context and with a view to their place in the overall statutory scheme.'"[1503]

Ch. III.C.3.a(1) showed that *Gregory* was a case in which the Court resolved an ambiguity that practitioners and the Board of Tax Appeals had not discerned. The Court frequently adds a supporting analysis of extrinsic evidence to a finding of plain meaning.[1504] The threshold issue of whether the statute is ambiguous arises in the area of *Chevron* deference, discussed below in Ch. VI.D., where it also has been recognized that evidence extrinsic to the statute may be examined to find that the statute is unambiguous. Therefore, the gloss about unambiguous statutes not requiring interpretation is itself ambiguous.

[1500] Crane v. Commissioner, 331 U.S. 1, 6 (1947).

[1501] *Cf.* Colonial American Life Ins. Co. v. Commissioner, 491 U.S. 244, 255-62 (1989) (in the dissent's view the majority created an ambiguity out of a clear statute because of a mistaken desire to reason from first principles instead of analyzing the Code's text); Helvering v. Morgan's, Inc., 293 U.S. 121 (1934) (the Court strained to find "taxable year" ambiguous so that it could rule it to refer to the calendar year and not a short fiscal year).

[1502] Boston Sand & Gravel Co. v. United States, 278 U.S. 41, 48 (1928).

[1503] King v. Burwell, 135 S. Ct. 2480 (2015).

[1504] United States v. Vogel Fertilizer Co., 455 U.S. 16 (1982) involved a "not completely unambiguous" statute. The Court read the statute to require that the same shareholders be counted in meeting the 50% and 80% tests for common control under section 1563. The statute seemed clear in that it required that persons be counted for the 50% test only to the extent their stock ownership was "identical with respect to each such corporation." Nevertheless, the Court examined the legislative history because of the deference required for Treasury regulations that the Court invalidated. *See also* Baral v. United States, 528 U.S. 431 (2000) (even though statute stated that estimated taxes were deemed paid on the return due date, which seemed to be its plain meaning, the Court discussed problems of administrability and other matters in supporting its plain reading); Freytag v. Commissioner, 501 U.S. 868 (1991) (stating that when a statute has no exception it means Congress meant no exception, but then going on to examine legislative history).

Sometimes the Court's assertion that a statute is clear is not a conclusion about statutory meaning but a fact finding. For example Justice Black in *Arrowsmith* stated that later payments that were related to a prior sale of a capital asset "fall squarely" within the definition of capital losses; Justice Jackson in dissent thought this was an issue of fact within the Tax Court's domain.[1505]

Taxpayers most frequently are the party asserting that the Code's words have a plain meaning identifying a form taxpayers can adopt to obtain a stated tax result. In these cases, taxpayers assert form over substance not as a method of fact finding (discussed below), but as a method of legal interpretation, often called literalism. When the government resists plain meaning, it is usually because it believes that either or both of (a) tax theory, or (b) Congress' presumed or stated purpose, requires a different result. The Court is fairly resistant to the need to enforce tax theory in the context of an apparently clear statutory directive,[1506] as illustrated by its most recent examples of a literal interpretation in taxpayers' favor, which produced results that do not comport with the government's asserted tax theories:

- *PPL*: Because the U.K. windfall tax formula utilized net income in its formula, it must be an income tax for purposes of allowing the foreign tax credit, even though it also could be viewed as a property tax in substance.[1507]
- *Home Concrete:*[1508] "Omits" from gross income means that taxpayer did not report its gross receipts, not that it overstated its basis in property sold. This is a literal interpretation of "omits," but not of gross income (receipts less basis), which is the word used in the statute.[1509]
- *Gitlitz*:[1510] The Court ruled that an S corporation's excluded discharge of indebtedness income passed through to the shareholder because (1) it was a "item of income" under Section 1366(a)(1)(A), and (2) such pass through occurred before rather than after the excluded income had been applied to reduce the shareholder's suspended losses under Section 108(b)(4)(A). As a result, the shareholder was able to deduct suspended S corporation losses due to the momentary stock basis increase under

---

1505 Arrowsmith v. Commissioner, 344 U.S. 6 (1952).

1506 *See, e.g.,* Koshland v. Helvering, 298 U.S. 441 (1936) (rejecting regulation requiring that basis of stock be apportioned to stock received in spin-off, because statute applicable to sale of the original stock says gain will be computed based on its cost; that clearly refers to its entire original cost).

1507 PPL Corp. v. Commissioner, 133 S. Ct. 1897 (2013). *See* Cummings, *Form, Substance, and* PPL, 140 Tax Notes (TA) 365 (July 22, 2013).

1508 United States v. Home Concrete & Supply, LLC, 132 S. Ct. 1836 (2012).

1509 *See* Doyle v. Mitchell Bros. Co., 247 U.S. 179 (1918) (the origin of the view that gross income from the sale of property requires the deduction of cost).

1510 Gitlitz v. Commissioner, 531 U.S. 206 (2001). *See* Zelenak, *The Court and the Code, supra* note 413, at 1788 (". . . the Court adopted a literal interpretation of the statutory language, producing a structurally absurd tax benefit . . . clearly not contemplated by Congress.").

Section 1367(a)(1)(A), without actually increasing its investment in the corporation or including any amount in gross income. All nine Justices agreed with conclusion (1), which is certainly a plausible, if not inevitable, reading. Eight of the Justices agreed with conclusion (2) on the basis of language clearly indicating that the attribute reduction occurred after the determination of tax liability for the year. The government could not point to any legislative history clearly refuting the ordering rule. Thus, the result was simply a perhaps unintended consequence of writing a complicated set of rules.

- *UDI*:[1511] In tax theory, the member of the corporate group that had specified liability losses also should have a net operating loss that would merit being carried back 10 years rather than the usual shorter period. However, the Court held the Treasury to its rule that so far as a consolidated group is concerned there are no separate NOLs, at least as long as the corporations are in the group; rather there is only a consolidated net operating loss. Therefore, because the group had a CNOL and a member of the group had specified liability deductions (but no net loss of its own), the group was allowed to carry back losses that were not specified liability losses for ten years.
- *Soliman*:[1512] Because the statute said "principal place of business," the Fourth Circuit was wrong in letting the taxpayer deduct the expenses of his principal office, which was not necessarily his place of business.

Conversely, where the government can point to legislative history, or other evidence, such as the ordinary meaning of words, that gives some basis to conclude that Congress thought about the problem and did not intend the result, the Court is more likely to reject the taxpayer's plain meaning interpretation in favor of a more substance driven interpretation. See Ch. VI.B.1.d. for discussion of decisions based on Congress' purpose. Three examples of antiliteral interpretation against the taxpayer include:

- *Burnet v. Guggenheim*: Taxpayer transferred his property in trust for his own benefit prior to the adoption of the gift tax, and released his reserved rights over the trust property after the adoption of the gift tax. Taxpayer argued that because a transfer for no consideration had occurred before the tax was adopted, another such gift could not occur again after the tax was adopted. The Court interpreted the gift tax not to apply to the form of a transfer for no consideration, but to the substance of a gift. Because the taxpayer had not made a gift to the trustee or even the potential beneficiaries of the trust besides himself, the gift occurred when he completely released the powers over the trust property. This is the opinion frequently

---

[1511] *See* United Dominion Industries, Inc. v. United States, 532 U.S. 822, 839 (2001) (Thomas, J., concurring).

[1512] Commissioner v. Soliman, 506 U.S. 168 (1993).

cited for Justice Cardozo's inquiry "which choice is it the more likely that Congress would have made?"[1513]

- *Corn Products*: The Court adopted an anti-literal interpretation of capital assets that had to be corrected in *Arkansas Best*.[1514]
- *Woods*: The Court interpreted overstatement of basis to encompass the consequences of ignoring a partnership.[1515]

The most difficult cases are those in which the purpose of Congress cannot be ascertained on the basis of legislative history or a known problem that the statute was intended to solve or common word usage or the like, but rather must rest *solely* on the belief that Congress would not have written an absurd statute, or a statute that sometimes produces absurd results. But these difficult cases are, in fact, the proper dividing line between the cases that can go off on plain and literal meaning (like *Gitlitz*) and those in which a facially clear statute is subject to interpretation to carry out Congress' purpose as discussed in the next subchapter. In other words, cases like this can fairly go either way. See Ch. VI.B.2.l. for discussion of absurdity maxim. The proper default treatment of such cases in which one party would rely solely on a perceived absurdity is stated in this *per curiam* opinion of the Court:

> Judicial perception that a particular result would be unreasonable may enter into the construction of ambiguous provisions, but cannot justify disregard of what Congress has plainly and intentionally provided.[1516]

When the government relies on plain meaning, it usually is making the interpretive argument that the Congress intended form to control substance. Obviously the government will have the better of these cases, not because the Supreme Court has a literalist bent, but because it has a legal bent. Moreover, Justice Brandeis justified following the government's literal interpretation of the statute because the words indicated Congress' intent to fully exercise the taxing power.[1517] The Court has stated that hard cases do not make plain meanings change.[1518] Nevertheless, the Court will adopt antiliteral interpretations in the taxpayers' favor, including, for example:

- *Haggar Co. v. Helvering*: The Code required the taxpayer to provide certain information on its "first return" for a year, but the taxpayer provided that information on an amended return filed before the due date of the

1513 Burnet v. Guggenheim, 288 U.S. 280, 285 (1933).

1514 Corn Products Refining Co. v. Commissioner, 350 U. S. 46 (1955); Arkansas Best Corp. v. Commissioner, 485 U.S. 212 (1988). *See* Tucker, *The Warren Court: Its Impact on the Capital vs. Ordinary Concept Under the Internal Revenue Code*, 17 Kansas L. Rev. 53 (1968).

1515 United States v. Woods, 134 S. Ct. 557 (2013) (underpayment was "attributable to" overstated basis).

1516 Commissioner v. Asphalt Prods. Co., Inc., 482 U.S. 117, 121 (1987). *See also* Iselin v. United States, 270 U.S. 245 (1926) (assuming that Congress inadvertently failed to apply the tax to the facts at hand but refusing to create such coverage).

1517 Helvering v. Midland Mutual Life Ins. Co., 300 U.S. 216 (1937).

1518 Deputy v. Du Pont, 308 U.S. 488 (1940).

original return but after it had filed an original return. The Court ruled unanimously that "first return" did not literally mean the first return filed, but rather a timely filed return for the first year.[1519] Although the opinion referenced the doctrine that statutes should not be interpreted to produce an absurd result, the result the government sought would not have been absurd in the usual sense, but would have required a strict compliance with a line drawn in the statute. The opinion found that Congress did not intend to draw the line where the statute's words placed it, and so moved the line to yield a more just, but not inevitable, result.

Finally, disputes about literal interpretation can come up on a hypothetical: the taxpayer argues that if the government's plain meaning reading is right then some hypothetical absurdity could result. The Court has rejected such an argument, saying it was unrealistic, but in any event, not the taxpayer's facts.[1520]

VI.B.1.d. *Congress' Purpose*

Congress' purpose in enacting a statute is clearly relevant to the process of interpreting the statute,[1521] which sometimes leads to rejecting the primacy of form in fact finding, as discussed in Ch. VI.E.1. *Gregory v. Helvering* is the prime example of the Court interpreting rather brief Code language to add an uncodified requirement into the statute based on its understanding of Congress' purpose, which led to a refusal to allow form to control the tax outcome.[1522] Similarly, in 1827 Chief Justice Marshall interpreted the constitutional prohibition on a state's taxation of imports to prevent a state from taxing importers; Marshall rejected the state's argument that it was not taxing imports by stating: ". . . this is varying the form, without varying the sub-

---

[1519] Haggar Co. v. Helvering, 308 U.S. 389 (1940); *cf.* Mother Lode Coalition Mines Co. v. Commissioner, 317 U.S. 222 (1942) (finding it not absurd to require that an election for depletion to be made on the first return after the property produced income even though there was no net income without depletion).

[1520] Atl. Mut. Ins. Co. v. Commissioner, 523 U.S. 382 (1998) (rejecting taxpayer insurance company's argument that "reserve strengthening" had a plain meaning, and deferring to the regulations).

[1521] The importance of purpose to tax shelter cases has been highlighted as a new discovery in McCormack, *Tax Shelters and Statutory Interpretation: A Much Needed Purposive Approach*, 2009 U. Ill. L. Rev. 697. As the article argues, it does have a role in a better alternative to the application of the economic substance doctrine, but it is hardly a new idea. Also touting a purposive reading of tax cases is Schumacher, *Macniven v. Westmoreland and Tax Advice: Using "Purposive Textualism" to Deal with Tax Shelters and Promote Legitimate Tax Advice*, 92 Marq. L. Rev. 33 (2008).

[1522] *See supra* Ch. III.C.3.a(1).

stance. It is treating a prohibition which is general, as if it were confined to a particular mode of doing the forbidden thing."[1523]

A reader must know the purpose of a Code section to understand even superficially clear words (see, for example, section 304). When the words are not clear, or seem less clear once purpose is examined, then the Supreme Court engages in interpretation of the ambiguous section, asking, according to Justice Cardozo, ". . . which choice is it the more likely that Congress would have made?"[1524] Perhaps not all of the Justiced today would subscribe to that statement of Justice Cardozo, but given his common law background it is not surprising that he took that view. The following discussion examines the use of statutory purpose not only to inform clear words, but also to interpret ambiguous words and fill gaps or change clear words by construction.[1525]

The purpose of a Code section is not the same as the intent of certain legislators who voted for it because, for example, the general goal may be noble but the legislator's particular purpose may have been to benefit some particular taxpayer or group of taxpayers.[1526] Some try hard to distinguish "intentionalism" from "purposivism" in discussions of interpretive schools.[1527] The current dislike of intentionalism is not based on any new discoveries: obviously a search for congressional intent in legislative histories and debates cannot provide a sure statement of so elusive a fact.[1528] Purposivism suffers some of the same criticisms as intentionalism, but fares better. The general purpose of a provision is usually more reliably determinable, and the use of a general purpose to infer a particular meaning is more probative than, for example, a sentence in a report stating that Senator X had a particular opinion about a particular gap in the bill. Pragmatic observers long have understood that the determination of legislative intent is really a question of what general underlying purpose motivated the enactment in its entirety.[1529] Inferring a specific result from the perceived general purpose of a statute sometimes is a possible and useful improvement over a plain meaning approach that woodenly (and

---

1523 Brown v. Maryland, 25 U.S. 419, 444 (1827). However, the Supreme Court seized on this citation to support its conclusion that taxing the income of corporations amounted in substance to impermissible unapportioned taxation of land in *Pollock v. Farmers' Loan & Trust Co.*, 157 U.S. 429, 581, *modified*, 158 U.S. 601 (1895).

1524 Burnet v. Guggenheim, 288 U.S. 280, 285 (1933).

1525 Professor Elhauge has examined how a court goes about estimating the preferences of that enacting Congress. Elhauge, *supra* note 66, at 2049.

1526 Barker, *supra* note 25, at 848.

1527 *See, e.g.*, Eskridge, Frickey and Garrett, *supra* note 1421, at 221-30.

1528 Paul, Prosperity, at 396-97; Elhauge, *supra* note 66, at 2061-65 (reviewing writings to this effect).

1529 Paul, Studies II, at 259.

unimaginatively) reads the statutory words. The use of purpose is often identified with the work of Professors Hart and Sacks.[1530]

The major boundary on purposive interpretation is, of course, the words of the statute. It is sometimes too easy to confuse Congress' specific purposes with a presumed general purpose that the Code be logical or fair. The Code is not uniformly logical or fair,[1531] or is fair only from a certain point of view. For example, why are certain expenses that are clearly ordinary and necessary business expenses not deductible?[1532] Indeed, the whole area of "tax expenditures" concerns a mass of Code provisions thought to be outside someone's norms.[1533]

Understanding Congress' purpose can aid all of the three major categories of statutory interpretation and construction: determining plain meaning, interpreting ambiguous sections, and even construction of unambiguous sections contrary to text. Fortunately, in almost every tax dispute one or both parties will have an interest in explaining the purpose(s) of the relevant provision to the court. Therefore while text may be the theoretically primary and sometimes exclusive focus, purpose is its inevitable companion. However valid are the criticisms of legislative history as evidence of intent or purpose,[1534] the "current law—reasons for change" analyses in legislative histories are almost always both correct and essential to understanding the purpose of the text.[1535] The Supreme Court does not rigidly avoid legislative history even when the statute appears clear.[1536]

The Supreme Court sometimes follows purpose and not the literal words of the Code because it believes that all statutes should be construed in light

---

[1530] Hart and Sacks attempted to synthesize a "legal process" for judging, to circumscribe the process and make it more rational. *See* Eskridge & Frickey, *Legislation Scholarship and Pedagogy in the Post-Legal Process Era*, 48 U. Pitt. L. Rev. 691, 699 (1987) ("Although the Supreme Court itself only sometimes adopts the Hart and Sacks assumption about purposive and rational legislative action, commentators often accept it as established orthodoxy.").

[1531] See opinions of both Justice Douglas and Frankfurter in *Lewyt Corp. v. Commissioner*, 349 U.S. 237 (1955).

[1532] Knight v. Commissioner, 552 U.S. 181 (2008) (describes the two percent floor as an administrative expedient); I.R.C. §§ 67(a) (two percent floor), 162(e) (lobbying expenses).

[1533] *See* Bittker & Lokken, at 3.6.

[1534] For a review of the criticism, see Elhauge, *supra* note 66, at 2065-72.

[1535] But the Court parses those discussions carefully. *See* United States v. Am. College of Physicians, 475 U.S. 834 (1986) (*citing* "Reasons for change").

[1536] *See* Putnam v. Commissioner, 352 U.S. 82 (1956) (statute was clear but opinion discussed Congress' purpose); Harrison v. N. Trust Co., 317 U.S. 476 (1943) (reversed the lower court because its holding was based upon the earlier case of *Edwards v. Slocum*, 264 U.S. 61 (1924); instructed the lower court to look to the legislative history behind the Revenue Act of 1932 because the section at issue "was intended as 'a legislative reversal of the decision' in Edwards v. Slocum."); United States v. Am. Trucking Associations, Inc., 310 U.S. 534 (1940); United States v. Dickerson, 310 U.S. 554, 562 (1940) (these two cases were cited in Revenue Ruling 2001-57, 2001-2 C.B. 488 on statutory interpretation).

of their purpose,[1537] usually their general purpose.[1538] Even a literalist Justice like Scalia stated in a tax opinion that he was finding a meaning for a wholly ambiguous provision by carrying out Congress' purpose.[1539] While the face of the statute is the most persuasive evidence of its purpose, when difficulties with arise the Court resorts to other evidence of purpose (discussed below as extrinsic evidence).[1540] The Supreme Court early articulated this approach in a famous tax case, *Stockholms Enskilda Bank*:

> The intention [of the Congress] being thus disclosed, it is enough that the word or clause is reasonably susceptible of a meaning consonant therewith, whatever might be its meaning in another and different connection. . . . The rule of strict construction is not violated by permitting the words of a statute to have their full meaning, or the more extended of two meanings. The words are not to be bent one way or the other, but to be taken in the sense which will best manifest the legislative intent.[1541]

The reliance on Congress' purpose sometimes overlaps with the maxim that a statute should not be construed to produce an absurd result, that is, one which Congress would not have intended.[1542] These cases generally involve some element other than just the absurdity of the result of plain meaning:

[1537] *Am. Trucking Association, Inc.*, 310 U.S. at 543; Haggar Co. v. Helvering, 308 U.S. 389, 394 (1940) ("All statutes must be construed in light of their purpose."); El Al Israel Airlines, Ltd. v. Tsui Yuan Tseng, 525 U.S. 155 (1999) (construed a Convention in light of its "text, purpose, and overall structure," where ambiguous).

[1538] *See, e.g.*, Provost v. United States, 269 U.S. 443 (1926) (ruling that stamp tax on transfers of legal title to stock applied to stock lending transactions because they were within the general purpose of Congress to tax all title transfers except as specifically exempted, even if Congress did not have a specific purpose to tax lending transactions; also when Congress changed the law to adopt a change suggested in an earlier Congress and then rejected, it intended to change the law).

[1539] United States v. Woods, 134 S. Ct. 557 (2013).

[1540] *Am. Trucking Associations, Inc.*, 310 U.S. at 543-44. This is said to be the Court's most famous statement of purposivism. *See* POPKIN, at 132.

[1541] Helvering v. Stockholms Enskilda Bank, 293 U.S. 84, 94 (1934). For more recent examples, see *Commissioner v. Keystone Consolidated Industries, Inc.*, 508 U.S. 152, 160 (1993) (finding that Congress intended to end abuses of employer sales of property to pension plans) and *United States v. Donruss Co.*, 393 U.S. 297 (1969) (where the statute is ambiguous, a broad congressional purpose required a narrowing of the escape route allowed to the taxpayer). Of course, the Supreme Court also has stated a rule that is virtually the converse:

> [A]lthough a court may have reference to . . . [the statutory] purpose when there is a genuine question as to the meaning of one of the requirements Congress has imposed, a court is not free to disregard [statutory] requirements simply because it considers them redundant or unsuited to achieving the general purpose in a particular case.

Commissioner v. Gordon, 391 U.S. 83, 93 (1968).

[1542] Willcuts v. Milton Dairy Co., 275 U.S. 215 (1927) (construing "undivided profits" not to exist if capital was impaired because otherwise taxpayer would get the "benefit" of a capital impairment twice, which Congress would not have intended). *See* Ch. VI.B.2.l.

they may involve words that are at least subject to varying meanings or evidence of Congress' purpose in legislative histories.

Other examples of the Supreme Court's reliance on Congress' purpose include the following:

- *Quality Stores* employed a variety of interpretive techniques to infer Congress' purpose to require withholding on severance pay, but without ever referring to the intent or purpose of Congress.[1543] Justice Kennedy may have intentionally avoided those words to placate literalists who joined the opinion.
- *Home Concrete* inferred Congress' purpose to give the Service more time to discover gross receipts that the taxpayer did not report at all (as contrasted with overstated basis), even though the legislative history did not support that purpose.[1544]
- *Mayo* relied on Congress' purpose to broadly apply the tax and benefits of Social Security to rule that *Chevron* deference should be applied to the regulation requiring withholding on pay to medical students who worked at least 40 hours a week.[1545]
- *Davis* reasoned that an actual dividend placed corporate property in the hands of the shareholder without changing his economic interest in the corporation, and so Congress meant for a redemption that had the same result to be essentially equivalent to a dividend.[1546]
- The entire regime for taxing trusts and their beneficiaries shows that Congress' purpose was for the trust income to be taxed to someone.[1547]
- *Harmel* ruled that oil lease rentals did not share the hardship at which Congress aimed the capital gain preference;[1548]
- *Edwards v. Douglas* interpreted "accumulated" as not excluding current year earnings and profits by relying heavily on the purpose of Congress to increase the taxation of dividends to finance the war,[1549] contrary to the eventual normal usage in the Code.
- *Chicago Portrait* ruled that the ambiguous term "foreign countries" whose taxes were eligible for the foreign tax credit included not only foreign governments with "international standing" but any foreign government

---

[1543] United States v. Quality Stores, Inc., 134 S. Ct. 1395 (2014).

[1544] United States v. Home Concrete & Supply, LLC, 132 S. Ct. 1836 (2012) (adopted the logic of the section as argued by the taxpayer and rejected a different purpose of Congress argued by the government). It followed The Colony, Inc. v. Commissioner, 357 U.S. 28 (1958) (moving from a determination of statutory ambiguity directly to legislative history).

[1545] Mayo Found. for Med. Educ. & Research v. United States, 562 U.S. 44 (2011).

[1546] United States v. Davis, 397 U.S. 301 (1970).

[1547] Helvering v. Butterworth, 290 U.S. 365 (1933).

[1548] Burnet v. Harmel, 287 U.S. 103 (1932).

[1549] Edwards v. Douglas, 269 U.S. 204 (1925).

with authority to collect taxes, because that would carry out the purpose of the credit to prevent double taxation.[1550]

- The Court was unswayed by the inclusion of 16 ½ months of partnership income on a partner's final return, because when Congress wrote that the partner should include his share of the income of "any" partnership year ending in the partner's year, "any year" did not mean any one year, because the purpose of Congress was not to limit the inclusion to one partnership year but to include any year ending in the partner's year.[1551]
- *Phipps* endorsed the "*Sansome* rule" of earnings and profits continuity in reorganizations but had to apply the underlying congressional purpose it perceived to prevent the taxpayer from netting down its earnings and profits by its liquidated subsidiary's deficit.[1552]
- *Jewett* carefully examined how the Treasury wrote a regulation for the purpose of creating a rule that would satisfy each of two appellate court opinions, as a step in the Court's own interpretation of the regulation.[1553]
- The Court may disagree with the taxpayer as to Congress' purpose, as it did in *Braunstein*.[1554] The taxpayer reasonably argued that even though it fit within the formal definition of a collapsible corporation, it was not in fact converting ordinary income into capital gain, which was the loophole at which Congress aimed. But the Court ruled that Congress decided to carry out its purpose by creating an objective rule that would not require investigation of ad hoc circumstances.
- The Court has relied on purpose most frequently in support of the plain meaning of the statute. For example, in *Malat v. Riddell* the Court ruled that the definition of capital asset refers to a principal and not just a substantial purpose to hold for sale to customers, thus coordinating the natural interpretation of "primarily" with what the Court understood to be the general purpose of Congress.[1555]
- But when the Code leaves a term, such as "recapitalization," wholly undefined, the Court also relies on congressional purpose.[1556]

1550 Burnet v. Chicago Portrait Co., 285 U.S. 1 (1932).

1551 Guar. Trust Co. v. Commissioner, 303 U.S. 493 (1938) (relying on a change in the bill before it was enacted).

1552 Commissioner v. Phipps, 336 U.S. 410 (1949).

1553 Jewett v. Commissioner, 455 U.S. 305, 314 (1982).

1554 Braunstein v. Commissioner, 374 U.S. 65 (1963).

1555 Malat v. Riddell, 383 U.S. 569 (1966); *see also* United States v. Rodgers, 461 U.S. 677 (1983) (applying the "plain meaning" as supported by the evident purpose); Virginian Hotel Corp. v. Helvering, 319 U.S. 523, 527 (1943) ("allowed" deduction is normally one that is claimed, and it would take clear and compelling indication from the Congress to hold otherwise, although Justice Jackson in dissent disagreed). *See also* Universal Battery Co. v. United States, 281 U.S. 580 (1930) (an accessory for a car is a part primarily used in cars).

1556 *See* Bazley v. Commissioner, 331 U.S. 737 (1947); *see also* United States v. Davis, 397 U.S. 301 (1970) (finding the meaning of "not essentially equivalent to a dividend" to be informed by the obvious congressional purpose).

- The Court held that an employer had not "paid" a contribution to a qualified plan by giving a note, relying on Congress' purpose.[1557]
- Congress must have had a purpose that at least some of the contents of tax returns be widely available to the public, and, therefore, the direction for the Commissioner to post the return information publicly implicitly modified the criminal penalty for publishing return information.[1558]
- The Court ruled that a debt was not "discharged" for section 108 purposes when the bank never owed it under the original terms of the agreement (an early withdrawal penalty), based on an analysis of the likely purpose of Congress.[1559]
- Surprisingly, the Court construed "capital stock" to mean the net value of the assets of a corporation that had no capital stock by inferring Congress' intent from the context of the section.[1560]
- Another surprising reliance on Congress' purpose to collect as much tax as possible from oil importers led the Court to define "first domestic processing" as the first processing after enactment, not the first processing of the oil owned by the taxpayer (which would seem to be more natural).[1561]
- *Correll* interpreted the deduction for "meals and lodging" to imply an unstated requirement of overnight travel because it understood Congress' purpose to be to allow deductions only when living expenses were unusually high due to being away from home overnight (plus the inference that the meals must be linked with the lodging).[1562]
- The Court applied inferred purpose to close a loophole as to which Congress had no specific intent and rejected another logical reading in *Woolford Realty*.[1563] It refused to find that "the taxpayer" that could carry over its losses included the consolidated group and the income of its other members that the loss company joined after the year of loss, despite acknowledging the fact that generally ". . . in a system of taxation so intricate and vast as ours there are many other loopholes unsuspected by the framers of the statute, many other devices whereby burdens can be lowered."[1564]

But when the Court in *Corn Products* followed perceived congressional purpose to depart from the plain words of the statute, it stepped into a bog from

[1557] Don E. Williams Co. v. Commissioner, 429 U.S. 569, 579 (1977) (finding a congressional intent to ensure payment to employees from qualified plans on the basis of statutory language and clearly expressed legislative history).

[1558] United States v. Dickey, 268 U.S. 378 (1925).

[1559] United States v. Centennial Savings Bank FSB, 499 U.S. 573, 583 (1991).

[1560] Hecht v. Malley, 265 U.S. 144 (1924).

[1561] Colgate-Palmolive-Peet Co. v. United States, 320 U.S. 422 (1943).

[1562] United States v. Correll, 389 U.S. 299 (1967).

[1563] Woolford Realty Co. v. Rose, 286 U.S. 319 (1932).

[1564] *Id.* at 330.

which it had to extricate itself.[1565] In that opinion, it restricted the definition of capital assets to rule for the government that taxpayer did not receive a capital gain, but when other taxpayers claimed ordinary losses it modified its interpretation in *Arkansas Best.* These opinions have been cited as examples for arguments against purposive reading of the Code.[1566] Ultimately the search for and reliance on Congress' purpose is a matter of degree; courts will not stop doing it, no matter how much academics protest.

The Court also has recognized the limits of purpose as follows:

- Justice O'Connor said the Court does not sit as a committee to perfect the administration of the tax laws.[1567]
- *Nash* declined to recast the word recovery in the tax benefit rule to include abandonment of a bad debt reserve.[1568]
- *Hendler Dairy* was a decision of the Court that created a "practical embargo" on use of the reorganization provisions, requiring that Congress reverse the decision retroactively.[1569]
- *Southwest Consolidated*[1570] stated that "'[s]olely' [for voting stock] leaves no leeway," without discussing the harshness of the consequences or the congressional intent or policies.
- In *Hanover Bank,* the Court was not moved by even a major statutory blooper. The case involved the deductibility of bond premium measured by the difference between the maturity price and an earlier call price on a special call date.[1571] The government protested, and the Court did not disagree, that to allow use of the special call date price would create a "tax loophole of major dimension." But this dire prediction ". . . may not, of course, have any impact upon our interpretation of the statute under review. We are bound by the meaning of the words used

---

[1565] Corn Prods. Refining Co. v. Commissioner, 350 U.S. 46, 52 (1955) ("The capital-asset provision of section 117 must not be so broadly applied as to defeat rather than further the purposes of Congress.") The Court retreated from the perception of the meaning of its earlier decision in *Arkansas Best Corp. v. Commissioner*, 485 U.S. 212 (1988).

[1566] Livingston, *Practical Reason, supra* note 3, at 706 et seq.

[1567] United States v. Cleveland Indians Baseball Co., 532 U.S. 200 (2001) (refusing to balance efficiency of administration and fairness). *See* Myron C. Grauer, *Justice O'Connor's Approach to Tax Cases: Could She Have Led the Court Toward a More Collaborative Role for the Judiciary in the Development of Tax Law*, 39 Ariz. St. L.J. 69 (2007).

[1568] Nash v. United States, 398 U.S. 1 (1970).

[1569] United States v. Hendler, 303 U.S. 564 (1938) (treating the acquirer's assumption of the reorganizing corporation's liabilities as potentially taxable boot, allowing a basis step for acquirer's that had not paid the tax on boot in the years before the Court's decision). *See* Paul, Studies III, at 39 (an "unusually logical" decision).

[1570] Helvering v. Southwest Consolidated Corp., 315 U.S. 194 (1942).

[1571] Hanover Bank v. Commissioner, 369 U.S. 672 (1962).

by Congress, taken in light of the pertinent legislative history."[1572] The Court found that Congress knew of the windfall and did not change it.

- In another case, the Court stated: "The relevant question is not whether, as an abstract matter, the rule advocated by petitioner accords with good policy. The question we must consider is whether the policy petitioner favors is that which Congress effectuated by its enactment of section 6501. Courts are not authorized to rewrite a statute because they might deem its effects susceptible of improvement."[1573]
- In *Iselin*, Justice Brandeis agreed that Congress probably had a purpose to tax the case at hand, but the words it used did not extend to the facts, and to apply the tax would go beyond statutory construction.[1574]
- In *Hall*, the majority refused to even attempt to see an ambiguity in the statutory words, which the four-Justice-dissent asserted could be used to carry out what they thought was the clear intent of Congress.[1575]
- In a case involving the tax law of the Phillipines, where Chief Justice Taft had been the Governor General, Taft refused to agree that the law requiring Chinese merchants to keep their books in English was a "nose of wax to be changed from that which the plain language imports," but having found it applicable by its terms, relieved the Chinese from the criminal penalty under the Phillipine Bill of Rights.[1576]

VI.B.1.e. *Administrability*

Administrability by the government of the tax law may support plain meaning.[1577] Administrability also is a primary reason for not construing equitable assistance for the taxpayer into the Code.[1578] Administrability of the law can trump plain meaning as in the following examples:

[1572] *Id.* at 682; *see also* Commissioner v. Korrell, 339 U.S. 619 (1950) (another bond premium case in which the Court acknowledged that its literal interpretation might result in a "tax loophole," but said that either Congress intended it or should fix it).

[1573] Badaracco v. Commissioner, 464 U.S. 386, 398 (1984).

[1574] Iselin v. United States, 270 U.S. 245 (1926).

[1575] Hall v. United States, 132 S. Ct. 1882 (2012).

[1576] Yu Cong Eng v. Trinidad, 271 U.S. 500 (1926).

[1577] La Belle Iron Works v. United States, 256 U.S. 377 (1921) ("invested capital" in the excess profits tax meant actual investments made by shareholders for stock and not subsequent revaluations of corporate assets, which the IRS could not effectively audit); Arkansas Best Corp. v. Commissioner, 485 U.S. 212 (1988) (pulled back from *Corn Products* Doctrine, which relied too heavily on taxpayer's motives); Girard Trust Co. v. United States, 270 U.S. 163 (1926) (payment of interest to date of allowance of taxpayer's claim rather than date of tax refund explained on grounds of plain meaning and administrability); United States v. Donruss Co., 393 U.S. 297 (1969) (refused to interpret the accumulated earnings tax to require a dominant tax avoidance motive because such a motive would be hard to ever prove and would undermine the purpose of Congress).

[1578] *See supra* Ch. V.E.1.f; *see, e.g.*, United States v. Brockamp, 519 U.S. 347 (1997) (no equitable tolling, and citing the 200 million returns and 90 million refunds that the Service has to administer).

- *Cleveland Indians* ruled back pay was includable in wages paid in the earlier year for purposes of computing social security benefits but not for income tax purposes, based in part on considerations of administrability.[1579]
- *Kowalski* stated that the boundaries of many exclusions and deductions must be arbitrary in order to be administrable.[1580]
- The Court would not adopt an approach to bond premium deduction that depended on knowing the market price of certain stock where the market was "thin" and the stock value was not reliably determinable.[1581]
- "In matters so practical as the administration of tax laws and in the decision of problems connected with them, a high degree of precision is often impossible to achieve. But it is far better to make such a rough estimate as the data will permit than completely to ignore the realities of the compromise because of the difficulties of evaluation."[1582]
- A second return need not be filed for a period for which an initial return has already been filed when no or minimal changes have been imposed by retroactive legislation.[1583]
- The Court refused to interpret a procedural tax statute as never applying to pending tax litigation, based in part on the propriety of Congress correcting an administrative error.[1584]
- The Court refused to read the "clearly to reflect income" exception of what is now section 446(b) to allow ad hoc deviations from the two limited choices between pure cash and pure accrual accounting.[1585]

Administrability motivates the Supreme Court's tax decisions more easily when the law is uncertain as in the following examples:

- The Court relied on administrability by an agency to refuse to allow a taxpayer to amend its claim for refund to ask for more, and on different grounds, after the statute had run.[1586]
- The *Moline Properties* principle that erected a very high threshold to disregarding a corporation as not being separate from its shareholders is

---

[1579] United States v. Cleveland Indians Baseball Co., 532 U.S. 200 (2001).

[1580] Commissioner v. Kowalski, 434 U.S. 77 (1977).

[1581] Commissioner v. Nat'l Alfalfa Dehydrating & Milling Co., 417 U.S. 134 (1974).

[1582] Helvering v. Safe Deposit & Trust Co., 316 U.S. 56 (1942) (the issue was how much of a settlement of a will dispute was an inheritance); *see also* United States v. Davis, 370 U.S. 65 (1962) (better to value amount realized as value of property sold than not to tax the sale).

[1583] Zellerbach Paper Co. v. Helvering, 293 U.S. 172, 178 (1934) (avoiding "complications and injustice").

[1584] Graham & Foster v. Goodcell, 282 U.S. 409 (1931).

[1585] Security Flour Mills Co. v. Commissioner, 321 U.S. 281 (1944).

[1586] United States v. Andrews, 302 U.S. 517 (1938).

based on the inherent ambiguity of the shareholder-corporation relationship and the need for the Service to have a clear rule to follow.[1587]
- *Midland Mutual* rejected the taxpayer's argument based on difficulty of administration, even though it did not seem all that difficult: the taxpayer was a creditor who thought that it should not recognize interest income when it bid on the debt for the security unless the property were worth more than the principal; Justice Brandeis thought recognition should not depend on the difficulty of proving value.[1588]
- The fundamental reason for the administratility concern is that the revenue must be protected so the government can function: "If there existed in the courts, State or National, any general power of impeding or controlling the collection of taxes, or relieving the hardship incident to taxation, the very existence of the government might be placed in the power of a hostile judiciary."[1589]

In ruling on the constitutionality of a tax, the Court has also emphasized the importance of being realistic about taxes: "Taxation is eminently practical, and is in fact brought to every man's door ..."[1590] In a sense, administrability played a role in Chief Justice Roberts' choice to save the Affordable Care Act from a strong argument that its "individual mandate" was an unconstitutional regulation rather than a constitutional tax, despite Congress' refusal to call it a tax.[1591] And sometimes the Court has more concern for administrability than Congress, as in *Home Concrete*, where it interpreted "omits from gross income" to mean omits reporting gross receipts because those are the cases in which the Service needs more time to find the omission.[1592] The opinion adopted the taxpayer's argument that this was a "logical" interpretation despite lack of any evidence in legislative history that Congress had that concern. In conclusion, there is more to administrability than practicality. Since at least the advent of the New Deal Court (see Ch. III.C.1), the Court's federal tax rulings have reflected a general, if somewhat waning, appreciation of the fact that if all technical arguments against taxes were accepted, the fisc would be severely affected. This can be seen in the creation of a more expansive definition of gross income in *Glenshaw Glass*,[1593] and in the Court's 2014 refusal to read a negative implication into different parts of the Code that

---

[1587] Commissioner v. Bollinger, 485 U.S. 340, 346 (1988) ("The Commissioner does not have the resources to audit and litigate the many cases in which agency status could be thought debatable.").

[1588] Helvering v. Midland Mutual Life Ins. Co., 300 U.S. 216 (1937).

[1589] Cheatham v. United States, 92 U.S. 85 (1876).

[1590] Nicol v. Ames, 173 U.S. 509 (1899); Knowlton v. Moore, 178 U.S. 41 (1900) (in ruling the inheritance tax constitutional, the Court construed it so as not to cause "great inconvenience").

[1591] Nat'l Fed'n of Indep. Bus. v. Sebelius, 132 S. Ct. 2566 (2012).

[1592] United States v. Home Concrete & Supply, LLC, 132 S. Ct. 1836 (2012).

[1593] Commissioner v. Glenshaw Glass Co., 348 U.S. 426 (1955).

seemed to treat the same income differently.[1594] But a waning can be seen in decision like *Clarke* on summons enforcement in 2014.[1595]

And yet, administrative efficiency has always had its limits as many of the decisions above showed and Justice Douglas explained in a case holding that last year's dependency exemption does not rationally determine this year's indigency: "The establishment of prompt efficacious procedures to achieve legitimate state ends is a proper state interest worthy of cognizance in constitutional adjudication. But the Constitution recognizes higher values than speed and efficiency. Indeed, one might fairly say of the Bill of Rights in general, and the Due Process Clause in particular, that they were designed to protect the fragile values of a vulnerable citizenry from the overbearing concern for efficiency and efficacy that may characterize praiseworthy government officials no less, and perhaps more, than mediocre ones."[1596]

VI.B.1.f. *Reluctance to Pursue Perceived Social Values*

Taxpayers, and sometimes the Service, often try to appeal to the Court's sympathy to favor one group or the other. Although Congress and the states can and do pursue many perceived social values in writing tax laws,[1597] the Supreme Court has been reluctant to interpret ambiguous Code sections to reflect various social values asserted by taxpayers.

- *Banks* rejected efforts of lower courts to pursue various imagined values in order to avoid taxing a tort plaintiff on the portion of her recovery that went to attorneys fees, by ruling that the taxpayer simply was assigning her income to her agent, the lawyer.[1598]
- *Burke* refused to find that back pay awards were excludable recoveries for personal injuries.[1599]
- *Schleier* refused to exclude age discrimination awards.[1600]
- *Sorensen* specifically declined to help out a recipient of an earned income credit, stating "[t]he ordering of competing social policies is a quintessentially legislative function."[1601]

[1594] United States v. Quality Stores, Inc., 134 S. Ct. 1395 (2014).

[1595] United States v. Clarke, 134 S. Ct. 2361, 2364 (2014). *See* Cummings, *Summons Enforcement and the Supreme Court*, 144 Tax Notes (TA) 835 (Aug. 18, 2014).

[1596] United States Dep't of Agriculture v. Murry, 413 U.S. 508 (1973).

[1597] For one of the most detailed defenses of the power of a state to more heavily tax large corporations for the purpose of restraining them, see dissent of Brandeis in *Liggett v. Lee*, 288 U.S. 517 (1933).

[1598] Commissioner v. Banks, 543 U.S. 426 (2005).

[1599] United States v. Burke, 504 U.S. 229 (1992).

[1600] Commissioner v. Schleier, 515 U.S. 323 (1995).

[1601] Sorensen v. Sec'y of Treasury, 475 U.S. 851 (1986).

Perhaps the exception that proves the rule is *Bob Jones University,*[1602] which held that tax exemption was inconsistent with racial segregation, citing *Duchesne*[1603] for the view of all enlightened courts that look to the entire statute and try to reach the legislature's purpose if possible. See discussion below of general public policy.

VI.B.2. *Finding Meaning from Text*

In the process of determining if a section is unambiguous (or what an unambiguous section means), the Court uses the methods discussed below. Ideally these methods should be applied in the sequence suggested.

VI.B.2.a. *Ordinary Meaning of Words*

The Court assumes Congress uses words in the Code in their common, ordinary, everyday meaning, unless otherwise indicated.[1604] This is not the norm, however, when the word is a "creature of the tax law."[1605] It also does not control when the term has a pivotal role in the tax law, such as "property" that can be levied on,[1606] "gift" that is not taxable as income,[1607] and of course "income" itself, no matter how common those terms may be. A major source

---

[1602] Bob Jones Univ. v. United States, 461 U.S. 574 (1983); *see* Elhauge, *supra* note 66, at 2118-19 (showing how the Court adopted the political preferences of the current political process as reflected in Service pronouncements).

[1603] Brown v. Duchesne, 60 U.S. 183, 194 (1857). The Supreme Court frequently cites *Duchesne. See* Helvering v. N. Y. Trust Co., 292 U.S. 455 (1934) (reading a section contrary to its plain meaning).

[1604] United States v. Home Concrete & Supply, LLC, 132 S. Ct. 1836 (2012) (applying dictionary meaning of "omits"); Commissioner v. Soliman, 506 U.S. 168, 174 (1993) (applying the dictionary definition of "principal"); Park 'N Fix, Inc. v. Dollar Park & Fly, Inc., 469 U.S. 189, 194 (1985); Malat v. Riddell, 383 U.S. 569 (1966); Hanover Bank v. Commissioner, 369 U.S. 672 (1962) (stating that words used in the Code should be given their ordinary, everyday sense, citing *Crane*); Commissioner v. Korell, 339 U.S. 619 (1950) ("bond premium" has common meaning in accordance with firmly established principle of tax law that ordinary meaning is persuasive of statutory meaning); Crane v. Commissioner, 331 U.S. 1 (1947) (applying the dictionary definition of "property"); Helvering v. William Flaccus Oak Leather Co., 313 U.S. 247 (1941) (finding that demolition is not a "sale or exchange" by ordinary meaning of the words); this interpretation produced an important rift between "sale or exchange" and "sale or other disposition" in section 1001, despite the absence of any evidence of a reason for the distinction or that Congress intended it; Old Colony R.R. Co. v. Commissioner, 284 U.S. 552, 560 (1932) (stating that "interest" is to be given to "usual, ordinary and everyday meaning"; this is a seminal cite in the area).

[1605] *See* Commissioner v. Brown, 380 U.S. 563, 569-71 (1965) (ruling that "sale," unlike "capital gain," is given its common meaning where "it is used in the Code without limiting definition and without legislative history indicating a contrary result"); United States v. Centennial Savings Bank FSB, 499 U.S. 573, 580 n. 6 (1991) (defining "discharge" by reference to Black's Law Dictionary). But "association" was not a creature of the tax law, and ordinary meaning was followed. Hecht v. Malley, 265 U.S. 144 (1924).

[1606] *See* United States v. Craft, 535 U.S. 274 (2002).

[1607] *See* Bittker & Lokken, at 10.2.1 (discussing Commissioner v. Duberstein, 363 U.S. 278 (1960)).

of tension is that the Service generally tends to view any word with a tax impact as being a creature of the tax law and thus requiring interpretation in the context of tax theory; the Court tends to resist such arguments,[1608] but less so where the Treasury has gotten out in front of the issue with regulations narrowing the meaning of a term.[1609]

Like canons of construction (discussed below), dictionary definitions are in low repute among academics.[1610] Nevertheless, the Court's usage of the common meaning of words is clear and persistent, including citations to dictionaries[1611] Perhaps the most famous example, which also teaches two other lessons (the importance of not cutting off tax jurisprudence from non-tax cases, and the pride the Supreme Court feels in its own decisions, no matter how old) is this passage from *Welch v. Helvering*, as the Court defined the word "necessary" in section 162 by reference to the 1819 opinion of the Supreme Court in one of the most important cases in American history:

> We may assume that the payments to creditors of the Welch Company were necessary for the development of the petitioner's business, at least in the sense that they were appropriate and helpful. McCulloch v. Maryland, . . . [17 U.S. 316 (1819)].[1612]

In addition to lower profile decisions, the Court has used the common meaning approach in many important tax decisions. These examples show that commonly understood meanings are not wooden meanings, but rather

---

[1608] *See, e.g.,* Brown Shoe Co. v. Commissioner, 339 U.S. 583 (1950) (community contribution to capital produced basis in property to corporation because Revenue Act said contributions to corporate capital result in carryover basis; the fact that the contributors were not shareholders and thus did not have such a relationship with the corporation that supports such vicarious sharing of "cost" did not sway the Court); *cf.* United States v. Chicago, Burlington & Quincy R.R. Co., 412 U.S. 401 (1973) (contribution to capital case, noting "anomalous result" of income exclusion plus basis addition).

[1609] *See, e.g.,* Textile Mills Sec. Corp. v. Commissioner, 314 U.S. 326 (1941) (enforcing regulation having no basis in the statute, which precluded deduction of lobbying expenses for a German group of manufacturers seeking to recover their property that the government had expropriated during World War I); Real Estate Land Title & Trust Co. v. United States, 309 U.S. 13 (1940) ("obsolescence" requires some change in the state of the art, not just abandonment by the particular taxpayer, as per regulations). But the regulation did not work in *Avery v. Commissioner*, 292 U.S. 210 (1934) (a dividend check normally mailed on December 31 both was not received in the year it was mailed and was not subject to the taxpayer's demand in that year; the Treasury regulation said being subject to demand equaled receipt, but the Court disagreed).

[1610] Use of dictionary definitions has come under attack by linguists who advocate an empirical study of actual usage. *See* Brudney & Baum, *Oasis or Mirage: The Supreme Court's Thirst for Dictionaries in the Rehnquist and Roberts Eras*, 55 W. & M. L. REV. 483 (2013); Cunningham et al., *Plain Meaning and Hard Cases,* 103 YALE L.J. 1561 (1994); Cunningham & Repetti, *supra* note 17, at 16 (citing Aprill, *The Law of the Word: Dictionary Shopping in the Supreme Court*, 30 ARIZ. ST. L.J. 275, 316-318 (1998)).

[1611] As recorded by Kirchmeier, *Scaling the Lexicon Fortress: The United States Supreme Court's Use of Dictionaries in the Twenty-First Century*, 94 MARQ. L. REV. 77 (2010-2011).

[1612] Welch v. Helvering, 290 U.S. 111 (1933).

essay to define the essence of the thing; thus, relying on common meaning is a method of statutory construction that looks to the purpose of Congress. Also, the common meaning is not limited to the dictionary definition, but can refer to a meaning common in the trade or business involved.

- *Gregory v. Helvering* turned on the meaning of corporate reorganization that was common in business circles.[1613]
- *Cambridge Loan & Bldg. Co.* ruled that a building and loan did not have to conform to rigid new standards of a Treasury regulation because Congress described them as "domestic," which term imported the common meaning ascribed by state legislatures in allowing their creation.[1614]
- *Deputy v. Du Pont* identified the importance of the popular import of statutory words particularly in cases of the interest deduction allowance, citing an 1854 opinion for ordinary meaning.[1615]
- *Lewis v. Reynolds* ruled that when the taxpayer claimed refund on account of "overpayment," that word referred to the payment made in relation to the payment actually owed, thus allowing the Service to redetermine the correct tax liability.[1616]
- *Florsheim Bros.* ruled that tax "return" as used in the revenue act was not a technical term, but rather meant a writing containing the normally expected contents of a tax return.[1617]
- *Le Gierse* ruled that a contract bearing all of the indicia of an insurance policy was not an insurance policy when it did not shift any risk (the soon-to-be-decedent paid more than the maturity value in an effort to take advantage of an estate tax exclusion).[1618]
- *Bob Jones University* held that functioning as a charity was inconsistent with racial segregation as commonly understood.[1619]
- *National Alfalfa* said that implicit in the concept of debt discount is the requirement that the debt be subject to the exigencies of the competitive money market.[1620]
- *Stockholms Enskilda Bank* distinguished narrower interpretations of "obligations" as for a different purpose.[1621]

[1613] Gregory v. Helvering, 293 U.S. 465 (1935). See Ch. III.C.3.a(1).

[1614] United States v. Cambridge Loan & Building Co., 278 U.S. 55 (1928).

[1615] Deputy v. Du Pont, 308 U.S. 488 (1940) (citing Maillard v. Lawrence, 57 U.S. 251 (1854) (for "the general rule that 'popular or received import of words furnishes the general rule for the interpretation of public laws,'").

[1616] Lewis v. Reynolds, 284 U.S. 281 (1932); Jones v. Liberty Glass Co., 332 U.S. 524 (1947).

[1617] Florsheim Bros. Drygoods Co. v. United States, 280 U.S. 453 (1930).

[1618] Helvering v. Le Gierse, 312 U.S. 531 (1941) ("Failure, even studious failure, in one contract to refer to the other cannot be controlling. Moreover, authority for such consideration is not wanting, however unrealistic the distinction between form and substance may be.").

[1619] Bob Jones Univ. v. United States, 461 U.S. 574 (1983).

[1620] Commissioner v. Nat'l Alfalfa Dehydrating & Milling Co., 417 U.S. 134 (1974).

[1621] Helvering v. Stockholms Enskilda Bank, 293 U.S. 84 (1934).

- In *Lewyt,* Justice Douglas interpreted "imposed" to mean "accrued" where both words were used in the section, ruling in the taxpayer's favor.[1622]
- Sometimes the ordinary meaning is ordinary meaning in the common law when the word is a legal word like "defraud."[1623]

Common usage informs minor and procedural rules as well as larger issues. For examples:

- *Billings* ruled that "annually" meant paid every year and not one time, and also meant the tax was due on the next month after enactment.[1624]
- Justice Holmes concluded that three years after the return was due was the day in the third year that matched the day after the day the return was due, observing that the taxpayer was allowed the entire last day to file the return.[1625]

The exception to common usage definitions for terms that are creatures of the tax law generally is triggered when the Service asserts such an exception. Nevertheless, the Court thought the word "incurred" was subject to a dictionary definition, even though it seems to have particular tax meanings.[1626] See discussion of development of "benefits and burdens" analysis of ownership in Ch. VI.F.2.b.

And sometimes the Court has said a word or phrase has no "fixed meaning" at all, in which case it allowed the Commissioner to craft a meaning unique to the taxpayer's facts.[1627] Conversely, sometimes the Court reads words directly contrary to their ordinary meaning, based on other interpretive cues.[1628]

[1622] Lewyt Corp. v. Commissioner, 349 U.S. 237 (1955).

[1623] Neder v. United States, 527 U.S. 1 (1999) ("accumulated settled meaning under the common law").

[1624] Billings v. United States, 232 U.S. 261 (1914).

[1625] Burnet v. Willingham Loan & Trust Co., 282 U.S. 437 (1931) (also affirmed the fiction that a day has no parts, but is a unit).

[1626] Hall v. United States, 132 S. Ct. 1882 (2012).

[1627] *See, e.g.*, Ray Consolidated Copper Co. v. United States, 268 U.S. 373 (1925) ("capital stock" has no fixed meaning and so Treasury could choose between stock value and asset value, and chose asset value because stock value was depressed at the relevant time).

[1628] United States v. Wells Fargo Bank, 485 U.S. 351 (1988) (exemption of housing bonds from "all taxes" did not include estate taxes because that would have been too great a change from prior law not to have been more clearly indicated).

VI.B.2.b. *Same or Similar Words in the Code*

The next interpretive step to clarify ambiguity should be to assess the internal context of the section and interrelated sections,[1629] the use of words in the Code generally,[1630] and common interpretations thereof.[1631] Frequently, the Supreme Court has described this step as a search for the plain meaning of the statute, and not a clarification of ambiguity by reference to extrinsic sources.[1632] This view underscores the ambiguity of the concept of plain meaning.

Accordingly, Justice Blackmun, speaking for eight members of the Court, stated (and applied) in a tax case that: "[It is a] normal rule of statutory construction . . . that identical words used in different parts of the same act are intended to have the same meaning."[1633] Blackmun based that view on a broader principle that the Code must be given "as great an internal symmetry and consistency as its words permit. . . ."[1634] The Court may specifically

---

[1629] *See* Davis v. United States 495 U.S. 472 (1990) (because "for the use of" charity has a range of possible meanings, the Court examined the history and usage of the term in tax statutes and agreed with a consistent administrative interpretation, though not stated in a regulation); United States v. Donruss Co., 393 U.S. 297, 302 *et seq.* (1969); *see, e.g.*, Begier v. Internal Revenue Service, 496 U.S. 53 (1990) (determining when a trust fund is "collected or withheld" for the Service by reference to other related sections); Church of Scientology of California v. Internal Revenue Service, 484 U.S. 9, 15-16 (1987) (interpreting the Code section by first examining its words, second examining other parts of the same section, and third examining legislative history).

[1630] *See* Crane v. Commissioner, 331 U.S. 1 (1947) (not finding any other instances of the Code changing the normal meaning of "property").

[1631] *See, e.g.*, United States v. Wells Fargo Bank, 485 U.S. 351, 355-56 (1988) (where the Supreme Court said that exemptions of property from taxation were well understood to refer only to property taxes and not excise taxes; however, this decision rejected the plain reading of the Code).

[1632] *See* Bufferd v. Commissioner, 506 U.S. 523 (1993) (not admitting that "after the return was filed" is ambiguous in the case of an S corporation's return and audit of its shareholders); Commissioner v. Asphalt Prods. Co., Inc., 482 U.S. 117 (1987) (refusing to agree that statute was ambiguous, while reversing Court of Appeals, which thought it was); Schauer, *Statutory Construction, supra* note 1458, at 242-43 (stating that even when the plain meaning is ambiguous, the Court principally debates the plain meaning); *Id.* at 246 (stating that plain language discourse dominates the Court's statutory construction in most cases).

[1633] Commissioner v. Keystone Consolidated Industries, Inc., 508 U.S. 152 (1993) (citing Sorenson v. Sec'y of Treasury, 475 U.S. 851, 860 (1986) (applying the same rule to construction of the Code). *See also* Commissioner v. Lundy, 516 U.S 235 (1996); Direct Marketing Assn. v. Brohl, 135 S. Ct. 1124 (2015) (Anti-Injunction Act and Tax Injunction Act may be interpreted in parallel because they serve same function, though they are not in the same Title of the U.S. Code); United States v. Bishop, 412 U.S. 346 (1973) (willfully meant same thing for felonies and misdemeanors; also considered context).

[1634] Commissioner v. Lester, 366 U.S. 299, 304 (1961) (quoting Justice Douglas in United States v. Olympic Radio & Television, Inc., 349 U.S. 232, 236 (1955)).

find that provisions are *in pari materia*.[1635] The Court used the phrase when one section was cut into two.[1636] Perhaps the most quoted support for Code symmetry came from Justice Douglas, who actually was referring to necessary limitations on symmetry imposed by the "plain meaning" of the statutory words:

> This taxpayer argues the inequity of the results which would follow from our construction of the Code. But as we have said before, "general equitable considerations" do not control the question of what deductions are permissible. . . . It may be that Congress granted less than some thought or less than was originally intended. We can only take the Code as we find it and give it as great an internal symmetry and consistency as its words permit. We would not be faithful to the statutory scheme, as revealed by the words employed, if we gave "paid or accrued" a different meaning for the purposes of section 122(d)(6) than it has in the other parts of the same chapter.[1637]

Sometimes this interpretive method is called the "whole act rule" or a presumption about cohesion or structural integrity of the text.[1638] Justice Brandeis said that the first definition given to a word in a statute is assumed to be the same throughout the statute.[1639] Statistical research has shown that the Supreme Court has demonstrated a very high degree of reliance on structural cohesion or integrity in federal tax cases, substantially greater than reliance on canons aimed at the meaning of particular words.[1640]

But any presumption of structural integrity gives way when the context compels a different definition.[1641] Sometimes the different usages of the same

---

[1635] *See, e.g.*, Merrill v. Fahs, 324 U.S. 308 (1945) (construing the estate and gift taxes as being *in pari materia*); U.S. v. Stewart, 311 U.S. 60 (1940) (resolving an ambiguity in the more specifically applicable statute by relying on the clearer statute *in pari materia*). But an early income tax opinion refused to allow the principle to overcome what the Court found to be the clear words of the statute. Barnes v. R.R., 84 U.S. 294 (1873).

[1636] King v. United States, 379 U.S. 329 (1964).

[1637] *Olympic Radio*, 349 U.S. at 236.

[1638] Brudney & Ditslear, *supra* note 59, at 1266.

[1639] Pampanga Sugar Mills v. Trinidad, 279 U.S. 211 (1929).

[1640] Brudney & Ditslear, *supra* note 59, at 1266.

[1641] *See* Malat v. Riddell, 383 U.S. 569 (1966) (stating that even a literal meaning can be changed by the "relevant internal evidence of the statute itself"); Commissioner v. Estate of Bedford, 325 U.S. 283 (1945) (refusing to apply a definition adopted for another purpose); Higgins v. Commissioner, 312 U.S. 212 (1941) ("business" did not have the same meaning for deduction purposes as in another tax usage); Helvering v. Stockholms Enskilda Bank, 293 U.S. 84 (1934) (declining to utilize meaning of term used in other parts of the act because different context required different meaning); Helvering v. City Bank Farmers Trust Co., 296 U.S. 85 (1935) (declined to apply a limitation appearing in another section that a committee report said was similar, because the words were different). Judge Henry Friendly often is quoted for the following observation on the interrelationship of the meanings of the same words used at different places in the Code: ". . . where the Internal Revenue Code is concerned, no controlling weight can be given to the usual presumption that, when the same words are used in several sections of a statute, they mean the same thing." Sirbo Holdings, Inc. v. Commissioner, 509 F. 2d 1220, 1223 (2d Cir. 1975).

word in the Code are clear.[1642] Or, two Code sections that originally were similar may lose their relationship to each other when one is changed and the other is not.[1643] *Quality Stores* ruled that the fact that one Code section had an overinclusive definition of wages to include severance pay did not mean that another Code section *in pari materia* but without the definition did not also include severance pay.[1644] Rather the Court considered the overall context and history of the withholding rule and found that the severance pay was wages for both purposes of withholding. The opinion did not preclude the cross-fertilization of construction of different taxing schedules, but the Court has stated that at least some principles applied to the estate tax should not be applied to the income tax.[1645]

Justice Douglas thought that the (then) other 60 Code appearances of "trade or business" had no bearing on its use in section 174 because that section added the words "in connection with."[1646] Similarly, the Court has taken note when the Code qualifies the same word in other sections but not the section at issue, finding Congress knew how to qualify if it wanted to.[1647] Perhaps the most famous cite for the potential for a single word to have different meanings is Justice Holmes' statement:

> It is not necessarily true that income means the same thing in the Constitution and the Act. A word is not a crystal, transparent and unchanged, it is the skin of a living thought and may vary greatly in color and content according to the circumstances and the time in which it is used.[1648]

[1642] United States v. Cleveland Indians Baseball Co., 532 U.S. 200 (2001) (back pay was includable in wages paid in the earlier year for purposes of computing social security benefits but not for tax purposes, where considerations of administrability prevailed).

[1643] Commissioner v. Stern, 357 U.S. 39 (1958) (the government was arguing that because the two sections originally were similar, the one that Congress did not later change should be interpreted to mean the same as the changed section; the Court rejected that argument); Hecht v. Malley, 265 U.S. 144 (1924) (income tax applied to associations no matter how organized but Congress intentionally limited excise tax to corporations organized under state law, so it could not apply to a trust).

[1644] United States v. Quality Stores, Inc., 134 S. Ct. 1395 (2014). This opinion contains a statement that may become a go-to cite: "The statement that, 'all men shall be treated as if they were six feet tall does not imply that no men are six feet tall.'" The earlier opinion establishing *pari materia* was Rowan Cos. v. United States, 452 U.S. 247 (1981).

[1645] United States v. Darusmont, 449 U.S. 292 (1981) (the constitutionality of tax retroactivity).

[1646] Snow v. Commissioner, 416 U.S. 500 (1974).

[1647] United States v. Reorganized CF&I Fabricators of Utah, 518 U.S. 213, 224 (1996) (Congress did not intend for Revenue Code meanings to apply in the Bankruptcy Code); United States v. Hemme, 476 U.S. 558 (1986) ("allowed" sometimes specifically requires a tax effect and sometimes does not); *see also* Central Ill. Pub. Serv. Co. v. United States, 435 U.S. 21 (1978) (relying in part on the presence of the modifier "if" in the income tax withholding section to rule that the meaning of "wages" was not congruent with all compensatory section 61 income; also citing the fact that the withholding rules are in a different subtitle from section 61).

[1648] Towne v. Eisner, 245 U.S. 418 (1918).

The highest profile, recent invocation of Holmes' rule occurred in the opinion of the Chief Justice ruling the individual mandate penalty in the Affordable Care Act to be constitutional as a tax.[1649] He first ruled that the Anti-Injunction Act did not prevent the suit because the penalty was a penalty, applying the maxim that Congress used the word tax elsewhere in the Care Act and so presumably intended not to call the penalty a tax, but then found the penalty to be a tax for purposes of constitutional analysis, applying substance over form reasoning.

VI.B.2.c. *Interpreting Section in Context*

Closely related to interpreting words in light of other usages of the same words is the interpretation of a section in light of related sections, and sometimes in relation to the entirety of one section.[1650] See also Symmetry of the Code, Ch. VI.B.2.f. One graduate of the Harvard Law School has reported to the author that the only thing he recalled from Dean Griswold's tax class was the warning: "Read to the end of the section." That is still good advice and is related to the need to read parts of the Code in their broader contexts.[1651] This process also relates to finding purpose, as discussed above. It is so intuitive that it is seldom remarked upon, but illustrations include the following:

- The Court has interpreted the gift tax in light of its purpose as a corollary or supplement to the estate tax.[1652] Similarly, it interpreted one ambiguous subsection of the early estate tax to be consistent with a general principle that it deduced from the other subsections.[1653]
- The Court has recognized the possibility of an interpretation at odds with plain meaning when the statute is read "as an organic whole."[1654] That is what happened in *King v. Burwell* in 2015.[1655]

1649 Nat'l Fed'n of Indep. Bus. v. Sebelius, 132 S. Ct. 2566 (2012).

1650 For a different but analogous point of view, see Walsh, *Formally Legal, Probably Wrong: Corporate Tax Shelters, Practical Reason and the New Textualism*, 53 Stan. L. Rev. 1541, 1565-79 (2001) (arguing that a "structural textualism" that looks at the overall structure and purpose of the income tax could possibly convince textualist judges to rule against corporate tax shelters on the basis of the text rather than judge created doctrines).

1651 This broad principle is supported by many statements of the Court outside the tax cases, including most recently the unanimous opinion in Sturgeon v. Frost, 577 U.S. __ (2016) (context and overall statutory scheme).

1652 *See, e.g.*, Jewett v. Commissioner, 455 U.S. 305, 309 (1982).

1653 Reinecke v. Northern Trust Co., 278 U.S. 339 (1929).

1654 *See* United States v. Foster Lumber Co., Inc., 429 U.S. 32 (1976) (citing Lewyt Corp. v. Commissioner, 349 U.S. 237 (1955)). *See also* Alexander v. Cosden Pipe Line Co., 290 U.S. 484 (1934) (the statute was not "happily phrased").

1655 King v. Burwell, 135 S. Ct. 2480 (2015) (tax credit available even though health insurance was not purchased on a state exchange, as required by statute). *See* Cummings, *The Supreme Court's 2014 Term in Tax*, 148 Tax Notes (TA) 1005 (Aug. 31, 2015).

- That a taxpayer is allowed to report on the "basis on which it keeps its accounts" obviously does not prevent the Service from correcting errors in accrual method reporting.[1656]
- In the seminal construction of the charitable exemption the Court rejected the notion that a charity could not also earn income, by noting that the statute itself referred to the charity's net income.[1657]
- Reserves "required by law" that were deductible by life insurance companies must refer to reserves for life insurance policies and not other types of insurance.[1658]
- Because Congress specifically precluded insurance companies from depreciating non-income-producing real estate, Congress must have intended the same treatment for personal property.[1659]
- Absence of a cross reference to definitions like "gain" (as now determined under section 1001) does not mean that the general provisions of a provision like section 1001 did not apply.[1660]
- The *White* opinion performed extensive analysis of the roles of multiple sections in defining sales and exchanges, gross income and applying tax rates to show that a liquidating loss was a capital loss.[1661]
- *Davis* ruled that the meaning of the term "not essentially equivalent to a dividend" in section 302(b)(1) was informed by the "plain language" of the section requiring a certain methodology to be used, disagreeing with Justice Douglas' dissent, which would have installed a business purpose exception to dividend treatment and unmoored "essentially equivalent" from the statute.[1662]
- The Court further extended this approach in *Clark*, when it read into section 356 the section 302 methodology for finding dividend equivalence.[1663]
- Both plain language and reading the two sections as being related in the legislative scheme led the Court to rule that the deficiency termination section required use of the deficiency assessment procedure of the defi-

---

[1656] United States v. Am. Can Co., 280 U.S. 412 (1930) (the Revenue Act also authorizes the government to take action essential to orderly enforcement of the obligations imposed on taxpayers).

[1657] Trinidad v. Sagrada Order de Predicadores, 263 U.S. 578 (1924) (also reading "exclusively" to be unconcerned with incidental sales).

[1658] Helvering v. Illinois Life Ins. Co., 299 U.S. 88 (1936); *see also* Helvering v. Inter-Mountain Life Ins. Co., 294 U.S. 686 (1935) (also excludes noninsurance reserves).

[1659] Rockford Life Ins. Co. v. Commissioner, 292 U.S. 382 (1934).

[1660] MacLaughlin v. Alliance Ins. Co. of Philadelphia, 286 U.S. 244 (1932).

[1661] White v. United States, 305 U.S. 281 (1938).

[1662] United States v. Davis, 397 U.S. 301 (1970). Murtagh cited *Davis* is a prime example of the willingness of the Supreme Court to "legislate" in uncertain areas of the tax law. Murtagh, *supra* note 105, at 539. For other examples, see Commissioner v. Acker, 361 U.S. 87 (1959) (references to estimated tax imply a return has been filed).

[1663] Commissioner v. Clark, 489 U.S. 726 (1989).

ciency section, because the word deficiency meant the same thing in both sections.[1664]

- The Court held the statute of limitations for assessments against an S corporation shareholder to run from the filing of the shareholder's return not the corporation's return because it is the shareholder's tax that is being assessed.[1665]
- *Hellman* read past the subsection that said all distributions to shareholder are taxed as dividends to see the subsection stating that payments in liquidations are gains, and inferred Congress' intent that the latter would trump the former in case of liquidations, based on the entire section.[1666]
- *Maryland Casualty* is an early decision that bridged the corporate excise tax of 1909 and the 1913 income tax act.[1667] The former taxed "income received" and the latter taxed income "arising or accruing," The Court ruled that the income tax also meant "received" because another part of the income tax act referred to income received.
- *Galletti* reasoned that based on the general function of the assessment the Court could determine that taxes and not taxpayers were assessed.[1668]
- *Beacon Brass* reasoned that the coexistence of several statutes criminalizing false statements showed that Congress did not intend to supplant the tax evasion statute's application to false statements by a single false statement criminal statute.[1669]
- The fact that the refund statutes expressly allow persons other than the taxpayer assessed to seek refund in one section indicates that a section without such a clear statement should be interpreted the same way.[1670]
- "As a general rule, where the legislation dealing with a particular subject consists of a system of related general provisions indicative of a settled policy, new enactments of a fragmentary nature on that subject are to be taken as intended to fit into the existing system and to be carried into effect conformably to it, excepting as a different purpose is plainly shown."[1671]
- In 2012, the Court interpreted "incurred by the estate" by reviewing the context of several Bankruptcy Code tax provisions.[1672]

1664 Laing v. United States, 423 U.S. 161 (1976). *See also* Hercules Gasoline Co. v. Commissioner, 326 U.S. 425 (1945) (phrase should mean the same thing in two related sections).

1665 Bufferd v. Commissioner, 506 U.S. 523 (1993).

1666 Hellmich v. Hellman, 276 U.S. 233 (1928).

1667 Maryland Casualty Co. v. United States, 251 U.S. 342 (1920).

1668 United States v. Galletti, 541 U.S. 114 (2004) (partner's liability is secondary).

1669 United States v. Beacon Brass Co., 344 U.S. 43 (1952).

1670 United States v. Williams, 514 U.S. 527 (1995).

1671 United States v. Jefferson Elec. Mfg. Co., 291 U.S. 386 (1934) (federal excise tax case).

1672 Hall v. United States, 132 S. Ct. 1882 (2012).

- In 2013, Justice Scalia said that a wholly ambiguous part of the Code could be interpreted by reference to the structure and other provisions of the act (TEFRA) by which it was added to the Code.[1673]

However, decisions involving property taxes or income taxes are not readily transferable to the estate tax.[1674] And the fact that interest is part of the tax for one purpose does not necessarily apply for all purposes of the Code.[1675]But as some of the decisions cited above show, interpreting a section in context requires identifying the relevant context; it may not be the general context of the related sections. In *Ogilvie Hardware,* the Court considered a retroactive amendment intended to relieve from the accumulated earnings tax corporations that had been unable to avoid the tax by paying out dividends because state law prevented them from paying out dividends due to a deficit of earnings. The statute referred to such corporations as having a "deficit of accumulated earnings and profits." The government interpreted the statute in the context of the corporate tax earnings and profits rules and found the corporation not to have had a deficit under the peculiar rules applied for that purpose. The Court disagreed, stating "the provision before us is not a general tax exemption to be interpreted in the framework of a currently operating general revenue law. It is a special retroactive relief measure [to be interpreted according to the context Congress considered and the purpose it wished to accomplish]."[1676]

Another type of context is the context of legal doctrines that existed at the time Congress legislated. The Court ruled that bonds had a situs where the physical certificates were kept, which was consistent with the legal view of the time of enactment.[1677] Likewise, a statute describing a geographic location should be interpreted from the viewpoint of Washington, D.C.[1678]

And sometimes the Court creates the context. In a ruling on the 1864 income tax as applied to corporations, the Court turned a one sentence tax on corporate interest and dividends into a fleshed out scheme (with the help of the tax collector) on annual earnings and profits of the corporation.[1679]

1673 United States v. Woods, 134 S. Ct. 557 (2013).

1674 United States v. Mason, 412 U.S. 391, 395 (1973).

1675 Manning v. Seeley Tube & Box Co., 338 U.S. 561 (1950).

1676 United States v. Ogilvie Hardware Co., 330 U.S. 709, 717 (1947).

1677 Burnet v. Brooks, 288 U.S. 378 (1933) ("Congress did not enact a maxim" referring to the later maximum that the stock moved with the owner).

1678 Hadden v. Collector, 72 U.S. 107 (1867) ("beyond the Cape of Good Hope").

1679 Bailey v. R.R. Co., 106 U.S. 109 (1882).

VI.B.2.d. *Single Taxpayer Consistency*

The Supreme Court has recognized that the Code generally (but not inevitably)[1680] strives for consistency in the treatment of one taxpayer.[1681] This broad concept has been used to resolve many ambiguities, as in the following examples:

- The calculation of property's adjusted tax basis strives to prevent double taxation of one taxpayer by adjusting basis in various ways, such as including a taxpayer's gain recognition in "tax cost basis" for the property received and otherwise reflecting a taxpayer's earnings history in basis in the taxpayer's property.[1682]
- The Supreme Court ruled that depreciation should reduce the basis of the depreciated property even before the statute required such reduction; otherwise the property owner would use a single capital cost twice to reduce income.[1683]
- In *Philadelphia Park*, the Court of Claims found the cost of property to be not what the taxpayer gave for it but what it was worth on receipt (and inclusion in taxpayer's income), because that result would properly shield the taxpayer from later double taxation on disposition of the acquired property.[1684]
- In *Crane*, the Supreme Court expanded the definition of amount realized to include the amount of the seller's nonrecourse mortgage on disposition of the security, to counterbalance the benefit the seller had enjoyed from the basis attributable to that mortgage.[1685] It based this on the related one taxpayer consistency rule that borrowing does not produce income

---

[1680] Commissioner v. Standard Life & Accid. Ins. Co., 433 U.S. 148, 160 (1977) ("Although we do not accept the notion that there must be perfect symmetry in the tax laws, there should be a measure of consistency in the accounting treatment of an item affecting interrelated elements in a formula such as that used to calculate the policyholders' share of investment income.").

[1681] *See generally* Shuldiner, *Consistency and the Taxation of Financial Products*, 70 TAXES (CCH) 781 (1992) (arguing that consistency and not symmetry is the hallmark of the Code).

[1682] Cummings, *The Silent Policies of Conservation*, *supra* note 1253, at 113. But this principle was not applied when it was cast as an argument of estoppel, in *Helvering v. Salvage*, 297 U.S. 106 (1936) (taxpayer nonfraudulently failed to include bargain element of stock purchase from employer in income in 1922 but was allowed to count 1922 value of stock as its basis for purposes of gain on later sale).

[1683] United States v. Ludey, 274 U.S. 295 (1927).

[1684] Philadelphia Park Amusement Co. v. United States, 126 F. Supp. 184 (Ct. Cl. 1954). *Cited with approval in* United States v. Davis, 370 U.S. 65 (1962). *See* Geier, *Commentary*, *supra* note 1455, at 445 (contending that Justice Scalia's plain meaning approach could have lead to an incorrect decision in *Philadelphia Park*).

[1685] Crane v. Commissioner, 331 U.S. 1, 10 (1947) ("Thus it appears that the applicable provisions of the Act expressly preclude an equity basis, and the use of it is contrary to certain implicit principles of income tax depreciation, and entails very great administrative difficulties"); *see* BITTKER & LOKKEN, at 4.3.2.

because the receipt is offset by the liability; but when the liability is discharged, the receipt is taxable.[1686]

- In *Tufts*, the Court actually labeled as "asymmetrical" the result of failing to include relief from a nonrecourse purchase money debt in the amount received on sale of the encumbered property, in light of the inclusion of the debt amount in the original cost basis for the property.[1687]
- The tax benefit rule is a single taxpayer consistency rule.[1688] *Nash* interpreted the tax benefit rule to be aimed at avoiding double benefit and found none was possible where the partnership that had deducted the loan loss reserve received for its assets stock worth the net value of the loans, thus not replicating the loss.[1689]
- *Palmer* refused to find a dividend when a corporation issued to its shareholders rights to buy corporate assets at their then current fair market value, despite the fact that the value of the assets rose by the time the rights were exercised, because the corporation never distributed its earnings, on the theory that it had contracted away the right to benefit from the increase in value of the assets; thus, the corporation's noninclusion of the assets' value gain was linked to its inability to distribute a dividend.[1690]

[1686] *See* United States v. Centennial Savings Bank FSB, 499 U.S. 573, 582 (1991); United States v. Kirby Lumber Co., 284 U.S. 1 (1931); Bowers v. Kerbaugh-Empire Co., 271 U.S. 170 (1926).

[1687] Commissioner v. Tufts, 461 U.S. 300 (1983); *see* I.R.C. § 7701(g), which effectively codifies *Tufts*. The only other tax opinion using asymmetrical in another sense is CSX Transp., Inc. v. Ala. Dep't of Revenue, 562 U.S. 277 (2011) (interpreting federal statute as applied to state tax).

[1688] *See* Hillsboro National Bank v. Commissioner, 460 U.S. 370, 383 (1983) ("transactional equity"). Another example of single-taxpayer symmetry is *Portland Golf Club v. Commissioner*, 497 U.S. 154 (1990). The golf club wanted to deduct its losses on sales to nonmembers from its investment income in determining its unrelated business income tax. The club computed the losses by allocating a portion of its overhead to the nonmember sales, on a gross-to-gross basis. The Court ruled that the losses were deductible if the nonmember sales were entered into for profit, but that factual question must be determined using the same method of overhead allocation the club wanted to use to quantify the deductible loss.

Single taxpayer symmetry failed, however, to overcome the plain meaning of the statute in *Helvering v. Bliss*, 293 U.S. 144 (1934) holding that the base for the 15% of net income limitation on the charitable deduction should include capital gains despite the fact that the capital gains would be taxed at preferential rates. Conversely, consistency prevailed in an evident rejection of plain meaning that was described by the Court as an ambiguity, where the taxpayer-trust attempted to both deduct 100% of a charitable contribution of gain and exclude 50% of the gain. United States v. Benedict, 338 U.S. 692 (1950). The Court acted similarly in United Cal. Bank v. United States, 439 U.S. 180 (1978) to avoid an "unfair and unintended result . . ."; literally the alternative tax did not allow a deduction for a charitable gift of capital gains; the Court said that to rule otherwise would allow form to rule over substance.

[1689] Nash v. United States, 398 U.S. 1 (1970) (*Hillsboro*, distinguished *Nash*, but appears to loosen the requirements for applying the tax benefit rule).

[1690] Palmer v. Commissioner, 302 U.S. 63 (1937). *But see* Rev. Rul. 80-292, 1980-2 C.B. 104 (rights to buy stock of subsidiary taxable).

- The tax accounting rules generally attempt to match income and expense of one taxpayer, although less rigorously than financial accounting.[1691]
- Congress has a policy of not allowing a taxpayer to report income on the cash method and deductions on the accrual method.[1692]
- *Burnet v. Guggenheim* effectively ruled that a single taxpayer cannot make but one taxable gift of the same property and proceeded to identify the point at which it is most logical to identify the gift: when the taxpayer parts with control of the property.[1693]
- *Phipps* ruled that one taxpayer consistency applied to two corporations when one was the successor of the other in a reorganization or tax free liquidation.[1694]

VI.B.2.e. *Symmetry: Two Taxpayer Consistency*

The Supreme Court has recognized another presumed congressional concern for matching tax consequences of the two taxpayers on opposite ends of one transaction so that they offset so far as the fisc is concerned. Examples of two taxpayer matching in the Code and case law include the following:

- The payor deduction and recipient inclusion treatment of alimony is an example that mirrors the more ubiquitous example of deduction/inclusion generally.[1695]
- Justice Brandeis justified including in the income of the mortgagee the accrued interest that was part of the amount it bid in to claim the property on foreclosure by citing the deduction the mortgagor certainly could claim.[1696]
- Inevitably, the use of the cash method by the payee and the accrual method by the payor makes timing mismatches endemic in the tax system.[1697] Many of the provisions primarily aimed at reversing that result, such as sections 267 and 1239, operate only where there is a close relationship between the taxpayers.
- The cloning of basis upon the exchange of property for stock in a section 351 exchange is an example of two taxpayer symmetry in which gain and loss generally can be replicated, and through the operation of sections

---

1691 *See generally* Crane, *Matching and the Income Tax Base: The Special Case of Tax-Exempt Income*, 5 AM. J. TAX POL'Y 191 (1986); Geier, *The Myth of the Matching Principle as a Tax Value*, 15 AM. J. TAX POL'Y 17 (1998). But the Supreme Court seems to think the myth exists. INDOPCO, Inc. v. Commissioner, 503 U.S. 79 (1992).

1692 Commissioner v. S. Texas Lumber Co., 333 U.S. 496 (1948).

1693 Burnet v. Guggenheim, 288 U.S. 280, 285 (1933).

1694 Commissioner v. Phipps, 336 U.S. 410 (1949) (earnings and profits)carryover).

1695 Commissioner v. Lester, 366 U.S. 299 (1961); *see also* Burton-Sutton Oil Co. v. Commissioner, 328 U.S. 25 (1946) (which noted that the treatment of a payment by the taxpayer at issue would be the same as the treatment of the payment's recipient (a royalty for oil property, or a capital investment)).

1696 Helvering v. Midland Mutual Life Ins. Co., 300 U.S. 216 (1937).

1697 *See* Don E. Williams Co. v. Commissioner, 429 U.S. 569 (1977).

358 and 362, the income recognized by the shareholder in the exchange affects the basis of the corporation in the property.[1698]

- The Court applied that cloning approach in *Fisher*,[1699] where it reasoned that a corporation's earnings and profits had to be determined on the basis of tax accounting rather than financial accounting so that built in gain upon contribution of appreciated property would, when recognized, permit taxable dividend distributions as a matter of two party tax logic.
- The partnership area has a variety of two taxpayer consistency concerns stemming from the fact that for some purposes the partners are treated as separate from the entity partnership.[1700]

But two taxpayer matching is not always required and is not always possible. The American Bar Association conducted an extensive study of whipsaw at the request of the Service in the 1970's and identified numerous potential whipsaw situations but concluded that the effort they devoted to the problem "may have been disproportionate to the actual magnitude of the problem."[1701]

The Supreme Court did not enforce two taxpayer matching in *Hillsboro National Bank*, where the Court refused to apply the tax benefit rule to deny a deduction granted to a bank by section 164(e) for its shareholders' taxes that it paid, when those taxes were refunded to the shareholders.[1702] Similarly, the Court in *Duberstein* stated that the deductibility of an employee gift did not require includability by the employee.[1703] The Court referred to the government's arguments for parity as:

> . . . not principles of law but rather maxims of experience. . . . Some of them represent truisms. . . . Others are overstatements of possible evidentiary inferences . . . it is doubtless relevant to the over-all inference that the transferor treats a payment as a business deduction. . . . But these inferences cannot be stated in absolute terms. Neither factor is a shibboleth. The taxing statute does not make nondeductibility by the transferor a condition on the "gift" exclusion; . . .[1704]

1698 Cummings, *The Silent Policies of Conservation, supra* note 1253, at 113.

1699 Commissioner v. Fisher, 327 U.S. 512 (1946).

1700 *See, e.g.*, I.R.C. § 704(c).

1701 *Final Report Special Committee on Whipsaw Section of Taxation American Bar Association*, 30 Tax Law. 127, 129 (1976).

1702 Hillsboro National Bank v. Commissioner, 460 U.S. 370 (1983).

1703 Commissioner v. Duberstein, 363 U.S. 278 (1960). For another case indicating the importance but noncontrolling nature of matching, see *Fulman v. United States*, 434 U.S. 528 (1978) (recognizing the general desirability of matching one taxpayer's deduction with the amount of another taxpayer's income from the same property, but bowing to contrary regulations).

1704 *Duberstein*, 363 U.S. at 287.

VI.B.2.f. *Symmetry of the Code*

The Supreme Court has recognized a third type of symmetry of the Code itself.[1705] For example, the Court looked for symmetry well beyond the section at issue and even into the legislative history of other sections in the important case of *Flora*, which was argued twice.[1706] The Court ruled five-to-four that the precondition to suit for refund of taxes by paying "any sum" did not mean less than all of the tax due, based on several considerations of overall symmetry of the Code. The Court justified this seemingly nonliteral interpretation largely on (1) legislative history of other sections (creation of Tax Court and declaratory judgments) in which an understanding that all of the tax would be paid was indicated, and (2) a 50–60 year history of judicial application, with no indication that the addition of "any sum" changed that. Undoubtedly the practical difficulties presented by taxpayers who might proceed in both the Tax Court and the district courts, which the opinion examined, strongly motivated the decision. Other examples follow:

- *Consumer Life* supported the interpretation of one section by inferences drawn from a separate section written at a different time but also addressing the same subject (insurance company taxation): the other section would not make sense if the first section were interpreted as the Service wanted.[1707]
- The Supreme Court has noted: "the true meaning of a single section of a statute in a setting as complex as that of the revenue acts, however precise its language, cannot be ascertained if it be considered apart from related sections, or if the mind be isolated from the history of the income tax legislation of which it is an integral part."[1708]
- *Groetzinger* explained how the overall structure of the income tax statute differentiates between transactions entered into for profit and a trade or business, and the Court supplied the meaning of trade or business, which appears nowhere in the Code.[1709]
- *Wheeler* ruled that it made no sense not to compute a corporation's earnings and profits on the basis of its taxable income as measured by the basis in contributed property transferred from the shareholder, as contrasted with stepping up the basis to value at the time of contribution for purposes of E&P calculation (although E&P was undefined in the Code).[1710]

1705 Manning v. Seeley Tube & Box Co., 338 U.S. 561 (1950) ("structure of the code").

1706 Flora v. United States, 362 U.S. 145 (1960).

1707 United States v. Consumer Life Ins. Co., 430 U.S. 725 (1977).

1708 Commissioner v. Engle, 464 U.S. 206, 223 (1984) (quoting Helvering v. Morgan's, Inc., 293 U.S. 121, 126 (1934)).

1709 Commissioner v. Groetzinger, 480 U.S. 23 (1987).

1710 Commissioner v. Wheeler, 324 U.S. 542 (1945).

- *New Colonial Ice* stated that the structure of the rules for determining taxable income indicated Congress' purpose to limit the deduction of losses to the person sustaining them.[1711]
- *Jefferson Electric* stated as to an excise tax: "As a general rule, where the legislation dealing with a particular subject consists of a system of related general provisions indicative of a settled policy, new enactments of a fragmentary nature on that subject are to be taken as intended to fit into the existing system and to be carried into effect conformably to it, excepting as a different purpose is plainly shown."[1712]

For further discussion, see Interpreting Section in Context, Ch. VI.B.2.c., above.

VI.B.2.g. *Ordering Rules*

The Court relies on the many signals in the Code that one of its rules should be subservient to another, including the following:

- The most fundamental signal is the statement of a general rule "except as otherwise provided [in this section or this Part of this Subpart or Chapter or Title].[1713] Sometimes these signals are labeled "general rule," as is section 312(a).
- Sometimes the signals are more subtle: A subsidiary stock purchase described in section 304(a)(2) trumps a brother sister stock purchase described in section 304(a)(1), because the former says "unless paragraph (2) applies."
- For a more fundamental example, the Court in *Idaho Power*[1714] gave great weight to the ordering rule in section 161 that the described deductions are allowed except as provided in Part IX, which includes section 263 requiring capitalization of certain amounts paid out, which the Court said applied to depreciation otherwise allowed in section 167. Thus, one could not stop with finding a deduction rule because the proper order of analysis required examining the exceptions to deduction.
- Also, to the extent another section or its regulations provides specific guidance for an item of income, the more specific section applies notwithstanding section 61 and its regulations.[1715]

1711 New Colonial Ice Co. v. Helvering, 292 U.S. 435 (1934), *cited in* Randall v. Loftsgaarden, 478 U.S. 647 (1986) (a securities case).

1712 United States v. Jefferson Elec. Mfg. Co., 291 U.S. 386 (1934).

1713 *See, e.g.,* Gitlitz v. Commissioner, 531 U.S. 206 (2001) (relying heavily on the phrase in section 108(a)); Boulware v. United States, 552 U.S. 421 (2008) (when section 301 otherwise provides, section 61 does not apply alone).

1714 Commissioner v. Idaho Power Co., 418 U.S. 1 (1974).

1715 Reg. § 1.61-1(b). *But see* Helvering v. Clifford, 309 U.S. 331 (1940) (the fact that Congress specifically included the income of revocable trusts in the settlor's income did not reduce the ability of section 61 to include the income from a short term trust in the settlor's income).

- In *Reo Motors*, the Court described the NOL statute as creating a sequential "trichotomy" that must be followed in sequence.[1716]

The Supreme Court has at times applied ordering rules of its own, or refused to upset normal ordering, as in *Turnbow*, where taxpayer admitted there was no B reorganization because he had received some forbidden "boot in a B," but argued that the related section 356 governing the taxation of boot when received in a reorganization should reinterpret the term reorganization to allow boot.[1717] The Supreme Court disagreed, ruling that the transaction had to be a reorganization first, before section 356 could be applied.

VI.B.2.h. *Specific Versus General*

Implicit in several of the latin maxims of construction is the concept that when Congress has dealt specifically with an issue, more general sections do not control it. Examples include the following:

- Section 119 did not leave room under section 61 for a different exclusion for meals.[1718]
- The Tax Lien Act of 1966 controlled because it was the later statute, more specific and more comprehensive in its treatment of federal tax liens.[1719]
- A "basic principle of statutory construction:" precisely drawn detailed statute preempts more general remedies.[1720]
- A publisher could not be prosecuted for publishing lists of taxpayers that Congress had directed be made public because the statute criminalizing publishing parts of returns applied only to the extent "not provided by law," and thus gave way to the specific Congressional intent to make names public (although the opinion did not discuss the generally versus the specific).[1721]

A different issue arises when a party contends that the existence of Code provisions dealing with a matter in certain cases implies that Congress did not intend it to be similarly treated in other cases. The taxpayer made this argument in *Midland-Ross*, contending that because the Code sections that specifically addressed original issue discount did not apply to its facts, it was

---

[1716] Reo Motors, Inc. v. Commissioner, 338 U.S. 442 (1950).

[1717] Turnbow v. Commissioner, 368 U.S. 337 (1961).

[1718] Commissioner v. Kowalski, 434 U.S. 77 (1977). *See also* Boulware v. United States, 552 U.S. 421 (2008) (the specific rules of section 301 apply to the exclusion of section 61).

[1719] United States v. Estate of Romani, 523 U.S. 517 (1998). *See also* EC Term of Years Trust v. United States, 550 U.S. 429 (2007) (more specific remedy precluded general remedy).

[1720] Hinck v. United States, 550 U.S. 501 (2007) (opinion by Chief Justice Roberts interpreting a statute that did not say it was exclusive, to be exclusive, because it was specific); HCSC-Laundry v. United States, 450 U.S. 1 (1981) (specific statute controls a general provision).

[1721] United States v. Dickey, 268 U.S. 378 (1925).

not taxable on original issue discount as ordinary income.[1722] The Court disagreed: ". . . they may demonstrate, not that the general rule was to the contrary, but that the general rule was unclear, . . . and that Congress wished to avoid any doubt as to its treatment of particular situations." This decision also reflects the vast ability of section 61 to encompass income also described in more targeted sections.[1723]

Justice Thomas rejected the preference for the more specific in *Kawashima*.[1724] The taxpayers admitted they had filed false returns but argued they could not be deported on this ground because (1) the revenue code did not specify that filing false returns was a crime of fraud, and (2) the other ground that specifically referred to tax crimes did not include the crime for which they were guilty. Justice Thomas rejected the argument that the two grounds were mutually exclusive and found that the government was a "victim" of a crime of fraud in which it lost more than $10,000 even though the taxpayers were not guilty of the tax crime in which the government also had to lose more than $10,000.

VI.B.2.i. *Strict Construction of Exemptions, Deductions, Exclusions, Nonrecognition, Credits, and Other Allowances*

This important set of presumptions is discussed in detail in Ch. II.B.2.c(4), but flagged here for completeness.

VI.B.2.j. *Penalty Provisions*

Related to the presumption for a broad construction of income and the correlative strict construction of deductions against the taxpayer is the strict construction of penalties against the government. This derives from the rule of lenity applied in the criminal law, as discussed in Ch. II.B.2.a(4). The Supreme Court strictly construes penalty provisions within the Code against the government, in most cases.[1725] The same is true of forfeitures.[1726] The Court refused to apply a tax penalty against a bankrupt estate because it would hurt the creditors of the taxpayers and so could not educate the taxpayer, thus ruling based on purpose.[1727]

1722 United States v. Midland-Ross Corp., 381 U.S. 54 (1965). *See also* Helvering v. Clifford, 309 U.S. 331 (1940) (the fact that Congress specifically included the income of revocable trusts in the settlor's income did not reduce the ability of section 61 to include the income from a short term trust in the settlor's income); Sims v. United States, 359 U.S. 108 (1959). *Compare* Helvering v. Wood, 309 U.S. 344 (1940) (same result could not be reached due to pleading error).

1723 *Cf.* Boulware v. United States, 552 U.S. 421 (2008).

1724 Kawashima v. Holder, 132 S. Ct. 1166 (2012).

1725 *See* Ivan Allen Co. v. United States, 422 U.S. 617, 627 (1975); Commissioner v. Acker, 361 U.S. 87, 91 (1959); *cf.* Fulman v. United States, 434 U.S. 528 (1978) (doctrine not applicable to personal holding company tax because the statute provides its own way out of the tax).

1726 United States v. Ryan, 284 U.S. 167 (1931).

1727 Simonson v. Granquist, 369 U.S. 38 (1962).

When the penalty is criminal prosecution for a tax crime, strict construction applies.[1728]

VI.B.2.k. *Superfluity and Surplusage*

The Supreme Court has applied in tax cases the maxim of construction that every part of the statute be given a meaning or function,[1729] and the courts should not interpret one provision in a way that would render another provision superfluous,[1730] or redundant,[1731] or effectively inoperative.[1732] In a related approach, the Court interpreted sections 302 and 318 to require attribution of stock ownership for one purpose in order to effect Congress' intent in clearly making it applicable for a closely related purpose.[1733] The Court called the six-year statute of limitations in the Tucker Act a "negative condition," so as to leave room for a shorter statute of limitations for tax refund claims; otherwise, the shorter limit would have been meaningless.[1734] Superfluity is an aspect of the jurisprudential fact that courts must decide cases. Whereas the agency might punt on an issue, when parties present an issue of statutory construction to the court, it cannot duck by calling the section meaningless.[1735]

But the important 2015 ruling in favor of Obamacare stated that the canon against surplusage was not absolute (the exchange "established by the State" left "by the State" as surplusage).[1736]

Example as surplusage. Also the Court allowed a part of the statute to be ignored as surplusage in *Chickasaw Nation.*[1737] It considered a section erroneous in that it was not an example of the rule, unless the statute were interpreted to state two rules, or a different rule from that specifically stated. The opinion evaluated the overall structure and purpose of the statute and relied on "common sense" reasoning in rejecting the expansion of the rule, finding the example to be surplusage. The taxpayer argued the statute was ambiguous,

---

[1728] United States v. Scharton, 285 U.S. 518 (1932), *cited in* Kawashima v. Holder, 132 S. Ct. 1166 (2012) (but strongly criticized in dissent by Justice Ginsburg); United States v. Habig, 390 U.S. 222 (1968) (citing *Scharton* for principle that criminal limitations rule is to be construed liberally in favor of repose, but not in this case).

[1729] *See* Atl. Mut. Ins. Co. v. Commissioner, 523 U.S. 382 (1998) (avoiding treating a clause as superfluous); Commissioner v. Estate of Hubert, 520 U.S. 93 (1997).

[1730] Freytag v. Commissioner, 501 U.S. 868, 877 (1991); Sunshine Anthracite Coal Co. v. Adkins, 310 U.S. 381 (1940) (Bituminous Coal Act tax); United States v. Quality Stores, Inc., 134 S. Ct. 1395 (2014).

[1731] Davis v. United States, 495 U.S. 472 (1990) ("to … or for the use of" have different applications).

[1732] Graham & Foster v. Goodcell, 282 U.S. 409 (1931) (narrow construction rejected because it would make statute virtually inoperative).

[1733] United States v. Davis, 397 U.S. 301 (1970).

[1734] United States v. A. S. Kreider Co., 313 U.S. 443 (1941).

[1735] United States v. Woods, 134 S. Ct. 557 (2013).

[1736] King v. Burwell, 135 S. Ct. 2480 (2015).

[1737] Chickasaw Nation v. United States, 534 U.S. 84 (2001).

which seems evident, and the Court seems to have proceeded on that basis. This combined with one other such decision suggests that examples are an exception to the rule: examples don't mean to change the basic rule of the section but are not surplusage when they answer one case.[1738]

VI.B.2.l. *Other Maxims and Canons*

Canons and maxims of statutory construction generally,[1739] like dictionary definitions, are in low repute among scholars and some judge-authors,[1740] and yet courts (including the Supreme Court), taxpayers and the Service apply them every day, whether they use the latin terms or not.[1741] This disconnect suggests that simply pointing out the faults of canons is not as useful as figuring out the virtues of canons.[1742] That they persist is probably due not only to their usefulness to busy judges but also to the fact that they probably are seldom determinative even when recited.[1743] Observers long have recognized their value in stabilizing the law by providing a ground of decision in cases of otherwise irresolvable uncertainty.[1744]

One analysis explained[1745] how that stabilization works by showing that canons and other methods of statutory interpretation and construction esti-

---

1738 United States v. Am. College of Physicians, 475 U.S. 834 (1986).

1739 For complete lists of canons, *see* Staudt et al., *Judging Statutes, supra* note 20, at 1933-34 (*e.g.,* avoid rendering language superfluous, *ejusdem generis, ejusdem unius*, ignore drafting mistakes, *nosciture a sociies,* placement has no relevance, placement has relevance, plain meaning/common usage, punctuation grammar and syntax, headings irrelevant, headings are relevant, technical meaning of words, whole act rule); Eskridge, Frickey and Garrett, *supra* note 1421, at Appendix; Eskridge & Frickey, *The Supreme Court, 1993 Term—Forward: Law as Equilibrium*, 108 Harv. L. Rev. 26, 97-108 (1994) (listing the maxims the Rehnquist Supreme Court used).

1740 *See* Cunningham & Repetti, *supra* note 17, at 16 (quoting the frequently quoted analysis by Karl Llewellyn that canons are useless because for every canon there is a potentially equally applicable conflicting canon, in *Remarks on the Theory of Appellate Decisions and the Rules or Canons about How Statutes Are to Be Construed,* 3 Vand. L. Rev. 395, 401-06 (1950) ("Latin maxims are honored only when all else fails in discerning Congress' purpose."); Murtagh, *supra* note 105, at 528 (citing Neuberger v. Commissioner, 311 U.S. 83, 88 (1940)); Popkin, at 145 (blaming the legal realists for contending that canons come in pairs that cancel each other out); Posner, The Federal Courts, *supra* note 125, at 276 et seq.; Ross, *supra* note 1464, at 561 (arguing that liberal and conservative judges alike misuse canons to justify their judicial activism).

1741 Posner, *Statutory Interpretation—In the Classroom and in the Courtroom*, 50 U. Chi. L. Rev. 800, 805 (1983) (negative academic views of maxims have had little impact on the courtroom).

1742 *See* Frankfurter, *Some Reflections on the Reading of Statutes*, 47 Colum. L. Rev. 527, 544 (1947) ("axioms of experience").

1743 Murtagh, *supra* note 105, at 538.

1744 *See* Shapiro, *Continuity and Change in Statutory Interpretation*, 67 N.Y.U. L. Rev. 921 (1992).

1745 Elhauge, *supra* note 66.

mate congressional preferences (Congress' purposes)[1746] and elicit them.[1747] Thus, linguistic canons (such as *ejusdem generis*) are quite important at the margins where the statute is truly ambiguous, despite the application of whatever interpretive techniques the court feels proper.[1748] This approach soundly justifies what most judges and other lawyers using the tax law do instinctively: base all interpretational methods directly or indirectly on the ultimate authority of the legislature.

Use of canons also can elicit legislative responses in the most unobjectionable way.[1749] Thus, for example, the rule of lenity applies for penalty provisions because it can encourage the legislature to redefine exactly how tough it wants the criminal law to be, as contrasted with forcing the judges to lean toward harshness, which decisions likely would be upheld;[1750] tax exemptions are strictly construed because the interest groups that lobby for them are likely to have had enough influence to achieve clear coverage if Congress had intended it.[1751].

Canons frequently are parsed as either linguistic or substantive.[1752] Several authors have studied the use of canons of construction by the Supreme Court in tax cases and concluded they have only marginal impact.[1753] That may be, but they are validated to some extent because the Court does recite them, and so they should be recognized as legitimate tools; or, if the Court does not cite them by name, it applies the same reasoning. The only linguistic canons that Professor Staudt found the Court to have relied on to any significant degree by name are *expressio unius est exclusio alterius* (five percent) and *noscitur a sociies* (three percent).[1754]

Expressio unius est exclusio alterius means that stated statutory conditions or alternatives can preclude others and can help estimate the preference (or

---

1746 *Id.*

1747 *Id.* Both articles are combined in ELHAUGE, STATUTORY DEFAULT RULES, *supra* note 1423.

1748 *See* Elhauge, *supra* note 66, at 2032, 2056.

1749 *Id.*

1750 *Id.* at 2194.

1751 *Id.* at 2207. But he erred in citing as a canon that taxing provisions are interpreted strictly against the government *Id.* at 2208. The cites are to Stevens' and Thomas' dissenting and concurring opinions in *United Dominion Industries, Inc. v. United States*, 532 U.S. 822 (2001), but only Thomas undertakes to cite cases, which are the abandoned strict construction cases discussed above in Ch. II.B.2.a. Thomas makes clear that he is writing in opposition to Stevens' dissent, which advocated deference to the administrator. As shown above, all of these cases predated the clear rejection of this doctrine in *White v. United States*, 305 U.S. 281 (1938).

1752 *See, e.g.,* Brudney & Ditslear, *supra* note 59, at 1239-40.

1753 Staudt et al., *Judging Statutes, supra* note 20, at 1932-35 (finding use of canons not to be common, but when used, by far the most important were to interpret the Code in accordance with background legal concepts and judicially developed terms of art, or the plain meaning); Mary L. Heen, *Plain Meaning, The Tax Code and Doctrinal Incoherence*, 48 HAST. L.J. 771, 778, n. 38 (1997).

1754 Staudt et al., *Judging Statutes, supra* note 20, at 1935.

purpose) of the legislature or elicit the preference of the legislature (by further enactments).[1755] The Court has been quite careful in applying the canon in tax cases,[1756] asking whether the Congress had a reason to consider the omitted item at the time the list was enacted, and if not, then deciding that the canon did not apply.[1757] The Court sometimes applies the maxim without using its term, stating that "some things too clearly evince a legislative enactment to call for a redundancy of utterance" that the section was intended to be exclusive.[1758] And in *Arkansas Best,* Justice Marshall stated that "the location" of the words stating that all property is a capital asset except for listed exceptions means that the list is exclusive.[1759]

The Court has rejected the *expressio unius* canon in favor of allegedly clear congressional intent where the canon could have been applied.[1760] But when it applied the canon it did so with a cite to a historic early tax decision of Justice Story.[1761] *Noscitur a sociies,* meaning that a word is known by the company it keeps, appears less often by its latin name, but is probably used more often due to its eminent sensibleness.[1762] Justice Scalia rejected application of the maxim without citing it where there was a conflict between a parenthetical (indicating sameness) and the use of the word "or" indicating difference.[1763]

Ejusdem generis (of the same kind) can be preference eliciting (Elhauge disagrees with Llewellyn who cited cases that were not preference eliciting).[1764]

[1755] Elhauge, *supra* note 66, at 2213. In *United States v. Wells Fargo Bank*, 485 U.S. 351 (1988) the Court reasoned how Congress wrote the law as it did in 1937 in anticipation of the application of the canon.

[1756] *See* Standefer v. United States, 447 U.S. 10 (1980) (refusing to apply the canon to a legislative report); Burnet v. Brooks, 288 U.S. 378 (1933) (canon proves too much).

[1757] United Dominion Industries, Inc. v. United States, 532 U.S. 822 (2001); Barnhart v. Peabody Coal Co., 537 U.S. 149 (2003).

[1758] Palermo v. United States, 360 U.S. 343 (1959). *See also* United States by & ex rel. IRS v. McDermott, 507 U.S. 447 (1993) (because Congress specifically let certain simultaneous liens trump the federal tax liens, the general rule is that they don't).

[1759] Arkansas Best Corp. v. Commissioner, 485 U.S. 212 (1988). *See also* United States v. Quality Stores, Inc., 134 S. Ct. 1395 (2014) (applied but not stated).

[1760] *See* Neuberger v. Commissioner, 311 U.S. 83 (1940) (ruling that a partner could deduct individual noncapital losses from the sale or exchange of his assets against partnership noncapital income from similar sales even though such income was not among the items that the Code specifically listed as retaining its character on a pass through basis).

[1761] *See* Lang v. Commissioner, 289 U.S. 109 (1933); (citing Bend v. Hoyt, 38 U.S 263 (1839) (Story, J.) (customs case, which did not cite the canon by name but did apply it; one exception precludes others)).

[1762] *See* Jarecki v. Searle & Co., 367 U.S. 303 (1961) (applying the maxim); United States v. Leslie Salt Co., 350 U.S. 383 (1956) (adopting Treasury application of the maxim); Direct Mktg. Assn. v. Brohl, 135 S. Ct. 1124 (2015) (a state tax case, but the Tax Injunction Act interpreted is similar to the federal Anti-Injunction Act).

[1763] United States v. Woods, 134 S. Ct. 557 (2013) ("the parenthesis cannot bear that much weight").

[1764] Elhauge, *supra* note 66, at 2216. The Court applied *ejusdem generis* in *Duffy v. Central R. Co.*, 268 U.S. 55 (1925).

Here, too, the Court has been sparing in its use.[1765] Therefore it appears to be a makeweight argument, used only when not inconsistent with the otherwise determined general purposes of the provision.[1766] When the statute states a list and includes "similar" items there is no need to apply the maxim, but similarity must be determined.[1767] The canon is not relevant when the Court decides that the two words or groups have different subject matters.[1768] Justice Scalia called this an "asymmetrical statute," being one with several subsections addressing one subject (property taxes) and containing limitations that do not apply to a fourth subsection that addresses a wholly separate tax.[1769] A similar argument can be made when a statute applies to a particular case and a general case, which would include the particular case and make it superfluous unless one were to limit the statute to the specific case. Chief Justice Marshall rejected this argument in an early tax opinion.[1770]

Catchall. The 2011 *CSX* opinion referred to above refines the ejusdem maxim by parsing between catchalls that are intended to summarize a list and catchalls that happen to be at the end of the list but refer to dissimilar things.

Absurdity. The canon that declines to adopt the usual or literal meaning of a statute when necessary to avoid an absurdity or to thwart the obvious purpose of the statute[1771] does not rely on preference eliciting because the preference is known (using Elhauge's terminology).[1772]

- The fountainhead of the absurdity doctrine in the Supreme Court (though not its first use) is the *Church of the Holy Trinity*.[1773]

1765 Helvering v. Stockholms Enskilda Bank, 293 U.S. 84 (1934) (application of canon would conflict with other evidence of purpose).

1766 *See* F. W. Fitch Co. v. United States, 323 U.S. 582 (1945). The Court applied *ejusdem* in *Bend v. Hoyt*, 38 U.S 263 (1839) (Story, J.) (customs case).

1767 Nicol v. Ames, 173 U.S. 509 (1899) (found a stock yard to be a "similar place" to a stock exchange for purposes of applying an excise tax to sales at the exchange).

1768 CSX Transp., Inc. v. Ala. Dep't of Revenue, 562 U.S. 277 (2011) (interpreting federal statute as applied to state tax).

1769 *Id.* But Justices Thomas and Ginsburg read the catchall at the end of a list of four to be informed by the limitations on the first three.

1770 United States v. Fisher, 6 U.S. 358 (1805) (lien on revenue officer and all persons not limited to revenue officer's tax debts).

1771 *See* United States v. Craft, 535 U.S. 274 (2002) (refusing to adopt the absurd interpretation that no one owned property); Commissioner v. Brown, 380 U.S. 563 (1965) (reciting but not finding the canon applicable); Helvering v. Hammel, 311 U.S. 504 (1941); Haggar Co. v. Helvering, 308 U.S. 389 (1940); Gulf States Steel Co. v. United States, 287 U.S. 32 (1932) ("manifestly unjust if not absurd"); United States v. Ryan, 284 U.S. 167 (1931). An opinion may not use the word "absurd" but in effect apply this maxim, as in Mansfield v. Excelsior Refining Co., 135 U.S. 326 (1890) (Congress would not say that only the taxpayer need receive notice of intent to see his interest in property to pay his taxes, if Congress intended the interests of other rights holders to be destroyed in the sale).

1772 Elhauge, *supra* note 66, at 2218.

1773 Church of the Holy Trinity v. United States, 143 U.S. 457 (1892) ("laborer" who could not immigrate did not include minister).

- But absurdity will override a clear statute only in "rare and exceptional circumstances," where the absurdity would shock the "general moral and common sense," and "there must be something to make plain the intent of the Congress that the letter of the statute is not to prevail."[1774] That "something" may be Congress' overall purpose.[1775] Mere inconvenience will not trigger the doctrine.[1776] For some reason the Court likes to cite the *Brown* opinion for the absurdity maxim outside the tax context, even though it found no absurdity in literally applying the statute.[1777]
- An example of such other evidence of Congress' intent was observed in *Flora*, which concluded that several additions to the Code must reflect Congress' assumption that the absurd interpretation for which the taxpayer argued was not the meaning of the statute.[1778]
- Sometimes absurdity is in the eye of the beholder, and does not include mere unreasonableness of legislation.[1779]
- Absurdity is often paired with an explanation that the statute simply is not referring to the issue at hand, although it makes a broad statement that would appear to cover the issue at hand.[1780]
- Often when the Court declines an absurdity argument made by the taxpayer it points out that this is a problem for Congress (preference eliciting).[1781]
- Shock-the-conscience absurdity in the tax law is illustrated by *Hill*,[1782] in which contrary to the plain meaning of the statute the Supreme Court rejected a construction sought by the taxpayer that would have produced an "astonishing" result: a capital item sheltering 10 times its cost.

[1774] Crooks v. Harrelson, 282 U.S. 55 (1930) (finding an incongruity not to be an absurdity).; Treat v. White, 181 U.S. 264 (1901). A similar formulation appears in United States v. Ron Pair Enters., Inc., 489 U.S. 235, 242 (1989) (". . . a result demonstrably at odds with the intentions of its drafters . . ."). In *Helvering v. Hammel*, 311 U.S. 504 (1941), Justice Stone stated courts have "some scope" to reject an absurd literal interpretation.

[1775] Gulf States Steel Co. v. United States, 287 U.S. 32 (1932).

[1776] United States v. Fisher, 6 U.S. 358 (1805) (early tax lien case).

[1777] Commissioner v. Brown, 380 U.S. 563 (1965).

[1778] Flora v. United States, 362 U.S. 145, 157 (1960).

[1779] *See* Commissioner v. Asphalt Prods. Co., Inc., 482 U.S. 117 (1987) (lower court judge thought applying the negligence penalty to much larger non-negligent portion of underpayment was absurd, but to the Supreme Court it was perhaps unreasonable but explainable; in any event the statute was clear).

[1780] *See, e.g.*, Gulf States Steel Co. v. United States, 287 U.S. 32 (1932) (Taxpayer gave a bond to prevent collection efforts just before the statute of limitations on collection ran. Taxpayer subsequently substituted other bonds. Then Congress enacted a statute saying that a decision of the Board of Tax Appeals that collection was barred by the statute was to be considered a ruling that there was no deficiency. The Court rejected the taxpayer's argument that this statute prevented the government's enforcement of the bond, both on grounds of absurdity of result and on the ground that the statute simply did not address bonds.).

[1781] White v. United States, 305 U.S. 281 (1938).

[1782] United States v. Hill, 506 U.S. 546, 560 (1993).

- *Badaracco*[1783] supported a plain meaning reading of the Code by stating that Congress could not have intended to treat a fraudulent taxpayer better than a nonfraudulent one.
- A version of absurdity is to state that Congress would not have written two provisions in the same law to conflict with each other, which the Court applied to the Constitution.[1784]Another version is that Congress is aware of reality and would not have written a statute in conflict with it.[1785]

As discussed in Ch. VI.B.1.c. above, the cases in which absurdity of result alone is the asserted ground for rejecting plain meaning are the cases that can go either way but are most likely to be decided based on plain meaning.

Other maxims applied by the Supreme Court in tax cases, which in some instances are applications of the maxims already discussed, include the following:

- *Pasquantino* considered and limited the application of the canon of strict construction of a statute thought to be in derogation of the common law. [1786]
- Repeals by implication are not favored.[1787]
- "Indian canon," which assumes Congress intends its statutes to benefit the tribes.[1788]
- *Knowlton v. Moore* decided an estate tax dispute by stating: "where a particular construction of a statute will occasion great inconvenience or produce inequality and injustice, that view is to be avoided if another and more reasonable interpretation is present in the statute."[1789]

1783 Badaracco v. Commissioner, 464 U.S. 386 (1984); *see also* Reinecke v. Northern Trust Co., 278 U.S. 339 (1929) (rejected "incongruous" interpretation that was inconsistent with rest of section); Ford Motor Co. v. Commissioner, 102 T.C. 87 (1994) (upholding the Commissioner's determination on clear reflection of income grounds due to the "incongruous" result sought by taxpayer that increased its net worth as its accrued tort liability grew).

1784 Brushaber v. Union P. R. Co., 240 U.S. 1 (1916).

1785 Helvering v. Canfield, 291 U.S. 163 (1934).

1786 Pasquantino v. United States, 544 U.S. 349 (2005) (calling the "revenue rule" that one country will not collect another country's taxes a common law rule and analyzing whether the tax lien statute was in derogation of a common law rule); *see* Stone, *The Common Law in the United States*, *supra* note 199, at 18 ("We need to be reminded, too, that in the construction of statutes establishing administrative agencies and defining their powers there is little scope for the ancient shibboleth that a statute in derogation of the common law must be strictly construed. . .").

1787 West India Oil Co. v. Domenech, 311 U.S. 20 (1940); EC Term of Years Trust v. United States, 550 U.S. 429 (2007) (called canon against implied repeals and rejected); Graham & Foster v. Goodcell, 282 U.S. 409 (1931). *But see* Steamboat Co. v. The Collector, 85 U.S. 478 (1873) (when Congress repealed the part of the statute that imposed the tax, the proviso fell with it).

1788 Chickasaw Nation v. United States, 534 U.S. 84 (2001) (the term is unique to this opinion)

1789 Knowlton v. Moore, 178 U.S. 41 (1900).

- Tax statutes are more likely to look to the future than the past, and so an ambiguity will be resolved in favor of the interpretation that applies the tax to an event that can occur in the future rather than one that occurred in the past.[1790]
- When an exception in a statute amounts to an affirmation of the application of its general provisions to all other cases not excepted;[1791] and when an exception also evidences that the thing excepted was in the larger group.[1792]
- Other sections show that Congress knew how to do something different if it wanted to.[1793]
- When a statute limits a thing to be done in a particular mode, it includes the negative of any other mode.[1794]
- Courts cannot create an exception in the Code where the Congress has declined to do so.[1795]
- The Court will read exceptions narrowly in order to preserve the primary operation of the policy of the provision (apparently without regard to whether it is a deduction or exclusion).[1796]
- Where two laws are irreconcilably in conflict, the later act will be treated as repealing the earlier.[1797]

[1790] Colgate-Palmolive-Peet Co. v. United States, 320 U.S. 422 (1943).

[1791] Kendall v. United States, 107 U.S. 123 (1883); Bend v. Hoyt, 38 U.S. 263 (1839) (exception applying different customs duty for sewing silk meant that all other silk was taxed at the common rate).

[1792] Brown v. Maryland, 25 U.S. 12 (1827)

[1793] United States v. Ron Pair Enters., Inc., 489 U.S. 235, 242 n. 5 (1989) ("When Congress wanted to restrict the application of a particular provision of the Code to such liens, it used the term 'security interest.'"); Commissioner v. Asphalt Prods. Co., Inc., 482 U.S. 117, 120 (1987) (observing that when Congress wanted to limit a penalty to a portion of the deficiency, it knew how to do so); Badaracco v. Commissioner, 464 U.S. 386, 395 (1984) (observing in construing a word in the Code that when Congress intends only a temporary suspension of the statute of limitations it knows how to say so); United States v. Rodgers, 461 U.S. 677, 696 (1983) (contrasting another section where the additional provision sought by the losing party was clearly stated); Helvering v. William Flaccus Oak Leather Co., 313 U.S. 247 (1941) (deciding that "demolition" was not a sale or exchange, the Court observed that other sections of the tax act deeming events to be a sale or exchange show Congress has expressly stated which ambiguous events are to be a sale or exchange); *but see* United States v. Wells Fargo Bank, 485 U.S. 351, 357 (1988) (recognizing the "familiar argument" but laboring rather heavily to avoid its application); United States v. Donruss Co., 393 U.S. 297 (1969) (declining to decide on the basis of greater specificity in other Code sections).

[1794] Botany Worsted Mills v. United States, 278 U.S. 282 (1929).

[1795] Freytag v. Commissioner, 501 U.S. 868 (1991).

[1796] Knight v. Commissioner, 552 U.S. 181 (2008).

[1797] EC Term of Years Trust v. United States, 550 U.S. 429 (2007); *see also* S. Rep. No. 445, 100th Cong., 321-22 (1988) (accompanying section 7852(d)(1) concerning tax treaties and U.S. statutes and making the same point).

For a further list of Supreme Court canons with citations see the Eskridge and Frickey article.[1798]

VI.B.2.m. *Word Definitions*

The Court has defined many words in tax opinions, both common and uncommon words.

- *And* requires both;[1799] conversely, the Court held a list of three possible grounds to impose withholding tax liability on a corporate officer joined by "and" did not require each of the grounds to be present;[1800] lists ending with "and" are conjunctive and not disjunctive.[1801]
- *Apportion* means to divide and assign in just, not necessarily equal, proportion.[1802]
- *Arising under* does not mean "based solely upon" [not a tax case].[1803]
- *As aforesaid* directs the reader to use the earlier reference in the sentence to specific legacies to find that a $10,000 amount applied per legacy and not to the entire estate.[1804]
- *As of* may not have a clear meaning and can mean either the facts as they actually existed or as they should have existed.[1805]
- *Capital stock* has been twice interpreted to mean net asset value, when the corporation does not have stock outstanding.[1806]
- *Directly or indirectly* was given an extremely broad reading in *McWilliams* to encompass a sale of stock into the market as being a sale to the wife.[1807]
- *Discretion*, when referring to the Commissioner's discretion, can be overcome only the taxpayer bearing the heavy burden of proving its approach reasonable and the Commissioner's approach unreasonable and arbitrary.[1808]

1798 Eskridge & Frickey, *The Supreme Court, 1993 Term, supra* note 1739, at 97-108 (listing the maxims the Supreme Court has used).

1799 McFeely v. Commissioner, 296 U.S. 102 (1935).

1800 Slodov v. United States, 436 U.S. 238 (1978).

1801 Crooks v. Harrelson, 282 U.S. 55 (1930), citing United States v. Field, 255 U.S. 257 (1921).

1802 Manhattan General Equipment Co. v. Commissioner, 297 U.S. 129 (1936).

1803 Jones v. R. R. Donnelley & Sons Co., 541 U.S. 369 (2004).

1804 Knowlton v. Moore, 178 U.S. 41 (1900).

1805 United States v. Quality Stores, Inc., 134 S. Ct. 1395 (2014); Barnhart v. Peabody Coal Co., 537 U.S. 149 (2003).

1806 Hecht v. Malley, 265 U.S. 144 (1924); Ray Consolidated Copper Co. v. United States, 268 U.S. 373 (1925) ("capital stock" has no fixed meaning and so Treasury could choose between stock value and asset value, and chose asset value because stock value was depressed at the relevant time). *See also* United States v. Loan & Bldg. Co., 278 U.S. 55 (1928).

1807 McWilliams v. Commissioner, 331 U.S. 694 (1947).

1808 Thor Power Tool Co. v. Commissioner, 439 U.S. 522 (1979); Lucas v. Kansas City Structural Steel Co., 281 U.S. 264 (1930).

- *Established to the satisfaction of the Commissioner*, when used in a refund rule, does not grant absolute unreviewable power to decide, but rather refers to normal decision making.[1809]
- *Example . . . is best construed as an illustration of one possible application*" of [in this case] the regulation, and not as a vehicle for Treasury to state an additional substantive rule or undo the substantive rule of the regulation;[1810] this is a recurring issue and the Court's refusal to read a substantive rule into an example runs contrary to a tendency among practitioners and the Service to read great significance into examples in regulations.
- *Exclusively* means that if there is any other reason "substantial in nature," then the requirement of exclusivity cannot be satisfied.[1811]
- *Hereafter*: dividends paid "hereafter" mean after the enactment of the taxing law;[1812]
- *If . . . then* is a fairly common construct in the Code, which can have more ambiguity than might be thought.[1813]
- *In the business* refers to the particular business of the taxpayer, not a hypothetical generic business.[1814]
- *Manufacturing* does not require that a person make the thing with his own hands, but rather Congress understands the world's division of labor (and this was in 1916).[1815]
- *May*, when used in a statute, usually implies some degree of discretion, and when the statute is changed from "shall" to "may," it is best construed as indicating Congress believed that equitable discretion existed all along.[1816]
- *Not any*: when the Court saw five "not any's" in one section, it thought Congress really meant it.[1817]
- *Of*: *Poe v. Seaborn* ruled that when the statute taxed income "of every individual," the word "of" imported state law ownership.[1818]
- *Or*: a list ending with "or" is disjunctive.[1819]

1809 United States v. Jefferson Elec. Mfg. Co., 291 U.S. 386 (1934).

1810 United States v. Am. College of Physicians, 475 U.S. 834 (1986).

1811 Better Business Bureau v. United States, 326 U.S. 279 (1945). If this meaning had been applied by the Treasury to section 501(c)(4) the current upset over campaigning by those organizations would not have arisen.

1812 Blake v. Nationl Banks, 90 U.S. 307 (1875).

1813 See competing tax examples by Justices Roberts and Sotomayor in Scialabba v. Rosalina Cuelar de Osorio, 134 S. Ct. 2191 (2014), not a tax case.

1814 Massey Motors, Inc. v. United States, 364 U.S. 92 (1960).

1815 Carbon Steel Co. v. Lewellyn, 251 U.S. 501 (1916).

1816 United States v. Rodgers, 461 U.S. 677, 706-08 (1983).

1817 United States v. Clintwood Elkhorn Mining Co., 553 U.S. 1 (2008).

1818 Poe v. Seaborn, 282 U.S. 101 (1930). The Court reaffirmed the significance of "of" in *United States v. Mitchell*, 403 U.S. 190 (1971).

1819 Porter v. Commissioner, 288 U.S. 436 (1933); United States v. Woods, 134 S. Ct. 557 (2013) ("as the case may be" sealed the interpretation).

- *Principal* means of first importance (see Ch. IV.A.1).[1820]
- *Purpose* of a taxpayer imports more than knowledge of facts and their tax consequences.[1821]
- *Relates to*, according to Justice Scalia in the *Woods* opinion, is "essentially indeterminate;"[1822] evidently this means wholly ambiguous.
- *Shall*: a direction that the Commissioner "shall" take an action within a defined period is not jurisdictional and does not authorize the Court to impose a sanction for failure to act in time.[1823]
- *Shares* refers to equity in partnerships and nonstock companies (and may also refer to stock), in contrast to "stock," which refers to stock corporations.[1824]
- *Sold* in a country means the place where the final act confirming and approving the price and other terms of sale occurred.[1825]
- *Subject to* tax is not limited to the taxpayer on whom the tax was originally assessed.[1826]
- *The*: Congress' choice to use the article "the" rather than "a" had no particular significance;[1827] this *Donruss* opinion is fairly unique in the tax opinions and remarkable in converting "for the purpose of" into a test that turned on one of several unranked purposes.[1828]
- *Transaction entered into for profit* is not limited to the acquisition of property but is a term of common usage that can encompass the conversion of residential property to rental use.[1829]
- *Wholly* may not mean 100%.[1830]
- *Would* may refer to what is customarily done.[1831]

VI.B.3. *Use of Extrinsic Evidence to Resolve Ambiguities and Gaps*

The following chapters discuss the Supreme Court's reliance on evidence extrinsic to the words of the Code, other than the interpretational tools discussed above, which principally means legislative histories.

[1820] Commissioner v. Soliman, 506 U.S. 168 (1993).

[1821] United States v. Donruss Co., 393 U.S. 297 (1969).

[1822] United States v. Woods, 134 S. Ct. 557 (2013). He cited *Maracich v. Spears*, 133 S. Ct. 2191 (2013), which is distinguishable.

[1823] Barnhart v. Peabody Coal Co., 537 U.S. 149 (2003).

[1824] Duffy v. Mutual Ben. Life Ins. Co., 272 U.S. 613 (1926).

[1825] Compania General de Tabacos v. Collector , 279 U.S. 306 (1929).

[1826] United States v. Williams, 514 U.S. 527 (1995).

[1827] United States v. Donruss Co., 393 U.S. 297 (1969).

[1828] *Cf.* United States v. Harriss, 347 U.S. 612 (1954) (not a tax case, but involving a similar liberal reading of an apparently absolute requirement).

[1829] Heiner v. Tindle, 276 U.S. 582 (1928).

[1830] United States v. Seattle-First Nat'l Bank, 321 U.S. 583 (1944) (a transfer can be wholly by operation of law even steps leading up to the operation of the statutory transfer are voluntary).

[1831] Knight v. Commissioner, 552 U.S. 181 (2008).

The Court has relied on evidence extrinsic to the face of the statute to (1) interpret facially ambiguous provisions,[1832] including interpreting facially ambiguous provisions to be unambiguous (meaning they can have only one meaning),[1833] (2) fill gaps,[1834] and (3) construe facially unambiguous provisions contrary to facial meaning.[1835] The prototypical ambiguities that the Supreme Court has clarified are the meaning of income as discussed above in relation to *Eisner v. Macomber*, the meaning of association in *Morrissey*,[1836] and several terms related to deductions and capitalization, including "trade or business," "ordinary and necessary," "away from home,"[1837] "betterments made to increase the value of any property" in section 263,[1838] and gifts. Beyond these grand examples, there is a never ending supply of lesser ambiguities to which the Court has applied extrinsic evidence of meaning.

A statute that seems to be ambiguous on its face can be found to allow only one interpretation through use of "traditional tools of statutory construction," which include legislative histories.[1839]

VI.B.3.a. *Judicial Versus Administrative Decisions*

Taxpayers often fail to recognize that the Service may approach statutory interpretation in ways that differ from those used by the courts. This book and other commentators usually focus on what the courts do; that presumes that all other parties interpret the law by projecting what the courts will do. While taxpayers should do that, administrative agencies, such as the Treasury and the Service, are not necessarily bound by this approach, because they are charged with interpreting the statutes as the coordinate executive branch of government, and also with making legislative regulations in some cases. The Constitution, Article II, section 3, tasks the executive branch with taking care that the laws are faithfully executed, which authorizes an independent judgment about the wise application of the laws.[1840] Therefore, despite whatever

---

[1832] *See, e.g.*, The Colony, Inc. v. Commissioner, 357 U.S. 28 (1958) (moving directly from a finding of ambiguity to legislative history).

[1833] *See supra* Ch. VI.B.1.c. and *infra* Ch. VI.C.

[1834] *E.g.*, Commissioner v. Standard Life & Accid. Ins. Co., 433 U.S. 148 (1977) (when Congress adopted NCIS accounting rules except where accrual accounting dictates a different result, and accrual rules did not cover the situation, the NCIS rules apply).

[1835] The prototypical example is *Gregory v. Helvering*, 293 U.S. 465 (1935).

[1836] Morrissey v. Commissioner, 296 U.S. 344 (1935) (the Court created the definition of "association" to be taxed as a corporation by the broadest sort of analogizing to chartered corporations; later rejected by regulations).

[1837] Commissioner v. Stidger, 386 U.S. 287 (1967) (ruling military officer's home was in Japan not California); United States v. Correll, 389 U.S. 299 (1967) (establishing "overnight rule"); Commissioner v. Flowers, 326 U.S. 465 (1946).

[1838] *See* INDOPCO, Inc. v. Commissioner, 503 U.S. 79 (1992); Commissioner v. Lincoln Savings & Loan Assoc., 403 U.S. 345 (1971).

[1839] Chevron U.S.A., Inc. v. Natural Resources Defense Council, Inc., 467 U.S. 837, 842-43 (1984); *see infra* Ch. VI.D.

[1840] Easterbrook, *Executive Branch Interpretation of the Law: Unitary Executive Interpretation*, 15 Cardozo L. Rev. 313, 315 (1993).

methods of statutory interpretation are currently in vogue in the courts, they will not necessarily be used by agencies.

Among other reasons for the agencies' greater latitude is that the vast amount of their guidance will never be reviewed by courts.[1841]

> . . . why should agencies, when given deference under the *Chevron* doctrine precisely because they are Congress's chosen delegate for implementing statutory policies, constrain themselves to act like courts when going about their quite separate business.[1842]

The agency's freer use of legislative history in interpreting the Code also fits nicely with any opposite institutional reluctance on the part of the courts: by giving *Chevron* deference to the agency interpretations (See Ch. VI.D. below), the courts obtain access to legislative history by the back door.[1843]

However, agencies like the Treasury and Service are accustomed to giving close attention to legislative histories, regardless of whether that is in vogue in the Supreme Court. Any person familiar with their processes will agree that they try very hard to extract every shred of evidence of legislative intent from all available sources—legislative histories, contemporaneous commentary, overall purpose, etc.—in interpreting ambiguous sections of the Code.[1844] They also give extraordinary credence to even the smallest indications in the words of the statute. The reason is institutional in the case of the Service: it says it does not have discretion to "make law" when the statutory meaning can be determined by objective indicia.[1845] The Treasury may exercise greater freedom, but that generally reveals itself only in regulations and is heavily constrained by the Service's institutional conservatism in parsing the Code. Also, the Service often bends its interpretations to the needs of litigation, both by its own Chief Counsel attorneys and Justice Department attorneys in Tax Division cases. Litigators, even government litigators, are bound to explore all avenues to victory, even if they mangle the law in the process.

The relevance of the distinction for tax is that (1) the Chief Counsel and Treasury perhaps should more clearly assess the basis on which they interpret the Code, and (2) taxpayers should beware that agency interpretation may differs from court interpretation.

1841 Mashaw, *Agency Centered or Court Centered Administrative Law: A Dialogue with Richard Pierce on Agency Statutory Interpretation*, 59 ADMIN. L. REV. 889 (2007).

1842 *Id.* at 900.

1843 Mashaw, *Norms, Practices and the Paradox of Deference: A Preliminary Inquiry into Agency Statutory Interpretations*, 57 ADMIN. L. REV. 501, 512 (2005).

1844 I.R.M. 4.10.7.2.2. *See* Mashaw, *Norms, Practices and the Paradox of Deference*, *supra*, at 501, 511 (*citing* Strauss, *When the Judge Is Not the Primary Official with Responsibility to Read: Agency Interpretation and the Problem of Legislative History*, 66 CHI.-KENT L. REV. 321 (1990)).

1845 Mashaw, *Norms, Practices and the Paradox of Deference*, *supra* note 1843. at 511 (". . . agencies might need to wrap themselves in the blanket of pre-legislative congressional utterances in order to maintain the integrity of the statutory scheme in the face of powerful political controllers intent of wrenching statutory schemes loose from their historical, contextual foundations.").

VI.B.3.b. *Legislative History*

VI.B.3.b(1) *Reliance on Legislative History in Interpreting the Code*

The Supreme Court's tax opinions in recent years have been relatively light on legislative histories; sometimes one Justice inserts a history reference sheepishly.[1846] But until late in the 20th century the Supreme Court more typically stated that "possible doubts as to the proper construction of the language [of a tax statute] should be resolved in light of its administrative and legislative history."[1847] The most prominent opinions commonly cited for the Supreme Court's reliance on legislative history are *Church of the Holy Trinity*[1848] (not a tax case) and *Stockholms Enskilda Bank*.[1849] The Court has commonly said it was relying on such information,[1850] not just in terms of Congress' statements about what it was doing, but in terms of tracing the history of the legislative process for clues to meaning, which may be a more acceptable process to foes of the histories.[1851]

[1846] *E.g.*, Hall v. United States, 132 S. Ct. 1882 (2012) (Justice Sotomayor put a history reference in a footnote, prefaced by "for those of us for whom it is relevant").

[1847] McCaughn v. Hershey Chocolate Co., 283 U.S. 488 (1931). *See* Bufferd v. Commissioner, 506 U.S. 523 (1993) ("While the views of a Congress engaged in the amendment of existing law as to the intent behind that law are "entitled to significant weight, …").

[1848] Church of the Holy Trinity v. United States, 143 U.S. 457, 459 (1892). This has been identified as the case marking the turn of the American courts to legislative history. Elhauge, *supra* note 66, at 2224 (citing Vermeule, *Legislative History and the Limits of Judicial Competence: The Untold Story of Holy Trinity Church*, 50 Stan. L. Rev. 1833, 1836 & n.15 (1998)); *see also* Popkin, at 121-22. Justice Scalia has cited the decision as proof of why statutes should be read literally. Scalia, Common Law Courts in a Civil Law System 18-23 (Amy Guttman ed. 1997). *See also* Blatt, *Missing the Mark: An Overlooked Statute Redefines the Debate over Statutory Interpretation*, 64 U. Miami L. Rev. 641 (2009-2010) (pointing out the relevance of the statutory change that occurred before the decision was rendered, approving its result retroactively).

[1849] Helvering v. Stockholms Enskilda Bank, 293 U.S. 84 (1934) (based on extensive analysis of legislative history concluded that words "annual and periodical" did not preclude taxation of a lump sum royalty).

[1850] *See, e.g.*, White v. Winchester Country Club, 315 U.S. 32, 41 (1942) ("… Substantially contemporaneous expressions of opinion are highly relevant and material evidence of the probable general understanding of the times and of the opinions of men who probably were active in the drafting of the statute."); The Colony, Inc. v. Commissioner, 357 U.S. 28 (1958) (moving from a determination of statutory ambiguity directly to legislative history).

[1851] *See, e.g.*, Helvering v. Nw. Steel Rolling Mills, Inc., 311 U.S. 46 (1940) (what appears to be an overly strict refusal to treat a corporate charter as a contract, explained by legislative history showing that Congress dropped from the bill the deduction for the category the taxpayer claimed); United States v. Quality Stores, Inc., 134 S. Ct. 1395 (2014) (reviewing the course of amendments).

Reliance on legislative histories has generated disagreements for a long time generally,[1852] and in tax cases in particular.[1853] In a 1949 dissent, Justice Frankfurter included an Appendix A listing well over 50 opinions of the Court in the past decade in which legislative history was "decisive."[1854] However contentious the practice may be, the reliance of most interested parties on legislative materials is not going away in the tax area. The Service directs its agents that the committee report accompanying the House bill generally states the reason for the amendment and "this reasoning establishes the legislative intent behind the finalized law;" it encourages the use of all three of the House, Senate, and Conference Reports, even by revenue examiners.[1855] The Service's Cumulative Bulletins have long carried legislative histories; the 1939 Volume cumulates the legislative histories of all prior Revenue Acts. But legislative history has a much broader meaning than House and Senate Reports on the enacted bill, although the weight of legislative materials less directly related to the enactment of the bill at hand may be relatively less.[1856]

Empirical studies show that in addition to coordinating with other statutes, citations of legislative history are by far the largest category of evidence of statutory meaning recited by the Supreme Court.[1857] The Court's use of legislative tax history increased over time and rose well above 50% of the cases.[1858] Of course the Court does not slavishly rule in accordance with some legislative history that is in conflict with the normal understanding of the statute.[1859] Because "normal understanding" is a term of art, the impact of

---

1852 For review, see Elhauge, *supra* note 66, at 2027-72 (defending uses of legislative history, at least when other interpretive methods fail to resolve ambiguity). For example of judicial disapproval, see opinion of Scalia, J. in *Conroy v. Aniskoff*, 507 U.S. 511, 518 *et seq.* (1993) (attacking use of legislative history).

1853 *See, e.g.*, Brudney and Ditslear, *supra* note 59, at 1242-44, 1262 (arguing that the Supreme Court relies on legislative history in tax cases for the particular reason of borrowing expertise from the Congressional staff); Ferguson, Hickman & Lubick, *Reexamining the Nature and Role of Tax Legislative History in Light of the Changing Realities of the Process*, 67 TAXES (CCH) 804 (1989); Lewis, *Viewpoint: The Nature and Role of Tax Legislative History*, 68 TAXES (CCH) 442 (June, 1990); Livingston, *Congress, the Courts and the Code, supra* note 1455, at 819; Murtagh, *supra* note 105, at 529-30 (citing Holmes statement in Pine Hill Coal Co. v. United States, 259 U.S. 191, 196 (1922): "It is a delicate business to base speculation about the purposes or construction of a statute upon the vicissitudes of its passage."); *see also* Piper v. Chris-Craft Indus., Inc., 430 U.S. 1, 26 (1977) (stating that reliance on legislative history is a "step that is to be taken cautiously").

1854 Commissioner v. Estate of Church, 335 U.S. 632 (1949).

1855 I.R.M. 4.10.7.2.2. But reliable legislative history does not include Joint Committee Reports. I.R.M. 32.2.3.5.1.2.3.3.

1856 *See generally* RICHMOND, FEDERAL TAX RESEARCH Ch. 7 (Foundation Press 2007).

1857 *See* Staudt et al., *Judging Statutes, supra* note 20, at 1942.

1858 *Id.* at 1944.

1859 *See, e.g.*, Commissioner v. Schleier, 515 U.S 323 (1995) (citing TWA, Inc. v. Thurston, 469 U.S. 111 (1985)); Helvering v. City Bank Farmers Trust Co., 296 U.S. 85 (1935) (committee report said a later enacted section was "in accord" with the section being interpreted, but the Court refused to find that they had the same meaning because the words differed; four justices dissented).

legislative history can never be certain. Empirical studies also show the types of legislative histories on which the Supreme Court has placed the most reliance between 1969 and 2008, in tax cases where legislative histories were cited: Senate Report (78.4%); House Report (68.2%).[1860] These percentages are significantly higher than for a comparison group of workplace law cases; in contrast the tax opinions place significantly less relative reliance on conference reports and floor debates.[1861] The authors argue that in citing tax legislative history the Supreme Court is "borrowing expertise."[1862]

Legislative history will continue to be relied on by all interested parties and so it is important to acknowledge that there is good theoretical support for that tool. Reliance on legislative history is a valid way to estimate the preferences of the enacting Congress, whether or not a particular report accurately reflects the unified will of Congress, or elicits the preferences of Congress.[1863]

However, Justice Scalia, often joined by other Republican appointed Justices, eschews legislative history.[1864] For that reason, when other Justices write opinions they tend to avoid using it. This can result in an amusing dance around legislative history as occurred in *Mayo.*[1865] Chief Justice Roberts' opinion made a statement about what Congress intended, for which it cited the Treasury's notice of proposed rule making for the regulation at issue. The particular page cited quoted a 1939 House Committee Report that supported the Treasury and the Court's ruling. Or disliked legislative history in the form of a single congressman's recorded statement can be dismissed because he "misspoke."[1866]

A different way to use legislative history is to differentiate between two parts of a section that were enacted at different times. *Minnesota Tea* stated that the two different ways to structure a tax free reorganization had separate legislative histories and were intended to be mutually excluive, but it if turned out they overlapped, the taxpayer could pick the more favorable rule.[1867]

Another use of histories is to infer what was known to Congress at the time of legislating. Justice Whitaker called this the "legislative environment" comprised of subject matter, context, legislative history and executive interpretation.[1868] For example, a 1945 opinion inferred that Congress would have

---

[1860] Brudney and Ditslear, *supra* note 59, at 1262.

[1861] *Id.*

[1862] *Id.* at 1283.

[1863] *See supra* Ch. VI.B.

[1864] *See* Hall v. United States, 132 S. Ct. 1882 (2012) (a bankruptcy tax decision written by Justice Sotomayor; because Justice Scalia joined, the majority opinion prefaced discussion of legislative history by saying "for those of us for whom it is relevant.").

[1865] Mayo Found. for Med. Educ. & Research v. United States, 562 U.S. 44 (2011).

[1866] United States v. Wells Fargo Bank, 485 U.S. 351 (1988).

[1867] Helvering v. Minnesota Tea Co., 296 U.S. 378 (1935).

[1868] Sims v. United States, 359 U.S. 108 (1959).

known about a Treasury regulation defining educational organizations for one purpose, when it used the term for another purpose.[1869]

Also, legislative history continues to be cited as a makeweight argument in support of what the opinion has already said to be the clear meaning of the statute. In one opinion, the history was a report on rules changes to the Court from its own rules committee.[1870]

Legislative history bears an important relationship to the *Chevron* doctrine (see Ch. VI.D.). It requires that the agency interpretation of the statute receive deference if the statute cannot be interpreted to have a clear meaning after applying normal tools of statutory interpretation. In 1984 when *Chevron* was written, the Court routinely relied on legislative history. That is much less true today. Some argue that should mean that the "normal tools" now do not include legislative history, which results in even greater room for administrative interpretation.[1871] That seems to be an odd view both because it is inconsistent with the basis on which the *Chevron* doctrine was invented and it tends to further diminish the role of courts, which, in the end, will not hold.[1872]

VI.B.3.b(2) *Effect of Subsequent Legislative History*

The Supreme Court states that the view of a subsequent Congress in legislative history cannot affect the interpretation of an earlier statute,[1873] but nevertheless the Court may cite it as support.[1874] This is particularly relevant to tax regulations because the tax legislative staffs always explain a change by first explaining the existing law.[1875] In one opinion, Justice Brennan simply stated that the congressional report was obviously mistaken in its summary of the law as it existed at the time of an amendment to the Code.[1876] The sub-

---

[1869] Better Business Bureau v. United States, 326 U.S. 279 (1945). Even opponents of legislative history admit to this usage. Manning, Chevron *and Legislative History*, 82 Geo. Wash. L. Rev. 1517, 1551 (2013) (a relevant term of the trade at the time of enactment may be preserved in the history).

[1870] United States v. Davila, 133 S. Ct. 2139 (2013).

[1871] Manning, Chevron *and Legislative History*, *supra* note 1869.

[1872] *See, e.g.*, United States v. Home Concrete & Supply, LLC, 132 S. Ct. 1836 (2012) (plurality opinion).

[1873] O'Gilvie v. United States, 519 U.S. 79 (1996) (citing earlier tax opinions; view of later Congress cannot control interpretation of earlier enacted statute); Penn. Mut. Life Ins. Co. v. Lederer, 252 U.S. 523 (1920) (forceful refusal of Justice Brandeis to give any weight to reenactment of the section at issue six years later, when the bill at first contained and there was sticken from the bill a phrase that the taxpayer contended had to be interpolated into the section for the government to win); United States v. Am. College of Physicians, 475 U.S. 834 (1986).

[1874] In addition, the Supreme Court has relied on later Congresses' intent to construe earlier acts in other cases. *See* Pipefitters Local Union No. 562 v. United States, 407 U.S. 385 (1972); Glidden Co. v. Zdanok, 370 U.S. 530, 541 (1962); Fed. Hous. Admin. v. Darlington, Inc., 358 U.S. 84, 90 (1958).

[1875] Bufferd v. Commissioner, 506 U.S. 523 (1993) (refused to accept report's account of "present law").

[1876] South Carolina v. Regan, 465 U.S. 367 (1984).

sequent history is even more suspect when the President vetoes a supposedly clarifying provision.[1877]

The issue has been quite actively debated by the Court outside of its tax cases, and a prominent cite is *Cipollone*, which addresses the preemptive effect of pre-1969 federal law.[1878] Justice Stevens, writing for four Justices, thought "the views of a subsequent Congress form a hazardous basis for inferring the intent of an earlier one,"[1879] quoting a 1960 opinion of Justice Harlan in an income tax case.[1880] The congressional reports discussed in the 1960 tax opinion identified one change as the only material change from existing law (a more specific reference than "clarification"), and the party argued that meant another change was not material, hence the amendment reflected prior law. Harlan's opinion rejected that reading as a "slender reed." Although three justices in *Cipollone* thought the amendment had not changed the law,[1881] their cited authority for relying on the views of a subsequent Congress was a case in which the amendment itself stated the meaning of the prior act.[1882]

In addition to *Cipillone*, the weight of Supreme Court authority is strongly against reliance on subsequent legislative history.[1883] This view is thought to stem from a shift from the Burger Court's readiness to accommodate congressional desires to the Rehnquist Court's relative unwillingness to bend to

---

1877 Waterman Steamship Corp.v. United States, 381 U.S. 252 (1965) (gain on sale of merchant ship).

1878 Cipollone v. Liggett Group, Inc., 505 U.S. 504 (1992). Congress had amended the tobacco warning statute in 1969 as to pre-emption of state law by federal law, and the Senate Report stated that the amendment "clarified" the earlier law. Both parties in *Cipollone* contended that the amendment did not materially alter prior law: the plaintiff viewed the amendment as not having wide preemption scope and the defendant viewed it as having wide preemption scope. Thus, each party used the "clarification" point to bolster its argument. The Stevens opinion in *Cipollone*, in which three other justices joined on this point, found the amendment to make a significant change and that the law had changed. The Blackmun opinion, in which two justices joined, did not find the amendment to make significant change and gave weight to the clarification reference.

1879 *Id.* at 520.

1880 United States v. Price, 361 U.S. 304, 313 (1960); *see also* Int'l Bhd. of Teamsters. v. United States, 431 U.S. 324, 354 n. 39 (1977) (discounting the views of a later Congress).

1881 Cipollone v. Liggett Group, Inc., 505 U.S. at 539.

1882 Red Lion Broad. Co. v. F.C.C., 395 U.S. 367, 380 (1969).

1883 *See* Cent. Bank, N.A. v. First Interstate Bank, N.A., 511 U.S. 164, 185 (1994) ("of little assistance," citing *Betts*); Pub. Employees Ret. Syst. v. Betts, 492 U.S. 158, 168 (1989) ("of little assistance"); Mackey v. Lanier Collection Agency & Serv., 486 U.S. 825, 839-40 (1988) (later opinion of Congress does not control the issue of interpretation of earlier enactment); *but see* Bell v. New Jersey, 461 U.S. 773, 785 (1983) ("the view of a later Congress does not establish definitively the meaning of an earlier enactment, but it does have persuasive value"; but this was a case where the plain statutory language as well as contemporaneous legislative history reached the same interpretation). The opinion in United States v. Quality Stores, Inc., 134 S. Ct. 1395 (2014) could have but did not cite post-enactment legislative history argued to it by a party, probably due to the low repute of such history.

congressional preference.[1884] However, the Supreme Court has given weight to legislative histories stating intent to change or clarify,[1885] and Mr. Justice Jackson gave weight to a legislative report on an unenacted bill that discussed Congress' dislike of the courts' interpretation of the Code.[1886]

There can be a question as to what histories are written after the fact. In a 2013 tax opinion, Justice Scalia dismissed a Blue Book written by the Joint Committee to describe tax legislation of the prior year as after the fact legislative history.[1887] This reflects ignorance of the tax legislative process in which the Joint Committee explanation usually embodies the prior committee reports that build on one another.

A special kind of subsequent legislative history arises when Congress changes the law the Court is interpreting before it renders decision or shortly thereafter. An analysis showed this occurred as to more than half of the Rehnquist Court's tax decision.[1888]

VI.B.3.b(3) *Change or Clarification?*

Sometimes the subsequent legislative history is not much more than a statement or a bill title stating an intent to clarify or change the law. That Congress sometimes "clarifies" a Code section by amending it does not mean Congress thought it was not changing the law. The word clarification generally means to make clear, suggesting a prior state either of ambiguity or absence of direction, or darkness.[1889] It also can be read as if preceded by the word "mere," as implying minor and nonsubstantive amendments.[1890] Alternately, it (along with the term "technical change") can refer to a "wide-ranging" change of law.[1891]

Whenever Congress has amended the Code in a way that supports the arguments of one side or the other to a tax dispute, even in the absence of congressional comment on what it thought the law used to be, the benefited party

---

[1884] *See* Eskridge, *Reneging on History? Playing the Court/Congress/President Civil Rights Game*, 79 CAL. L. REV. 613, 668-69 (1991); *cf.* Farber & Frickey, *Legislative Intent and Public Choice*, 74 VA. L. REV. 423, 466-68 (1988) (weight given to later history varies; should receive some weight); Eskridge, *The New Textualism*, 37 UCLA L. REV. 621, 635-36 (1990) (sometimes receives weight); Posner, *Economics, Politics, and the Reading of Statutes and the Constitution*, 49 U. CHI. L. REV. 263, 275 (1982) (agreeing with the "traditional answer" that subsequent history should be ignored).

[1885] *See* Hartley v. Commissioner, 295 U.S. 216 (1935).

[1886] City of New York v. Saper, 336 U.S. 328 (1949).

[1887] United States v. Woods, 134 S. Ct. 557 (2013).

[1888] Boyle, *The Rehnquist Court: Nineteen Years of Tax Decisions*, 25 VA. TAX REV. 451, 456 (2005).

[1889] WEBSTER'S THIRD NEW INTERNATIONAL DICTIONARY 415 (1971).

[1890] *See* Cipollone v. Liggett Group, Inc., 505 U.S. 504, 539 (1992); *see also Bell*, 461 U.S. at 789 (finding stated intent to clarify law, coupled with statement that amendment did not radically change the law, to support interpretation that prior law included part of amendment).

[1891] *See* Freytag v. Commissioner, 501 U.S. 868, 875 (1991) (ruling that a change in the authority of special Tax Court judges, which was meant by Congress "to clarify," actually constituted a wide-ranging power that changed prior limits).

inevitably argues that Congress merely clarified what the law always meant, while the other party counters that Congress surely thought it was changing the law. The best solution to these considerations is to view them as nugatory because offsetting, in the absence of additional probative evidence. However, the courts sometimes appear to be swayed by these arguments. These cases often overlap with cases involving the immediately preceding subject: later comment in legislative history on the meaning of an existing statute.

Where the Court considered only the changed statute and not a later legislative history, it has done the following:

- In *Colony, Inc.*, the Court said there seems to be no consistency in the decisions and little utility in the analysis.[1892]
- In *Babbit v. Sweet Home Chapter*, it stated that when Congress amends a statute it means to change something in a real and substantial way.[1893]
- In *Jewett*, it stated that "Congress may seek to clarify the future without affecting the past."[1894]
- In *Helvering v. N.Y. Trust Co.*, the Court observed that a change of language does not necessarily indicate a change of meaning but may be a clarification.[1895]
- In *Fairbanks*, it ruled that the adoption of the predecessor of section 1271(a) in 1934 changed and did not clarify the law as it had previously existed.[1896]
- In *Fisher*, it viewed a statutory change as a clarification (evidently because it was the same as an existing regulation) and that a statement in the act that it should not apply to pending cases did not prevent the prior regulation from applying to the instant case because it was the law without regard to the act.[1897]

[1892] The Colony, Inc. v. Commissioner, 357 U.S. 28 (1958) (avoiding the "speculative debate").

[1893] Babbitt v. Sweet Home Chapter, 515 U.S. 687, 701 (1995); *see also* Rutkin v. United States, 343 U.S. 130 (1952) (indicating that when the original definition of income was changed to delete "lawful" the Congress intended that unlawful income also be taxed; the dissent argued that the failure of Congress to act to reverse a contrary case decided six years earlier showed that the unlawful income was not taxable).

[1894] Jewett v. Commissioner, 455 U.S. 305 (1982).

[1895] Helvering v. N.Y. Trust Co., 292 U.S. 455 (1934).; Jewett v. Commissioner, 455 U.S. 305 (1982).

[1896] Fairbanks v. United States, 306 U.S. 436 (1939), as also explained in *Dixon v. United States*, 381 U.S. 68 (1965). Other cases of change rather than clarification include *Smeitanka v. First Trust and Savings*, 257 U.S. 602 (1922) and *Spring City Foundry Co. v. Commissioner*, 292 U.S. 182 (1934).

[1897] Commissioner v. Fisher, 327 U.S. 512 (1946). The treatment of pending cases probably was a great disappointment to someone's lobbyist; the opinion implied skepticism that "Congress intended by the proviso to pick out a small group of taxpayers and award them special tax exemptions which the whole Act was designed to deny all other taxpayers who did not happen to have tax litigation pending in September 1940."

- In *Watson*, it viewed a later enacted section to change the law, whereas the dissent thought it clarified what had been the law previously.[1898]
- In *Higgins v. Smith*, it purported to be unmoved by the enactment of section 267, but still ruled as if it had always existed, while the dissent protested that the enactment showed Congress meant to change the law;[1899]
- In *Jacobson*, relied on Congress' creation of an exemption to infer prior taxability.[1900]
- In *Knetsch*, it held that the enactment of a modified prohibition on the deduction of interest did not bless a pre-enactment deduction, both because legislative history did not reveal any such intent and because the act could not affect the deductibility of interest on debt that did not fit the statutory definition because the taxpayer did not owe a debt in fact.[1901]
- In *O'Gilvie*, it interpreted an amendment to section 104 making clear that punitive damages for nonphysical injuries were not excluded, not as proving that punitive damages for physical injuries were excluded, but as leaving such damages in a state of unclarity;[1902] this is an unusual approach.
- In *American Hide & Leather*, it ruled that when *Congress* dropped reference to the return as filed from the refund statute it meant to require that the period for claiming refund run from the correct due date only.[1903]
- In *Griffiths*, Congress seemed to purposefully punt back to the courts to determine whether it was changing or restating prior law.[1904] *Eisner v. Macomber* had ruled that a stock dividend was not includible in gross income as a constitutional matter. In 1936, Congress enacted a statute stating that stock dividends were not taxable to the extent not income under the constitution. The Court addressed the meaning of the statute for a 1939 stock distribution and viewed the statute as essentially ambiguous. Justice Jackson applied what could be viewed as a three part test to rule that Congress had not intended to change the result in *Macomber* (indeed, how could it): (1) consistent administrative treatment of stock dividends as not taxable; (2) similar consistent judicial treatment; and

---

1898 Watson v. Commissioner, 345 U.S. 544 (1953) (ruled portion of farm sale attributable to growing crops produced ordinary income; later enacted statute to treat as capital gain was needed to change the law; this case stated the principle that business assets must be comminuted and not treated as a mass for purposes of characterization).

1899 Higgins v. Smith, 308 U.S. 473 (1940).

1900 Commissioner v. Jacobson, 336 U.S. 28 (1949) (exemption created for corporate taxpayers buying debt for less than face showed that Congress thought that solvent debtors did not receive exempt gifts when creditors settled for less than face).

1901 Knetsch v. United States, 364 U.S. 361 (1960).

1902 O'Gilvie v. United States, 519 U.S. 79 (1996) (this result was so odd that Justice Alito used it in dissent in Texas Dept. of Housing v. Inclusive Communities Project, 135 S. Ct. 2507 (2015)).

1903 American Hide & Leather Co. v. United States, 284 U.S. 343 (1932).

1904 Helvering v. Griffiths, 318 U.S. 371 (1943).

(3) legislative history failing to disclose any intent to change *Macomber's* result.

VI.B.3.b(4) *Legislative Inaction and Reenactment and Court Rulings*

Legislative inaction in the face of a court's interpretation of a statute is not sufficient to bind a coordinate or higher court to that interpretation,[1905] but such an interpretation carries some weight once it has been brought to the attention of Congress and Congress has reenacted or amended the statute without changing the interpretation.[1906] Where reenactment has occurred, giving that fact weight is called the "reenactment doctrine" by the Supreme Court itself.[1907] Of course reenactment is less frequent in the tax statutes than it was before the 1939 Code, when the Revenue Act was reenacted every two years.[1908] Commentators have mostly agreed that the contention is a make-weight justification for a decision already arrived at on other grounds.[1909] The cases are inconsistent:

- As might be expected, the Court has a high opinion of reenactment after its own opinions interpreting Code terms.[1910] And re-enactment may mean just failure to amend.[1911]
- But the Court has also reversed its own holdings despite reenactment.[1912]
- The issue created much discussion in the area of estate taxation of gifts in trust with various retained or reversionary interests. In *Hallock*, the Court extensively discussed the implications of reenactment without consideration of court interpretation or of changes by Congress and found it

---

[1905] United States v. Price, 361 U.S. 304 (1960); Simonson v. Granquist, 369 U.S. 38 (1962) (court decisions went both ways).

[1906] Elhauge, *supra* note 66, at 2112.

[1907] Cent. Bank N.A. v. First Interstate Bank, N.A., 511 U.S. 164, 185 (1994) (stating that failed legislative proposals are a particularly dangerous ground on which to rest an interpretation of the prior statute).

[1908] Also, shifting from a biannual revenue law to a continuing Code had consequences for statutory interpretation. *See* Reo Motors, Inc. v. Commissioner, 338 U.S. 442 (1950) (change in way Code referred to prior law, in comparison with revenue laws, had no significance).

[1909] Solimine & Walker, *supra* note 91, at 429 (concluding that the Supreme Court gives little weight to the congressional inaction canon); Caron, *Tax Myopia or Mamas Don't Let Your Children Grow up to Be Tax Lawyers*, 13 VA. TAX REV. 517, 563-73 (1994) (concluding reenactment doctrine is a makeweight justification for a decision made on other grounds).

[1910] *See, e.g.*, Commissioner v. Keystone Consolidated Industries, Inc., 508 U.S. 152 (1993) (referring to a half century of court and administrative usage in treating transfer of property for cancelation of debt as a sale or exchange); Hecht v. Malley, 265 U.S. 144 (1924).

[1911] Arkansas Best Corp. v. Commissioner, 485 U.S. 212 (1988) (placing some weight on Congress' failure to express disfavor with Supreme Court's 25-year interpretation of capital gains).

[1912] James v. United States, 366 U.S. 213 (1961) *reversing* Commissioner v. Wilcox, 327 U.S. 404 (1946) (embezzled income taxable).

to have no bearing and so overruled its own prior decision.[1913] Later, in *Spiegel's Estate*, Justice Frankfurter's dissent included an Appendix B listing decisions of the past decade resting on the rule that reenactment carried the gloss of the Court's rulings.

- In *Phipps*, the Court noted that Congress had cited the *Sansome* rule with approval in legislative history and so continued to apply it.[1914]
- In *American Automobile*, the Court implied that Congress had approved, or at least not acted in light of the Court's decision in, *Automobile Club of Michigan*, and so affirmed its earlier decision.[1915]

For reenactment and Treasury regulations, see chapter VI.D.6.b.

VI.B.3.c. *Other Extrinsic Evidence*

VI.B.3.c(1) *General Public Policy*

Probably the Court's most important reliance on general public policy to decide a tax case came in *Bob Jones University*,[1916] which effectively created a new requirement for exemptions to satisfy the public policy against racial segregation.[1917] The Court ruled that public policy implicitly adopted by Congress required all section 501(c)(3) organizations to comply with the standards of racial nondiscrimination that applied to charities, even though section 501(c)(3) does not appear to require an educational institution like the University to be charitable to be exempt.[1918] The *Bob Jones* opinion cited the early decision in *Duchesne*, which held that Congress would not have intended to create patent protection to run against foreigners for acts outside the United States, even though the statute seemed to so provide.[1919] That decision was based in part on protecting vital public interests by preventing individuals from exercising foreign affairs powers.

[1913] Helvering v. Hallock, 309 U.S. 106 (1940) (where the Court declined to give weight to inaction on matter not brought to Congress' attention, and lack of reenactment of section 302(c), even though other parts of section 302 were amended).

[1914] *See, e.g.*, Commissioner v. Phipps, 336 U.S. 410 (1949) (Congress specifically endorsed the *Sansome* rule in legislative history).

[1915] Am. Auto. Assn. v. United States, 367 U.S. 687 (1961) (In the prepaid income cases the Court stated a doctrine that it had a "long established policy" of deferring where possible to congressional procedures in the tax field, evidently referring to timing matters in particular.); *see also* Schlude v. Commissioner, 372 U.S. 128 (1963).

[1916] Bob Jones Univ. v. United States, 461 U.S. 574 (1983).

[1917] *See* Eskridge & Frickey, *Statutory Interpretation as Practical Reasoning*, *supra* note 92, at 355-56 (stating it is the paradigm example); Stefan, *Bob Jones University v. United States: Public Policy in Search of Tax Policy*, 1983 SUP. CT. REV. 33 (1983).

[1918] The *Bob Jones* decision was motivated by the Court's basic understanding that: ". . . there can no longer be any doubt that racial discrimination in education violates deeply and widely accepted views of elementary justice." *Bob Jones*, 461 U.S. at 592. "We emphasize, however, that these sensitive determinations should be made only where there is no doubt that the organization's activities violate fundamental public policy." *Id.*

[1919] Brown v. Duchesne, 60 U.S. 183, 194 (1857) (the invention was brought into the United States, but on a boat on which it was installed outside the United States).

Broad public policy comes up less frequently in tax cases than in many other areas,[1920] but sufficient examples exist to make this a relevant extrinsic interpretive source in tax cases; they sometimes are called "frustration of public policy."[1921] To be relevant the public policy must be "sharply defined."[1922] Other examples include the following:

- In *Clarke v. Haberle Crystal Springs Brewing Co.*, the Court denied an obsolescence deduction for loss of a brewing business, which it "extinguished as noxious under the Constitution."[1923]
- In *Tank Truck Rentals, Inc. v. Commissioner*, the Court denied a business expense deduction for fines on the ground that a "finding of 'necessity' cannot be made . . . if allowance of the deduction would frustrate sharply defined national or state policies proscribing particular types of conduct, evidenced by some governmental declaration thereof."[1924]
- In *Cammarano v. United States* and also in *Textile Mills Sec. Corp. v. Commissioner*, the Court denied a business expense deduction for lobbying expenses under long-standing regulations expressing "a sharply defined national policy."[1925]
- In *McDonald v. Commissioner*, the Court refused to find that a political party assessment was a business expense of being a judge;[1926]
- But, in *Arthur Young*, the Court declined to enforce a nontax policy goal.[1927]

[1920] *See, e.g.*, United States v. Am. Trucking Assocations, Inc., 310 U.S. 534 (1940) (relying on broad public policy in employment regulations).

[1921] Bittker & Lokken, at 20.3.3.

[1922] Commissioner v. Tellier, 383 U.S. 687 (1966) (Court refused to deny deduction for costs of defense of crime arising in the taxpayer's business); Lilly v. Commissioner, 343 U.S. 90 (1952) (allowing deduction of what might be called "kickbacks" by opticians to referring eye doctors).

[1923] Clarke v. Haberle Crystal Springs Brewing Co., 280 U.S. 384 (1930).

[1924] Tank Truck Rentals, Inc. v. Commissioner, 356 U.S. 30, 33-4 (1958) (which is cited for the "public policy doctrine" or "frustration of public policy" doctrine).

[1925] Cammarano v. United States, 358 U.S. 498 (1959); Textile Mills Sec. Corp. v. Commissioner, 314 U.S. 326 (1941) (no deduction for lobbying for return of German's property seized during World War I).

[1926]

> The relation between money and politics generally—and more particularly the cost of campaigns and contributions by prospective officeholders, especially judges—involves issues of far-reaching importance to a democracy and is beset with legislative difficulties that even judges can appreciate. But these difficulties can neither be met nor avoided by spurious interpretation of tax provisions dealing with allowable deductions.

McDonald v. Commissioner, 323 U.S. 57 (1944).

[1927] United States v. Arthur Young & Co., 465 U.S. 805 (1984) (finding that possible "chilling effect" on accountants was not a significant public concern that should affect the interpretation of the scope of the government's discovery process).

- In *Hernandez*, the Court refused to evaluate the centrality of the taxpayer's religious beliefs to the claimed charitable deduction, but only evaluated whether there was a quid pro quo.[1928]
- In *Regan et al. v. Taxation with Representation of Washington*, the Court refused to require the tax law to subsidize lobbying and political expenditures.[1929]

The Code and regulations use concepts of public policy very sparingly. The primary instance is section 162(c), (f) and (g), denying deductions for certain expenses Congress believes frustrate public policy; and Regulation section 1.212-1(p), which imports those rules into section 212.

VI.B.3.c(2) *Tax Raising Public Policy*

In contrast, general public policy that supports the collection of tax can be a ground of decision. This occurred in a 1950 ruling that a taxpayer had to pay interest on a tax liability for 1941 even though a carried back 1943 loss wiped out the principal tax liability; to rule otherwise "would be to place a premium on failure to conform diligently with the law."[1930] In the tax accounting area, "It is the essence of any system of taxation that it should produce revenue ascertainable, and payable to the government, at regular intervals. Only by such a system is it practicable to produce a regular flow of income and apply methods of accounting, assessment, and collection capable of practical operation."[1931] An early opinion reasoned that the revenue must be protected so the government can function.[1932]

VI.C. Construction of the Code

VI.C.1. *Ambiguous Sections: Filling Gaps*

The tools and methods of interpretation discussed above also apply to construction of the Code. Whereas interpretation may help to discern the one true meaning of a facially ambiguous statute, construction is of two different types: filling gaps (where there may be no single correct answer) and construing the Code contrary to its literal meaning, the latter of which is discussed separately in Ch. VI.C.2. below. Gaps must be filled when the statute is not just ambiguous, but either does not address a subject that one of the parties now thinks it should have addressed, or addresses it in conflicting ways, or in an absurd way. Codes can never fully address all needful subjects and most problems of statutory interpretation don't involve ambiguities at all but gaps.[1933]

[1928] Hernandez v. Commissioner, 490 U.S. 680 (1989).

[1929] Regan et al. v. Taxation with Representation of Washington, 461 U.S. 540 (1983).

[1930] Manning v. Seeley Tube & Box Co., 338 U.S. 561 (1950).

[1931] Burnet v. Sanford & Brooks Co., 282 U.S. 359 (1931).

[1932] Cheatham v. United States, 92 U.S. 85 (1876).

[1933] *See* Christy, *Prolegomena to Federal Statutory Interpretation: Identifying the Sources of Interpretive Problems*, 76 Miss. L.J. 55, 64 (2006).

Gaps in the Code are necessarily identified in hindsight, except for (1) gaps the Code directs Treasury to fill by regulations, and (2) gaps that are so obvious from the outset that Congress had to expect courts to fill,[1934] as for example the very important term income, for which section 61 contains an obviously inadequate and nonexclusive list of examples. As discussed in Ch. I.B. Congress may leave more gaps than legislatures in other countries due to a tradition of expectation in this country that courts fill gaps left by Congress.

Professor Zelenak proposed a rather obvious approach for dealing with congressional inadvertence in tax cases in a 1986 article:

> If the factual pattern to which the statute must be applied is one that Congress did not specifically consider or address in enacting the statute, and if the inadequacy of the statutory language to support the logical result is due to congressional inadvertence rather than design, then a nonliteral interpretation may be appropriate under either an intent-based or meaning-based theory of interpretation.[1935]

In fact this is what the Supreme Court frequently has done,[1936] while protesting that it occurs only in "rare and exceptional circumstances."[1937] In any event, the Court cannot avoid the duty to give meaning to every tax law the Congress has seen fit to enact, no matter how ambiguous.[1938]

Gap filling necessarily implicates the discussion of *Chevron* in Chapter VI.D., below. To grossly oversimplify that matter, when Congress has left a gap in the substantive law so wide as to inevitably require agency amplifica-

---

[1934] *See* Commissioner v. Fink, 483 U.S. 89 (1987) (Stevens, J., dissenting) (stating that Congress leaves intentional gaps to be filled by judicial construction).

[1935] Zelenak, *Thinking About Nonliteral Interpretations of the Internal Revenue Code*, *supra* note 1455, at 658.

[1936] Commissioner v. Clark, 489 U.S. 726 (1989) (essentially creating a methodology for applying section 356 by adopting the approach of section 302); United States v. Generes, 405 U.S. 93 (1972) (establishing a "dominant" rather than "significant" purpose requirement for finding a shareholder-employee's loss on guaranteeing corporation's debt to be a business rather than a nonbusiness bad debt, based on a construction of Congress' intent); Morrissey v. Commissioner, 296 U.S. 344 (1935) (defining association).

[1937] United States v. Clintwood Elkhorn Mining Co., 553 U.S. 1 (2008); Freytag v. Commissioner, 501 U.S. 868 (1991); *see also* Barnhill v. Johnson, 503 U.S. 393 (1992) ("appeals to legislative history are well-taken only to resolve 'statutory ambiguity'"); Connecticut Nat'l Bank v. Germain, 503 U.S. 249 (1992); Estate of Cowart v. Nicklos Drilling Co., 505 U.S. 469 (1992); Demarest v. Manspeaker, 498 U.S. 184, 190 (1991); Union Bank v. Wolas, 502 U.S. 151, 156 (1991) (an "exceptionally heavy" burden must be carried to overturn the plain language); United States v. Ron Pair Enters., Inc., 489 U.S. 235, 242 (1989) ("rare cases"); United States v. James, 478 U.S. 597, 606 (1986) (requiring "rare and exceptional circumstances" and "clearly expressed legislative intent to the contrary" to overturn the unambiguous words of the statute); Am. Tobacco Co. v. Patterson, 456 U.S. 63, 74-5 (1982) ("Going behind the plain language of a statute in search of a possibly contrary congressional intent is a 'step to be taken cautiously' even under the best of circumstances."); Crooks v. Harrelson, 282 U.S. 55 (1930) (finding an incongruity not to be an absurdity).

[1938] Webre Steib Co. v. Commissioner, 324 U.S. 1 (1945) (Justice Jackson in a sugar processing tax decision).

tion that is so extensive that it seems to create the law, the amplification is accorded the greatest deference because Congress authorized it; and sometimes Congress adds to the fact of the gap a specific direction to write the regulation. Conversely, when the true meaning of the statute can be determined by the lawyerly tools of statutory interpretation, there is no such gap and the agency's views on the meaning of the statute are entitled to some but not as much deference. Hence the distinction between interpretation and construction, unambiguous and ambiguous statutes, and lesser or greater deference.

VI.C.2. *Unambiguous Sections*

The most difficult cases are those that result in ignoring the apparently unambiguous words of the Code. The general rule is that the Supreme Court will not create an exception to an unambiguous statute when the Congress has declined to do so,[1939] and will not enlarge the reach of a taxing statute based on presumed Congressional intent, when the statute is detailed and "drawn with care."[1940] Of course the issue is the clarity of Congress' words. Outside the tax area the Supreme Court has stated[1941] or found[1942] that it could rely on evidence of statutory meaning that is extrinsic to the words of the statute of the same sorts used to interpret ambiguous statutes, when that evidence shows the literal result to be demonstrably at odds with the intent of the drafters; this results in overturning the plain meaning of the statute as in the following examples in tax cases:

- Even though the statute defined a consolidated group in terms of "ownership or control," the Court ruled that control was not enough; there had to be direct or beneficial common ownership.[1943]
- Even though the charitable deduction was limited to a percentage of "net income" and the statute defined net income as net of capital loss, the Court computed net income without the capital loss because another special rule limited the tax effect of capital losses to a 12½% credit against the tax on net income without the loss.[1944]
- Even though the Court stated the Code was "silent" on the point, it ruled that the 50% deduction of a capital gain for purposes of computing net

---

[1939] Freytag v. Commissioner, 501 U.S. 868 (1991) (refused to limit the power of the Tax Court to assign cases to special trial judges, after examining legislative history).

[1940] Iselin v. United States, 270 U.S. 245 (1926) (Justice Brandeis rejected application of federal excise tax to sale of theater ticket given to shareholder but not sold at the box office).

[1941] For a primary cite outside the tax area, see United States v. Am. Trucking Associations, Inc., 310 U.S. 534, 543 (1940) (stating that not only absurd, but also unreasonable results of the plain meaning will be avoided, when contrary to the clear policy of the legislation as a whole; but the cases cited by the Court did not involve literally unambiguous statutes).

[1942] *See, e.g.,* Ozawa v. United States, 260 U.S. 178 (1922).

[1943] Handy & Harman v. Burnet, 284 U.S. 136 (1931).

[1944] United States v. Pleasants, 305 U.S. 357 (1939).

income also applied to reduce gross income, so as to limit the base against which a charitable contribution deduction could be claimed.[1945]

- The Court did not believe Congress intended to tax net capital gains without a charitable deduction, even though the Code said just that.[1946]
- The "*Corn Products* doctrine" could be viewed as an unfortunate example of the Court disregarding the words of the Code.[1947]
- The Court refused to read words that limited a depletion allowance to actual producing wells because of extensive analysis of prior law and legislative history.[1948]
- The Court interpolated a requirement that the percentage depletion deduction be reversed when a deduction was taken under section 1341, over dissents pointing out that doing what Congress might have wanted is not justification for disobeying the law.[1949]
- The Court read "distributed [from decedent's estate] to the taxpayer" to mean the date the executor distributed the property to a testamentary trustee, rather than the date the trustee distributed the property to the remainderman.[1950]
- By allowing a comma to isolate a phrase from a modifier, the Court avoided having to rule contrary to the words of the statute.[1951]
- The Court's decisions grounded on public policy discussed in Ch. VI.B.3.c. mostly overrode the statute.
- In *Wodehouse*, the Court ruled that the term "periodical" did not exclude lump sum royalty payments, based on legislative history and prior practice.[1952]
- The Court's development of the continuity of interest and continuity of business enterprise requirements for corporate reorganizations (in addition to the business purpose requirement)[1953] could be viewed as changing the statute (and were so viewed at the time).[1954]
- Even though a trustee clearly had not held the property for the time necessary to report a long term capital gain, and the Court admitted the

---

[1945] United States v. Benedict, 338 U.S. 692 (1950).

[1946] United Cal. Bank v. United States, 439 U.S. 180 (1978) (literally the alternative tax did not allow a deduction for a charitable gift of capital gains; the Court said that to rule otherwise would allow form to rule over substance).

[1947] Corn Prods. Refining Co. v. Commissioner, 350 U.S. 46 (1955) (substantially limited by Arkansas Best Corp. v. Commissioner, 485 U.S. 212 (1988)).

[1948] Commissioner v. Engle, 464 U.S. 206, 223 (1984) (stating that the meaning of the revenue statute can be determined only in light of related sections and the history of the statute).

[1949] United States v. Skelly Oil Co., 394 U.S. 678 (1969).

[1950] Maguire v. Commissioner, 313 U.S. 1 (1941).

[1951] *See* United States v. Ron Pair Enters., Inc., 489 U.S. 235, 242 (1989).

[1952] Commissioner v. Wodehouse, 337 U.S. 369 (1949).

[1953] Bittker & Eustice, at 12.61. But this book views *Gregory v. Helvering's* business purpose requirement as an example of interpretation.

[1954] The same could be said of *Bazley v. Commissioner*, 331 U.S. 737 (1947) in which the Court treated boot in a reorganization not as boot but as a dividend.

statute was literally unambiguous, it construed it to allow tacking of the trustor's holding period based on various evidences of Congress' intent and the Service's similar conclusion in an analogous situation.[1955]

- In some cases the Code so obviously does not mean what it says that the Court hardly feels the need to explain, as when it denied a deduction for "taxes paid" to the buyer of real estate who assumed and paid taxes that had already become a lien on the property and for which the seller was personally liable; the Court intuitively understood that the taxes had to be taxes *vis a vis* the payor, whether or not they were taxes in general.[1956]

VI.D. Courts' Deference to Administrative Interpretation

VI.D.1. *Overview*

The judicial function of statutory interpretation and construction changes when the Treasury writes regulations (and to a lesser extent when the Service issues other published guidance).The job of courts then may involve interpreting and applying the regulations, and sometimes deciding if they are valid when challenged by taxpayers. There has been a huge amount of academic, as well as professional, writing about judicial deference to agency action generally, and the degree of deference accorded Treasury regulations after the 1984 *Chevron* opinionparticularly.[1957] Most practitioners will not need to surmount this mountain of analysis because (a) much of the academic literature addresses political science issues that are interesting but irrelevant in practice, (b) the case law provides ample diversity to support almost any position on deference, and (c) although greater judicial deference is finally taking hold three decades after *Chevron*, judges remain likely to do what they would have done under any version of the principles.[1958]

The deference principles can affect the outcome of federal tax disputes over seemingly ambiguous provisions of the Code in three broad ways:

- If a regulation is an interpretation of a statute that can be rendered non-ambiguous by normal methods of statutory interpretation, then a court may be able to substitute its interpretation of the statute with more ease.
- If not, and a regulation is a so-called legislative (as opposed to interpretive) regulation that fills a gap left by Congress, then the regulation is said

---

[1955] Helvering v. N. Y. Trust Co., 292 U.S. 455 (1934).

[1956] Magruder v. Supplee, 316 U.S. 394 (1942).

[1957] Chevron U.S.A., Inc. v. Natural Resources Defense Council, Inc., 467 U.S. 837 (1984). *See generally* BITTKER & LOKKEN, at 110.4; SALTZMAN & BOOK, at 3.02[4].

[1958] *See* PIERCE, at §3.4 (statistical evidence of increasing deference); Paul, *Use and Abuse of Tax Regulations in Statutory Construction*, 40 YALE L.J. 660, 662-63 (1940) (n. 13 states that the various formulations the courts use to describe their deference could be "abolished from the judicial lexicon with little loss . . ."). Judge Posner observes that the deference doctrines are cited more than they really matter and that deference to agencies makes sense only when they have expertise in the area. POSNER, at 338.

to have the "force of law,"[1959] unless a court is asked and is willing to find that it fails a fairly low threshold of reasonableness that can be called an abuse of discretion, "arbitrary or capricious" action by the Treasury.

- If a statute or regulation is ambiguous, the government's further interpretations in rulings or other guidance of lesser import than regulations receives little deference.[1960]

But the seemingly critical dividing line between interpretive versus legislative regulations is muddied in two ways. First, there is some doubt whether it is possible to distinguish interpretive from legislative regulations, or whether the Supreme Court now supports such a distinction. The most recent Supreme Court opinion involving an intense review of *Chevron* deference in a tax case, *Mayo*, did not use the interpretive versus legislative terminology, but only asked whether the statute was ambiguous so that the regulation was subject to *Chevron* deference.[1961] The most recent Supreme Court tax opinion mentioning *Chevron* and *Home Concrete* explained that the relevant ambiguity was one constituting a gap that Congress implicitly or explicitly said should be filled by the agency.[1962] Therefore, it appears that the Supreme Court is trying to change the terms of the distinction into one of ambiguity or not. But because ambiguity is itself ambiguous—as the Court proved in *Home Concrete*—it is more useful to equate legislative regulations with those filling gaps so large that Congress can be charged with knowing it was authorizing legislative regulations that would receive *Chevron* deference, leaving all others to be interpretive.

The second source of confusion is that, up to 2011, the federal tax law was muddled by the endurance of what is sometimes called the *National Muffler*[1963] standard of deference to Treasury regulations, supposedly reflecting a special rule for all tax regulations,whether they were in the presumably interpretive category or clearly legislative. It was thought to be justified by the complexity of the subject matter, the expertise of the Treasury and similar considerations.[1964]

When the *Chevron* doctrine stating the Court's view of deference to legislative regulations appeared in 1984 in a nontax case, it drove a wedge between legislative regulations that were entitled to "*Chevron* deference" and interpretive regulations that were entitled to lesser deference, called "*Skidmore*

1959 United States v. Mead Corp., 533 U.S. 218 (2001).

1960 *See infra* Rulings, etc., Ch. VI.D.6.c.

1961 Mayo Found. for Med. Educ. & Research v. United States, 562 U.S. 44 (2011); Chevron U.S.A., Inc. v. Natural Resources Defense Council, Inc., 467 U.S. 837 (1984).

1962 United States v. Home Concrete & Supply, LLC, 132 S. Ct. 1836 (2012).

1963 Nat'l Muffler Dealers Assn., Inc. v. United States, 440 U.S. 472 (1979). *See also* Zenith Radio Corp. v. United States, 437 U.S. 443 (1978) (a tariff decision upholding a Treasury interpretation of 80 years standing, and relying on earlier tariff and not income tax decisions for deference to the regulation).

1964 *See, e.g.*, United States v. Cleveland Indians Baseball Co., 532 U.S. 200 (2001).

deference."[1965] Rather than apply *Skidmore* deference to interpretive tax regulations, for some years the Supreme Court continued to cite *National Muffler* in tax cases and the lower courts were confused about whether tax regulations were special.

But in a somewhat surprising turn of events, the *Mayo* opinion in 2011 announced that *National Muffler* actually had been according less deference to Treasury regulations than they merited under the *Chevron* standard.[1966]

Mayo removed *National Muffler* as a special standard for tax laws, but in effect the Court smay be continuing to conduct analysis similar to that of *National Muffler* by employing the full range of statutory interpretive tools.[1967]

Until the Supreme Court more clearly resolves the confusion about deference to Treasury regulations, the best characterization of its current view is a more fluid differentiation between interpretive and legislative regulations. This means that regulations issued under the general authority of section 7805(a) can be of either kind, even though in the past that section was thought to authorize only interpretive regulations. To the extent such "general authority" regulations are legislative, *Chevron* deference can be applied. The net effect is to mostly collapse all of the tests of regulations into a facts-and-circumstances analysis wherein deference increases as the need for the regulatory guidance increases (when statutory ambiguity or gaps are found plus some reason to think Congress intended Treasury to supply the specificity), and deference decreases as the instructions provided by Congress increase in specificity and scope (or at least the Court thinks it knows what the statute means).

And, in some unusual cases, the gaps are just too great to fill. The Court identified such a case in 2015: it declined to give *Chevron* deference to the Treasury regulation equating state and federal insurance exchanges because the statutory ambiguity was not one Congress left with intent that the administrator fill it.[1968] In other words, such a choice is above the pay grade of the agency, even though the Court effectively agreed with the regulation.

Finally, the Court has given some indications that it is tiring of the uproar over *Chevron*. It has decided tax cases in which the doctrine might have been

---

[1965] Skidmore v. Swift & Co., 323 U.S. 134 (1944).

[1966] The problem with the *National Muffler* standard was that it could be read to give the court more ways to reject a regulation, based on the ways it had been adopted and the like. *Mayo* purported to sweep those considerations away and install the single *Chevron* standard.

[1967] *See* United States v. Quality Stores, Inc., 134 S. Ct. 1395 (2014) (involving revenue rulings). Another aspect of *National Muffler* that the *Mayo* opinion said it did not like was second guessing the process by which the Treasury reached its final regulation, which in the case of *Mayo*, came late in the litigation process. The Court applied the same view in a 2013 decision refusing to hold against the Treasury the fact that it took a long time issuing a regulation that contained the interpretation of the statute the Court agreed with. United States v. Woods, 134 S. Ct. 557 (2013). Therefore, the Court's complaint against *National Muffler* seems to be more one of process than substance.

[1968] King v. Burwell, 135 S. Ct. 2480 (2015).

relevant, without mentioning it.[1969] And *Chevron* deference may be falling out of favor with the Republican Justices more than with the Democratic appointed Justices. The doctrine can best be viewed as one of those New Deal ideas related to robust administrative agencies, which should be anathema to the current group of Republican-appointed Justices: Why would they want to defer to federal agencies, in preference to Congress or themselves?

VI.D.2. Chevron *Doctrine*

The imprint of the Supreme Court is crucial to deference because its rulings define and presumably have enhanced the power of regulations under its 1984 *Chevron* doctrine.[1970] However, its original basic statement in *Chevron* was unremarkable:

> If the intent of Congress is clear, that is the end of the matter; for the court, as well as the agency, must give effect to the unambiguously expressed intent of Congress . . . . [However,] if the statute is silent or ambiguous with respect to the specific issue, the question for the court is whether the agency's answer is based on a permissible construction of the statute."[1971]

Thus, judicial deference to administrative interpretation of a statute is not "due" if Congress has made its intent "clear" in the statutory text. But if the statute is "silent or ambiguous," the courts are to show special deference, now called *Chevron* deference. Courts do so by asking whether the agency's rule is a permissible construction of the statute, rather than asking whether it is the one right construction.[1972] *Chevron* has risen to the status of doctrine, at least in the lower courts,[1973] and to a lesser extent in the Supreme Court's own opinions, where the Republican-appointed Justices are more likely to call it a standard or a framework for analysis "often" applied.[1974]

Post-*Chevron* opinions, including Supreme Court opinions, have not substantially clarified the law, although deference has increased.[1975] The leading justification for the doctrine is the practicality of courts' dealing with thou-

---

[1969] United States v. Quality Stores, Inc., 134 S. Ct. 1395 (2014) (although the administrative action was rulings and not regulations; nevertheless, Professor Hickman filed an amicus brief on her own behalf, which the opinion did not address one way or the other); Hall v. United States, 132 S. Ct. 1882 (2012). *See* Cummings, *Negative Implications and Code Interpretation*, 143 Tax Notes (TA) 931 (May 26, 2014).

[1970] *See generally* Cummings, *The Supreme Court's Deference to Tax Administrative Interpretation*, 69 Tax Law. 419 (2016).

[1971] 467 U.S. at 842-43.

[1972] This is really not a new idea, as evidenced by Paul, *Use and Abuse of Tax Regulations*, *supra* note 1958, at 662 ("the regulation does not have to be the best of all possible interpretations in the court's opinion").

[1973] The lower courts refer to the doctrine as such. *See, e.g.*, Arnett v. Commissioner, 473 F.3d 790 (7th Cir. 2007).

[1974] King v. Burwell, 135 S. Ct. 2480 (2015).

[1975] *See* Jellum, *Chevron's Demise: A Survey of Chevron from Infancy to Senescence*, 59 Admin. L. Rev. 725 (2007); Beermann, Chevron *at the Roberts Court: Still Failing after All These Years*, 83 Fordham L. Rev. 731 (2014).

sands of regulations. [1976] In theory, the choice for deference seems to be political in the broadest sense.[1977] The classic *Chevron* doctrine as applied today by the Supreme Court is reflected in these seven Supreme Court opinions (with emphasis on tax):

1. *Skidmore*: This pre-*Chevron* opinion is still cited for a lesser degree of deference to merely interpretive regulations.[1978]
2. *Mead*: Congress shows its intention for the agency to write guidance with greater force than merely interpretive regulations, which is called the force of law, not only by specific delegations of authority in the statutes to write specific rules (the classic example of a specific delegation being "The Secretary shall prescribe such regulations as he shall deem necessary in order that the tax liability of any affiliated group of corporations . . ." in section 1502).[1979] When Congress leaves a gap in the statute, that also can signal its intent for the agency to fill the gap.
3. *Mayo*: Such gaps include scenarios to which the statute must be applied that can go either way, and as to which someone simply has to make a decision.[1980]
4. *Brand X*: *Chevron* deference extends to allowing an agency's legislative regulation to overturn judicial precedents.[1981]
5. *Home Concrete*: But deference will not control after the Supreme Court has established a statute's meaning by announcing its interpretation,[1982] which means more generally that deference will not control when the court can interpret the statute contrary to the agency interpretation.[1983]

[1976] Pierce, at § 3.4.

[1977] Professor Elhauge (discussed further in Ch. VI.B.), has explained the *Chevron* doctrine as designed to rely on executive and politically accountable agencies that interpret statutory words as appropriate sources of official current interpretation of previously enacted ambiguous statutes. Elhauge, *supra* note 66, at 2126. He views the agency interpretation not as having interpretive precedence due to expertise, but as due deference on account of the agency's indirect political accountability, once all other interpretive methods have failed to resolve the ambiguity.

[1978] Skidmore v. Swift & Co., 323 U.S. 134 (1944); United States v. Mead Corp., 533 U.S. 218 (2001) (entitled to deference according to its persuasiveness).Christopher v. SmithKline Beecham Corp., 132 S. Ct. 2156 (2012).

[1979] United States v. Mead Corp., 533 U.S. 218 (2001).

[1980] Mayo Found. for Med. Educ. & Research v. United States, 562 U.S. 44 (2011) (when is a full time student an employee is a sort of gap).

[1981] Nat'l Cable & Telecomm. Assn. v. Brand X Internet Services, 545 U.S. 967 (2005) . *See* Gifford, *Emerging Outlines of a Revised Chevron Doctrine, supra* note 748, at 783, 828-32.

[1982] United States v. Home Concrete & Supply, LLC, 132 S. Ct. 1836 (2012) (plurality opinion, joined as to this point by Justice Scalia). *See* Cummings, *Tax Decisions of the Supreme Court's 2011 Term*, 137 Tax Notes (TA) 93 (Oct. 1, 2012).

[1983] For example, Freeman v. Quicken Loans, Inc., 132 S. Ct. 2034 (2012) (Justice Scalia said that was no reason to address *Chevron* when he could see that the statute could not support the agency interpretation).

6. *King v. Burwell*: Sometimes the discretionary issue is above the pay grade of the administrator.[1984]
7. *Judulang v. Holder*: The Court will examine the facts and factors the agency considered and can refuse to grant *Chevron* deference when the agency did not consider or properly weight factors the Court deemed relevant, or hinged the interpretation on irrelevant factors.[1985] The standard for *Chevron* deference is whether the regulation is arbitrary or capricious.

The *Chevron* doctrine is an expression of the fundamental constitutional separation of powers, which forbids Congress to delegate its law making authority to the executive branch.[1986] But Congress can properly grant to agencies general authority to write rules interpreting a statute, meaning stating the agency's view of what the statute meant, which a court could reject or not, with no special deference.[1987] This is the authority that section 7805(a) originally was thought to grant. Separation of powers also is not breached by Congress' specific grant of authority to the executive to write rules carrying out Congress' expressed or implied general purposes and policies, policies and standards, so long as the stated standards are sufficiently intelligible for the courts to determine whether the executive has abused its discretion.[1988]

Historically, grants of specific tax rule making, rather than interpretational, authority were narrowly targeted, as in authorizing the Secretary of the Treasury to organize a panel of seven tea experts to define unwholesome teas.[1989] Initially, the Supreme Court struck down efforts under New Deal legislation to authorize the executive to write Codes of industrial conduct on the theory that they were improper delegations; they were neither interpretive nor were they sufficiently bounded by specific legislative standards.[1990]

[1984] King v. Burwell, 135 S. Ct. 2480 (2015).

[1985] Judulang v. Holder, 132 S. Ct. 476 (2011). *See also* Michigan v. EPA, 135 S. Ct. 2699 (2015) (failed to weight the impact of cost; Scalia opinion rejecting agency action); Christopher v. SmithKline Beecham Corp., 132 S. Ct. 2156 (2012) (agency interpretation announced in amicus briefs not entitled to deference; Alito opinion).

[1986] *See, e.g.,* Dixon v. United States, 381 U.S. 68 (1965) (explaining that this is why the Service can retroactively change its position, because it is not changing the law it is interpreting).

[1987] Hickman, *Coloring Outside the Lines: Examining Treasury's (Lack of) Compliance with Administrative Procedure Act Rule Making Requirements,* 82 Notre Dame L. Rev. 1727, 1762 (2007).

[1988] *See* Util. Air Regulatory Group v. EPA, 134 S. Ct. 2427 (2014). However, Congress need not have had an intent about the specific question being answered by the delegated rule making. Chevron U.S.A., Inc. v. Natural Resources Defense Council, Inc., 467 U.S. 837, 845 (1984).

[1989] *See,* Buttfield v. Stranahan, 192 U.S. 470 (1904).

[1990] *See, e.g.,* A.L.A. Schechter Poultry Corp. v. United States, 295 U.S. 495 (1935). Stanley Surrey described the view of this case as the "traditionalist" view, and observed that the traditionalist would not think that an ambiguous statute could be subject to "interpretive" regulations because the standard in the statute would necessarily be too indefinite for interpretation. Surrey, *Scope and Effect of Treasury Regulations under the Income, Estate and Gift Taxes,* 88 U. Pa. L. Rev. 556, 576 (1940).

However, the Supreme Court came to recognize that the sheer complexity of New Deal legislation and of the 20th century world required substantial executive rule making if the laws were to function as Congress intended, with two consequences: (1) the courts viewed specific grants of authority to write rules with more lenience, meaning generally stated standards could be sufficient to support regulations;[1991] and (2) later the courts recognized that general grants of rule making authority, which previously had been viewed as authorizing only interpretive regulations, necessarily also authorized filling in some gaps in laws and also authorized making clear the ambiguous statute, in ways that previously had been thought to require a more specific delegation of rule making authority.[1992]

Brand X highlighted the two steps involved in the *Chevron* analysis. The first step is to determine if the statute has one clear meaning; if it does not, then the second step is to determine whether the administrative interpretation is within the parameters set by Congress. *Chevron* deference defines the second step. The first step is not merely a matter of reading the words of the statute; rather, all traditional tools of statutory interpretation can be employed to determine if the statute has one meaning. If so, and if a court (at least the Supreme Court) has announced that meaning, then the administrative interpretation cannot vary from it. This happened in *Home Concrete.* Obviously this puts a lot of pressure on the way a court characterizes its determination of ambiguity, which can be particularly hard to interpret in opinions that preceded the *Brand X* decision.

Mayo shows that the court must go to the second *Chevron* step only when it cannot interpret the statute to mean one thing using all the normal tools of statutory interpretation.[1993] The statute at issue was inherently ambiguous as applied to the facts, and could not be interpreted because it created the possibility that a student being paid was both a student and an employee, without providing guidance for which was which. To rely on predominance of one over the other was no help when the medical student both worked 40 hours and studied 40 hours. The Treasury regulation said that if the student worked as much as 40 hours, the student was an employee and the Court gave that regulation *Chevron* deference.

VI.D.3. *Similarity of* Chevron *Doctrine and Traditional Deference to Treasury Regulations*

The second step of the *Chevron* Doctrine is similar to the deference that traditionally was accorded to all Treasury regulations (i.e.,*National Muffler* deference) in that they are both high levels of deference. But *Chevron* deference

---

1991 *See, e.g.*, Wickard v. Filburn, 317 U.S. 111 (1942) (breezing past the delegation issue on the grounds that the federal legislation contained prescribed limits and standards for the exercise of administrative power).

1992 Hickman, *supra* note 1987, at 1772-73 (citing *Chevron*).

1993 Mayo Found. for Med. Educ. & Research v. United States, 562 U.S. 44 (2011).

may be less intrusive on Treasury's decision making process. Legislative regulations, which presumably are the category subject to *Chevron* deference, are to be upheld unless "arbitrary, capricious, an abuse of discretion, or otherwise not in accordance with law," as required by 5 U.S.C. section 706. In contrast, the following statement appeared and was applied in the *Fulman* opinion involving a section 7805(a) interpretive regulation in the same year as *National Muffler*:

> [I]t is fundamental . . . that as 'contemporaneous constructions by those charged with administration of' the Code, [Treasury] Regulations 'must be sustained unless unreasonable and plainly inconsistent with the revenue statutes,' and 'should not be overruled except for weighty reasons.' Bingler v. Johnson, . . . , quoting Commissioner v. South Texas Lumber Co., . . . accord, United States v. Correll, ... This rule of deference is particularly appropriate here, since, while obviously some rule of valuation must be applied, Congress, as we shall see, failed expressly to provide one. See United States v. Correll, *supra*; 26 U.S.C. §7805(a).[1994]

Later, *National Muffler* said:

> A regulation may have particular force if it is a substantially contemporaneous construction of the statute by those presumed to have been aware of congressional intent. If the regulation dates from a later period, the manner in which it evolved merits inquiry. Other relevant considerations are the length of time the regulation has been in effect, the reliance placed on it, the consistency of the Commissioner's interpretation, and the degree of scrutiny Congress has devoted to the regulation during subsequent re-enactments of the statute.[1995]

The Supreme Court historically considered Treasury regulations to occupy a rank beneath its own tax jurisprudence and the purpose of Congress.[1996] It has seldom invalidated a regulation in the last half century (but did so earlier

---

[1994] Fulman v. United States, 434 U.S. 528 (1978); *see also* Thor Power Tool Co. v. Commissioner, 439 U.S. 522 (1979).

[1995] Nat'l Muffler Dealers Assn. v. United States, 440 U.S. 472 (1979).

[1996] Staudt et al., *Judging Statutes, supra* note 20, at 1911.

with more frequency),[1997] and has more frequently upheld Treasury regulations.[1998]

Published guidance on the Code long has enjoyed a claim of exceptionalism,[1999] relative to other agencies' interpretations of their own laws, which loosely translated into a real or expected enhanced degree of deference.

[1997] The Supreme Court invalidated Treasury regulations in: United States v. Home Concrete & Supply LLC, 132 S. Ct. 1836 (2012); United States v. Vogel Fertilizer Co., 455 U.S. 16 (1982); Rowan Cos. v. United States, 452 U.S. 247 (1981); Commissioner v. Standard Life & Accid. Ins. Co., 433 U.S. 148 (1977); United States v. Cartwright, 411 U.S. 546 (1973); Ne. Pa. Bank & Trust Co. v. United States, 387 U.S. 213 (1967); Commissioner v. Acker, 361 U.S. 87 (1959); Trust Co. v. Commissioner, 325 U.S. 365 (1945); Helvering v. Credit Alliance Corp., 316 U.S. 107 (1942); Helvering v. Sabine Transp. Co., 318 U.S. 306 (1943); Helvering v. Or. Mut. Life Ins. Co., 311 U.S. 267 (1940) (invalidating retroactivity of regulations); Helvering v. Janney, 311 U.S. 189 (1940); Taft v. Helvering, 311 U.S. 195 (1940) (regulation failing to treat husband and wife filing joint return as a unit, as Congress had directed); Helvering v. R. J. Reynolds Tobacco Co., 306 U.S. 110 (1939) (rejecting retroactive effect of regulation); Rasquin v. Humphreys, 308 U.S. 54 (1939) (rejected retroactivity); Koshland v. Helvering, 298 U.S. 441 (1936); Manhattan General Equipment Co. v. Commissioner, 297 U.S. 129 (1936); United States v. Cambridge Loan & Building Co., 278 U.S. 55 (1928) (in effect); Lynch v. Tilden Produce Co., 265 U.S. 315 (1924) (a very restrictive ruling on the Treasury's power to define adulterated butter for purposes of a stamp tax).

[1998] The Supreme Court upheld Treasury regulations in: Mayo Found. for Med. Educ. & Research v. United States, 562 U.S. 44 (2011); Boeing Co. v. United States, 537 U.S. 437 (2003); Atl. Mut. Ins. Co. v. Commissioner, 523 U.S. 382 (1998); Nat'l Muffler Dealers Assn., Inc. v. United States, 440 U.S. 472 (1979); Fulman v. United States, 434 U.S. 528 (1978); Bingler v. Johnson, 394 U.S. 741 (1969); United States v. Correll, 389 U.S. 299 (1967); United States v. Catto, Jr., 384 U.S. 102 (1966); Hertz Corp. v. United States, 364 U.S. 122 (1960); United States v. Cannelton Sewer Pipe Co., 364 U.S. 76 (1959); Cammarano v. United States, 358 US 498 (1959); United States v. Allen-Bradley Co., 352 U.S. 306 (1957) (opinion makes the classic *Chevron* statement that the statute is ambiguous and either interpretation is possible, so interpretation of regulation governs); Commissioner v. Estate of Sternberger, 348 U.S. 187 (1955) (this opinion contains the inaccurate statement that there are no opportunities for the public to be heard on proposed regulations); Commissioner v. S. Texas Lumber Co., 333 U.S. 496, 501 (1948) ("regulations. . .should not be overruled except for weighty reasons); Commissioner v. Wheeler, 324 U.S. 542 (1945); Douglas v. Commissioner, 322 U.S. 275 (1944); Robinette v. Helvering, 318 U.S. 184 (1943); Magruder v. W. B. and A. R. C., 316 U.S. 69 (1942); Textile Mills Sec. Corp. v. Commissioner, 314 U.S. 326 (1941); Helvering v. Wilshire Oil Co., 308 U.S. 90 (1939) (containing an unusually strong endorsement of the power of Treasury to change regulations prospectively, over a "reenactment" argument); Helvering v. Winmill, 305 U.S. 79 (1938); Koshland v. Helvering, 298 U.S. 441 (1936); Helvering v. Rankin, 295 U.S. 123 (1935) (regulation could impose first in first out rule for sales of stock where taxpayer had not identified any shares as sold); Morrissey v. Commissioner, 296 U.S. 344 (1935); United States v. Dakota-Montana Oil Co., 288 U.S. 459 (1933); Fawcus Machine Co. v. United States, 282 U.S. 375 (1931); Universal Battery Co. v. United States, 281 U.S. 580 (1930 (excise tax regulation).

[1999] Since at least 1940 knowledgeable observers had realized that tax regulations were "different." Surrey, *Scope and Effect of Treasury Regulations, supra* note 1990, at 577. Surrey described the "traditionalist view" of *A.L.A. Schechter Poultry Corp. v. United States,* 295 U.S. 495 (1935), and said that while the traditionalists may be right, "they are talking of another world; as respects Federal taxation they have all the law books on their side except the United States Reports."

Academic writing criticized the claims of tax exceptionalism.[2000] The confusion nominally ended when *Mayo* applied *Chevron* to a tax regulation in 2011, without any special treatment, dismissing the *National Muffler* standard.[2001] And an opinion outside of the tax area confirmed that *Chevron's* standard is the same as that of the Administrative Procedure Act.[2002]

However, the rejection of the *National Muffler* standard was more about procedural purity than about the degree of deference. *Chevron* plus the Administrative Procedure Act said there was one standard, and the Court was not interested in muddying the waters further for tax regulations. Therefore, evidence about how long it took the Treasury to write a regulation and the like would not be relevant.[2003] The Court in 2013 refused to hold against the Treasury the fact that it took a long time issuing a regulation that contained the interpretation of the statute the Court agreed with, which fact might have cut the other way under *National Muffler*.[2004] But in *Quality Stores* Justice Kennedy wholly ignored *Chevron* and *National Muffler* while proceeding to agree with the Service's revenue rulings' interpretation of the statute by using all of the standard tools of statutory interpretation, some of which referred to the interaction of Congress with the rulings.

It may be that the types of considerations used in *National Muffler* will be replaced by a very similar type of examination of the process and considerations leading to the published guidance.[2005]

VI.D.4. *Summary of Current Deference Principles*

A summary of the current general principles on judicial deference reflected in the Supreme Court's opinions follows:[2006]

- Federal courts can interpret federal statutes as competently as federal agencies for the purpose of determining their *unambiguous meaning*, using traditional tools such as text, precedent, and legislative history, and

---

[2000] *See* Hickman, *Need for Mead: Rejecting Tax Exceptionalism in Judicial Deference*, 90 MINN. L. REV. 1537 (2005). *See also* Hoffer and Walker, The Demise of Tax Court Exceptionalism, 99 Minn. L. Rev. 221 (2014).

[2001] Mayo Found. for Med. Educ. & Research v. United States, 562 U.S. 44 (2011).

[2002] Judulang v. Holder, 132 S. Ct. 476 (2011).

[2003] *But see* Stephenson, *Strategic Substitution Effect*, 120 HARV. L. REV. 528, 536-37 (2006) (viewing agency fidelity to the statutory text not to be a typical motivating force). Many early revenue decisions held that contemporaneous application by revenue officers of an ambiguous statute should be respected. *E.g.*, Schell's Ex'rs v. Fauche, 138 U.S. 562 (1891).

[2004] United States v. Woods, 134 S. Ct. 557 (2013).

[2005] See Proof of Nonarbitrariness, below.

[2006] *See generally* PIERCE, at § 3.2 through 3.6.

the courts have no reason to cede that power to agencies;[2007] indeed, they have the duty to exercise the power to interpret federal statutes. A statute may have an unambiguous meaning even though it initially appears to be ambiguous. Although this may seem a contradiction in terms, it is simply the practical observation that if courts can't finally interpret statutes, they will lose one of the two lines of work they were created to do (the other is find facts).[2008]

- However, when Congress indicates in a statute that it intends an agency to fill a gap by deciding matters of policy or somehow achieving a defined end result, rather than simply interpreting the statute, then the agency may appropriately construct a rule where none exists, based on its presumed expertise in the general policy that Congress intends by the law it administers, its knowledge of the practicalities involved, and its familiarity with certain materials extrinsic to the statute, including the common law and legislative history. Thus, a court can confront a facially ambiguous statute and interpret it finally, or can find that the degree of ambiguity is so great as to indicate a gap,[2009] which has the cliff effect of permitting substantially greater deference to regulatory interpretation under *Chevron*.
- Such second category of agency constructions is entitled to a degree of deference (*Chevron* deference) by the federal courts because they are policy making activities explicitly or implicitly authorized by Congress. The deference requires only that the regulation not be arbitrary or capricious;[2010] but the Court allowed an essentially arbitrary choice between two rules in *Mayo*;[2011] *Mayo* also said that considerations previously applied under *National Muffler* (such as giving weight to long standing regulations or less weight for changed regulations) supposedly are not to

---

[2007] The plurality opinion of the Court applied this principle in United States v. Home Concrete & Supply, LLC, 132 S. Ct. 1836 (2012), which ruled that even if the statute once was unclear, after the Supreme Court interpreted it in the earlier *Colony* opinion, it had an unambiguous meaning that a Treasury regulation could not change. *See* Smith, *Brand X*, supra note 747, at 665 (showing that the administrative interpretation cannot overturn a court finding that the statute unambiguously had only one meaning, based on all traditional tools of statutory construction, including legislative histories).

[2008] This is essentially what the plurality held in United States v. Home Concrete & Supply, LLC, 132 S. Ct. 1836 (2012).

[2009] This occurred in *Mayo Found. for Med. Educ. & Research v. United States*, 562 U.S. 44 (2011).

[2010] Judulang v. Holder, 132 S. Ct. 476 (2011) (at note 7) (treating the *Chevron* standard as effectively the same as that in 5 U.S.C. section 706, the Administrative Procedure Act rule applicable to legislative regulations, which the act calls informal rule making).

[2011] Mayo Found. for Med. Educ. & Research v. United States, 562 U.S. 44 (2011) (seeming to approve of a choice, any choice, because without it there would be wasteful litigation and uncertainty in case by case applications).

be considered, because the regulation should be considered in its totality as arbitrary or capricious or not.[2012]

- Although such degree of deference is not accorded to mere agency interpretations of statutes, the courts still may accord some lesser deference, known as *Skidmore* deference,[2013] to some agency interpretations, particularly regulations.
- This summary ill conceals several substantial areas of confusion and disagreement in the law, including principally: (1) how do statutes show that Congress granted the agency power to make rules having the effect of law, (2) what is the practical difference between the two levels of deference, (3) what is the relevance of reenactment of the statute after the agency has issued regulations, and (4) is deference due rulings and other guidance not embodied in regulations?

The questions of whether and how much deference the courts should give to the Service's and Treasury's published guidance have probably reached a level of abstraction that places its current resolution beyond the realm of practical applicability by the lower courts.[2014] Empirical studies show that "there is only slightly more than a chance probability that the Supreme Court will mention and apply *Chevron* in cases raising issues of agency statutory interpretation,"[2015] and suggest there may be little practical difference between *Chevron* and *Skidmore* deference.[2016] Therefore, as noted above, the intense dissection of the *Chevron* doctrine may not mean much to practitioners. But its application can be important in episodic applicationst: the Supreme Court even uses *Chevron* to give extra weight to an agency's interpretation (even in briefs) of its own regulations.[2017]

[2012] The theory is that if the agency can change a court's interpretation it should be able to change its own interpretation.

[2013] *See* United States v. Mead Corp., 533 U.S. 218, 229 (2001) (entitled to deference according to its persuasiveness); Skidmore v. Swift & Co., 323 U.S. 134 (1944).

[2014] *See* Posner, at 113-14 (stating that deference or no deference is about as complex a choice as the real world can apply; and that as applied to lower court opinions, that means legal rulings receive no deference and factual rulings receive some deference, and deference generally means that the opposite ruling would also have been affirmed).

[2015] Eskridge & Baer, *The Supreme Court's Deference Continuum, an Empirical Analysis (from* Chevron *to* Hamdan*)*, unpublished manuscript cited in Mashaw, *Agency Centered or Court Centered Administrative Law, supra* note 1841, at 899.

[2016] Barnett, *Codifying Chevmore*, 90 N.Y.U. Law Rev. 1, 66 (2015).

[2017] *See, e.g.*, Long Is. Care at Home Ltd. v. Coke, 551 U.S. 158 (2007); Auer v. Robbins, 519 U.S. 452 (1997) (holding that an agency's interpretation of its own regulations is "controlling unless plainly erroneous or inconsistent with the regulation" (internal quotation marks omitted)); Bowles v. Seminole Rock & Sand Co., 325 U.S. 410, 414 (1945) (same). *See infra* Ch. VI.D.6.c.

VI.D.5. *The Difficult Distinction Between Legislative and Interpretive Regulations*

VI.D.5.a. *Summary*

Although some think the distinction between legislative and interpretive regulations is no longer controlling,[2018] or even employed today by the Supreme Court in its opinions, it is not possible to discuss Treasury regulations without understanding the perceived distinction. In summary:

- Legislative regulations "implement"[2019] and construe the statute and have the "force of law."[2020]
- Legislative regulations may address policy rather than legal determinations, or may apply the statute's stated general policy in detailed ways, but in either event are based on the view that the agency has sufficient expertise to make the policy judgments Congress did not have time to address.[2021]
- The Treasury must adopt legislative regulations (called substantive rules) with notice, comment, and hearing under the Administrative Procedure Act.
- But legislative regulations do not quite have the "force of law" because they are subject to courts second guessing whether they exceed the authority granted by Congress,[2022] hence *Chevron* deference; and legis-

---

[2018] Rogovin & Korb, *supra* note 754, at 327 (former Chief Counsel Korb states the Supreme Court in *Mead* eliminated the distinction). The Solicitor General now argues with frequency that all Treasury regulations are entitled to *Chevron* deference. Brief of United States, 2014 U.S. Briefs 114 (January 21, 2015), in King v. Burwell, 135 S. Ct. 2480 (2015). *See* Hickman, *Coloring Outside the Lines*, supra note 1987, at 1767 (arguing that the very fact of adopting a regulation with notice and hearing makes it a substantive regulation).

[2019] 5 U.S.C. § 551(4) (rules ". . . implement, interpret . . .").

[2020] Attorney General's Manual on the Newly Enacted Administrative Procedure Act, §4, n. 3. The Supreme Court excludes some agency materials from the force of law category based on their format. *See* Christensen v. Harris County, 529 U.S. 576, 587 (2000) ("interpretations . . . such as those in policy statements, agency manuals, and enforcement guidelines, all of which lack the force of law . . . ."). The Court earlier stated other grounds for giving a regulation the force of law, the most prominent being reenactment of the statute while the regulation was outstanding. Crane v. Commissioner, 331 U.S. 1, 8 (1947); Helvering v. R. J. Reynolds Tobacco Co., 306 U.S. 110 (1939).

[2021] Pierce, at § 6.2.

[2022]

> Indeed, long before the tax year here in question this Court had made it clear that 'The power of an administrative officer or board to administer a federal statute and to prescribe rules and regulations to that end is not the power to make law . . . but the power to adopt regulations to carry into effect the will of Congress as expressed by the statute. A regulation which does not do this, but operates to create a rule out of harmony with the statute, is a mere nullity.'

Dixon v. United States, 381 U.S. 68, 74 (1965).

lative regulations are not necessarily "law," as Congress uses that term to refer to its own statutes.[2023]

- Interpretive regulations issued under section 7805(a) interpret and thereby merely state the Treasury's view on the meaning of statutes and are entitled to some but lesser deference (*Skidmore* deference) than legislative regulations;[2024] for this reason the Treasury could change interpretive regulations retroactively,[2025] at least up to the "Taxpayer Bill of Rights 2" in 1996, which reversed the rule of retroactivity, subject to certain exceptions in section 7805(b); moreover, the Treasury is under no duty to assert a particular position as soon as authorized by the statute.[2026]
- The Code's general grant of regulatory authority in section 7805(a) primarily grants authority for interpretive regulations, but can support legislative regulations.[2027]
- Hundreds of specific grants of authority in substantive Code sections mostly authorize legislative regulations, depending on the terminology used.[2028]
- The "dominant standard" for whether a regulation is legislative was said to be the "*American Mining Congress* test," which assesses whether the regulation functions like a statute;[2029] but the *Mayo* opinion occupied the field for tax law, stating that "the ultimate question is whether Congress would have intended, and expected, courts to treat [the regulation] as within, or outside, its delegation to the agency of 'gap-filling' authority."[2030]
- Legislative regulations (but not interpretive regulations) can be subject to what is called *Chenery* review, which requires support in the administrative record of the notice and hearing proceeding for the choices made

---

[2023] Dep't of Homeland Sec. v. MacLean, 135 S. Ct. 913 (2015).

[2024] Hickman, *Three Phases of Mead,* 83 Ford. L. Rev. 527, 528 (2014).

[2025] *Dixon*, 381 U.S. at 76; Helvering v. Reynolds, 313 U.S. 428 (1941) (Court applied regulation adopted under amended statute after the date of the transaction at issue); Manhattan General Equipment Co. v. Commissioner, 297 U.S. 129 (1936).

[2026] Dickman v. Commissioner, 465 U.S. 330 (1984).

[2027] I.R.M. 32.1.1.2.8; Mayo Found. for Med. Educ. & Research v. United States, 562 U.S. 44 (2011). *See* United States v. Mead Corp., 533 U.S. 218, 229 (2001); Chevron U.S.A., Inc. v. Natural Resources Defense Council, Inc., 467 U.S. 837, 844 (1984). The Court identified the regulation at issue in *National Muffler* as issued under section 7805, but described it as supplying the definition of a term having no well understood meaning, which sounds like a legislative regulation. Nat'l Muffler Dealers Assn., Inc. v. United States, 440 U.S. 472 (1979).

[2028] Attorney General's Report on the Administrative Procedure Act, sec II.A(4) (1941), S. Doc. No. 8 (1941).

[2029] Am. Mining Cong. v. Mine Safety & Health Admin., 995 F.2d 1106 (D.C. Cir. 1993) (never cited by the Supreme Court). *See* Hickman, *Coloring Outside the Lines, supra* note 1987, at 1766; *see also id.* at 1769 (discussion of similar "substantial impact test"); Hickman, *Unpacking the Force of Law*, 66 Vand. L. Rev. 465, 481 (2013).

[2030] *Mayo*, 562 U.S. at 58.

in the final regulation;[2031] also called the hard look.[2032] But the Court has not applied these tests in a tax case.

- The principal reason the legislative-interpretive dichotomy may no longer be controlling is that the Supreme Court's decision in *Mead*[2033] is thought to have fuzzed up the distinction and focused instead on Congress' intent about agency guidance with the force of law, however that intent might be evidenced, and in whatever form the agency might give guidance. In fact the Court's opinions now rarely refer to legislative and interpretive regulations except when stating the parties' arguments; rather, they talk about ambiguity of the statute.[2034] This term brings its own confusions because the Court has been willing to interpret ambiguous statutes so as to have an unambiguous meaning, without giving regulations *Chevron* deference: the 2012 *Home Concrete* decision is the prime example. Therefore, for everyday practice purposes it continues to be useful to use the dichotomy.

VI.D.5.b. *Development of the Distinction*

In 1921, "rulings" were the predominant published guidance on tax and were generally viewed as either administrative (procedural) or interpretive; a quasi-legislative "regulation" category did exist and was used, for example, for accounting standards.[2035] The concept of legislative regulations in Supreme Court tax opinions dates at least back to 1934 in *Ilfeld*,[2036] which quoted a Senate Report referring to the consolidated return regulations as "regulations legislative in character." In 1936, the Court observed the difference between the two types of regulations and stated that the courts apply the "same principle" of giving "great weight" to the tax regulations.[2037] However, in 1940 Randolph Paul did not discuss the legislative versus interpretive distinction for Treasury regulations, but rather noted that the courts mouthed some degree of deference to agencies, while doing what they wanted.[2038] Stanley Surrey (later to be Assistant Secretary of the Treasury) wrote on this topic

---

[2031] Chenery I, 318 U.S. 80 (1943); Chenery II, 332 U.S. 194 (1947). *See* Murphy, Chenery *Unmasked: Reasonable Limits on the Duty to Give Reasons*, 80 U. CIN. L. REV. 817 (2011). Legislative rule making is somewhat confusingly called informal rule making. *Id.* at 839.

[2032] *See* Motor Vehicle Mfrs. Assn. v. State Farm Mut. Auto. Ins. Co., 463 U.S. 29 (1983).

[2033] *Mead Corp.*, 533 U.S. at 229. *See* Coverdale, *Chevron's Reduced Domain: Judicial Review of Treasury Regulations and Revenue Rulings after Mead*, 55 ADMIN. L. REV. 39, 82 (2003).

[2034] United States v. Home Concrete & Supply, LLC, 132 S. Ct. 1836 (2012).

[2035] HAIG ET AL., *The Legal Force and Effect of Treasury Interpretation*, *in* THE FEDERAL INCOME TAX 91-113 (Columbia Univ. Press 1921). The article likened such regulations to those setting standards for imported teas in *Buttfield v. Stranahan*, 192 U.S. 470 (1904).

[2036] Charles Ilfeld Co. v. Hernandez, 292 U.S. 62 (1934). *See also* Maryland Casualty Co. v. United States, 251 U.S. 342 (1920) (a federal tax opinion applying the "force of law" principle to state insurance regulations).

[2037] Koshland v. Helvering, 298 U.S. 441 (1936).

[2038] PAUL, STUDIES III, at 424-25, n. 15 (noting Supreme Court deference statements from great weight to force of law); *see also* PIERCE, at § 3.1.

in 1940 and thought that all general authority regulations (issued under the predecessor of section 7805(a)) were interpretive simply because of the contrasting existence of specific grants of regulatory authority in the Code.[2039] In 1944, Dwan discerned the difference, but later concluded that the legislative regulations had not been so well received.[2040]

The distinction received heightened significance when Congress enacted the Administrative Procedure Act in 1946. Section 4(a) of the Act exempted interpretive rules from the notice and hearing requirements that were applicable to "substantive rules."[2041] The same distinction continues today in 5 U.S.C. section 553, and is the principal basis for Treasury's belief that notice and hearing is not required for most of its regulations, though it commonly treats all but temporary regulations as if they were APA regulations (and more recently has started to assert all area subject to *Chevron* deference). The 1947 Attorney General's Manual on the newly enacted Administrative Procedure Act, Note 3 in Section 4 on Rule Making, supplied definitions for "substantive rules," which "implement the statute . . . and have the force and effect of law," versus "interpretive rules, which advise the public of the agency's construction of the statutes and rules which it administers."

The Act's terminology can be traced back at least to the 1941 Attorney General's Report on the Administrative Procedure Act,[2042] which proposed the enactment that occurred in 1946. Section II of that Report distinguished interpretations, which it referred to as "interpretive rules" or "rulings" that had only an advisory nature, from "substantive regulations," which were identified by the nature of the legislative language authorizing them. When the authorization indicated that the law would not work or be complete without the regulation, it was like "subordinate legislation." The 1941 Report probably described particularly well the rulings and regulations of the Treasury because its official author was Robert H. Jackson, who was intimately familiar with revenue practices, having been Chief Counsel and Assistant Attorney General for Tax.

Thus, Jackson's 1941 Report implied that all Treasury regulations were substantive whereas interpretive materials were "rulings," of which the Service authored many by that and other names (general counsel memorandum, office decisions, solicitor's opinion, mimeographed letter, etc.). When the Administrative Procedure Act dropped the term "regulation" in favor of an all purpose term "rule," it effectively forced an effort to distinguish interpretive

---

[2039] Surrey, *Scope and Effect of Treasury Regulations, supra* note 1990, at 556-58 (specifically referring to regulations issued under the authority of section 62, which was the predecessor of section 7805(a); Surrey stated the issuance of interpretive regulations would be equally valid without the statutory grant).

[2040] Dwan, *Some Technical Aspects of the Internal Revenue Statutes and Regulations*, 28 MINN. L. REV. 377, 380-83 (1944) (Dwan was then Assistant Chief Counsel of the Internal Revenue Service); Dwan, *Internal Revenue Code of 1954, supra* note 1468, at 829.

[2041] Pub. L. No. 404, ch. 324, 60 Stat. 237 (1946).

[2042] S. Doc. No. 8 (1941).

rules in the form of regulations from substantive rules in the form of regulations. That distinction produces much of today's confusion in the tax arena and also may explain why the earlier case law accorded all Treasury regulations high deference (the *National Muffler* standard).

Based on this origin of the distinction in relation to the notice and hearing requirement, it might seem that the two types of regulations could be differentiated based on whether that process was employed, and several prominent commentators read the law that way.[2043] But the Supreme Court has not adopted that answer, both because it would be over inclusive and under inclusive.[2044] The Treasury in practice uses the notice and hearing procedure for most of its non-temporary regulations, without analyzing whether they require it or not.[2045] The Court has stated that *Chevron* deference is not limited to regulations adopted with notice and hearing.[2046] For example, *Mayo* did not say that notice and hearing were required for what were clearly legislative regulations, but did weight the specificity of the statutory grant of authority and the use of notice and hearing in promulgating regulations as a significant sign that the regulation merited *Chevron* deference.[2047] *Mayo* derived the reference to notice and comment from *Mead*, which contained a frankly illogical statement that the agency's use of notice and comment somehow informed what Congress' words in the statutory grant of regulatory authority intended, with a citation only to a law review article.[2048]

Even before the APA was adopted, Randolph Paul asserted that all Treasury regulations should be issued with notice and hearing.[2049] From the earliest days of the APA the Treasury tried to err on the side of application of the notice and hearing requirement, even though it was understood that purely interpretive regulations were not subject to it, and the Service considers most regulations to be interpretive.[2050] The Treasury issues all but about four percent of its final regulations with notice and hearing, but frequently states it is not required to do so because they are interpretive. Treasury issues about one

---

[2043] *See* SALTZMAN & BOOK, at 3.02[4]–3.02[4][a], referring to that view and both stating and questioning it.

[2044] *See* Gersen, *Legislative Rules Revisited*, 74 U. CHI. L. REV. 1705, 1708-13 (2007).

[2045] *See N.Y.S.B.A. Tax Sec., Report No. 1121 on Legislative Grants of Regulatory Authority*, 2006 TAX NOTES TODAY 215-22 (Nov. 3, 2006).

[2046] Barnhart v. Walton, 535 U.S. 212 (2002); United States v. Mead Corp., 533 U.S. 218 (2001).

[2047] Mayo Found. for Med. Educ. & Research v. United States, 562 U.S. 44 (2011).

[2048] *Mead*, 533 U.S. at n. 11.

[2049] Paul, *Use and Abuse of Tax Regulations in Statutory Construction*, *supra* note 1958, at 684 ("all proposed interpretive and legislative regulations. . . .").

[2050] Dwan, *Internal Revenue Code of 1954*, *supra* note 1468, at 831. I.R.M. 32.1.5.4.7.5.1.

third of its regulations in temporary and proposed form.[2051] The Treasury does not hold hearings on temporary regulations (but does call for hearings on the proposed regulations that are slated to replace them). Therefore, some have raised questions about the propriety of substantive temporary regulations for the period they are in force as temporary.[2052] The practical consequence of failure of notice and hearing when required is to entitle the temporary regulation only to *Skidmore* and not *Chevron* deference.[2053]

Section 7805(a) authorizes interpretive regulations, whether or not it also authorizes legislative regulations. Section 7805(a) states:

> Except where such authority is expressly given by this title to any person other than an officer or employee of the Treasury Department, the Secretary shall prescribe all needful rules and regulations for the enforcement of this title, including all rules and regulations as may be necessary by reason of any alteration of law in relation to internal revenue.[2054]

The Supreme Court has assumed without discussion that certain regulations issued under the authority of section 7805(a) are interpretive,[2055] and in other cases has effectively said so.[2056] As such, they should not enjoy *Chevron* deference but would receive *Skidmore* deference.[2057] Nevertheless, prior to *Mayo*, the Court generally accorded such interpretive regulations the tradi-

---

[2051] *See* Hickman, *Coloring Outside the Lines, supra* note 1987, at 1727 (arguing that the very fact of adopting a regulation with notice and hearing makes it a substantive regulation); *see also* The Congressional Review Act (CRA), 5 U.S.C. §§ 801-808 (1996). The CRA is intended to provide Congress notice of both "major" and non-major rulemaking and even provides a procedure whereby Congress could nix rulemaking of which it disapproves. Although it is very rare for Congress to disapprove of agency rulemaking through this process, it still provides a dependable means by which the Service and Treasury Department inform Congress of its rules. Nonetheless, it appears that the Service and Treasury Department interpret the CRA as not applying to most regulations.

[2052] *See* Coverdale, *Chevron's Reduced Domain, supra* note 2033, at 69-70 (speculating that Treasury believes it is impracticable or contrary to the public interest); Hickman, *Coloring Outside the Lines, supra* note 1987, at 1727.

[2053] Coverdale, *Chevron's Reduced Domain, supra* note 2033, at 81 (speculating that Treasury believes it is impracticable or contrary to the public interest).

[2054] I.R.C. § 7805(a). The section contains a curious reference to regulations including those made necessary by reason of an alteration of law in relation to internal revenue. One court has interpreted these words to refer to regulations coordinating nontax laws and law changes with the tax law. *See* Ying v. Commissioner, 99 T.C. 273 (1992*), aff'd in part and rev'd in part*, 25 F.3d 84 (2d Cir. 1994). Section 7805 is to be distinguished from 5 U.S.C. § 301, which authorizes regulations governing agency operations.

[2055] Boeing Co. v. United States, 537 U.S. 437 (2003) (citing Cottage Savings Assn. v. Commissioner, 499 U.S. 554, 560-61 (1991) (which cited Nat'l Muffler Dealers Assn., Inc. v. United States, 440 U.S. 472 (1979) (which found an interpretive regulation to have been issued under section 7805(a) where the role of the regulation appears to be legislative, which cited United States v. Cartwright, 411 U.S. 546 (1973), which cited United States v. Correll, 389 U.S. 299 (1967), which was cited in the statement of the traditional standard quoted from *Fulman* in the text above)).

[2056] United States v. Vogel Fertilizer Co., 455 U.S. 16, 24-25 (1982).

[2057] *See* United States v. Mead Corp., 533 U.S. 218, 231-32 (2001).

tional pre-*Chevron* level of higher deference.[2058] Indeed, the Court's decisions on Treasury regulations rarely cited *Chevron*,[2059] and rather reached back to the historic cites (thus giving rise to the claim of speciality), up to the *Mayo* decision, which rejected the *National Muffler* test as applied to legislative regulations. However, the Court did apply the historic standard on a sliding scale depending on how fulsome is the Congress' guidance in the statute itself, or stated another way, how ambiguous is the statute.[2060]

The *Mayo* ruling that a section 7805(a) regulation could be entitled to *Chevron* deference is consistent with rulings that statutes like section 7805(a) in other titles of the U.S. Code grant authority for legislative regulations.[2061] Conversely, the regulation issued under a more specific direction to fill in a gap in the statute is the prototypical legislative regulation. Therefore, after *Mayo* most disputes are likely to relate to regulations issued under section 7805(a): when are they legislative and when are they interpretive?

The Supreme Court's usage of the legislative versus interpretive distinction is inconsistent, and relatively infrequent in tax cases. The Supreme Court discussed the distinction before *Chevron* in *Batterton v. Francis* (not a tax case).[2062] The first time the Supreme Court recognized two categories of deference for

---

2058 Boeing Co. v. United States, 537 U.S. 437 (2003); United States v. Cleveland Indians Baseball Co., 532 U.S. 200 (2001) (section 7805(a) regulations accorded *National Muffler* deference; no reference to *Chevron*).

2059 As of 2016, there were five cites in federal tax opinions of the Court. In addition to *Mead*, *Mayo*, and *Home Concrete*, see *At'l. Mut. Ins. Co. v. Commissioner*, 523 U.S. 382 (1998) (citing *Chevron* for the primacy of the issue of ambiguity of the statute, but then citing *Cottage Savings* for the not best but reasonable standard); United States v. Boyle, 469 U.S. 241 (1985) (giving the Treasury regulation "deference").

2060 *See Vogel Fertilizer Co.*, 455 U.S. at 24-5 (citing *National Muffler* and stating that because the statute already defined the term "with considerable specificity . . . the Commissioner's authority is consequently more circumscribed than would be the case if Congress had used a term 'so general as to render an interpretive regulation appropriate . . .'").

2061 *See* Nat'l Cable & Telecomm. Assn. v. Brand X Internet Services, 545 U.S. 967 (2005) (evaluating regulations issued under as statute authorizing the agency to ". . . prescribe such rules and regulations as may be necessary in the public interest to carry out the provisions of this Act. . . ." *Brand X* held that *Chevron* deference applied to the definition at issue because the statute was ambiguous on the point and the agency had authority to fill in the gap; the opinion read the statute as giving the agency the authority to write "binding legal rules"; presumably this means the same as having "the force of law."); *Mead*, 533 U.S. at 229; Chevron U.S.A., Inc. v. Natural Resources Defense Council, Inc., 467 U.S. 837, 844 (1984).

The Court accorded *Chevron* deference to a regulation issued under 42 U.S.C. § 12116, which states that the commission shall issue regulations to carry out the title. EEOC v. ARAMCO, 499 U.S. 244 (1991). Indeed, in *EEOC v. ARAMCO* Justice Scalia concurred, stating that *Chevron* had eliminated the distinction between legislative and interpretive regulations and applied a single test. However, the case is confusing because Congress did not grant the EEOC any rule making power and the case was about non-rule interpretations. So Scalia was trying to extend *Chevron* deference.

2062 Batterton v. Francis, 432 U.S. 416, 425-26 (1977) (contrasting "mere deference" for interpretive regulations with an arbitrary, capricious or abuse of discretion standard for legislative regulations); *see also* Alessi v. Raybestos-Manhattan, Inc., 451 U.S. 504 (1981) (citing *Batterton*).

Treasury regulations appears to have been in *Rowan Cos.*[2063] The degree of deference attributed to legislative regulations was that of *Fulman* quoted above. But *Fulman* addressed and upheld under that "particularly appropriate" rule of deference a section 7805(a) regulation that had no other "specific grant of authority," which *Rowan* said was needed for the enhanced deference.[2064] So, in a sense, *Fulman* predicted *Mayo*. Similarly, *Atlantic Mutual*[2065] rejected an attack on the Treasury regulation's definition of "reserve strengthening" because it was reasonable and passed the *Chevr*on test. T.D. 8433 says the Treasury issued the regulation under section 7805.

The Court addressed the distinction in the tax opinion *Boeing Co.*,[2066] which was unfortunately imprecise. The opinion recognized the convention of describing regulations issued under section 7805 as "interpretive," and contrasted that with "a specific grant of authority" (the opinion did not use the phrase "legislative regulation"). The opinion upheld the regulations because they were not arbitrary and not in conflict with any statute. The government argued they were specific authority regulations even though nominally issued under section 7805; the taxpayer said section 7805 applied and the Court appeared to agree with the government.[2067] However, the opinion stated that interpretive regulations were accorded deference, citing *Cottage Savings.*[2068] That case also involved section 7805 regulations and accorded them deference if reasonable, citing *National Muffler,*[2069] which referred indirectly to the Treasury as the "masters of the subject" and the heavy reliance Congress had placed on it to write rules; but on the other hand it described a variety of considerations that courts may rely on to evaluate rules, which appear to indicate a fair amount of discretion in the courts. It appears that *Mayo* and *Mead* clarified the confusion about *Chevron* deference applying to interpretive regulations not by saying it does, but by saying section 7805 authorizes both kinds of regulations, which creates a different ambiguity.

If the foregoing seems confusing and somewhat irrelevant, it is both. The most useful synthesis of the legislative/interpretive dichotomy is that, as a practical matter, it does not matter:

[2063] Rowan Cos. v. United States, 452 U.S. 247 (1981) (cited for this point by United States v. Vogel Fertilizer Co., 455 U.S. 16 (1982)).

[2064] *Rowan* also cited *Batterton*, 432 U.S. at 424-25, which did say that a specific grant would lead to more deference, and *Commissioner v. Portland Cement Co.*, 450 U.S. 156 (1981), which did involve a specific grant of authority but stated that "these regulations command our respect" citing I.R.C. § 7805(a).

[2065] Atl. Mut. Ins. Co. v. Commissioner, 523 U.S. 382 (1998).

[2066] Boeing Co. v. United States, 537 U.S. 437 (2003). Curiously, section 904 contained a specific grant of regulatory authority, on which the Treasury did not rely in issuing the regulations at issue.

[2067] *See* Hickman, *Need for Mead, supra* note 2000, at 1585.

[2068] Cottage Savings Assn. v. Commissioner, 499 U.S. 554 (1991).

[2069] Nat'l Muffler Dealers Assn., Inc. v. United States, 440 U.S. 472 (1979).

- What matters is the interplay between (a) the words of the grant of authority, (b) the size of the hole to be filled in the statute, (c) the extent of congressional guidance on the hole, (d) the boldness of the regulation Treasury writes, and (e) the reasonableness of that regulation in the light of these considerations.
- The most practical view of section 7805(a) is that it may be primarily a grant of Treasury's interpretive authority, but Congress has granted sufficient authority through section 7805 for Treasury to write legislative rules in all cases where the Code is sufficiently ambiguous or silent to leave a gap to be filled.[2070]
- Thus, "needful" regulations as authorized by section 7805 include not only mere interpretations, but also regulations (1) addressing very general terms like the word "income" in section 61, for which the Supreme Court said an "interpretive regulation" was appropriate,[2071] and (2) addressing terms like "carrying on or doing business" (used in the capital stock tax in the 1930's) that have created a "nebulous field of confusion" evidenced by courts trying to fit cases into one category or the other,[2072] as well as regulations (3) that are not obviously interpretive but rather fill gaps under section 7805(a) and not under specific authority such as section 1502, which may have been the case in *Boeing Co.*[2073]
- Whether 5 U.S.C. 706 applies or not, the Supreme Court historically has applied an arbitrariness standard to Treasury Regulations, without citing the Administrative Procedure Act.[2074]

Professor Hickman concludes that nearly all Treasury regulations (and even lesser guidance) are "binding" on taxpayers, and *for that reason* are necessarily "legislative" regulations because they have the force and effect of law.[2075] Her

---

[2070] This view is based on *United States v. Mead Corp.*, 533 U.S. 218 (2001); applied in *Swallows Holding Ltd. v. Commissioner*, 515 F.3d 162 (3d Cir. 2008). For fuller explanation of the view, see Cummings, *Treasury Violates APA?*, 117 TAX NOTES (TA) 263 (Oct. 15, 2007).

[2071] Helvering v. R. J. Reynolds Tobacco Co., 306 U.S. 110 (1939) (upholding a regulation under section 61 that a corporation did not realize income on dealing in its own stock, despite the fact that the Treasury had attempted to adopt a retroactive regulation to the contrary during the pendency of the suit).

[2072] Magruder v. W.B. & A.R.C., 316 U.S. 69 (1942).

[2073] Boeing Co. v. United States, 537 U.S. 437 (2003) (regulation was issued under section 7805 but the Service argued it also had specific authority, it filled a gap).

[2074] *E.g.*, United States v. Catto, Jr., 384 U.S. 102 (1966) (neither arbitrary nor contrary to the statute).

[2075] Hickman, *Coloring Outside the Lines, supra* note 1987, at 1762-64 (Sec. III, A, 1, last para.; Introduction: "most if not all"; procedural regulations are binding but excepted from the APA); Hickman Amicus Brief in *Quality Stores*, 2012 U.S. Briefs 1408 (Nov. 15, 2013) (the Court did not share the professor's concern with the "mess" which is the issuance of revenue rulings without notice and hearing); Hickman Amicus Brief in *Home Concrete*, 2011 U.S. Briefs 139 (Dec. 22, 2011) (although the Court did not follow the temporary regulation, it did not adopt her theory); Hickman Amicus Brief in Mayo Found. v. United States, 2009 U.S. Briefs 837 (Oct. 4, 2010) (the Court agreed that the regulation was entitled to *Chevron* deference, but not on the ground asserted by the professor).

analysis is not based on the nature of the gap left in the statute but on the agency's choice to write a regulation or even a revenue ruling with the force of law. She finds that an agency makes such a choice when it uses notice and hearing to promulgate the regulation. But even when it does not use notice and hearing, it cannot avoid issuing guidance that appears to have the force of law; but, if caught, the Court should deny that force.

This convoluted theory is not only impractical, it also is wrong. In the case of revenue rulings, it sets up a paper target and then knocks it down: revenue rulings will never be, and should not be, issued with notice and hearing because they never should have preclusive effect on legal interpretation. As to temporary regulations that are not issued with notice and hearing, she argues they should be stripped of *Chevron* deference as punishment and coercion to make the Treasury do right. The theory makes *Chevron* deference turn on either a fairly meaningless procedural choice or an unreasonable application of the force of law concept. No one should be fooled by lack of formal hearings: interested taxpayers have ways of making their wishes known, right up to and including waiting on the Secretary of the Treasury.

The theory may seem to be supported by some sentences in *Mead,* essentially copied in *Mayo*, when read in isolation. But those sentences are preceded by an initial premise that Congress left a gap in the substantive rule in the Code, which gap is the grant of regulatory authority, when combined with a specific or general grant of authority such as section 7805. The *Home Concrete* plurality opinion makes the distinction clear: if a court can figure out what the statute meant, there is no gap and no *Chevron* deference.

The main problem with Professor Hickman's theory is that it gets the logic exactly backward; it starts in the wrong place. The right place to start is the words of Congress. If Congress shows that it intends for an agency to issue rules with the binding effect of law (what was once called legislative regulations), then yes, the rules should be issued with notice and hearing, and if so, receive *Chevron* deference. But you don't reverse engineer a notice and hearing requirement from the fact that a taxpayer that reports contrary to published guidance is likely to receive a deficiency assessment: the IRS agent has no choice but to follow the agency's published guidance, even if it is a mere Notice or Announcement. Rather, you must inquire exactly what "binding" means in this context: a rule that cannot be contested as an inferior interpretation because Congress left a gap that it intended the Treasury to fill.

The tax system cannot run without some level of baseline deference to the tax administrator, which has no option but to speak through something "less" than regulations issued after notice and hearing. Indeed, practitioners in the corporate area are accustomed to learning the law from letter rulings and technical advice memoranda (and the Supreme Court cited a technical advice memorandum in its *Quality Stores* opinion). You can call this *Skidmore* deference or whatever, but what the IRS thinks matters. The Supreme Court has said so several times, including in *Nierotko*,[2076] an important FICA opinion also cited in the *Quality Stores* opinion.

The practical explanation for the continuing relevance of the interpretive/legislative distinction lies in turf protection by the courts and the fact that the terms very well encapsulate what is going on. When Treasury is performing what looks more like a judicial function of interpreting the meaning of a Code provision, its views are entitled to less weight and such guidance is called "interpretation," so as to preserve to the courts the ultimate power over the meaning of the laws. There is a growing view that core legal issues, as contrasted with issues more related to facts, are not presumed to have been delegated to the agency.[2077] Put another way, normal statutory interpretation is what courts do, and the Supreme Court, at least, is not going to give up that role.[2078]

The second Supreme Court decision upholding the Affordable Care Act, in 2015, revealed another way that an ambiguous statute can escape *Chevron* deference: the statutory conundrum may be so great that it is above the political power of an agency to resolve.[2079]

VI.D.5.c. *The I.R.M.'s Unusual View*

The Internal Revenue Manual originally stated the distinction in a very straightforward manner: if the Code states that the Treasury "shall provide" regulations, the regulations are legislative, otherwise they are interpretive, clarifying presumed ambiguities in the Code, and issued under section 7805(a).[2080] It acknowledged that the Service is bound by all regulations and the courts are not, without distinguishing between the two types of regulations.[2081] It referred to regulations generally as the Service's "position" on the interpretation of the law.[2082] This implies what is indicated more directly in connection to revenue rulings and procedures: that while the revenue agents are bound by interpretive regulations, the taxpayers are not required to follow them but may rely on them.[2083]

[2076] Social Sec. Bd. v. Nierotko, 327 U.S. 358 (1946).

[2077] *See* Gifford, *Emerging Outlines of a Revised Chevron Doctrine*, *supra* note 748, at 809-21.

[2078] Applied, in effect, in *United States v. Quality Stores, Inc.*, 134 S. Ct. 1395 (2014), which cited and relied on *Social Sec. Bd. v. Nierotko*, 327 U.S. 358 (1946), which was cited for this point in *Chevron* at footnote 9; United States v. Home Concrete & Supply, LLC, 132 S. Ct. 1836 (2012);

[2079] King v. Burwell, 135 S. Ct. 2480 (2015).

[2080] I.R.M. 4.10.7.2.3.2. However, the Service does not view the directive "shall" as the only way Congress can authorize legislative regulations. *See* MSSP TRAINING GUIDE ON INVENTORY PART 2, stating that section 472(a) authorizing taxpayer action "as the Secretary may provide" to authorize legislative regulations having the force of law.

[2081] I.R.M. 4.10.7.2.3.4.

[2082] I.R.M. 31.1.1.1.1. No other form of published guidance can change a regulation but another regulation. I.R.M. 32.1.1.4.

[2083] I.R.M. 4.10.7.2.6.

In reaction to the 2011 *Mayo* ruling, the Service added to the I.R.M. a further definition of legislative rules: "Legislative rules are required when Congress simply provided an end result, without any guidance as to how to achieve the desired goal or when a statutory provision does not provide adequate authority for the regulatory action taken."[2084] Then it carves back on the "specific grant" approach in recognition of the Supreme Court's inferences of authority from gaps in the statute. But it then states that if Congress provided specific rules and merely left gaps for the Secretary to fill, regulations filling those gaps are considered interpretative.[2085]

This view of "gaps" substantially misunderstands the Supreme Court's direction in *Mayo* that regulations entitled to *Chevron* deference fill gaps left by Congress in various ways in the Code.

VI.D.6. *Other Issues*

VI.D.6.a. *How Is Authority Granted?*

One of the facts and circumstances bearing on the measurement of deference to regulations is the wording and nature of the grant of authority itself. Here we focus on those words of authorization in the Code, which are of two types: (1) section 7805(a), which relates to all of the Code, and (2) hundreds of other more specific grants located in the sections to which they relate. Generally, section 7805(a) has been thought to authorize "interpretive regulations" entitled to *Skidmore* deference, and the rest to authorize mostly "legislative regulations" entitled to the full *Chevron* deference (subject to many questions and confusions discussed above). But when the statutory gap is so great as to make its meaning a conundrum of choices, a regulation issued under section 7805(a) can be treated as a legislative regulation and receive *Chevron* deference.[2086]

Outside section 7805, there appears to be no consistency[2087] to the ways Congress has authorized the Treasury and the Service to enlarge upon the Code (counted electronically as at least 550). They include by groups the following:[2088]

2084 I.R.M. 32.1.1.2.7.

2085 I.R.M. 32.1.1.2.8.

2086 *E.g.*, Mayo Found. for Med. Educ. & Research v. United States, 562 U.S. 44 (2011).

2087

> Nor has the Congress done anything to simplify the problem, but instead has strewn the Revenue Acts with a miscellany of references to administrative action without in any way indicating if the different modes of expression are intended to imply differences in the degree of power conferred upon the Commissioner.

Surrey, *Scope and Effect of Treasury Regulations, supra* note 1990, at 577-78.

2088 *See generally* Bittker & Lokken, at 110.4; N.Y.S.B.A. Tax Sec., *Report No. 1121, supra* note 2045, at 215-22 (containing the 550 count); Grewal, *Substance over Form: Phantom Regulations and the Internal Revenue Code*, 7 Hou. Bus. and Tax L.J. 42, 43-4 (2004) (focusing on directions to issue regulations that are not issued, *i.e.*, phantom regulations).

- The clearly "legislative" regulation authority grants: (1) a few Code sections clearly authorize legislative regulations;[2089] including sections that cannot even become operative without regulations;[2090] or cannot become operative without regulations for which the Code prescribes certain "principles";[2091] (2) sections that can be turned off in specific cases at the Secretary's election with little guidance in the Code;[2092] (3) sections that specifically refer to carrying out the "purposes" of the section or portion thereof;[2093] (4) sections that import one section's approach into other sections to which Congress has not specifically applied it;[2094] (5) sections that describe an abusive situation to be prevented by regulations;[2095] (6) sections that exempt a less problematic case from a rule aimed at abuse;[2096] or that prevent over taxation;[2097] or that moderate an absolute rule that may not work properly in all situations.[2098]
- Other sections authorize regulations necessary or appropriate for carrying out the section without reference to purposes specifically;[2099] and for adopting procedures for some reporting, election or other taxpayer activity.[2100]

2089 *See, e.g.*, I.R.C. §§ 472(a) (clearly reflect income), 704(c)(2) (even though the parameters are relatively extensive, the regulations built thereon are even more substantial), 7701(l) (anti-abuse regulations for all purposes of title), 1502. Douglas v. Commissioner, 322 U.S. 275, 281 (1944) (upheld the Service's authority to promulgate certain depletion Regulations, saying that Congress placed interpretative authority with the Service in recognition of the unforeseeable variety of depletion questions). The Supreme Court had earlier stated in *Helvering v. Wilshire Oil Co.*, 308 U.S. 90, 103 (1939), that because of the complexity of administering the depletion provisions the courts should interpret the statute authorizing depletion regulations so as to strengthen the Service's administrative powers.

2090 *See, e.g.,* I.R.C. § 336(e); *see* Notice of Proposed Rule Making, 73 Fed. Reg. 49,965 (Aug. 25, 2008).

2091 *See, e.g.,* I.R.C. § 597. The Supreme Court has stated that special deference is in order when regulations are written in response to a Code directive that a benefit not be accorded taxpayers except as provided in regulations written by the Treasury. *See* Commissioner v. S. Texas Lumber Co., 333 U.S. 496, 503 (1948) (the installment method would be available "under regulations prescribed . . .).

2092 *See, e.g.,* I.R.C. §§ 41(d)(4)(E) (discussed in FedEx Corp. v. United States, 103 A.F.T.R. 2d 2722 (W.D. Tenn. 2009), 165(j)(3), 172(f)(3), 367.

2093 *See, e.g.,* I.R.C. §§ 1(g)(7)(C), 21(f), 25(h)(1), 165(e)(6), 168(h)(8),197(g), 274(o), 301(e)(4), 304(b)(5)(B), 337(d) (referring to the purposes of a section of an act rather than the Code), 346(b) (similar reference), 355(b)(3)(D), 355(e)(5), 357(d)(3), 384(f), 409A(e), 864(e)(7), 1221(b)(4).

2094 *See, e.g.,* I.R.C. §§ 1(h)(9), 29(d)(8), 357(d)(3).

2095 *See, e.g.,* I.R.C. §§67(c)(1), 108(c)(5), 165(e)(6), 197(g), 355(g)(5), 361(b)(3), 384(f) (prevent circumvention through use of any other law or regulation).

2096 *See, e.g.,* I.R.C. §§ 274(d)(4), 332(d)(4).

2097 *See, e.g.,* I.R.C. § 304(b)(6).

2098 *See, e.g.,* I.R.C. § 1361(b)(3)(A) (QSSUB not a separate corporation except as regulations provide).

2099 *See, e.g.,* I.R.C. §§ 25A(i), 35(g)(9).

2100 *See, e.g.,* I.R.C. §§ 25(e)(3)(C) and (4), 31(b)(1), 38(c)(5)(B), 63(e)(3), 83(d)(2)(B), 446(c)(4).

- Other sections authorize regulations that fill in details in accordance to the overall plan of the statute.[2101]
- Sections authorize regulations that are more in the nature of defining events or conditions, as are more typical for other regulatory agencies.[2102]
- A section, such as 482, that does not authorize any regulations but under which the Treasury has written extensive regulations, essentially making the law in cross border transactions.

The New York State Bar Association Tax Section, in 2006, proposed a uniform menu of phrases to be used by Congress in granting various degrees and types of authority to write Treasury regulations.[2103] It has made no impact on Congress, and is not likely to, absent a complete rewrite of the Code (and probably not then), due to the massive review that would be required and the institutional tendency to retain words in the Code. The Report also stated how the principal affected parties, Treasury and practitioners, view authority grants and the nomenclature used, as quoted in the preceding Section.

VI.D.6.b. *Relevance of Reenactment?*

The reenactment doctrine received a substantial setback in 2011 when the *Mayo* opinion rejected the *National Muffler* considerations to be applied to legislative regulations, including "the degree of scrutiny Congress has devoted to the regulation during subsequent re-enactments of the statute."[2104] Nevertheless, it can be argued as to interpretive regulations and may continue to come up generally.

Dean Griswold considered the bearing of the reenactment of a section on the validity of regulations under that section to be a "well-trodden" issue in 1941, and concluded that it was foolish to treat the reenactment of a Code provision as congressional affirmance of an existing Treasury regulation.[2105] The Chief Counsel once agreed.[2106] Nevertheless, the sort of statements in Supreme Court opinions giving weight to reenactments that preceded

---

[2101] *See* Burnet v. S. & L. Bldg. Corp., 288 U.S. 406 (1933) (complications in installment reporting Congress could not readily forsee; authorized Treasury to fill in details).

[2102] *See, e.g.*, I.R.C. §§ 25C(d)(2)(B) (qualified energy property), 118(c)(3)(A), 246(c)(4)(C) (diminished risk of stock ownership), 305(c) (appropriate conversion ratio adjustments), 385 (definitions of debt and equity).

[2103] N.Y.S.B.A. Tax Sec., *Report No. 1121*, *supra* note 2045, at 215-22.

[2104] *Mayo*, 562 U.S. at 64.

[2105] Griswold, *A Summary of the Regulations Problem*, 54 Harv. L. Rev. 398, 423 (1941). *See generally* Bittker & Lokken, at 110.4.3.

[2106] One authority has correctly pointed out that:

> The fallacy in the frequently expressed rule that reenactment of a statute gives the force of law to prior interpretation is that it is unreasonable to assume that Congress was familiar with such interpretation unless it verbally or in committee reports indicated familiarity with such 'interpretation.'

G. C. M. 37,405 (Feb. 6, 1978) (citing 1 J. Mertens, Law of Federal Income Taxation § 3.24 (1969)).

Griswold's article[2107] continued to appear after his article,[2108] with some rejections.[2109] The Court tends to state the principle of not drawing an inference from reenactment but explains why it should not apply in a variety of ways, including the ancient status of the regulation and lower court enforcement.[2110] Other specific examples from the Supreme Court include the following:

- Arguably the highest profile tax case in which the Court applied the reenactment doctrine is *Bob Jones University* (which mostly involved Service rulings).[2111] The Court later distinguished it, saying that its facts showed "overwhelming evidence of acquiescence" on account of congressional hearings on the precise issue and 13 failed bills to overturn the Service position.[2112]
- The Supreme Court has applied the "force of law" term to interpretive regulations deemed to have been adopted by legislative reenactment,[2113] and to consolidated return regulations.[2114] Indeed, it is possible that the now defunct *National Muffler* standard for Treasury regulations derives not from an inherent respect for the Treasury but from the happenstance that Treasury regulations related to a set of statutes that Congress reenacted every two years, up to the 1939 Code.
- The Court has stated that repeated reenactment of statutory provisions without significant change constitutes congressional approval of prior longstanding and consistent administrative practice[2115] and administrative interpretations.[2116]
- The same is more true when Congress has legislated in the area and presumably was aware of the regulation but did not change it.[2117]
- The Court ruled that the codification of prior law in the 1954 Code, even when partial or appearing to deviate in various ways from prior law,

2107 *See, e.g.*, Lang v. Commissioner, 304 U.S. 264 (1938); Helvering v. Winmill, 305 U.S. 79 (1938); United States v. Safety Car Heating & Lighting Co., 297 U.S. 88 (1936); Zellerbach Paper Co. v. Helvering, 293 U.S. 172 (1934) (regulations had called returns filed to account for law changes amended returns and Congress relied on that treatment and so the statute of limitations for assessments should run from the original return); Mass. Mut. L. Ins. Co. v. United States, 288 U.S. 269 (1933); United States v. Kirby Lumber Co., 284 U.S. 1 (1931) (agreeing with the regulations that had survived reenactments); Provost v. United States, 269 U.S. 443 (1926).

2108 United States v. Hill, 506 U.S. 546 (1993); United States v. Correll, 389 U.S. 299 (1967); Cammarano v. United States, 358 U.S. 498 (1959); United States v. Leslie Salt Co., 350 U.S. 383 (1956); Corn Prods. Refining Co. v. Commissioner, 350 U.S. 46 (1955).

2109 *See, e.g.*, Commissioner v. Acker, 361 U.S. 87 (1959).

2110 *E.g.*, Cammarano v. United States, 358 U.S. 498 (1959).

2111 Bob Jones Univ. v. United States, 461 U.S. 574, 599-602 (1983).

2112 Solid Waste Agency v. U.S. Army Corps of Engineers, 531 U.S. 159, 169-70 (2001).

2113 Helvering v. R. J. Reynolds Tobacco Co., 306 U.S. 110 (1939).

2114 Old Mission Portland Cement Co. v. Helvering, 293 U.S. 289 (1934).

2115 *See, e.g.*, Fribourg Navigation Co. v. Commissioner, 383 U.S. 272, 283 (1966).

2116 *See* Costle, *Judicial Deference to Interpretive Regulations in the Face of Inconclusive Legislative History: The Example of Nalle v. Commissioner*, 47 TAX LAW. 259 (1993).

2117 *See, e.g.*, Boeing Co. v. United States, 537 U.S. 437 (2003).

could be treated by Treasury as a continuation of prior interpretations;[2118] but the Court gave particular attention to the legislative history of the 1954 Code in discerning a change from prior law.[2119]

- Reenactment did not affirm a Treasury regulation where the Congress would have known that many courts had invalidated the regulation.[2120]
- Reenactment does not preclude the Treasury from changing its interpretation.[2121]
- As a result of the reenactment authorities, the Treasury could not adopt a regulation retroactively changing its long standing regulation when Congress was presumed to have reenacted the law (the definition of income) in light of the prior regulation, even though Congress generally had authorized retroactive regulations.[2122]
- The reenactment doctrine cannot extend to the Service's interpretation of foreign law, to findings of fact by the Service, or to the Service's interpretation of a statute whose meaning is plain on its face.[2123]
- Claims of legislative acquiescence may be extended to lower court rulings, but the Court has stated this is at best only an auxiliary tool for use in interpreting ambiguous statutory provisions.[2124]

Of course the strongest form of reenactment is codification of a regulation. *Wheeler* discussed the codification of a regulation and ruled that showed it was valid all along.[2125]

VI.D.6.c. *Degree of Deference to Interpretation of Regulations, Rulings, and Lesser Published Guidance*

In practice the Supreme Court has not accorded much deference to the Service's interpretation of Treasury regulations, both before and after the

---

[2118] Fulman v. United States, 434 U. S. 528 (1978) (citing cases).

[2119] Commissioner v. Bilder, 369 U.S. 499 (1962) (only travel expenses of the patient are deductible medical expenses).

[2120] Commissioner v. Acker, 361 U.S. 87 (1959).

[2121] Helvering v. Reynolds, 313 U.S. 428 (1941).

[2122] Helvering v. R. J. Reynolds Tobacco Co., 306 U.S. 110 (1939); *see* PAUL, STUDIES III, at 420 (discussing the related cases Helvering v. Wilshire Oil Co., 308 U.S. 90 (1939) and Helvering v. Hallock, 309 U.S. 106 (1940)).

[2123] Biddle v. Commissioner, 302 U.S. 573 (1938).

[2124] Jones v. Liberty Glass Co., 332 U.S. 524 (1947) ("We do not expect Congress to make an affirmative move every time a lower court indulges in an erroneous interpretation.").

[2125] Commissioner v. Wheeler, 324 U.S. 542 (1945).

1984 *Chevron* decision.[2126] However, *Chevron* marked something of a dividing line in the rhetoric of the opinions, and announcements of deference increasingly are made based on *Chevron.*

The Court's principal pre-*Chevron* statement on the issue in a nontax case appeared in *Seminole Rock & Sand,*[2127] ruling that the agency's interpretation of its regulation is controlling unless plainly erroneous or inconsistent with the regulation, which continues to be the standard.[2128] The exceptions for erroneous or inconsistent interpretations potentially raise all of the same issues that arise in statutory interpretation (plain meaning, etc.), but for one major difference. The Treasury, unlike Congress, conducts a continuous interaction with taxpayers in audits, letter rulings, litigation and published guidance; also, as discussed above in Ch. VI.D.6.b., Congress can be deemed to interact with the Service and Treasury interpretations of the Code. This difference explains why in pre-*Chevron* tax opinions the Court frequently linked some version of the *Seminole* presumption of deference with the fact that the Treasury interpretation had been consistent over a period of years.[2129]

[2126] *See, e.g.,* United Dominion Industries, Inc. v. United States, 532 U.S. 822 (2001) (rejected Service's interpretation of consolidated return regulation); Commissioner v. Schleier, 515 U.S. 323, 336 n.8 (1995) (similar to *Bartels, infra,* referring both to interpretation of the regulation and the statute); Newark Morning Ledger Co. v. United States, 507 U.S. 546 (1993) (the Court disregarded decades of Service interpretation of its regulation forbidding the depreciation of goodwill to rule that the exclusion did not encompass customer lists of newspapers, because they fit what the Court ruled to be the broader definition of depreciable assets); United States v. Am. College of Physicians, 475 U.S. 834 (1986) (rejecting government's contentions about Treasury's intention in words of UBIT regulation); United States v. Hughes Properties, Inc., 476 U.S. 593 (1986) (overruled the Service interpretation of the Treasury regulation); Bartels v. Birmingham, 332 U.S. 126, 132 (1947) (interpretations published in the Cumulative Bulletin of regulations did not have the force and effect of a Treasury Decision).

[2127] Bowles v. Seminole Rock & Sand Co., 325 U.S. 410, 414 (1945); *see also* Ford Motor Credit Co. v. Milhollin, 444 U.S. 555, 566 (1980) ("[a]n agency's construction of its own regulations has been regarded as especially due [considerable respect]"); Coverdale, *Chevron's Reduced Domain, supra* note 2033, at 90 (discussed the doctrine of Bowles v. Seminole Rock & Sand Co., 325 U.S. 410 (1945)).

[2128] Coeur Alaska, Inc. v. Se. Alaska Conservation Council, 557 U.S. 261,, 275 (2009); Chase Bank USA, N.A. v. McCoy, 562 U.S. 195 (2011).

[2129] *See, e.g.,* Jewett v. Commissioner, 455 U.S. 305, 318 (1982); United States v. Swank, 451 U.S. 571(1981); Nat'l Muffler Dealers Assn., Inc. v. United States, 440 U.S. 472, 484 (1979)("The regulation has stood for 50 years, and the Commissioner infrequently but consistently has interpreted it to exclude an organization like the Association that is not industry-wide. The Commissioner's view therefore merits serious deference."); *cf.* Helvering v. Owens, 305 U.S. 468 (1939) (which stated that the Treasury had vacillated and adopted the approach the Treasury finally adopted in regulations). But the proliferation of government interpretation of a regulation may cause it problems when the interpretations are inconsistent. *See* Robinson Knife Mfg. Co. v. Commissioner, 600 F.3d 121 (2d Cir. 2010) (n. 11 notes that the agency brief is not the only interpretation).

The possibility or degree of deference has received increased attention since the 1984 decision in *Chevron*.[2130] In several nontax opinions post-*Chevron*, the Court has accorded deference to government interpretations of regulations in essentially the same way as *Seminole Rock*,[2131] including deference to the agency's interpretation of its own regulations in a legal brief filed in the instant action and to internal memoranda of the agency.[2132] But the Court rejected the Service's interpretation of the consolidated return regulations, which are legislative regulations.[2133] Such rejection may be easier when neither the Treasury nor the Service has issued a prior interpretation of a Code section but only develops a view in response to a taxpayer's position; such rejection can occur even as to the most arcane matters.[2134] But it rejected another interpretation as simply overreach.[2135]

Therefore, even though *Chevron* may now be cited to support deference to Service interpretation of Treasury regulations, it is hard to say that the advent of *Chevron* deference changed much in the field of deference to government interpretation of Treasury regulations. Indeed, the Supreme Court sometimes applies the Administrative Procedure Act deference (arbitrary or capricious) to the agency's interpretation of its own regulations.[2136] The Court has stated that the Administrative Procedure Act standard of arbitrary or capricious is the same as the *Chevron* standard.[2137] The Court proceeds directly to the APA standard when there is no question of statutory ambiguity, but rather the statute grants administrative discretion.[2138]

Of course the interpretation of regulations most often appears in revenue rulings. In post-*Chevron* tax opinions, the Court has declined to engage in a deference rating analysis of rulings, but nevertheless accorded them some weight in conjunction with the regulations they interpret and reenactment

---

[2130] *See* Coverdale, *Chevron's Reduced Domain, supra* note 2033, at 76, 78 (stating that the Supreme Court has never granted Chevron deference to a Revenue Ruling); Vasquez & Lowy, *Judicial Deference for Revenue Rulings in a Post-Mead World*, 6 J. TAX PRAC. AND PROC. 27 (2005).

[2131] *See, e.g.*, Long Is. Care at Home Ltd. v. Coke, 551 U.S. 158 (2007); Auer v. Robbins, 519 U.S. 452 (1997) (holding that an agency's interpretation of its own regulations is "controlling unless plainly erroneous or inconsistent with the regulation" (internal quotation marks omitted)).

[2132] *Long Is. Care at Home Ltd.*, 551 U.S. at 158 (unless plainly erroneous or inconsistent with the regulation being interpreted); *Auer*, 519 U.S. at 452.

[2133] United Dominion Industries, Inc. v. United States, 532 U.S. 822 (2001) (rejected Service's interpretation of consolidated return regulation).

[2134] *See, e.g., United Dominion Industries, Inc.*, 532 U.S. at 822; Gitlitz v. Commissioner, 531 U.S. 206 (2001) (not viewing a regulation as applicable).

[2135] United States v. Am. College of Physicians, 475 U.S. 834 (1986) (declining to let the import of one Example change the regulation's stated rule).

[2136] Thomas Jefferson Univ. v. Shalala, 512 U.S. 504, 512 (1994).

[2137] Judulang v. Holder, 132 S. Ct. 476 (2011) (at note 7).

[2138] *Id.*

by Congress.[2139] The Court has analogized this to *Skidmore* deference.[2140] And the revenue rulings that are given some deference may not be interpreting a regulation but the statute itself.[2141] The Court avoided the issue in *Quality Stores*, even though a professor filed an amicus brief to argue that revenue rulings have the "force of law" and are not issued with notice and hearing and so should be ignored; instead the Court basically enforced the position of the rulings, without discussing deference.[2142]

For compilation of cases invalidating and upholding Treasury regulations, see Ch. VI.D.3., above.

VI.D.6.d. *Proof of Nonarbitrariness*

Although the APA standard for regulations is relatively low, a regulation can be found to be arbitrary or capricious if the agency has no explanation for adopting the regulation.[2143] The opinions cited for this principle were either contemporaneous with or predated *Chevron*, but several post-*Chevron* opinions of the Court have relied on *State Farm*. Therefore, until the Court says otherwise, types of arbitrariness described in *State Farm* could be applied as standards; after all, if the *Chevron* standard is going to be just arbitrariness, that has to mean something definable.

That standard can raise additional questions about how such evidence should be memorialized (the administrative record), and whether after the fact explanations count, and when is a factual basis for a regulation relevant. This is unexplored territory for Treasury regulations in the Supreme Court, but can be expected to become contested.[2144] It provides a trap for the unwary agency that believes some points are obvious and fails to document them.

[2139] *See* United States v. Cleveland Indians Baseball Co., 532 U.S. 200, 220 (2001) ("We need not decide whether the Revenue Rulings themselves are entitled to deference. In this case, the Rulings simply reflect the agency's longstanding interpretation of its own regulations. Because that interpretation is reasonable, it attracts substantial judicial deference."); Commissioner v. Schleier, 515 U.S. 323, n. 8 (1995) (". . . we note that 'the Service's interpretive rulings do not have the force and effect of regulations,' Davis v. United States, . . . , and they may not be used to overturn the plain language of a statute. *See, e.g.*, Bartels v. Birmingham . . .").

[2140] Christensen v. Harris County, 529 U.S. 576, 587 (2000). But a statement by an individual before becoming an agency employee is not entitled to any deference. United States v. Wells Fargo Bank, 485 U.S. 351 (chief economist).

[2141] Davis v. United States, 495 U.S. 472 (1990) (considerable weight when they involve contemporaneous construction and have been in long use).

[2142] United States v. Quality Stores, Inc., 134 S. Ct. 1395 (2014).

[2143] *See* Motor Vehicle Mfrs. Assn. v. State Farm Mut. Auto. Ins. Co., 463 U.S. 29 (1983); Chenery I, 318 U.S. 80 (1943); Chenery II, 332 U.S. 194 (1947). *See* Murphy, Chenery *Unmasked: Reasonable Limits on the Duty to Give Reasons*, 80 U. Cin. L. Rev. 817 (2011). Legislative rule making is somewhat confusingly called informal rule making. *Id.* at 839.

[2144] *See* Cummings, *Holding Treasury to Its Word:* Altera *and Capricious Regulations*, 149 Tax Notes (TA) 519 (2015).

VI.D.6.e. *The Politics of Deference*

The politics of Chevron deference is peculiar and has not been much noted in the literature focusing on jurisprudence, political science, and the theories of administrative law.[2145] Justice John Paul Stevens wrote Chevron for a unanimous court of six (lacking Justices Thurgood Marshall, William H. Rehnquist, and Sandra Day O'Connor), giving deference to a regulation and holding in favor of Chevron Oil against an environmental group that thought the regulation was too lax and unauthorized.[2146] That is, in Chevron (1984) the interests of the administrator and the regulated industry happened to coincide, and you might say that the Reagan administration won through Chevron deference. The next major Chevron landmark is Mead (2001), an opinion written by Justice David H. Souter for all but Scalia.[2147] The holding is thought to have expanded the potential for deference in a case of little practical consequence (in contrast to Chevron),[2148] but Scalia, in dissent, believed it had limited deference.

Then Thomas wrote Brand X (2005), indicating that a regulation could reverse a court interpretation and approving a fairly arbitrary regulatory distinction between different types of cable services. Scalia dissented with Souter and Ginsburg joining in part. The case involved an intense intra-industry fight in a big wealthy industry over a Bush-era regulation that Thomas upheld.

In Home Concrete, we now find the Republican appointed Justices beginning to coalesce against deference, even to a regulation written by the Bush administration; the Democratic appointed Justices mostly coalescing around a theory of administrative law and political science;[2149] and Scalia went his own way as usual. This emerging pattern may suggest that it is dawning on the Republican-appointed justices that they have no policy reason (aside from the happenstance of which administration is in office) to promote the executive branch over the representative Congress and the courts themselves.[2150] As proof, in 2015 the conservative columnist George F. Will noticed the reaction against Chevron deference, which he attributed to Justice Thomas' concern about institutional separation.[2151]

[2145] However, see Beermann, Chevron *at the Roberts Court: Still Failing after All These Years Symposium:* Chevron *at 30: Looking Back and Looking Forward*, 83 FORDHAM L. REV. 731 (2014) (finding a slight but not significant tilt away from *Chevron* in the Roberts group).

[2146] *Chevron*, 467 U.S. 837.

[2147] *Mead*, 533 U.S. 218.

[2148] It involved the tariff on day timers. In contrast, many states filed amicus briefs in *Chevron*.

[2149] "Our legal system presumes there will be continuing dialogue among the three branches of Government on questions of statutory interpretation and application." *Home Concrete*, 132 S. Ct. at 1852.

[2150] For example, Chief Justice Roberts expressed discomfort with the growth of agency power in *City of Arlington v. FCC*, 133 S. Ct. 1863 (2013).

[2151] George F. Will, *Standing Athwart the Administrative State*, THE NEWS AND OBSERVER, 16A (Nov. 30, 2015).

That view also happens to be institutionally conservative in that it preserves the Courts' historic role of saying what the law is. It did not hurt that the result in Home Concrete was both pro-taxpayer and against a somewhat sneaky attempt by the government to bootstrap its litigating position in a pending case by adopting a retroactive regulation after sitting on its hands for 50 years. If Treasury does not understand the perils of this kind of conduct, it is tone-deaf. At least where the federal government is concerned, winning tax shelter cases does not justify just any conduct, particularly when you don't win.

Finally, Mayo was the rare tax case in which Chevron deference was applied.[2152] On the surface it appears to be a large shift of power to the administrator, but it is not. It leaves the Court with complete discretion to say, yes, we know what the statute means. And only if the Court chooses not to do that, and finds ambiguity, need it allow deference, but then the deference is fairly unconstrained. The finding of ambiguity or not in the statute remains within the sole control of the courts.

The most recent opinions of the Court referring to Chevron do not reflect a feeling that it has limited the judicial authority of at least the Supreme Court.[2153] When relied on to uphold agency action, the Justices involved are most likely to be Democratic appointed.[2154]

VI.E. Fact Finding: as Applied to the Code and as Peculiar to the Code

This book undertakes to show that the two (and only two) core legal processes—standard statutory interpretation and construction, and fact finding—can, when properly applied, explain all court decisions on federal taxation that may appear to apply rules peculiar to tax, except for those cases decided under the economic substance doctrine (which usually functions as a lower-court-generated positive rule of law). This subchapter addresses the second of the two standard processes: fact finding. Experienced lawyers know that cases more often turn on the finding of facts than on the interpretation of law.[2155] Obviously the facts that need to be found are dictated by interpretation and construction of the statute. For example, Ch. V.E.1.c. on Usury shows how the law of usury was construed to require liberal fact findings to show the existence of loans and heavy interest where neither existed in form. No less should that occur in tax, as discussed in Ch. V.E.

Fact finding is not a popular subject in the tax law,[2156] probably because it is hard to do and tax professionals would much rather work with the law (until litigation occurs). Indeed, the unpopularity of fact finding is just another way

---

2152 Mayo Found. for Med. Educ. & Research v. United States, 562 U.S. 44 (2011).

2153 Mellouli v. Lynch, 135 S. Ct. 1980 (rejected on agency interpretation because it made "scant sense").

2154 Scialabba v. De Osorio, 134 S. Ct. 2191 (2014).

2155 *See* Speiser v. Randall, 357 U.S. 513 (1958).

2156 *Cf.* Fuller, *Business Purpose*, *supra* note 762, at 335 (examining private law fact finding).

in which the tax law is more like the general law than is usually thought: it is surprising that even Justice Holmes said, "I hate facts."[2157] The tax doctrines applied to what are thought to be tax shelters tend to rely on hard to prove facts, such as intent; it is typical for an opinion in such a case to start with pages of seemingly irrelevant detail about how educated the taxpayer was, what good advice he did or did not receive, and what tax scheme he intended to carry out. This subchapter addresses the standard fact finding methodologies most typically applied in tax cases. It shows that observing case clusters, or poles around which fact finding methods cluster, is a more useful methodology for resolving doubtful cases than attempting to create universal rules.

Justice Brandeis captured the essence of the fact finding problem when he said:

> . . . in the investigation of the facts the lawyer differs very materially from the scientist or the scholar. The lawyer's investigations into the facts are limited by time and space. His investigations have reference always to some practical end. Unlike the scientist, he ordinarily cannot refuse to reach a conclusion on the ground that he lacks the facts sufficient to enable one to form an opinion. He must form an opinion from those facts which he has gathered; he must reason from the facts within his grasp.[2158]

Justice Cardozo, however, reminds us of the duty to find hard facts in tax cases:

> The mind rebels against the notion that Congress . . . was willing to foster an opportunity for juggling so facile and so obvious. . . . To such an attempt the reaction of an impartial mind is little short of instinctive that the deduction is unreasonable . . . .[2159]

Of course, it is often a legal question whether a tax case is to turn on fact finding or statutory interpretation (including applying the statute to undisputed facts). Therefore, for example, while the Court might think that strike benefits paid to union members are income under the Code, if the issue goes to a jury as a fact question and the jury decides the benefits are a nontaxable gift, the Court will affirm.[2160]

The Federal Rules of Evidence apply to all federal tax disputes, including disputes in the Tax Court.[2161]

[2157] Tushnet, *The Logic of Experience: Oliver Wendell Holmes on the Supreme Judicial Court,* 63 VA. L. REV. 965, 979 n. 12 (1977) (quoting Holmes-Pollock letters).

[2158] BRANDEIS, THE OPPORTUNITY IN THE LAW, "BUSINESS—A PROFESSION," 332 (1933).

[2159] Woolford Realty Co. v. Rose, 286 U.S. 319, 330 (1932).

[2160] *See* United States v. Kaiser, 363 U.S. 299 (1960).

[2161] *See* LARSON, TAX EVIDENCE, *supra* note 1024; *supra* Ch. V.E.1.d. (discussing the parol evidence rule).

VI.E.1. *Substance and Form*

VI.E.1.a. *Substance and Form Outside of Tax Law*

Many of the maxims of equity emphasize reliance on finding substance and not relying solely on form, as discussed in Ch. V.E. This equitable origin is not peculiar to the tax law,[2162] and even older evidence shows it is not peculiar to law.[2163] In tax cases, equitable fact finding frequently involves piecing together steps that might seem unconnected. The sampling below from a variety of areas of the law reflects rules of evidence, equity maxims and rules specific to the legal issues involved. They have in common the inherent and traditional ability of the law (both law and equity) to look beyond form and in many cases to employ an integration of multiple steps in order to apply the law to facts properly. The purpose of reviewing them here is to reinforce the point that tax law is not "special" when it looks to substance:

- Tort law—negligence: The core concept of proximate cause is a step transaction concept that links together a chain of events that can make an actor liable for damages at the end of the chain based on reasonable foreseeability.[2164]
- Contract law—entirety of the contract: Many principles and doctrines allow what is in form an unconditional promise to be made conditional or dependent on mutuality;[2165] the courts allowed multiple writings to be combined under a variety of circumstances showing their integration into one contract;[2166] the substance, not the form, of a private contract

[2162] *See, e.g.*, Paulsen v. Commissioner, 469 U.S. 131 (1985) (the opinion stated that in construing the securities laws in SEC v. W.J. Howey Co., 329 U.S. 293, 301 (1946), and similarly in the case at hand, the Court examined the economic substance and not just the formal terms of a contract to determine if it was a security, although different tests might be applied).

[2163] For example in the 27th chapter of Genesis, Jacob got his father's blessing by wearing a hairy coat and so seeming to be hairy like his brother, who was supposed to get the blessing. Thus form prevailed over substance (and there was no undoing the blessing when the truth came out). But in the 22nd chapter of Genesis God found the substance of obedience to God was present in Abraham's willingness to sacrifice his son Isaac, so God did not demand the form of the sacrifice: substance prevailed over form. The 21st chapter of Exodus gives several examples of how culpability would not result from damage alone without the necessary purpose, intent or knowledge linking an earlier act (leaving the bull unfenced, etc.); thus steps were linked based on the actor's purpose. Genesis 18:16-33 shows that economic substance was not God's standard, because he was willing to spare Sodom if only 10 righteous men could be found there (down from the original requirement of 50); thus economic substance is not the only determinant of substance. And sometimes form controls, period: circumcision was required of the Jewish males in Genesis 17.

[2164] *See* HILLIARD, THE LAW OF TORTS 94 (Little Brown 1859) (referring to a chain of events case); Palsgraf v. Long Island R.R., 248 N.Y. 339 (1928) is the standard cite for this doctrine.

[2165] *See* PARSONS, *supra* note 172, at Vol. 1, Part II, Ch. 1.

[2166] *See* WILLISTON, LAW GOVERNING SALES OF GOODS AT COMMON LAW AND UNDER THE UNIFORM SALES ACT §§ 107-111 (Baker, Voorhis 1909).

determines its meaning.[2167] Randolph Paul discussed how the doctrine was used in the identification of a "contract" for tax purposes.[2168]

- Contract law—consideration: The common law required consideration to support a contract and tried to straddle a line between having to evaluate whether the consideration on both sides of the contract was of equal value, and allowing purely formal consideration to control; courts of equity would not enforce a contract with purely formal consideration; courts of law required some real value in the consideration.[2169]
- Contract law—performance: The common law required substantial performance and not a "mere literally accurate performance."[2170]
- Contract law—consequential damages: A plaintiff can recover consequential damages from breach of contract when the damages are sufficiently linked to the breach.[2171]
- The Uniform Commercial Code codifies many such principles of contract law that can have tax effects: a lease may be a security instrument (UCC § 1-203); a sale that is unconditional in form may be a security transaction (UCC § 2-102); a contract does not have to be contained in a single document and can be evidenced by unwritten rules (UCC § 2-103 (definition of "record") and §§ 2-106, 2-201, 204, 207 (contract)); even negotiable instruments can be comprised of multiple documents part of the same transaction (UCC § 3-117).
- Criminal law—*mens rea*: The core maxim of the criminal law in England was *actus non facit reum nisi mens sit rea*, meaning an act does not make a person guilty unless their mind is also guilty.[2172]
- Wills—satisfaction of gift: A devise in a will need not be effectuated after death if the testator has satisfied it by gift during life.[2173]
- Real property—statute of frauds: The statute of frauds required written evidence of a trust in land, but the absence of a writing did not prevent the formation of such trusts and a writing could later evidence the earlier formation of a trust.[2174]
- Real property—evidence of title: Title to real property could be proved by a variety of methods ranging from pure substance (seizin) to pure form (written deed).[2175]

[2167] Heryford v. Davis, 102 U.S. 235 (1880).

[2168] PAUL, STUDIES II, at 232-35.

[2169] *See* PARSONS, *supra* note 172, at Vol. 1, 436 *et seq.*

[2170] *See id.* at Vol. 2, 656 *et seq.*; Levin, *The Substantial Compliance Doctrine*, *supra* note 1043 at 1605 *et seq.*; Chouest, *supra* note 1043, at 269.

[2171] Hadley v. Baxendale, 9 Exch. 341 (1854) (the standard cite for this doctrine).

[2172] STEPHEN, HISTORY OF THE CRIMINAL LAW OF ENGLAND 94, Vol. II (Macmillan 1883).

[2173] BIGELOW, LAW OF WILLS FOR STUDENTS 370 (Boston 1898).

[2174] REEVES, TREATISE ON THE LAW OF REAL PROPERTY, Vol. 1, 436 (Little Brown 1909).

[2175] BURTON, ELEMENTARY COMPENDIUM OF THE LAW OF REAL PROPERTY, § 7 (Littell 1839) ("Of Evidence of Title to Land in Fee Simple.").

- Real property—equity of redemption: Even though a mortgage has been foreclosed and the mortgagee is in possession, the mortgagor had the right to redeem the property for 20 years, an equitable right.[2176]
- The concept of rebate ties a refund of part of a purchase price with the accurate determination of the price.

A powerful proof of substance over form from the Supreme Court in the commercial law area is Justice Holmes' opinion in *Rankin*.[2177] The receiver of a plaintiff bank sued to recover a $30,000 deposit in the defendant bank. The deposit was the proceeds of a borrowing from defendant bank ostensibly by the plaintiff's president on plaintiff's behalf. The president and the lending bank had made a side agreement that the deposit could not be drawn upon. The arrangement was designed to make the plaintiff bank appear to have $30,000 more assets than it had, to fool the bank examiner. The Court determined that the plaintiff never had any right to the deposit. Justice Holmes relied entirely on the state commercial law to see through the subterfuge: "If the Guthrie bank had sued . . . it could not have recovered, . . ." The *Rankin* decision would have come out the same way on the same reasoning if it had been a tax case about a deduction for any interest the plaintiff might have claimed it paid on the "loan." Justice Holmes stated that even though the plaintiff bank had an account in its name in the defendant bank as the result of a purported loan (through the agency of its president), "as between the banks no one got any money." In other words, substance prevailed over form as a matter of normal commercial litigation fact finding.

An earlier case argued in the Supreme Court by Francis Scott Key showed the Court looking through a similar artifice to find that a ship captured as a prize of war was not owned by Russians, as purportedly shown by a document (in form), but was probably English (and thus subject to capture).[2178] One of the facts on which the Court relied was that the purported Russian owner "never exercised a single act of ownership over the vessel." This approach dating from 1816 is perfectly congruent with the fact finding that occurs in tax cases today when the court asks who really acted as if they owned the property or ran the business.[2179] This is not a tax-specific fact finding methodology, nor does it reflect a special construction of the Code; it is a normal fact finding process based on common sense understanding of what statutes mean in general.Congress surely knew the ability of the courts of law and

[2176] *Id.* at 209; Peugh v. Davis, 96 U.S. 332 (1878) (equity will treat a deed absolute on its face as a mortgage); *see* discussion of *F. & R. Lazarus supra* Ch. V.E.1.f(2).

[2177] Rankin v. City Nat'l Bank, 208 U.S. 541 (1908) (the opinion refers to the "first step of the transaction").

[2178] The St. Nicholas-Meyer, et al. claimants, 14 U.S. 417 (1816).

[2179] *See, e.g.*, Roubik v. Commissioner, 53 T.C. 365, 381 (1969) ("Nor do we think that the corporation was ever, as a practical matter, given the right to direct any of its "employees" in their professional activities.").

equity to determine the substance of a matter, when it enacted the tax laws, and assumed the courts would apply those tools.

VI.E.1.b. *Tax Law; Nomenclature*

In 1978 Yale tax law professor Boris Bittker wrote that 50 years earlier an author had written that form and substance were "the most overworked words in the tax vocabulary" and the same could be proved in 1978.[2180] It it true today. Several terms swirl around the substance versus form confusion: "substance versus form," "step transaction doctrine," "economic substance," "economic substance doctrine," "business purpose," and "business purpose doctrine." They fit together as follows:

- A system of statutory rules applicable to financial events (like a tax law) necessarily operates on the forms of those events, but generally assumes that common sense and common meaning of common words and terms will be applied to determine if the *substance* of a thing or event or transaction, rather than its legal or commercial *form*, complies with an applicable requirement of the rules.[2181]
- In such cases the relevant substance is the *economic substance*; the focus of the tax law on money tends to require that economics inform the variety of substance that is relevant.[2182]
- The proper goal of such resort to substance in tax cases is to strive toward *uniformity* by taxing like things in a like manner, nationwide.[2183] In effect, this is the same reason that substance over form is a principle of equity, so that the seeker of equitable relief can be treated equally with everyone else.
- Hence, statements in court opinions that the *substance not the form* of transactions controls the tax results should be understood as made in the context of normal fact finding; such statements in income tax cases first arose when the Supreme Court was trying to identify income.[2184]
- Even though discussed here as a fact finding issue, the dominance of *substance over form* almost always is preceded, implicitly or explicitly, by a statutory interpretation that Congress did not intend for form to control

---

[2180] Bittker, *Pervasive Judicial Doctrines in the Construction of the Internal Revenue Code*, 21 How. L.J. 693, 703 (1978), quoting Underwood, *Form and Substance in Tax Cases*, 16 Va. L. Rev. 327 (1930).

[2181] *See, e.g.*, Diedrich v. Commissioner, 457 U.S. 191 (1982) (when donee pays donor's gift tax it has economically benefited donor and converted the gift into a part sale).

[2182] *Cf.* United States v. Byrum, 408 U.S. 125 (1972) (holding that retention of stock voting rights was not the sort of economic benefit with which the law was concerned).

[2183] *See* Reiling, *supra* note 26, at 567 (author was Assistant Chief Counsel of the Service).

[2184] *Id.* (because income may arise from a variety of means, substance not form must control its determination); *see supra* Ch. II.B.2.c(3).

for purposes of the particular provision at issue;[2185] but in many cases Congress does intend for form to control, or has no intent one way or the other, and that is the root cause of the substance/form problems.[2186]

- One common sense tool applied to categorize events for the purpose of statutes like the Code is to collapse multiple steps into one event, to better identify the substance of a multi-step event, from beginning to end;[2187] this is called the *step transaction doctrine* analysis.
- Such collapsing, and other tools used to identify substance not revealed by form, frequently rely on evaluating a participant's purpose or intent, most often the *business purpose* or lack thereof in income tax cases, both when the statute requires a business purpose,[2188] and when the taxpayer's purpose informs what it did (just as Congress' purpose can inform the words of the statute); sometimes the Service or a court gets carried away and asserts a *business purpose doctrine*, which purports to require a business purpose for all favorable tax results; those requirements tended to coalesce into the *economic substance doctrine*.
- Although *substance versus form* issues can arise in any area of tax (for example, such issues in the estate and gift area were very contentious in the first half of the 20th century), most of the more recent substance versus form tax disputes involve the income tax and business taxpayers (corporations and partnerships), or at least ostensible profit making transactions; such businesses and transactions are normally pursued for profit making purposes, of which saving taxes is certainly one, but is thought to be a suspect purpose if it is the only purpose (see discussion in Ch. II.C.1. of the "natural state" of taxpayer conduct without regard to taxes, to which the tax law can be applied as written, as contrasted with tax reduction conduct, which is thought to require doctrines like the *economic substance doctrine*, or at least more strict scrutiny of facts and law).
- Confusion necessarily results from the fact that sometimes form must control in the application of rules to events, either because (1) that is the default rule, or (2) that is all we have to go on as a practical matter, or (3) that is what Congress intended (as for example entities formed as corporations are generally respected as separate taxpayers despite their total dominance by other taxpayers).

2185 *See, e.g.,* Bingler v. Johnson, 394 U.S. 741 (1969) (ruling that nominal "scholarships" were not the type of scholarships intended for exemption by section 117); Haynes v. United States, 353 U.S. 81 (1957) (exemption for "health insurance" depended first on interpretation of the statute and second on analysis of the substance of the payments provided to the taxpayer).

2186 See Ch. II.B.2.c(3) discussing *Isham.*; also, for example, form controlled in *Cottage Savings*, though to a lesser extent.

2187 *See, e.g.,* Commissioner v. Jacobson, 336 U.S. 28, 40 (1949) (when a debtor discharges an obligation by paying the debt of the creditor, the tax law treats the creditor as receiving the payment).

2188 *See* Gregory v. Helvering, 293 U.S. 465 (1935) (there was no purpose to reorganize a corporation and so there was no reorganization).

This summary shows that the tax specific doctrines should be fact finding approaches that would be common to all statutes and terms in common usage, such as ownership, debt obligation, and interest. Although terms used in the Code do not necessarily have the same meaning for tax purposes as they have generally, to the large extent they share the common meanings, and they are subject to the common law courts' ability to discern that a pig with a tail is not a horse.

To the extent it is correct to say that substance generally controls over form, that means that the norm for tax rules is to include an assumption of common sense fact finding. That does not deny the rule of law but rather fulfillsit. For example, in the Supreme Court's decision in *Hansen*,[2189] the issue was who borrowed money and the Court applied standard fact finding methods to determine that fact; as a result the Court held the taxpayer to its form but the opinion is commonly cited nevertheless as a substance over form authority.[2190]

VI.E.1.b(1) *Origins and Overview*

The question of form versus substance in tax usually asks whether private law characterizations (meaning labels applied by the parties) control tax outcomes.[2191] NYU Law School Professor Harvey P. Dale said "substance controls form all of the time in the tax law . . . except when it doesn't." The challenge is to tell when it doesn't, which involves one or more of these three factors:

1. The ubiquitous assertion that substance controls puts the emphasis in exactly the wrong place.[2192] The initial presumption of the tax law must be that form controls because (a) the statute generally is written with respect to forms, (b) forms are congruent with substance most of the time—that is why they exist, and (c) the tax system could not operate if form were not the default determinant.
2. The correctly identified starting presumption that form controls gives way to two opposing principles: (a) the ability of the common law to look past form to substance, which most frequently has occurred in tax in

---

[2189] Commissioner v. Hansen, 360 U.S. 446 (1959).

[2190] *See, e.g.*, Exche. Sec. Bank v. United States, 492 F.2d 1096 (5th Cir. 1974).

[2191] *See* INT'L FISCAL ASSOC., FORM AND SUBSTANCE IN TAX LAW, *supra* note 114, at 23. *See also Treasury White Paper on Corporate Tax Shelters*, *supra* note 14, at sec. IV.B.1; *Symposium on Business Purpose, Economic Substance and Corporate Tax Shelters*, 54 SMU L. REV. (2001) (containing 11 papers).

[2192] For examples of the ease with which the Treasury asserts that substance controls form, see Reg. §§ 1.355-6(c)(3)(i) ("This paragraph (c)(3) does not affect the determination of whether an instrument is an option or stock under general principles of tax law (such as substance over form."); 1.382-4(d)(9)(v) (same); *cf.* United States v. Williams, 514 U.S. 527 (1995) (where the Court described its opinion in another case as choosing "substance over form," but not stating that such was always the right result; the issue was who was paying taxes when a business collected the taxes from its customers and the Court found the customers to be taxpayers).

cluster areas such as sale-leaseback, assignment of income, loans, etc., and (b) the tax specific principle that state law labels cannot finally control federal tax outcomes, for a variety of reasons.[2193]

3. The decisions that promote substance over form sometimes do so on the basis of common law and equity methods (for example, *F. & R. Lazarus*, involving a sale and leaseback, treated as a loan[2194]), and sometimes do so on the basis of an interpretation of the Code to require a unique factual standard be met, which cannot be determined simply based on common law terminology (for example, ownership for depreciation purposes requires an equity investment).

Unfortunately, tax practitioners and generalist federal judges have taken to viewing the applications in tax cases of traditional fact finding methods as special (sometimes called "tax exceptionalism"). This has led, for example, to the conversion of the relevance of economic substance from a fact finding method to a "doctrine" of substantive law: the economic substance doctrine (See Ch. V.F.). Substance versus form matters have become more confused in the tax law than in other areas of the law for several reasons, including:

- The narrow specialization of tax professionals;
- The relatively greater specificity of the tax law, which promotes the view that forms should have more dominance in fact finding;
- The tendency to replace cluster approaches to specific factual questions with the economic substance doctrine; and
- The predominance of entities, whose reality as separate taxpayers as contrasted with agents has been a core problem of form in the tax law.

The substance over form approach to the income tax is a fact finding approach whose origins as discussed in Ch. II.B.2.c(3) in cases like *Eisner v. Macomber* belie both its current ubiquity and its current application almost exclusively against taxpayers. Before the Civil War, the Supreme Court applied the principle of substance over form to determine the real object of a property tax. For example, *McCulloch v. Maryland* ruled a state tax on the notes of the Bank of the United States to be a tax on the United States.[2195] Before the 1913 income tax was adopted, the statement and concept that "it is the substance and not the form which controls" was used in the taxpayer's favor in an infamous Supreme Court decision that has since been repudiated and roundly condemned: *Pollock v. Farmers' Loan & Trust Co.*[2196] The Court

---

[2193] *See infra* Ch. VI.E.2.

[2194] *See supra* Ch. V.E.1.f(2).

[2195] McCulloch v. Maryland, 17 U.S. 316 (1819). The same principle was applied in other intergovernmental tax immunity decisions. *E.g.*, Collector v. Day, 78 U.S. 113 (1871), and was not abandoned until the 1940s. *See* CUMMINGS, CONSTITUTION. Similarly, the Court ruled that a state tax on imports was not a tax on occupations. Brown v. Maryland, 25 U.S. 419 (1827) ("this is varying the form, without varying the substance.").

[2196] Pollock v. Farmers' Loan & Trust Co., 157 U.S. 429, 581, *modified*, 158 U.S. 601 (1895); *see* BURNS, *supra* note 159, at 109-11.

ruled that the tax on the corporation's income was in substance a tax on its land and therefore unconstitutional as an unapportioned direct tax. Similarly in *Fairbank* in the same era the Court struck down a stamp tax on bills of lading on the ground that in substance they were impermissible taxes on exports.[2197] However, by rephrasing the same economic exaction as an tax on the corporate privilege, Congress enabled the 1909 federal corporate income tax to escape the fate of the *Pollock* decision.[2198]

These pre-1913 opinions were precursors of early Supreme Court decisions under the 1913 income tax like *Macomber, Southern Pacific*, and *Turrish*, which applied substance over form in taxpayers' favor in the process of trying to define the amorphous concept of income (principally for constitutional purposes) and whether it was earned before or after the constitutional cut off date of 1913.[2199] The Supreme Court explained this origin in *Weiss v. Stearn*, also a taxpayer victory, which became the most often cited source of the substance over form concept:

> *Eisner v. Macomber*, . . . gave great consideration to the nature of income and stock dividends. It pointed out that, within the meaning of the Sixteenth Amendment, income from capital is gain severed therefrom and received by the taxpayer for his separate use; that the interest of the stockholder is a capital one, and stock certificates but evidence of it; . . . The conclusion was that, "having regard to the very truth of the matter, to substance and not to form, he has received nothing that answers the definition of income within the meaning of the Sixteenth Amendment."[2200]

Similarly, the Court stated in *Kerbaugh-Empire*, also a seminal early decision on the breadth of the concept of income and also ruling for the taxpayer: "In determining what constitutes income substance rather than form is to be given controlling weight (citing *Macomber*)."[2201] The Court's early invocations of substance clearly were not part of an anti-taxpayer reading of the Code that denied to taxpayers the right to rely on the Code as written. Rather, they were

---

[2197] Fairbank v. United States, 181 U.S. 283 (1901) (Justice Harlan dissented, joined by three other Justices). That the maxim was going down in defeat as a protector of taxpayers is reflected by its use in dissent by Justice Sutherland in *Bromley v. McCaughn*, 280 U.S. 124 (1929).

[2198] Flint v. Stone Tracy Co., 220 U.S. 107 (1909).

[2199] Eisner v. Macomber, 252 U.S. 189 (1920) (the Court similarly disregarded the form of a stock dividend and said that in substance the shareholder got nothing of value; but the Court then relied on form by treating the legal skin of the corporation as preventing the passage of its income to its shareholders); Lynch v. Turrish, 247 U.S. 221 (1918) (the form of a corporate liquidation after 1913 could not mask the substance of the increase in value of the corporation as having occurred before 1913); S. Pac. Co. v. Lowe, 247 U.S. 330 (1918) (the Court found that a post-1913 dividend from a controlled subsidiary was actually pre-1913 income of the parent corporation, and thus not taxable, because in substance the parent earned the income of its subsidiary before 1913 and the dividend was post-1913 income only as a matter of form).

[2200] Weiss v. Stearn, 265 U.S. 242 (1924). *See also* United States v. Phellis, 257 U.S. 156 (1921) (recognizing the importance of substance in relation to form).

[2201] Bowers v. Kerbaugh-Empire Co., 271 U.S. 170 (1926)

part of an effort to supply meaning to the amorphous constitutional concept of income. That is a cluster area, albeit hugely important in an income tax. In addition, these early grand pronouncements about substance and form are basically pronouncements about the importance of the facts, not statements of additional rules of law peculiar to the Code. For example, Justice Black wrote the opinions in both *Court Holding Co.*[2202] (a frequently cited substance over form authority) and *Cumberland Public Service*,[2203] and in those and other opinions had much to say about tax reduction devices and contrivances.[2204] But when the Service brought *Cumberland* to the Court, thinking it involved the same facts as *Court Holding* in which the Service was victorious, Justice Black disagreed on the basis of very careful, if difficult, factual analysis. The lower courts, however, have tended to use the substance over form rubric in ways that differ profoundly from the early Supreme Court usages: (1) more like a rule of law than a reference to general fact finding, (2) usually viewing the concern for substance as peculiar to the tax law, (3) applying substance over form generally to prevent the application of detailed and specific Code provisions as they are written, and (4) limiting substance over form to be a tool of the Service.

The result has been confusion. Randolph Paul wrote in 1938:

> Nothing is more misleading than the attempt of the courts in these days to fetter tax law by 'almost invariably misleading' maxims. One of the most overworked of maxims is the tiresome slogan used by Mr. Justice Pitney of the Supreme Court in an early income tax case [*Southern Pacific Co.*[2205]] when he referred to the test of 'truth' and 'substance' as distinguished from 'form' and 'appearance.' Ever since . . . *Macomber* . . . the courts have been learnedly pretending to apply this test, thus avoiding by the use of pompous generalities the task of distinguishing between form and substance in particular cases. An ubiquitous distinction is obviously impossible.[2206]

There is a ranking of fact finding that can cause labels and forms not to control,[2207] including (discussed more fully in Ch. VI.E.1.e.):

- Fraud and sham (for example, the taxpayer "paid" the expense and the payee secretly rebated half of it; or the payee was the taxpayer's agent, so the taxpayer paid himself);[2208]
- Nonfraudulent mislabeling (the debt is really stock), which depends on analysis of substance in economic terms;[2209] and

---

2202 Commissioner v. Court Holding Co., 324 U.S. 331 (1945).

2203 United States v. Cumberland Pub. Serv. Co., 338 U.S. 451 (1950).

2204 Paul, *Justice Black and Federal Taxation*, *supra* note 418, at 514-15.

2205 S. Pac. Co. v. Lowe, 247 U.S. 330 (1918).

2206 PAUL, STUDIES II, at 200-02.

2207 Warren observed a somewhat similar ranking in 1981. Warren, *The Requirement of Economic Profit*, *supra* note 1182, at 985.

2208 *See infra* Ch. VI.E.1.e(2).

2209 INT'L FISCAL ASSOC., FORM AND SUBSTANCE IN TAX LAW, *supra* note 118, at 29-36.

- Finding the facts of no profit potential and/or no business purpose as grounds for denying the normal tax consequences of transactions that otherwise would be respected (the "economic substance doctrine").[2210]

The first two types of mislabeling are forbidden and reversed if found out by the government, based on factual analysis of "economic substance";[2211] the third is the "economic substance doctrine," discussed in Ch. V.F., which imposes a positive rule of law and does not just find facts (although it depends on facts). In most countries other than the United States that do not have broad anti-tax-avoidance statutory rules, the function of the doctrines is served more frequently by the sham and mischaracterization approaches.[2212] In the United States, the doctrines have taken the place of findings of agency and other common sense methods of determining that money was not actually borrowed, etc.

There is a range of facts that may be employed by courts in form versus substance analyses, including:

- Evidence that is natural or primary or "pure facts;"[2213]
- Secondary or legal facts or "legal substance" or "legal reality" (private law rights and obligations, such as a loan), which reject shams and mischaracterizations, and which may rely more or less heavily on form depending on the norms of the legal system;[2214] *F. & R. Lazarus* is an example of legal reality prevailing in tax;[2215]
- Tax facts (including factual concepts unique to taxation, such as "loss sustained" or "gain realized");[2216] and
- Economic facts (economic substance), which may or may not be determinative of tax results (for example, the shareholder economically enjoys the corporation's income but the corporation's income will not be attributed to the shareholder unless he disrespects the corporation).[2217]

In carrying its burden of proof in any type of tax dispute the taxpayer should be required to assert that the ultimate fact the Code requires existed at the relevant time and to prove that:

- The fact existed in terms of formal indicia (for example, a corporate charter actually was issued by the Secretary of State); and

---

2210 *See supra* Ch. V.F.

2211 Int'l Fiscal Assoc., Form and Substance in Tax Law, *supra* note 118, at 30.

2212 *Id.*

2213 *Id.* at 28.

2214 *Id.* at 24, 30, 33.

2215 *See supra* Ch. V.E.1.f(2).

2216 Int'l Fiscal Assoc., Form and Substance in Tax Law, *supra* note 118, at 27. *See* Cummings, *Form versus Substance in the Treatment of Taxable Corporate Distributions,* 85 Taxes (CCH) 119 (2007) (discussing application of substance considerations in one area).

2217 Int'l Fiscal Assoc., Form and Substance in Tax Law, *supra* note 118, at 25, 28-9, 32.

- The formal indicia comported with the state of affairs that the required form is expected to reflect (i.e., the chartered corporation actually operated the business whose income it reported, meaning the attribution of the income to the corporate entity was not a sham in fact).[2218]

At the margins questions of form versus substance turn into pure questions of statutory construction, when the courts determine that there is no form that satisfies the statute at all, but only a certain substance. Such was true of the troubled history of the statute including gifts in contemplation of death in a decedent's estate. In 1931, the Supreme Court had no trouble deciding that when death terminated the decedent's life estate, the prior gift of the remainder was included in the estate.[2219] But in later cases the Court relied on form, only to be brought back to its original approach nine years later.[2220]

VI.E.1.b(2) *Step Transactions*

The "step transaction doctrine" is the most common application of the substance over form approach to fact finding.[2221] The doctrine describes the method of fact finding that integrates two or more events to find a fact that is usually the single event that controls the tax outcome. The reorganization regulation and a few others invoke the step transaction doctrine by name.[2222]

For example: A may make a gift to B, a single event. Alternately, A may deliver the gift to C as an agent to deliver a gift to B. That is still a single event because the actions of C are treated as the actions of his principal. Alternately, A may try to disguise the fact that he has made a gift to B by characterizing the delivery to C as a gift to C, and secretly instructing C to deliver the gift to B. Because the A-C transaction looks like one event and the C-B transaction looks like a second event, the collapsing of the two events to determine their tax treatment is said to apply the step transaction doctrine (even though C is actually an agent in the last case too).

The term "step transaction" is commonly applied in, and evidently peculiar to, the application of the federal tax laws; but the concept is not. The most important point is that, like substance over form, step transaction analysis is a common law fact finding method that is not peculiar to tax disputes, although it has cluster applications as discussed in Ch. VI.E.1.b(2). The Service is never precluded from asserting the doctrine except where published

---

2218 *See, e.g.*, Roubik v. Commissioner, 53 T.C. 365 (1969) ("Nor do we think that the corporation was ever, as a practical matter, given the right to direct any of its "employees" in their professional activities."); *see infra* Ch. VI.F.3.b(2).

2219 Klein v. United States, 283 U.S. 231 (1931).

2220 Helvering v. Hallock, 309 U.S. 106 (1940).

2221 *Treasury White Paper on Corporate Tax Shelters*, *supra* note 14, at sec. IV.B.1.

2222 Reg. §§ 1.338(h)(10)-1(c)(2), 1.355-6(a)(1), 1.367(a)-8(q)(1), 1.368-1(a), 1.1041-1T Q&A 2, 1.1361-4(a)(2)(i), 1.1361-5(b)(1)(i), 301-7701-3(g)(2)(i).

guidance has specifically declined to apply it.[2223] However, taxpayers also can assert a step transaction when it reflects a normal way to determine legal consequences, for example as by combining several writings to establish the terms of a contract.

The example above introduces the most difficult aspect of the step transaction doctrine: the element of purpose or intent. If in the third case A really intended to make the gift to C, and C acted on his own to pass it along to B, then there is no step transaction from A to B. Alternately, if the law being applied only calls for a literal transfer of record title, and A transfers record title to C, whether or not as an agent, then there also is no step transaction. But few tax rules are dependent on so mechanical a step as transferring record title without equitable ownership.[2224]

The best illustrations of the step transaction doctrine in action in nontax fields can be found in the law of usury (discussed in Ch. V.E.1.c. above), which bears similarities to tax in being statute based, relating to commercial or financial transactions, and being influenced by avoidance efforts. An early treatise on usury stated:

> The usury statutes contemplate that a search for usury shall not stop at the mere form of the transaction, but that all shifts and devices intended to cover usury should be brushed aside and the real dealings and intentions of the parties inquired into.[2225]

Another treatise began its discussion of usury with a section entitled "Immateriality of the form of the contact."[2226] Thus the underlying law presumed the application of something like the step transaction doctrine.

Randolph Paul canvassed the subject of step transactions in 1938 and stated that the step transaction doctrine refers to whether a thing that appears to be isolated must be characterized in conjunction with another thing and whether a thing that appears to be alone must be divided into parts for characterization.[2227] He concluded: (1) step transactions were the principal form of substance versus form analysis; (2) many such cases are decided on the basis of the constructive receipt doctrine; (3) the parol evidence rule does not apply to the determination of the terms of a contract not involving the parties to the litigation; and (4) interdependence of steps was the best determinant

---

2223 *See, e.g.*, Reg. §1.368-2(k)(1) (no recharacterization of a first step reorganization on account of certain later related steps); Rev. Rul. 1996-29, 1996-1 C.B. 50 (delinks reincorporation from related events).

2224 One such case was *Provost v. United States*, 269 U.S. 443 (1926).

2225 Webb, *supra* note 113, at 228.

2226 Parsons, *supra* note 172, at Vol. 3, 108.

2227 *See* Paul, Studies II, at 202-03.

for combining steps.[2228] Other commentators also have analyzed step transactions extensively.[2229]

In addition to questions of intent, most of the uncertainty surrounds two questions: (1) when does the search for related steps stop, and (2) what are the tests for conjoining separate facts, of which the binding commitment is thought to be the strongest, the interdependence test thought to be the best,[2230] and the "end result" test sometimes applied.[2231] There is no area of the tax law in which the method cannot be applied (unless the Service turns it off), because normal fact finding requires it. In the tax area the step transaction doctrine should not be dictated by a judge's views on statutory interpretation,[2232] because as noted above it is a department of fact finding rather than legal interpretation. However, Justice Harlan in *Gordon* identified one aspect of step transactions that is peculiar to the income tax: the need to determine "the essential character of a transaction" by the end of the annual reporting period rather than leaving it unfixed, awaiting other events.[2233] For this reason, *Gordon* required that the linkage of the later steps be proved somehow to have existed at the time of the first step.

Other Supreme Court applications of step transaction fact finding include the following:

- In *Lazarus*, as noted above, the Supreme Court applied a step transaction analysis in the taxpayer's favor,[2234] which integrated a deed (to the bank) and a lease back to be a mortgage, as discussed in Ch. V.E.1.f(2), above.
- The Supreme Court has applied the step transaction doctrine by name only once in a tax case, *Clark*, by reading it into the Code, where Congress wanted the whole of a unified transaction to be tested.[2235] *Clark* cited *Minnesota Tea*,[2236] which found that a distribution was to creditors when it was in form to shareholders who were required to pay it over to credi-

---

[2228] *Id.*

[2229] *See* BITTKER & LOKKEN, at 4.3.5; Mintz and Plumb, *Step Transactions in Corporate Reorganizations*, 1954 N.Y.U. INST. ON FED. TAX'N 247; Eisenberg, *Musings on Form and Substance in Taxation*, 49 CHI. L. REV. 859 (1982). For more recent comment, *see* Keinan, *Rethinking the Role of the Judicial Step Transaction Principle, and a Proposal for Codification*, 22 AKR. L.J. 45 (2007); Cummings, *What Were They Thinking? Rev. Rul. 2003-51: A New Gloss on the Step Transaction Doctrine?* 2003 TAX NOTES TODAY 246-34 (Dec. 22, 2003).

[2230] PAUL, STUDIES II, at 235-54.

[2231] BITTKER & EUSTICE, at 3.09[2].

[2232] Cunningham & Repetti, *supra* note 17, at 23.

[2233] Commissioner v. Gordon, 391 U.S. 83 (1968) (also states there must be a "binding commitment" in the first year to do the second step in the later year).

[2234] Helvering v. F. & R. Lazarus & Co., 308 U.S. 252 (1939).

[2235] Commissioner v. Clark, 489 U.S. 726, 738 (1989) (citing the "well-established 'step-transaction doctrine'," which is most often relied on by the government, as an additional justification for applying a plain meaning of "exchange" in determining the character of reorganization boot).

[2236] Minnesota Tea Co. v. Helvering, 302 U.S. 609 (1938).

tors. *Clark* also cited *Court Holding Co.*,[2237] which viewed a series of steps "as a whole" and found that in substance the corporation rather than its shareholders had made a sale. Both of these earlier decisions were unremarkable cases of fact finding in which the shareholders acted as agents of the corporations.

- Earlier, in *Dobson*, the Court recognized that such integration frequently was necessary in deciding tax cases.[2238]
- *Alabama Asphaltic* ignored intervening steps to find creditor continuity and uphold reorganization treatment as desired by the taxpayer.[2239]
- *Arrowsmith*, in effect, applied a step transaction approach (sometimes called the relation back doctrine) by treating a later payment as integrated with an earlier sale for characterization purposes because the parties contracted for the two events to be linked.[2240] An entirely different tax principle can link events without regard to the parties' intent, when the linkage is needed to provide symmetry in the tax law.[2241]
- *Knetsch* determined that no borrowing occurred in substance based on the sequence of events and payments.[2242]
- *Le Gierse*[2243] integrated an annuity contract and a purported life insurance policy that were bought at the same time, for purpose of evaluating whether insurance was purchased.
- *Frank Lyon* involved the government's effort to step together the rent payments received by the taxpayer with the debt service payments it made, for the purpose of treating taxpayer as an agent of the tenant; the Court disagreed.
- *McWilliams* linked a sale of stock on the market by one family member with a purchase of the same stock on the market by another family member within less than a month.[2244]

Although some have said that the doctrine is always dependent on a prior determination that the statute requires integrative fact finding,[2245] as shown in *Clark* the Supreme Court appears to think that Congress generally assumes it will be applied except as otherwise provided. Therefore, the more useful question is to ask when does Congress' intent show it should *not* be applied. The most obvious limiter on the step transaction doctrine in the Code is the

---

[2237] Commissioner v. Court Holding Co., 324 U.S. 331 (1945).

[2238] Dobson v. Commissioner, 320 U.S. 489 (1943).

[2239] Helvering v. Alabama Asphaltic Limestone Co., 315 U.S. 179 (1942).

[2240] Arrowsmith v. Commissioner, 344 U.S. 6 (1952).

[2241] Hillsboro National Bank v. Commissioner, 460 U.S. 370 (1983) (tax benefit rule).

[2242] *See infra* Ch. VI.E.1.e(2)(c).

[2243] Helvering v. Le Gierse, 312 U.S. 531 (1941) ("Failure, even studious failure, in one contract to refer to the other cannot be controlling. Moreover, authority for such consideration is not wanting, however unrealistic the distinction between form and substance may be.").

[2244] McWilliams v. Commissioner, 331 U.S. 694 (1947).

[2245] *See* Jensen, *Of Form and Substance: Tax-Free Incorporations and Other Transactions under Section* 351, 11 VA. TAX REV. 349, 372-75 (1991).

annual accounting principle; only in "rare and extraordinary cases" can the character of a transaction or the amount of income or loss be postponed by stepping together events across the year end.[2246] Although the Supreme Court has not given any guidelines for waiting periods that insure two events will not be stepped together, two years is a good rule of thumb.[2247]

The Supreme Court has had to back away from at least two step transaction-type rulings: *Bowers v. Kergaugh Empire* (which attempted to shoehorn too many intervening events into the analysis of income from cancelation of indebtedness); and *Corn Products* (which too easily disregarded the meaning of inventory by analyzing what the taxpayer did with its corn futures).[2248]

VI.E.1.b(3) *Economic Substance*

Tax opinions have used the words "economic substance" in two very different ways:[2249]

1. The Supreme Court has used it in the traditional sense as a conclusion from the evidence considered in the process of fact finding to categorize or identify things or events based on their economic effects ("economic substance"), which may differ from their forms;
2. Some lower federal courts have used the phrase as part of the economic substance doctrine.[2250]

And, of course, since 2010, the phrase has appeared in section 7701(o)(1), undefined, but limited by certain boundaries.

There is a third usage of economic substance in relation to tax, the Haig-Simons conception of income, which has not been used by the Supreme Court.[2251] It refers to the economic income that is thought to be the proper determinant of an income tax base, but clearly is not used by the Code. This conception of economic income has little if any relevance to the two usages focused upon here. An effort to base tax upon it inevitably conflicts with the fundamental fact that the Code is written in terms of transactions, as ably explained by Rosenberg:

2246 BITTKER & LOKKEN, at 48.1.9 (open transactions), 4.8.8 (rescission); *see* Rosenberg, *supra* note 378, at 400-17 (analyzing the step transaction doctrine generally and pointing out the annual accounting problem).

2247 *See* Cummings, *Avoiding Linked Events: How Long Must We Wait?*, 148 TAX NOTES 781 (Aug. 17, 2015).

2248 Bowers v. Kerbaugh-Empire Co., 271 U.S. 170 (1926); Corn Prods. Ref. Co. v. Commissioner, 350 U.S. 46 (1955).

2249 *Cf.* Oei, *supra* note 106, at 635, 656 (similarly describing the two tax uses of economic substance as procedural and substantive).

2250 *See supra* Ch. V.F.2; *see generally* Pietruszkiewicz, *supra* note 8.

2251 *Cf.* Hillsboro National Bank v. Commissioner, 460 U.S. 370, 404 n. 1 (1983) (which does contain a *cf.* cite to Haig-Simons in a concurrence); *see* Weiss v. Wiener, 279 U.S. 333, 335 (1929) ("The income tax laws do not profess to embody perfect economic theory.").

> While the substance of series of transactions might be seen as the overall change in economic status of the taxpayer involved, tax transactions are always defined by reference to the means (i.e., exchanges) used to reach the ends (economic changes) rather than by the ends themselves.[2252]

Economic substance as fact-finding method. The "economic substance" of a formal set of events is how one would characterize the events based on evidence of their economic effects, as contrasted with characterization based on their form or possibly some other criteria as in the following examples:

- As discussed in Ch. V.E.1.f(2), the courts of equity early were able to discern that a formal deed was in economic substance a mortgage and, moreover, that the mortgagor had the equitable right to redeem the property deeded when he had paid the sum owed.
- As discussed in Ch. V.E.1.c., the common law was able to apply the usury statutes to transactions that either did not have the form of borrowings or did not at first appear to be usurious (because the extra interest was hidden or obscured).
- In the *Rankin* case discussed in Ch. VI.E.1.a., Justice Holmes found that the substance of debt outside the tax context was not what its form purported to be.
- In *Knetsch*, the Supreme Court determined that a borrowing in form was not a borrowing in economic substance because, as in *Lazarus*, the taxpayer was not obtaining an equity. *See* Ch. VI.E.1.e(2)(c).
- In *Palmer*, the Court observed that the distribution of a right to buy corporate assets below their current value would be treated as a dividend as a matter of economic value, even though not in form (but on the facts of the case the rights were at current value when issued and so no dividend occurred, either then or when later exercised after the optioned property had appreciated).[2253]

The use of economic substance as a method of fact finding originally entered the tax law in cases defining income in favor of the taxpayer (*Southern Pacific Co. v. Lowe* and *Eisner v. Macomber*).[2254] In contrast, now economic substance is asserted almost solely by the government in efforts to reject the taxpayers' forms in connection with specialized areas of the Code; taxpayers generally are held to the form they choose. The fact finding cases can be divided for purposes of discussion into two groups, which admittedly can be hard to separate: cases involving common usage terms and cases involving terms that are more peculiar to the tax system (such as income or loss realization) or have come to be viewed as requiring special definitions for tax purposes (such as depreciation).

[2252] Rosenberg, *supra* note 378, at 429.

[2253] Palmer v. Commissioner, 302 U.S. 63 (1937).

[2254] *See supra* Ch. II.B.2.c(3).

The common usage cases. The common usage cases ask, for example, whether the note really establishes an indebtedness;[2255] whether the sale leaseback is really a loan;[2256] whether the deed is really security for a loan;[2257] whether the transfer of property to A is indirectly a transfer to B because it was for the benefit of B;[2258] whether the association member made a charitable contribution equal to the amount of the insurance premium and received the insurance for free;[2259] whether the nominally low interest rate is really higher when other payments are taken into account, and many more. The common usage cases sometimes employ the term economic substance simply as the long form of the word substance in the substance versus form dichotomy, on the unstated assumption that economic substance is the only sort of substance with which the tax law should be concerned (as contrasted with the substance of love and affection, effective management, voting control,[2260] *etc.*); in earlier times the economic substance of capital versus income was closely studied.[2261]

The Supreme Court has used the term in fact finding in this way in several cases:

- *Paulsen* discusses whether an interest in a corporation is debt or equity.[2262]
- *Boulware* used the term in finding whether a shareholder had received a distribution from his corporation when none was declared and paid in form; this did not reflect an "economic substance doctrine," but rather the common understanding that a dividend is a benefit flowing from a corporation to a shareholder in her capacity as such.[2263]
- *Aluminum Castings* ignored the taxpayer's labeling of its return as made on the cash method, and saw that it was on the accrual method as a matter of substance.[2264]
- In *Consolidated Edison*, the Court was not impressed by the fact that a tax payment was labeled "payment" and ruled it a deposit.[2265]
- *De Ganay* ruled that stock existed where the certificates were located not where the owner was located, based on ordinary meaning.[2266]

2255 *See* BITTKER & LOKKEN, at 33.2

2256 *Id.* at 48.1.6. *E.g.*, Helvering v. F. & R. Lazarus & Co., 308 U.S. 252 (1939).

2257 *Id.* at 40.7.

2258 *See* BITTKER & EUSTICE, at 5.8.1.

2259 United States v. Am. Bar Endow., 477 U.S. 105 (1986) (the Court refused to believe this explanation).

2260 *Cf.* United States v. Byrum, 408 U.S. 125 (1972) (holding that retention of stock voting rights was not the sort of economic benefit with which the law was concerned).

2261 *See, e.g.*, Lynch v. Turrish, 247 U.S. 221 (1918) (income did not include gain on liquidation of corporation because it had gradually accrued to capital).

2262 Paulsen v. Commissioner, 469 U.S. 131 (1985) (the opinion stated it would examine economic substance and not just formal terms of an instrument).

2263 Boulware v. United States, 552 U.S. 421 (2008).

2264 Aluminum Castings Co. v. Routzahn, 282 U.S. 92 (1930).

2265 United States v. Consol. Edison Co., 366 U.S. 380 (1961) (effectively reversed by I.R.C. § 461(f)).

2266 De Ganay v. Lederer, 250 U.S. 376 (1919).

- The Supreme Court applies the same approach outside of tax cases, based on common law fact finding methods.[2267]

The example of original issue discount. The history of how the Supreme Court has treated original issue discount shows its conservatism in applying economic substance even as a fact finding tool in the income tax.

- By at least 1916, the Treasury allowed a annual deduction for original issue discount as a loss, but by at least 1934, it admitted it was an element of computing interest expense.[2268]
- In 1932, the Court labeled as an "esoteric concept derived from subtle and theoretical analysis," the government argument that the cash basis debtor's stated interest payments should be treated as two payments: a lesser amount of interest and repayment of extra capital it had received before 1913 in the form of bond issue premium.[2269] The opinion called this "effective rate" analysis esoteric.
- But, in 1934, the Court assumed the ability of an issuer to amortize and deduct original issue discount.[2270]
- *Deputy v. Du Pont* applied the dislike of the esoteric to payments by a borrower of stock and refused to treat them as interest.[2271]
- But, in 1965, the Court recognized that when the holder sells non-interest-bearing notes of a third party borrower for more than its cost, the holder receives the equivalent of interest income and not capital gain.[2272] The Court reasoned that original issue discount is compensation for the use of money, which is the definition of interest as a matter of substance.

This history shows that the Court allowed economic substance to determine interest only to the extent consistent with the most broadly accepted commercial usage. It would not extend economic analysis to find interest in other transactions just because (a) money was received and periodic payments made, or (b) mathematic computations could demonstrate a similarity to interest (or not, in the case of issue premium).

The cases involving terms that are more peculiar to the tax system. Even if common law fact finding as normally applied would not allow economic substance to control form, the tax law can because state law never entirely controls federal tax results.[2273] This occurs in the cases of core terms used in the tax law, such as income and gift, even though they have common under-

---

[2267] *See, e.g.*, the nontax case of Catalano, Inc. v. Target Sales, Inc., 446 U.S. 643, 648 (1980) ("it is virtually self-evident" that extending interest free credit for the purchase of goods amounts to giving a discount), *cited in* Dickman v. Commissioner, 465 U.S. 330 (1984) to support gift tax liability.

[2268] *See* Helvering v. Union Pac. R.R. Co., 293 U.S. 282 (1934).

[2269] Old Colony R.R. Co. v. Commissioner, 284 U.S. 552 (1932).

[2270] Old Mission Portland Cement Co. v. Helvering, 293 U.S. 289 (1934).

[2271] Deputy v. Du Pont, 308 U.S. 488 (1940).

[2272] United States v. Midland-Ross Corp., 381 U.S. 54 (1965).

[2273] *See infra* Ch. VI.E.2.

standing definitions.[2274] For example, in common usage taxpayer Knetsch had an obligation to pay an amount as a matter of law; but for tax purposes Knetsch did not owe an "indebtedness" for which an interest "deduction" was allowable, because for tax purpose a real expectation of actual net payment is applied and obtaining the economic use of the money borrowed is expected.[2275]

However, the cases seem to indicate that when the term at issue is not one of common usage and more peculiar to the Code, it may be less likely to be applied based on substance. For example, in *Weiss v. Wiener* Justice Holmes denied depreciation to the owner of 99-year leases, stating:

> The income tax laws do not profess to embody perfect economic theory. They ignore some things that either a theorist or a business man would take into account in determining the pecuniary condition of the taxpayer. . . . It does not matter that in Ohio, where the properties lie, these long leases are treated as in many respects like conveyances of the fee. The Act of Congress has its own criteria, irrespective of local law, that look to certain rather severe tests of liability and exemption and that do not allow the deductions demanded whatever the lessees may be called.[2276]

Similarly, Justice Brandeis in *Midland Mutual* ruled that the creditor that bid in the principal and interest owed for the property securing the debt realized interest income without regard to whether the property value exceeded the principal amount; his reasoning was very similar to that underlying *Cottage Savings*, discussed below.[2277] It was based on the peculiar tax concept of realization, which required income inclusion even though economically the taxpayer did not seem to get anything.

In *Fribourg*, the Court refused the government's argument that the taxpayer could not deducte the scheduled depreciation because the property obviously had not depreciated as evidenced by its sale in the year for a high price.[2278]

Although realization of gain or loss is similar to accounting accrual, the Court has refused to hinge it on economic analysis, instead looking to form and legal rights. In its most direct treatment of the government's argument based on "economic substance" in a tax avoidance transaction (*Cottage Savings Assn.*[2279]), the Supreme Court did not embrace the opportunity to recognize a special sort of fact finding that would be peculiar to tax, and dismissed the argument to the extent the government meant to question anything other than the bona fides of the state law transaction:

[2274] *See, e.g.*, Dickman v. Commissioner, 465 U.S. 330 (1984) (ruling an interest free loan to a family member to be a gift; this case is now controlled by section 7872).

[2275] *See infra* Ch. VI.E.1.e(2)(c) (discussing the *Knetsch* decision).

[2276] Weiss v. Wiener, 279 U.S. 333 (1929).

[2277] Helvering v. Midland Mutual Life Ins. Co., 300 U.S. 216 (1937).

[2278] Fribourg Navigation Co. v. Commissioner, 383 U.S. 272 (1966).

[2279] Cottage Savings Assn. v. Commissioner, 499 U.S. 554 (1991).

> The Commissioner contends that the losses were not sustained [by Cottage Savings] because they lacked "economic substance," by which the Commissioner seems to mean that the losses were not bona fide. We say "seems" because the Commissioner states the position in one sentence in a footnote in his brief without offering further explanation. . . .The only authority the Commissioner cites for this argument is *Higgins v. Smith* . . . In *Higgins*, we held that a taxpayer did not sustain a loss by selling securities below cost to a corporation in which he was the sole shareholder. We found that the losses were not bona fide because the transaction was not conducted at arm's length and because the taxpayer retained the benefit of the securities through his wholly owned corporation. . . . Because there is no contention that the transactions in this case were not conducted at arm's length, or that Cottage Savings retained de facto ownership of the participation interests it traded to the four reciprocating S & L's, *Higgins* is inapposite.[2280]

Similarly, in *Clay Brown* the Service admitted the taxpayer had sold property in a way that was not a "sham" and that was accepted for state law purposes, but contended there was no sale because the benefits and burdens of ownership of the property had not shifted, because the buyer had made no investment and the seller's price was to be paid from the property's earnings.[2281] The Court disagreed, stating that while that may be a rational analysis, it had never been the law; absent specific indicia to the contrary, common words are used in their common and ordinary sense. The Court took the same position in *San Joaquin Fruit*, rejecting the taxpayer's claim that it had acquired the property prior to 1913 by virtue of owning a lease and an option to purchase.[2282]

In both *Cottage Savings* and *Clay Brown* the Supreme Court declined Service invitations to create a special, tax specific, way to find tax facts based on economic substance. Although *Cottage Savings* focused on "loss sustained," a term peculiar to the Code, both cases fundamentally involved the identification of a sale and both cases applied standard methods of fact finding. In *Cottage Savings*, the Court implied that the economic substance argument can prove too much: for example, all arm's length sales leave the seller in the same economic position as before the sale: he owns the same value. Rather, the standard tax approach is to stop with intermediate evidence: in *Cottage Savings* the taxpayer legally disposed of the loss property. For another example, Mr. Justice Holmes showed that actuarial tables, rather than the way a life expectancy actually turned out, were the proper measure of value as of a given date, despite the initial absurdity of resorting to statistical probabilities when you knew the actual facts.[2283] And *Tufts* refused to be swayed by the fact that the nonrecourse debtor's security was not worth the amount of debt from which the debtor had been relieved when he sold the property to the creditor

---

2280 *Id.* at 568.

2281 Commissioner v. Brown, 380 U.S. 563 (1965).

2282 Helvering v. San Joaquin Fruit & Investment Co., 297 U.S. 496 (1936).

2283 Ithaca Trust v. United States, 279 U.S. 151 (1929).

for the debt.[2284] These cases suggest that the Supreme Court knows how to apply economic substance fact finding to unseat form where appropriate, and that there is nothing unusual or tax specific about the process, but it is mostly common law fact finding.

Although this Chapter addresses substance versus form as an issue in fact finding, the fact may be a law and the issue may be a legal one, as in the 2012 decision upholding the "individual mandate penalty" in the Affordable Care Act because the penalty was in substance a tax, even though Congress studiously avoided labeling it as such.[2285] Likewise, the 2013 *PPL* opinion purported to look to the substance rather than the form of the U.K. windfall tax to determine that it was an income tax for foreign tax credit purposes, although in the end the opinion relied on the form of the tax by emphasizing that it included net income in part of its formula.[2286]

The *PPL* opinion went further to rely on a variant of substance over form: economic realities rather than legal abstractions. Unfortunately, it cited for this new found principle a 1956 opinion deciding who was entitled to claim the oil depletion allowance, and because the Court had previously ruled that the allowance depended on economic ownership, it repeated the point in the 1956 opinion.[2287] Properly understood, the depletion allowance opinions state a cluster rule for the depletion allowance and not a new principle to be applied throughout the Code.

VI.E.1.b(4) *Business Purpose*

The concept that a taxpayer must prove that it had a business purpose for at least some types of transactions as a condition for a tax benefit originated in *Gregory*,[2288] although its roots were earlier.[2289] As shown below, Second Circuit Judge Learned Hand is most responsible for trying to cross-fertilize this requirement into all other Code provisions allowing tax benefits in profit making transactions.[2290] But *Gregory* was limited solely to the nonrecognition benefits of corporate reorganizations; indeed, the holding had an even more limited focus because (1) the Court had evidence that Congress intended the Code's words to require a business purpose, and (2) the taxpayer had attempted to use a transitory corporation (having no business purpose) in

---

2284 Commissioner v. Tufts, 461 U.S. 300 (1983).

2285 Nat'l Fed'n of Indep. Bus. v. Sebelius, 132 S. Ct. 2566 (2012). *See* Cummings, *Health Insurance Tax Upheld*, 136 TAX NOTES (TA) 599 (July 30, 2012).

2286 PPL Corp. v. Commissioner, 133 S. Ct. 1897 (2013). *See* Cummings, *Form, Substance, and* PPL, 140 TAX NOTES (TA) 365 (July 22, 2013).

2287 Commissioner v. Southwest Exploration Co., 350 U.S. 308, 315 (1956).

2288 Gregory v. Helvering, 293 U.S. 465 (1935); *see* discussion of *Gregory v. Helvering supra* Ch. III.C.3.a(1).

2289 Weiss v. Stearn, 265 U.S. 242 (1924) (conditioned a reorganization on business purposes and conduct).

2290 *See also* Cummings, *Quote Learned but Cite Gus*, 142 TAX NOTES (TA) 993 (March 3, 2014).

the conduct of the purported reorganization.[2291] No opinion written for the Supreme Court in deciding a case has ever cited *Gregory* as establishing an all encompassing business purpose test for the Code. There is no such requirement.[2292]

Nevertheless, lower courts came to cite *Gregory* in support of various sorts of business purpose requirements for many tax benefits other than nonrecognition in a corporate reorganization. Such cases mostly involved investigations of economic substance as a matter of traditional fact finding, with the taxpayer's purpose (business or tax saving) being part of the relevant evidence on whether the transaction matched the Code's requirements.[2293] Also, such cases frequently involved an effort by the Service to secure the aid of the courts in filling a loophole in some particular tax allowance provision. Hence, business purpose properly is neither a "doctrine" outside of corporate reorganizations, nor a separate requirement of all tax benefits created by the Supreme Court. Rather it is an evidentiary aspect of fact finding that is almost always examined when the court conducts a substance versus form investigation; and, of course, it has become a "prong" of the "economic substance doctrine," where it does not act alone but as part of a set with the requirement of substantial profit or profit potential (which, properly understood, originated as a tax finding tool).

A good example of the limited scope of the alleged business purpose requirement is the fact that the section 163 interest deduction requires no business purpose for incurring the indebtedness (See Ch. VI.F.6.). Thus, cases like *Stanton* in 1960 said that interest was deductible as long as the debt was really owed, regardless of whether the debt was tax motivated.[2294] Lower court rulings like *Goodstein* (1959) denied an interest deduction not because the taxpayer had no business purpose but because standard fact finding showed no indebtedness on which interest could be paid.[2295] However, *Goldstein* in 1966 interpreted a business requirement into the law for allowance of an interest deduction; it cited no Supreme Court opinion but *Knetsch*, which in contrast found as a fact that the taxpayer simply did not obtain the use of

---

2291 *Helvering*, 293, U.S. at 465; *see also* Eisenstein, *Book Review*, *supra* note 866, at 227-28 (skewering the ease with which casual observers claimed *Gregory* pervaded the entirely of the tax law).

2292 In addition to the proof of this point in the following discussion, see Rosenberg, *supra* note 378, at 394-97 (also observing the inappropriate extension of the limited *Gregory* approach).

2293 *Id.* at 399-400 (observing that the absence of business purpose may indicate that a transaction is not what it purports to be, but not in all cases).

2294 Stanton v. Commissioner, 34 T.C. 1 (1966).

2295 Goodstein v. Commissioner, 267 F.2d 127 (1st Cir. 1959). Justice Douglas in dissent in *Knetsch* argued that the majority had in effect required a business purpose for an interest deduction, but it did not say that; it said no indebtedness existed. *See* Kanter, *Interest Deduction: Use, Ruse and Refuse*, 46 Taxes (CCH) 794, 825 (1968).

any borrowing and so there was no indebtedness on which interest could be due.[2296]

The confused citations of *Gregory* can be partly justified by the Supreme Court's hindsight references to the transitory corporation used in that transaction as a sham or disregardable corporation.[2297] That might have been another reason to deny reorganization treatment, but it was not the one used in 1935.

As a result of *Gregory*, business purpose, plus continuity of proprietary interest and continuity of business enterprise became requirements for section 368 reorganization treatment even though they did not literally appear in the Code;[2298] the Supreme Court interpreted or construed each of the three requirements into the statute.[2299] Congress has never amended the Code to incorporate these requirements, but the Treasury incorporated them into Regulation section 1.368-1 controlling reorganizations. In other situations where Congress had wanted to focus on business purpose it has said so, as in sections 355 and 269,.[2300] or its words have been interpreted to say so (section 162 requires a trade or business, which imports a profit motive).

Not long after *Gregory v. Helvering* the lower courts began to speak of lack of business purpose in denying various tax deductions and allowances. This expansion of the "business purpose doctrine" outside the realm of reorganizations went mostly unnoticed.

- A 1947 article that focused on the measurement of a corporate business purpose identified a 1943 Tax Court Memorandum decision, *Humko*, as the first to apply the concept to an interest deduction, without even noticing that the transaction did not involve a reorganization.[2301]
- Bittker & Lokken attribute the expansion to (or see it as announced in) the 1949 opinion of Learned Hand in *Transport Trading*,[2302] also not

---

[2296] *See* Goldstein v. Commissioner, 44 T.C. 284 (1965), *aff'd*, 364 F.2d 734 (2d Cir. 1966).

[2297] Nelson v. Adams, USA, Inc., 529 U.S. 460, 471 (2000); Helvering v. Alabama Asphaltic Limestone Co., 315 U.S. 179 (1942).

[2298] Actually, Treasury stated these requirements in a 1934 regulation. *See* Spear, *Corporate Business Purpose in Reorganizations*, 3 TAX L. REV. 225, 232 (1947).

[2299] *See* BITTKER & EUSTICE, at 12.61.

[2300] For analysis of business purpose generally, see Silverman, West & Nocjar, *Establishing Business Purpose in a Transparent World*, 2004 TAX NOTES TODAY 159-17 (Aug. 16, 2004).

[2301] Spear, *Corporate Business Purpose in Reorganizations*, *supra* note 2298, at 240 (citing Humko Co. v. Commissioner, 2 T.C.M. (CCH) 1121 (1943); Fuller, *Business Purpose, supra* note 762, at 362 (also identifying *Humko* as the point of expansion). *Humko* illustrates the confusions of "doctrines" with fact finding. *Humko* redeemed preferred stock proportionately from its two shareholders for demand obligations bearing interest at twice the going rate and claimed interest deductions, which the court denied by finding as a fact that the parties did not intend to create a demand debt, because the corporation could not have paid off the debt on demand without liquidating its inventory and jeopardizing its existence.

[2302] Transp. Trading & Terminal Corp. v. Commissioner, 176 F.2d 570 (2d Cir. 1949); BITTKER & LOKKEN, at 4.3.4. Making the same connection is Miller, *Federal Courts as Makers of Income Tax Law, supra* note 524, at 160, and Schlesinger, *Gregory Guards the Code*, 28 TAXES (CCH) 1085 (1950).

a reorganization case. As explained more fully in the footnote, Hand's opinion in *Transport* is highly suspect and should not serve as the ground for reading a business purpose into all Code provisions.[2303] In summary, Judge Hand's opinion was brief on analysis and purported to discover that the business purpose requirement that *Gregory v. Helvering* interpreted into the reorganization section also attached to all tax provisions governing all "commercial and industrial transactions," including specifically the payment of dividends. Indeed *Gregory* and another opinion written by Hand were the only cases *Transport Trading* cited. Hand seems to have had a mission to convert all cases into *Gregory* cases, probably due to his role as the author of the Second Circuit opinion in that important case. His opinion did not even cite *Court Holding Co.,*[2304] which was the Supreme Court opinion directly on point. His opinion essentially ignored the separation between a parent corporation and its wholly owned subsidiary, for example stating that "Parent, acting through the

---

[2303] Transport Trading was the subsidiary of a parent that had sold stock in Pacific to Transport in 1937 for $20,000, causing the parent to recognize a $480,000 loss. Allegedly the fortunes of Pacific turned around by 1940 when a buyer offered to buy Pacific stock for nearly $600,000. If Transport sold Pacific stock it would recognize nearly $600,000 in gain (having a basis of $20,000). But if it dividended Pacific stock to parent, it would not recognize *General Utilities* gain (Bittker & Eustice, at 8.20), parent would take a fair market value basis in the Pacific stock and would pay tax on 15% of its value after an 85% dividends received deduction, and parent could sell the stock for no gain. So parent caused Transport to distribute the Pacific stock and parent sold the stock. The Tax Court applied *Court Holding Co.* and ruled that Transport had not negotiated the sale to the point that it must be treated as having sold it before it liquidated. Transp. Trading & Terminal Corp. v. Commissioner, 9 T.C. 247 (1947). The Second Circuit reversed in a peculiarly reasoned opinion, that essentially rejected the locus of negotiations as a ground for decision. Despite the fact that *Court Holding* was cited by the Tax Court and was the Supreme Court authority that was clearly on point, Judge Hand insisted on citing only his opinion in *Fairfield S.S. Corp. v. Commissioner*, 157 F.2d 321 (2d Cir. 1946) and the Supreme Court in *Gregory v. Helvering* (affirming his opinion). In *Fairfield*, he also took the Tax Court to task for misinterpreting *Court Holding* to apply where the subsidiary had not made a binding contract of sale. But he affirmed the Tax Court in *Fairfield* by creating the alternate ground that there had been no distribution of the asset to be sold because the liquidating distribution was not for a business purpose, citing *Gregory*. Hence arose the idea that reached flower in *Trading Transport* that all business transactions needed a business purpose to be respected. Actually what Hand had done was to find a way around the *General Utilities* doctrine.

It would surprise taxpayers today to know that dividends need business purposes; or that a corporate liquidation needs a business purpose. Moreover, that idea was no more than a makeweight in *Trading Transport* where Hand concluded that (1) the sale was binding on the subsidiary because the buyer was bound (thus satisfying *Court Holding*), and (2) he implied an application of *Higgins v. Smith* by emphasizing the control the parent exercised over the subsidiary and their oneness. Professor Chirelstein, in his signature analysis of Judge Hand's tax cases, found the *Fairfield* and *Trading* opinions to be confusing and not reflective of any important new and cogent rule of law. Chirelstein, *supra* note 368, at 452 *et seq.* (he also reported that contemporaneous observers found the cases "radical"). *See* Cummings, *Quote Learned but Cite Gus*, 142 Tax Notes (TA) 993 (March 3, 2014).

[2304] *See infra* Ch. VI.F.2.e.

taxpayer, had on October 21 declared the dividend to itself. . . ." In fact Hand could have decided *Transport Trading* on the basis of traditional fact finding, as the Supreme Court did in an analogous decision one year later: *Cumberland Public Service*.[2305]

- That Judge Hand conducted a one-judge mission to implant a business purpose requirement throughout the Code also is reflected in *Hoey*,[2306] discussed in Ch. VI.F.3.b(1).
- A 1952 article about business purpose in reorganizations did not discern any broader "doctrine," but noted that the Service and courts had applied an analogous argument to shore up the "essentially equivalent to a dividend" language of the predecessor of section 302.[2307]
- The Supreme Court's *Knetsch* opinion in 1960 appears to have marked a shift from primary emphasis on a "business purpose doctrine" (deriving from *Gregory v. Helvering)* to a focus on economic substance in fact finding, in the sense that it later was called a doctrine related to lack of business purpose and profit.[2308]
- By 1961, the business purpose doctrine was observed to have spread from corporate reorganizations to corporate distributions, disregard of partnership entities, and sales and leasebacks.[2309] A more recent study of Supreme Court rulings concluded business purpose played a less important role in decisions than generally thought.[2310]

The better explanation of the role of business purpose is that the Supreme Court has construed a business purpose requirement into a limited number of Code rules (including reorganizations, and respecting corporations and partnerships), the Congress has included such requirement in a limited number of sections (for example sections 162, 269 and 355), and beyond that the Court sometimes assesses business purpose as evidence with respect to the broader inquiry into facts.

Examples of the Supreme Court's approach to business purpose outside of reorganizations include the following:

- *Portland Golf Club* construed a business purpose requirement into a particular Code usage of the term "trade or business." The issue was whether a social club could deduct losses realized on nonmember sales against

---

2305 United States v. Cumberland Pub. Serv. Co., 338 U.S. 451 (1950).

2306 Nat'l Investors Corp. v. Hoey, 144 F.2d 466 (2d Cir. 1944).

2307 Michaelson, *Business Purpose and Tax-Free Reorganization*, 61 YALE L.J. 14, 38 (1952).

2308 Summers, *A Critique of the Business Purpose Doctrine*, *supra* note 522, at 47 ("appreciably affect his beneficial interest . . . the future of this formulation is difficult to predict"); Fuller, *Business Purpose, supra* note 762, at 362 (also identifying *Knetsch* as not like the earlier "business purpose cases"); Eisenstein, *Book Review*, *supra* note 866, at 228-29 (explaining *Knetsch* as specifically not based on business purpose for debt); *see also* Smith, *Business Purpose: The Assault upon the Citadel*, 53 TAX LAW. 1 (2000) (titling the article "business purpose" but devoting text to "economic substance doctrine");

2309 Summers, *A Critique of the Business Purpose Doctrine*, *supra* note 522, at 43.

2310 Blank & Staudt, *Corporate Shams*, *supra* note 4, at 1642.

investment income. The Court ruled it could not because it could not make a profit on the nonmember sales when the fixed costs were counted, as they must be.[2311]

- The Supreme Court assessed a taxpayer's business purposes for a transaction as one fact bearing on whether the form of a transaction comported with its substance, where the substance was determinative (insurance).[2312]
- In *Hanover Bank*,[2313] the Supreme Court cited both *Knetsch* (indebtedness) and *Gregory* (reorganizations) as examples of when absence of business purpose can evidence a sham in fact.
- The Court required a business purpose for the formation of a partnership, a cluster area.[2314]
- Business purpose can be at issue in the business versus personal distinction.[2315]
- The Court specifically rejected the significance of business purpose in making some determinations in the corporate area.[2316]

In conclusion, the fact finding of economic substance sometimes depends on the intent of the parties, just as intent informs contract construction, and intent is evidenced by presence or absence of business purpose; and in isolated cases the Supreme Court and Congress have placed a substantive requirement of business purpose into certain tax rules, most importantly the corporate reorganization rules. Beyond that, the economic substance doctrine purports to employ business purpose as one of its two-pronged test, but it actually is the root source of that doctrine.

VI.E.1.b(5) *The General Requirement of Bona Fides*

The Supreme Court has referred to bona fides in tax opinions, reflecting the fact that the federal tax laws (like commercial law, etc.) implicitly require bona fides. The term likely originated in the rights of a bona fide purchaser for value of property[2317] To be a bona fide purchaser one had to give actual

---

2311 Portland Golf Club v. Commissioner, 497 U.S. 154 (1990) (The Court applied the long held interpretation of "trade or business" in section 162 to require an intent to earn a profit; this is akin to the *Gregory* interpretation of "reorganization" as involving a business undertaking.).

2312 United States v. Consumer Life Ins. Co., 430 U.S. 725 (1977).

2313 Hanover Bank v. Commissioner, 369 U.S. 672 (1962).

2314 Commissioner v. Culbertson, 337 U.S. 733 (1949).

2315 *See, e.g.*, Rudolph v. United States, 370 U.S. 269 (1962) (whether salesman's expenses of attenting a convention are primarily personal or business); Commissioner v. Flowers, 326 U.S. 465 (1946).

2316 United States v. Chicago, Burlington & Quincy R.R. Co., 412 U.S. 401 (1973) (the Court criticized its earlier two non-shareholder-contribution-to-capital decisions as setting up a distinction based on the motives of the property contributors and not the "economic and business consequences" for the corporation); United States v. Davis, 397 U.S. 301 (1970) (dividend equivalence).

2317 *See* Williams v. Gibbes, 61 U.S. 535 (1858).

value and not just legal consideration, such as a peppercorn or an uncollectible promise to pay.[2318]

John Adams and John Jay wrote a requirement of bona fides of debt into the Paris Peace Treaty of September 30, 1783, and the Supreme Court interpreted it to mean "contracted with good faith, or honestly, and without covin, and not kept on foot fraudulently. Bona fide is a legal technical expression; and the law of Great Britain and this country has annexed a certain idea to it. It is a term used in statutes in England, and in acts of Assembly of all the States, and signifies a thing done really, with good faith, without fraud, or deceit, or collusion, or trust. The words bona fide are restrictive, for a debt may be for a valuable consideration, and yet not bona fide."[2319] This statement reflects two important points: (1) the Court assumed the law could tell when "a thing [was] done really," and (2) a debt could be for a valuable consideration and still not be bona fide.

Thus, bona fides reflects economic substance, discussed above, and can be viewed as an earlier term for the same idea. The term appears in the Court's tax opinions as follows:

- Bona fides were present where there was arm's length dealings and the form of a transaction reflected a real disposition of property ownership.[2320]
- Bona fides were present where the parties intended to effect the transaction that was documented in *Frank Lyon*[2321] referring to "bona fide negotiations."
- Litigation between adversaries who were actually adverse was bona fide in *Bosch.*[2322]
- A sale that occurred for state law purposes at an arm's length price was bona fide in *Clay Brown.*[2323]
- An agreement in which family members really meant to act as partners was bona fide in *Culbertson.*[2324]

2318 Frederick A.Whitney, Value and the Doctrine of Bona Fide Purchase, 7 St. John's Law Rev. 181, 188 (1933).

2319 Ware v. Hylton, 3 U.S. 199, 241 (1796).

2320 Cottage Savings Assn. v. Commissioner, 499 U.S. 554 (1991).

2321 Frank Lyon Co. v. United States, 435 U.S. 561 (1978).

2322 Commissioner v. Estate of Bosch, 387 U.S. 456 (1967) (quoting congressional report that had referred to "*bona fide* adversary proceedings").

2323 Commissioner v. Brown, 380 U.S. 563 (1965).

2324 Commissioner v. Culbertson, 337 U.S. 733 (1949).

- However, the Supreme Court does not allow a finding of bona fides to substitute for compliance with the Code.[2325]

The most difficult cases are those in which there are few if any nontax consequences of the transaction or status. That is why residence involves many disputes as to *bona fides*. It is also why "tax shelters" spawn doctrines. When faced with those cases the Supreme Court usually defaults to standard legal analysis:

- In *Cottage Savings*, referred to above, the taxpayer actually disposed of legal ownership of a discrete group of mortgage investments, and so its sale was bona fide.
- In *Knetsch*, the taxpayer did not really borrow any money because he could never pay the $4,000,000 in notes he signed; the "interest" paid the "lender" was really a fee.[2326]
- In *Frank Lyon*, referred to above, the taxpayer bore certain of the risks of ownership, albeit hedged by the lease, and so the Court allowed the form to control as a default.

The federal courts generally and the Service commonly apply the Code by construing into it a requirement of bona fides, without using the term.[2327] This is an appropriate legal construction, leading to the appropriate application of equitable methods of fact finding. It also reflects the principle, discussed in Ch. II.C.1., that the Code is written to apply to transactions in their natural (bona fide) states. Sometimes, however, the courts act as if a requirement of bona fides requires a special rule, such as the economic substance doctrine.

The Code and regulations contain many specific requirements of bona fides; the large number does not mean that when bona fides is not specifically required it is unnecessary; rather the large number supports the view that the tax law generally requires bona fides. The Code contains 55 specific requirements of bona fides, and the final, temporary and proposed regulations con-

---

[2325] United States v. Davis, 397 U.S. 301 (1970) (rejected the argument of Justice Douglas that the bona fides of a business transaction could prevent application of a rule taxing it a certain way in the absence of tax avoidance); Commissioner v. Gordon, 391 U.S. 83 (1968) (rejected the argument that bona fides could substitute for complying with the requirements of section 355); National Carbide Corp. v. Commissioner, 336 U.S. 422 (1949) (rejected the argument that bona fide business purposes could make a corporation the agent of the shareholders without following the strict test applied by the Court); Deputy v. Du Pont, 308 U.S. 488 (1940).

[2326] Knetsch v. United States, 364 U.S. 361 (1960).

[2327] *See, e.g.*, Du Pont v. Commissioner, 118 F.2d 544 (3d Cir. 1941) ("The attachment of an artificial importance to the fact of sale placed a powerful weapon in the hands of the taxpayer. In its selection of this arbitrary criterion, the Congress used the bare phrase 'sale or exchange'. Standing alone, it imported too much unreality. The courts filled in the outline with the obviously indicated *bona fides*.").

tain 273 requirements of bona fides,[2328] and the Revenue Rulings since 1954 contain 533 assumptions of bona fides.

One may deduce from these specific requirements of bona fides that Congress recognizes there may be cases in which an event or a status has an important bearing on the tax outcome, the taxpayer may have an interest in faking the event or status and doing so may be relatively easy, and proving the event to be fake may be relatively hard. The Code and regulations generally do not define bona fides; rather they assume the law has much experience with this concept. Regulation section 1.368-1(c) explains that each act making up a corporate reorganization must bona fide occur. In other instances, a definition may reflect the fact that "real" and "actual" often show up with the term "bona fide": for example, the lower of cost or market selling price must be a price at which the taxpayer actually offered the inventory for sale in a recent period.[2329] This example reflects a construction of the purpose of the rule to get at what the taxpayer is really willing to sell the inventory for, not an arbitrary price set in a vacuum that the taxpayer was not willing to live by. Randolph Paul took the same approach to tax avoidance generally:

> Escape from tax is permitted if he has actually done what he pretends to have done, and his acts have placed him in the position of being responsible for the consequences.[2330]

VI.E.1.c. *The Primacy of Form*

It is not self contradictory to hold that (1) the law generally has always known how to determine the relevant substance contrary to form as discussed in the preceding Sections, and (2) the tax law is no exception, but (3) the tax law operates as a matter of default upon the form of transactions, while sometimes applying "substance over form" primarily in the government's favor. The focus of the lower courts on the tax specific doctrines generally and the ESD in particular tends to obscure the more fundamental point that the Congress has built the Internal Revenue Code and its application on form.

The obvious reason for the primacy of form is administrability: taxpayers must report based on form and the Service is unable to audit all taxpayers to determine whether form comports with substance. Indeed, this fact is the reason for the proliferation of reporting and disclosure requirements, aimed at bringing to the Service's attention transactions that the Service might think should not be taxed according to form. Most of the law on this subject relates to corporate transactions, and subchapter C necessarily exalts form more

---

2328 *See, e.g.*, Reg. § 1.267-1(c) (deductions are not allowable in transactions that lack bona fides even if section 267 does not apply); Reg. § 1.166-1(c) (debt must be bona fide).

2329 *See* Thor Power Tool Co. v. Commissioner, 439 U.S. 522 (1979).

2330 Paul, Studies II, at 114.

than the tax law generally, because corporations are merely forms.[2331] This reaches it apogee in the complex foreign tax rules, which are primarily built on the ability of U.S. persons to artificially cut themselves off from foreign income by interposing the skin of a foreign corporation between themselves and the foreign income (resulting in deferral of U.S. taxation of the foreign income).[2332]

In 1937 Randolph Paul identified the statement "that the substance, not the form controls" as a bromide and that lawyers who do not know that sometimes form controls should not be practicing law.[2333] Cahn observed in 1942 that it is not correct to say that substance rather than form controls the application of the tax law; the default starting point is form.[2334] Learned Hand said that "form" and "substance" are "anodynes for the pains of reasoning."[2335] Justice Brandeis stated: "There is nothing unfamiliar in taxing on the basis of the legal effect of a transaction. Income may be realized upon a change in the nature of legal rights held, though the particular taxpayer has enjoyed no addition to his economic worth."[2336] Boris Bittker agreed that "there are times" when form wholly determines the tax treatment, declining to admit it was the real default.[2337]

Generally it is not possible for Congress to describe the multitude of facts on which it bases tax obligations and benefits in terms other than the forms the transactions take. Forms are shorthand tools for fact finding. There are clear exceptions to reliance on form, like the wash sale rule of section 1091. Then there are the cases in which the courts apply a purposive reading to the statute and interpret substantive requirements into the statute, as in *Gregory v. Helvering*.

[2331] The examples of the exaltation of form in the corporate area are ubiquitous: Rev. Rul. 1984-111, 1984-2 C.B. 88 (incorporation of partnership has three possible tax treatments depending on form used); I.R.C. § 108(e)(6), (8) (shareholder's contribution of corporation's debt to corporation treated differently depending on whether additional stock received in exchange).

[2332] *See generally* Bittker & Eustice, at 15.60.

[2333] Paul, Studies I, at 89.

[2334] Cahn, *Taxation, supra* note 362, at 593 ("Form is essential to effective administration of tax laws. It is the handle by which men's affairs are grasped and held and moved about. Form makes intelligent taxonomy possible."); *see also* Steinberg, *supra* note 548, at 459:

> . . . substance does not always control in Subchapter C, both because proper form is sometimes a necessary condition for the desired tax treatment and because, where the substance of a transaction is ambiguous or capable of being achieved through more than one transactional approach, form frequently becomes the dispositive factor in determining the tax treatment of the parties.;

U.S. Treasury, Report on Tax Shelters, 46-7 (1999) (generally tax results are based on form).

[2335] Commissioner v. Sansome, 60 F. 2d 931, 933 (2d Cir.) (1932).

[2336] Helvering v. Midland Mutual Life Ins. Co., 300 U.S. 216 (1937).

[2337] Bittker, *Pervasive Judicial Doctrines in the Construction of the Internal Revenue Code*, 21 How L.J. 693, 704 (1978).

However, as only a default choice, form can give way to fact finding of substance. The traditions of law and equity, as shown above in Ch. V.E.1., have never limited fact finding to form. The common law has never blinkered fact finding to focus only on one step at a time in an integrated transaction. The common law's tools to see through form to fact are many, and can be difficult to apply, but no more so in tax than elsewhere. Tax, however, does have the peculiar limitation that generally taxpayers cannot claim their substance controls their form, even though the common law and equity might so allow.[2338]

As further evidence of the dominance of form, Congress has failed to adopt an all purpose anti-form (or anti-avoidance) rule in the Code for its 100-plus year life, but rather has introduced targeted anti-form rules where it wanted (see discussion of section 269, above), and has chosen to respect form at all of the critical junctures: corporations are treated as separate entities liable for their own taxes; corporations are domestic or foreign on the basis of the purely formal fact of where they are chartered, without regard to management and control or any other indicia of reality;[2339] ownership of property is not generally attributed to another person on the basis of their being related, but rather attribution occurs only where specifically required, as in section 302 and 316.

The Supreme Court generally has agreed to the primacy of form, and the examples are many, from 1923 forward. These are grouped below as taxpayer wins-on-form cases, and the Service wins-on-form cases.

Taxpayer wins on form:

- *Merriam* ruled that form controlled substance by exempting as a gift and not compensation a bequest made to the executors in lieu of any compensation. (But note this was one of the last Supreme Court opinions applying the presumption of strict construction against the government in tax cases.).[2340]
- Justice Holmes relied on state chartering of building and loans to classify the entity in all but the "extravagant cases" where dealings with nonmembers predominated and the entity could be called a "mask."[2341]
- The Court ruled that the dividend is not unqualifiedly subject in the prior year to the demand of even the corporation's president when the formal method of distribution was to place it in the interoffice mail to be received on January 2.[2342]
- As Justice Frankfurter pointed out in dissent, a formal state court order consented to by the trust beneficiaries was allowed to control the taxation

[2338] *See infra* Ch. VI.E.1.e(4).

[2339] I. R. C. § 7701(a)(4).

[2340] United States v. Merriam, 263 U.S. 179 (1923); Bogardus v. Commissioner, 302 U.S. 34 (1937) (similar). Where the taxpayer did not try so hard to make compensation look like a gift the Court found compensation. Commissioner v. Duberstein, 363 U.S. 278 (1960).

[2341] United States v. Cambridge Loan & Building Co., 278 U.S. 55 (1928).

[2342] Avery v. Commissioner, 292 U.S. 210 (1934).

of the trust income in a way that could not have been achieved by a simple agreement of the parties.[2343]

- Justice Brandeis affirmed the very formal ability of a shareholder to designate which of uncertificated shares he intended to sell, because that is one of the "important attributes of ownership," even though in substance there likely is no reality to the tracing implied in such designation.[2344] Ever since, the Treasury has allowed the same approach (now in Regulation section 1.1012-1(c)).
- In *Palmer*, the Court ruled that a corporation does not pay a dividend by distributing to shareholders a right to buy corporate assets for then current fair market value, despite the fact that the value of the assets went up by the time the rights were exercised.[2345]
- In *Lester*, the Court refused to infer that a payment to the wife was really child support because it stepped down in amount as children reached adulthood, reading the statutory words "specifically designated" to exclude such inferences.[2346]
- The Court has established a fine distinction based on form for depletion purposes between a lessee having an economic interest in the natural resource and a person having a right to mine the natural resource.[2347]
- The Court cogently explained why form must control in *Brown*[2348] when it considered the Commissioner's argument that the identification of a "sale" should always rely on the shifting of the benefits and burdens of ownership of the property. The Commissioner contended they had not shifted because the purchase price would be paid only from the earnings of the property. The Court said such analyses did not control the outcome, stating: "The term 'sale' is used a great many times in the Internal Revenue Code and a wide variety of tax results hinge on the occurrence of a 'sale.' To accept the Commissioner's definition of a sale would have wide ramifications, which we are not prepared to visit upon taxpayers, absent congressional guidance in this direction."[2349]
- *Byrum* rejected the Service's attempt to show that the decedent had practical control over property by relying on the status of various parties as fiduciaries and their presumed fiduciary obligations.[2350]

[2343] Freuler v. Helvering, 291 U.S. 35 (1934).

[2344] Helvering v. Rankin, 295 U.S. 123 (1935). This principle remains in Regulation section 1.1012-1(c)). But the shareholder must create some evidence of his designation other than his own intent. Snyder v. Commissioner, 295 U.S. 134 (1935).

[2345] Palmer v. Commissioner, 302 U.S. 63 (1937). *But see* Rev. Rul. 80-292, 1980-2 C.B. 104.

[2346] Commissioner v. Lester, 366 U.S. 299 (1961).

[2347] Paragon Jewel Coal Co. v. Commissioner, 380 U.S. 624 (1965).

[2348] Commissioner v. Brown, 380 U.S. 563 (1965).

[2349] *Id.* at 575.

[2350] United States v. Byrum, 408 U.S. 125 (1972).

- *Frank Lyon* initially stated the tax law's ability to look past form to find the facts of a transaction, but then based its ruling on form by stating that it would not look past what actually occurred to rule on the basis of what might have occurred.[2351]
- The Court rejected the Service's argument that the lessor's right of termination upon 30 days notice undercut the economic interest of the lessee-taxpayer in the oil leases so as to preclude lessee's depletion allowance.[2352]
- *Cottage Savings* decided that a sale was a disposition despite the fact that the sale proceeds were economically identical to the property sold.[2353] The opinion stated that considerations of workability and administrative convenience supported identifying a realization based on form rather than substance.
- *Centennial Savings* respected the form of the designation of an "early withdrawal penalty" as precluding there ever having been an obligation to return the full deposit that could give rise to discharge of indebtedness income.[2354]
- *Home Concrete* was a sort of taxpayer win based on form because in form the taxpayer did not omit gross income, even though in substance the overstatement of basis had the same effect.[2355]
- The taxpayer won in *Hobby Lobby* based on the form of the Affordable Care Act insurance requirement (enforced by a tax), because in substance the taxpayer was not asked to pay for the care to which it objected.[2356]
- *PPL* ruled for the taxpayer based largely on the form of the foreign tax as being nominally based on net income, even though it could be viewed in substance as a property tax.[2357]

Service wins on form:

- *Provost* ruled that a stock loan was a disposition of ownership of the stock (for purposes of a stock transfer tax), despite the economic similarity of the transaction to a borrowing with a pledge of the stock to the lender.[2358]

2351 Frank Lyon Co. v. United States, 435 U.S. 561 (1978).

2352 United States v. Swank, 451 U.S. 571(1981).

2353 Cottage Savings Assn. v. Commissioner, 499 U.S. 554 (1991).

2354 United States v. Centennial Savings Bank FSB, 499 U.S. 573 (1991).The government wanted to treat a one step transaction (the bank's collection of an early withdrawal penalty) as a two step transaction, analogizing it to the depositor paying the penalty and getting all of his deposit back; the Court of Appeals disagreed, stating that this would "elevate form over substance.; the Court reversed."

2355 United States v. Home Concrete & Supply LLC, 132 S. Ct. 1836 (2012).

2356 Burwell v. Hobby Lobby Stores, Inc., 134 S. Ct. 2751 (2014). *See* Cummings, Hobby Lobby *and Federal Taxes*, 145 Tax Notes (TA) 519 (Nov. 3, 2014).

2357 PPL Corp. v. Commissioner, 133 S. Ct. 1897 (2013).

2358 Provost v. United States, 269 U.S. 443 (1926). *See also* Goodyear Tire & Rubber Co. v. United States, 273 U.S. 100 (1927) (recapitalization treated as a stock disposition for purposes of the same stock transfer tax); Founders General Corp. v. Hoey, 300 U.S. 268 (1937).

- In a decision that seems odd today, the Court ruled that a corporation owed the Civil War income tax on its dividends paid because it declared the dividends, regardless of the possibility that they might have been in excess of the legal amount. The opinion stated that the law disregards "what is merely exceptional," evidently meaning that normally a declared dividend will be assumed to be legitimate.[2359]
- The establishment of the annual accounting concept prevents resort to claims that in substance no income was earned over a multi-year period.[2360]
- The cash method of accounting operates purely on the basis of form; payment with a note is not payment.[2361]
- In *Atlantic City Elec. Co.*, the Court refused to enter into an evaluation of the reality of the "control" of a holding company but rather adopted a "more certain" test based on actual current voting rights.[2362]
- The *Groman*[2363] and *Bashford*[2364] opinions specifically rejected taxpayers' appeals to look at the "realities" rather than the form because the reorganization statute depended on form.
- Even though the stock seller told his broker to sell the last purchased shares (thus intending to sell those shares and communicating that intent to the broker), he was held to have sold the earlier purchased shares that the banker mistakenly delivered to the broker for sale.[2365]
- *McClain* ruled that a bond retired for five cents on the dollar was "retired" and so the taxpayer suffered a capital loss, even though he could have made a trifling change in the form of the transaction (abandoning it for nothing) and deducted an ordinary loss.[2366]
- The Court ruled that a marital settlement agreement that purported to be absolute on its face would be treated as such despite having "some earmarks" as a security device, absent evidence that it was "only" a secu-

---

2359 Central Nat. Bank v. United States, 137 U.S. 355 (1890).

2360 Burnet v. Sanford & Brooks Co., 282 U.S. 359 (1931) (Sixteenth Amendment adopted to enable the government to raise revenue and no other known method of doing that except on a periodical basis, thus establishing the taxable year concept).

2361 Helvering v. Price, 309 U.S. 409 (1940); Eckert v. Burnet, 283 U.S. 140 (1931).

2362 Atlantic City Elec. Co. v. Commissioner, 288 U.S. 152 (1933). It held that "stock" in the then applicable affiliation definition was not limited and so included all kinds of stock, including preferred stock. Because the taxpayer's parent holding company held only 77% of the voting stock—all of the common—the public held most of the preferred, they could not consolidate. The taxpayer argued that the voting preferred should be ignored because the taxpayer had the power to redeem it and the holding company could cause the redemption at any time.

2363 Groman v. Commissioner, 302 U.S. 82 (1937).

2364 Helvering v. Bashford, 302 U.S. 454 (1938).

2365 Davidson v. Commissioner, 305 U.S. 44 (1938).

2366 McClain v. Commissioner, 311 U.S. 527 (1941).

rity device; and quoting Justice Holmes: "[Difficult questions are] pretty much everything worth arguing about in the law."[2367]

- *Southwest Consolidated* refused to treat creditors who had stepped into the shoes of stockholders as "stockholders," because they did not own a specified class of stock. [2368]
- *Marlborough* would not disregard *mesne* conveyances so as to render an asset transfer in bankruptcy as corporation to corporation and thus a reorganization. [2369]
- The formal power to invade the trust for the benefit of the widow, no matter how frugal she might be or how conservative the trustee might be, was enough to prevent the charitable bequest from being sufficiently exact to deduct.[2370]
- A civil service government lawyer was seconded to the Coast Guard during the war to serve as a lieutenant commander without pay "other than compensation of their civil positions, in case of government employees." The question was whether he received exempt military pay. The Court said no because he received his compensation in his capacity as a civilian under the documentation, even though his work was entirely military (in substance).[2371]
- An auto dealer that discounted installment paper received from car buyers could not treat the finance company as lending directly to the buyers.[2372]
- *Davis* rejected the taxpayer's argument that application of the attribution rules for purposes of defining a dividend exalted form over substance; the Court observed that "the difference between form and substance in the tax law is largely problematical . . .".[2373]
- Justice Marshall stated that "At some point, however, the form in which a transaction is cast must have considerable impact."[2374]
- The Court rejected taxpayer efforts to prove the lack of intent of a decedent to retain interests in trust property, even though the statute referred

---

[2367] Pearce v. Commissioner, 315 U.S. 543 (1942).

[2368] Helvering v. Southwest Consolidated Corp., 315 U.S. 194 (1942).

[2369] Bondholders Comm., Marlborough Inv. Co. v. Commissioner, 315 U.S. 189 (1942). But the lower court in *Helvering v. Southwest Consolidated Corp.*, 119 F. 2d 561 (5th Cir. 1941), *reversed*, 315 U.S. 194 (1942) had ruled just the opposite and the issue was not discussed in the Supreme Court's reversal.

[2370] Merchant's Nat'l Bank v. Commissioner, 320 U.S. 256 (1943); Henslee v. Union Planters Nat'l Bank & Trust Co., 335 U.S. 595 (1949) ("What common experience might regard as remote in the generality of cases may nonetheless be beyond the realm of precise prediction in the single instance.").

[2371] Commissioner v. Connelly, 338 U.S. 258 (1949).

[2372] Commissioner v. Hansen, 360 U.S. 446 (1959).

[2373] United States v. Davis, 397 U.S. 301 (1970).

[2374] United States v. Mississippi Chem. Corp., 405 U.S. 298 (1972) (cost of shares that bank purchased in Bank for Cooperatives from which it principally borrowed money was not additional interest because Congress chose to call it investment for shares).

to the decedent's intent; the Court said that reliance on subjective intent as opposed to the possibilities of events would "create[s] substantial obstacles to the proper application of the federal estate tax laws."[2375]

- The partner must report income that the partnership allocates to the partner, regardless of whether the partner will ever receive it as a matter of substance.[2376]
- The primacy of form is most clear in the area of deductions and allowances; as a general rule the Court will not recharacterize a transaction to a form that qualifies for a deduction despite the fact that the two forms are economically equivalent.[2377]
- The Court in effect ruled on form rather than substance in *Fink*.[2378] It held that majority shareholders' contribution of some of their stock to the corporation should be treated according to what it was in form, a contribution to capital, regardless of the economic fact that the shareholders might thereby reduce their interest in the corporation relative to other shareholders and suffer an economic loss.
- *Hall* ruled for the Service based on form—the taxpayer was the individual bankrupt—and not the substance that the sale occurred during the existence of the bankruptcy estate.[2379]

These opinions do not prove that form always or even generally controls over substance in the tax law but they do disprove the misstatement that substance always controls over form and they show that form is the default determinant outside areas of common law fact finding.

VI.E.1.d. *Relevance of Alternate Transactions*

A common way of asserting the substance of a transaction is to analogize it to another transaction that might instead have occurred—an alternate transaction. As noted immediately above, in the case of deductions the Supreme Court does not allow a taxpayer to report as if its transaction had been done in an alternate form, with no economic differences from the one he chose; rather the taxpayer must report according to the chosen form. But this principle is not limited to deductions: the Court generally does not rule on the

---

2375 United States v. Grace Estate, 395 U.S. 316 (1969); Estate of Spiegel v. Commissioner, 335 U.S. 701 (1949).

2376 United States v. Bayse, 410 U.S. 441 (1973) (Kaiser made retirement contributions to a plan for the doctor partnership, which the partnership had to include as received according to the Court, regardless of whether the doctor partner ever got the retirement payment).

2377 *See* Commissioner v. Nat'l Alfalfa Dehydrating & Milling Co., 417 U.S. 134 (1974) (taxpayer redeemed $50 par value stock that was worth less than $50 for $50 notes; the Court refused to view the transaction as if the taxpayer had redeemed the stock for its value and then the former shareholders bought the notes for the same lower price).

2378 Commissioner v. Fink, 483 U.S. 89 (1987) (The Court seemed to be heavily motivated by preventing discretionary loss recognition.).

2379 Hall v. United States, 132 S. Ct. 1882 (2012).

basis of what might have been, and most commonly applies that approach against taxpayers.[2380]

The Supreme Court opinion in *Centennial Savings* rejected an "as if" approach applied by the Court of Appeals.[2381] The Court refused to recast a transaction away from the form the taxpayer has chosen, also citing the irrelevance of what might have been done as contrasted with what actually was done in *Frank Lyon.*[2382]

Exceptions to the rule, also against the taxpayer, can occur when the Court decides to analogize a taxpayer's form to another form in order to identify its substance. For example, it ruled original issue discount to be interest, though the opinion did not say it was applying an alternative way to pay interest.[2383] Also the Court thwarted an unintended use of a nonrecognition (or deduction, allowance, etc.) rule in *Southwest Consolidated*,[2384] where the acquiring corporation literally assumed the liability of the reorganizing corporation (which would not have resulted in recognition), but the Court treated the transaction as if the acquirer had paid the cash borrowed as part of the reorganization to pay off the security holder creditors (which did not result in nonrecognition). Similarly, in *Hendler*[2385] the Court viewed the assumption of a liability the same as paying cash to the taxpayer who then paid of its liability.

VI.E.1.e. *When Form Does Not Control*

The Supreme Court's tax decisions based on finding facts that differ from forms can be placed in six categories listed here. The first two have been discussed in detail in Ch. II.B.2.c(3), and III.C.3.a and b. The last four are discussed in this subchapter.

[2380] *See* Boulware v. United States, 552 U.S. 421 n. 7 (2008); Don E. Williams Co. v. Commissioner, 429 U.S. 569 (1977) (the similarity of a secured note to a cash payment did not make it so); Cent. Tablet Mfg. Co. v. United States, 417 U.S. 673, 690 (1974) (analogizing a fire loss to a consual sale does not make it so); Founders Gen. Corp. v. Hoey, 300 U.S. 268 (1937) (may be a special case of this rule because it involved the highly formal stamp tax); United States v. Davis, 397 U.S. 301 (1970) (taxpayer argued it could have chosen a different form and avoided tax; Court said not relevant). *See also* Abramski v. United States, 134 S. Ct. 2259 (2014) (not a tax case; Scalia's dissent argued the transaction could have been another way that would not have been a crime).

[2381] The government wanted to treat a one step transaction (the bank's collection of an early withdrawal penalty) as a two step transaction, analogizing it to the depositor paying the penalty and getting all of his deposit back; the Court of Appeals disagreed, stating that this would "elevate form over substance." United States v. Centennial Savings Bank FSB, 499 U.S. 573 (1991).

[2382] Frank Lyon Co. v. United States, 435 U.S. 561 (1978) ("No matter how the transaction could have been devised otherwise,...")

[2383] United States v. Midland-Ross Corp., 381 U.S. 54 (1965).

[2384] Helvering v. Southwest Consolidated Corp., 315 U.S. 194 (1942).

[2385] United States v. Hendler, 303 U.S. 564 (1938).

1. *Income definition.* Seminal definition of income decisions relying on substance both in the taxpayer's favor (*Southern Pacific Co.*[2386] and *Macomber*[2387]) (an approach that generally has not endured in terms of favoring the taxpayer) and in the government's favor (*Old Colony Trust Co.*[2388] and *Diedrich*[2389]) (an approach that has endured).
2. *Statutory interpretation and construction.* Decisions relying on construction of a nonformal requirement into the statute (*Gregory*[2390] and *McWilliams*[2391]). This category actually applies to all of the cases in which form does not control (other than the economic substance doctrine cases) because the courts must explicitly or implicitly find the purpose of Congress to rely on some facts other than the forms in which the facts are cast. When the method of fact finding is a common law method, such as using agency or principles of equity, the interpretation of the Code to adopt such methods is implicit because the Code contemplates the use of normal fact finding methods. When the deviation from form is more stark, as in *Gregory* and *McWilliams*, the Court generally admits explicitly that it is construing an unstated requirement into the Code.
3. *Normal fact finding.* Decisions employing traditional common law and equitable fact finding methods (such as *Lazarus & Co.*[2392]). This category covers the multitude of ways a taxpayer can be found to have mischaracterized transactions, which may be either legitimate disagreements about ambiguous facts or may result from intentional efforts to disguise facts through the use of undisclosed agents, related steps, offsetting steps and other factual disguises. For example, tax advisors were pretty sure Mrs. Gregory's plan worked in the early 1930s, as was the Tax Court, which ruled for her.
4. *Fraud.* Frauds and misrepresentation of entity (*Higgins v. Smith*[2393]), which sometimes are referred to as "sham in fact."
5. *Shams.* Shams for tax purposes ("sham in law or in substance") involving unrelated parties (*Knetsch,* discussed in Ch. VI.E.1.e.2(c)). There is a form, meaning documents were signed and sometimes payments were made, but there was no mutual intent to enforce the transaction as documented. These decisions actually just apply normal fact finding, but sometimes apply a special label for that process. Unlike *Gregory*, which

[2386] Southern Pacific Co. v. Lowe, 247 U.S. 330 (1918); *see supra* Ch. II.B.2.c(3).

[2387] Eisner v. Macomber, 252 U.S. 189 (1920); *see supra* Ch. II.B.2.c(3).

[2388] Old Colony Trust Co. v. Commissioner, 279 U.S. 716 (1929) (finding that when the employer paid the employee's taxes the employee had received compensation income).

[2389] Diedrich v. Commissioner, 457 U.S. 191 (1982) (donor recognized sale gain when donee was required to pay gift tax for which donor was liable).

[2390] Gregory v. Helvering, 293 U.S. 465 (1935); *see supra* Ch. III.C.3.a(1).

[2391] McWilliams v. Commissioner, 331 U.S. 694 (1947) (which Ch. III.C.3.b. *supra*, views as overreaching).

[2392] Helvering v. F. & R. Lazarus & Co., 308 U.S. 252 (1939); *see infra* Ch. V.E.1.f(2).

[2393] Higgins v. Smith, 308 U.S. 473 (1940); *see supra* Ch III.C.3.a(2).

the Tax Court decided in the taxpayer's favor because there was no common law fact to find to the contrary,[2394] the federal district judge in *Knetsch* ruled against the taxpayer by applying common law methods to determine there was no loan on which interest could have been paid.[2395]

6. *Non-arm's-length.* Related party transactions.

VI.E.1.e(1) *Normal Fact Finding*

Supreme Court deviations from the control of form primarily reflect normal fact finding for two categories of facts:

1. Applications of common law principles such as agency,[2396] fraud, integration of contracts to determine the obligation of parties, implied contracts, assignments, trusts, bailment, estoppel,[2397] identifying interest (as for usury purposes), identifying mortgages, novation, reformation and rescission—all as they would be applied in state courts to determine state law rights.[2398] Ch. V.E.1. discusses the specific instance of the equity of redemption and equitable fact finding generally.
2. Applications of generally the same fact finding approaches to determine the existence of any additional facts that the tax law requires for its results, which are not required for state law purposes. The Supreme Court has referred to the differentiation between the two types of facts as the state law sticks in the tax law bundle, in a case finding property to be subject to a federal tax lien even though it was not considered to be property subject to claims of the taxpayer's general creditors.[2399] Similarly, many common law facts bear on whether an employer's transfer to an employee is a gift or compensation, but the test applied is not the common law definition of gift.[2400]

2394 Gregory v. Commissioner, 27 B.T.A. 223 (1932).

2395 Knetsch v. United States, 58-2 USTC P 9935 (S.D. CA, 1958).

2396 *See* Miller, *Federal Courts as Makers of Income Tax Law, supra* note 524, at 154 (explaining how an entirely proper and normal role of courts in tax cases is to see the straw man or conduit or dummy as an agent; Miller was the founder of Miller & Chevalier). *See* Commissioner v. Court Holding Co., 324 U.S. 331 (1945) (sale by one person cannot be transformed into sale by another person by passing title through the latter as a conduit).

2397 R. H. Stearns Co. v. United States, 291 U.S. 54 (1934) ("He who prevents a thing from being done may not avail himself of the non-performance which he has himself occasioned…").

2398 *See, e.g.,* Arthur Andersen LLP v. Carlisle, 129 S. Ct. 1896 (2009) (in which Justice Scalia stated in the opinion of the Court: ". . . 'traditional principles' of state law allow a contract to be enforced by or against nonparties to the contract through 'assumption, piercing the corporate veil, alter ego, incorporation by reference, third-party beneficiary theories, waiver and estoppel,' 21 R. Lord, Williston on Contracts, sec. 57:19, p. 183 (4th ed. 2001))."

2399 *See* United States v. Craft, 535 U.S. 274 (2002).

2400 *See* Bittker & Lokken, at 10.2.1, discussing the fact intensive opinion in *Commissioner v. Duberstein*, 363 U.S. 278 (1960).

In such cases the taxpayer may argue that the Service has pursued a practice of ignoring the "economic realities.," The Court has strongly implied that while a taxpayer may properly rely on such practice, the taxpayer faces a heavy burden of proving the practice.[2401]

A general unstated principle of Code application is that as a matter of fact finding the tax collector can determine the nature of the thing for tax purposes contrary to its form by using traditional fact finding methods such as those listed above, except as otherwise provided in the Code.[2402] This is inferred to be the intent of Congress, as the Court recognizes when it says, as it repeatedly has:

> In interpreting the meaning of the words in a revenue act we look to the "ordinary, everyday senses" of the words.[2403]

For examples:

- *Miles* held that the distribution to shareholders of a right to buy more stock was analogous to a stock dividend and so should be taxed (or not) in the same way.[2404]
- The provision of telegraph services was not "free" and thus exempt from the tax on transmission simply because the telegraph company and the railroad contracted to swap services without payment up to a fixed amount.[2405]
- *Old Colony Trust* held the payment of the employee's taxes (form) to be compensation (substance).[2406]
- Similarly, the Court ruled that when the lessee contracts to pay the lessor's income tax on the rent, the payment to the tax collector is a "short cut" to paying the lessor and so is also rent.[2407]
- The statutory term "ordinary and necessary expenses" of a trade or business does not encompass excessive payments denominated as compensation,[2408] but rather should follow the general rule that "popular or received import of words furnishes the general rule for the interpretation of public laws."[2409]
- The saga of *May v. Heiner* shows an exception that proves the rule.[2410] It ruled that "possession and enjoyment" of property placed in trust with

---

2401 United States v. Midland-Ross Corp., 381 U.S. 54 (1965).

2402 *See generally* Levmore, *Recharacterizations and the Nature of Theory in Corporate Tax Law*, 136 U. Pa. L. Rev. 1019 (1988) (arguing that recharacterizations should be complete, consistent, brief and direct).

2403 Commissioner v. Soliman, 506 U.S. 168 (1993).

2404 Miles v. Safe Deposit & Trust Co., 259 U.S. 247 (1922).

2405 Hellmich v. Mo. Pac. R.R. Co., 273 U.S. 242 (1927).

2406 Old Colony Trust Co. v. Commissioner, 279 U.S. 716 (1929).

2407 United States v. Boston & Maine R.R., 279 U.S. 732 (1929).

2408 Botany Worsted Mills v. United States, 278 U.S. 282 (1929).

2409 Deputy v. Du Pont, 308 U.S. 488 (1940). *See* Ch. VI.F.11.

2410 May v. Heiner, 281 U.S. 238 (1930).

a retained life estate passed to the remainderman because title formally passed to the trustee. Nineteen years later the Court overruled *Heiner* because substance and not form should govern.[2411] It is odd that the statutory words could have been interpreted to describe a formal transfer in the first place.

- Mr. Justice Holmes said in creating the "doctrine of constructive receipt of income" (a later term, not his): "If a man directed his bank to pay over income as received to a servant or friend, until further orders, no one would doubt that he could be taxed upon the amounts so paid. It is answered that in that case he would have a title, whereas here he did not. But from the point of view of taxation there would be no difference."[2412]
- *Superior Oil* is a state tax case addressing whether the consignment of a delivery of oil to a buyer at its out of state address (form) controlled the factual determination whether the sale of the oil was in intrastate or interstate commerce when all other events concerning the sale occurred in the state.[2413] The Court held it did not (substance). Rather than being a substance over form case, this is simple fact finding, based on an interpretation of the meaning of the constitutional term "interstate."
- *Raybestos* ruled that a stock for stock exchange occurred in a reorganization even though the reorganizing corporation did not literally receive the acquirer's stock and exchange it for its own shares held by its shareholders, because the "generating source" of the shareholder's right to receive the stock was the asset transfer by the corporation.[2414]
- *Bogardus* disregarded a recital of a payment being in recognition of past services (form) and found a gift (substance).[2415]
- *Lyeth* found that the form of a contractual settlement of an inheritance dispute did not change the substance that the taxpayer received the property by inheritance, and thus it was exempt because all of the rights of the taxpayer derived from his status as an actual or potential heir;[2416]
- *Magruder* ruled that a land buyer who agreed to pay the property taxes that had already attached as a lien on the property was not paying deductible taxes because they were not a tax liability as to him.[2417]
- In *Wilmington Trust Co.*, the taxpayer had long and short accounts with a brokerage company in the same stock in generally the same amounts, but the brokerage company had not denominated the long positions as having been sold; the Court affirmed a Tax Court finding that the long positions had been sold.[2418] Thus, the Court rejected an extreme reliance

---

[2411] Commissioner v. Estate of Church, 335 U.S. 632 (1949).
[2412] Corliss v. Bowers, 281 U.S. 376 (1930).
[2413] Superior Oil Co. v. Mississippi, 280 U.S. 390 (1930).
[2414] Raybestos-Manhattan, Inc. v. United States, 296 U.S. 60 (1935).
[2415] Bogardus v. Commissioner, 302 U.S. 34 (1937).
[2416] Lyeth v. Hoey, 305 U.S. 188 (1938).
[2417] Magruder v. Supplee, 316 U.S. 394 (1942).
[2418] Wilmington Trust Co. v. Helvering, 316 U.S. 164 (1942).

on form imposed by a third party that probably should be viewed as a related agent.

- *Southwest Consolidated* ruled that the exception from boot treatment for liabilities assumed in a reorganization did not apply to the a liability created in the reorganization to obtain cash to pay boot, because that was in substance cash and not liability assumption.[2419]
- *Detroit Edison* ruled that taxpayer's cost for construction had to be netted down by the amount of nontaxable contributions to capital it had received as inducements for the construction, because they reduced its cost in substance.[2420]
- A corporation could not deduct state taxes withheld on dividends because they were not "imposed" in substance on the corporation even though it paid them.[2421]
- Whether a corporation should be taxed on sales of treasury stock should not depend on the formalities of whether it was retired but on the real nature of the transaction.[2422]
- *LoBue* ruled that the fact that an employer granted stock options in order to enable employees to become shareholders (form) did not prevent their characterization as compensation (substance).[2423] In a related decision, *Smith* ruled that worthless options granted by an employer were not intended to be zero value compensation because the intended compensation was the option spread to be realized by the employee potentially when the property appreciated in value and the employee exercised the option.[2424]
- *Dickman* said that Congress intended the gift tax to cover "all the protean arrangements which the wit of man can devise . . .".[2425]
- *Paulsen* addressed the factual distinction between stock and debt.[2426] After concluding that a passbook savings account did not represent a continuity of interest (stock) for reorganization purposes, the Court stated that in determining whether a person has a substantial proprietary interest the Court looks to economic substance rather than form. The distinction

---

2419 Helvering v. Southweset Consolidated Corp., 315 U.S. 194 (1942).

2420 Detroit Edison Co. v. Commissioner, 319 U.S. 98 (1943).

2421 Wisc. Gas & Elec. v. United States, 322 U.S. 526 (1944).

2422 United States v. Anderson, Clayton & Co., 350 U.S. 55 (1955) (the regulation contained that requirement).

2423 Commissioner v. LoBue, 351 U.S. 243 (1956).

2424 Commissioner v. Smith, 324 U.S. 177 (1945). The opinion made a "cf" cite to *Palmer v. Commissioner*, 302 U.S. 63 (1937), which had concluded there was no distribution to shareholders under similar facts.

2425 Dickman v. Commissioner, 465 U.S. 330 (1984) (quoting Commissioner v. Wemyss, 324 U.S. 303 (1945)). *See also* United States v. Mfrs. Nat'l Bank, 363 U.S. 194 (1960) ("transfer" not limited to direct person to person transfer but obviously can include payment made to a third party for the benefit of the heir).

2426 Paulsen v. Commissioner, 469 U.S. 131 (1985); *see infra* Ch. VI.F.7.

between stock and debt is a long-standing factual issue that has never depended on the form of the instrument.

- *Clark* refers to economic substance because sections 302 and 356 do, as a way to determine the fact of whether a redemption is a dividend.[2427]
- *Indianapolis Power* involved the application of traditional legal analysis to the determination of income as a fact.[2428] The question was whether customer deposits (in form) were advance payments and thus income to the taxpayer. The Court believed that such payments are inherently ambiguous in fact and can be characterized as income or not only by close analysis of both the factual and legal consequences of the transaction.
- *Bartels v. Birmingham* treated as an independent contractor a party denominated by contract as employee, based on common law principles.[2429]

Several of the foregoing examples involve construing a rule about which Congress had no purpose, by selecting a rule that is administrable and not easily avoidable by taxpayer's choice of form. Additional examples include:

- In the tax benefit area, the Court rejected an overly formal meaning for recovery of an item that had produced a tax benefit in order to achieve the rule's purpose.[2430]
- In the "origin of the claim" cases, the Court rejected a rule based on purpose of the payment as being overly subject to formal manipulation.[2431]

Sometimes there is an overlap of substance fact finding with legal interpretation as in 1827 when Chief Justice Marshall interpreted the constitutional prohibition on a state's taxation of imports to prevent a state from taxing importers; Marshall rejected the state's argument that it was not taxing imports by stating: ". . . this is varying the form, without varying the substance. It is treating a prohibition which is general, as if it were confined to a particular mode of doing the forbidden thing."[2432]

VI.E.1.e(2) *Fraud and Shams*

Federal tax opinions involving "tax shelters" frequently use the word "sham,"[2433] but less so the word "fraud." Indeed, none of the high profile "tax shelter" Service victories of the "corporate tax shelter" era beginning with *ACM Partnership*[2434] involved even the assertion of fraud penalties. Perhaps

---

[2427] Commissioner v. Clark, 489 U.S. 726 (1989).
[2428] Commissioner v. Indianapolis Power & Light Co., 493 U.S. 203 (1990).
[2429] Bartels v. Birmingham, 332 U.S. 126 (1947).
[2430] *See* Hillsboro National Bank v. Commissioner, 460 U.S. 370 (1983).
[2431] Woodward v. Commissioner, 397 U.S. 572 (1970).
[2432] Brown v. Maryland, 25 U.S. 419, 444 (1827).
[2433] *See, e.g.,* Frank Lyon Co. v. United States, 435 U.S. 561(1978) (where the Court found the transaction was not a sham).
[2434] ACM P'ship v. Commissioner, 157 F.3d 231 (3d Cir. 1998).

this reflects a caution attributable to the practical impediments to imposing the 75% fraud penalty of section 6663, as contrasted with the 20% (or 30% or 40%) accuracy related penalties of sections 6662 and 6662A. Also, fraud generally imports concealment; most "tax shelter" cases do not depend on concealment.[2435] Unlike the accuracy related penalties, the Service has the initial burden of proof at a "clear and convincing" level; the accuracy related penalties cannot apply if the fraud penalty is imposed; and fraud typically is asserted in cases of bald failure to file or report income or other actions involving active concealment.[2436]

Despite the good reasons for the Service not to assess the fraud penalty or even assert fraud, confusion ensues when the word sham serves as a de facto fraud indicator. Courts and the Service employ the words sham and sham transaction as if everyone knows their meaning, when in fact the words simply signal the conclusion that the taxpayer's form will be ignored.

VI.E.1.e(2)(a) *Fraud*

Fraud generally is a intentional misrepresentation or concealment of a relevant fact for the purpose of obtaining some benefit from the defrauded person.[2437] In earlier times, the Supreme Court occasionally used the term "fraud on the revenue," mostly related to customs duties, but has not used the term recently.[2438] Because fraud is grounded in concealment for improper purposes, the Court has recognized in tax cases the broad relevance and admissibility of evidence needed to prove it.[2439] In the *Isham* opinion, discussed in Ch. II.B.2.a(2) above, the Court said that even if the taxpayer's actions were

---

[2435] *See* Fuller, *Business Purpose, supra* note 762, at 367-68 (distinguishing concealment from simulation in which the character of a transaction is obscured, as in the case of debt).

[2436] *See generally* BITTKER & LOKKEN, at 114.6; SALTZMAN & BOOK, at 7B.02. On the other hand, facts that would support fraud allow the Service to apply section 446(b). United States v. Hughes Properties, Inc., 476 U.S. 593 (1986) (stating that if the Service determined that a taxpayer manipulated its slot machines so as to not properly reflect income, section 446(b) could be applied).

[2437] *Cf.* Strong v. Repide, 213 U.S. 419 (1909) (not a tax case; there appear to be no modern era tax cases in which the Supreme Court has had the need to define fraud). *See also* Kawashima v. Holder, 132 S. Ct. 1166 (2012) (construing a deportation statute and ruling that the willful filing of a false return is fraudulent).

[2438] "Fraud on the revenue" evidently could have a less odious meaning than fraud, as it was applied to carrying mail in conflict with the monopoly of the Post Office, which the Supreme Court characterized as a government revenue raiser. United States v. Bromley, 53 U.S. 88 (1851). But it also applied to intentional efforts to evade tax. Merritt v. Welsh, 104 U.S. 694 (1882) (adding color to sugar to make it appear of a different type for tax purposes); The John Griffin, 82 U.S. 29 (1873) ("segars" unloaded at night to avoid customs).

[2439] Wood v. United States, 41 U.S. 342. 360-61 (1842) (customs duties case in which intentional failure to show correct value on invoice could result in forfeiture of the goods: "for fraud being essentially a matter of motive and intention, is often deducible only from a great variety of circumstances, no one of which is absolutely decisive; but all combined together may become almost irresistible as to the true nature and character of the transaction in controversy.").

a "fraud on the revenue" they were "legal" and worked to avoid the tax liability. Congress at least once has realized that imposing the standard of finding fraud was too difficult for normal use in collecting taxes.[2440] The traditional earmarks of fraud include badges of fraud and efforts to disguise.[2441] Tax fraud generally imports lying.[2442]

But aside from purposeful concealment of income and the like, the rarity of fraud in even the historic tax avoidance cases of the 20th century is remarkable. In addition to the reasons listed in the preceding Section, the Service's hesitancy to assert fraud may date back to the refusal of the Board of Tax Appeals to uphold the assessments, including fraud penalties, proposed in the high profile six month trial of Andrew W. Mellon, based on conduct very similar to that in *Higgins v. Smith*.[2443]

As discussed in Ch. III.C.3.a(2) above, *Higgins v. Smith* is one of the most prominent cases in which the Service imposed the civil fraud penalty for a shareholder's trying to claim a loss on a sale to his wholly owned corporation (which was conduct that probably was accepted practice at the time, as evidenced by the fact that the Secretary of the Treasury Mellon did essentially the same thing); but the jury rejected the fraud penalty and the government did not appeal on that issue.[2444] A similarly prominent civil fraud penalty case (taxpayer also was indicted, but got off, and the issue was whether the civil fraud penalty could nevertheless apply; it could) involved Mr. Mitchell, chairman of the National City Bank, who in 1929 purported to recognize a loss on selling some bank stock to his wife.[2445] The fraud penalty was sustained in the *Mitchell* case for these reasons:

- The stock was in a margin account with J.P. Morgan, the wife/buyer assumed the margin loan, the stock remained pledged, but Morgan was not notified of the sale.
- The wife owed Mitchell interest on the loan, which exceeded the dividends on the stock, so Mitchell had to make birthday, etc. "gifts" to the wife so she could pay him the interest.
- The wife had no way to repay the principal of the debt.
- Mr. Mitchell represented to third parties that he had not sold any of his stock in the bank.
- Three months later, the wife purported to resell the stock to him for $212 per share (her buying price), even though it had declined in value to $45.

2440 *See* Ivan Allen Co. v. United States, 422 U.S. 617, 625 n. 8 (1975) (describing amendment to accumulated earnings tax).

2441 *See* Saltzman & Book, at 7B.02, 8.08[4][a].

2442 *See* I.R.M. 20.1.5.14.1 (listing "badges of fraud").

2443 Mellon v. Commissioner, 36 B.T.A. 977 (1937) (prosecuted by Robert H. Jackson).

2444 See description of taxpayer's actions in Smith v. Higgins, 102 F.2d 456 (2d Cir. 1939).

2445 Helvering v. Mitchell, 303 U.S. 391 (1938).

- Mitchell also fraudulently failed to report $666,666.67 in compensation for the same year.[2446]

By contrast, the more normal cases of tax evasion do not attract a fraud penalty, as Bittker & Lokken observed:

> Deficiencies caused by dividends disguised as salary, improper allocations between personal and business expenses, expensing items that should be capitalized, excessive depreciation, unwarranted bad debt deductions, and other items involving the exercise of judgment are seldom the basis for a fraud penalty unless the intent to evade tax is almost inescapable.[2447]

For example, in *Court Holding Co.*, the Tax Court specifically rejected the fraud penalty.[2448] Both the *Smith* and *Mitchell* cases involved situations in which state law probably would treat the taxpayers as the owners of the property they purportedly sold (vis a vis creditors, *etc.*). Presumably knowing this, the taxpayers nevertheless counted on what they hoped was the bare minimum of paperwork to allow them to tell the government that they had sold their property for tax purposes. In contrast, the only persons ever entitled to the cash sale proceeds in *Court Holding* were the shareholders, and so the tax report that they sold the stock was more in line with legal rights.

It is likely that the term "sham" when used in tax cases actually covers some fraud cases. Indeed, the "sham in fact" variety of shams (as contrasted with "sham in substance") appears necessarily to be frauds. See further discussion below. Randolph Paul similarly struggled with the difference between evasion and avoidance, and concluded that evasion must involve some element of deceit but need not amount to fraud.[2449]

VI.E.1.e(2)(b) *Shams*

Properly understood, a sham is a fraud, which is an intentional lie about a fact.[2450] In early opinions, the Supreme Court used the word sham to describe a lender's attempt to hide usury, for example.[2451] The confused usage in tax began when the Supreme Court employed the term sham in *Moline* in 1943 to describe both a fraudulent use of the corporate form in *Higgins v. Smith* and the very different *Gregory* case, which was based on statutory construc-

---

2446 Mitchell v. Commissioner, 89 F.2d 873 (2d Cir. 1937).

2447 Bittker & Lokken, at 114.6.

2448 Court Holding Co. v. Commissioner, 2 T.C. 531 (1943); *see* Butler, *Income Tax Fraud—Basic Principles*, 33 Or. L. Rev. 199, 208-09 (1958) (observing that not hiding facts helps avoid fraud).

2449 Paul, Studies I, at 16.

2450 *See* Cummings, *The Sham Transaction Doctrine*, 145 Tax Notes (TA) 1239 (Dec. 15, 2014).

2451 *E.g.*, Houghton v. Burden, 228 U.S. 161 (1913); Home Bond Co. v. McChesney, 239 U.S. 568 (1916).

tion that the Court later noticed might also have involved a sham corporation (thoughnot a fraud_ (.[2452]

Gregory construed a business purpose requirement into the reorganization statute and compared the facts with the requirement and found that no reorganization of a business corporation had occurred. Therefore it was a sham reorganization because the facts did not meet the definition. Some later opinions of the Supreme Court confirmed this view.[2453] But in other, offhand, references to *Gregory* the Court referred to a sham corporation.[2454] However, the *Gregory* opinion itself (and the government argument) clearly did not disregard or sham the transitory corporation that was supposed to be the result of the reorganization, but only found the transaction involving a real corporation not to meet the statutory definition of a reorganization. Properly understood, that holding did not make the corporation a sham.

Traditionally the word sham outside the tax law, and even in earlier tax cases, probably meant outright fraud.[2455] But more commonly in tax cases today the term sham refers to conduct short of fraud;[2456] in these cases the word sham is no more than a derogatory adjective; it does not carry additional meaning. But even this view was questioned by an early IRS official, further showing the inutility of the concept:

> By sham I mean that it is not necessary to examine into the state of mind of the particular person who conceived the sham. It is sufficient if by the actions and views of reasonable men it is generally recognized as a sham.[2457]

When the Court found no sham in *Frank Lyon*,[2458] it likely meant there was no legal fraud in that the taxpayer had not disguised a transaction with an undisclosed agent as an arm's length transaction.

More recently tax opinions have developed a terminology that distinguishes "shams in fact" from "shams in substance."[2459] While usage varies, the most reasonable explanation of the distinction is the simplest: the sham in

---

[2452] Moline Properties, Inc. v. Commissioner, 319 U.S. 436 (1943) (saying both cases involved "shams or unreal" corporations).

[2453] Bazley v. Commissioner, 331 U.S. 737 (1947); Helvering v. Gowran, 302 U.S. 238 (1937).

[2454] In addition to *Moline*, Nelson v. Adams USA, Inc., 529 U.S. 460 (2000); Hanover Bank v. Commissioner, 369 U.S. 672 (1962) (cf. cite to *Gregory*); National Carbide Corp. v. Commissioner, 336 U.S. 422 (1949); Helvering v. Minnesota Tea Co., 296 U.S. 378 (1935).

[2455] See insightful analysis and cites in Donahue, *supra* note 18, at 166-67. Dictionaries are not in agreement on the origin of the term "sham," but some suggest that it derives from the terms "shame" or "ashamed," as in the cases of a persons who is disguised and is ashamed of it.

[2456] *Cf.* THE COAL INDUSTRY RETIREE HEALTH BENEFITS ACT OF 1992 (which enacted § 9722 entitled Sham transactions: "If a principal purpose of any transaction is to evade or avoid liability under this chapter, this chapter shall be applied (and such liability shall be imposed) without regard to such transaction.").

[2457] *See* Reiling, *supra* note 26, at 567 (author was Assistant Chief Counsel of the Service).

[2458] Frank Lyon Co. v. United States, 435 U.S. 561 (1978).

[2459] Keinan, *The Economic Substance Doctrine*, *supra* note 1131, at Ch.§ IIIC, Portfolio 508-1.

fact is fraud and the sham in substance is any other form that the tax law will disregard because it does not meet the statutory definition. The "sham in fact" terminology is reminiscent of the original wording of Federal Rule of Civil Procedure 12(f), which up until 1983 allowed a motion to strike a pleading that is "false or sham."[2460] A sham in law (or substance) is best viewed as a nonfraudulent (no parts are hidden) but intentional effort to mischaracterize a transaction for tax purposes.

The earliest use of the sham in fact or law dichotomy in a tax case was in 1965, apparently in response to a Service assertion that the taxpayer had committed a sham in fact or law.[2461] The earliest appearance in the Tax Court was in 1999, citing a 1989 11th Circuit definition: "Courts have recognized two basic types of sham transactions. Shams in fact are transactions that never occur. In such shams, taxpayers claim deductions for transactions that have been created on paper but which never took place. Shams in substance are transactions that actually occurred but which lack the substance their form represents."[2462] Also in 1999 the Joint Committee on Taxation distinguished sham transactions that did not occur (sham in fact), from transactions that did actually occur but would not receive the desired treatment under the economic substance doctrine.[2463]

Contrary to what the 11th Circuit said, courts had not recognized the two types of shams by those names, but, as illustrated by *Higgins v. Smith* and *Gregory*, there were cases of fraud in which the events the taxpayer reported did not occur (which is simply lying), and there were other cases in which the taxpayer's events were all known and appeared to meet the Code's requirements, but the court applied the law on some other basis of fact finding (as in *Gregory*, because the Court construed the statute to require a business purpose). The sham in substance term sometimes is used as an alternate name for the economic substance doctrine.[2464]

One way to separate the subcategories of shams follows:[2465]

- *The definitional fraud or sham (in fact):* Most all of the sham cases involve an analysis of whether some Code definition is met, and one group of these concerns a state of facts, without regard to transactions with other persons. An example is the existence of an "office"; the Court agreed

---

[2460] 2-12 Moore's Federal Practice Civil § 12.37[3][A].

[2461] Cen-Tex, Inc. v. Campbell, 16 A.F.T.R. 2d 5364 (N.D. Tex. 1965) (court found no sham in law or fact), *aff'd*, 377 F.2d 688 (5th Cir. 1967).

[2462] Kirchman v. Commissioner, 862 F.2d 1486 (11th Cir. 1989) (cited by *Winn-Dixie Stores, Inc. v. Commissioner*, 113 T.C. 254 (1999) and *U.P.S. v. Commissioner*, 1999 T.C.M. (RIA) 1999-268).

[2463] Joint Comm. on Taxation, Description and Analysis of Present Law Tax Rules, *supra* note 1158, at § II(A)(2)(b), (c).

[2464] I.R.M. 4.32.1-4 ("sham in substance (lacks business purpose and economic substance").

[2465] Others have similarly attempted to categorize gradations of shams and this list is somewhat similar to those by Warren, *The Requirement of Economic Profit*, *supra* note 1182, at 985; and Fuller, *Business Purpose*, *supra* note 762, at 393.

the taxpayer's office was not a sham due to real activities of the taxpayer involving it.[2466]

- *The unrelated party transaction fraud or sham (in fact):* These cases involve the taxpayer's transaction with an unrelated party, which either (a) was not even papered in the way the taxpayer reported it (a rare case of blatant misrepresentation), or (b) was so papered, but the papering did not reflect the enforceable agreement as a matter of state law, of which *Goodstein* [2467] (discussed in more detail below) should be viewed as a prime example. Distinguishing such cases from shams in substance can be difficult; moreover, courts seem to avoid the distinction, probably because of the ready availability of the tax specific sham in substance approach discussed below, which can overlap the sham in fact.
- *The related party transaction (or agency) fraud or sham (in fact):* These cases involve a special kind of fraud: concealing from the Service the status of a related party as the taxpayer's agent. *Higgins v. Smith* is the classic example. The taxpayer's purported transaction with a related party may have (a) not actually occurred as reported, or (b) may have been misrepresented because the status of the related party as an agent was hidden from the Service. The Court found *Frank Lyon* did not involve a sham because the unrelated lessor really was an unrelated lessor and not the taxpayer's agent. See Ch. VI.F.2.c. The *Court Holding*[2468] and *Cumberland* [2469] cases are in this category because the real issue was whether the sales were made by the shareholders as the agents for the liquidating corporations, but were misrepresented to the Service as corporate sales. *National Carbide* [2470] and *Moline Properties* [2471] both recognized *Gregory* [2472] and *Higgins v. Smith*[2473] as such agency cases involving controlled entities that at best were agents of the taxpayers and probably did not meet the *Moline* standard to be recognized at all.[2474] In the case of *Higgins*, the purported transactions with the corporation did not occur at all. Rather, the corporation was a "desk drawer" corporation and the Court upheld the fraud penalty. The sham and agency cases frequently are also assignment of income cases.[2475]

[2466] Commissioner v. Scottish-Am. Inv. Co., 323 U.S. 119 (1944).

[2467] Goodstein v. Commissioner, 267 F.2d 127 (1st Cir. 1959).

[2468] Commissioner v. Court Holding Co., 324 U.S. 331 (1945).

[2469] United States v. Cumberland Pub. Serv. Co., 338 U.S. 451 (1950).

[2470] National Carbide Corp. v. Commissioner, 336 U.S. 422 (1949).

[2471] Moline Properties, Inc. v. Commissioner, 319 U.S. 436 (1943).

[2472] Gregory v. Helvering, 293 U.S. 465 (1935); Helvering v. Minnesota Tea Co., 296 U.S. 378 (1935) (agreed as to *Gregory*).

[2473] Higgins v. Smith, 308 U.S. 473 (1940).

[2474] Nelson v. Adams USA, Inc., 529 U.S. 460, 471 (2000) (recognized this fact as to *Greogry*, 65 years later).

[2475] All of these elements came together in Commissioner v. Culbertson, 337 U.S. 733 (1949), where the issue was whether the father, the original rancher, ran the ranch or the partnership ran it.

- *The sham (in substance) tax characterization:* This is the most commonly used category, which is misused when actual fraud or agency or failure to meet state law standards might fit the facts better. It frequently is applied to transactions with an unrelated party involving real and binding obligations that are not recognized for tax purposes because the income tax has its own requirements for terms and concepts that may have a different common law meaning. See Ch. VI.E.2. For example: an "investment" is required for depreciation as discussed below; an indebtedness with real intent to repay for money actually borrowed is required for an interest deduction;[2476] a restructuring for business purposes is required for a reorganization.[2477] *Frank Lyon*[2478] stated this concept while ruling for the taxpayer, as did *Consumer Life*[2479] and *Hanover Bank.*[2480] *Knetsch*[2481] is the prime example of a Supreme Court decision finding a sham in substance (there were presumably binding legal obligations but no borrowing in fact and no indebtedness for tax purposes, discussed below); *Goldstein*[2482] is an often cited example, but the court declined to call it a "sham."
- *Cases where some other tax rule should be applied:* Other rules such as that of section 482 frequently could have been applied in sham cases.[2483]
- *Taxpayer planning contrary to Congress' intent:* The term sham is overused when it is applied to a transaction Congress did not intend to cover with a benefit, as in *Carlton,*[2484] where Congress intended a tax benefit for stock purchased from decedents, but decedents' executors appropriated the benefit by buying stock after the death and having it redeemed. The Court was unmoved by talk of sham, and did not even consider trying to construe the original statute to preclude such planning.

The foregoing analysis suggests that the term "sham transaction doctrine" (which the Supreme Court has never used and does not appear in Treasury Regulations) is useless and confusing, as several commentators have observed.[2485]

Though not a Supreme Court decision, *Goodstein* is a case that cannot be avoided in discussing shams, because it and related cases involving the M.

[2476] *See* Equitable Life Assur. Society v. Commissioner, 321 U.S. 560 (1944).

[2477] Gregory v. Helvering, 293 U.S. 465 (1935).

[2478] Frank Lyon Co. v. United States, 435 U.S. 561 (1978).

[2479] United States v. Consumer Life Ins. Co., 430 U.S. 725 (1977).

[2480] Hanover Bank v. Commissioner, 369 U.S. 672 (1962).

[2481] Knetsch v. United States, 364 U.S. 361 (1960).

[2482] Goldstein v. Commissioner, 44 T.C. 284 (1965), *aff'd*, 364 F. 2d 734 (2d Cir. 1966); *see infra* Ch. VI.F.6. "Indebtedness and Interest."

[2483] *See, e.g.*, Shell Petroleum, Inc. v. United States, 102 A.F.T.R. 2d 5085 (S.D. Tex. 2008) (in which the Service argued sham transaction and lost and did not argue the obviously applicable section 482 until it was too late); *see also* Reg. § 1.482-1(f)(1)(i) (stating that the Commissioner is not limited to fraud and sham in asserting section 482).

[2484] United States v. Carlton, 512 U.S. 26 (1994).

[2485] *See* Cummings, *The Sham Transaction Doctrine*, 145 Tax Notes (TA) 1239 (Dec. 15, 2014).

Eli Livingston tax shelter of the 1950's formed a bridge from the New Deal tax shelter cases discussed in Ch. III.C. to the invention of the "economic substance doctrine" and other approaches to tax shelters in the late 20th century.[2486] Supposedly taxpayer bought $10 million worth of securities on 100% margin and pledged the securities for the margin loan. Taxpayer prepaid the interest for six months, intending to claim a large deduction against his income then taxed in the 83% bracket. But in reality the taxpayer never obtained ownership of the securities, the lender never obtained a pledge of the securities and did not advance the $10 million to anyone.[2487] Thus, the "loan" in *Goodstein* probably would not have been enforceable under state law, which would ask the same question about a contract; is this what the parties intended? The Service correctly agreed in one case that a transaction is a sham when it is not binding under state law. [2488]

VI.E.1.e(2)(c) *Knetsch*

Knetsch[2489] deserves more analysis because it and *Frank Lyon* are the last two Supreme Court opinions to decide a tax case using the word "sham," and it is the first Supreme Court tax opinion to refer to a "sham transaction," and the last Supreme Court substantive law decision to rule against the taxpayer involved in what might be called a "tax shelter."[2490] *Knetsch* is not an application of the economic substance doctrine, but rather a case of fact finding.

Taxpayer Knetsch claimed deductions for interest purportedly paid under nonrecourse notes for $4 million. The notes were the purchase price of "annuity bonds" to pay off in the future in the amount of $4 million; the bonds secured the nonrecourse notes. Thus, the taxpayer promised to pay the issuer so it could pay him, but taxpayer had no means of paying the principal and his conduct showed that he was not even going to effectively pay the interest, because he borrowed his payments back immediately. The trial judge found as facts that neither party intended to create an indebtedness owed by

[2486] Goodstein v. Commissioner, 267 F.2d 127 (1st Cir. 1959) (affirming the Tax Court).

[2487] As shown by a variety of evidence including: (1) the margin lender had no capital with which to finance anything; (2) the margin lender was owned by the brother of the planner of the scheme, M. Eli Livingston, (3) the taxpayer borrowed back his interest payments, (4) the stock sale was documented by the friendly broker as having occurred even though the court could find no evidence that it actually occurred, and for these and other reasons the court found as a fact that (5) the parties never intended that an indebtedness be created.

[2488] *See* Commissioner v. Brown, 380 U.S. 563 (1965) (implying that Service agreed sale in that case was not a sham because it was binding under state law).

[2489] Knetsch v. United States, 364 U.S. 361 (1960); *see* Donahue, *supra* note 18, at 168 (citing *Knetsch* and *Goldstein* as the second generation of sham cases); *see also supra* Ch. V.F.2. above discussing *Knetsch* in relation to economic substance doctrine.

[2490] United States v. Woods, 134 S. Ct. 557 (2013) ruled against the taxpayer on a penalty issue and referred to the sham transaction but did not decide the substantive issue.

Knetsch.[2491] It was the trial opinion that said the transaction was a sham, and the Supreme Court only recited that statement.

"Sham" referred to a nonfraudulent disguise: no facts were hidden and the question was one of legal characterization. It is a decision in the cluster area of indebtedness, as discussed in Ch. VI.F.6. It affirmed the trial court's finding of fact that the taxpayer did not pay interest on indebtedness as required for a deduction under section 163(a),[2492] because taxpayer owed no debt: mutually offsetting obligations vitiated the borrowing in form. The debt was sham debt, meaning it was not debt intended to be paid.

The opinion did not deny that legally binding contracts existed (if the insurance company went into bankruptcy, the trustee could have tried to enforce the notes), but rather ruled that the identification of an indebtedness for purposes of the interest deduction allowance requires fact finding to determine if the debtor owes money. This places *Knetsch* in the fact category of cases, not the ambiguous statute category.[2493] The unrelated third party lender entered into binding contracts with the taxpayer that called for the payment of "interest," but they did not constitute a true forbearance.[2494] This can be called a sham in substance.

[2491] Knetsch v. United States, 2 A.F.T.R. 2d 6115 (S.D. Cal. 1958) (The findings of fact included:

> (XIV.) The plaintiff and Sam Houston did not intend that plaintiff become indebted to Sam Houston. (XV.) No indebtedness of the plaintiff was created by any of the plaintiff's transactions with Sam Houston. (XVI.) The plaintiff's payments were no more than annual premiums, the purchase price of a contract on a deferred payment plan. (XVII.) No money or other economic benefit was received by the plaintiff from Sam Houston. (XVIII.) Neither the $143,465 paid by the plaintiff to Sam Houston in 1953 nor the $147,105 paid in 1954, was a payment of interest.).

[2492] *Id.*

[2493] *See* Warren, *The Requirement of Economic Profit*, *supra* note 1182, at 985 (arguing that *Knetsch* was a sham case and did not depend on some broader profit motive requirement, at least where the deduction benefit is made available by Congress); Madison, *supra* note 15, at 726 (stating that *Knetsch* was resolvable by looking at whether the debt was actual or not, rather than by applying a judicial doctrine to override the statute). In the context of the nonrecourse note used, taxpayer had nothing to protect by paying the note. Rev. Rul. 1982-94, 1982-1 C.B. 31 (cites *Knetsch* on similar facts and holds that no debtor creditor relationship existed).

[2494]

> For it is patent that there was nothing of substance to be realized by Knetsch from this transaction beyond a tax deduction. What he was ostensibly 'lent' back was in reality only the rebate of a substantial part of the so-called "interest" payments. The $91,570 difference retained by the company was its fee for providing the facade of "loans" whereby the petitioners sought to reduce their 1953 and 1954 taxes in the total sum of $233,297.68. There may well be single premium annuity arrangements with nontax substance which create an 'indebtedness' for the purposes of section 23(b) of the 1939 Code and section 163(a) of the 1954 Code. But this one is a sham.

Knetsch v. United States, 364 U.S. 361, 366 (1960).

For tax deduction purposes, the Court had consistently ruled that more than a paper writing reciting an obligation to pay was required.[2495] The lower courts and the Service understand this by examining the underlying relationship of the parties: whether the lender really owned the borrowed funds and whether the borrower really borrowed them, despite literal flows of funds and loan documents.[2496] This factual view came to full flower in the stock v. debt arena, where nominal debt is frequently disregarded as such.[2497]

By using the word "sham" the Court clearly did not mean that there were no contracts or that the taxpayer had hidden a fact as in a fraud, but rather that he had presented real facts to portray a picture that was false for tax purposes.[2498] It meant that there was nothing of value bought by taxpayer with a true purchase money obligation, which is a federal tax law requirement for an interest deduction. Taxpayer, as the putative borrower, intended to get nothing and got nothing from the insurance company for his principal debt (which would always reduce any payout on the annuity).

The *Knetsch* decision came just prior to a spate of decisions holding nondeductible the interest paid on nonrecourse debt secured by property worth considerably less than the debt.[2499] For example, *Estate of Franklin*[2500] denied a deduction for interest actually paid on a nonrecourse obligation (as in *Knetsch*) on the ground that either the obligation was not enforceable, based on all the surrounding circumstances, or was too indefinite or tentative to create debt (because the value of the security was far less than the amount of the obligation). *Franklin* reached this conclusion under section 163. Neither the Tax Court nor the Ninth Circuit found it necessary in *Franklin* to resort to off-Code rules to find that there was no debt to the extent the taxpayer would not be economically interested in paying nonrecourse debt in an amount that exceeded the value of the security. There is no reason to think that the Supreme Court in *Knetsch* was doing anything different from what the lower

---

2495 *See, e.g.,* Deputy v. Du Pont, 308 U.S. 488 (1940) (ruling that the remission of dividends received on borrowed stock was not interest); Old Colony R.R. Co. v. Commissioner, 284 U.S. 552, 560 (1932) ("And as respects 'interest,' the usual import of the term is the amount which one has contracted to pay for the use of borrowed money.").

2496 *See, e.g.,* Rev. Rul. 1987-69, 1987-2 C.B. 46 (refusing to treat as a loan the loan back of funds given by parent to child, reasoning that the child never obtained ownership of the funds through the initial "gift" due to the obligation to lend it back; citing Guar. Trust Co. v. Commissioner, 98 F.2d 62 (2d Cir. 1938) (husband transferred funds to his wife under a prearranged agreement for the wife to create a trust with herself as trustee, and the trust returned the money to the husband as a purported loan)); *accord,* Elbert v. Commissioner, 45 B.T.A. 685 (1941) (In the context of the nonrecourse note used, taxpayer had nothing to protect by paying the note.).

2497 *See* 1432 Broadway Corp. v. Commissioner, 4 T.C. 1158 (1945*), aff'd,* 160 F.2d 885 (2d Cir. 1947) (viewed as upsetting all tax planning by Flack, *Where Tax Savings Is Behind Business Purpose*, 23 TAXES (CCH) 910 (1945)).

2498 *See* Warren, *The Requirement of Economic Profit, supra* note 1182, at 985 (which views this as a sham in fact case).

2499 *See* Rev. Rul. 1977-110, 1977-1 C.B. 58.

2500 Estate of Franklin v. Commissioner, 544 F.2d 1045 (9th Cir. 1976).

courts did in *Franklin*. Thus, *Knetsch* stands for a limited cluster rule for defining indebtedness, even though the Court cited *Gregory*.

Other commentators agree to a modest view of *Knetsch*. Shapiro viewed *Knetsch* as a good example of the Warren Court's gingerly and modest approach, desiring to avoid over involvement in complex tax matters.[2501] The Warren Court also avoided establishing legal standards as opposed to case by case decisions in which it stressed facts rather than law (with the major exception of *Glenshaw Glass*).[2502] As evidence, *Knetsch* refused to confirm or deny the appellate court's view that the total absence of nontax purpose itself voided the interest deduction. The Court may have felt its easiest course was to defer to the Service, and to avoid making rules because more detailed rules can be avoided.[2503]

Professor Blum[2504] criticized *Knetsch*, while agreeing that it was different from *Gregory*, which construed the statute. Professor Warren[2505] described *Knetsch* as both finding facts based on substance, and also possibly asserting that whatever the facts might be, the tax results could not stand due to the absence of profit potential. He characterized this suggestion as the "central stage" in the development of the "economic profit doctrine," which had been picked up by the Second Circuit in *Goldstein* (which is better viewed as interpreting a business purpose requirement into the interest deduction).[2506] As discussed in Ch. V.F.2, *Knetsch* is indeed the turning point of the economic substance doctrine, even though it did not apply it, identify it, or label it.

VI.E.1.e(3) *Related Party Transactions*

No discussion of cases refusing to accept a taxpayer's version of the facts can avoid recognizing the special issues surrounding a taxpayer's transactions with persons who are related by interest or family. Section 482 is the first among many Code sections that applies additional scrutiny to related party transactions. All courts will examine the facts of related party transactions more closely because they lack the presumption of arm's length dealings that usually (but by no means always) assures the bona fides of transactions with unre-

---

[2501] Shapiro, *The Warren Court and Federal Tax Policy*, *supra* note 435, at 208; *see, e.g.*, Aquilino v. United States, 363 U.S. 509 (1960) (remanding to the New York courts a tax lien dispute so that New York could determine the property rights of the federal taxpayer, before reaching the issue of the primacy of the federal tax lien).

[2502] *See* Barker, *supra* note 25, at 857 ("the almost mystical power of Chief Justice Warren's words").

[2503] *Id.* at 223.

[2504] Blum, *Knetsch v. United States: A Pronouncement on Tax Avoidance*, 1961 SUP. CT. REV. 135.

[2505] Warren, *Requirement of Economic Profit*, *supra* note 1182, at 986.

[2506] Goldstein v. Commissioner, 44 T.C. 284 (1965), *aff'd*, 364 F.2d 734 (2d Cir. 1966).

lated parties.[2507] The importance of relatedness is illustrated by two signature taxpayer victories in the Supreme Court:

1. The Supreme Court ruled for the taxpayer in *Frank Lyon* because it was involved in a "multiparty transaction," which apparently meant in part that the counterparties were unrelated, which was true only after the Court found Lyon was not its lessee's agent.[2508]
2. Similarly in *Cottage Savings*, the Court relied heavily on the fact that the taxpayer actually transferred property to an unrelated party, despite its receipt of economically identical property in the exchange. [2509]

Related party transactions could be listed as one of the cluster areas discussed below except for the fact that the tax case law has not developed a cohesive approach to related party transactions to accompany the suspicion usually applied to them. The reasons may be that (1) the suspicion is so well engrained in the common law that common law fact finding meets all the needs not otherwise supplied by (2) the many Code and regulation related party rules.[2510]

Other cluster areas discussed below are subsets of related party transactions, for example: most assignment of income cases, transactions between taxpayers and their agents, and transactions between taxpayers and their controlled entities (*Higgins v. Smith*, involving an alter ego). The tax specific doctrines most frequently involve transactions between related persons,[2511] or tax-indifferent persons. It is more useful to identify a related party transaction as such and to apply nontax evidentiary and substantive methods and principles before or in lieu of applying tax specific doctrines. Those methods and principles include the following categories.

[2507] *See* Blank & Staudt, *Corporate Shams*, *supra* note 4, at 1642, 1685 (reporting a statistically significant finding that the Supreme Court is more likely to rule for a corporate taxpayer whose transaction involves third parties).

[2508] Frank Lyon Co. v. United States, 435 U.S. 561 (1978).

[2509] Cottage Savings Assn. v. Commissioner, 499 U.S. 554 (1991).

[2510] Examples of Code limitations on related party transactions include: section 108(e)(4) (related person discharging debt of taxpayer); section 267 (disallowing losses and deferring deductions between related parties); sections 302 (a sufficiently high level of share ownership can cause a redemption to be treated as a dividend), 304 (a sufficient high level of share ownership can cause a stock sale to be treated as a dividend), 1561 (related corporation limitations); section 453(e) (second disposition by related person stops installment method);section 482 (the Code's principal general attack on related party transactions, discussed in Ch. IV.B.); subchapter K's many anti-avoidance rules, such as section 704(c) and Regulation section 1.701-2, which are based on the inherent relatedness of partnerships, usually with a small number of members who know each other; section 1031(f) (like kind exchanges limited); section 1239 (capital gains limited); the subpart F rules that apply special limitations on shareholders of controlled foreign corporations, defined as foreign corporations more than 50% of the vote or value of which is owned by United States shareholders owning 10% or more; andsection 7872 (interest free loans between related persons recharacterized).

[2511] *See* BITTKER & LOKKEN, at 4.3.3.

Estate tax cases. The Supreme Court struggled in many opinions with whether a transfer took effect in possession or enjoyment at death. These are always related party transactions. At first the Court relied primarily on form and legal title, but in *Hallock* plainly stated that in determining whether a transfer becomes complete only at death it looks to substance not form.[2512]

Family Partnerships. The Court ruled that a family partnership could not be disregarded out of hand. See Ch. VI.F.3.d.

Evidentiary truthfulness. The Supreme Court has not stated a presumption generally that transactions between related parties are not bona fide.[2513] The Federal Rules of Evidence do not limit the competency of related witnesses. But evidence offered by biased or interested persons has always been subject to attack in court as bearing on its credibility.[2514] In *Helvering v. Clifford,* Justice Douglas said that "special scrutiny" was required due to the close relation of the taxpayers.[2515] That statement illustrates the point that in related party transactions the Court's concern is not grounded on tax saving motives, but in the more generic suspicion of the arm's length nature of transactions between closely related parties and of the evidence such parties supply.

Arm's length prices. The Supreme Court recognizes without discussion that related persons, such as related corporations, may deal with each other on non-arm's-length basis.[2516] The Code is especially concerned with these cases, as reflected in section 482, which gives the Service substantial discretion to adjust the reporting of business taxpayers engaging in related party transactions. To the extent the taxpayers represent the non-arm's-length prices to be fair to the Service, such representations also can be fraudulent.

Griffiths v. Helvering ignored the attempted form of the shareholder transferring stock to his wholly owned corporation and the corporation selling the stock for $100,000 both because (1) it was a *Court Holding* type of case in which the trial court found as a fact that the sale occurred in the hands of the shareholder, and (2) it was an assignment of income case in that the $100,000 received was not for the stock at all (the stock had just been bought for $8,000 and presumably that was its value, not $100,000), rather it was in settlement of a tort claim based on the earlier purchase of the stock by the shareholder.[2517] The Board of Tax Appeals rejected the fraud penalty, surprisingly.[2518]

[2512] Helvering v. Hallock, 309 U.S. 106 (1940); Commissioner v. Estate of Church, 335 U.S. 632 (1949).

[2513] *See* Shauer v. Alterton, 151 U.S. 607 (1894) (fraudulent conveyance).

[2514] *See* WIGMORE, *supra* note 1083, at § 943.

[2515] Helvering v. Clifford, 309 U.S. 331 (1940).

[2516] Container Corp. of Am. v. Franchise Tax Bd., 463 U.S. 159, 190 (1983) ("closely related corporations can engage in a transfer of values that is not fully reflected in their formal ledgers.").

[2517] Griffiths v. Helvering, 308 U.S. 355 (1939).

[2518] Griffiths v. Commissioner, 37 B.T.A., 314 (1938).

Treating two or more taxpayers as one. With the few exceptions of true "alter ego" situations that prove the rule, like *Higgins v. Smith*,[2519] the tax law does not treat two taxpayers as one, as shown by the absence of attribution of ownership of property from one taxpayer to another except as specifically stated in the Code.[2520]

Control. Related parties frequently control one another's actions. This fact underlies the assignment of income doctrine.[2521] It was a spurious ground for treating two taxpayers as one in *Higgins v. Smith*.[2522] It applies appropriately in cases of transactions between the taxpayer and its agent (which *Higgins v. Smith* may be viewed as).

VI.E.1.e(4) *Taxpayer's Ability to Reject Form*

Generally the taxpayer does not have the same latitude to reject the form of its transactions that the government enjoys.[2523] The reason is that the taxpayer generally has chosen the form of its transactions, or at least has been a party to those choices, and so suffers from a sort of estoppel.[2524] Also, allowing a taxpayer to reject its form would amount to the application of equity in the taxpayer's favor, and as discussed in Ch. V.E.1.f., there generally is no equity for taxpayers in the application of the federal tax laws. However, if the taxpayer rejects the form it has chosen as by not respecting it, the Service also may hold it to the "form" of that rejection.[2525]

Example: Doctor properly forms corporation to operate her medical practice and maintains a set of books reflecting the practice's income as the corporation's income, but holds herself out to patients and the rest of the world as operating as a sole practitioner. In this case, the form chosen by the doctor is not the form she actually used to practice medicine. Therefore, when the Service treats the income as her personal income, it is not disregarding the form she chose, rather it is holding her to the form she used.

[2519] *See supra* Ch. III.C.3.a(2).

[2520] *See, e.g.,* I.R.C. § 318. The exclusivity of the Code's attribution rules is implied in *United States v. Davis*, 397 U.S. 301 (1970).

[2521] *See* BITTKER & LOKKEN, at 75.2.1.

[2522] *See supra* Ch. III.C.3.a(2).

[2523] *See* BITTKER & LOKKEN, at 4.3.6; Blatt, *Lost on a One Way Street*, *supra* note 885, at 381; *Treasury White Paper on Corporate Tax Shelters*, *supra* note 14, at sec. IV.B.1.c.

[2524] *See* Commissioner v. Nat'l Alfalfa Dehydrating & Milling Co., 417 U.S. 134, 149 (1974) (". . . once having done so he must accept the tax consequences of his choice . . ."); Helvering v. Coleman-Gilbert Associates, 296 U.S. 369 (1935) (terms of trust controlled over how it might have been actually operated).

[2525] The first indication that substance over form probably would be a one way street in favor of the government was when *Higgins v. Smith*, 308 U.S. 473, 477 (1940) (no loss on sale to controlled corporation), distinguished *Burnet v. Commonwealth Improvement Co.*, 287 U.S. 415 (1932) (but gain must be recognized in analogous case). *See, e.g.,* Commissioner v. Hansen, 360 U.S. 446 (1959) (auto dealer could not recast his financed auto sales as borrowings by car buyers directly from lender).

Except for early cases like *Macomber*, which sometimes ignored form in finding income as a matter of constitutional interpretation,[2526] most of the decisions that have allowed taxpayers to reject their forms have applied common law and equitable fact finding. The primary example is *F. & R. Lazarus*,[2527] which ruled that the substance of a conveyance absolute in form should control to allow the conveyor to depreciate the property because the integrated transaction was a secured loan. Another example is *Tex-Penn*,[2528] discussed in Ch. VI.E.3.b., which used standard methods of interpretation of contracts to get at the intent of the parties, contrary to form. Such approaches most frequently arise in cases of corporate reorganizations.[2529] As late as 1936 it was thought that the courts applied substance over form in favor of taxpayers "with absolute impartiality."[2530] But that view is no longer the norm.

A recent empirical study of the use of judicial doctrines (with substance over form being the principal doctrine examined) in tax cases from 1993 to 2006 did not find evidence of a "one-way" rule in the courts.[2531] It concluded that taxpayers frequently do raise the judicial doctrines, although often to argue against them, and sometimes prevail in applying them.[2532] However, the specifics of the study did indicate a bias in favor of the Servicewith doctrines like substance over form.

A slightly different issue arises when a taxpayer argues substance over form in the determination of the nature of a law. The taxpayer PPL argued successfully that in substance the U.K. windfall tax was an income tax that should be creditable and the Court agreed, but actually based its reasoning on the formal fact that the tax fomula included net income.[2533]

[2526] *See supra* Ch. II.B.2.c(3); *see also* Weiss v. Stearn, 265 U.S. 242 (1924) ("when applying the provisions of the Sixteenth Amendment and income laws enacted thereunder we must regard matters of substance and not mere form.").

[2527] Helvering v. F. & R. Lazarus & Co., 308 U.S. 252 (1939); *see also* U.S. Trust Co. v. Commissioner, 296 U.S. 481 (1936) (upholding taxpayer's treatment of a single trust in form as three trusts because the property and income was operated as three trusts in accord with the intent of the grantor); *see supra* Ch. V.E.1.f(2).

[2528] *See, e.g.*, Helvering v. Tex-Penn Oil Co., 300 U.S. 481 (1937) (the Court allowed circumstantial evidence to controvert the deal agreement that identified a $350,000 cash payment as part of the reorganization exchange proceeds); Thomas v. Perkins, 301 U.S. 655, 659 n. 2 (1937) (granting clause of conveyance appeared to transfer ownership of oil, but other parts of document showed that transferor retained ownership of part of the oil, for example that he was to be paid only in the oil); Anderson v. Wilson, 289 U.S. 20 (1933) (trustee had ownership of property that it sold under a power of sale, and thus was the only party that could report the loss, despite the fact that it did not hold title; it held powers amounting to ownership).

[2529] *See Tex-Penn Oil Co.* 300 U.S. at 481; *see also* Helvering v. Minnesota Tea Co., 296 U.S. 378 (1935); Weiss v. Stearn, 265 U.S. 242 (1924).

[2530] Layman, *supra* note 224, at 576.

[2531] Schneider, *supra* note 885, at 35.

[2532] *Id.*

[2533] PPL Corp. v. Commissioner, 133 S. Ct. 1897 (2013). *See* Cummings, *Form, Substance, and* PPL, 140 Tax Notes (TA) 365 (July 22, 2013). *See also* Nat'l Life Ins. Co. v. United States, 277 U.S. 50 (1928) (agreeing with taxpayer that exempt bonds in substance were taxed by denial of deductions).

VI.E.2. *State Law*

Normally the federal courts find facts in tax cases in the same ways, using the same tools, that state courts would use when faced with the same factual issues.[2534] See Ch. VI.E.1.e(1) on "Normal Fact Finding." The discussion of equity in Ch. V.E.1. above shows how the Supreme Court relied on state and federal equity court's methods to determine who owned nominally leased real property.[2535] The Court sometimes takes a shortcut to the terms of a state law rule by citing a Restatement of the law.[2536] This provides a sort of nationwide uniformity, but not a uniformity attributable to creating a unique federal rule.[2537] However, the Supreme Court frequently has stated that "The labels applied to a transaction for purposes of State law are not binding for Federal tax purposes."[2538] These departures from state law in the federal tax cases have grown over time and have marked a shift from the early formalism with which some federal tax rules (for example the definition of corporate reorganizations, before *Gregory v. Helvering*) were applied.[2539]

There are several sound reasons for the Court's refusal to be bound by state law characterizations, and one spurious reason:

- The spurious reason is that sometimes the statement that state law does not control only means that state law "labels" do not control, which the state law itself well might agree with, depending on the function performed by the labels.
- The Court wants to avoid state control of the federal taxing power.[2540]

[2534] *See* Arthur Andersen LLP v. Carlisle, 129 S. Ct. 1896 (2009) (in which Justice Scalia stated in the opinion of the Court: ". . . 'traditional principles' of state law allow a contract to be enforced by or against nonparties to the contract through 'assumption, piercing the corporate veil, alter ego, incorporation by reference, third-party beneficiary theories, waiver and estoppel,' 21 R. Lord, Williston on Contracts, sec. 57:19, p. 183 (4th ed. 2001).").

[2535] *See also* Helvering v. Stuart, 317 U.S. 154 (1942) (this opinion also expressed a strong preference to respect the determination of state law as made by the court of appeals that sits for the circuit in which the state is located). As to state law and federal taxes, see generally Bittker & Lokken, at 4.1.

[2536] Commissioner v. Banks, 543 U.S. 426 (2005).

[2537] Kolstad v. ADA, 527 U.S. 526 (1999); Burlington Indus. v. Ellerth, 524 U.S. 742 (1998).

[2538] Commissioner v. Estate of Bosch, 387 U.S. 456 (1967); Morgan v. Commissioner, 309 U.S. 78, 81 (1940) (whether power of appointment is "general" is question of federal law).

[2539] *See* Klarmann, *Metamorphosis of the General Principles in Federal Income Taxation*, 36 Taxes (CCH) 179, 180-81 (1958) (increasing number of tax specific concepts); Reiling, *supra* note 26, at 564-65 (author was Assistant Chief Counsel of the Service).

[2540] Burnet v. Harmel, 287 U.S. 103 (1932) (state law characterization of oil property leases as sales cannot control the plenary power of Congress to tax).

- The Court believes that federal taxation should apply on a uniform basis throughout the country.[2541] However, it is inevitable that state law differences will produce different federal tax results, as occurred in the treatment of property divisions in community property states versus common law states.[2542] On the other hand, the Court specifically declined to pursue uniformity as to tax lien enforcement,[2543] which is typical of the Court's refusal to create nationwide uniformity through federal common law for many collection issues.[2544]
- The Court has refused to be bound by lower state court decisions involving the taxpayer, but decisions of the highest state court can control certain fact findings for federal tax purposes.[2545]
- Related to the desire for nationwide uniformity, the Court realizes that the Code frequently uses common terms that must carry a special or different import for federal tax purposes, in one of two ways:
  - Satisfying the state law meaning of a specific term usually is a necessary but not sufficient ground for applying the Code rule using the term because other considerations are relevant to an income tax: for example, the existence of binding legal obligations to pay money denominated as interest does not prove that the payment is interest on an indebtedness that qualifies for a deduction allowance under sections 162 or 163 (see *Knetsch*).
  - Alternately, satisfying the state law meaning is irrelevant to the application of a tax rule. For example: (i) the fact that one spouse legally owns the right to receive the husband's salary does not prevent the other spouse from being taxed on her receipts, under the assignment of income doctrine;[2546] (ii) the fact that a state views a 99 year lease as equal to fee ownership does not bind the federal tax laws because

---

2541 United States v. Irvine, 511 U.S. 224 (1994); Estate of Putnam v. Commissioner, 324 U.S. 393, 395-396 (1945) (meaning should be uniform unless Congress indicates an intent to be governed by state law); Helvering v. Stuart, 317 U.S. 154 (1942); Lyeth v. Hoey, 305 U.S. 188 (1938) (inheritance exclusion must provide nationwide uniformity and so cannot depend on state law characterization); Thomas v. Perkins, 301 U.S. 655 (1937). *See* Reiling, *supra* note 26, at 564-65 (author was Assistant Chief Counsel of the Service). But lack of uniformity caused by varying state laws does not cause the tax law to be unconstitutional on grounds of nonuniformity of application. Fernandez v. Wiener, 326 U.S. 340 (1945).

2542 United States v. Davis, 370 U.S. 65 (1962) (the Court rejected the taxpayer's contention that to treat property divisions in divorces differently depending on the state law would make the outcome turn on "elusive and subtle casuistries which . . . possess no relevance for tax purposes.").

2543 Commissioner v. Stern, 357 U.S. 39, 44 (1958); Phillips v. Commissioner, 283 U.S. 589 (1931).

2544 *See generally* Cummings, *Nationwide Uniformity and the Common Law of Federal Taxation*, 66 Tax Law. 1 (2012).

2545 Commissioner v. Estate of Bosch, 387 U.S. 456 (1967) (stating that the doctrine of *Erie v. Tompkins* is not controlling); *see* Bittker & Lokken, at 4.1.5.

2546 Lucas v. Earl, 281 U.S. 111 (1930).

the Congress has different concerns;[2547] and (iii) the fact that a devise to an alien is void under state law did not prevent application of a federal inheritance tax.[2548]

The Court has tried to explain the relationship of state law to fact finding in federal tax cases in different ways:

- The Court has stated that for purposes of a federal tax lien on property, state law determines which sticks are in a person's bundle and federal tax law determines whether those sticks are property for federal tax purposes. These statements most frequently appear in decisions involving tax liens, which decisions should be separated for purposes of analysis because the Court is most deferential to state law property rules in the area of tax liens.[2549]
- The Court stated in an early association decision: "It is true that Congress cannot convert into a corporation an organization which by the law of its state is deemed to be a partnership. But nothing in the Constitution precludes Congress from taxing as a corporation an association which, although unincorporated, transacts its business as if it were incorporated."[2550]
- The Court stated: "Congress establishes its own criteria and the state law may control only when the federal taxing act by express language or necessary implication makes its operation dependent on state law."[2551]

Of course the law is otherwise when the Code specifically depends on an event as defined by state law: the classic example is the "statutory merger" that

---

[2547] Weiss v. Wiener, 279 U.S. 333 (1929).

[2548] Scholey v. Rew, 90 U.S. 331 (1875) (taxpayer had asserted ownership regardless of lack of right, and so was estopped).

[2549] United States v. Craft, 535 U.S. 274 (2002); *see also* Drye v. United States, 528 U.S. 49 (1999) (disclaimer ineffective to divest taxpayer's property interest for lien purposes); United States v. Nat'l Bank of Commerce, 472 U.S. 713 (1985) (state creates right in bank account and federal law determines whether the Service can levy); Henneford v. Silas Mason Co., 300 U.S. 577 (1937) ("bundle of privileges"). Very early in a case not involving liens, Burnet v. Harmel, 287 U.S. 103 (1932), the Court stated:

> For the purpose of applying this section to the particular payments now under consideration, the act of Congress has its own criteria, irrespective of any particular characterization of the payments in the local law. . . .The state law creates legal interests, but the federal statute determines when and how they shall be taxed.

Unfortunately the "bundle of sticks" analogy has a questionable lineage: it was part of the Eighth Circuit's reasoning in Frank Lyon Co. v. United States, 536 F.2d 746 (8th Cir. 1976), *reversed,* 435 U.S. 561 (1978) (the Supreme Court recited the Circuit's theory but did not apply it as such). For further discussion, see Ch. VI.F.2.a.

[2550] Burk-Waggoner Oil Assn. v. Hopkins, 269 U.S. 110 (1925); *see* Reiling, *supra* note 26, at 566 (identifying this case as the first major example of the need to ignore state law in certain cases to create uniformity across the country in the application of the tax laws).

[2551] Lyeth v. Hoey, 305 U.S. 188 (1938).

can be a tax reorganization.[2552] In *Metropolitan Edison*, the Court allowed the fact that a state court viewed a subsidiary liquidation into its parent as a "de facto merger" to determine whether it was a merger for federal tax purposes, despite the failure to comply exactly with either of the state's two merger/consolidation statutes.[2553] Presumably the explanation is that the Code looked to whether the transaction occurred under the state's merger statutes and if a state court said it did in effect, then it did for tax purposes. This case is somewhat out of step with other authorities.[2554]

Finally, reliance on state law labels can become a constitutional issue, as occurred in a decision holding the Defense of Marriage Act unconstitutional, and allowing the tax law (and other federal laws) to incorporate state determinations of marriage.[2555]

VI.E.3. *The Last Word in Fact Finding*

The degree to which the trial court's fact findings (in a Tax Court or other non-jury trial) control the outcome of a case that is appealed is supposed to be governed by Rule 52(a) of the Federal Rules of Civil Procedure, which directs that trial court findings of fact are not be rejected unless "clearly erroneous." This exception is broad enough to allow appellate courts to have great latitude to decide appeals based on a different view of the facts.

VI.E.3.a. *In the Tax Court:* Dobson

The Tax Court always rules without a jury and its decisions are reviewed in the same manner as decisions of the district courts sitting without a jury, under section 7482(a)(1). However, it has not always been so. For about 20 years, the fact findings of the Board of Tax Appeals (renamed the Tax Court of the United States in 1942) were, or were supposed to be, unreviewable, under what came to be called the "*Dobson* rule," named after the case that belatedly enforced a statute making the Tax Court fact finding unreviewable.[2556] The *Dobson* rule was based on deference to administrative action, because, until 1969, the Tax Court functioned as an administrative agency that reviewed the actions of another administrative agency, the Service; in 1969, Congress made it a court of law exercising the judicial power, albeit within the Executive Branch.[2557]

The current relevance of these prior rules is twofold: (1) to show that they worked and could work again, and (2) to suggest a linkage of the repeal in 1948 of the statute on which the *Dobson* rule was based to the rise of the

---

2552 I.R.C. § 368(a)(1)(A).

2553 Helvering v. Metropolitan Edison Co., 306 U.S. 522 (1939). A similar regulatory relaxation of the merger definition did not occur until 2003 in T.D. 9038, 2003-1 C.B. 524.

2554 Bittker & Lokken, at 4.1.3, 4.1.4.

2555 United States v. Windsor, 133 S. Ct. 2675 (2013).

2556 *Dobson v. Commissioner*, 320 U.S. 489 (1943); *see* Paul, Dobson v. Commissioner*: The Strange Ways of Law and Facts*, 57 Harv. L. Rev. 753 (1944); Stark, *supra* note 417, at 214.

2557 *See* Freytag v. Commissioner, 501 U.S. 868 (1991).

ESD some decades later.[2558] The ESD was created in the lower courts to deal with a wave of "tax shelters." If the Tax Court had been allowed to retain its nearly absolute ability to find facts, it might have defeated various perceived tax shelters by normal methods of fact finding.[2559] Instead, largely as a result of vague language in opinionsof the courts of appeal (see *Goldstein*, *Goodstein*, *Rice's Toyota*) the ESD was developed and took the place in many cases of basic fact finding methods.[2560]

Justice Jackson wrote the *Dobson* opinion. He was the Justice most knowledgeable about federal tax administration, having litigated an astounding number of big tax cases as Chief Counsel, Assistant Attorney General, Attorney General and Solicitor General. The *Dobson* opinion emphasized that the 1926 statute allocated fact finding responsibility to the Tax Court based on the view of Congress that "administrative finality" in taxation was desirable.[2561] By "administrative" Congress referred to the fact that the Board of Tax Appeals was viewed as an administrative agency at that time. When Congress revised the law in 1948 to reduce that administrative finality, it laid the groundwork for the burgeoning influence of the other federal courts in the creation of the doctrines and for the forum flexibility that has helped to propel complexity in the tax law.

The Revenue Act of 1924 created the Board of Tax Appeals as an independent agency in the executive branch; the Revenue Act of 1926 limited review of its decisions by the appellate courts to questions of law.[2562] The 1926 legislative history confirmed that Congress intended to limit review to questions of law, which included "the existence of at least some evidence to support the findings of fact and the validity of any ruling upon the admissibility of evidence."[2563] Justice Jackson rejected the recommendation of his clerk that fact versus law distinctions are not very meaningful; he evidently was motivated by two practical views he had derived from his close association with the New Deal and with the Bureau of Internal Revenue: (1) taxes were too

---

[2558] Goldberg, *supra* note 175, at 27 (attributing to the *Dobson* rule three of four key pro-government tax decisions of the period, which marked a turning toward less freedom for taxpayers).

[2559] As it did in *Glass v. Commissioner*, 87 T.C. 1087 (1986), reviewed, affirmed by nine circuits including the 6th Circuit, *Ratliff v. Commissioner*, 865 F.2d 97 (1989), and not reversed by any circuit. This involved a securities straddle that has reappeared in various forms of tax shelters. Later cases had much more difficulty applying fact finding. *See, e.g.*, Wright v. Commissioner, 809 F. 3d 877 (6th Cir. 2016).

[2560] For a discussion of how fact finding was replaced by the ESD in one type of cases, see Cummings, *The New Normal, supra* note 769, at 521 (contrasting the Tax Court's reasoning in *Palm Canyon* in 2009 with the London Option Cases in the 1980's).

[2561] John Kelley Co. v. Commissioner, 326 U.S. 521 (1946).

[2562] Revenue Act of 1926, § 1003(b), 44 Stat. 110 (codified at 26 U.S.C. 1141) (directed the appellate court to "affirm, or if the decision of the Board is not in accordance with law, to modify or reverse the decision of the Board, with or without remanding . . .").

[2563] S. FIN. COMM., 69th Cong. Report No. 52 36 (Jan. 16, 1926).

much litigated, and (2) the expertise of federal agencies should be accorded enhanced deference.[2564]

In other words, for Jackson to say that review of the Tax Court's decisions should be limited to issues of law was not so much a focus on the law versus fact distinction as it was using the statutory tool at hand to enforce deference to the Tax Court and to limit tax litigation. *Thus, Jackson was using the limit on the scope of appeal in a way similar to the Service's currentuse of the tax specific doctrines: as a rough thumb on the scales in favor of the government.* Jackson could do nothing about the more likely cause of lack of deference to the Board: the existence of two other refund routes of tax cases to the appellate courts, which had pre-dated the Board, and the appellate courts' inevitable tendency to review all tax appeals on the same basis.[2565]

Dobson even proclaimed that mixed questions of law and fact (and "ultimate facts") that could not be teased apart should be treated as fact questions.[2566] Justice Jackson based this expansive concept of the expertise of the Tax Court on the fact that it was an administrative agency that was accorded deference, not on a conclusion about the meaning of mixed questions. He joined Justice Frankfurter in concurring in *Bingham's Trust*, where they contended that the interpretation of the Code was a matter within the Tax Court's expertise, as was its application to facts it found.[2567] However, the opinion of the Court rejected the idea that the Tax Court could finally decide which were questions of fact.

Dobson was to be short lived for two reasons. First, it employed a questionable rationale that (a) questions of accounting fell into the fact category, and that (b) the tax benefit rule was a question of accounting and therefore one of fact.[2568] Second, and probably more important, it failed to, indeed it could not, solve the problem that the taxpayer could avoid the Board by paying the tax and suing for refund in either of two trial courts. This exacerbated the practical problem that limiting review of the Board meant limiting the chances of both the Bureau and of taxpayers (and their advocates) to prevail

---

[2564] Barrett, *Justice Jackson on "What the Law's Going to Be—At Least Until Its 'Gelding',"* 6 Green Bag 2d 123 (2003); Paul, *Dobson v. Commissioner, supra* note 2556, at 754-55.

[2565] *Id.* at 760-61.

[2566] 320 U.S. at 501.

[2567] Bingham's Trust v. Commissioner, 325 U.S. 365 (1945). Justice Frankfurter similarly expressed his view of the Tax Court's administrative expertise in the *McDonald* opinion. McDonald v. Commissioner, 323 U.S. 57 (1944). For another example where the Tax Court effectively created the very important distinction between business and investing, without assistance from the Supreme Court, see *Higgins v. Commissioner*, 312 U.S. 212 (1941), which affirmed the Board of Tax Appeals.

[2568] Paul, *Dobson v. Commissioner, supra* note 2556, at 765, 797.

through appeals; commentators said that all of taxpayers, the government and the courts disliked *Dobson*.[2569]

This chorus caused Congress to be dissatisfied with *Dobson* (which had simply applied the language Congress had written) and, in 1948, to adopt what became section 7482(a) of the Code, requiring that Tax Court decisions be reviewed in the same manner as decisions of district courts sitting without a jury.[2570] Jackson was not happy.[2571] Other Justices sided with him and cited *Dobson* to emphasize how complex was the tax law and how the general courts should defer to the specialty court.[2572]

Had *Dobson* survived unchanged, it could have limited the development of the tax specific doctrines, at least in Tax Court matters, because they frequently are approaches to fact finding.[2573] In fact Jackson's opinion in *Dobson* went far in proclaiming that step transaction and other fact integrative methods, and all matters of accounting, were issues of fact. When a court applies the doctrines as fact finding tools, or applies earlier tools to combat tax avoidance,[2574] or applies more traditional common law fact finding methodologies, the court properly emphasizes the fact finding function and heavily weights the case outcome toward the work of the trial courts. Consequently, there is

---

[2569] Note, *Dobson Rule Abolished by New Statute Governing Review of Tax Court Decisions*, 1 Stan. L. Rev. 305, 306 (1948); Note, *Legislative Correction of the Dobson Rule*, 10 U. Pitt. L. Rev. 83 (1948); Wattles, *Federal Tax Cases upon Appeal: The Rise and Demise of the Dobson Rule*, 1 U. Fla. L. Rev. 333 (1948).

[2570] *See* Note, *Interpretation of the Internal Revenue Code: Courts v. Commissioner*, 32 Ind. L.J. 400, 409 (1956).

[2571] Mr. Justice Jackson, whom Mr. Justice Frankfurter joined, dissented in *Arrowsmith v. Commissioner*, 344 U.S. 6 (1952), stating:

> Solicitude for the revenues is a plausible but treacherous basis upon which to decide a particular tax case. A victory may have implications which in future cases will cost the Treasury more than a defeat. This might be such a case, for anything I know. Suppose that subsequent to liquidation it is found that a corporation has undisclosed claims instead of liabilities and that under applicable state law they may be prosecuted for the benefit of the stockholders. The logic of the Court's decision here, if adhered to, would result in a lesser return to the Government than if the recoveries were considered ordinary income. Would it be so clear that this is a capital loss if the shoe were on the other foot? Where the statute is so indecisive and the importance of a particular holding lies in its rational and harmonious relation to the general scheme of the tax law, I think great deference is due the twice-expressed judgment of the Tax Court. In spite of the gelding of *Dobson* . . . by the recent revision of the Judicial Code . . . I still think the Tax Court is a more competent and steady influence toward a systematic body of tax law than our sporadic omnipotence in a field beset with invisible boomerangs. I should reverse, in reliance upon the Tax Court's judgment more, perhaps, than my own.

[2572] *See* Flora v. United States, 362 U.S. 145, 178 (1960) (Whitaker, J., Frankfurter, J., Harlan, J., and Stewart, J. dissenting).

[2573] Paul, *Dobson v. Commissioner*, *supra* note 2556, at 766.

[2574] Rice, *supra* note 377, at 1050.

a strong argument that the *Dobson* rule and the statute on which it was based should be reinstated.[2575]

VI.E.3.b. *Mixed Questions of Fact and Law*

The *Dobson* view that mixed questions of law and fact decided by the Tax Court were entitled to deference because the Tax Court's rulings were administrative ceased in 1969 when the Tax Court clearly became a judicial court, subject to the full force of the Federal Rules of Civil Procedure. Rule 52(a) authorizes review of determinations of fact on a "clearly erroneous" basis; of course questions of law are reviewed de novo. The distinction is necessarily confused when issues are called mixed question of law and fact. The Supreme Court has struggled with this but repeatedly has stated that applying law to facts is usually a law finding and not a fact finding operation.[2576] In an accurate statement that unfortunately promotes rather than diminishes the confusion, Justice Scalia stated that the Court has observed that "the characterization of a mixed question of law and fact for one purpose does not govern its characterization for all purposes."[2577]

A turning point of the Court's approach to the distinction was *Pullman-Standard.*[2578] That opinion rejected a distinction, or at least the terminology, that had been used in many tax opinions of the Court: "ultimate findings" (reviewable as law) and "evidentiary findings" (reviewable as facts). *Pullman* said: "[Rule 52(a)] . . . does not divide facts into categories; in particular it does not divide findings of fact into those that deal with 'ultimate' and those that deal with 'subsidiary' facts."[2579] *Pullman* ruled that discriminatory intent was a fact, even though it was the ultimate fact that caused the law to apply.

The Court has never cited *Pullman* in a tax case. Footnote 19 of that opinion states that the Court did not need to address the confused issue of mixed questions of law and fact, and the Court has not subsequently resolved that issue. However, the footnote indicates that the Court believed mixed questions are reviewable as questions of law, citing three of the Court's tax opinions.[2580] The key to the conundrum may lie in *Pullman's* definition of a mixed question: the court applies the law to "established" facts. By defining it that way, the fact finding element is entirely removed or at least separated, and the

---

2575 Shores, *Deferential Review of Tax Court Decisions: Dobson Revisited*, 49 TAX LAW. 629 (1995).

2576 *See* Thompson v. Keohane, 516 U.S. 99 (1995); *see generally* Pietruszkiewicz, *supra* note 8, at 339.

2577 United States v. Gaudin, 515 U.S. 506 (1995). For example, when constitutional issues are involved the Court generally believes it reviews as a matter of law. Lilly v. Va., 527 U.S. 116 (1999).

2578 Pullman-Standard v. Swint, 456 U.S. 273 (1982).

2579 *Id.* at 287.

2580 Bogardus v. Commissioner, 302 U.S. 34 (1937); Helvering v. Tex-Penn Oil Co., 300 U.S. 481 (1937); Helvering v. Rankin, 295 U.S. 123 (1935). Then a "cf" cite named Commissioner v. Duberstein, 363 U.S. 278, 289 (1960); Commissioner v. Heininger, 320 U.S. 467, 475 (1943).

mixed question must be a legal question. That juries decide mixed question is entirely consistent, because they sit as the judge.[2581]

The three tax opinions with which *Pullman* agreed (and the two contrasting tax opinions cited) provide the basis for a practical rule of thumb: (1) when the primary issue of decision is not the meaning of a term in the Code (such as gift) but is a fact—intent, as in *Duberstein*, or which shares were sold, as in *Rankin*, or whether a business' expense is ordinary and necessary, as in *Heininger*—the question is one of fact; but (2) when the primary issue is the meaning of a Code term (do these facts constitute compensation?), which may be informed by multiple factual findings, the question is a mixed one treated as a law issue,as in *Tex-Penn;* but (3) the third decision, *Bogardus*, which was similar to *Duberstein* and reversed the Tax Court on the gift finding, was later rejected by the Supreme Court.[2582]

The *Tex-Penn*[2583] decision well illustrates the distinction and how tax opinions may have stopped referring to ultimate findings as law, but can reach the same result by calling them mixed questions of law and fact.,[2584] The opinion also is worth analysis because it is in the same small group as *Macomber* and *F. & R. Lazarus*: the ultimate finding is contrary to form and in the taxpayer's favor. The Court found compliance with the reorganization section by allowing the taxpayer to rely on facts that were contrary to the terms of a contract it entered into; but the opinion basically interpreted the meaning of reorganization.

Shareholders owned oil leases and also had conveyed some oil leases to Tex-Penn for its stock. A newly formed and capitalized corporation, Transcontinental, was to acquire all of the leases, paying shareholders for theirs and Tex-Penn for its. Tex-Penn was to pay its own debts of about $350,000. Tex-Penn was to receive Transcontinental stock for its assets. Tex-Penn reported the asset transfer as a nontaxable reorganization under what was the predecessor of section 368(a)(1)(C), at a time when it did not allow any boot. The following facts tended to show that Tex-Penn received boot:

- Its return showed that it had received Transcontinental stock and $350,000 cash.
- The contract between Tex-Penn and Transcontinental stated that Tex-Penn was receiving stock and $350,000 cash from Transcontinental for its assets.

[2581] *See, e.g.*, Hana Fin., Inc. v. Hana Bank, 135 S. Ct. 907 (2015).

[2582] *Duberstein,* 363 U.S. at 289, n. 11.

[2583] Helvering v. Tex-Penn Oil Co., 300 U.S. at 481; *see* PAUL, STUDIES II, at 239-45 (extensive discussion of case, focusing on whether it goes beyond the interdependence test for combining steps).

[2584] *See also* Rudolph v. United States, 370 U.S. 269 (1962), (the most recent reference to ultimate facts in a tax case).

The Board of Tax Appeals ruled for the government and the Third Circuit reversed as a matter of law.[2585] The key to the Third Circuit's opinion was that it discerned that Transcontinental had put the reference to the cash in the offer to Tex-Penn and in the contract because it wanted to make sure it got the assets debt free.[2586]

The Third Circuit backed this up by analysis of how the money actually flowed and how the shareholders' receipts were reduced by the $350,000, as would occur if that were part of what they received in exchange for their individually owned leases. The Supreme Court agreed with the Third Circuit.[2587]

VI.E.3.c. *Fact Versus Law and Footnote 16*

Another take on the mixed question of law and fact/ultimate fact confusion in tax cases appeared in footnote 16 of the important *Frank Lyon* opinion, which is often cited in connection with the economic substance doctrine, even though that case did not involve that doctrine, which had not yet been invented. The footnote seems to be describing the same type of case as *Tex-Penn*, discussed above. It means that when the tax law does not turn simply on a common law fact such as the payment of compensation, but rather requires the interpretation of the Code (depreciation requires ownership and ownership requires an investment or growing equity), the latter is a question of law.

Footnote 16 in *Frank Lyon* states:

> The general characterization of a transaction for tax purposes is a question of law subject to review. *See* American Realty Trust v. United States, 498 F.2d 1194, 1198 (CA4 1974).[2588]

It is odd that the Supreme Court would cite a lower court opinion for such a seminal observation, particularly when the lower court opinion relied for this point on a Supreme Court opinion, which it did not follow. The explanation seems to be that the Supreme Court intended to side with *American Realty*'s statement because it was the lower court opinion that created a split in the circuits leading to the *Frank Lyon* opinion and with which the Court agreed on the merits

American Realty stated "In *Helvering v. Lazarus & Co.*, the Supreme Court suggested that the determination of the bona fides of a sale-and-lease-back

---

2585 Tex-Penn Oil Co. v. Commissioner, 83 F.2d 518 (3d Cir. 1936).

2586 "But notwithstanding these recitations in the papers, all of the parties to these negotiations and agreements perfectly well understood that the lessees were individually supplying the $350,000 for the purpose of paying the debts of Tex-Penn so that its properties might be transferred free and clear of debt." *Id.*

2587 The Supreme Court relied on ". . . what in fact was done rather than the mere form of words used in the writings employed . . . no weight as evidence can be given to mere recitals, directions, engagements and admissions of respondents contained in the documents relied on by the Board." *Tex-Penn Oil Co.*, 300 U.S. at 481.

2588 Frank Lyon Co. v. United States, 435 U.S. 561 (1978).

transaction involves, ultimately, a legal conclusion, albeit one grounded in underlying findings of fact."

The *Frank Lyon* case was tried to a federal district judge without a jury.[2589] The trial judge found as a fact that the intent of the parties to the contracts was consistent with the form of the contracts as a sale leaseback, and so the buyer-lessor, Lyon, owned the building and could depreciate it. That tax law conclusion was entirely consistent with the way a contract would be interpreted under state contract law. It considered the economic argument that Worthen Bank would be compelled to exercise the option to purchase and rejected it as a matter of fact.

The Eighth Circuit reversed.[2590] It dismissed the trial judge's findings about intent as irrelevant in face of what it thought was the clear economic import of the contracts, which it ruled to place ownership in the tenant; it rejected the Fourth Circuit view in *American Realty Trust* that extrinsic evidence of intent of the parties was relevant to determining the nature of the contract between the parties; and it agreed with the government's contention that the ultimate question of ownership was a question of law, which allowed it more easily to reverse.[2591] The government had learned better after claiming it was a question of fact in *American Realty*.

In *American Realty*, the taxpayer landlord in a sale-leaseback case had won a jury verdict; the government's primary position was that the issue of ownership was a factual issue;[2592] the government came to regret this approach since the jury found the fact for the taxpayer. The Supreme Court stated in *Frank Lyon* that it granted certiorari "because of an indicated conflict with *American Realty Trust*...."[2593] The Supreme Court sided with *American Realty* because it refused to upset the trial court's finding of fact: "We cannot indulge in such speculation [about whether lease options would be exercised] in view of the District Court's clear finding to the contrary."[2594] The finding to which the Court referred was not the finding of ownership but the refusal to find that that Worthen would exercise the option. At the end of that sentence appears footnote 16, which cites *American Realty* and not its own opinion in *Lazarus*.

So, in both *Frank Lyon* and *American Realty*, the courts of appeals had thought the issue was one of law. The Supreme Court approved of the way the *Frank Lyon* circuit court respected the trial court fact finding based on the

---

2589 Frank Lyon Co. v. United States, 75-2 U.S. Tax Cas. (CCH) P9545 (E.D. Ark. 1976).

2590 Frank Lyon Co. v. United States, 536 F.2d 746 (8th Cir. 1976).

2591 Professor Wolfman wrote the definitive article on *Frank Lyon* and stated that the Eighth Circuit treated the issue as one of law not fact. Wolfman, *Supreme Court in the Lyon's Den*, *supra* note 413, at 1075, 1083. Wolfman, no doubt, obtained inside insight about the case from Erwin Griswold, his former dean at the Harvard Law School, who represented Frank Lyon in the Supreme Court.

2592 American Realty Trust v. United States, 498 F.2d at 1197.

2593 Frank Lyon Co. v. United States, 435 U.S. at 572. Professor Wolfman stated that the alleged conflict was that "the approaches of the Fourth and Eighth Circuits were inconsistent. Wolfman, *Supreme Court in the Lyon's Den*, *supra* note 413, at 1093.

2594 435 U.S. text at fn. 16.

intent of the parties, while realizing that ultimately interpreting a contract contrary to its terms is a judicial act of law finding in the common law,[2595] which occurred in *Lazarus*, and that is what the *American Realty* statement meant. But the finding of facts on which such interpretation might rest—the parties' intent, which might be inferred from the economics of the transaction – is fact finding for the trial judge.

One of the few appellate court tax opinions to actually delve into the footnote 16 issue disagrees with the foregoing analysis.[2596]

VI.E.4. *Burden of Proof*

The courts often state that their decisions are impelled by the taxpayer's failure to carry its burden of proof of facts relevant to tax liability, but it is difficult to know the real impact of the assignment of the burden of proof to the taxpayer.[2597] The rules on burden of proof can be categorized by reference to the procedural posture of the cases, and derive from two Supreme Court decisions (*Welch* and *Lewis*) as modified by statutes:

Rules applicable to all actions in which taxpayer is plaintiff or petitioner or otherwise has the burden of proof on a factual issue:

- Burden of proof: The taxpayer has the burden of persuasion to prove its claim (i.e., "burden of proof") by the preponderance of the evidence.[2598] This allocation of the burden grew out of the sole original way that a taxpayer could contest federal taxes by a common law action for money had and received, in which the taxpayer had the plaintiff's traditional burden of proving its case; that burden was adopted in pre-payment Tax Court litigation to insure equality of procedure, which procedure the Supreme Court views as a substantive rule.[2599]
- Section 7491 may apply to reallocate to the government the burden of proof with respect to "factual issues" relevant to the determination of tax liability, after the taxpayer has introduced "credible evidence," subject to

[2595] Restatement of Contracts, Second, § 212. See 9-52 Moore's Federal Practice - Civil § 52.33; Corbin on Contracts § 24.30.

[2596] Wellpoint, Inc. v. Commissioner, 599 F.3d 641 (7th Cir. 2010). Judge Posner seems to be saying that applying a relatively clear legal standard to facts is fact finding. But he would probably agree that applying an unclear legal standard to facts may be a legal conclusion, and the ownership required for the right to depreciate is an unclear legal standard.

[2597] *See* Jones, *The Burden of Proof 10 Years after the Shift*, 121 Tax Notes (TA) 287 (Oct. 20, 2008).

[2598] *See* United States v. Janis, 428 U.S. 433 (1976); Saltzman & Book, at 7B.11[2][a]; *see also* Lynch, *Burden of Proof in Tax Litigation Under I.R.C. § 7491—Chicken Little was Wrong!*, 5 Pitt. Tax Rev. 1 (2007). For an unusual prior rule creating a *prima facie* case for either side, see *Webre Steib Co. v. Commissioner*, 324 U.S. 164 (1945) (opinion by Justice Jackson on refund of a sugar processing tax).

[2599] Lynch, *supra* note 2598, at 12, 14.

certain limitations in section 7491(a)(2).[2600] "Factual issues" evidently do not include mixed questions of law and fact, which should take a lot of issues out of the rule.[2601]

Rules applicable to Tax Court actions:

- Because Tax Court cases always start with the Commissioner's assessment of additional tax, the rule of *Welch v. Helvering* applies in all Tax Court cases.[2602] It recognizes a presumption that the Commissioner's determination of tax is correct. However, it is a procedural presumption only, placing the burden of going forward on the taxpayer.[2603]
- U.S. Tax Court Rule 142(a)(1) provides: "The burden of proof shall be upon the petitioner, ..."
- The ultimate issue on which the taxpayer has the burden of proof is the correctness of the Commissioner's deficiency assessment.[2604] However, when the assessment is a "naked assessment," without any basis whatsoever, the taxpayer need only demonstrate that the Commissioner's determination of gross income is arbitrary and excessive; thereafter, the burden of going forward with the evidence shifts to the Commissioner, who is then required to prove the correct amount of gross income.[2605]

Rules applicable to taxpayers' actions seeking refund of taxes paid under deficiency assessment:

- The presumption of correctness of the deficiency assessment (*Welch v. Helvering*, discussed above) applies.[2606]
- The ultimate issue on which the taxpayer has the burden of proof is whether the taxpayer's correct tax liability for the year is less than the amount he has paid and by how much.[2607]

[2600] Section 7941 (which by cross reference contains other exceptions). *See generally* Saltzman & Book, at 7B.11[2][a]; Lynch, *supra* note 2598.

[2601] Lynch, *supra* note 2598, at 17-8, 25 *et seq.* (suggesting how mixed questions should be handled); *see* Chapter VI.E.3.b.

[2602] Welch v. Helvering, 290 U.S. 111 (1933); *see also* United States v. Fior D'Italia, Inc., 536 U.S. 238 (2002); Bittker & Lokken, at 115.4.2.

[2603] Saltzman & Book, at 1.05[2][b].

[2604] *Welch*, 290 U.S. at 111.

[2605] Helvering v. Taylor, 293 U.S. 507 (1935) (explained in United States v. Janis, 428 U.S. 433 (1976)); *see also* Lynch, *supra* note 2598, at 15 (describing another exception for assessments based on allegedly unreported income without any factual support). There is also some indication that income and deduction issues are treated differently. *See generally* United States v. Anderson, 269 U.S. 422 (1926); Bittker & Lokken, at 115.4.2 (Tax Court burden of proof).

[2606] *Welch*, 290 U.S. at 111; *see also* United States v. Fior D'Italia, Inc., 536 U.S. at 238; Niles Bement Pond Co. v. United States, 281 U.S. 357 (1930); Bittker & Lokken, at 115.4.2.

[2607] United States v. Gen. Dynamics Corp., 481 U.S. 239 (1987).

Rules applicable to taxpayers' actions seeking refund of taxes paid without deficiency assessment:

- The ultimate issue on which the taxpayer has the burden of proof is whether the taxpayer's correct tax liability for the year is less than the amount he has paid and by how much.[2608]

Rules applicable to Service counterclaims in refund actions:

- There is conflict in the circuits about whether the Service has the burden of proof on its counterclaims to collect assessments in the taxpayer's refund suit.[2609]

VI.F. Factual Clusters

A factual cluster is a fact pattern or transaction that frequently recurs in problematic tax cases, presents difficult issues of factual characterization or legal interpretation or both, and which the courts have addressed by effectively fashioning some sort of rule of law ("cluster rules"), or method of fact finding or presumption, which frequently involves a substance over form approach. For example, the treatment of corporations as taxpayers separate from their shareholders and the erection of a relatively high barrier to prevent shareholders from treating their corporations as their agents is a classic factual cluster and cluster rule, discussed in Ch. VI.F.3.

VI.F.1. *Utility of Identifying Factual Clusters*

By recognizing and respecting the limited scope of factual cluster cases, one can both distinguish them from vaguer all purpose doctrines (such as the economic substance doctrine), and limit their application to the transactions for which they were developed. Unfortunately the lower federal courts have tended to convert some cluster rules into universal doctrines (the economic substance doctrine being the primary example). This subchapter focuses on Supreme Court decisions in cluster areas, but obviously clusters are best informed by a larger number of lower court decisions, some of which are cited below.

By focusing on caselaw in discrete areas, this subchapter follows the advice of Randolph Paul. who said of the step transaction doctrine: "The cases come first and build toward the rule."[2610] But as Justice Holmes said of judicial legislation: "I recognize without hesitation that judges must and do legislate, but they do so only interstitially; they are confined from molar to molecular motions."[2611] The federal tax cases often build toward serviceable rules in

[2608] Lewis v. Reynolds, 284 U.S. 281 (1932).

[2609] *See* Segal, *Who Bears the Burden of Proof in Taxpayer Suits Against the Service?,* 4 PITT. TAX REV. 155 (2007).

[2610] PAUL, STUDIES II, at 252.

[2611] S. Pac. Co. v. Jensen, 244 U.S. 205, 221 (1917) (Holmes, J., dissenting).

cluster areas by being observed in hindsight as cases addressing similar factual issues in a similar way.

Several astute observers have predicted that the tax law would develop around such clusters:

- Relying on Justice Holmes' description of the way the common law developed, Paul speculated in 1940 that new cases might cluster around opposite poles and begin to approach each other, so as to permit a line to be drawn between them,[2612] and predicted that "some rule more definite than the broad generalization that substance, and not form, controls will eventually develop from the cases."[2613]
- Professor Rice recommended in 1953 that (1) the need for anti-avoidance tools was real and appropriate, but that (2) the search for an overarching rule was futile, and so (3) the better approach was to chart what the courts had actually done in specific areas.[2614]
- Assistant Chief Counsel Reiling in effect described clusters when he explained how the co-existence of opposing extreme positions (the example being family partnership cases, but the same point applies to the *Court Holding*, *Cumberland Public Service* extremes) sometimes leads to legislative creation of a cluster rule.[2615]
- William F. Nelson observed in 1995 that the "common law doctrines" had not been applied uniformly across the tax law, but rather applied with "high voltage" to reorganizations, business expenses and deductions.[2616]

Cluster rules have a better claim on the authority of common law making than generalized doctrines because their "creation" is in hindsight, as induced from a volume of case law, rather than deduced from the current needs of the revenue collector, or created out of a single lower court opinion that improperly analyzed precedents. The interpretive principles outlined in Ch. VI.B. above also can be viewed as cluster rules. Cluster rules today need to develop in the lower courts due to the difficulty of obtaining review of a tax case by the Supreme Court. However, in earlier times the Supreme Court decided a sufficient volume of tax cases to develop, or put its imprimatur on, cluster rules and most of the following examples reflect those decisions.

[2612] PAUL, STUDIES III, at 129 (citing HOLMES, THE COMMON LAW 127 (1881)).

[2613] *Id.* at 130.

[2614] Rice, *supra* note 377, at 1051-52.

[2615] *See* Reiling, *supra* note 26, at 567.

[2616] Nelson, *Limits of Literalism*, 73 TAXES (CCH) 641, 644 (1995).

VI.F.2. *Ownership and Sale of Property*

VI.F.2.a. *General*

The ownership of property, including property that is income, is one of the most fundamental concepts in the income tax.[2617] It arises in connection with a variety of tax rules that depend on property ownership: who must pay tax on the income from the property, when must the disposition of property be taxed, who is entitled to the depreciation of wasting property and to the interest deduction from financed purchases of property, and what property is subject to the federal tax lien. The meaning of ownership in the tax law can vary depending on which of these uses is at issue.

Randolph Paul studied the question in the 1930s and stated that however much leeway the Supreme Court might accord Congress in areas of taxation, "it is axiomatic that Congress is without power to tax one person on the income of another."[2618] He observed that income that does not come from labor necessarily comes from property, which makes its ownership critical, and ownership determines from whom the tax shall be collected.[2619] *Poe v. Seaborn* ruled that when the statute taxed income "of every individual," the word "of" imported state law ownership.[2620]

But several considerations require going beyond state law, or at least formal ownership under state law:

[2617] *See* Bittker & Lokken, at 4.4.1A. *See also* Cunningham, *Taxation without Realization: A "Revolutionary" Approach to Ownership*, 47 Tax L. Rev. 725, 726 (1992); Faber, *Determining the Owner of An Asset for Tax Purposes*, 61 Taxes (CCH) 795 (1983); Gideon, *supra* note 41, at 839-46 (arguing that ownership rather than profit motive should have been at issue in *Rice's Toyota*); Faber et al., *Ownership and Disposition of Property: New Rules for Old Problems*, 75 Taxes (CCH) 768 (1997); Marsh, *Tax Ownership of Real Estate*, 39 Tax Law. 563 (1985) (concluding that there is no agreed upon rule of ownership); Miller, *Taxpayers' Ability to Avoid Tax Ownership: Current Law and Future Prospects*, 51 Tax Law. 279 (1997); Cummings, *A Tax Common Law Approach to Property Ownership*,139 Tax Notes (TA) 1059 (May 27, 2013).

[2618] Paul, Studies II, at 44 (The Effect on Federal Taxation of Local Rules of Property). *See also* Knowlton v. Moore, 178 U.S. 41 (1900) (expressing doubt that one person's property could be taxed at a rate dependent on another person's attributes); Hoeper v. Tax Com. of Wisconsin, 284 U.S. 206 (1931) (state tax opinion, citing *Knowlton*); Randall v. Loftsgaarden, 478 U.S. 647 (1986) (and generally deductions and losses are limited to the person that sustained them).

[2619] *Id.*, at 40-8. *See also* Miller, *Nominee Conundrum: The Live Dummy Is Dead but the Dead Dummy Should Live*, 34 Tax L. Rev. 213 (1978) (relating the ownership issue to dummy corporations and cases like *Higgins v. Smith*; identified four kinds of ownership—record, title, substantive law and common speech; viewed *Higgins* as deciding that an overriding public policy prevents a taxpayer from enjoying a tax benefit (loss) when there is no change in common speech ownership; the Supreme Court could distinguish *Commonwealth Improvement Company* because it involved gains and a taxpayer can be held to the tax advantages flowing from his choice of form).

[2620] Poe v. Seaborn, 282 U.S. 101 (1930). The Court reaffirmed the significance of "of" in *United States v. Mitchell*, 403 U.S. 190 (1971).

- The Supreme Court has stated that state law is not completely dispositive for tax purposes because it only determines which sticks are in a person's bundle and federal tax law determines whether that bundle is property ownership,[2621] for the reasons discussed in Ch. VI.E.2.
- The justification for the sticks and bundle dichotomy is that state law concepts of ownership, and other state law characterizations and forms, can be overridden by federal tax principles (such as the assignment of income doctrine), and other concepts specific to particular tax rules.[2622] For another example, the Supreme Court ultimately concluded that illegally obtained property could constitute income even though the possessor did not have legal title to the property, which would usually prevent state law ownership.[2623]
- The common law and equitable methods of fact finding, and detecting fraud, trusts, agency,[2624] security, etc., can override bare title even for state law purposes.[2625]
- In contrast, the federal tax usage of property that hews most closely to the state law is the application of the federal tax lien to property of the taxpayer, where the state is always allowed to define whether the taxpayer has interests in property, but the federal law defines the nature and enforcement of the federal tax lien on those property interests.[2626]
- However, even a tax law can be interpreted to look to bare title, when Congress so intended.[2627]

The greatest uncertainties in the ownership area arise in the same two types of cases as in the debt versus corporate equity area:[2628] (1) related party transactions, and (2) factually ambiguous unrelated party transactions. In the related party cases, questions of assignment of income, trust, and agency issues arise, all of which are separate cluster areas. The Court addressed own-

---

[2621] United States v. Craft, 535 U.S. 274 (2002).

[2622] *See, e.g.*, Weiss v. Wiener, 279 U.S. 333 (1929) (Holmes, J.) (the owner of a 99 year lease that the state law treated as fee ownership not allowed to depreciate the buildings on the property when lease began because he paid nothing for the lease other than annual rent, which he was allowed to fully deduct).

[2623] James v. United States, 366 U.S. 213 (1961) (embezzled income taxable; reversing *Commissioner v. Wilcox*, 327 U.S. 404 (1946)).

[2624] Commissioner v. Bollinger, 485 U.S. 340 (1988); *see infra* Ch. VI.F.3.

[2625] *See supra* Ch. V.E.1.f(2) (as to the equity of redemption).

[2626] *See* Cummings, *Nationwide Uniformity and the Common Law of Federal Taxation*, 66 Tax Law. 1 (2012).

[2627] *See* Provost v. United States, 269 U.S. 443 (1926) (holding stamp tax to apply to transfer of legal title to borrowed shares of stock and refusing to consider economic equivalencies); Goodyear Tire & Rubber Co. v. United States, 273 U.S. 100 (1927) (recapitalization treated as a stock disposition for purposes of the same stock transfer tax); Founders General Corp. v. Hoey, 300 U.S. 268 (1937).

[2628] *See* Bittker & Eustice, at 4.03 (arm's length ambiguities), 4.04 (non-arm's-length shareholder-held debt).

ership in depth in the trust cases, culminating in *Clifford*.[2629] It reasoned that the grantor's continued dominion and control of property could justify ignoring the formal ownership by the trust, whether or not that ground would suffice to change the ownership of property of a related corporation, or between unrelated parties, due to the particular cluster treatments of both trusts and corporate entities. The Court was careful to say in *Clifford* that it was not deciding on assignment of income grounds (although that seemed powerfully implicated). Thus, the trust cases took an approach to property ownership that should be viewed as a cluster area, not necessarily having universal application to fact finding even within the area of property ownership.

Finally, the Supreme Court held in *Crane* that property owned is not the equity in the property but the physical thing subject to ownership or the rights inherent in ownership.[2630] That definition cuts against the benefits and burdens definition discussed next.

VI.F.2.b. *Benefits and Burdens*

The term "benefits and burdens" (of ownership) is one of those terms that tax practitionerrs have come to use so freely that they implicitly accept it as a shorthand way to identify the owner of property for all federal tax purposes.[2631] However, the Supreme Court has never stated that benefits and burdens was the proper indicator of property ownership for income tax purposes, although it has frequently relied on equitable ownership and beneficial ownership, state law concepts.[2632] It referred to beneficial ownership in an early

---

[2629] Helvering v. Clifford, 309 U.S. 331 (1940). *Clifford* was the genesis of the term "Clifford Trust" whereby a spouse placed certain property in trust for a short term in order to attempt to shift the incidence of taxation of the property's income to the other spouse for that term without ultimately moving ownership of the property. Justice Douglas said that "special scrutiny" was required due to the close relation of the taxpayers. But close scrutiny was not the only principle relied upon to disregard the trust for income tax purposes; in addition the Court cited the fact that the statute's definition of "gross income" carried within it a legal conception of considerable breadth.

[2630] Crane v. Commissioner, 331 U.S.1 (1947).

[2631] *See* Cummings, *A Tax Common Law Approach to Property Ownership*, 139 Tax Notes (TA) 1059 (May 27, 2013).

[2632] *E.g.*, Helvering v. Horst, 311 U.S. 112, 118 (1940); Duffy v. Central R. Co. of N.J., 268 U.S. 55 (1925) (the opinion did not use the term "equitable ownership," but the taxpayer claimed it did not have equitable ownership of lessee improvements under a 999-year lease, and it lost); Propeller Co. v. United States, 81 U.S. 670 (1872) (equitable ownership, not a tax case); Drexel v. Berney, 122 U.S. 241, 254 (1887); Zantzingers v. Gunton, 86 U.S. 32 (1874) (equitable ownership in borrower); Stoehr v. Wallace, 255 U.S. 239 (1921) (equitable ownership in Germans who nominally sold stock in U.S. subsidiary to avoid Trading with the Enemy Act). *See also* Montana Catholic Missions v. Missoula County, 200 U.S. 118, 127-128 (1906). Frank Lyon Co. v. United States, 435 U.S. 561 (1978) (referred to the lower court's use of benefits and burdens, but did not adopt the standard). But in an estate tax decision the Court refused to include property in the taxable estate when the decedent did not have legal ownership, although equity would subject it to her creditors under some circumstances. United States v. Field, 255 U.S. 257 (1921).

decision addressing the meaning of owning substantially all of the stock of another corporation for purposes of filing consolidated returns: it said ownership was not determined by control but by beneficial ownership or the power to acquire it.[2633] No version of the term "benefits and burdens" appears in any Supreme Court federal tax opinion deciding the ownership of property, except for *Frank Lyon* (discussed below), and two early estate tax opinions.[2634]

The benefits and burdens concept has a questionable foundation and is more relevant to some tax issues than others. It properly has been used to identify the moment of transfer of ownership for purposes of the holding period, for section 1001 timing, and for estate and gift transfer tax purposes, where it is clear that one person at a time owns the property. Beyond the timing cases, there is no proper all purpose benefits and burdens test for ownership in the federal tax law. The reason is simple: the common law spent too many centuries developing formal means for identifying ownership (deeds, bills of sale, contracts, trusts, partnerships) for the income tax to completely ignore them.

The first uncertainty about the term "benefits and burdens" is to what benefits and burdens does it refer, with the principal alternatives being control[2635] versus profit and loss potential. For income tax purposes it is almost always assumed to mean ongoing profit potential and risk of loss.[2636] However, control has been determinative in some cases.[2637] But historically there was a further differentiation: ultimate profit and loss as contrasted with current income and current burdens of ownership. The Treasury showed this in 1920 when it used "benefits and burdens" to refer to ultimate risk of loss by destruction and long term gain potential, as contrasted with a "commercial usage" view of ownership to refer to a right to current income from property and obligation for current expenses.[2638]

Attention to who has benefits and burdens with respect to property arises in at least three cluster areas: (1) the timing or *when* cases in the income tax—there clearly is only one owner at a time and the issue is when the transfer of ownership occurred (referred to above); (2) the *who* cases in the income tax—two or more persons have ambiguous owner like interests in the same property at the same time; and (3) the estate and gift tax cases, which have

---

2633 Handy & Harman v. Burnet, 284 U.S. 136 (1931).

2634 Coolidge v. Long, 282 U.S. 582 (1931); Chase National Bank v. United States, 278 U.S. 327 (1929).

2635 *See* Chase National Bank v. United States, 278 U.S. 327 (1929) (lising for transfer tax purposes the relevant benefits and burdens of power to dispose of the property and use the proceeds, pledge the property, have the property subjected to the claims of creditors).

2636 *See, e.g.,* Reg. § 1.141-7(c) (states a "benefits and burdens test").

2637 Helvering v. Horst, 311 U.S. 112 (1940).

2638 A.R.R. 13, 1920 No. 2 C.B. 78; O.D. 751, 1920 No. 3 C.B. 118; A.R.M 189, 1922 I-2 C.B. 68.

developed a separate cluster of their own.[2639] The who cases most frequently involve depreciation, which is a cluster discussed separately below in Ch. VI.F.2.c. As shown there, the Supreme Court in *Frank Lyon* refused to allocate ownership based on a generalized estimate of who was most likely to derive the most benefits and burdens from property. Unfortunately, since the 1980's the Treasury and Service have applied the concept of benefits and burdens indiscriminately, without regard to the origins of the concept, which are explained below.[2640]

When/Timing. The tax origin, and principal appropriate cluster use of benefits and burdens of ownership as indicia of substance to trump form of ownership, is in the when cases, ascertaining holding periods, including timing of sale:

- The Court ruled that the holding period for capital gains purposes started when the heir acquired title under state law subject to the administration of the estate, prior to actual distribution.[2641] This is a special case in which the state laws long have fixed rights upon death.
- Similarly, the Court ruled that a distribution from an estate had occurred when the estate conveyed property to a trustee for the beneficiary; the beneficiary had obtained an equitable interest and did not have to directly receive the property for purposes of the tax basis determination.[2642] This ruling was at odds with an earlier ruling that "acquired" was a common meaning word that meant obtained as one's own.[2643]
- The Service has long ruled that in cases of an unconditional contract of sale, the sale occurs on the earlier of the transfer of title or delivery of possession and control, which later came to be called benefits and burdens, not because the "test" was ultimate profit and loss, but because the

---

[2639] *See, e.g.*, Chase National Bank, 278 U.S. at 327 (stating that the shifting of benefits and burdens and not technical distinctions determine when a succession tax is due); *see also* Saltonstall v. Saltonstall, 276 U.S. 260 (1928) (Justice Stone).

[2640] *See, e.g.*, Reg. § 1.701-2(c)(7) ("The benefits and burdens of ownership of partnership property are in substantial part shifted . . ."). The concept entered the partnership regulations in 1986, T.D. 8099, 1986-2 C.B. 84, which for the first time determined the partner's interest in the partnership by reference to the partners' agreement to share the economic benefit or burden of items of income or loss. Reg. § 1.704-1(b)(3)(i).

[2641] Helvering v. Gambrill, 313 U.S. 11 (1941); McFeely v. Commissioner, 296 U.S. 102 (1935); *see also* Brewster v. Gage, 280 U.S. 327 (1930) (heir's basis was value at death not when property was distributed).

[2642] Maguire v. Commissioner, 313 U.S. 1(1941).

[2643] Helvering v. San Joaquin Fruit & Investment Co., 297 U.S. 496 (1936).

person who got possession and control in these cases necessarily also had the ultimate profit and loss.[2644]

- But benefits and burdens transfer coincides with form in sales when there is no pre-closing shift. *North Texas Lumber Co.* held that a seller who retained title and possession of the property did not accrue the sale in the year when the contract was binding, the buyer was ready will and able to pay and the only thing standing in the way of closing was within the seller's total control: the preparation and delivery of the deed.[2645]

The original source of the relation of "benefits and burdens" to property is in English property law that had nothing to do with the current usage. Wharton's Maxims No. 80 stated: "He who enjoys the benefit ought also to bear the burden; and the contrary."[2646] It goes on to explain that the maxim is primarily used in relation to real property to identify the rights and obligations obtained by a successive owner.[2647] Thus, the common law was not concerned with identifying a fee owner based on who had benefits and burdens (the typical tax use), as much as it was concerned with the transferee getting the benefits and burdens of the particular estate transferred (which might be less than fee ownership).

The tax law use turns this maxim on its head when it assumes that having a particular sort of benefits and burdens, for example the risk of loss and potential of profit from property, reflects 100% of the benefits and burdens of fee ownership, and attempts to reverse engineer ownership from that fact. This approach is the signal of a true cluster in tax, because it selects facts that have significance for tax purposes (profit and loss) but are not necessarily the

---

[2644] The terminology traces to Treasury choices made in 1920. *See* Rev. Rul. 1954-607, 1954-2 C.B. 177 (The "burdens and privileges of ownership") (citing O. D. 751, 3 C. B. 116 (1920) (possession and control); Rev. Rul. 1958-101, 1958-1 C. B. 233 (prize)). The pivotal early Tax Court application appears to have been *Merrell v. Commissioner*, 40 T.C. 66 (1963), where the court held the Service to earlier rulings relying on the earlier of title transfer or acquisition of benefits and burdens, citing BROWN ON REAL PROPERTY (1950) for the view that ownership was indicated by benefits and burdens. This was a new discovery by Brown, as a 1918 treatise had not discerned that concept, rather citing possession as the prima facie indicia of ownership. SCHOULER, TREATISE ON THE LAW OF PERSONAL PROPERTY §2 (1918) (also the index reveals no emphasis on benefits and burdens). *See also* S. R. A., Inc. v. Minnesota, 327 U.S. 558 (1946) (possession under executory contract of purchase constituted ownership); Major Realty Corp. v. Commissioner, 749 F.2d 1483 (11th Cir. 1985) (title passes upon earlier of title or benefits and burdens).

[2645] Lucas v. N. Texas Lumber Co., 281 U.S. 11 (1930) (the Court specifically addressed accrual of income and not ownership of property); *see also* Helvering v. San Joaquin Fruit & Investment Co., 297 U.S. 496, 499 (1936) (lease plus irrevocable option to purchase at end of lease term was not ownership; "the word 'acquired' is not a term of art in the word of property but one in common use. The plain import of the word is 'obtain as one's own.' Language used in tax statutes should be read in the ordinary and common sense.").

[2646] WHARTON, LEGAL MAXIMS WITH OBSERVATIONS AND CASES, Part I, ch. 80 (Law Times Office 1865).

[2647] *See, e.g.,* In re Estate of Porter, 138 Cal. 618 (1903) (the issue was which devisee should bear a certain burden).

same facts with which the property law would concern itself (for examples: control, enjoyment, possession).

The tax timing cases find one source in nontax law aside from the equity maxim. The very first Board of Tax Appeals opinion that used the phrase "benefits and burdens" in assessing timing of transfer of ownership cited a Supreme Court bankruptcy decision.[2648] It held that a margin buyer of stock was the owner by virtue of having benefits and burdens (though not using that term) even though the broker did not retain the exact shares that were bought and pledged.[2649]

Sale or not? When the issue is not timing but whether a transfer occurred at all, the Court rejected a benefits and burdens test in *Clay Brown*,[2650] on reasoning very similar to that it applied in *Frank Lyon*, discussed below. The Service admitted the taxpayer had sold property in a way that was not a sham and was respected for state law purposes, but contended there was no sale because the benefits and burdens of ownership of the property had not shifted, based on the fact that the buyer had made no investment and the seller's price was to be paid from the property's earnings. The Court stated that while rational, this had never been the law because, absent specific indicia to the contrary, common words are used in their common and ordinary sense.[2651] The Court specifically rejected the contention that a person buying property on the installment method must have wealth apart from the property purchased in order to be a bona fide purchaser of that property. The best proof that the retention of benefits and burdens of a particular piece of property does not determine its ownership is the tax treatment of stock lending. As explained by the Chief Counsel, the Service and the courts consistently treated a lender of securities who is entitled to receive all of the economic benefits and burdens of the securities during the period of the loan as not the owner; rather the lender has made a disposition of the stock, although it might not be taxable under section 1001, or otherwise (prior to enactment of section 1058).[2652]

[2648] S. Cal. Rock & Gravel Co. v. Commissioner, 26 B.T.A. 296 (1932) *(citing* Richardson v. Shaw, 209 U.S. 365 (1908)).

[2649] In *Richardson*, the customer bought the stock through a broker that went bankrupt. The Court ruled the customer could recover the stock upon payment of the margin loan not as a preference to a creditor but as a reclaiming of property pledged, despite the fact that the shares recovered were not literally the shares pledged, because the broker had itself pledged them for its own loan. Justice Holmes reluctantly concurred, stating: "A just deference to the views of my brethren prevents my dissenting from the conclusion reached, although I cannot but feel a lingering doubt." *Richardson*, 209 U.S. at 385. But when the Tax Court later confronted a similar issue in the context of an agreement to sell fungible agricultural products from inventory, it ruled no sale occurred until delivery, refusing on the facts to apply the state law "fungible goods doctrine." Pac. Grape Co. v. Commissioner, 17 T.C. 1097 (1962).

[2650] Commissioner v. Brown, 380 U.S. 563 (1965).

[2651] *See also* McFeely v. Commissioner, 296 U.S. 102 (1935) (to hold means to own which means to acquire, all of which have their common meaning).

[2652] G.C.M. 36,948 (Dec. 10, 1976).

This treatment was based on the Supreme Court ruling that a stock loan was a disposition for excise tax purposes.[2653]

Other Supreme Court rulings in the benefits and burdens area include the following:

- An early ruling on the Civil War inheritance tax said that an alien inheritor was estopped by claiming the benefit of the property to set up alienage as a ground for avoiding the tax; state law made inheritance by an alien null and void.[2654]
- Sometimes a formal transfer of title must be examined to determine if it amounts to a transfer of ownership at law generally.[2655]
- The Court has recognized ownership without title.[2656]
- *Cottage Savings* found a sale of one set of mortgage interests and acquisition of another set, despite the fact that the benefits and burdens of the property ownership had not economically changed.[2657]

VI.F.2.c. *Burdens and Depreciation:* Frank Lyon

VI.F.2.c(1) *Depreciation*

The cluster approach to ownership for depreciation purposes is to ask whether the taxpayer has made or will make the investment in the property, so as to potentially own an equity.

Property ownership is the fundamental precondition of property depreciation. Identifying the person entitled to a deduction for the depreciation of property for tax purposes is a type of benefits and burdens of ownership analysis that has produced several sub-clusters of case authorities, the most prominent of which are the sale leaseback and leveraged lease cases.[2658] The cluster involves the intertwining of the economic analysis of who has born or will bear the legal burden of the presumed decline in value of the investment (usually meaning the person who is at risk if the investment funds are bor-

---

2653 Provost v. United States, 269 U.S. 443 (1926); *see* S. Rep. No. 95-762, 1978-2 C.B. 357, 359 (1978) (explaining the purpose of section 1058). Also, taxpayers are allowed to postpone closing of a sale so that their long term holding period for the property matures. MacMurray v. Commissioner, 21 T.C. 15 (1953) nonacq., 1958-2 C. B. 9; Dyke v. Commissioner, 6 T. C. 1134 (1946).

2654 Scholey v. Rew, 90 U.S. 331 (1875).

2655 *See* Thomas v. Perkins, 301 U.S. 655, 659 (1937) (granting clause of conveyance appeared to transfer ownership of oil, but other parts of document showed that transferor retained ownership of part of the oil, for example that he was to be paid only in the oil).

2656 Anderson v. Wilson, 289 U.S. 20 (1933) (trustee had ownership of property that it sold under a power of sale, and thus was the only party that could report the loss, despite the fact that it did not hold title; it held powers amounting to ownership).

2657 Cottage Savings Assn. v. Commissioner, 499 U.S. 554 (1991).

2658 *See* Bittker & Lokken, at 4.4.2-3 (treating these as clusters of authorities); Gideon, *supra* note 41, at 839; *infra* Ch. VI.F.2.c(3).

rowed), and traditional notions of legal ownership of the fee as seen through the lens of federal taxation.[2659]

Section 167(c)(1) bases depreciation on cost of property, which is property presumably owned by the taxpayer and to whom the cost basis is attributed (subject to many special rules for carryover of property basis for gifts, *etc.*).[2660] But the Supreme Court long ago recognized that the common law and equity, without the aid of the federal courts in tax cases, understood that ownership was not governed by record title. The Court made clear in a seminal sale leaseback case, *F. & R. Lazarus*, that in determining who makes such an investment the courts should look to substance and not form, but substance of a particular well recognized type that was enforceable in courts of equity.[2661] The Court in *Lazarus* did not set sail on an unconstrained search for substance, as reflected by this concluding statement distinguishing another case:

> Whatever the significance of [the *Braden*] case, it can have no application here. In the *Braden* case, the equitable doctrine—here controlling—of looking to extrinsic evidence behind a transfer absolute on its face to determine whether only a security transaction was contemplated by the parties, was neither invoked nor passed upon.[2662]

As shown in Ch. V.E.1.f(2), the Court in *Lazarus* relied on the way a court of equity would determine equitable rights to identify the owner of the property. The Service failed to understand that when it came to argue *Frank Lyon*, and convinced the Circuit Court that it could rely on a looser economic analysis of who might ultimately benefit the most from the property,[2663] thereby leading to the wrong conclusion largely based on the potential for the lessee to profit from the property and the limited profit potential for the lessor. The Supreme Court rejected the Court of Appeals' approach to substance in *Lyon* and focused on the investment the lessor was legally obligated to make in the property, as discussed in the next subchapter.

2659 Weiss v. Wiener, 279 U.S. 333 (1929) (owner of 99-year lease not entitled to depreciation of property on the leased estate, even though state law and accounting would so allow).

2660 *See* Detroit Edison Co. v. Commissioner, 319 U.S. 98, 102 (1943):

> But we think the statutory provision that the 'basis of property shall be the cost of such property' § 113(a) normally means, and that in this case the Commissioner was justified in applying it to mean, cost to the taxpayer. A property may have a cost history quite different from its cost to the taxpayer. It may have been purchased for less or more than original cost, or built by contract which called for payments on which the builder profited greatly or suffered heavy loss. But generally and in this case the Commissioner was in no error in ruling that the taxpayer's outlay is the measure of his recoupment through depreciation accruals.

2661 Helvering v. F. & R. Lazarus & Co., 308 U.S. 252 (1939) (discussed in Ch. V.E.1.f(2)).

2662 *Id.* at 255.

2663 Frank Lyon Co. v. United States, 536 F.2d 746 (8th Cir. 1976).

Lazarus cited *Duffy* for the proposition that he who pays for and suffers the loss by depreciation of property is the one who can depreciate it.[2664] *Frank Lyon* in turn cited *Lazarus* in characterizing that person as the one whose capital was committed, and thus was being consumed by the depreciation in value of the property that was assumed to occur.[2665] *Lazarus*' outcome depended on how a court of equity would treat the sale leaseback; the connection to equity is echoed in section 162(a)(3), which allows deduction for rent paid for property in which the taxpayer has no title or "equity."[2666] As applied to a lessee, the term "benefits and burdens" most commonly relates to whether the lessee's payments create a fund of value in the property for the permanent benefit of the lessee, just as equity is generated to the owner when the secured indebtedness is paid.[2667] The issue of the right to depreciation also arises in cases of contingent purchase money debt, with the question being the same: will the owner make an investment that is really at risk?[2668]

At the common law, at least the current benefits and burdens of ownership were enjoyed by the bare title holder, the mortgagee for example, even though the mortgagor had an equitable right to reacquire the property because the mortgagor was making the investment.[2669] Thus, at least up to some point in legal history, the equitable owner-borrower *did not* have the benefits and burdens of the property, but rather a right that could be enforced at equity to reacquire legal title, based on his burden of payment. Citing *F. & R. Lazarus* for proof that benefits and burdens proves ownership (as the Service has done)[2670] turns the concept on its head.

VI.F.2.c(2) Frank Lyon

Special attention must be paid to *Frank Lyon*[2671] due to its many citations in lower federal court opinions for various doctrines purporting to exalt economic substance in tax fact finding. In fact it was a pro-taxpayer decision that determined as a fact that the lessor taxpayer did not function as an agent of the lessee, and so the form controlled. It is the only Supreme Court tax opinion

---

2664 *F. & R. Lazarus & Co.*, 308 U.S. at 254 n. 6 (citing Duffy v. Central R. Co. of N.J., 268 U.S. 55 (1925)).

2665 *Frank Lyon Co.*, 435 U. S. at 562 ("depreciation fund" created by rent payments in *Lazarus*). The *Frank Lyon* opinion also requires an investment, and cited at this point *United States v. Chicago, Burlington & Quincy R.R. Co.*, 412 U.S. 401 (1973).

2666 The Chief Counsel investigated the history of the rental deduction in depth and concluded that the legislative history was unrevealing, but that the reference to equity did relate to rights enforceable at equity. G.C.M. 37,812 (Jan. 5, 1979) However, simply having a right enforceable by equity courts with respect to the property did not prevent the right holder from leasing the property; for example, a remainderman could lease the life tenant's interest.

2667 *See* G.C.M. 34,164 (July 14, 1969).

2668 *See* Bittker & Lokken, at 41.2.2.

2669 Stone, *The Equitable Mortgage in New York*, 20 Colum. L. Rev. 519 (1920).

2670 *See* Sun Oil Co. v. Commissioner, 562 F. 2d 258 (3d Cir. 1977) (the Service argued that *Lazarus* required basing ownership on benefits and burdens).

2671 Frank Lyon Co. v. United States, 435 U. S. 561 (1978).

addressing the very confusing and seldom identified issue of when an independent party (sometimes called a "middleman") that appears to be engaged in two independent transactions with two other parties is to be treated as the agent of one of them, with the result that the two other parties are actually the principals in a single transaction.[2672] The opinion basically rejected free floating economic substance analysis in favor of finding no reason to reject the form; even the Supreme Court is not certain what the opinion means.[2673]

Facts. The undisputed facts of the *Frank Lyon* case are that Worthen wanted to build a bank building; it couldn't borrow the money at the rate it needed to pay due to banking regulations and the usury laws; therefore, it arranged for Lyon to borrow the money, build the building, and lease it to Worthen at a rental that would exactly cover the debt payments and provide Lyon a six percent return, subject to various assumptions about Worthen's exercise of its lease extension and purchase options; the trial court found as a fact that all of the rental and option amounts were fair and arm's length. Lyon claimed to be entitled to depreciate the building and the government disagreed. The core of the government's case was that Lyon was a "conduit" (agent) for the bank loan to Worthen; in other words, no matter how fair and arm's length the rental and purchase prices might be, at the end of the day the government argued Lyon was just borrowing money for Worthen, to help Worthen subvert the banking and usury laws.

In contrast with the earlier *Lazarus* case (discussed in Ch. V.E.1.f(2)), which involved only a borrower (formal lessee) and a lender (formal lessor) that had legal title, *Frank Lyon* involved a lender that did not have legal title, a borrower (Lyon), and lessee (Worthen), each of whom appeared to have economic interests in the property. The Service viewed such three party transactions as more difficult than the two party lease sale cases for which it had issued a safe harbor;[2674] in contrast it had set out ruling guidelines for the three party transactions.[2675] The three party leveraged lease guidelines emphasized what would be called today economic substance, rather than state law principles like equitable ownership.[2676] *Frank Lyon* cited and summarized the Service's leasing ruling and procedures but purported not to pay them much

---

[2672] *Cf.* Notice 2001-16, 2001-1 C.B. 730 ("intermediary transactions"); *see infra* Ch. VI.F.8 on conduits. *Court Holding Co.* and *Cumberland Public Service Co.* are analogous but did not involve an independent middleman.

[2673] *See* Nebraska Dept. of Revenue v. Loewenstein, 513 U.S. 123 (1994) ("Whatever the language relied on by respondent may mean, our decision in that case to honor the taxpayer's characterization of its transaction as a "sale-and-leaseback" rather than a "financing transaction" was founded on an examination of "the substance and economic realities of the transaction." 435 U.S. at 582. This examination included identification of 27 specific facts.").

[2674] Rev. Rul. 1955-540, 1955-2 C. B. 39.

[2675] Rev. Proc. 1975-21, 1975-1 C. B. 715 (limited rulings on leases) (superceded by Rev. Proc. 2004-34, 2004-1 C. B. 991).

[2676] *Cf.* Oei, *supra* note 106, at 635 (contrasting the different ways in which bankruptcy law and tax law recharacterize leases, and explaining the differences on the basis of the interests to be protected).

attention because they were not applicable to real estate by their terms (which likely was not a logical distinction). Later when the case to which they would apply (equipment leases) arose in the Fourth Circuit in *Rice's Toyota* (discussed in Ch. V.F.2.), instead of citing them the Fourth Circuit cited *Frank Lyon*, and its vague "standards."[2677] This illustrates how pivotal *Frank Lyon* is to the entire cluster area of depreciation, leases and borrowings.

Although the taxpayer won on the basis of its form (it owed the debt that mostly funded the building being depreciated), the Service commonly cites *Frank Lyon* for its general dictum[2678] about substance controlling form (the Court could not tell who "owned" the building economically).[2679] *Frank Lyon,* like *Knetsch*,[2680] is (1) an ambiguous facts case, and (2) a cluster area case, but it came out the other way for reasons that no one (including the Supreme Court) has ever been quite able to explain logically, aside from observing that it involved unrelated third parties (which *Knetsch* also did).[2681]

One explanation for the confusion surrounding *Frank Lyon* is that it is part of four separate cluster areas in the income tax, including:

- Ownership and depreciation discussed here,
- Shams (Ch. VI.E.1.e(2)(b)),
- Agency and conduits (Ch. VI.F.8.), and
- Indebtedness (Ch. VI.F.6.).

In addition, it involved the confused procedural issue of whether characterization of a transaction is a question of law or fact, discussed in Chapter VI.E.3.c.

Court's analysis. The Court adopted the trial court's findings that Frank Lyon was not the agent of its lessee for purposes of borrowing from the third party, but rather was acquiring an equity in the property by making an investment in it.[2682] If instead the Court had found Frank Lyon to have been the

---

[2677] Rice's Toyota World, Inc. v. Commissioner, 752 F.2d 89 (4th Cir. 1985) (adopted the *Frank Lyon* reference from the Tax Court opinion, 81 T.C. 184 (1983)).

[2678] Certainly the Court's reasoning can be binding. *See* Maney v. United States, 278 U.S. 17, 23 (1928) ("The reasoning that prevailed in those cases must govern this."). But the rule is otherwise for dictum, which is precedentially irrelevant to the reasoning, both of which are subservient to the opinion's holding. *See* Gen. Elec. Co. v. Gilbert, 429 U.S. 125, 146 (1976) (Brennan, J., dissenting).

[2679] *See, e.g.,* Rev. Rul. 2002-69, 2002-2 C.B. 760.

[2680] Knetsch v. United States, 364 U.S. 361 (1960).

[2681] When a party quoted language from the *Frank Lyon* opinion to the Court in support of an argument that its sale repurchase agreement was that rather than a loan the Court said:

> Whatever the language relied on by respondent may mean, our decision in that case to honor the taxpayer's characterization of its transaction as a 'sale-and-leaseback' rather than a 'financing transaction' was founded on an examination of 'the substance and economic realities of the transaction.' This examination included identification of 27 specific facts.

Nebraska Dept. of Revenue v. Lowenstein, 513 U.S. 123, 134 (1994).

[2682] Frank Lyon Co. v. United States, 36 A.F.T.R. 2d 5154 (E.D. Ark. 1975).

agent of its lessee, Lyon would have lost not only its depreciation deduction, but also its interest deduction (because the lessee would have been the real borrower from the third party lender), and would have been involved in a sham transaction (an agent masquerading as an independent counterparty). But the term agent did not appear in any of the three opinions from trial court to Supreme Court. Rather, the Service asserted that Frank Lyon was a "mere conduit," with which the Supreme Court and the trial court disagreed. Sometimes the Supreme Court uses "conduit" to refer to agent,[2683] but Lyon was neither. See Ch. VI.F.8.

The Supreme Court rejected the court of appeals' view that the lessee owned the property because the lessee "enjoyed all benefits and bore all burdens."[2684] The Court of Appeals thought the lessee bore the burdens because it was obligated to pay rent that would cover the taxpayer's debt payments.[2685] The Supreme Court did not rely on a benefits and burdens analysis at all in reaching its decision that the lessor owned the property and could depreciate it, but rather on the ultimate responsibility of Lyon to pay the mortgage. Some commentators correctly observed that benefits and burdens are only one of several considerations in sale leaseback cases, and an unsatisfactory one.[2686]

The key points about the trial, court of appeals, and Supreme Court opinions in the case are as follows:

- The district court ruled for the taxpayer based on fact findings that seemed hard for a court of appeals to either ignore or overturn; the Service did not even put up any evidence on the fairness of the rental and purchase prices.[2687] The district court found as a fact that Lyon was not a "conduit" for a loan to Worthen from the bank.
- Nevertheless, the Eighth Circuit reversed on the facts, finding that Lyon was a "conduit," but going farther to construct an imaginary set of dealings between Worthen and Lyon that did not actually occur but that were consistent with its "conduit" finding.[2688]
- The case reached the Supreme Court because the Eighth Circuit arguably had created a conflict with the standard view of similar cases expressed in *American Realty Trust*,[2689] although both said the characterization was an

2683 The Court frequently equates the word conduit with agent. *See* United States v. Bayse, 410 U.S. 441 (1973); *accord*, Farmer's Reservoir & Irrigation Co. v. McComb, 337 U.S. 755 (1949); Mayo v. United States, 319 U.S. 441 (1943); Gen. Util. & Op. Co. v. Helvering, 296 U.S. 200 (1935) (quoting lower court opinion); United States v. Cal. & Or. Land Co., 148 U.S. 31 (1893); Irvine v. Lowry, 39 U.S. 293 (1840); Commissioner v. Court Holding Co., 324 U.S. 331 (1945).

2684 Frank Lyon Co. v. United States, 435 U.S. 561, 571 (1978).

2685 Frank Lyon Co. v. United States, 536 F.2d 746, 752 (8th Cir. 1976).

2686 *See* Harmelink & Shurtz, *Sale-Leaseback Transactions Involving Real Estate: A Proposal for Defined Tax Rules*, 55 S. Cal. L. Rev. 833, 844 *et seq.* (1982).

2687 *Frank Lyon Co.*, 36 A.F.T.R.2d at 5154.

2688 *Frank Lyon Co.*, 536 F.2d at 746.

2689 Am. Realty Trust v. United States, 498 F.2d 1194 (4th Cir. 1974).

issue of law[2690] (and perhaps in part because the petitioner's counsel was Erwin Griswold, who had been Solicitor General up to four years earlier). Griswold's brief on the merits for Frank Lyon is compelling on the facts and the law.[2691] He rebutted the government's "conduit" argument: that Lyon was an "accommodation party" or a "straw man."[2692]

- The Court first concluded the transaction was not a "sham," which presumably meant Lyon was not a "conduit" or agent for Worthen in getting a loan; it then stated that did not automatically determine the result (which was a way of reserving, as the Court consistently has done, to the federal tax law the final say as to what facts are required for federal tax results; see Ch. VI.E.2.); but it said that on the facts of the case it "readily follows" that finding Lyon not to be a sham decided the case.
- The opinion indicated that it was applying the meaning of depreciation that was peculiar to the federal tax law by this statement: "The right to depreciate for tax purposes presumes investment; that is why a taxpayer cannot depreciate contributions to capital that it did not take into income."[2693]
- The dictum that the Service likes to cite from the opinion states: "In applying the doctrine of substance over form, the Court has looked to the objective economic realities of a transaction rather than to the particular form the parties employed."[2694]
- But the Court did not rely on such economic realities in the *Lyon* case, because it said: "It is clear from the facts, none of the parties to this sale-and-leaseback was the owner of the building in any simple sense." Therefore, the Court did not apply the substance over form statement, at least based on economics, because the economics did not provide an answer; this is the core of its rejection of the Eighth Circuit's view.
- The Court in effect applied a "tie goes to the runner" approach of respecting the taxpayer's form where there was no agency and economically it could not be said that anyone was invested in the property, but the formal owner was formally obligated to pay for it, while citing 27 possible considerations that later cases might choose to apply (or not).

[2690] *See* Ch. VI.E.3.c.

[2691] Brief for the Petitioner, Frank Lyon Co. v. United States, 435 U.S. 561 (1976) (No. 76-624), 1977 WL 189155.

[2692] Brief for the Petitioner, Frank Lyon Co. v. United States, 435 U.S. 561 (1976) (No. 76-624), 1977 WL 204922.

[2693] The Court cited at this point *United States v. Chicago, Burlington & Quincy R.R. Co.*, 412 U.S. 401 (1973).

[2694] *See, e.g.*, Rev. Rul. 2002-69, 2002-2 C.B. 760. The Supreme Court said it was relying on economic realities rather than legal abstractions in the *PPL* opinion, but actually ruled based on the form of the foreign tax, and did not cite *Frank Lyon* for the principle. PPL Corp. v. Commissioner, 133 S. Ct. 1897 (2013).

Many commentators have called the *Lyon* opinion "confused" (or less charitable terms).[2695] However, when stripped to its bare essentials (and reordered), the opinion can be explained this way:

- The two issues are whether Lyon was Worthen's agent, and if not, whether Worthen nevertheless should be treated as the owner of the building it was renting, for tax depreciation purposes.
- As a matter of fact, Lyon was not Worthen's agent for borrowing money to build the building. Therefore the transaction as not a "simple sham" to disguise a borrowing through a conduit.
- The right to claim depreciation for property goes to the party that has made, or is obligated to make, an investment in the property (which is another way of saying that person reasonably expects to obtain an equity in the property).
- Lyon had made or would make an investment in the property,[2696] because it was solely liable as a matter of law to the lender to pay for the property; hence it bore the risk of loss. That it also had a legal right to collect rent from Worthen that would cover the debt payments was not relevant. *This is a hugely important point because that right can be viewed as a type of defeasance of Lyon's payment obligations and defeasance is the Service's primary ground for arguing that obligations are not real in the leasing tax shelter context.*[2697]
- It could be relevant if Worthen had been economically accruing an equity in the property (benefits of ownership) by the combination of its lease payments and purchase rights, but the Court rejected the 8th Circuit's method of guessing that might occur as too speculative to influence the decision. In this regard, the decision was quite similar to *Clay Brown*, which was cited.[2698]

The Court evaluated economic reality primarily in finding that Lyon was not an agent because Lyon was a real business that actually owed the debt. The same facts that made Lyon an independent actor also made it an investor of its own credit in the property. As in *F. & R. Lazarus*, but for different reasons, the Court did not pursue a free floating economic analysis of who stood to gain the most from the property, and specifically refused to do so at two points:

1. "There is no simple device available to peel away the form of this transaction and to reveal its substance."[2699]

[2695] *See, e.g.*, Del Cotto, *Sale and Lease Back: A Hollow Sound When Tapped*, 37 TAX L. REV. 1, 40 (1981); Faber et al., *Ownership and Disposition of Property*, *supra* note 2617, at 773.

[2696] *See* Madison, *supra* note 15, at 727.

[2697] *See, e.g.*, BB&T Corp. v. United States, 523 F.3d 461 (4th Cir. 2008).

[2698] Commissioner v. Brown, 380 U.S. 563 (1965).

[2699] Frank Lyon Co. v. United States, 435 U.S. 561, 562 (1976).

2. "As is clear from the facts, none of the parties to this sale-and-leaseback was the owner of the building in any simple sense."[2700]

Both parties heavily relied on *F. & R. Lazarus*,[2701] which applied traditional principles of equity to find that a nominal lessee was the owner of the equity of redemption vis a vis a mortgagee. *Frank Lyon* distinguished *F. & R. Lazarus* because it was a two party rather than a multi party transaction; this must have meant that the equity of redemption principle could not apply because the other party that might be the owner was not the lender. This distinction was technically correct, but misleading. The *Frank Lyon* opinion unfortunately failed to observe the unique role that equitable rights had played in the *Lazarus* decision (see Ch. V.E.1.f(2)) and instead characterized it as a finding of "substance." Evidently it meant to invoke the broader principle of *Lazarus* as asking who was acquiring an equity in the property (Lyon).

The decision's iconic status is largely awarded in hindsight. Contemporaneous commentary did not find *Frank Lyon* to be groundbreaking, and was mostly negative as to its "reasoning." Hoffman Fuller thought that *Frank Lyon* was pro-taxpayer (which it is: the taxpayer won based on form).[2702] He noted that before the decision the Service had frequently won sale leaseback cases involving related parties but not unrelated parties. As to the opinion's 27 "realities," he rejected the view of some that taxpayers would lose such cases unless they could show most or all. Weinstein and Silvers thought that the Court decided first that the arrangement was not a "sham," apparently meaning that Lyon was not Worthen's agent to borrow money, and then listed a "torrent" of factors to support ruling for the taxpayer.[2703] Scott thought the opinion "did little more than articulate untractable [sic] standards."[2704] Solomon and Fones observed that the Court refused to rest its decision on pure economic analysis, and that the main difficulty it posed for the tax advisor was lack of predictability.[2705] Finally, Professor Wolfman strongly criticized both the outcome and the reasoning of the case, as well as the Service's means of pursuing it.[2706]

Arguably *Rice's Toyota's* cite to *Frank Lyon* played a pivotal role in diverting the Tax Court, and hence the appellate courts, away from an understanding of *Frank Lyon* as a cluster rule for depreciation cases, and converted it into a broader authority that led indirectly to the economic substance doctrine. It happened like this: Until that time the Tax Court generally had addressed cases involving nonrecourse debt-financed depreciable property by asking

---

[2700] *Id.* at 565.

[2701] Helvering v. F. & R. Lazarus & Co., 308 U.S. 252 (1939).

[2702] Fuller, *Sales and Leasebacks and the Frank Lyon Case*, 48 GEO. WASH. L. REV. 60 (1979).

[2703] Weinstein & Silvers, *Sale and Leaseback Transactions after The Frank Lyon Co.*, 24 N.Y.L. SCH. L. REV. 337 (1978).

[2704] Scott, *Sale-Leaseback v. Real Financing: Lyon's Roar and the Aftermath*, 1982 U. ILL. L. REV. 1075, 1089 (1982).

[2705] Solomon & Fones, *Sale-Leasebacks and the Shelter Oriented Investor*, 56 TAXES (CCH) 618 (1978).

[2706] Wolfman, *The Supreme Court in the Lyon's Den*, *supra* note 413, at 1075.

whether an investment in property had in fact been made so as to create a depreciable investment, and whether true debt had been incurred for its purchase so as to support an interest deduction; these are factual issues under sections 167 and 163.[2707] But after *Frank Lyon*, the Service's attorneys evidently urged the Tax Court in such cases to go to a different level and "sham" the entire transaction, which presumably allowed the court to entirely disregard the purchase (with very little if any difference in result from the prior approach). Thus, in *Rice's Toyota World* the Tax Court stated:

> *Respondent's primary argument* is that petitioner's purchase and leaseback was a tax-avoidance scheme which should be *disregarded in its entirety* for Federal income tax purposes because it is without economic substance. . . . It is well established that a transaction entered into solely for the purpose of tax reduction and which has no economic or commercial objective to support it is a *sham* and without effect for Federal income tax purposes. *Frank Lyon Co. . . . The sham transaction theory is broader in scope than an analysis of whether a nonrecourse debt is properly includable in basis.* Rather, its focus is on the entire transaction. Is the taxpayer actually acquiring an asset or any non-tax benefit? Is the asset likely to be forfeited after the tax benefits are reaped? . . . *Drawing a precise line of demarcation between valid and invalid transactions is invariably difficult. . . . The leading case supporting the existence of a sham transaction theory is Gregory v. Helvering* . . . Mr. Rice's failure to focus on the business or non-tax aspects of the transaction is not necessarily fatal to petitioner's claim. If an objective analysis of the investment indicates a realistic opportunity for economic profit which would justify the form of the transaction, it will not be classified as a sham.[2708] [emphasis added]

On appeal the Fourth Circuit seemed to restate the Tax Court's concerns in the infamous "two-pronged" test, attributed to *Frank Lyon*: "The tax court read Frank Lyon Co. v. United States, 435 U.S. 561 (1978), to mandate a two-pronged inquiry to determine whether a transaction is, for tax purposes, a sham."[2709] That was a breathtaking conclusion for the Fourth Circuit to make in a brief opinion for two reasons: (1) because *Frank Lyon* did not find a sham, its discussion was dictum; and (2) the Court listed 27 factors and not two.

In conclusion, *Frank Lyon* was a case decided on the basis of fact finding concerning agency, in which the Supreme Court put down its customary marker reserving to the federal tax law the power uniquely to define its own terms (including substance over form), but in the end it found the facts as any state court would find them (adopting the facts found by the trial judge in a bench trial). The relevant facts were whether Lyon was Worthen's agent and whether Lyon was acquiring a depreciable equity in the property. As

---

2707 *See, e.g.*, Estate of Franklin v. Commissioner, 64 T.C. 752 (1975), *aff'd*, 544 F.2d 1045 (9th Cir. 1976); Pleasant Summit Land Corp. v. Commissioner, 1987 T.C.M. (RIA) 1987-469 (which post-dated *Rice's*, but reflected the traditional approach).

2708 Rice's Toyota World, Inc. v. Commissioner, 81 T.C. 184 (1983).

2709 Rice's Toyota World, Inc., v. Commissioner, 752 F.2d 89 (4th Cir.1985).

discussed in Ch. VI.F.8., agency is a hard factual question. It unfortunately gets obscured in tax cases by use of euphemisms like "sham" or "conduit." The clearest example of the difficulty of agency fact findings in the tax area is the *Moline Properties*, *National Carbide*, *Bollinger* trilogy.[2710] It took the Supreme Court two tries to state a workable rule for when a shareholder could treat its corporation as its agent. In *Bollinger*, Justice Scalia made a statement about *National Carbide* that we should have the boldness to make about *Frank Lyon*: "In any case, we decline to parse the text of *National Carbide* as though that were itself the governing statute."[2711]

As to equity, *Frank Lyon* applied exactly the same standard *Lazarus* had applied: asking who is acquiring an equity to determine property ownership, which also determined who was liable on the debt.

VI.F.2.c(3) *Subleasing and Leasebacks*

In addition to *Frank Lyon*, discussed immediately above, the Supreme Court has considered sale leasebacks in at least two other cases. This group of three decisions forms a cluster rule that the tax law generally respects the form of the sale leaseback, probably because it is a much used commercial transaction. Sale leasebacks between unrelated persons generally are respected according to their form except when the form is understood in commercial usage to be a loan. *Clay Brown* was even more heavily freighted with tax avoidance than *Frank Lyon,* as the taxpayer sold its business assets to a charity and leased them back; but the Court respected the form and the taxpayer won.[2712] *F. & R. Lazarus* is the exception that proves the rule of the three decisions, because the Court held that the taxpayer had the equity of redemption of the property it appeared to have sold to the bank, and so the taxpayer won and could depreciate the property.[2713]

A variation on this theme involves tax benefits sought by a party that leases property from its owner and subleases the property back to that owner. These transactions tend to be even more complicated than the purchase leaseback because the indicia of property ownership are even more confused when the property owned is a lease. The lower court decisions in this area tend to apply the economic substance doctrine as if it were the positive rule of law for which it is generally advertised, rather than embodying techniques (asking is there a business purpose; is there a profit potential) that may be better suited to difficult fact finding where the form of a lease is particularly unlikely to reflect its reality for federal income tax purposes.[2714]

2710 Bittker & Lokken, at 85.2.4.

2711 Commissioner v. Bollinger, 485 U.S. 340 (1988).

2712 Commissioner v. Brown, 380 U.S. 563 (1965).

2713 Helvering v. F. & R. Lazarus & Co., 308 U.S. 252 (1939); *see* Ch. V.E.1.f(2).

2714 *See* Cummings, *SILOs and LILOs in the Tax Court*, 140 Tax Notes (TA) 1413 (Sept. 23, 2013).

VI.F.2.d. *Assignment of Income*

Cases to which the assignment of income doctrine is applied comprise a large and diffuse cluster for which substance controls form, as indicated in Ch. III.C.4.c. This doctrine is the most important judge-made positive rule of law in the income tax and the most important cluster rule in general, as well as the most important cluster rule concerning ownership of income. It also is the most important example of how a cluster rule can be quite radical within its limited scope, without being reinterpreted as a general principle that substance always rules over form. Assignment of income principles figured prominently in the struggle over income splitting in the community property states.[2715]

The doctrine prevents state law ownership rights from determining taxable income in order to prevent shifting of income to a nontaxpayer or lower bracket taxpayer.[2716] The interconnections of the doctrine with the income tax are so pervasive that they should be teased apart for better understanding:

The doctrine entered the tax law, most prominently, in the pre-New Deal year 1930 in *Lucas v. Earl,*[2717] where Mr. Justice Holmes disregarded the technicalities of state law to require compensation to be taxed to the wage earner, not the wage owner.

- Ten years later the New Deal Court decided a series of four cases extending the doctrine to assignment of income from property.[2718]
- The doctrine illustrates in true common law fashion the prototypical way a tax cluster rule relies on the substance of facts that is relevant for federal

---

[2715] *See* Commissioner v. Harmon, 323 U.S. 44 (1944); Poe v. Seaborn, 282 U.S. 101 (1930).

[2716] Bittker & Lokken, at ch. 75; *see also* Barker, *supra* note 25, at 853-54 (pointing out that the doctrine did not develop in England where income taxes were mostly collected by withholding at the source, which obviously could not involve progressive rates based on the recipient's overall income level; when rates become more progressive in England, the pattern of strict construction by the courts had been set).

[2717] Lucas v. Earl, 281 U.S. 111 (1930).

[2718] Helvering v. Clifford, 309 U.S. 331 (1940); Helvering v. Eubank, 311 U.S. 122 (1940); Helvering v. Horst, 311 U.S. 112 (1940); Harrison v. Schaffner, 312 U.S. 579 (1941). The most controversial of these was *Clifford.* In *Clifford,* the taxpayer declared himself the trustee of his property for the benefit of his wife for five years. It was thought that this arrangement was a proper way to shift income, because Congress had twice amended the Revenue Law to prevent such results from other types of trust, but not this one. The Supreme Court disagreed, ruling that the income belonged to the trust settlor, under the predecessor of section 61. The opinion rested principally on the lack of any change in the husband's "dominion and control" over his property. But the Court also relied to an extent on disbelief that the husband had really divested himself of anything as a matter of fact, given the close family relationship with the trust beneficiary and the short term of the trust. Justice Douglas cited *Lucas v. Earl* and stated that he need not reach the assignment doctrine to decide the case. Despite this statement, it is hard to tease *Clifford* apart from the other three cases that did rely on *Earl.* Moreover, *Schaffner* lumped *Clifford* with the assignment of income cases.

tax purposes.[2719] The Supreme Court admitted in *Sunnen* that it generated the assignment of income doctrine over a series of cases that arose to meet the "attenuated subtleties" created by taxpayers.[2720]

- The Court primarily cited and relied on the doctrine in *Higgins v. Smith*, discussed in Ch. III.C.3.a(2).[2721]
- The assignment of income doctrine is proof of why a progressive income tax cannot rely solely on state law rights,[2722] as discussed in Ch. VI.E.2. The doctrine does not depend on title, either to the income or to property from which the income flows, but rather on command over the income as determined broadly.[2723] Generally, the control over income indicates ownership of the income, which has a variety of tax imports.[2724] Thus, the doctrine emphasizes a different aspect of ownership from the benefits and burdens cluster of ownership generally discussed in Ch. VI.F.2.c., above.
- It usually involves related persons (another cluster area) as assignor and assignee,but not always. *P.G. Lake* ruled that the purchaser of oil production payments had not converted ordinary income into capital gains, thereby using assignment of income to create an exclusion from the literal definition of capital asset.[2725]
- It can be viewed as an application of the principles of agency (a broader cluster area). This fact is often obscured because the opinions emphasize control of the income as the operative element, but control is also a cardinal evidence of agency.[2726] The Supreme Court most clearly recognized this linkage in *Banks*,[2727] ruling that a lawyer receiving a contingent fee in litigation was not a partner of the plaintiff but an agent. Commentators

---

[2719] *See* Fuller, *Business Purpose, supra* note 762, at 393 (identifying the assignment of income doctrine as a real success in the tax law dealing with private law, in contrast with the business purpose doctrine).

[2720] Commissioner v. Sunnen, 333 U.S. 591, 607 (1948); *see also* United States v. Bayse, 410 U.S. 441 (1973) (doctors could not avoid inclusion by assigning income to profit sharing trust).

[2721] *See* Tarleau, *supra* note 653. (The article focuses on *Higgins* because of language that seems to allow the government to disregard form when a transaction does not change the control of flow of economic benefits, relying on the view that ownership of property is determined for tax purposes not just by title but by considering who receives or commands the economic benefits, citing Burnet v. Wells, 289 U.S. 670. But *Wells* was a case testing the constitutionality of a grantor trust statute, not simply addressing taxation based on control.)

[2722] *See* Plumb, *The Problem of Related Taxpayers: A Procedural Study*, 66 Harv. L. Rev. 225 (1953).

[2723] *See Sunnen*, 333 U.S. at 604-05 (citing Corliss v. Bowers, 281 U.S. 376 (1930)).

[2724] *See* Commissioner v. Lester, 366 U.S. 299 (1961) (finding no portion of payment to wife was for child support because wife's ability to use the money was unlimited); Helvering v. Horst, 311 U.S. 112 (1940).

[2725] Commissioner v. P. G. Lake, Inc., 356 U.S. 260 (1958). *See* Tucker, *The Warren Court: Its Impact on the Capital vs. Ordinary Concept Under the Internal Revenue Code*, 17 Kansas L. Rev. 53 (1968).

[2726] Restatement (Third) of Law of Agency § 1.01 (2006).

[2727] Commissioner v. Banks, 543 U.S. 426 (2005); *see* Hellwig, *The Supreme Court's Casual Use of the Assignment of Income Doctrine*, 2006 U. Ill. L. Rev. 751, 762.

have not generally identified the importance of the principles of agency to assignment of income cases.[2728]

VI.F.2.e. Court Holding Co.

Court Holding Co. is the most famous and influential Supreme Court decision on the ownership of property in the context of the question who sold the property when the property has been transferred between related parties as an initial step in its ultimate disposition to unrelated persons.[2729]

VI.F.2.e(1) *Who Sold the Property?*

Second only to the assignment of income cases is the cluster of cases turning on the answer to the question who sold the property? These cases can treat formal sales by one taxpayer as made by another taxpayer, hence substance appears to control form, but that is not the best explanation of what is going on. Rather they are cases of assignment of income between related parties,[2730] involving income generated by property rather than services (as in *Lucas v. Earl*), and can be best explained in terms of agency.[2731] The following discussion addresses the facts of the *Court Holding* case in detail and the cluster in general.

A surprisingly large number of important Supreme Court tax decisions involve who sold the property: in 1935, *Gregory*,[2732] in 1935, *General Utilities*,[2733] in 1938, *Minnesota Tea*,[2734] in 1939, *Griffiths*,[2735] in 1940, *Horst*,[2736] in 1945, *Court Holding Co.*,[2737] in 1947, *McWilliams*,[2738] and in 1950, *Cumberland Public Service Co.*[2739] The confusion generated by these

---

[2728] *But see* Jensen, *Schneer v. CIR: Continuing Confusion over the Assignment of Income Doctrine and Personal Service Income*, 1 Fla. Tax Rev. 623, 646 (1993) (stating the linkage).

[2729] Commissioner v. Court Holding Co., 324 U.S. 331 (1945); *see* Cummings, *Form versus Substance*, *supra* note 2216; Bittker & Eustice, at 10.05[5][a], 10.06[4]; *cf.* Reg. § 1.346-3 (indirectly references the issue in the case in the context of partial liquidations).

[2730] *See* Ferguson v. Commissioner, 108 T.C. 244 (1997) (a gift to charity and sale case like *Applestein*, discussed below, in which the Tax Court linked those acknowledged assignment of income cases with *United States v. Cumberland Public Service Co.*, 338 U.S. 451 (1950), the twin of Court Holding Co.), *aff'd*, 174 F.3d 997 (9th Cir. 1999); *cf.* Kingson, *The Deep Structure of Taxation: Dividend Distributions*, 85 Yale L.J. 861, 884 (1975) (similarly arguing that *Court Holding* is not about substance, but not linking the assignment of income issue).

[2731] *See* Commissioner v. Banks, 543 U.S. 426, 436 *et seq* (2005) (the attorneys fee in a contingency case is first taxed to the client even though paid directly to the attorney by the defendant becaue the attorney is not a joint venturer with the client but rather is the agent of the client).

[2732] Gregory v. Helvering, 293 U.S. 465 (1935).

[2733] Gen. Util. & Op. Co. v. Helvering, 296 U.S. 200 (1935).

[2734] Minnesota Tea Co. v. Helvering, 302 U.S. 609 (1938).

[2735] Griffiths v. Helvering, 308 U.S. 355 (1939).

[2736] Helvering v. Horst, 311 U.S. 112 (1940).

[2737] Commissioner v. Court Holding Co., 324 U.S. 331 (1945).

[2738] McWilliams v. Commissioner, 331 U.S. 694 (1947).

[2739] United States v. Cumberland Pub. Serv. Co., 338 U.S. 451 (1950).

cases had substantial impact on the development of the Code, leading to the enactment of section 334(b)(2) in 1954, and then of section 338 in 1982, and the amendment of section 338 and finally the repeal of the *General Utilities* doctrine in 1986.[2740]

In general, the Court views the owner and seller of property as the one who controls the property and its sale. This is different from the widely applied "benefits and burdens" tests, but consistent with the way accountants differentiate between agents and principals.[2741]

VI.F.2.e(2) *Evidence of Who Sold*

A primary indicator of a cluster is the use of a specific fact finding method to resolve a particularly difficult factual question, and the rule of *Court Holding* does that in relying heavily on identifying who conducted the negotiations of sale.[2742] Randolph Paul, discussing the tax opinions of Justice Black, identified *Court Holding*[2743] and *Cumberland Public Service Co.*[2744] as examples of how Justice Black based his tax decisions on careful examination of the facts, rather than on the generalizations for which his opinions are frequently cited.[2745] However, the courts err when they fail also to take into account considerations of agency and purport to apply the parol evidence rule to ignore the formation of contracts by parol. That rule does not apply as to a third party like the Service, as discussed in Ch. V.E.1.d.

Court Holding Co. treated a corporate liquidation preceding a sale in form by the shareholders of the corporate assets received in the liquidating distribution as if the corporation had sold the assets and distributed the sale proceeds in liquidation. As a result, the corporation recognized the gain in the assets that otherwise would not have been taxed under the then extant *General Utilities* doctrine.[2746] *Court Holding Co.* is miscast when cited as an

---

[2740] *See generally* BITTKER & EUSTICE, at 10.41.

[2741] *See* FASB Accounting Standards Update No. 2016-08, Revenue from Contracts with Customers, Principal versus Agent Considerations (Topic 606) (March 2016).

[2742] *See, e.g.,* Rev. Rul. 1996-30, 1996-1 C.B. 36 (reading the two cases as establishing a locus of negotiations test).

[2743] Commissioner v. Court Holding Co., 324 U.S. 331 (1945).

[2744] *Cumberland Pub. Serv. Co.*, 338 U.S. at 451.

[2745] Paul, *Justice Black and Federal Taxation, supra* note 418, at 515.

[2746] *See* BITTKER & EUSTICE, at 8.20[3]; Cummings, *Where Did Court Holding Go?*, 121 TAX NOTES (TA) 1435 (Dec. 22, 2008). The technique attempted in *Court Holding* aimed to exploit a gaping loophole allowing the corporation to distribute its assets (as opposed to selling the assets to third parties and distributing the proceeds) without recognizing built-in gain, and the shareholders to take a fair market value basis after paying a capital gains tax on the stock redemption. *See* Tye, *Corporate Distributions—Some Current Trends*, 4 TAX L. REV. 459 (1948) (analyzed the cases and observed that the Tax Court judges were split three ways, with the majority believing that the corporation is taxable on the sale due to mere sale negotiations by the officers, others believing that the negotiations must have progressed to a point of substantial agreement, and the third group believing that form controls; and explains *Court Holding* by the fact that the sale had already started (part of the proceeds received) before the liquidating distribution).

all purpose substance over form authority.[2747] It is an application of the doctrine combating assignment of income between related parties.[2748] The opinion asked which of two interested and related taxpayers made a sale that one negotiated and the other completed. It relied on the fact that the corporate officers "negotiated" the sale,[2749] which is essentially the same as asking which of the two parties controlled the income; relying on control is common in assignment of income cases that trace their origin to the breadth of the section 61 concept of income.[2750] Relying on who conducted the negotiations also is a way of saying that others would reasonably believe that the party doing the negotiating was the principal in the sale, thus in a sense holding the taxpayers to their real "form" rather than their formal form.

The Tax Court found as a fact that the corporation entered into an *unenforceable* oral contract to sell its real property and directly received a small part of the purchase price ($1,000) (which receipt did not make the contract enforceable).[2751] It found that the shareholders carried out that oral contract by themselves entering into a written contract on the same terms. It refused to view the oral contract as having been called off and a new arrangement substituted. *It found that the shareholders acted as the corporation's agents* in completing the sale the corporation contracted for orally.[2752] The Tax Court was correct in finding the oral contract to be probative even though maybe not binding, because the parol evidence rule does not bind a third party like the Service.[2753]

The Court of Appeals in *Court Holding*[2754] reversed with one dissent, finding the unenforceability of the oral contract to be dispositive. This view

[2747] *See* Cummings, *Midco Transactions Resurface*, 103 TAX NOTES (TA) 1061 (May 24, 2004); *see also* Notice 2003-46, 2003-2 C.B. 53 (illogically importing *Court Holding* into a check-the-box sale case); Cummings, *Form versus Substance*, *supra* note 2216 (proposal for proper treatment of this type of transaction).

[2748] BITTKER & LOKKEN, at 5.2, 75.1.

[2749] Kingson, *supra* note 2730, at 881-84 (characterizing negotiation as establishing the substance of the transaction).

[2750] BITTKER & LOKKEN, at 75.3.4.

[2751] Court Holding Co. v. Commissioner, 2 T.C. 531 (1943). The Tax Court opinion contrasted a true conduit-type case: Tully Trust v. Commissioner, 1 T.C. 611 (1943). There taxpayer sold stock to a middleman for $100.50, who resold to the corporation for $101. Because the middleman had complete freedom of what to do with the property, the court did not impute his sale to the taxpayer. This case came out differently from *Court Holding* both because the transferee was not related to the taxpayer by some affinity (family, etc.), and because the transferee controlled the sale, which had not been pre arranged by the original owner, thus preventing his identification as a related agent of the taxpayer.

[2752] The Tax Court refused to impose the fraud penalty, finding that the corporation could legitimately have thought that its technique would work to avoid the tax.

[2753] *See supra* Ch. V.E.1.d.

[2754] Commissioner v. Court Holding Co., 143 F.2d 823 (5th Cir. 1944).

accorded form and state law primacy over substance, even in a related party context.[2755]

The Supreme Court reversed, agreeing with the Tax Court. Its opinion can and should be read as based on the trial court's finding that the shareholders made the sale *as agents of the corporation*, which also would have solved any statute of frauds problem with the written contract because their sale contract was in writing and a writing was not necessary to prove agency.[2756] In a sense, this finding seems wrong because the shareholders had no intent to execute the contract as the agent of the corporation.[2757] But it is right because the shareholders really cared only that they not *appear* to act as agents of the corporation. The Tax Court refused to allow the taxpayer's machinations to obscure the fact that its shareholders were closing the sale as agent for the corporation. As discussed in Ch. VI.E.1.b(4), Judge Learned Hand tried mightily to ignore the cluster rule based on negotiations established by *Court Holding* (before the *Cumberland* opinion).

Therefore, *Court Holding* is not an all purpose substance over form authority but reflects a cluster rule in the assignment of income cluster, which is applied when the change in, or creation of, a contract (binding or not) changes the identity of the taxpayer. But unfortunately, *Court Holding* is not normally recognized as an assignment of income case,[2758] probably due to the authorities it cited, principally *Gregory*.[2759] Although *Gregory* did involve a similar effort to move the location of the sale, neither the government nor the Court tried to make one party the seller of property formally sold by the

[2755] The sandwiching of the form driven Court of Appeals opinion between (1) the workmanlike Tax Court finding of an agency, and (2) the sweeping generalization of the Supreme Court opinion, illustrates a classic division of labor in tax litigation. The Tax Court does the heavy lifting of trying to help the Rube Goldberg Code work; the Court of Appeals is likely to rule as if tax cases are like any commercial law case; and the Supreme Court episodically pronounces doctrines that reverberate in unknowable ways down the decades. *See generally* Cummings, *Statutory Interpretation and* Albertson's, *supra* note 9.

[2756] *Court Holding Co.*, 2 T.C. at 538 ("executed for it by its stockholders as its agent").

[2757] They had been advised that they, not the corporation, had to sell the property in order to obtain the tax advantage, and they made every effort to reach that result under state law. Judge Learned Hand made the same observation in *Fairfield S.S. Transport v. Commissioner*, 157 F.2d 321 (2d Cir. 1946) ("the shareholders had most carefully provided the contrary").

[2758] *Cf.* Helvering v. Eubank, 311 U.S. 122 (1940) (disregarded assignments of rights to insurance renewal compensation); Helvering v. Horst, 311 U.S. 112 (1940) (disregarded gift of interest coupons attached to bonds that donor retained). *Commissioner v. Oates*, 207 F.2d 711 (7th Cir. 1953) *acq.* 1960-1 C.B. 5, pointed out that lacking the element of assignment of income to a third party, those authorities do not apply.

[2759] Gregory v. Helvering, 293 U.S. 465 (1935).

other party.[2760] *Gregory* is properly viewed as a case about statutory interpretation: what does "reorganization mean"?[2761] *Court Holding's* other cites were to cases having no bearing on assignment of income, but for one: *Griffiths v. Helvering*.[2762] In that brief opinion, the Supreme Court reiterated its view that assignment of income cases depended on who controlled the income.

It is well known that the antithesis of *Court Holding* is *Cumberland Public Service Co.*[2763] Its facts showed that *as a matter of tax planning to avoid the corporate level tax*, the corporation never intended to sell its assets and never contracted to do so, even though it did receive an offer to buy its assets. The facts were unclear whether the officers of the corporation in their capacity as such negotiated on behalf of the shareholders, or negotiated as shareholders (which they were). Presumably, the Supreme Court thought they negotiated as shareholders to sell assets.

Like *Court Holding*, *Cumberland* affirmed the factual finding of the trial court as to who made a sale: "Here as in the *Court Holding Co.* case we accept the ultimate findings of fact of the trial tribunal."[2764] Subsequently, the Supreme Court described the dichotomy of the two cases as depending on who *negotiated* the sale and stated that where the management and owner-

---

[2760] In *Gregory*, a corporation dropped Monitor shares into Averill, all the stock of which it distributed to Mrs. Gregory, who liquidated Averill and sold the Monitor shares. The Bureau asserted that Mrs. Gregory should be taxed as if she had received the Monitor shares as a dividend and sold them; the Court of Appeals, affirmed by the Supreme Court, believed, instead, that the shareholder had received the Averill shares, but as a dividend, not in a reorganization. Neither court viewed the corporation as having sold the Monitor stock and distributed the cash, which would have been consistent with *Court Holding*. *Id.*

[2761] *See supra* Ch. III.C.3.a(1).

[2762] Griffiths v. Helvering, 308 U.S. 355 (1939).

[2763] United States v. Cumberland Pub. Serv. Co., 338 U.S. 451 (1950) (which concluded as a matter of law that the shareholders sold the property).

[2764] *Id.* at 456. Beyond that, the guidance given by the opinion is that (1) the factual determination of who made the sale in the case of a closely held corporation and its shareholders is "particularly shadowy and artificial when the corporation is closely held"; (2) but the fact finding cannot be avoided because Congress has made tax consequences turn on it (a rule that Congress later changed in the case of liquidating corporations); (3) there is no taint involved in escaping the corporate level tax through the liquidation route provided by Congress; and (4) in a footnote the Court stated that:

> What we said in the *Court Holding Co.* case was an approval of the action of the Tax Court in looking beyond the papers executed by the corporation and shareholders in order to determine whether the sale there had actually been made by the corporation. We were but emphasizing the established principle that in resolving such questions as who made a sale, fact finding tribunals in tax cases can consider motives, intent, and conduct in addition to what appears in written instruments used by parties to control rights as among themselves.

Id. at 455 n.3.

ship overlapped, that was an unsatisfactory determinant.[2765] Thus, despite the principle that generally there is no taint in fashioning a transaction to minimize taxes, special scrutiny applies to income shifting between related parties: that results in a cluster rule for who sold the property situations.

The obvious point of difficulty is identifying the degree of maturation of the sale needed to invoke the doctrine. *Cumberland* relied in part on the fact that the seller arguably never pursued a sale of the assets by the corporation. Thus, even though there was an identity of interest as to the corporation and its shareholders, the Court allowed the formalities of the negotiations and the way the parties set up the deal to control, *so long as the parties were consistent* in acting as if the shareholders were making the sale and the shareholders actually made the sale. This suggests that even in these related party cases, the taxpayer can make form control if the taxpayer consistently respects the form it has chosen. The Court reasoned that it could not be said that income accrued to the corporation because the corporation itself never negotiated to sell the property.

Gregory could have been a who sold the property type of case but probably was not because the ultimate property sale evidently was on a public market and so did not have to be arranged in advance.[2766] Therefore, the government did not argue that United sold the Monitor stock and distributed the sale proceeds to its shareholder, Mrs. Gregory;[2767] rather the government argued that United distributed the Monitor stock to Mrs. Gregory and she sold it.[2768] The Court of Appeals held that United distributed to her the Averill (i.e. Spinco) stock, but not in a reorganization (which the Supreme Court affirmed).

General Utilities also is not normally recognized as a who sold the property case, but in fact would have been decided on the same basis as *Court Holding Co.* and *Cumberland* but for the fact that the Supreme Court held that the government had not properly asserted below the argument that the shareholders sold the corporate property as agents of the corporation. The corporation owned half of the stock of a corporation with one other shareholder; a third party approached them and wanted to buy all of the stock and General Utilities' president said that could be done only after the corporation distributed the stock to its shareholders because it did not want to incur a corporate

---

[2765] Central Tablet Mfg. Co. v. United States, 417 U.S. 673 (1974). That case involved a corporation's casualty loss by fire, which occurred before the adoption of the plan of liquidation of the corporation, but the insurance recovery occurred thereafter. The Court ruled that then section 337 did not apply to exclude the gain because the disposition of the property occurred before the corporation adopted the plan of liquidation.

[2766] *See* Brief Amicus Curiae, Gregory v. Helvering, 293 U.S. 465 (1935) (No. 127), 1934 WL 60142.

[2767] But the Board's opinion suggests that. Gregory v. Commissioner, 27 B.T.A. 223 (1932) (government contended that "the petitioner must be taxed as upon a dividend consisting of the amount received upon the sale of the Monitor shares as if such amount had been distributed by the United corporation directly to her.").

[2768] *See* Brief for Petitioner, Gregory v. Helvering, 293 U.S. 465 (1935) (No. 127), 1934 WL 60333.

level tax. The Board of Tax Appeals found that General Utilities never agreed to sell the stock orally or in writing even though it negotiated the sale, and the Supreme Court rejected the Court of Appeals' effort to modify that finding. Hence General Utilities succeeded in avoiding the double tax, indeed becoming the brand name for such a ploy.

Minnesota Tea might seem to be out of place in this group, but is not: instead of asking who sold the property, it asks an analogous question, who paid the corporate debts?[2769] Minnesota Tea attempted a reorganization without liquidating. Rather, it distributed some of its assets (other than the stock it received in the reorganization) and required its shareholders to agree to pay its debts as its agents, so that it could satisfy the requirement of the predecessor of section 361(b) that it must distribute to its shareholders any boot received in a reorganization rather than keeping the boot and paying corporate debts. The opinion answered the question on the same basis that *Court Holding* determined who sold the property, by finding the shareholders to be agents of the corporation, but this time to be agents for purposes of paying its debts. Because the opinion is frequently cited as an anti-conduit authority, it is important to recognize the narrowness of its holding. It appears at first to make the radical conclusion that when a corporation liquidates and distributes its assets to its shareholders and they assume or become liable for and pay its debts then the corporation actually paid its own debts. Instead, the facts of the contracts showed the shareholders to be paying agents, not assumers of liability who were left to pay them or not.[2770]

The Supreme Court opinion in *Minnesota Tea* cited only *Gregory* for the point that the shareholders were a conduit for corporate payment to creditors, also uttering the unfortunate line:

> A given result at the end of a straight path is not made a different result because reached by following a devious path. The preliminary distribution to the stockholders was a meaningless and unnecessary incident in the transmission of the fund to the creditors, all along intended to come to their hands, so transparently artificial that further discussion would be a needless waste of time. The relation of the stockholders to the matter was that of a mere conduit.[2771]

[2769] Minnesota Tea Co. v. Helvering, 302 U.S. 609 (1938).

[2770] Minnesota Tea Co. v. Commissioner, 28 B.T.A. 591 (1933). The Board originally did not think the corporation had reorganized; the Supreme Court reversed and remanded. 296 U.S. 378 (1935). Then the Board found that the corporation had distributed the assets to its shareholders, but government counsel changed on the second appeal to Robert H. Jackson, and he convinced the Court of Appeals that as a matter of law the corporation paid the shareholders to assume its debts in 89 F.2d 711 (8th Cir. 1937), which the Supreme Court affirmed. 302 U.S. 609 (1938). The Court of Appeals opinion clearly thought there was nothing unusual in treating a contract to pay a debt as an agency: "There is nothing unfamiliar in taxing on the basis of the legal effect of a transaction." 89 F.2d at 715.

[2771] Minnesota Tea Co. v. Helvering, 302 U.S. at 609.

This is an entirely overblown way of saying that someone who happened to also be a shareholder functioned as an agent.

Minnesota Tea is remarkably similar to *Hendler Dairy*.[2772] Hendler transferred all of its assets to Borden in exchange for Borden stock and Borden's assumption of Hendler's debts. The debts included a half million dollar bond that Hendler had called for redemption, which was to occur nine days after the date of the acquisition. Borden did pay off the bonds as scheduled. The Supreme Court found that the assumption and payment was in substance a payment of the half million to Hendler, which then used the funds to pay its creditors; it might as well have called Borden a paying agent. This caused Hendler to recognize half million of its gain in the assets it transferred to Borden. If the facts had involved a more typical assumption of a debt not near retirement, the conclusion of the case might have been different.

Horst also is a who sold the property case (the property being interest coupons), which differed from *Gregory* and *General Utilities* in that the legal right to the income from the property already existed: the taxpayer gave away the interest coupons on his bonds. The Court viewed this as a pure assignment of income case.

McWilliams addressed who sold the property in another sense (was it the husband or some nameless market seller): husband sold shares on the market and wife bought the same number of shares at the same time on the market, presumably for the same price. Husband wanted to recognize a loss and circumvent section 267. The Court, in effect, ruled that the husband sold to the wife, rather than some unidentifiable market seller selling to the wife. Although Ch. III.C.3.b. discusses *McWilliams* critically, at least the Court read and applied a statutory anti-abuse rule purposively, in contrast to reading it literally and then relying on an amorphous doctrine like the economic substance doctrine.

Although several of these cases gave rise to some broad language, none of them involved anything other than standard fact finding in the cluster area where the timing of the sale or payment must be identified as between related parties.

A related cluster area involves identifying the seller when there has been a unilateral tender from a buyer (as in cases of an offer to redeem, a liquidation, or a merger). In these cases, often involving a gift to a charity that completes the sale, the courts have directly recognized the assignment of income issue in the cases, but have tended to identify the seller based how much the donor

[2772] United States v. Hendler, 303 U.S. 564 (1938).

controlled the sale process, which is consistent with the *Court Holding Co.* approach.[2773]

VI.F.2.f. *Triangulation*

The Supreme Court pioneered the fact finding method of triangulating payments through a taxpayer even though the actual payments involved two other persons.

- When a corporation paid the officer's taxes, it paid compensation to the officer, who would be treated as paying his own taxes.[2774]
- *Lucas v. Earl* created the assignment of income doctrine by treating the compensation that the husband direct to be paid to the wife as paid to the husband, who presumably then gave it to his wife.[2775]
- Joliet Railroad leased its entire road to another railroad in 1864 for payments including annual payments of a $7 per share dividend to its shareholders. By 1931, Joliet began to wonder why it should report the $105,000 in dividends that never passed through its hands as income to it; the Court held it was income under the assignment of income doctrine, even without Joliet serving as a conduit.[2776]

[2773] These cases generally find an assignment of income when the sale has advanced so far as to have turned the property into a right to receive income as a practical matter, and the legal possibility that the sale would not occur is "remote and hypothetical." Jones v. United States, 531 F.2d 1343 (6th Cir. 1976) (stating that the Sixth Circuit was aligning with the Second and Eighth Circuits in adopting a "realities and substance" test rather than a hypothetical possibility test); Kinsey v. Commissioner, 477 F.2d 1058 (2d Cir. 1973); Hudspeth v. United States, 471 F.2d 275 (8th Cir. 1972); Salvatore v. Commissioner, 434 F.2d 600 (2d Cir. 1970). The Ninth Circuit agreed. Ferguson v. Commissioner, 174 F.3d 997 (9th Cir. 1999). All of these cases involved gifts to charities, unlike *Estate of Applestein v. Commissioner*, 80 T.C. 331 (1983), which involved a gift to children but also relied on *Jones. See also* Petersen v. Commissioner, 1986 T.C.M. (RIA) 1986-267 (gift to children). However, *Rauenhorst v. Commissioner*, 119 T.C 157 (2002), rejected the *Jones, Kinsey, Hudspeth* line of cases in a charity case because it was superceded by Revenue Ruling 78-197, which ruled that where the donor controlled the corporation that was going to redeem the stock from the charity the donor would be taxed on the sale only if the donee was bound to go through with the sale. This practical realty standard is consistent with *Court Holding* and with *Cumberland*, in that even though there was little chance the sale would not occur, that was not due to the fact that the corporation had acted to turn the property into sale proceeds to itself. That is, no matter how likely the sale may be, if the original owner has not itself brought the sale to near fruition, the sale by the shareholders cannot be attributed to it.

[2774] Old Colony Trust Co. v. Commissioner, 279 U.S. 716 (1929). *See also* Diedrich v. Commissioner, 457 U.S. 191 (1982) (donee's payment of gift tax treated as payment to donor); Commissioner v. Hansen, 360 U.S. 446 (1959) (treating payment of one's income to a third party as constructive receipt).

[2775] Lucas v. Earl, 281 U.S. 111 (1930).

[2776] United States v. Joliet & C.R. Co., 315 U.S. 44 (1942).

VI.F.3. *The Separateness of Entities*

The tax law, like the general law, normally treats entities as separate from their owners based on form, with certain exceptions.[2777] The Supreme Court has called this a separate entity doctrine as to corporations.[2778] The tax law's exceptions are not necessarily broader that those of the general law, only different. Consequently, it can be said (a) that form controls the separateness of entities in the tax law to the extent expected generally, and (b) that to the extent the tax law has different standards, they form cluster areas in the income tax in which substance overrides form to a limited extent, and in different ways for corporations, partnerships and trusts because they are taxed under different taxing regimes.

VI.F.3.a. *Concerns Unique to an Income Tax*

Every person is potentially a United States taxpayer, and section 7701(a)(10) defines person to include a "trust, estate, partnership, association, company or corporation." Therefore, the tax system has a need to keep persons and taxpayers separate from each other, except, and to the extent the Code adopts a passthrough regime or otherwise ameliorates double taxation of the same income. Because of this need, particularly as to corporate entities, cluster rules have developed to define the separation.

The separateness of corporations has an important place in the history of U.S. law generally. Through an obscure addition by the reporter of the Supreme Court's opinions, corporations gained the constitutional protections accorded to "persons," and hence even more separateness:

> The Court does not wish to hear argument on the question whether the provisions of the Fourteenth Amendment to the Constitution . . . applies to corporations. We are all of the opinion that it does.[2779]

That case and the U.S. Constitution may explain why the Code uses "persons" as the all purpose denominator.

The Supreme Court explained the general federal treatment of entities in a 1983 opinion by Justice O"Connor outside the tax arena:[2780]

- In 1819, Chief Justice Marshall described private corporations as existing only in contemplation of law.

[2777] New Colonial Ice Co. v. Helvering, 292 U.S. 435 (1934).

[2778] Commissioner v. Bollinger, 485 U.S. 340, 349 (1988).

[2779] Santa Clara County v. S. Pac. R.R. Co., 118 U.S. 394 (1886) (a state tax case); *see generally* NACE, GANGS OF AMERICA ch. 9 (Berrett-Koehler 2003). The Court dramatically expanded the concept of corporations as persons in *Burwell v. Hobby Lobby*, 134 S. Ct. 2751 (2014). *See* Cummings, Hobby Lobby *and Federal Taxes*, 145 TAX NOTES (TA) 519 (Nov. 3, 2014).

[2780] First Nat. City Bank v. Banco Para, 462 U.S. 611 (1983); superceded in the foreign government context by statute, as explained in *Weinstein v. The Islamic Republic of Iran*, 624 F. Supp. 2d 272 (E.D.N.Y. 2009).

- They are not to be regarded as separate from their owners in all circumstances.
- One such exception is when the corporation is the agent of the owner because it is "so extensively controlled by its owner."
- A second exception is the equitable principle that the separateness of entities will be disregarded if it works fraud or injustice.
- An example of the equitable principle is that a corporation that is interposed to defeat legislative policies can be disregarded.

Thus, the Court identified agency and equity as the core tools for disregarding the separateness of legal entities. The Court also has applied these principles in the tax area, but they operate differently due to the different interests involved and the purpose of Congress to recognize corporations as separate taxpayers.

The earliest evidence of the difference between the general law and the tax view of entities is that it took the tax law longer to treat corporations as separate from their owners for purposes of the income tax. In *Collector v. Hubbard*, the Court upheld Congress' choice to tax shareholders on the undivided profits of corporations under the Civil War income tax.[2781] The income tax was first successfully levied on corporations in 1909, after the 1894 act taxing corporate income was held unconstitutional in *Pollock*.[2782] Nevertheless, in *Southern Pacific* in 1918,[2783] the Court ignoted the separateness of a corporation and its subsidiary. As discussed in Ch. II.B.2.C.3., by the time of *Eisner v. Macomber* in 1920, the Court shifted from the look through analysis that supported its decision in *Hubbard* to the view that the corporate shell blocked the shareholders from the corporation's undistributed income. Thus, the tax law trended away from substance over form in the area of corporate taxation, both by the choices made by Congress and the approaches taken by the Court in applying the statutes.

The second evidence of the difference is that the Code defines various entities in its own terms (for example, a corporate charter is not necessary to be a tax corporation, which is called an "association"), and provides different taxing regimes, the most prominent being: corporations or associations;[2784] partnerships;[2785] trusts and estates;[2786] cooperatives;[2787] insurance compa-

---

[2781] Collector v. Hubbard, 79 U.S. 1 (1871).

[2782] Pollock v. Farmers' Loan & Trust Co., 157 U.S. 429, *modified*, 158 U.S. 601 (1895); Bittker & Lokken, at 2.5.1.

[2783] S. Pac. Co. v. Lowe 247 U.S. 330 (1918); *cf.* National Carbide Corp. v. Commissioner, 336 U.S. 422 (1949) (vehemently denying that *Lowe* was based on agency, or at least agency as normally understood, and indicating that the law had passed *Lowe* by).

[2784] I.R.C. §§ 7701(a)(3) (the definition), 11 (the taxing provision); Subchapters C and S define special rules for corporations.

[2785] I.R.C. §§ 7701(a)(2), 701 (provides that partners not partnerships are taxed); Subchapter K defines special rules for partnerships.

[2786] I.R.C. §§ 641-692.

[2787] I.R.C. §§ 1381-1388.

nies;[2788] and banks.[2789] Trusts and corporations have produced by far the most disputes about the separate treatment of entities, because they can deflect income away from owners, but in the case of corporations also can result in two tiers of tax on the same income. The Court recognized the importance of entities as separate sources of revenue for the government in *Bellis*, as an explanation for refusing to extend to them the protection against self-incrimination.[2790] Indeed the multiplication of taxation of corporate income is a third reason for the tax law to more readily recognize the separateness of a corporation than the common law.

Mr. Justice Holmes captured the essential problem posed by entities when he said that to call them fictions leads nowhere, because they are fictions created by law and intended to be acted on as if true.[2791] His statement also reflects the fundamental reason that the tax law tends to respect the corporate form more than the general law: Congress intends them to be acted on by the Code as if true.

VI.F.3.b. *Corporations*

The tax law had to develop a cluster rule *to prevent* substance over form from too easily treating the corporation as the agent of its shareholders, because such treatment would defeat the potential double taxation of corporate income, which is the fundamental reason for the corporate income tax. Therefore, equitable rejection of the use of the corporation is not common for federal tax purposes because Congress intended corporations to be taxed separately from their shareholders, and for corporate income to be doubly taxed when distributed. Indeed, the legislative history of proposals to codify the economic substance doctrine state that corporate organization is a protected transaction.[2792]

However, the federal tax law's enhanced respect for the separateness and independence of corporations from their shareholders creates a deep confusion in the case of closely held corporations, particularly one shareholder corporations and wholly owned subsidiaries of other corporations. Closely held corporations inevitably are agents of their shareholder or shareholders in practice. They exist solely to carry out the shareholder's will and only rarely does a subsidiary of another corporation have officers and directors who act independently of the parent. Therefore, the fact of shareholder control of the corporation cannot be allowed to undo the separateness of the corporation. Even in these cases the tax law refuses to treat the corporation as the agent of its parent corporation, absent a fairly careful effort by the taxpayer to overcome the presumption of separateness and independence. In stating this clus-

2788 I.R.C. §§ 801-848.

2789 I.R.C. §§ 581-601.

2790 Bellis v. United States, 417 U.S. 85 (1974).

2791 Klein v. Board, 282 U.S. 19, 24 (1930).

2792 *See supra* Ch. V.F.7.b(1).

ter rule, the Supreme Court recognized the control exercised by shareholders of closely held corporations and stated that such control could not be allowed to prevent the treatment of the corporation as a separate taxpayer for reasons of administrability: it would just be too hard for the Service to determine on a case by case basis when such control spelled agency and when it did not.[2793]

Inevitably this tilt of the law away from admitting the obviousness of agency allows corporations and their shareholders to avoid agency status when they don't want it; the principal example is the whole regime for deferring foreign income earned by subsidiaries of the U.S. shareholder, which is based on a formal separation of ownership.

The 2014 *Hobby Lobby* decision introduced a wild card into the tax treatment of corporations.[2794] On the one hand it confirmed the normal federal income tax treatment of a corporation as a person, but on the other hand it invested the corporate person with the status and interests of its shareholders, at least when the corporation is closely held, for the purpose of claiming religious liberties. By treating the corporation as the alter ego of its shareholders, the opinion basically reversed the entire history of corporate taxation. The only possible limits of the opinion's theory are (1) it may apply only to closely held corporations (undefined), and (2) it may only apply to protect certain constitutional rights of individual shareholders.

The current state of the corporation cluster rules is as follows:

- The federal income tax law will respect the form of a state law corporation as a separate person,[2795] which can have its own tax items and attributes.[2796]
- The owner of the corporation must take the bad with the good of its corporation's separateness, meaning that it cannot appropriate to itself the corporation's tax attributes (usually losses) when it chooses,[2797] and that the corporation will be taxed on income from dealing with its shareholder as if it were an unrelated person.[2798]

[2793] Commissioner v. Bollinger, 485 U.S. 340, 345 (1988).

[2794] Burwell v. Hobby Lobby Stores, Inc., 134 S. Ct. 2751 (2014) (holding that a closely held for profit corporation could assert rights under the Religious Freedom Restoration Act and so avoid paying penalty taxes under the Affordable Care Act). *See* Cummings, *Hobby Lobby* and Federal Taxes, 145 Tax Notes (TA) 519 (Nov. 3, 2014).

[2795] Reg. § 301.7701-2(b)(1); *see* Burnet v. Clark, 287 U.S. 410, 415 (1932) ("A corporation and its stockholders are generally to be treated as separate entities. Only under exceptional circumstances—not present here—can the difference be disregarded.").

[2796] *See generally* Cleary, *The Corporate Entity in Tax Cases*, 1 Tax L. Rev. 3 (1947).

[2797] *See* Interstate Trans. Lines v. Commissioner, 319 U.S. 590 (1943) (a parent utilizing a shell subsidiary to book certain portions of its business cannot deduct the subsidiary's expenses); Dalton v. Bowers, 287 U.S. 404 (1932) (inventor who assigned his invention to a corporation was not in the corporation's losing business; he could claim only a capital loss).

[2798] Burnet v. Commonwealth Improvement Co., 287 U.S. 415 (1932).

- The owner can treat its corporation as the owner's agent only with difficulty, under rules worked out by the Supreme Court in *National Carbide* and *Bollinger*.[2799]
- The Service can disregard a corporation that does not conduct a business at all, as announced in *Moline Properties, Inc.*[2800]
- Also under *Moline Properties*, the Service can disregard the nominal conduct of business by a corporation, meaning that if the owner (shareholder) disregards its own corporation as the entity conducting the business, then the Service can choose to follow the form of what the shareholder in fact does with the business rather than the form of some minimal paperwork that says the business belongs to the corporation.[2801]

VI.F.3.b(1) *Corporations: Business vel Non?*

Moline Properties, Inc.[2802] generally is viewed as establishing the rule that a corporation (later extended to other entities including specifically partnerships) that either was set up for a business purpose or activity, or carried on a business activity, must be respected as an entity by both the Service and the taxpayer.[2803] It was preceded by *Chile Copper Co.*, which had called a pure holding company the "brain or at least the efferent nerve" of its operating subsidiary, and for that reason a separate taxable entity.[2804] *Moline* raised the bar for either the government or the taxpayer to treat income nominally earned by (or deductions of) the corporation as the income (or deductions)

[2799] *See* Bittker & Eustice, at 2.10 (discussing Commissioner v. Bollinger, 485 U.S. 340, 345 (1988) (easing the *National Carbide* test); National Carbide Corp. v. Commissioner, 336 U.S. 422 (1949)).

[2800] Moline Properties, Inc. v. Commissioner, 319 U.S. 436 (1943).

[2801] This is essentially what happened in *Higgins v. Smith*, 308 U.S. 473 (1940); *see* the text immediately following Ch. VI.F.3.b(1).

[2802] *Moline Properties, Inc.*, 319 U.S. at 436.

[2803] *See, e.g.*, N. Indiana Pub. Serv. Co. v. Commisioner, 105 T.C. 341 (1995):

> The alternative requirements of business purpose or business activity have been restated many times. With respect to the latter requirement, the quantum of business activity may be rather minimal. . . . Even where a corporation is created with a view to reducing taxes, if it in fact engages in substantive business activity, it will not be disregarded for Federal tax purposes. . . . This is true even if the primary reason for the corporation's existence is to reduce taxes.

See also Madison, *supra* note 15, at 735.

[2804] Edwards v. Chile Copper Co., 270 U.S. 452 (1926).

of the shareholder.[2805] Unfortunately *Moline* was followed by decades of confusion about the related issue of when a shareholder could treat a corporation as the agent of its shareholder,[2806] marked principally by the Supreme Court's opinions in *National Carbide* (which appeared to create a very stringent requirement for treating a corporation as its shareholder's agent) and *Bollinger* (which somewhat relaxed the requirement).[2807]

The *Moline* test came to be called a two-pronged test,[2808] which is unfortunate terminology because it allows confusion whether the two prongs are conjunctive or disjunctive. By referring to a purpose that "is the equivalent of business activity . . ." the *Moline* opinion evidently intended that even if the entity did not get around to conducting business due to organizational problems or the like, or was created to avoid creditors (which it recognized as a valid purpose), or to serve as a holding company with no business of its own,

---

[2805] The Court had vacillated on the issue. In 1937, Randolph Paul could still say that the Court would disregard an established corporate entity, citing *Southern Pacific Co. v. Lowe*, 247 U.S. 330 (1918) and *Gulf Oil Corp. v. Lewellyn*, 248 U.S. 71 (1918). In the former, the subsidiary owned the railroad and leased it to the parent and paid the parent dividends, which the parent claimed were not taxable because they were paid out of pre-1913 earnings of the subsidiary. It was undisputed that the dividends were paid out of pre-1913 earnings but the law had no concept of tracing dividends for this purpose and so the trial court had ruled that the receipt of the dividends was post-1913 income as to the parent. The Supreme Court reversed for the stated reason that the subsidiary's income had been the parent's income when earned, not for all purposes, but for the special purpose of applying the constitutional limitation. In doing so, the Court recited facts showing that the subsidiary was little more than a bookkeeping entity, for which the parent kept the books. However, the Supreme Court later disavowed *Southern Pacific* in *National Carbide*, stating that "it lays down no rule for tax purposes." National Carbide Corp. v. Commissioner, 336 U.S. 422, 432 (1949). In *National Carbide*, the Supreme Court imposed what came to be viewed as a super limitation on a corporation's claim that it earned income as an agent for its shareholders. That decision repudiated *Lowe's* approach that had treated shareholder and corporation as one, without regard to agency, based solely on "complete domination and control" by one of the other. National Carbide Corp., 336 U.S. at 426. *Commissioner v. Bollinger*, 485 U.S. 340 (1988) further modified the rule.

[2806] *See* Bittker & Eustice, at 1.05[1][b]; *see generally* Lainoff, Bates & Bowers, *Attributing the Activities of Corporate Agents Under U.S. Tax Law*, 38 Ga. L. Rev. 143, 152-58 (2003).

[2807] *See* immediately preceding subchapter.

[2808] *See, e.g.*, Bertoli v. Commissioner, 103 T.C. 501, 511-12 (1994) ("When called upon to determine whether or not a particular entity (i.e., a partnership) will be recognized for tax purposes, the courts subsequent to *Moline Properties*, have used a two-prong test—the entity (1) must be created for a business purpose, or (2) must carry on a business activity. *See* Hagist Ranch, Inc. v. Commissioner, 295 F.2d 351 (7th Cir. 1961), *aff'g*, 1960 T.C.M. (RIA) 1960-206; O'Neill v. Commissioner, 271 F.2d 44, 49 (9th Cir. 1959), *aff'g*, 1957 T.C.M. (RIA) 1957-193; Jackson v. Commissioner, 233 F.2d 289 (2d Cir. 1956), *acq., aff'g*, 24 T.C. 1 (1955); Paymer v. Commissioner, 150 F.2d 334 (2d Cir. 1945); Lomas Santa Fe, Inc. v. Commissioner, 74 T.C. 662, 674 (1980), *aff'd*, 693 F.2d 71 (9th Cir. 1982); Cooper v. Commissioner, 61 T.C. 599, 602 (1974); Shaw Constr. Co. v. Commissioner, 35 T.C. 1102, 1114 (1961), *aff'd*, 323 F.2d 316 (9th Cir. 1963), *acq.*; Aldon Homes, Inc. v. Commissioner, 33 T.C. 582, 597 (1959)."); *cf.* United States v. Joliet & C.R. Co., 315 U.S. 44 (1942) (corporation remained in existence from 1864 to 1931 solely to maintain stock books so that its shareholders could collect the proceeds of the sale of its properties in 1864 directly from the purchaser; nevertheless, the Court upheld taxing the annual sale proceeds to the corporation).

it could nevertheless be respected if there were an intent to conduct business or business was facilitated. That view makes the purpose prong helpful to taxpayers wanting the entity to be respected, rather than hurtful.

However, that view has been turned on its head by an approach of the D.C. Circuit that carrying on some business activity is not sufficient to require respect of the business entity where business purpose is lacking.[2809] The D.C. Circuit states that "courts have understood the 'business activity' reference in *Moline* to exclude activity whose sole purpose is tax avoidance.[2810] The opinion reasoned that shortly after *Moline* the Second Circuit held per Judge Learned Hand in *National Investors Corp. v. Hoey* "that the retention and sale of securities, after the date when the corporate holding had served its nontax goals, could not be considered for tax purposes."[2811]

Hoey[2812] does not so hold. Moreover, *Hoey* should be recognized as part of Judge Learned Hand's one-judge effort to convert all tax avoidance cases into *Gregory* cases by expanding the requirement of business purpose across the entire Code, an effort also reflected in his opinion in *Transport Trading*, discussed in Ch. VI.E.1.b(4). In *Hoey*, a parent caused its subsidiary to begin to liquidate, and then delayed the liquidating distribution to increase the loss to be recognized on the stock due to the continued decline in the value of the subsidiary. Hand's opinion said that the taxpayer failed to prove the value of the liquidating dividend at the time it became taxable under constructive receipt analysis. But the opinion went on to discuss the lack of business purpose for the subsidiary's holding assets after deciding to liquidate. Whatever Judge Hand meant by this analysis, he did not order that the corporation be disregarded; he merely ordered that the shareholder had to prove when it should be treated as receiving the distribution for purpose of valuation and loss. The tax law has rejected the notion that the cure for an ambiguous liquidating distribution is to ignore the corporation; rather it is to treat the distribution as a dividend.[2813]

Thus, the extreme approach of the D.C. Circuit has no firm footing in *Hoey*. Moreover, *Hoey's* verbiage seems to be an overreaction of Learned Hand to being on the panel that was overturned by the Supreme Court in *Higgins v. Smith*,[2814] and to writing the opinion in *Morris & Essex R. Co.*,[2815] which he

---

[2809] *See* Jackel, *For Better or Worse*, *supra* note 1131, at 96-33 (discussing *Moline Properties*).

[2810] ASA Investerings P'ship v. Commissioner, 201 F.3d 505 (D.C. Cir.), cert. denied, 531 U.S. 871 (2000); *see also* Saba P'ship. v. Commissioner, 273 F.3d 1135 (D.C. Cir. 2001).

[2811] *ASA* relied on *Hoey* in a peculiar fashion, stating: "So too, for ASA: Although its investment in LIBOR notes might have had a business purpose, the prior three-week investment in and subsequent sale of PPNs was, like the retention of assets in *Hoey*, a business activity merely conducted for tax purposes." *ASA Investerings*, 201 F.3d at 513. This parses up an entity's activities so that some are not business motivated and so not of the entity.

[2812] Nat'l Investors Corp. v. Hoey, 144 F.2d 466 (2d Cir. 1944).

[2813] Olmstead v. Commissioner, 1984 T.C.M. (RIA) 1984-381.

[2814] Higgins v. Smith, 308 U.S. 473 (1940).

[2815] United States v. Morris & Essex R.R. Co., 135 F.2d 711 (2d Cir. 1943).

felt was reversed in reasoning by *Moline*.[2816] However, the *National Carbide* opinion cited *Hoey* in a "see" footnote for the dictum: "Escaping taxation is not a "business" activity."[2817]

The original statement in *Moline* is still the law: the corporation will be respected as a separate entity if it carries on business or was organized for the equivalent of a business activity, and holding assets is carrying on a business, and doing so in a corporate form purely to reduce tax liability does not negate the use of the corporation. Of course when there is a business but the corporation does not conduct it, the corporation can fail the *Moline* test, as discussed below.

The disregardable transitory corporation. A special category of corporation that effectively fails the *Moline* test is the corporation that is disregardable because it is transitory. The Service rather than the Supreme Court has pioneered the disregard of the transitory corporation in helping taxpayers effect triangular reorganizations before the Code allowed them.[2818] In hindsight, the one day corporation used in *Gregory v. Helvering* should have been disregarded because it was transitory, but that was not the ground of the ruling.[2819]

VI.F.3.b(2) *Corporations: Who Conducts the Business?*

In most cases applying the *Moline Properties* test, there is indisputably a business conducted by someone (the shareholders or a related person), the corporation reports to the Service that it earned the income of that business, and the Service questions whether the corporation conducted the business. This question is analogous to the question asking who owns property (discussed in

---

[2816] The Second Circuit opinion in *Higgins v. Smith* upheld the separateness of the corporation in reliance on *Burnet v. Commonwealth Improvement Co.*, 287 U.S. 415 (1932). The Supreme Court reversed the Second Circuit, as discussed *supra* in Ch. III.C.3.a(2). Then the Second Circuit cited the Supreme Court's decision in *Higgins* to support a conclusion in *Morris & Essex* that the separation between the corporation and its shareholders be ignored ("Courts will not allow the fictitious personality of a corporation to be used as a means for avoiding public duties." *Morris & Essex*, 135 F.2d at 713.). Then Hand apparently felt that *Moline* (decided less than a month after *Morris*) upset the reasoning of *Morris & Essex* (but surely not the result, which should have depended on the "dividend" being triangulated through the corporation) by stating that a corporation will be respected if it has any business activities, regardless of motive. Hand purported to apply the *Moline* principle with a vengeance in *Hoey* by stating that the loss on the shareholder's investment in the subsidiary stock terminated at the moment the subsidiary ceased conducting business, which was when the decision to liquidate occurred and it no longer engaged in any business activity. Moline Properties, Inc. v. Commissioner, 319 U.S. 436 (1943).

[2817] National Carbide Corp. v. Commissioner, 336 U.S. 422 (1949).

[2818] Rev. Rul. 1967-448, 1967-2 C.B. 144.

[2819] Gregory v. Helvering, 293 U.S. 465 (1935) should have been decided on the basis that the spun off corporation was transitory and disregardable, but the Supreme Court did not notice the significance of that until later. *See supra* Ch. VI.F.3.b(1); *cf.* Helvering v. Alabama Asphaltic Limestone Co., 315 U.S. 179 (1942) (observing that disregardable transitory steps often occur in bankruptcy reorganizations); John Kelley Co. v. Commissioner, 326 U.S. 521 (1946) (referring to *Gregory* as a case of "temporary compliance with statutory literalness").

Ch. VI.F.2., above), and has produced many disputed cases in the income tax law. These cases frequently also could be decided under section 269 (acquisition of control of a corporation for the principal purpose of tax avoidance) or section 482.[2820]

Unfortunately a serviceable cluster rule has not developed, because the Service refuses to believe that taxpayers should be allowed to use corporations principally to reduce taxation.[2821] The rule should be that the corporation's legal ownership of the property or the business or the income (outside assignment of income cases), plus general holding out of the corporation as doing so (which requires the owners of the corporation to be consistent in their regard for the corporation), is sufficient to insure that form and substance coincide. However, there seems to be more pressure on the taxpayer to prove the substance of its corporation as the tax avoidance motive becomes more obvious. For example, in *Shaw Constr. Co.* eighty six corporations, which were created to "build and sell" groups of houses that were actually constructed by another corporation owned by the same shareholders, were found not to have conducted the business of owning and selling the houses under the *Moline* test; the controlling shareholder clearly was using the multiple corporations to obtain eighty six surtax exemptions and runs up the rate scales.[2822]

The following list suggests the range of possibilities for a one shareholder corporation. The point of the list is to ask where the line should be drawn, and the suggested line is indicated. All cases assume the corporation owns legal title to its assets and could defend that title against creditors of its shareholder, and that its own creditors would have first claim on those assets (if the corporation does not own the business assets for those state law purposes, then it very likely cannot own the income from them for federal tax purposes, absent clear leasing, etc. arrangements). The same analysis applies to a corporation with a small number of owners and directors, as in *Roubik*.[2823]

1. Corporation has "independent" board and management that make their own decisions and clearly operate the corporation's business in its name with its own assets and employees and in its own offices. Of course these facts are the gold standard, they describe most publicly traded corporations, and almost never exist in the very closely held context.

2820 *See, e.g.,* Foglesong v. Commissioner, 691 F.2d 848 (7th Cir. 1982).

2821 *See, e.g.,* Nat'l Harrison Associates, Inc. v. Commissioner, 42 T.C. 601, 618 (1964):

> Whether the primary reason for its existence and conduct of business was to avoid U.S. taxes or to permit more economical performance of contracts through use of native labor, or a combination of these and other reasons, makes no difference in this regard. Any one of these reasons would constitute a valid business purpose for its existence and conduct of business as long as it actually conducted business.

2822 Shaw Constr. Co. v. Commissioner, 35 T.C. 1102, 1114 (1961), *aff'd,* 323 F.2d 316 (9th Cir. 1963), *acq.* (declined to apply sections 269 and 482 after finding *Moline* to have been flunked).

2823 Roubik v. Commissioner, 53 T.C. 365 (1969).

2. Corporation board and management is the sole shareholder (or its employees or agents, acting at its direction), who maintains separate corporate books and records for the corporation and operates its business in the corporate name with the corporation's own assets and employees and in the corporation's offices.

2A. Same as 2 except that the corporation is legally located in another jurisdiction where independent contractors (usually accountants and lawyers) are employed to perform accounting and legal functions and where the board assembles periodically to act. (This scenario is typical of "intellectual property holding companies" and many controlled foreign corporations, organized to reduce state taxes or take advantage of deferral of foreign income.)[2824]

3. Corporation board and management is the sole shareholder (or its employees or agents, acting at its direction), who maintains separate corporate books and records for the corporation and operates its business in the corporate name with the corporation's own assets, but out of the shareholder's office and using the shareholder's shared employees who are compensated by the corporation.

4. Corporation board and management is the sole shareholder (or its employees or agents, acting at its direction), who maintains separate corporate books and records for the corporation and operates its business in the corporate name with the corporation's own assets, but out of the shareholder's office and using the shareholder's shared employees who are not compensated by the corporation.

* * *

5. Corporation board and management is the sole shareholder (or its employees or agents, acting at its direction), who maintains separate corporate books and records for the corporation, but operates the corporation's business in the shareholder's name with his assets (or in the name of an affiliate), out of his office and using his employees who are (or are not) compensated by the corporation.[2825]

6. Corporation board and management is the sole shareholder (or its employees or agents, acting at its direction), who does not properly maintain separate corporate books and records and operates the corporation's business in his name with his assets, out of his office and using his employees who are not compensated by the corporation.

Clearly, the first scenario cannot be the only way to maintain the separateness of corporation and shareholder, because it will rarely occur in the closely

[2824] *See, e.g.,* Bass v. Commissioner, 50 T.C. 595 (1963) (the court seemed unconcerned that all of the foreign functionaries were ministerial in character).

[2825] These are essentially the facts of *Roubik,* 35 T.C. at 365, and *Shaw Construction Co.*, 35 T.C. at 1102, and *Aldon Homes, Inc. v. Commissioner*, 33 T.C. 582 (1959), which had more assets than *Shaw*, but still was not held out as doing the business.

held case. Clearly the fact of the shareholder's total control is irrelevant to the issue.[2826] *National Carbide* made clear that total control of the minutest detail, supplying all its assets, and taking all its profits, did not destroy the veil between corporation and shareholder; indeed the Court indicated that is what sole shareholders commonly do.[2827] Because subsidiaries are controlled, as is a ventriloquist's dummy, they inevitably are "dummies" in that sense, but still separate tax persons for tax purposes.[2828]

Moreover, the Court in *National Carbide* was unmoved by the fact that the subsidiary's alleged "purchase" of all of its business assets from the shareholder was accomplished entirely through the creation of intercompany receivables and payables (apparently non-interest-bearing). The Court turned the assignment of income principle against the subsidiary, saying that it could not escape taxation of its income by agreeing to distribute it to the shareholder. The Court's 1949 decision was based principally on the inherent ambiguity of the corporation shareholder relationship: it always can be claimed to be principal and agent, and that may be economic reality, but in *Moline Properties, Inc.* the Court decided it is not tax reality, for reasons of administrability of the tax system as it relates to entities.

Any of scenarios 2-4 should be sufficient to maintain separateness, although 4 may require some deemed payment by the corporation. Scenarios 5 and 6 are problematic. Even if the corporation not only has corporate documents and board minutes, but also enters into contracts to have others conduct activities for it, the critical missing element in the cases that fail the *Moline* test most often is being held out to third parties as conducting the business.[2829]

The corporate business can be attributed to the shareholder under various state law principles, for example if the corporation is not "bankruptcy remote" from the shareholder, in the sense that its shareholder's bankrupt estate will not include the corporation's assets.[2830] Presumably state law will control tax law in these cases. However, the relevance of another state law

---

2826 Commissioner v. Bollinger, 485 U.S. 340, 345 (1988); *cf. Higgins v. Smith*, 308 U.S. 473 (1940) (discussed *supra* Ch. III.C.3.a(2)). *Higgins* implied an impractical standard by saying that the shareholder's control of the corporation resulted in no economic exchange when the shareholder sold property to the corporation. That is true in 100% of all corporations. So *Higgins* makes sense only as a precursor of the *Moline* test and obsoleted by that decision. For more recent efforts of the Service, see *Foglesong v. Commissioner*, 691 F.2d 848 (7th Cir. 1982); Bittker & Eustice, at 2.07.

2827 National Carbide Corp. v. Commissioner, 336 U.S. 422 (1949).

2828 *See* Bittker & Eustice, at 2.10 ("Nominee and Dummy Corporations").

2829 *Higgins, Roubik, Shaw* and *Aldon* all suffered from this failing.

2830 *See, e.g.*, Principal Life Ins. Co. v. United States, 70 Fed. Cl. 144 (2006) (describing the use of bankruptcy remote "special purpose entities").

concept, piercing the corporate veil, is less clear. Piercing the corporate veil[2831] is the classic common law method for treating the shareholders as operating a corporate business (and for treating them as liable for its debts), but has made little impression on the law of tax aside from collection cases.[2832] The Court's most recent discussion of the general subject in *Bollinger*[2833] did not mention creditors' rights or bankruptcy outcomes, thus suggesting that for tax purposes a corporation's business may be attributed to its shareholders for reasons short of legal rights, dependent mostly on acts inconsistent with the corporation's ownership of the business and how the corporation is held out to third parties (thus holding the taxpayer to the conduct part of its "form" that acts contrary to its paper "form").

Higgins v. Smith. More confusion enters when the corporation is described as the shareholder's "alter ego" and for that reason not owning the business whose income it reports. The Supreme Court later characterized *Higgins* as an alter ego situation.[2834] *Higgins* was a category 5 or 6 case. The ambiguous term "alter ego" really means either that (a) the corporation existed on paper but would not be recognized by the tax law at all because it flunked the *Moline Properties* test, or (b) in any event it was the shareholder's agent insofar as earnings were concerned.

We know that (a) is correct as to *Higgins* because the Court in *Moline Properties*[2835] identified Smith's corporation as not meeting the low bar set for corporate activity. Moreover, in the final part of the *Higgins* litigation on June 9, 1943, the Second Circuit reversed as to the income inclusion by Smith's corporation in the appeal from the Board of Tax Appeals case (meaning that the corporation did not even earn the interest and dividends attributed to

---

[2831] *See* Nelson v. Adams, USA, Inc., 529 U.S. 460 (2000) (stating that piercing the corporate veil had not been asserted in the case and that one person corporations are not to be lightly disregarded, citing *Gregory* as an exception that proves the rule); United States v. Bestfoods, 524 U.S. 51, 63 (1998) (failure to speak to the matter of parent liability for subsidiary torts at all evidences no intent to abrogate common law doctrine of piercing the corporate veil). *See generally* Cummings, *Nationwide Uniformity and the Common Law of Federal Taxation*, 66 TAX LAW. 1 (2012).

[2832] *See, e.g.*, Sparks Farm, Inc. v. Commissioner, 1988 T.C.M. (RIA) 1988-492 (piercing the corporate veil is supplanted by *Moline*).

[2833] Commissioner v. Bollinger, 485 U.S. 340 (1988).

[2834] G.M. Leasing Corp. v. United States, 429 U.S. 338, 351 (1977); *see* Cleary, *supra* note 2796, at 1. The use of the term alter ego is very loose. For example, *Campbell County State Bank, Inc. v. Commissioner*, 37 T.C. 430 (1961) stated that *Moline Properties, Inc.* said that a corporation could be its sole shareholder's alter ego and still be respected as a separate entity, when in fact *Moline* said no such thing. It simply stated that at one time the entity at issue was not the shareholder's alter ego.

[2835] Moline Properties, Inc. v. Commissioner, 319 U.S. 436 (1943).

it), citing *Moline.*[2836] Thus, Smith's corporation was the prototypical corporation that had no business, not because there was no business to be had, but because that entity did not own and operate it.[2837]

Because *Higgins v. Smith* is such a high profile decision and is emblematic of the corporation with no business of its own, it is instructive to identify the facts that supported that conclusion. The reversed Board of Tax Appeals opinion in the companion case was a classic summation of the respect then given to corporations, even with minimal formalities:[2838]

- The corporation failed to "pay for" the stock except by book entries, but the Board was impressed by the fact that over time the balance in the book account went both ways.
- Smith retained the certificates for the stock sold to the corporation, but that was commercially reasonable.
- Smith had no reason *not to want* the corporation to take title to the stock because Smith knew that was key to his tax savings plans.
- Smith "dominated and controlled" the corporation, but that did not mean that his dealings with it were "improper" in the state law sense, including being at non-arm's-length prices, and allowing the corporation to have the benefits and burdens of its purchases.

However, the five-judge dissent to the Board's opinion cited a wide variety of more and less probative facts, but its core ground was that the corporation never obtained ownership of the stocks allegedly sold to it *because the corporation was Smith's agent*, as a matter of fact under state law, stating:

> I maintain, taking an extremely hypothetical case, that if any stranger had obtained a judgment against Innisfail and attempted to levy execution upon the stocks and their dividends, which are alleged to have been owned by Innisfail, the corporation would have had as a defense that the stocks were

---

[2836] Commissioner v. Smith, 136 F.2d 556 (2d Cir. 1943). The Second Circuit also called the corporation a "personal agency." It directed a "consolidation" of the two incomes. It made no mention of the possibility of applying Revenue Acts section 45 (current section 482) or section 104 (accumulated earnings tax), either of which would have seemed applicable. It rejected the Board's distinction between losses and dividends as "illusory" in light of the complete lack of business purpose or business conduct by the corporation and ordered the Commissioner to "consolidate" the income of the corporation with the shareholder. *Id.*

[2837] *See* Commissioner v. Laughton, 113 F.2d 103 (9th Cir. 1940) (explaining that in *Higgins v. Smith* there was a business, it just was not the corporation's business).

[2838] Smith v. Commissioner, 40 B.T.A. 387 (1939); *see supra* Ch. III.C.3.a(2) (explaining that Smith won a case before the Board for one year and lost a refund cases on a jury trial, which verdict was reinstated by the Supreme Court decision).

> at all times owned by Smith, that the dividends at all times were his, and that it was a mere agent of Smith.[2839]

The dissent would have ruled for the taxpayer if these facts had been different:

> He could easily have contributed to his wholly owned corporation working capital; he could easily have permitted Innisfail to own and control its assets, receive income therefrom, and carry on a corporate business in the true sense. He could have done with exactness and fidelity all the things which he now protests he did but, which the facts show, were not done, i. e., convey to Innisfail title to stocks and lend to and borrow from his corporation.[2840]

The Second Circuit opinion on the appeal (released after the Supreme Court's opinion in the companion case) viewed the same facts differently from the Board:[2841]

- The shareholder "... kept its securities with his own and his wife's in his safe deposit boxes."
- "No notes were issued for advances made by himself or Innisfail to one another and no interest was charged by either on balances ...".
- The total absence of assets in the corporation, but rather the corporation bought stock from Smith on credit and borrowed, creating a running account, to which the dividends on the stock the corporation bought were conveniently credited to Smith's benefit as debt repayment and not dividends.

2839 *Smith*, 40 B.T.A. at 403-04. The dissent went on to say:

> While we are not bound by requirements of local law in applying the revenue acts, it is extremely doubtful whether, in applying the revenue acts, we should give recognition to transactions undertaken without strict and literal compliance with local law, particularly where the taxpayer admits that an important purpose was to circumvent the Federal revenue acts and where the evidence shows such purpose to be the only one. It makes a stronger case against a taxpayer that he has ignored the literal requirements of local law in transactions held out to have been with a separate business entity. If petitioner's ingenuity fails at any point we should not resolve doubts in his favor. *Morsman v. Commissioner,* 90 Fed. (2d) 18. A taxpayer can hardly expect us to regard transactions as complete, so as to exempt him from tax liability under the revenue acts, where he has chosen to leave the transactions incomplete and subject to defenses under local law and executed in a manner in which no real business transaction would be executed. So I would hold that the transactions fail, not only because they were not real under the tax law, but also because the transactions would fail if, instead of Innisfail, they had been with, for example, the hypothetical XYZ Co. in which petitioner did not own any stock, albeit the XYZ Co. would not, by any stretch of the imagination, ever carry on such transactions with a stranger in the normal course of business.

2840 *Id.* at 423.

2841 *Smith*, 136 F.2d at 556.

These facts of *Higgins v. Smith* reveal about as good a cluster rule as might be found in such a difficult scenario: for the business and assets to belong to the closely held corporation for income tax purposes, they must be legally conveyed to and titled in the corporation and it should operate those assets in its own name. Failure to do so means that at best the corporation is the shareholder's agent; at worst it does not itself do enough to be a *Moline Properties* separate entity; and in any event, the shareholder will have created an alternate form by his conduct of ignoring the corporate separateness, to which the Service may choose to hold him.

In contrast with *Smith* is former Secretary of the Treasury Andrew W. Mellon's similar sales to corporations co-owned with his brother or other close associates, which resulted in civil fraud assessments by the Roosevelt Treasury; the Board of Tax Appeals ruled for Mellon after a half year trial and tremendous public interest and scrutiny.[2842] The Board found Mellon did not control the family corporation that bought his stock and said even if he had controlled it that would not have vitiated the sales to it absent fraud or special circumstances. Mellon's family corporation evidently operated with more attention to detail, and actually had separate family member owners, in contrast with Smith's corporation. These differences show an application of the separate cluster rule that related party transactions should be strictly scrutinized.

In conclusion it appears that the "one man" corporation is a cluster area as to which the Service would like to, but has been unable to, effectuate a clear cluster rule,[2843] though suspicion of shareholder and corporation dealings will be inevitable.

VI.F.3.c. *Trusts*

Although it is difficult now to believe, the issue of whether a temporary transfer to a trust effectuated a shifting of income was a huge problem in the 1930's. The Court applied a cluster rule in *Clifford*[2844] to undo a transaction that was effective for state law purposes, but planned for tax savings, not because it lacked business purpose or economic substance per se, but because of the tax-specific doctrine against assignment of income.[2845] Today a trust's characterization is controlled by Regulation section 301.7701-4, and the grantor trust rules govern the income taxation of transfers in trust with

---

2842 A.W. Mellon v. Commissioner, 36 B.T.A. 977 (1937) (Mellon had sold stock at a loss to his controlled bank and to a "family corporation" and then reacquired the stock; in no case was he the sole shareholder of the buyer).

2843 *See, e.g.*, Foglesong v. Commissioner, 691 F.2d 848 (7th Cir. 1982). *See generally* Bittker & Eustice, at 2.07.

2844 Helvering v. Clifford, 309 U. S 331 (1940).

2845 *See* Bittker & Lokken, at 80.1.1; *supra* Ch. VI.F.2.d.

retained interests.[2846] Also, the Court has adopted a broad view of the existence of a trust and a fiduciary of a trust, in the bankruptcy context.[2847]

VI.F.3.d. *Partnerships*

The Court has ruled that persons create partnerships by the natural consequences of their actions, and if those actions turn out to match the common conception of a partnership, they have created a tax partnership.[2848] Just as trusts experienced a development of a cluster rule for entity treatment, the Court developed a cluster rule for identifying partners in the category of "family partnerships," now controlled by section 704(e). In *Tower*, the Court ruled that the Service can both (a) challenge the state law existence of a partnership on the same grounds any other third party might assert, and also (b) challenge the existence of a partnership for tax purposes whether or not it passes the state law test.[2849] This is an application of the assignment of income doctrine: the *Tower* opinion's first cite to support the facts found by the Tax Court was to *Lucas v. Earl*, the seminal assignment of income authority.[2850] Then in the important *Culbertson* decision the Supreme Court rejected the Service's efforts to completely ignore the state law creation of a partnership among family members for tax reduction motives,[2851] although it left the law unclear.[2852] The result has been an unsatisfactory cluster rule for the identification of partnerships relying on this handful of decisions that were fact specific, in an area the Court has not revisited for over half a century. Nevertheless, lower courts persistently cite *Culbertson* for what a partnership is.

As in the case of trust characterization, today the treatment of partnerships as entities is subject to Regulation section 301.7701-2(a), which is thought to adopt what is in effect the *Moline Properties* threshold for business activity in

---

[2846] *See* Bittker & Lokken, at 83.2.

[2847] Holywell Corp. v. Smith, 503 U.S. 47 (1992).

[2848] Lusthaus v. Commissioner, 327 U.S. 293 (1946).

[2849] Commissioner v. Tower, 327 U.S. 280 (1946). The Tax Court found that the husband and wife never formed a partnership where the husband purportedly made a gift of part of his property to his wife, who purported to then join with him in organizing a partnership with the intended result of splitting the property income between them through the partnership distributions. 3 T.C. 396 (1944). The Supreme Court did not rely on a general law definition of partnership, but resorted to the special rules for tax purposes asking whether the conduct, intent and acts of the partners belied the formal arrangement; and asking specifically whether the husband still controlled the income for tax purposes. In this relational context, the Court stated that intent to avoid taxes was relevant. The Court did not rely on the Tax Court finding that the husband had not legally effectuated the gift; the opinion cited *Court Holding Co.* as an assignment of income case. *See* McKee, Nelson & Whitmire, at 3.03.

[2850] Also *Tower* was a companion to Lusthaus v. Commissioner, 327 U.S. 293 (1946), which was an assignment of income case that found that the husband's gift of the partnership interest to the wife, not the partnership, was a sham.

[2851] Commissioner v. Culbertson, 337 U.S. 733 (1949).

[2852] *See* McKee Nelson & Whitmire, at 3.02[2].

order to be respected as an entity.[2853] The regulation defines business entities as entities recognized for federal tax purposes, and a state law entity (such as an LLC) can be either a partnership or a corporation, and to be a corporation it must pass the *Moline* test, and therefore the *Moline* test must apply to all business entities (or else some other standard test must be derived).[2854]

Regulation section 1.701-2(b) attempts to impose a regulatory business purpose requirement on partnerships, which, if enforced, would effectuate a cluster rule more directly than application of the assignment of income doctrine to reject the formation of a partnership.

VI.F.4. *Reorganizations*

The cluster rules that the Supreme Court created for corporate reorganizations were among the first tax cluster rules; they now are written into regulations.[2855] Subchapter C defines corporate reorganizations that can permit tax deferred nonrecognition exchanges of property. Because nonrecognition transactions are to be strictly construed as exceptions to the general rule of recognition,[2856] the Supreme Court construed the Code to contain rules that evaluate whether the alleged reorganization has the substance of transactions Congress intended to benefit. These requirements, along with the assignment of income doctrine, were the earliest important cluster areas to develop in the income tax case law. For purposes of this discussion reorganizations include tax deferred distributions of stock known as spin offs, whether they involve a section 368 reorganization or not.[2857] *Gregory v. Helvering* was a spin off and reorganization case, and profoundly affected the administration of the law in both areas[2858]

The Supreme Court created three judicial requirements for qualifying reorganizations: business purpose, continuity of business activity, and continuity of proprietary interest.[2859] It did so by construing these requirements into the statutes to effectuate the intent of Congress. In addition, the Supreme Court affirmed the *Sansome* rule in *Phipps,* thereby in effect creating the predecessor of section 381 providing for carryover of earnings and profits (and other tax attributes) of a reorganized corporation.[2860] The reorganization cluster has benefited from an unusually large amount of care and attention by both

---

[2853] McKee Nelson & Whitmire, at 3.03. *See also* Nelson, *Limits of Literalism, supra* note 2616, at 649.

[2854] McKee Nelson & Whitmire, at 3.03[1] and [2] (however, the *Culbertson* test for partnerships still plays an uncertain role).

[2855] Reg. § 1.368-1.

[2856] *See* Reg. § 1.1002-1.

[2857] *See* Bittker & Eustice, at 11.02[1].

[2858] *Id.*; *supra* Ch. III.C.3.a(1). However, at that time a spin off could not occur without a preparatory asset reorganization. When the reorganization requirement was dropped in the 1954 Code, the Treasury did not delink spinoffs from the reorganization requirements.

[2859] *See* Bittker & Eustice, at 12.03.

[2860] Commissioner v. Phipps, 336 U.S. 410 (1949) (explained in G.C.M. 36,406 (Feb. 6, 1978)).

Congress and Treasury, due to the interplay between massive private sector lobbying for more freedom to enjoy the benefits of reorganizations, and acute audit and ruling attention, at least in earlier years, on this important tax-deferral area. In revising the reorganization rules in 1954, the Senate rejected the more detailed rules in the House bill in favor of more general rules, stating:

> . . . such certainty is not to be achieved at the expense of the legislative flexibility necessary to provide a statutory pattern which will tax, in an equitable manner, the myriad business transactions with which this area of law is concerned. [Therefore we reject rules that] . . . would make it difficult for necessary business transactions to be carried out with a minimum of interference from the tax laws.[2861]

Accordingly, the post-1954 regulations and statute contain the following general doctrines that Congress intended to do the work of more specific statutory provisions, which it eschewed. They reflect the cluster rules established by the Supreme Court for reorganizations as well as other cluster rules used by the Court:

- Regulation section 1.368-1(a), (b) and (c):
  - Invoke the "step transaction doctrine" (and section 368(a)(2)(C) and Regulation section 1.368-2(k)(1) turns it off);
  - Limit reorganizations to the precise forms approved, and to changes caused by "business exigencies"—that is, it embodies the business purpose doctrine;
  - Require a continuity of proprietary interest and business activity, which bolster the business exigencies requirement;
  - Require satisfaction of the Code's underlying assumptions and purposes; a transaction will not qualify based purely on mechanics (which embodies substance over form);
  - Require that the execution of the approved forms of reorganization must be bona fide and the reorganization must be an ordinary and necessary activity (which also enforces the business purpose requirement);
  - Provide that a reorganization cannot be imposed on a transaction on which the imposition of tax is imminent by attempting to conceal the real character of the transaction (another substance over form statement).
- Regulation section 1.1002-1 imposes a requirement of strict construction and purposive interpretation for all nonrecognition provisions, of which the reorganization provisions are the most prominent.
- Section 355(a)(1)(B) imposes the "device" requirement, among many others, on spin offs, which backstops the business purpose requirement.

[2861] S. Rep. No. 1622 at 41-2 (1954).

- Regulation section 1.355-2 imposes strict additional rules concerning device, business purpose and continuity.
- Section 269 (which predates 1954) was designed to have a primary impact on acquisitive reorganizations, by its focus on acquisitions of control and on carryover basis in assets of corporations.[2862]

Granted these rules and many others controlling reorganizations are the result of nearly 100 years of trial and error; nevertheless most informed persons would agree that they work, at least to the extent of limiting the tax deferral allowed in reorganizations to the transactions Congress intended. Because they work, for the most part the broader doctrines that have been applied by lower courts in other areas of the tax law generally have not been applied as such to reorganizations.

VI.F.5. *The Statutory Requirement That Loss Be Sustained*

Not only are deductions generally strictly construed against the taxpayer (Ch. II.B.2.c(4)), and loss deductions subject to numerous specific Code limitations (such as the limit on deducting capital losses in section 1211),[2863] but loss deductions also are subject to the general Code requirements that losses must be (a) sustained, (b) realized, (c) recognized, (d) allowed, and (e) not disallowed. This multiplicity of limitations shows that deduction of losses is the most heavily guarded allowance in the income tax, and so it is not surprising that it has been the lightening rod for cluster treatments that look to substance rather than form. The economic substance doctrine has been most commonly applied to transactions designed to generate losses.[2864] Creation of an economic substance doctrine as a positive rule of law might have been avoided if the courts had given more meaning to the statutory requirement that loss be sustained.

The income tax laws have required since the beginning that losses be "sustained," now in section 165(a).[2865] Section 165(c)(2) limits loss deductions (other than for casualties) to profit making investments when outside the business area. Regulation section 1.166-1(c) requires that a debt be *bona fide* to support a bad debt deduction; the requirement of *bona fides* hardly needs to be stated separately in any rule of the Code—it is an inherent requirement of all transactions.[2866] But Regulation section 1.165-1(b), dating from at least 1934, goes much farther when it states: "Substance and not mere form shall

---

2862 *See supra* Ch. IV.A.

2863 *See* Cummings, *Discontinuities in Corporate Recognition of Loss*, *supra* note 822. Also, section 183 limits hobby losses of individuals and S corporations to activities engaged in for profit.

2864 *See, e.g.*, Palm Canyon Invs. LLC v. Commissioner, 2009 T.C.M. (RIA) 2009-228 (as explained in Cummings, *The New Normal*, *supra* note 769).

2865 The Tariff Act of 1913, ch. 16, 38 Stat. 114, 167 (1913).

2866 Ch. VI.E.1.b.5.

govern in determining a deductible loss."[2867] This terminology very likely was drawn from the much cited opinion of the Supreme Court in *Weiss v. Stearn*, discussed in Ch. VI.E.1.b(1).

The regulatory reference to "substance and not mere form" is a rare one and should be viewed as a cluster rule entrusted to the courts and the Service to protect the loss area, rather than a reference to a universal doctrine. Put another way, any time a loss deduction is at issue the control of form is called off by regulation. Thus, Treasury clearly signaled that loss allowance is different from other areas of the tax law where form can control; substance "shall" control as to loss allowance. As a result, there never has been a reason to apply the economic substance doctrine or any court made positive rule of law to the loss disallowance cases, which comprise the majority of the ESD cases.

But the power of these statutory and regulatory statements has not been generally observed, nor has the requirement that a loss be "sustained" been given special prominence. The Supreme Court has said that it imports a practical and not a legal test,[2868] and requires that the loss be "actual and present."[2869] These definitions are fully sufficient to justify a heightened requirement, although it is likely that "sustained" originally referred mostly to matters of timing rather than economic measurement of loss.[2870] Timing is the sense in which the Court has most recently used it.[2871]

The loss is the most problematic of deductions, featured heavily in many tax shelters.[2872] Indeed, it is hard to see how a transaction can come under the control of the economic substance doctrine without being a loss or deduction (or credit) generator, although the doctrine also has been applied to credits. Some have proposed that the regulation and even the ESD are so incapa-

---

[2867] The regulation applicable in 1934 is quoted in *Stuart v. Commissioner*, 38 B.T.A. 1147 (1938); *see* 1 Fed. Reg. No. 175 (1936) § 3.23(e)-1. The Supreme Court quoted this sentence in *Cottage Savings Assn. v. Commissioner*, 499 U.S. 554, 556 (1991), where it contrasted the loss in *Higgins v. Smith* and found that the loss in *Cottage Savings* was "*bona fide*."

[2868] *See* Boehm v. Commissioner, 326 U.S. 287 (1945); Lucas v. Am. Code Co., 280 U.S. 445 (1930) ("The general requirement that losses be deducted in the year in which they are sustained calls for a practical, not a legal, test.").

[2869] Burnet v. Huff, 288 U.S. 156 (1933).

[2870] *See* Lewellyn v. Electric Reduction Co., 275 U.S. 243 (1927) (business loss not sustained until facts show loss of value). The requirement that a loss be "actually sustained" appeared in the 1909 corporate income tax. Corporate Income Tax Act of 1909, 36 Stat. 11, 113 (1909). The accounting profession had preferred the terminology tht the loss be ascertained. Haig et al., *supra* note 189, at 30. Evidently the requirement that loss be sustained to be deductible has long been thought to refer to a closed transaction. *See* Paul, Studies III, at 301; T.B.R. 55, 1919 Cum. Bull. No. 1, 123 (refers to the year in which it occurs). Perhaps the failure to attach a further requirement was due to the times, in which the reality of the losses was not often a problem.

[2871] *See* Cottage Savings Assn. v. Commissioner, 499 U.S. 554 (1991) (stating that the loss was not sustained in *Higgins v. Smith*, even though the seller certainly had an unrealized loss in the property sold).

[2872] Tightening of section 165 was recommended by McMahon, *Beyond a GAAR*, *supra* note 19, at 1738.

ble of dealing with abusive loss recognition that a special non-economic-loss rules should be written into section 165.[2873] A better interpretation of "loss sustained" and better application of the regulations on the books could serve that purpose.

The Supreme Court's track record in allowing losses upon property dispositions is quite instructive:

Higgins v. Smith disallowed a loss that *had economically accrued* but was not sustained because the seller did not part with the property: the shareholder's purported sale to a wholly owned corporation did not produce recognition because the sale was fraudulent, meaning it did not occur because the corporation did not exist for tax purposes, or at most was the seller's agent; but the seller did not lose the potential to recognize the loss properly by a later transaction.[2874]

- *McWilliams* disallowed a loss that *had economically accrued* by deeming a sale on the public market to be a related party sale to a relative who bought the same amount of stock at the same time that the other relative sold on the public markets; the Court construed the disallowance statute to produce this result.[2875] Under the statute at that time, the loss was totally lost.[2876]
- In *Generes*, the Court created a higher standard for proof of the business relationship of a debt to claim a bad debt deduction, reasoning that Congress created a distinction between business and non business bad debts and so must have intended the distinction to be meaningful.[2877]
- In *Fink*, the Court ruled that a non-pro-rata contribution to capital by a majority shareholder of the corporation's own stock was *not deductible* as a loss but rather was a contribution to capital.[2878] The opinion acknowledged that the shareholder had experienced a reduction in the value of his stock, but because there was no reliable way to tell the amount of loss in the case of a closely held corporation (meaning it was an open transaction), he had not sustained a loss that could be deducted. Thus, the loss was *economically incurred in part*, but not to the extent claimed by the taxpayer.
- In *Cottage Savings*,[2879] the Court *allowed* a deduction for losses *economically incurred* and actually sustained by allowing recognition to occur

---

[2873] Johnson & Zelenak, *Codification of General Disallowance of Artificial Losses*, 122 Tax Notes (TA) 1389 (Mar. 16, 2009); *see also* Chirelstein & Zelenak, *Tax Shelters and the Search for a Silver Bullet*, 105 Colum. L. Rev. 1939 (2005) (making essentially the same recommendation).

[2874] *See supra* Ch. III.C.3.a(2).

[2875] *See supra* Ch. III.C.3.b.

[2876] However, if the relative held the stock until 1953 and recognizes a gain, the loss may be allowed to that extent. IRC § 267(d).

[2877] United States v. Generes, 405 U.S. 93 (1972).

[2878] Commissioner v. Fink, 483 U.S. 89 (1987).

[2879] Cottage Savings Assn. v. Commissioner, 499 U. S. 554 (1991).

upon swapping mortgages for economically identical mortgages in *arm's length* transactions. Thus, the Court found that the legal transfer of ownership was the economic substance required for loss recognition.

These authorities suggest that losses from property dispositions must be at least economically incurred, which means the taxpayer has bona fide receipts or value less than adjusted basis, and that ownership of the property must be legally terminated in a closed transaction; but that in related party transactions the Supreme Court asks whether the loss has been sustained by looking for agent buyers and by strictly construing the relevant Code provision. Loss allowances are subject to the canon of strict interpretation of deductions and allowances discussed in Ch. II.B.2.c(4) and to Regulation section 1.165-1(b). Therefore, these rules and canons comprise a sort of cluster rule and should preclude the need for a doctrine to deny abusive losses in most cases.

The most difficult aspect of determining whether the taxpayer has sustained a loss is the determination of basis. In the problematic cases, the taxpayer often claims a basis that does not reflect the cost of the property due to some timing mismatch (for example, *ACM Partnership*[2880]), or shifting of basis from another persons that is likely not to be a taxpayer (for example, Notice 2001-45[2881]), or confusion involving the interrelationship of liability assumption and basis (for example, the Son of Boss cases[2882]). In such cases, the amount realized is undisputed but the basis seems unreasonably high. The best approach is that the requirement that loss be sustained should be applied after all mechanical tax rules have been exhausted (which might have obviated the use of the ESD in all three examples), and when that point is reached the question should be whether the claimed use of basis is authorized by the appropriate published guidance.[2883] If it is, then the solution should be to change the published guidance, because basis rules are inevitably somewhat mechanical.

VI.F.6. *Indebtedness and Interest*

The identification of indebtedness and interest thereon rivals the assignment of income doctrine for importance as a cluster area that promotes substance over form.[2884] The Supreme Court early defined interest as money owed for

---

[2880] ACM P'ship v. Commissioner, 1997 T.C.M. (RIA) 1997-115, 157 F.3d 231 (3d Cir. 1998).

[2881] Notice 2001-45, 2001-2 C.B. 129.

[2882] *See, e.g.,* United States v. Home Concrete & Supply LLC, 132 S. Ct. 1836 (2012) (which did not involve the substantive question).

[2883] Although the Supreme Court did not decide the merits of the case, tax basis was at issue in *United States v. Woods*, 134 S. Ct. 557 (2013). The lower courts missed good chances to decide the case on better grounds. *See* Cummings, *The Supreme Court's 2013 Term in Tax*, 145 Tax Notes (TA) 65 (Oct. 6, 2014).

[2884] *See generally* Asimov, *The Interest Deduction*, 24 UCLA L. Rev. 749 (1977).

the use or forbearance of money,[2885] or somehow the taxpayer must have the "use of funds" to justify the interest deduction.[2886] But the Supreme Court early stated in a tax opinion that it had declined and would continue to decline to give debt a peremptory definition, evidently due to the multiplicity of forms in which interest might appear.[2887] For that reason, a substantial sub-cluster area addresses the distinction between debt and equity, discussed in the following Chapter.[2888]

The tax law has come relatively easily to treat the identification of debt and interest as a matter of substance and not form because the common law did so, as the discussion of usury in Ch. V.E.1.c. above shows. The Treasury Regulations treat the resort to substance for debt identification as the norm.[2889] An early example of looking past form to find debt in a Supreme Court commercial law case is Justice Holmes' opinion in *Rankin*.[2890] The plaintiff bank sued to recover from the defendant bank a $30,000 deposit, which was the proceeds of a borrowing from defendant bank ostensibly by the plaintiff's president on plaintiff's behalf. The president and the defendant bank had made a side agreement that the deposit could not be withdrawn. The purpose for this arrangement was to make the plaintiff bank appear to have $30,000 more assets than it had, for the benefit of the bank examiner. The Court ruled for the defendant by finding as a fact that the plaintiff never had any right to the deposit: in other words no loan occurred where the loan proceeds were left with the lender. Justice Holmes relied entirely on the state commercial law to see through the subterfuge, stating: "If the Guthrie bank [the defendant] had sued . . . it could not have recovered, . . ." The *Rankin* decision would have come out the same way on the same reasoning if it had been a tax case about a deduction for any interest the plaintiff might have claimed it paid on the loan. Justice Holmes stated that even though the plaintiff bank had an account in its name in the defendant bank as the result of a purported loan (through the agency of its president), "as between the banks no one got

---

2885 Deputy v. Du Pont, 308 U. S. 488 (1940) (refusing to allow an interest deduction for payments a short seller of stock had to make to the lender of the stock, representing dividends received). This opinion likely derived the "for the use or forbearance of money" from Justice Field's statement in *Brown v. Hiatts*, 82 U.S. 177 (1873). Indeed, the first appearance of the phrase in any federal court opinion was in that opinion. *See also* Old Colony R. Co. v. Commissioner, 284 U.S. 552, 560 (1932) ("the usual import of the term is the amount which one has contracted to pay for the use of borrowed money").

2886 Manning v. Seeley Tube & Box Co., 338 U.S. 561 (1950).

2887 United States v. Childs, 266 U.S. 304 (1924) (but the Court respected the difference between amounts the tax law denominated as penalty and interest on unpaid taxes).

2888 *See* John Kelley Co. v. Commissioner, 326 U.S. 521 (1946) (discussing stock that was a hybrid instrument because paying of interest was conditional on corporate earnings). For other sub-clusters, *see* Cummings, *Searching for Indebtedness*, 146 TAX NOTES (TA) 899 (Feb. 16, 2015).

2889 *See* Reg. §§ 1.141-5(c)(1) (loans); 1.148-1(c)(3)(i) (pledge).

2890 Rankin v. City Nat'l Bank, 208 U.S. 541 (1908) (the opinion refers to the "first step of the transaction").

any money." In other words, substance prevailed over form as a matter of normal commercial litigation fact finding.

The common law approach to fact finding of debt in the tax law is reflected in several decisions of the Supreme Court:

- In a state tax case, the Supreme Court indicated no distinction between its ability in tax and nontax cases to categorize a sale repurchase as a borrowing;[2891] indeed, there is an additional reason to do so in the income tax because deductions are strictly construed.[2892]
- In *John Kelley*, the Court said: "These cases now under consideration deal with well understood words as used in the tax statutes—'interest' and 'dividends. [2893] They need no further definition."
- In *Putnam*, the Court easily recognized that when a guarantor paid on the guarantee, it did not have a loss but a debt claim against the original obligor, which could become a bad debt. [2894]
- In *National Carbide*, the Court easily discerned that the total absence of provision for interest meant that a nominal loan was a contribution to capital.[2895]
- However, because the federal tax law does not defer totally to state law, there is an additional income tax requirement for allowing an interest deduction: section 163(a) requires an "indebtedness."[2896] The tax cluster rule that has developed from the special requirements of the interest deduction require the obligor to satisfy the following series of requirements. Not only must the repayment be enforceable under state law (for example, the *Rankin* case, discussed above) as an indebtedness;[2897] but also: the obligation must not be characterized as something else under rules that may be peculiar to the tax law (like equity or an option, etc., as was discussed, for example, in *Paulsen*);[2898]

[2891] Nebraska Dept. of Revenue v. Lowenstein, 513 U.S. 123 (1994) (addressed the *Frank Lyon* 27 factors test).

[2892] *See, e.g.,* Commissioner v. Nat'l Alfalfa Dehydrating & Milling Co., 417 U.S. 134 (1974) (rejected the claim that bond issue premium arose upon exchange of a $50 note for $50 preferred stock worth less than $50). This is true despite the fact that many Code sections address the inherent uncertainties about interest: section 7872, the original issue discount rules, the AHYDO rules, section 267.

[2893] John Kelley Co. v. Commissioner, 326 U.S. 521 (1946).

[2894] Putnam v. Commissioner, 352 U.S. 82 (1956).

[2895] National Carbide Corp. v. Commissioner, 336 U.S. 422, 435 n.16 (1949).

[2896] *See generally* Asimov, *supra* note 2884, at 784-93 (Asimov does not identify these categories as such, but they are included in his review).

[2897] *See, e.g.*, Equitable Life Assur. Society v. Commissioner, 321 U.S. 560 (1944) (creation of purported obligation was discretionary with the taxpayer, so it was not deductible interest). The debt must be "real," or not a "factual sham," which means that in substance the interest paid is upon an obligation for money actually owed upon a borrowing by the taxpayer, which is usually a matter of intent. *See, e.g.*, Goodstein v. Commissioner, 267 F.2d 127 (1st Cir. 1959).

[2898] Paulsen v. Commissioner, 469 U.S. 131 (1985); *see also* BITTKER & LOKKEN, at 40.7 (sales characterized as loans and vice versa).

- In the case of nonrecourse or other contingent debt repayment must be likely as a matter of economic compulsion;[2899] and
- In the case of original issue discount, the particularized tax rules must be satisfied (which is interest and not capital gain, despite the lack of denomination as interest).[2900]

The state law might or might not have characterized the transactions in *Knetsch*[2901] as a debt with interest, depending on the purpose for which the characterization was made (maybe no for purpose of usury, probably yes for purposes of enforceability of the literal obligations). But because there was no actual borrowing, meaning funds or credit for the use of the taxpayer (similar to *Rankin*), there was no indebtedness for income tax purposes and no interest deduction allowed. The same was true in the *Goodstein* line of cases.[2902] But confusion entered in *Goldstein* where the Tax Court found as a fact that no indebtedness existed (which was thought not to require a business purpose), but the Second Circuit's affirmance added some language about a "purposive activity" being required to make debt real for tax purposes, which is best viewed as the interpretation of a business purpose requirement similar to the interpretation of the reorganization section in *Gregory v. Helvering*.[2903] See Ch. III.C.3.a(1).

Some assert that *Knetsch* stands for some tax specific rule other than the fact of the existence of an indebtedness based on intent to repay a borrowing.[2904] For example, the first federal district court opinion to use the phrase "economic substance doctrine," involved an interest deduction on debt that should have been found simply not to be an indebtedness as normally determined.[2905] Properly understood, the cluster approach to finding the fact of indebtedness in the income tax is not a new general purpose economic substance doctrine.

VI.F.7. *Debt Versus Equity*

The debt versus equity issue is an important tax specific cluster due to the ability of corporate debtors to deduct interest paid but not dividends paid.[2906] Like the treatment of debt, the identification of a distribution with respect to stock (the ordinary understanding of a dividend described in section 301) is understood to be a matter of substance and not necessarily controlled by

---

2899 *See, e.g.*, Estate of Franklin v. Commissioner, 64 T.C. 752 (1975), *aff'd*, 544 F.2d 1045 (9th Cir. 1976).

2900 United States v. Midland-Ross Corp., 381 U.S. 54 (1965).

2901 *See supra* Ch. VI.E.1.e(2)(c).

2902 *Goodstein*, 267 F. 2d at 127.

2903 Goldstein v. Commissioner, 44 T.C. 284 (1965), *aff'd*, 364 F.2d. 734 (2d Cir. 1966); *see* Kanter, *supra* note 2295, at 826-27.

2904 Asimov, *supra* note 2884, at 789.

2905 Peerless Indus., Inc. v. United States, 73 A.F.T.R. 2d 1242 (E.D. Pa.), *aff'd*, 37 F.3d 1488 (3d Cir. 1994) ($20M 50 year OID note issued to charity for $21,000).

2906 *See generally* Bittker & Eustice, at 4.

form. But agreeing exactly what that substance is has been near impossible, and so the cluster approaches that have developed are not particularly satisfactory.

Section 385 authorizes regulations defining debt, but the Treasury has never been able to produce them; section 385(b) states factors that mostly relate to the debt versus equity dichotomy. Like other cluster areas, the most trouble in corporate debt versus equity cases is caused by (1) ambiguous facts,[2907] and (2) related party transactions.[2908]

The Supreme Court has illustrated these points about the debt equity cluster as follows:

- In *Kelley* the Court stated in finding securities to be stock: "There is no one characteristic, not even exclusion from management, which can be said to be decisive in the determination of whether the obligations are risk investments in the corporations or debts. So-called stock certificates may be authorized by corporations which are really debts and promises to pay may be executed which have incidents of stock."[2909]
- Conversely, similar notes in the companion cases of *Talbot Mills* were debt.[2910]
- *Paulsen* stated about savings and loan members: "The fact that dividends rather than interest are paid is by no means controlling."[2911] It weighed the equity and debt characteristics and found the debt to prevail.

VI.F.8. *Agency and Conduit*

Taxpayers necessarily receive income and incur expenses through agents and so the income tax could not function if ordinary agency principles were not applied.[2912] However, when the taxpayer uses a concealed agent (meaning a person whose status as agent is concealed) a substance over form approach to fact finding based on all of the facts and circumstances must be applied. Initially the use of entities as disguised agents in real estate transactions probably arose innocently enough, at least as far as the income tax was concerned,[2913] and the party wanting the tax law to treat the agent as an agent

---

[2907] *Id.* at 4.03.

[2908] *Id.* at 4.04; *see* Plumb, *The Federal Income Tax Significance of Corporate Debt: A Critical Analysis and Proposal*, 26 Tax L. Rev. 369, 579 (1971) (recognizing that debt-equity rules must be different in cases of shareholder debt); Asimov, *supra* note 2884, at 775 *et seq.*

[2909] John Kelley Co. v. Commissioner, 326 U.S. 521 (1946) (but the Court simply punted the decision to the Tax Court under the *Dobson* rule).

[2910] Talbot Mills v. Commissioner, 326 U.S. 521 (1946). *Kelley* and *Talbot* were decided together; they were *Dobson* cases in which the Court relied on the Tax Court's fact findings.

[2911] Paulsen v. Commissioner, 469 U.S. 131 (1985).

[2912] *E.g.*, Maryland Casualty Co. v. United States, 251 U.S. 342 (1920) (agent's receipt of income attributed to the taxpayer).

[2913] *See, e.g.*, Note, *Tax and Business Considerations in Use of Corporations for Real Estate Ownership*, 5 Real Prop. Prob. and T. J., 518 (1970) (entities used to disguise the real party in interest).

was the taxpayer, not the Service. Out of this issue arose the important cluster areas marked by Supreme Court opinions in *Moline*, *National Carbide* and *Bollinger*, as discussed in Ch. VI.F.3.b. But both in that cluster, and outside it where the real parties in interest did not want to be collapsed with the entities, the courts and the Service have seemed reluctant to address the issue in terms of agency by name, and instead employ terms like "sham" (which the Supreme Court applied in *Higgins v. Smith*) and "conduit" (which the Supreme Court discussed in *Frank Lyon*), or "dummy," "straw" or "strawman," "nominee," or the judicial doctrines, probably because of the agency fact-finding difficulties.[2914] These terms reflect an unfortunate cluster rule that confuses rather than clarifies the point that the real issue is whether there is an agency, and if not, whether there is a reason why another party should be treated as if it were the taxpayer's agent despite lack of usual indicia of agency.

The Supreme Court has sometimes based tax decisions on finding an undisclosed agent to be an agent.

- This occurred but was not made clear in the *Court Holding Company* and *Cumberland Public Service* cases, as discussed in Ch. VI.F.2.e. above.
- *Southern Pacific*, one of the origins of the substance over form slogan, was really based on viewing a subsidiary as an agent of the parent;[2915] but the Court in *National Carbide* vehemently denied that the subsidiary was an agent as it normally used that term.[2916]
- The Supreme Court applied agency findings in *Banks*, and rejected efforts of lower courts to pursue various imagined values in order to avoid taxing a tort plaintiff on the portion of her recovery that went to attorneys fees, by ruling that the taxpayer simply was assigning her income to her agent, the lawyer;[2917] indeed, the assignment of income doctrine is based on agency (the actual recipient of the income is treated as receiving it on behalf of the assignor).
- And the Court faced up to the difficult task of establishing how and when a corporation can be treated as the agent of its shareholders in *National Carbide* and *Bollinger*.[2918]

As Randolph Paul noted in 1938, tax lawyers probably have forgotten what they ever knew about the common law of agency, and that may indirectly have contributed to shying away from directly examining agency in tax cases.[2919] A brief review of the traditional law of agency shows that no formal or

2914 *Id.* (listing the terms); *see also* National Carbide Corp. v. Commissioner, 336 U.S. 422 n. 6 (1949) (listing such names for corporations serving an agency function).

2915 S. Pac. Co. v. Lowe, 247 U.S. 330 (1918).

2916 National Carbide Corp. v. Commissioner, 336 U.S. 422 (1949).

2917 Commissioner v. Banks, 543 U.S. 426 (2005).

2918 Commissioner v. Bollinger, 485 U.S. 340 (1988).

2919 Paul, Studies II, at 216, n. 66.

particular act is necessary to confer the power of agency, and it may be proved by parol evidence.[2920]

> In the vast majority of cases [the authority of agency] . . . is informally conferred, or is presumed from the acts and conduct of the principal. A large portion of the transactions of the modern business world [as of 1914] is carried on by simple and informal means. A word or look or gesture often suffices to give assent to great undertakings or to set in motion the complicated machinery of commerce. Little, often, is said or written, but that little carries with it a train of legal consequences no less certain and definite then if the whole were included in the spoken or written words. Hence it is that in many cases the existence of an agency is implied or presumed from the words or conduct of the parties, although the creation of an agency was not within their immediate contemplation.[2921]

> The general rule may, indeed, be layed down the other way; that an agent or attorney may ordinarily be appointed by parol, in the broad sense of that term at the common law; that is, by a verbal declaration, in writing not under seal, or by acts and implications. And it is absolutely indispensable for the exigencies of commercial business, that the rule should be so; . . . .[2922]

> . . . the most usual mode of appointment [of an agent] is by an unwritten request, or by implication from the recognition of the principal, or from his acquiescence in the acts of the agent.[2923]

> Parol evidence is admissible, however, to show that someone not named in the contract as the obligor was in fact the principal contracting party; and whatever may be the merits of the doctrine, it is now firmly settled that the admission of parol evidence is not in violation of the rule mentioned. The evidence is not admitted to vary or contradict the written contract; it is admitted in such case to prove by the testimony offered, not that the instrument is not binding on those whom it purports to bind, but that it is binding also upon another. . . .[2924]

It is possible that the Service fails to argue agency when it could because (a) it is more comfortable with the euphemisms used in tax opinions that tend to obscure discussions of agency in tax cases (sham, conduit) and (b) it may realize the difficulty presented by the core definition of agency as a fiduciary relationship resulting from a manifestation of consent by both principal and agent.[2925] The sort of cases where the Service would want to prove that the taxpayer was someone's agent, or vice versa, are the very cases where there was no holding out of agency. But agency clearly can be created by the principal's

---

[2920] Meacham, Treatise on the Law of Agency § 228 (Callaghan 1914).

[2921] *Id.* at § 241.

[2922] Story, Commentaries on the Law of Agency § 47 (1874).

[2923] *Id.* at § 54.

[2924] Reinhard, Treatise on the Law of Agency in Contract and Tort 329 (Bobbs-Merrill 1902); *see also* Paul, Studies II, at 216, n. 66 (as to parol evidence).

[2925] Restatement of (second) Agency, §§ 1, 15 (1958).

conduct that reasonably causes the agent to believe he has authority, and third parties can similarly come to rely on implied agency.[2926]

VI.F.8.a. *Agent Versus Independent Contractor*

The common law used agency principles primarily to decide when the torts or contracts of one person would be *attributed* to another. Both the torts of and the contracts made by an agent normally will be attributed to the principal, unless the agent is an independent contractor, which is determined principally by a finding that the principal does not control the contractor. Lacking such control, an independent contractor's torts normally are not attributed to the principal. But if the principal has by contract given the independent contractor the power to contract on behalf of the principal, then normally the contractor will be treated as an agent for that purpose, and its contracts will be attributed to the principal.[2927] Because the tax law usually is concerned with contracting rather than tortious activities, activities of another can be attributed to the taxpayer either through a finding of control or specific granting of authority to the contractor.

The practical problems in evaluating an independent contractor's status are in finding the existence of control or of a power to act for the principal as a matter of fact. These problems need not implicate any special fact finding methods in the tax law, which can employ evidence such as (a) conduct of the principal that would reasonably lead the contractor to believe that it was being controlled by the principal (for example, the principal told it what to do and paid it a fixed fee for doing it); or (b) conduct of the principal that would reasonably lead other parties involved in the transaction to believe the same. The Supreme Court, in effect, has applied these methods in the *Court Holding Co.* and *Cumberland Public Service Co.* line of cases, discussed in Ch. VI.F.2.e., by focusing on who negotiated the sale of property to determine who made the sale for tax purposes.

Is some other tax specific cluster rule for analyzing agency required by the needs of the tax system? If so, logically it would focus not only on control and apparent authority, as does the common law approach, but also the economic consequences to the contractor; that is, does the contractor act for a fee as an agent would, or for a profit with the possibility of a loss as an owner would? Most of these cases of this sort involve use of the term "conduit," discussed next.

VI.F.8.b. *Independent Contractor Versus Conduit*

The tax law has struggled with the cases in which a taxpayer uses what appears to be an independent contractor to carry out a transaction seemingly on behalf of the taxpayer for what seems to be a nominal fee; often those contractors are found to be agents, but the confusing label of conduit is applied.

[2926] *Id.* at §§ 26, 27.

[2927] *See generally* Lainoff, Bates & Bowers, *supra* note 2806, at 149-51.

The prototypical example of the success of such strategy is *Clara M. Tully Trust*, which was contrasted by the lower court in *Court Holding Co.*[2928] In other cases, the actions of similar contractors are attributed to the taxpayer because they are conduits. But calling a person a conduit should not end the analysis. The use of the label conduit in tax cases involves three sorts of confusions: (1) it implies that the conduit cannot act for itself as a separate taxpayer, but that is clearly too simplistic a view; (2) it confuses agency with conduit status; and (3) it masks the real issue of identifying those cases in which the actions of an independent party should be imputed to the taxpayer, which may justify a cluster rule for tax, but that rule requires more than the word conduit.

Labeling a person a conduit generally indicates the inertness of a pipeline, which often is assumed to mean the pipeline does not act for its own interests.[2929] Such assumption is incorrect; after all, pipelines are owned by someone who profits from the liquid carried. Thus, calling a person a conduit does not necessarily mean either that the person does not act for itself or that it is engaged in an improper transaction. For example in the important case of *Deputy v. Du Pont*, the Supreme Court labeled Pierre S. Du Pont as a conduit for the payment of dividends he received on borrowed stock to the lender of the stock, but being a conduit did not prevent his payments from having tax consequences for Mr. Du Pont (just not the ones he wanted).[2930]

Sometimes a conduit is an agent of another taxpayer and sometimes not. In the former case, the agent's acts within the scope of the agency are always imputed to the principal. For example, in *General Utilities* the Supreme Court tended to agree with the Circuit Court that the corporation should be taxed on the shareholders' sale of corporate property distributed to them because they were "agents or conduits through whom the transfer of title was effected."[2931] But the Court reversed because the argument had not been considered by the trial court. The conduit acted for itself in a 1942 case where a railroad had leased all of its railroad property to another railroad in 1864, and ever since the other railroad had been paying the first railroad's dividends directly to the first railroad's shareholders.[2932] In fact, the opinion stated that the conduit was not even a conduit because the lessee railroad paid the divi-

---

[2928] Court Holding Co. v. Commissioner, 2 T.C. 531 (1943). The Tax Court opinion contrasted a true conduit-type case: Tully Trust v. Commissioner, 1 T.C. 611 (1943). There taxpayer sold stock to a middleman for $100.50, who resold to the corporation for $101. Because the middleman had complete freedom of what to do with the property, the court did not impute his sale to the taxpayer. This case came out differently from *Court Holding* both because the transferee was not related to the taxpayer by some affinity (family, etc.), and because the transferee controlled the sale, which had not been pre arranged by the original owner, thus preventing his identification as a related agent of the taxpayer.

[2929] *See, e.g.*, Hancock v. Louisville and N. R.R. Co., 145 U.S. 409 (1892) (stating a corporation was not a conduit because it acted independently in its own right).

[2930] Deputy v. Du Pont, 308 U.S. 488 (1940).

[2931] Gen. Util. & Op. Co. v. Helvering, 296 U.S. 200 (1935).

[2932] United States v. Joliet & C.R. Co., 315 U.S. 44 (1942).

dend directly; nevertheless the Court taxed the first railroad on the dividends. So the lessee railroad was in effect a paying agent.

Frequently when the Court calls a person a conduit it clearly means an agent that has entered into a voluntary relationship with the taxpayer and perhaps others to perform a certain role. For example, the Court has used the common dichotomy of treating a partnership as an entity and a conduit for different purposes.[2933] The Court has said one person is not the conduit for another (to borrow) without discussing agency, but meaning agency.[2934] In *Frank Lyon*, the Court never mentioned the word agency but rather took up the Service's assertion that Frank Lyon was a "conduit" and cited many considerations to determine it was not, but said that the most important was the primary liability of Frank Lyon to the third party lender.[2935] The ruling necessarily meant Frank Lyon was not the property seller's agent, but rather acted on its own behalf and owned the building it leased.

But "conduit" often refers to a person who performs a certain known role that can be counted on by the taxpayer who is planning a step transaction, even though the person is not employed as an agent; the nonagent conduit often is said to be "passive,"[2936] (in contrast to an agent who is at least active in the principal's interests). In other words, a nonagent conduit can tie a taxpayer to an end result of several steps in the same way the desktop toy works: on ball strikes a second ball, which causes a third adjacent ball to swing. For a nontax example, the Court early recognized that a suit in the name of a governor *ex relatione* a citizen of another state was a proper diversity action because the governor, who appeared in name only, was a conduit (even though he obviously was not an agent).[2937]

The regulations under section 351 have embraced the nonagent conduit concept after trying unsuccessfully to rely on agency principles. The issue is whether "control [of the corporation] immediately after" an asset for stock exchange is affected by the use of stock underwriters. Initially the Service took the position that if the underwriter was an agent of the corporation to sell its stock, not it but the public who bought from it was the original investor in the corporation (best efforts underwriting); conversely, if the underwriter was at risk in buying the stock, it was not an agent and its resale could break the

---

2933 United States v. Bayse, 410 U.S. 441 (1973).

2934 Edwards v. Chile Copper Co., 270 U.S. 452 (1926) (parent formed to issue bonds and relend proceeds to exploration company was not conduit for the subsidiary but rather was its brain; therefore the parent had a business and was not excluded from the income tax as a nonbusiness entity; the fact that two corporations would have to pay tax was just the way the system worked); *see* S. Texas Rice Whse. Co., 43 T.C. 540 (1965), *aff'd*, 366 F.2d 890 (5th Cir. 1966) (lower court example) (taxpayer's long time counsel and trial attorney in instant case volunteered his son, also an attorney, to perform the conduit role described in Notice 2001-16, 2002-1 C.B. 730; trial court had little trouble finding that he never controlled the stock he bought in form, and so disregarded his actions).

2935 Frank Lyon Co. v. United States, 435 U.S. 561 (1978); *see supra* Ch. VI.F.2.c.

2936 *See, e.g.*, Miami Herald Pub. Co. v. Tornillo, 418 U.S. 241 (1974).

2937 McNutt v. Bland, 43 U.S. 9 (1844).

chain of "control immediately after."[2938] The current regulation rejects the distinction based on agency and treats the public as the original transferor if the underwriter is either the agent of the issuer or its holding is "transitory."[2939] The shift to reliance on "transitory" holding is a shift to "conduit" treatment without using that term.

At least in the Supreme Court and some fairly high profile appellate court decisions, assertions of conduit status by the Service have not fared well:

- *Cumberland Public Service* ruled in effect that the fact that the shareholders might have been expected to sell the corporation's property after it was distributed to them did not require imputation of their sale to the corporation, in contrast with the *Court Holding Company* case where the shareholders were treated as agents of the corporation;[2940] the Service asserted that the shareholders were conduits in both cases, but neither of the opinions really embraced the conduit concept.
- *Chamberlin* ruled in effect that the contemplated activities of a nonagent life insurance company (called a conduit) that planned to buy the preferred stock issued pro rata to the corporation's shareholders could not be attributed to the corporation.[2941]
- *Esmark* ruled in effect that the market purchase of a block of corporation's stock, followed by swap of that block for a corporate asset, could not be attributed to the corporation.[2942]

In contrast, perhaps the most well known taxpayer loss based on conduit theory is *Aiken Industries*, which involved a related party financing conduit.[2943] Congress authorized regulations to deal with "conduit financing arrangements" in section 7701(l) in 1993.[2944] The resulting regulations are limited; they refer only to section 881, imposing the 30% withholding tax on fixed and determinable annual and periodical income paid to foreigners.[2945] The conduit approach depends on the end result or interdependence branches of the step transaction doctrine.[2946] But when the result would be attributing a nonagent's actions to a taxpayer, the norm is *Frank Lyon*, where that did not occur. For discussion of specific types of conduits not discussed here see Bittker & Lokken at para. 6.2 (including nominees, cost companies and cooperatives).

2938 Rev. Rul. 1978-294, 1978-2 C.B. 141, obsoleted by T.D. 8665, 1996-1 C.B. 35.

2939 Reg. § 1.351-1(a)(3); *see* BITTKER & EUSTICE, at 3.09[2].

2940 United States v. Cumberland Pub. Serv. Co., 338 U.S. 451 (1950); Commissioner v. Court Holding Co., 324 U.S. 331 (1945); *see supra* Ch. VI.F.2.e.

2941 Chamberlin v. Commissioner, 207 F.2d 462 (6th Cir. 1953).

2942 Esmark Inc. v. Commissioner, 90 T.C. 171 (1988), *aff'd*, 886 F.2d 1318 (7th Cir. 1989).

2943 Aiken Indus., Inc. v. Commissioner, 56 T.C. 925 (1971) (successive borrowings used in treaty shopping).

2944 *See* BITTKER & LOKKEN, at 67.3.

2945 Reg. § 1.881-3.

2946 *See supra* Ch. VI.E.1.b(2).

VI.F.9. *Natural Resources Extraction*

Sometimes Congress' treatment of an entire subject area is so unusual as to reflect its desire that the rules be somewhat peculiar to that subject, which amounts to authorizing a cluster rule.[2947] For example, the Supreme Court recognized the extracting of natural resources to be such an area, and so declined to cross fertilize precedents from that area into general tax.[2948] It has given the depletion allowance a broad, purposive, reading rather than a strict reading.[2949] Most importantly for purposes of identifying the area as a cluster, the Court has identified the persons entitled to the depletion allowance based on economic analysis rather than title ownership.[2950] But it has also recognized the allowance as a rule of thumb that does not permit investigation of actual depletion.[2951] Perhaps this favorable treatment is partly due to the persistence of the industry in litigating its rights: 32 Supreme Court decisions on natural resources up to 1990. These decisions reflect an intense iterative process whereby the Congress changed the statute, Treasury changed regulations and the Supreme Court was required to interpret both.

VI.F.10. *Timing of Receipts and Payments; Tax Accounting*

The entire area of timing, which is tax accounting, is a large cluster overarching the whole of the income tax; it sometimes relies on substance (e.g., the constructive receipt doctrine),[2952] and sometimes relies on form (e.g., the cash method of accounting generally). The Supreme Court has played a seminal role in fashioning the tax accounting rules for timing of reporting of receipts and payments.[2953] Section 446 empowers the Secretary to modify a taxpayer's method of accounting so that it clearly reflects income.[2954] The Supreme Court has recognized that this means something different from generally

[2947] *See generally* BNA Tax Management Portfolios nos. 601, 603, 605, 610 on natural resources taxation.

[2948] Commissioner v. Brown, 380 U.S. 563 (1965).

[2949] Commissioner v. Engle, 464 U.S. 206 (1984); Lynch v. Alworth-Stevens Co., 267 U.S. 364 (1925) (lessee as well as lessor had property interest in depleting minerals and so fit within the purpose of the depletion allowance). *But cf.* Burton-Sutton Oil Co. v. Commissioner, 328 U.S. 25 (1946) (espousing a less formal determination of ownership, and causing Justice Frankfurter to protest about gossamer distinctions).

[2950] *See, e.g.*, Palmer v. Bender, 287 U.S. 551 (1933).

[2951] Helvering v. Mountain Producers Corp., 303 U.S. 376 (1938) (the evident purpose of the statute controls).

[2952] Bittker & Lokken, at 5.9.

[2953] *See* Hanes, *supra* note 413 (The definitive article on Supreme Court and Tax Accounting, it concludes that the accrual rules are illogical as the consequence of an initial incoherence in the statute and necessary intervention by the Court beyond its expertise and episodic intervention by Congress to benefit certain business interests: "Basically the responsibility for raising revenue is legislative and executive rather than judicial." *Id.* at 74).

[2954] Bittker & Lokken, at 105.1.4.

accepted accounting principles,[2955] and thus truly reflects tax specific rules.[2956] The Court interprets the section generously,[2957] and has accorded the Treasury wide latitude.[2958]

The basic point the Court has established is that tax accounting is different from financial accounting because it has different goals.[2959] The Court has emphasized economic rather than formal considerations in tax accounting.[2960] Both of these factors identify the accounting rules as a cluster area. The Court's most important rulings in the area include:

- The search for "identifiable events" to mark the year of a loss deduction generally;[2961]
- The rule that the taxpayer need not be an incorrigible optimist or Stygian pessimist to deduct worthless securities;[2962]
- The "all events test" for accrual accounting;[2963]
- The open transaction doctrine;[2964]
- The doctrine that upon the sale of a going business the sale price must be comminuted into fragments;[2965]
- The rule that an accrual method taxpayer cannot deduct business taxes it is contesting;[2966]
- The rule that items are not to be taken out of the normal annual treatment under the cash or accrual methods and treated in a particular way

---

2955 *See generally* Hanes, *supra* note 413.

2956 Thor Power Tool Co. v. Commissioner, 439 U.S. 522 (1979).

2957 *See* United States v. Fior D'Italia, Inc., 536 U.S. 238 (2002); Detroit Edison Co. v. Commissioner, 319 U.S. 98, 102 (1943) (as to depreciation, "The Congress wisely refrained from formalizing its methods and we prescribe no over-all rules.").

2958 *See, e.g.*, United States v. Catto, Jr., 384 U.S. 102 (1966) ("It is not the province of the court to weigh and determine the relative merits of systems of accounting.")

2959 *See* Schlude v. Commissioner, 372 U.S. 128 (1963) (cannot defer prepayments) and the two decisions preceding it; *Thor Power Tool Co.*, 439 U.S. at 522 (distinguishing goals of tax accounting and financial accounting); N. Am. Oil Consol. v. Burnet, 286 U.S. 417 (1932) (importance of taxable year).

2960 *See, e.g.,* United States v. Anderson, 269 U.S. 422 (1926) (munitions tax expense accrued when economically arose).

2961 Reg. § 1.165-1(d)(1); Bittker & Lokken, at 25.4.1.

2962 Bittker & Lokken, at 25.4.4.

2963 United States v. Anderson, 269 U.S. 422 (1926) (although the fact involve a reserve as a deduction, it was appropriately deducted to match the income).

2964 Burnet v. Logan, 283 U.S. 404 (1931); Bittker & Lokken, at 43.2.1.

2965 Watson v. Commissioner, 345 U.S. 544 (1953) (ruled portion of farm sale attributable to growing crops produced ordinary income; later enacted statute to treat as capital gain was needed to change the law; this case stated the principle that business assets must be comminuted and not treated as a mass for purposes of characterization); United States v. Hill, 506 U.S. 546 (1993) (similarly, the cost of property bought as a unit must be apportioned among the parts as required for different taxing regimes as to the various parts).

2966 Dixie Pine Prod. Co. v. Commissioner, 320 U.S. 516 (1944).

in a particular case because it is deemed more equitable to either the taxpayer or the government;[2967]

- The assumption that the amount realized can be measured by the value of the property the taxpayer sold when the parties act at arm's length;[2968]
- The guidelines requiring that deductible casualty losses must be sudden, unexpected and unusual;[2969] and
- The time and amount of includibility of compensation from options granted by employers.[2970]

VI.F.11. *Business Expense Deduction Rules*

The section 162 business expense deduction has generated several cluster rules, no doubt because of its ubiquity and importance to business taxpayers. Most importantly, the Court has construed into the section a profit purpose requirement, much as it construed a business purpose requirement for reorganizations in *Gregory*, based on interpreting the words "trade or business."[2971] The statutory term "ordinary and necessary expenses" of a trade or business does not encompass excessive payments denominated as compensation,[2972] but rather should follow the general rule that "popular or received import of words furnishes the general rule for the interpretation of public laws."[2973]

The most well-known cluster rule is the *Cohan* rule. In the case of George M. Cohan in 1930, the Second Circuit held that where a taxpayer is clearly entitled to deductions but cannot show their exact amounts, rather than deny

---

2967 Security Flour Mills Co. v. Commissioner, 321 U.S. 281, 286 (1944).

2968 United States v. Davis, 370 U.S. 65 (1962) (wife's marital rights given up deemed worth the value of the property husband conveyed to wife).

2969 Bittker & Lokken, at 34.2.

2970 The Supreme Court created much of the law in this area. *Commissioner v. Smith*, 324 U.S. 177 (1945) involved an employer that gave its employee options to buy from the employer stock of another corporation with a strike price then below its value. It held that the exercise of the option at a later time when the employee could realize a profit from the option was the intended compensation and so the employee was in receipt of compensation income when he exercised the option at a price below its value. *Commissioner v. Lo Bue*, 351 U.S. 243 (1956) involved an employer that gave its employee options to buy its own stock from the employer for less than value. In later years, the employee exercised the options and claimed the value realized was not compensatory income because the options were not granted for the purpose of compensation but rather for the purpose of giving him a proprietary interest in the company. The Court rejected that argument, stating that the only alternative to compensation was a gift, and there was no basis to treat the options as gifts. Then the Court ruled that the receipt of an option that was in the money but did not have a "readily ascertainable market value" was not income upon receipt but rather upon exercise. The final issue was whether the taxability date was the date of exercise of the option and giving a note or the date the optionee paysthe note in cash and receives the stock. The Court remanded on this issue. The lower courts held the date of exercise to be the measurement date. Commissioner v. Lo Bue, 256 F. 2d. 735 (3d Cir. 1958).

2971 Commissioner v. Groetzinger, 480 U.S. 23 (1987). Applied in Portland Golf Club v. Commissioner, 497 U.S. 154 (1990).

2972 Botany Worsted Mills v. United States, 278 U.S. 282 (1929).

2973 Deputy v. Du Pont, 308 U.S. 488 (1940). See Ch. VI.F.11.

all deductions, the court can determine the proper amount, weighing its judgment heavily against the taxpayer.[2974] The Supreme Court has acknowledged the existence of the *Cohan* rule.[2975] Although the scope of the *Cohan* rule has been reduced by Code amendments, it still can be applied in some cases.[2976] It is a good example of a cluster rule, because it addressed difficult issues of fact, operated in a fairly circumscribed area, and employed a special level of fact finding presumption.

Other business expense deductions cluster rules include:

- The overnight rule for the away from home expense deduction;[2977]
- The convenience of the employer doctrine;[2978]
- The standard for a trade or business;[2979] and
- The various methods for identifying whether expenses are ordinary and necessary under section 162(a), including the reasonableness rule for transactions between related parties,[2980] and whether they are nondeductible personal or capital expenditures, for which the Supreme Court has created meaning out of the most limited of congressional guidance.[2981]

A particular reason for seeking cluster rules in this area is that it is burdened by Justice Cardozo's famous statement: "The standard set up by the statute is not a rule of law; it is rather a way of life. Life in all its fullness must supply the answer to the riddle."[2982] But Bittker and Lokken counsel against seeking an additional cluster rule to identify ordinary and necessary business expenses because finding a business connection and an absence of the nondeductible purposes should be sufficient; if more is required then Congress should say so.[2983]

VI.F.12. *Insurance*

The defining of insurance by the Supreme Court is very similar to its approach to defining the corporate reorganization in *Gregory v. Helvering* (Ch. III.C.3.a(1), above): Congress intended the commonly employed mean-

---

2974 Cohan v. Commissioner, 39 F.2d 540 (2d Cir. 1930); *see* Bittker & Lokken, at 21.4.1.

2975 Ry. Express Agency v. Virginia, 358 U.S. 434 n. 4 (1959).

2976 *See, e.g.,* United States v. Norlem, 104 A.F.T.R. 2d 2009-6956 (D. Minn. 2009) (Service agreed that *Cohan* Rule could be applied where there is a basis for approximation, which court found to exist).

2977 United States v. Correll, 389 U.S. 299 (1967) (establishing "overnight rule").

2978 Commissioner v. Kowalski, 434 U.S. 77 (1977) (prior rule for excluding supper money given to employees).

2979 Commissioner v. Groetzinger, 480 U.S. 23 (1987) (gambler was in a trade or business; rejected Frankfurter's gloss requiring selling goods or services as not achieving "the status of a Court holding").

2980 Bittker & Lokken, at 20.1.5.

2981 *Id.* at 20.3.2. *E.g.*, Commissioner v. Lincoln S&L Assn., 403 U.S. 345 (1971).

2982 Welch v. Helvering, 290 U.S. 111 (1933).

2983 *Id.* Their principal concern is that there not be undue emphasis on the unusual nature of an expense, which they consider to be irrelevant to the business connection.

ing of the word "insurance" when it referred to insurance in various sections, which takes account of but is not controlled by form and state law regulatory treatment and labels, and imports a substantive inquiry into the shifting and distribution of an insurance risk.[2984] Thus, this cluster starts with a statutory interpretation that has migrated across unrelated insurance provisions as a fact finding cluster (affecting various forms of insurance, in particular life insurance, and insurance companies and the identification of life insurance contracts).

The most commonly cited Supreme Court authority on the meaning of insurance for tax purposes is *Helvering v. Le Gierse*, which reversed the Board of Tax Appeals and the Second Circuit to find that the proceeds of a $25,000 life insurance policy did not qualify for an estate tax exclusion; therefore, they were includible in the decedent's gross estate as transfers intended to take effect at death.[2985] The facts of the case show how the Court both integrated the two contracts that the decedent entered with the insurer and analyzed their economic reality to find their effect, but did so after first interpreting the words of the statute and finding the presumed legislative purpose.

Decedent was an 80-year-old woman who had no reason apart from age to anticipate an immediate demise. She owned a home and securities that had declined in value to between $25,000 and $30,000 by December, 1935 and wanted to avoid further deterioration of the value of her investments. With the aid of an insurance agent she decided to liquidate the investments and paid from the proceeds $27,125 to Connecticut General Life Ins. Co. for the simultaneous purchase of two contracts:

1. For $4,179, a "standard form" "single premium life annuity nonparticipating," to pay $49.15 monthly for life; and
2. For $22,946, a "standard form" "single premium life policy nonparticipating" to pay to her daughter $25,000 upon the insured's death; the policy permitted the owner to borrow the cash value of the policy, a defined amount, which began at $19,550 and increased yearly in a modest amount.

The decedent was not required to take a physical examination or to answer certain questions that were normally required. The primary reason the dece-

[2984] For a current statement of the Service's definition of insurance based on *Le Gierse*, discussed below, see Revenue Ruling 2009-26, 2009-38 I.R.B. 336. *See also* Miller, *Distinguishing Risk: The Disparate Tax Treatment of Insurance and Financial Contracts in a Converging Marketplace*, 55 TAX LAW. 481, 507 (2001) (identifying what is viewed as a four part test).

[2985] Helvering v. Le Gierse, 312 U.S. 531 (1941); *see* PAUL, STUDIES III, at 351, 374-391 (Life Insurance, Annuities and Income Tax) (discussing the *Le Gierse* and *Keller* cases at length, between the Court of Appeals and Supreme Court decisions); Miller, *Distinguishing Risk*, *supra* note 2984, at 504 *et seq.* (concluding that the decedent failed the insurance test because she did not transfer the risk of her death to the insurance company). The Court has cited *Le Gierse* in extending the insurance definition from life insurance to other forms of insurance, as in *Haynes v. United States*, 353 U.S. 81 (1957) (disability insurance self-insured by employer).

dent bought the contracts was to preserve the principal of her estate for her daughter; she was aware of estate tax considerations. Eighteen days after she bought the contracts she suffered a mortal stroke and died six days later, on January 1, 1936. Although the insurer treated and priced the two contracts separately, the BTA opinion found that the insurer would not have issued the insurance without the annuity due to the insured's age; but it would have issued the annuity without the insurance.[2986]

The estate tax return excluded the life insurance. The notice of deficiency asserted: (1) the $25,000 contract was not insurance, and (2) the decedent's purchase of the contract was a transfer in contemplation of death. The BTA rejected both contentions, relying on a reviewed decision it had issued the day before, *Keller*, which also went to the Supreme Court as a companion case to *Le Gierse.*[2987] The BTA relied primarily on a Supreme Court bankruptcy decision, *Legg. v. St. John*, which ruled that a disability rider on a life insurance policy produced payments upon the bankrupt's disability (which had occurred) that were property of the bankrupt estate because they were not excludable life insurance policy cash value.[2988] *Legg* observed certain formal linkages between the two contracts, but stated they did not make the disability insurance life insurance because there were different risks and separate premiums. *Legg* did not have to define life insurance because the disability insurance was clearly payable as such.

The BTA in *Keller* focused almost entirely on the separability of the terms of the two contracts and gave little attention to the statute requiring inclusion of property that the decedent transferred property in contemplation of death and also retained the right to income. The Supreme Court similarly did not focus on the contemplation of death provision. It distinguished *Legg* on the ground that the two contracts were not necessarily issued together. Rather it focused on the word insurance in the statute and the evident purpose of Congress in excluding life insurance proceeds from the gross estate. It relied

---

2986 Le Gierse v. Commissioner, 39 BTA 1134 (1939). The insurer could not reliably underwrite the policy alone due to the insured's age, but could determine "with almost certainty" that it would not lose money on the combination of contracts as priced to decedent. The premium for the insurance policy as a stand alone policy for an 80-year-old person could not be said to be the standard premium because the insurer did not issue such policies to persons of such an age without the annuity contract; age 70 was normally the top age for stand alone insurance.

2987 Estate of Keller v. Commissioner, 39 BTA 1047 (1939), *reversed*, 113 F.2d 833 (3d Cir. 1940), *affirmed*, 312 U.S. 543 (1941). The Third Circuit decision created a conflict between the circuits. The policies in *Keller* were issued by The Equitable, and the insured survived for 15 months, but otherwise the facts were very similar.

2988 Legg v. St. John, 296 U.S. 489 (1936). The *Legg* decision involved a close but different issue from that in *Keller*. In form and substance the disability policy was a disability policy that happened to be issued as a supplement to a life insurance policy. In the context of *Keller* it was as if the issue was the taxation of the annuity payments. Just as there was nothing of substance that resembled life insurance in the disability payments, surely the Board of Tax Appeals would have required the annuity payments to be taxed as annuity and not life insurance receipts.

on the "commonly accepted" meaning of the word insurance in the statutory exemption:

> . . . it is logical to assume that when Congress used the words "receivable as insurance" in § 302(g), it contemplated amounts received pursuant to a transaction possessing these features [of risk shifting and risk distribution]. . . . usually insurance payable to specific beneficiaries is designed to shift to a group of individuals the risk of premature death of the one upon whom the beneficiaries are dependent for support. Indeed, the pith of the exemption is particular protection of contracts and their proceeds intended to guard against just such a risk.

Thus, the Court figured out what the Congress thought it was doing: it did not wish to diminish by the estate tax those funds intended to replace the unexpected loss of income of the breadwinner, where the funds did not represent wealth the decedent owned, but rather were funds that she could provide only through the risk shifting mechanism of insurance. Two later Supreme Court opinions on essentially the same single premium annuity and insurance plan used in *Le Gierse* left intact that opinion's definition of insurance, but showed that the two contracts did not have to be linked for all tax purposes.[2989]

The *Le Gierse* decision has been implicated in almost all of the major categories of Code provisions dealing with insurance. The subsequent Supreme Court rulings include:

- Section 101 excludes from gross income the proceeds of life insurance paid on account of death.[2990]
- The employee health insurance exclusion cases; and[2991]

[2989] *Goldstone v. United States*, 325 U.S. 687 (1945), involved essentially the same plan except the decedent insured gave the two policies to his wife, and the issue was whether the transfer took effect at death; the Court ruled it did and the life insurance proceeds were includable in the gross estate. *Fidelity-Philadelphia Trust Co. v. Smith*, 356 U.S. 274 (1958), differed in that the decedent had irrevocably assigned only the life insurance policies before her death. The Court ruled that the assigned policies were not includible in her gross estate because her retention of the annuity policies was not a retention of income from the property that was the insurance policies. The government relied on *Le Gierse* to argue that the annuity and the life policy were inseparable. The Court distinguished *Le Gierse* on the ground that there the government relied for inclusion on the transfers to take effect at death rule, whereas here the government relied on the retained interest rule. The Court did not modify its definition of insurance, but rather found that the two contracts that constituted the issuer's noninsurance obligation were still two contracts, and that when the insured disposed of one, the other represented an independent separable right against the insurer, that was not an aspect of the property of insurance given away.

[2990] *See* United States v. Supplee-Biddle Hardware Co., 265 U.S. 189 (1924) (life insurance proceeds not income).

[2991] *See, e.g.*, Haynes v. United States, 353 U.S. 81 (1957) (ruling that health insurance was not limited to the forms of insurance typically provided by insurers).

- The treatment of reinsurance agreements between insurance companies, which the Court almost wholly made up by reasoning from basic principless.[2992]

However, *Le Gierse* is not the beginning of the Court's effort to define insurance. Earlier the Court said life insurance was "an indemnity for, and repayment of, an economic loss," as contrasted with the profit realized upon cashing in life insurance policies before death.[2993] Also the Court decided that Congress had referred to insurance as commonly understood, and therefore would not be bound by state law labels. In *Bowers*, the Court ruled that a taxpayer who predominantly brokered and guaranteed mortgage loans, but issued no mortgage insurance, did not qualify for the insurance company exemption from the general corporate tax because "the character of the business actually done in the tax years determines whether it was taxable as an insurance company."[2994] The cites for this statement were general "substance" cites, and so this opinion originated the words that still appear in a Regulation.[2995] The opinion refused to be influenced by the formal classification of the corporation as an insurer because it viewed Congress as intending tax categorization to be based on business done and not the fact of organization under state insurance laws. The opinion distinguished an earlier decision that had allowed an exempt savings and loan to have certain other activities, indicating that the issue was what was the core business.[2996]

In conclusion, the Court has treated insurance like it has treated reorganizations and interest and other major generic terms used in the Code: as intended by Congress to carry their ordinary meaning as a matter of statutory interpretation, and not to be governed by state law labels.

VI.F.13. *International*

Cluster rules have arisen in tax cases involving nonresidents and domestic taxpayers with foreign income due in part to the sensitive nontax issues that can be implicated.

[2992] Colonial American Life Ins. Co. v. Commissioner, 491 U.S. 244 (1989); United States v. Consumer Life Ins. Co., 430 U.S. 725 (1977).

[2993] Lucas v. Alexander, 279 U.S. 573 (1929).

[2994] Bowers v. Lawyers' Mortgage Co., 285 U.S. 182 (1932); *cf.* United States v. Home Title Ins. Co., 285 U.S. 191 (1932) (decided the same day as *Bowers* and coming out the other way on the facts, citing *Bowers*).

[2995] Reg. § 1.803-3(a)(1).

[2996] United States v. Loan & Bldg. Co., 278 U.S. 55 (1928) (Justice Holmes applied the approach that Congress intended to use words as then commonly understood, and then states commonly allowed building and loan associations to deal with nonmembers and have capital stock).

- The Supreme Court sometimes has enforced a so-called "revenue rule," holding that the United States will not enforce the revenue laws of another nation.[2997]
- The Court looks to domestic concepts of an income tax for purposes of determining creditability of foreign taxes.[2998]
- The Court early established that treaties and federal statutes are on an equal footing and the later in time prevails unless otherwise specified.[2999] This is called the doctrine of treaty override.
- The *PPL* opinion purported to find a foreign tax to be a creditable income tax based on substance, but the reasoning was flawed, reflecting a dislike for the politics that produced the foreign tax.[3000]

VI.F.14. *Tax Crimes*

The Supreme Court has interpreted the handful of Title 26 criminal sections in ways that create a cluster rule for tax crimes.[3001] A primary example is *Cheek*, which raises a fairly high bar to convict a tax protester.[3002] The appellant was convicted of tax evasion. He was a "tax protester" who did not believe the income tax was constitutional, did not believe wages were income and did not believe he was a taxpayer required to file a return. The opinion focused on the statutory requirement of willfulness, which it explained as an element required to prove the crime because of the complexity of the tax laws. However, the opinion drew a distinction between the right to rely on a belief that the tax law was unconstitutional and a belief, however, irrational, that the defendant was not required to pay tax under the words of the Code. Evidence of the former could be withheld from the jury; evidence of the latter could not. Therefore, willfulness meant what the defendant actually thought, up to a line drawn by the Court based on the purpose it found the willfulness requirement to serve.

[2997] Pasquantino v. United States, 544 U.S. 349 (2005) (extensively analyzing the revenue rule and finding it not to apply to a crime of fraud wholly committed in the United States to evade the foreign tax). For the revenue rule, see BITTKER & LOKKEN, at 65.4.7. The rule is an extension of the rule of nations that one nation does not enforce another nation's criminal statutes.

[2998] Biddle v. Commissioner, 302 U.S. 573 (1938). But the D.C. Circuit applied the act of state doctrine to accord weight to the foreign country's interpretation of its tax laws. Riggs Nat'l Corp. v. Comm'r, 295 F.3d 16, 23 (D.C Cir. 2002). *See also* PPL Corp. v. Commissioner, 133 S. Ct. 1897 (2013) (which incorrectly claimed that the *Biddle* opinion supported the view that a foreign tax's economic effects determined whether it was creditable; the Court improperly interlineated "[a tax]" in a quote).

[2999] *See, e.g.*, The Cherokee Tobacco, 78 U.S. 616 (1870) (a tax case). *See generally* Sachs, *Is the 19th Century Doctrine of Treaty Override Good Law for Modern Day Tax Treaties?* 47 TAX LAW. 867 (1994).

[3000] PPL Corp. v. Commissioner, 133 S. Ct. 1897 (2013). *See* Cummings, *Form, Substance, and* PPL, 140 TAX NOTES (TA) 365 (July 22, 2013).

[3001] *See generally* BITTKER & LOKKEN, at 114.9.

[3002] Cheek v. United States, 498 U.S. 192 (1991).

The most recent tax crime decision involving deportation, on the other hand, went far out of its way to classify filing a false return as fraud to uphold deportation of the taxpayers.[3003]

The applicability of the rule of lenity to civil tax matters that could lead to criminal prosecution is discussed in Ch. II.B.2.a(4).

VI.G. Supreme Court Procedures

Like the Circuit Courts, the Supreme Court will not consider for the first time a ground for tax liability asserted by the Commissioner that is not fairly within the issues decided below.[3004] However, the Court has remanded for development of facts on a newly proposed issue.[3005] But, in the high profile decision in *General Utilities*, the Court rebuked the Circuit Court for such a remand.[3006] The Court has recognized the ability of an appellate court to consider a newly raised issue to prevent a plain miscarriage of justice.[3007]

When the Court wanted to base a ruling on a finding of fact that the trial court had not exactly made, it said it should remand but went ahead and ruled as if the fact had been found.[3008]

[3003] Kawashima v. Holder, 132 S. Ct. 1166 (2012).

[3004] Helvering v. Wood, 309 U.S. 344 (1940) (income was not taxable to trust grantor under the revocable trust rule and so Commissioner could not assert on appeal that it was gross income under the predecessor of section 61). *See also* Helvering v. Cement Investors, Inc., 316 U.S. 527 (1942) (it was not clear whether the Commissioner was trying to assert an alternate ground or an alternate tax liability).

[3005] *See* Estate of Spiegel v. Commissioner, 335 U.S. 701 (1949) (dissent); Helvering v. Gowran, 302 U.S. 238 (1937). *But see* Helvering v. Stuart, 317 U.S. 642 (1942) (allowing ground argued in Court of Appeals but not in answer to Tax Court petition to be considered in the Supreme Court).

[3006] General Utils. & Operating Co. v. Helvering, 296 U.S. 200 (1935), discussed in Helvering v. Pfeiffer, 302 U.S. 247 (1937).

[3007] Hormel v. Helvering, 312 U.S. 552 (1941). Cited as still good law in Henderson v. United States, 133 S. Ct. 1121 (2013).

[3008] United States v. Wells, 283 U.S. 102 (1931).

Ch. VII. Other Solutions to Problems of Application of the Code

VII.A. The Government's Recourse to Published Guidance

This book primarily addresses the Supreme Court's interpretations of the Code because they are the most authoritative, and up to fairly recently, have been sufficiently numerous to form a discrete body of law, as discussed in Ch. III.A., above. Yet its tax decisions are only a small fraction of all court interpretations. Consequently our tax law has been largely created in the lower courts under the episodic supervision of the Supreme Court.[3009] Robert H. Jackson complained in 1937 that tax cases were too much litigated and in too many courts.[3010] Randolph Paul agreed in 1947.[3011] Martin D. Ginsburg in 1984 stated his famous maxim that frequently the Commissioner's club turns into a large green snake to bite the Commissioner on the hind parts, with the club being wielded primarily in the multifarious venues of tax litigation.[3012] Nothing has changed since. The voluntary diminution of the Supreme Court's supervision over the tax laws, as well as the rise of the *Chevron* doctrine (see Ch. VI.D.) suggest that the Treasury should increase its output of published guidance.

[3009] *See* Dailey, *supra* note 410. Mr. Justice Jackson, with whom Mr. Justice Frankfurter joined, dissented in *Arrowsmith v. Commissioner*, 344 U.S. 6 (1952), and coined the term "sporadic omnipotence."

[3010] Jackson, *Equity in the Administration of Federal Taxes*, *supra* note 166, at 641.

[3011] Paul, Prosperity, at Ch. 44.

[3012] Ginsburg, *supra* note 972, at 76.

Thoughtful observers have long agreed.[3013] Dean Griswold thought that tax law is or should be largely a matter of administration rather than litigation.[3014] Robert W. Wales, Tax Legislative Counsel from 1946-1952 wrote a perceptive analysis of the Supreme Court's tax decisions from 1937 to 1948.[3015] He concluded that the Court had spent a lot of effort on tax cases that in retrospect it felt should never have reached it. Wales proposed these solutions:

- The Bureau, the DOJ, and the Treasury's legislative function should better coordinate how the government wanted to solve issues in the tax law; he saw too much of an institutional tendency to solve by litigation rather than regulations or legislation.
- He advocated basic legislative solutions that could undercut a lot of disputes, such as joint returns; he would have applauded the passive loss rules.
- The Supreme Court should not be called upon to provide the final answer to every hard tax issue.
- The Treasury has been too timid in meeting problems in regulations.[3016]

However, little attention has been given, at least in the federal tax area, to how the Executive Branch should perform its own administrative duties with regard to statutory interpretation. Indeed, the existence of the *Chevron* doctrine[3017] creates an interesting paradox: the Treasury presumably interprets the Code based on how a court would interpret it, realizing that a court would give a certain amount of deference to the Treasury's judgment.[3018]

The Service's own policies on this subject include the following:

- The Service essays to "try to find the true meaning of the statutory provision and not to adopt a strained construction in the belief that it is

---

[3013] Paul, Prosperity, at 395. Paul observed that the federal courts handle a large number of tax cases, both in absolute and relative numbers; that the administration has mostly abdicated interpretation of the laws to the courts; that the courts are seen as too hard on tax avoidance, by "judicial legislation." Paul rejected the complaints because modern times require flexibility in the law, particularly when the object of the flexibility is to thwart tax avoidance. His objection is that the courts should not be doing this in most case; the treasury should do it. "The choice is between the present unsatisfactory method of litigation and more administrative finality." *Id.* at 398. *See also* Eisenstein, *Some Iconoclastic Reflections, supra* note 598 (urging more published guidance and less litigation).

[3014] Griswold, *A Summary of the Regulations Problem, supra* note 2106, at 423.

[3015] Wales, *supra* note 278, at 84-7.

[3016] *See also* Dubroff, The United States Tax Court: An Historical Analysis, *supra* note 713, at 31 (quoting a 1926 Senate Select Committee report recommending more published guidance for taxpayers).

[3017] *See supra* Ch. VI.D.

[3018] *See supra* Ch. VI.B.3.a.

"protecting the revenue." The revenue is properly protected only when "we ascertain and apply the true meaning of the statute."[3019]

- However, the Service does not feel itself bound by the strict terms of the Code. For example a General Counsel Memorandum intentionally construed a section contrary to its plain meaning and justified that because in "other instances in the subchapter C area, the Service has likewise not followed the plain meaning of a statutory phrase when to do so would produce an illogical result."[3020]
- "Published guidance generally refers to that body of guidance that sets forth the definitive position of the Service, as approved by the Commissioner and the Department of the Treasury. Published guidance must be followed by all components of the Service and can be relied upon by taxpayers in litigation. For purposes of this section, published guidance includes Treasury Decisions, notices of proposed rulemaking, revenue rulings, revenue procedures, and Internal Revenue Bulletin notices and announcements."""[3021]
- "The proper method for conveying the positions of the Office and the policies of the Service is through published guidance. In contrast, litigation should be used as an enforcement tool to advance and defend established positions, not as a vehicle for making policy."[3022]
- "Also, where an appellate court has decided an issue in a case contrary to the Service position, it may be necessary to settle or concede the issue in cases appealable to that court until an appropriate case can be litigated in another circuit."[3023]
- "The nationwide jurisdiction of the Federal Circuit is one factor in considering a recommendation for certiorari. A loss in this circuit may mean that the Government will not litigate another case with the issue." [3024]
- Nonacquiescence signifies that, although the decision was not appealed or was not reviewed by the Supreme Court, the Service does not agree with the holding of the court and will not follow it nationwide in disposing of other cases. With respect to opinions of an appellate court,

---

3019 Rev. Proc. 64-22, 1964-1 C.B. 689; *see also* I.R.M., 31.1.1.1(3)(" It is our responsibility to find the true meaning of the statutory provision and not to adopt a strained construction with the goal of maximizing revenue. We properly protect the revenue only when we ascertain and apply the true meaning of the statute."); I.R.M. 31.1.1(3) (same).

3020 G.C.M. 39,102, at n. 8 (Dec. 21, 1983) (The Chief Counsel Memorandum cited for this point); Rev. Rul. 1964-73, 1964-1 C.B. 142; Rev. Rul. 1978-442, 1978-2 C.B. 143; Rev. Rul. 1981-41, 1981-1 C.B. 121.

3021 I.R.M. 31.1.1.2.1. This is a narrower list than the list of authorities that constitute "substantial authority." Reg. § 1.6662-4(d)(3)(iii). The Tax Court will follow the decisions of the circuit court of appeals to which the case would be appealable unless it believes the precedent has become outmoded. Golsen v. Commissioner, 54 T.C. 742 (1970), *aff'd*, 445 F.2d 985 (10th Cir.); Kent v. Commissioner, 61 T.C. 133 (1973).

3022 I.R.M. 31.1.1.1.3(1).

3023 I.R.M. 31.1.1.1.3(3).

3024 I.R.M. 36.2.2.5.1.4.

> the Service generally will follow the holding in cases appealable to that circuit due to the binding nature of the opinion on lower courts even when the office concludes that the opinion is erroneous. The AOD may include a statement that the holding will not be followed in future cases in the circuit if the case can be distinguished on the facts. Any decision to not follow circuit court precedence in that circuit is a strategic decision, which can only made after consultation with the Department of Justice Tax Division.[3025]

These policies show how the Treasury and Service can be constrained by the adverse interpretive opinion of a single court, trial or appellate. Getting out ahead of such decisions with regulations is the single most effective (but not foolproof) method for the Treasury to follow. A useful beginning point could be to ramp up section 269.[3026]

But the Treasury, through the Service, has a history of trying to make law through litigation, in addition to the economic substance doctrine as discussed in Ch. V.F., above. Some unsuccessful examples include the following:

- Wage withholding: The Supreme Court rejected Service efforts to litigate contrary to Treasury regulations and force employers to "withhold" income tax on lunch money that was not deductible by the employee; the Service belatedly issued a Revenue Ruling stating its newly discovered view of the law, but the Treasury never even tried to assert the position in regulations.[3027]
- Customer based intangibles: The government's response to a 1973 case holding that the court made "mass asset rule" did not always apply to customer based intangibles was only a conclusory revenue ruling in 1974, which led eventually to the Supreme Court's agreeing with the 1973 holding 1993.[3028]
- The *United Dominion* opinion took the Service back to the basics of its own regulations that it had not amended to assert the position it argued for in court.[3029]
- The Court's *Gitlitz* decision likely resulted in part from the Service's attempt to rely on a regulation that did not speak to the issue, and the Treasury's failure to adopt a regulation that did speak to the issue.[3030]

On the other hand, sometimes the government wins after many losses, which emboldens the desire to make law through litigation. A significant

---

[3025] I.R.M. 31.3.1.
[3026] Recommended by McMahon, *Beyond a GAAR*, *supra* note 19, at 1741.
[3027] Cent. Ill. Pub. Serv. Co. v. United States, 435 U.S. 21 (1978).
[3028] Newark Morning Ledger Co. v. United States, 507 U.S. 546 (1993).
[3029] United Dominion Industries., Inc. v. United States, 532 U.S. 822 (2001).
[3030] Gitlitz v. Commissioner, 531 U.S. 206 (2001).

example is *Cannelton*.[3031] It involved an interpretation of the depletion allowance and the government had lost in the Tax Court and at least six circuits, but finally won when the Supreme Court agreed to hear one of the cases.[3032] At least the Treasury had written its interpretation into a regulation, although the Supreme Court's majority opinion did not give the regulation much weight. The Treasury also sought a statute change, which occurred almost simultaneously with the Supreme Court decision.[3033] Perhaps the series of litigated cases was required to prompt Congress to act; or perhaps it was required to prompt Treasury to seek the law change?

Of course Treasury regulations run the risk of going beyond the statute, at least in the eyes of some court.[3034] And in some cases the task is just impossible: Professor Bittker counseled the Treasury not to write more regulations after the Kintner Regulations of 1960 but rather to litigate the corporate nature of professional associations, because it would be too hard for Treasury to figure out the factual state law issues involved.[3035] As it turned out, the Treasury eventually just gave up and let business entities choose to be corporations for tax purposes, or not.

VII.B. Systemic Changes

VII.B.1. *Tax Appeals*

Almost all observers interested in good tax administration have decried the complexity of routes in tax litigation: four possible types of trial courts (Tax Court, United States District Court, Claims Court, United States Bankruptcy Court, only one of which is devoted exclusively to tax),[3036] 13 possible appel-

---

3031 United States v. Cannelton Sewer Pipe Co., 364 U.S. 76 (1959). Another example is *Quality Stores*, 134 S. Ct. 1395 (2014), which the Service won, but it could have helped itself out a lot by writing a regulation.

3032 *See* Taubeneck, *The Depletion Base Controversy*, 46 A.B.A. 1136 (1960).

3033 *Id.*

3034 *See, e.g.,* Commissioner v. Acker, 361 U.S. 87 (1959) (rejecting Treasury regulation that said filing no estimated return should be treated as filing a zero return);

3035 Bittker, *Professional Association and Federal Income Taxation: Some Questions and Comments*, 17 Tax L. Rev. 1, 32 *et seq.* (1961).

3036 *See generally* Greenaway, *supra* note 760.

late courts, and then the Supreme Court.[3037] Many have recommended the creation of a Court of Tax Appeals. For example, Professor Traynor proposed giving the Board of Tax Appeals exclusive jurisdiction over refund claims and having a court of tax appeals from the Board.[3038] Charles Lowndes was ready to rescue the Supreme Court from tax cases in 1960.[3039] Martin D. Ginsburg recommended the same.[3040] Professor Boyle recommended a national court of tax appeals after studying the tax opinions of the Rehnquist Court and finding that more than half of the issues the Court decided either had already been or would be resolved by administrative or legislative action.[3041] Arguably these proposals went nowhere because the current menu of choices better suits practitioners' and taxpayers' desire for maximum flexibility in all directions.

The current non-system of appeals of tax disputes evolved without a plan. Originally suits for the recovery of taxes had to be initiated in the state courts, unless diversity of citizenship could be established between the taxpayer and the tax collector.[3042] "The jurisdiction of the Court of Claims . . . . over suits to recover taxes is based on the clause in the original Act of February 24, 1855, c.122, 10 Stat. 612, empowering it to determine 'all claims founded

---

[3037] *See* Bland, *Federal Tax Appeals*, 25 COLUM. L. REV. 1013 (1925); Del Cotto, *The Need for a Court of Tax Appeals, An Argument and a Study*, 12 BUFF. L. REV. 5 (1962); Easterbrook, *Ways of Critiquing the Court*, 95 HARV. L. REV. 802 (1982); Eustice and Lyons, *Federal Income Taxation*, 1960 ANN. SURV. OF AM. L. 226, 227 (1960); Griswold, *The Need for a Court of Tax Appeals*, 57 HARV. L. REV. 1153 (1944); Jackson, *Equity in the Administration of Federal Taxes, supra* note 166; Miller, *A Court of Tax Appeals Revisited*, 85 YALE L.J. 228 (1975); Note, *Interpretation of the Internal Revenue Code:, supra* note 2570 (arguing for a national court of tax appeals). *But see* Craig, *Federal Income Tax and the Supreme Court: The Case against a National Court of Tax Appeals*, 1983 UTAH L. REV. 679 (1983); NYSBA, *Response to Proposals for a National Court of Appeals*, TAX NOTES (TA) 819, 823 (Feb. 12, 1990)
But this view ignores the fact that the tax laws are passed by non specialist legislators, even if they are written by tax specialists on the staffs of the tax-writing committee and the Joint Committee on Taxation. It also adopts a narrow view of what factors should dictate the development of the tax law.

[3038] *See* Schlaffer, *Criticism of the Jurisdiction of the Board of Tax Appeals*, 20 TAXES (CCH), 420, 424 (July 1942).

[3039] Lowndes, *Federal Taxation and the Supreme Court, supra* note 433, at 222 (reporting that there had been 524 income tax decisions, 75 estate tax, 19 gift tax, the vast majority of which involved only construction; he agreed with Brandeis that ". . . more important that the applicable rule of law be settled, than that it be settled right." [Brandeis dissenting in Burnet v. Coronado Oil and Gas Co., 285 U.S. 393 (1932)] and pointed to *Court Holding* and *Cumberland* as examples of the Court's unwillingness to set a rule).

[3040] Ginsburg, *supra* note 972; *see also* Dawson, *Should the Federal Tax Litigation System Be Restructured?* TAX NOTES (TA) 1427 (Sept. 26, 1988) (recommending that all matters be tried in the Tax Court and appealed to one court of tax appeals).

[3041] Boyle, *The Rehnquist Court: Nineteen Years of Tax Decisions*, 25 VA. TAX REV. 451, 506 (2005).

[3042] *See* Collector v. Hubbard, 79 U.S. 1 (1871) (although claims court jurisdiction evidently was available at the time of this case).

upon any law of Congress.'"[3043] Statistics show that tax cases form only a small and declining part of the Claims Court's recent case load,[3044] although that belies its importance.

The Tax Court is thought to do a consistently good job applying the Code, and that fact should support the creation of a court of tax appeals to supplant the Circuit Court. Professor Shores has studied appeals from the Tax Court and concluded that "in many if not most instances the reasoning and conclusions of the Tax Court on questions of law is superior to that of the courts of appeal that overturn them."[3045] For example, the Tax Court had figured out at least by 1997 that the presumption of the *Gould* case was overturned by *White*.[3046] The Federal Circuit was still unaware of that in 2005.[3047]

The Board of Tax Appeals was created to perform the administrative functions theretofore discharged by the Committee on Appeals and Review, which the Commissioner of Internal Revenue had established in his office.[3048] The

---

3043 *Compare* Williamsport Wire Rope Co. v. United States, 277 U.S. 551 (1928) (citing United States v. Kaufman, 96 U.S. 567, 569 (1878); *and* Dooley v. United States, 182 U.S. 222 (1901); *with* United States v. Emery, Bird, Thayer Co., 237 U.S. 28 (1915)).

3044 1997 418/3023 (14%), 1998 528/2944 (18%), 1999 562/2871 (19.5%), 2000 431/2919 (15%), 2001 420/2848 (15%), 2002 259/2572 (10%), 2003 254/3189 (8%), 2004 248/5470 (4.5%), 2005 272/6909 (4%), 2006 348/7529 (4.6%), 2007 434/7760 (5.5%), 2008 408/7738 (5%). From the annual reports of the Claims Court.

3045 Shores, *Deferential Review of Tax Court Decisions, supra* note 2575, at 707-08.

3046 Booth v. Commissioner, 108 T.C. 524 (1997); *see supra* ChII.B.2.c.

3047 Falconwood Corp. v. United States, 422 F.3d 1339 (Fed. Cir. 2005).

3048 *See* H. Rep. No. 179, at 7 (1924); S. Rep. No. 398, at 8 (1924). The Revenue Act of 1918, § 1301(d), 40 Stat. 1057, 1141, created an Advisory Tax Board to be appointed by the Commissioner with the approval of the Secretary of the Treasury. *See* H. Rep. No. 767, at 38 (1918); S. Rep. No. 617, at 58 (1918). The Commissioner might submit to the Board, and on the request of a taxpayer must submit, any question relating to the interpretation or administration of the income, war-profits or excess-profits tax. The functions of the Board were, in some degree, similar to those of the excess-profits tax advisers and reviewers who had aided the Commissioner in applying the 1917 act. *See* Annual Report of the Commissioner of Internal Revenue, 13 (G.P.O. 1918). Procedure was established by Regulation 45. See T.D. 2881, 21 Treas. Dec. 214, art 1701 (1918). The Board, which was organized on March 13, 1919, came to an end on October 1 of that year. Annual Report of the Commissioner of Internal Revenue, 12-4 (G.P.O. 1919).

The work that had been performed by the Advisory Tax Board was, however, immediately taken over by a committee of lawyers and accountants organized by the Commissioner in the Bureau. *Id.* at 14. The procedure for taking appeals to this committee, which was known as the Committee on Appeals and Review, was laid down in O.D. 709, 3 C.B. 370. The nature of the work of this body is described in the Annual Report of the Commissioner of Internal Revenue, 14-5 (G.P.O. 1920); Annual Report of the Commissioner of Internal Revenue, 14-5 (G.P.O. 1921).

Section 250(d) of the Revenue Act of 1921, 42 Stat. 227, 265-66, provided that if on examination of a return under the Acts of 1916, 1917, 1918, or 1921, a tax or deficiency in tax should be discovered, the taxpayer should be notified and given a period of not less than 30 days in which to file an appeal. *See* H. Rep. No. 350, at 14 (1921); S. Rep. No. 275, at 20-1 (1921). The procedure for perfecting appeals under this section was laid down by Regulation 62, art. 1006 (T.D. 3409, Nov. 13, 1922); and T.D. 3492. Appeals under this section appear to have been commonly handled by the Committee on Appeals and Review. *See* Rules of

Board and the Tax Court faced three pivotal shifts in their powers over the years: (a) the life and death of the *Dobson* rule, as discussed in Ch. VI.E.3.a., (b) the court's adoption of the *Golsen*[3049] rule: the Tax Court will follow the precedent of the Court of Appeals to which the case can be appealed.; and (c) the removal of the Tax Court from the Executive Branch.

It would be too much to expect politically for trial jurisdiction to be removed from the district courts and the claims court. The bar probably would not support any change, as the current system maintains maximum flexibility in all directions.[3050] But channeling all appeals from all trial courts through one tax court of appeals is a reasonable compromise. The Court of Appeals for the Federal Circuit was never intended to approximate the Tax Court in tax expertise, but rather to be a generalist court through which a type of cases would flow,[3051] hopefully with some unifying influence.[3052] Nevertheless, the Circuit's work is heavily weighted toward patent cases.

Practitioners have tended to oppose a court of tax appeals for the stated reason that non-specialist judges bring a desirable perspective to the process.[3053] That is undeniably true. However, the varying considerations must be balanced, and at some point the value added by the generalist appellate judges may not be worth the expense of delay and confusion in the law engendered by the multiple routes of appeal. Many generalists would retain an influence on the tax system, including the United States District judges,

---

Procedure before the Committee, A.R.M. 219, Int. Rev. Cum. Bull. III-1, 319; Annual Report of the Commissioner of Internal Revenue, 15 (G.P.O. 1922); Annual Report of the Commissioner of Internal Revenue, 8-9 (G.P.O. 1923); Annual Report of the Commissioner of Internal Revenue, 10-2 (G.P.O. 1924).

The Board of Tax Appeals was created by section 900 of the Revenue Act of 1924, 43 Stat. 253, 336. Section 1100 of the same act, 43 Stat. 253, 352, repealed section 250 of the Revenue Act of 1921. By Treasury Decision 3616 (1924), all cases pending before the Committee and the Special Committee on Appeals and Review were transferred to the Solicitor of Internal Revenue, and the Committees were abolished. *See also* Report of the Commissioner for 1924, *supra,* at 12. The Board of Tax Appeals was not a part of the Bureau of Internal Revenue; it was an independent agency. But by specific provision of the Revenue Act of 1924, § 900(k), 43 Stat. 253, 338, it was defined as an agency "in the executive branch of the Government." *But cf.* Goldsmith v. Board of Tax Appeals, 270 U.S. 117, 121-22 (1926) (Board refused admission to a certified public accountant; remanded for hearing on his request). Its sole function consisted in reviewing, on appeal, determinations of the Commissioner under the revenue laws. For a further report of the working of the Committee on Appeals and Review, see Talbert, *Relief Provisions and Appeals, in* Haig, et. al, *supra* note 189, at 257; Dubroff, The United States Tax Court: An Historical Analysis, Part I, *supra* note 713.

[3049] Golsen v. Commissioner, 54 T.C. 742 (1970), *aff'd,* 445 F.2d 985 (10th Cir.).

[3050] *See* Janicke, *To Be or Not to Be: The Long Gestation of the U.S. Court of Appeals for the Federal Circuit (1887-1982),* 69 Antitrust L.J. 645, 653 n. 43 (2002) (candid observers admitted the multiple routes to appeal created business for practitioners).

[3051] *See* Plager, *A Review of Recent Decisions of the United States Court of Appeals for the Federal Circuit,* 56 Am. U. L. Rev. 751, 754 (2007).

[3052] *See* Janicke, *supra* note 3050, at 653 (goal of Hruska Commission).

[3053] *See* Miller, *The Courts of Last Resort in Tax Cases: A Specialized Court of Tax Appeals,* 40 A.B.A. 563 (1954); Miller, *Can Tax Appeals Be Centralized,* 23 Taxes (CCH) 303 (1945).

the Bankruptcy judges, the Claims Court judges, the Supreme Court, the Treasury's politically sensitive offices and the Congress. The theory that the creation of conflicts in the circuits to be resolved by the Supreme Court is a valuable exercise in fleshing out all possibilities is just that—a theory—and even if once true, it is no longer possible due to the paucity of the Supreme Court's recent tax decisions.

Removing the other Circuits from the appeal process does not mean removing the Supreme Court. Its unique role in the nation's laws should not be excluded from the tax system.[3054]

VII.B.2. *Other Proposals*

Systemic proposals for improvement of the matters of application of the federal tax laws on which this book has focused are in short supply. One good source of recommendations about tax matters generally, some of which address interpretive issues, is the National Taxpayer Advocate's Annual Report to Congress. The Reports list the most litigated legal issues, and its analysis of those issues could be used to pursue more administrable interpretations. Professor Bernard Wolfman recommended that Federal Rule of Civil Procedure 44.1 be amended to state: "The court, in determining foreign or domestic law, may consider any relevant material or source, including testimony, whether or not submitted by a party or admissible under the Federal Rules of Evidence . . ." [3055] The New York State Bar Association Tax Section recommended standardized language in the Code for authorizations of treasury guidance.[3056]

VII.C. Conclusion

This book has shown how the application of the federal tax laws both suffers and benefits from the absence of a cohesive view of the relationship of taxpayers to tax paying. That void has been filled by many doctrines, principles, canons, presumptions, burdens, etc., which when viewed together form an impressive anti-taxpayer regime. The most prominent of the tax specific doctrines in recent years has been the economic substance doctrine. With its partial codification in 2010, the application of the federal tax laws may undergo a further sharp turn against taxpayer electivity and flexibility. It is not by accident that this turn occurs at a time of dire national need for revenue, as did the New Deal era shift in favor of the tax collector, but this time without Congress having to take the blame.

The current turn will not produce the benefits to the fisc produced by the New Deal turn. That failure, if coupled with continued high revenue needs and the encrusting process of a hundred years of experience with the income

---

[3054] *See* Staudt et al., *Judicial Decisions as Legislation, supra* note 412, at 1402.

[3055] Wolfman, *Expert Testimony on the Law,* 57 TAX LAW. 709 (2004) (Twelfth Annual Erwin N. Griswold Distinguished Lecture).

[3056] N.Y.S.B.A. Tax Sec., *Report No. 1121, supra* note 2045, at 215-22.

tax (and perpetual political opposition to it), could lead in our lifetimes to its partial replacement by a tax system that would be allegedly simpler to apply. Good luck with that.

Table of Federal Cases